THE UNTOLD STORY OF WESTERN CIVILIZATION

Vol. 5

THE UNTOLD STORY OF WESTERN CIVILIZATION

VOLUME 5

CONTEMPORARY HISTORY

PAX AMERICANA

Chuck and Tom Paprocki

Inner World Publications
San German, Puerto Rico
www.innerworldpublications.com

Copyright 2019 by Chuck & Tom Paprocki
All rights reserved undeer International and
Pan-American Copyright Conventions

Published in the United States by
Inner World Publications
P.O. Box 1613, San German, Puerto Rico, 00683

Library of Congress Control Number:
2018948333
ISBN: 978-1-881717-76-8

Cover Design: Tom Paprocki

All rights reserved. This book, or parts thereof, may not be reproduced in any form or by any means, electronic or mechanical, including photocopying, recording, or by any information storage or retrieval system, without the permission of the publisher except for brief quotations.

Cover photo: David Rockefeller spearheaded American capitalism around the world, leaving billions in abject destitution and the planet's eco-system in ruins. As the dark lord of American imperialism and the grandson of John D. Rockfeller, who illegally captured control of the oil industry at the beginning of American industrialism, David inherited media, pharmaceutical, and banking empires. He controlled the Council on Foreign Relations, which dictated foreign policy to several presidents and the CIA which destroyed left-leaning governments around the world seeking to protect their own resources. After the cultural revolution delegitmized his activities, he formed the Trilateral Commission, adding Japanese and European capitalists to his consultant group. To understand the rise of post-WWII American imperialism and its role in creating globalization, one must understand the role of David Rockefeller in bringing it about.

Dedication

To the memory of Prabhat Rainjan Sarkar,
our spiritual guide

Contents

Part One: The Ruling Class

Introduction   2

Why Is History Important To Know?   4
The Intention of the Capitalist Elite   5
The Impact of Capitalist Plans on the American People   8
The Role of Public Education in Blaming the Victim   10
The Elimination of Social Concerns from Public Education   13
The Role of TV in Capitalist Society   13
The Role of the Two-Party System   14
The Right Wing   16
The Left Wing   17
Common Ground   19

Chapter One: American Capitalists in the Global Economy   25

Federal Reserve Bank   26
Who Controls the Bank Today?   28
How Do the Bankers Control the US Government?   29
Debt: An Overview   33
How the Bank Makes the Money   35
The Connection between Work and Debt   37
Inflation and Deflation   38
Bad Debts   39
The Bankers' Play Book   41
    The Perpetual Debt Play   41
    The Debt Roll-Over Play   42
    The Up-The-Ante Play   42
    The Rescheduling Play   43

The Protect-The-Public Play	43
The Big Bailout	44
The Guaranteed Payment Play	45
Money is the Federal Reserve Banks' IOU	46
The Ebb and Flow of the Economy is Based on Aggregate Supply and Demand	49
The Role of Politicians in the Debt Game	52
Bretton Woods: The Federal Reserve Note Goes International	54
The Birth of "Undeveloped" and "Developing" Countries	58
The Third World (Perpetually Undeveloped Countries)	60
Making an Example of Chile	62
The US-Based Multinational Corporation	67
International Banks and the Expansion of American Imperialism	69
The World Bank	71
The International Monetary Fund	76
The GATT	78
The Principle upon Which International Capital Works	79
The United Nations and Resistance to International Monopoly Capitalism	82
Global Power Blocs	84
The OECD	85
The Union of Soviet Socialist Republics (USSR)	85
Organization of Petroleum Exporting Countries (OPEC)	88
The Group of 77	89
The Brandt Report	92
The UN General Assembly 11th Special Session, 1980	93
The Brundtland Report (Our Common Future)	96
The Domestic Consequences of US Imperialism	101
How the US-based Multinational Corporations Control Us	104
I'm Forever Blowing Bubbles	108
Who Owns the Money Today?	116
How Much Money Are We Talking About?	119
Are We On The Brink Of Financial Collapse?	120
Domestic Debt	124

What is the Solution to This Existential Crisis?   127
The End Game Strategy of the Capitalist Countries
(Plan A)   130
The Capitalist Plan   133
Conclusion   136

Chapter Two: The American Intellectuals   138

Policy-Oriented Intellectuals vs Value-Oriented
  Intellectuals   139
The Origins of the Council on Foreign Relations   141
The Trilateral Commission   144
The Trilateral Commission and the US Presidency   148
  The Carter Administration   149
  The Reagan Administration   151
  The George H. W. Bush Administration   152
  The Bill Clinton Administration   155
  The George W. Bush Administration   156
  The Barak Obama Administration   165
    Trans-Pacific Partnership   168
The Trilateralist Media   169
The Crisis of Democracy   172
The Trump Administration   181
The Ideology of American Conservatism   182
  What is a Conservative?   182
  The Tenets of Conservatism   185
The Protestant Religion and the Rise of American
  Conservatism   191
  Evangelicals   192
  Southern Baptists   194
  Fundamentalists   198
  The Christian Voice   200
  The Moral Majority   202
  Charismatic Christianity   205
  The Tea Party   207
  Christian Dominionism   211
Lessons Learned   214

The Ideology of American Liberalism	218
What is a Liberal?	220
Liberal Groups	224
The Tenets of Liberalism	227
The Rise of American Liberalism	233
Liberal Christians	234
Secular Liberals	236
Neo-Liberals	238
The Progressives	239
Teddy Roosevelt	241
Franklin D. Roosevelt	242
The Cold War	244
The New Left	247
The Greens	249
The Occupy Movement	253
Non-Violence	255
Failings of the Occupy Movement	257
Conclusion	259

Chapter Three: The American Warriors: Nation as Empire — 260

What is Militarism?	261
The Military-Industrial Complex	265
The Korean War	267
The Vietnam War	269
The End of the Cold War	270
The Fall of the Union of Soviet Socialist Republics (USSR)	273
The End of the US Cold War Containment Strategy	279
Peak Oil	281
Enter the Neo-Cons	285
Domestic Policy: Eavesdropping and the Militarization of Local Law Enforcement	289
Secure Communities	289
The Militarization of the Domestic Police	292

The Patriot Act	297
National Defense Authorization Act (NDAA)	298
Executive Order 13603	299
Foreign Policy: The War on Terrorism	304
The Definition of Terror	305
The Impact of US Imperialism on Exploited People and on the Imperialists Themselves	308
Capitalism in the Middle East	310
The Growth of Islamic Fundamentalism	312
Al-Afghani	314
Post-World War I in the Middle East	315
The Muslim Brotherhood	315
The Devotees of Islam	317
Jamaat-e-Islami	318
World War II	319
Post World War II	320
Sayyid Qutb	321
Muammar Qaddafi	323
The Ayatollah Khomeini	325
Afghanistan and the Rise of the Taliban	328
Osama bin Laden and al-Qaeda	332
The War on Terror Unleashed	339
The Pentagon's New Map	341
Rules and Their Importance	342
American Wars in the Middle East	345
Public Enemy #1	347
The US Army in Saudi Arabia	347
Economic Sanctions on Iraq	348
The Second Wave of Islamic Fundamentalism	350
The Dogmatism of Islamic Fundamentalism	354
The Arab Spring	356
The Civil War in Syria	359
Assad's Strategy	361
Combatant Groups	362
The Free Syrian Army (FSA)	362
The Syrian Democratic Forces (SDF)	363
The Southern Front	363
Jabhat Fateh al-Sham	363

Harakat Ahrar al-Sham al-Islamiyya	364
ISIS	364
Shiite/Sunni Conflict in Syria	365
Foreign Intervention	366
The United States	366
Turkey	368
Russia	370
Refugee Migration	375
Yemen	379
Civil War in the North	380
Yemeni Unification, 1990	381
Impact of the Gulf War, 1990-91	381
The Oil Factor	383
The Houthi Rebellion	384
US Counterinsurgency in Iraq	386
The Field Manual	387
Nation-Building	389
Welcome Home!	395
What was it Like to Be an American Soldier in Iraq?	396
The Department of Veteran Affairs (VA)	402
Despite the Chaos, the "Good Guys" Are Winning	405
Subterfuge	407
Revolving Doors	408
Leverage	409
Making Money	410
Bad Strategy, Bad Tactics	411
The Flawed Vision of Global Dominance	412
Our Idea of American Greatness Is Too Small	413

Part Two: The American People

Introduction   419

Chapter 4: The American People   422

Who We Are	422
Sex and Gender	424

The Generations ... 429
  The GI Generation ... 430
  Silent Generation ... 431
  Baby Boomers ... 432
  Generation X ... 433
  Generation Y/Millennials. ... 436
  Generation Z ... 440
Race ... 444
Class ... 454
  The Upper, Middle, and Lower Classes ... 456
  Marxist Class Analysis ... 459
Class by Social Psychology ... 461
Religion ... 466
National Origin ... 475

Chapter Five: Social Forces — 478

Unemployment and Debt ... 478
  The Impact on the Family Structure ... 482
  The Unemployment Rate and the Employment Rate ... 483
  The Trump Economy ... 490
  Family Debt ... 495
Political Polarization ... 498
  The 2016 Election ... 502
  Enter Trump ... 503
  Consequences for the People ... 505
  Facts to Cool Tempers ... 506
  What Can Well-Intentioned Americans Do to Begin to Heal the Rift Between Us? ... 509
National Security ... 515
  Corporate Spying on US Citizens ... 521
  Micro Chipping People ... 525
  Micro Chipping Clothes ... 526
Immigrants and Refugees ... 528
  Western Reaction to the Mass Migration ... 529
  The Life of Refugees ... 534
  Mexican Immigrants ... 539
  The Immigrant and Refugee Problem Will Not Go Away. ... 545

What is the Solution to the Problem of Refugees and
    Immigrants?   547
Destruction of the Environment   548
  Ozone   549
  Air Pollution   550
    Fossil Fuel Pollution   555
  Water Pollution   558
    The Politics of Water in the US   561
  Land Pollution   563
  Loss of Species   565
    Bees   565
    Monarch butterflies   567
    Birds   567
    Cats and Dogs   569
    Farm Animals   570
    Wild Animals   573
    Loss of Large Mammals Around the World   578
    Loss of Plant Species   582
  Climate Change   583

Chapter Six: Meeting Basic Needs   593

What is Right Livelihood?   593
The Right to Food   595
  Industrial Agriculture   596
  The Green Revolution   597
  GMOs (Genetically Modified Organisms)   600
  What Is Food?   607
  Processed Food (Fast Food and Junk Food)   609
  Availability of Real Food   614
  False Propaganda   616
Shelter   617
  Homelessness   620
Clothing   623
Health Care   628
  State of Health of Americans   629
  A Brief History of American Health Care   631
  The Flexner Report   633

Big Pharma	636
Government Regulation	638
Mental Health	640
Health Insurance	644
Education	649
What is Education?	649
The Important Need for Education	650
The Goal of Education	652
The History of US Education	653
The Profit Motive	655
Education Reform	657
Debt Collection	660
The Impact on Student Loan Borrowers	661
The Primary and Secondary School System	662
Conclusion	672

Conclusion to Book One   680

Appendix A: Ten Key Values of the US Green Party   690

Appendix B: Declaration of the Occupation of New York City   693

Appendix C: 9/11/2001, the Day That Shook the World   696

Appendix D: Immigrants to US by Country

of Origin	710
Appendix E: Function and Sources of Nutrients	722
Endnotes	728
Illustration Credits	824
Index	830
About the Authors	839

List of Figures

Fig. 5-1: Interest vs Certain Government Programs	32
Fig. 5-2: Shrinking Middle Class	39
Fig. 5-3: $20 Gold Certificate	47
Fig. 5-4: IMF/World Bank Protest Sign	75
Fig. 5-5: Inter-Connectedness of Largest Companies	118
Fig. 5-6: State and Local Debt Per Capita	125
Fig. 5-7: Density of World Population in 2019	131
Fig. 5-8: Recent Federal Debt	135
Fig. 5-9: Home Owners Equity in Real Estate: 2000-2010	167
Fig. 5-10: Afghanistan Before and After	330
Fig: 5-11: The Arabian Peninsula	335
Fig. 5-12: Map of the Middle East	392
Fig. 5-13: US Warfare Expenditures vs Other Countries	411
Fig. 5-14: Ratio of Men and Women in the Fifty States	425
Fig. 5-15: Comparison of Human Skulls to Those of Animals	447
Fig. 5-16: Questions of Race in the 2000 Census	453
Fig. 5-17: National Ancestry	476
Fig. 5-18: Federal Debt By President & Political Party	480
Fig. 5-19: What Republicans and Democrats Say About Each Other	500
Fig. 5-20: Top Ten Origins of People Applying for Asylum in the EU	530
Fig. 5-21: New Orleans After Hurricane Katrina	546
Fig. 5-22: Emissions from Oil Extraction and Refining for Petroleum Products Used in the US (CO_2e) Compared to CO_2	

Emissions from the Use of Major Transportation Fuels in
the US. 556

Fig. 5-23: Rise in Greenhouse Gases Over Last Two Thousand
Years 589

Fig. 5-24: Ingredients of a Typical Protein Bar 613

Part One: The Ruling Class

Introduction

The Untold Story of Western Civilization is the first part of a trilogy entitled *History, Ideology, and Revolution*. This book, which is History's fifth volume, examines contemporary history from the perspective of the United States after WWII during which time it began its quest to establish its global economic empire.

In Volume I of *The Untold Story of Western Civilization*, we explored our ancestral beginnings in the agricultural civilizations of matriarchal society. We looked at the social psychology at a time when women played the dominant role in society. We explored the beliefs and rituals and the politics and economics of this age.

In Volume II, we witnessed how matriarchal society was replaced by patriarchal society, initially by the Aryan nomadic tribes that poured out of the Caucasus mountains and spread across India, the Middle East, and Northern Europe, and then how matriarchal society was virtually eliminated by the succession of male-dominated civilizations that began in the Middle East with the Sumerians and ended with the Greek and Roman occupations. During this period, which is considered to be Ancient History, we watched how the warrior psychology became dominant and those, who best exemplified the warrior spirit, became the ruling class.

In Volume III, we moved westward and explored the history of Eastern and Western Europe. We traced the origins of tribal society among the Slavs, Germans, and Celts and watched how these tribes were uprooted by the mass invasions of nomadic tribes from Mongolia and the Russian Steppes. We saw how these massive invasions, coupled with the expansion of the Roman Empire northward into the mainland, created the need for the European tribes to centralize authority under local kings (warlords) and build larger armies to protect themselves. We saw how this arrangement led to the breakdown of the tribal system and with it men's regard for women and the important roles they played in tribal society, including those of priestess, warrior, healer, and keeper of the tribal wealth. We saw how this transition set the stage for the emergence of the male-dominated nation-states of Europe. We also explored life inside the Roman Empire and looked at its impact on Western Europe and the Near East. We then examined the rise of the Catholic Church that arose from the ashes of Rome to become the supreme power in Western Europe. During this period in history, called the Middle Ages, we traced how the intellectual psychology came to dominate life in Europe and how those, who best exemplified the skills of this psychology, became the new ruling class in the form of the Church clergy.

In Volume IV, we explored the rise of capitalism through the Renaissance, Reformation, and the Enlightenment periods. We watched the vice-like grip of the Church begin to loosen as new intellectual thought and a proliferation of artists began to create secular ideas among the people. We watched how this new freedom, inspired a revolution within the Church itself and set the stage for a hundred years of religious wars, in which Protestant sects, founded on conflicting dogmas, battled the Catholic Church to lay waste to Europe during what became known as the Protestant Reformation. In the vacuum of power caused by the fall of the Church and the aristocracies of Europe, who were also caught up in these wars, we saw the middle class merchants rise to power and eventually come to dominate western society. We saw how the capitalist psychology came to control this period of Modern History and how those who possessed this psychology became the new ruling class. The capitalists still constitute the ruling class of Western society today, while the intellectual class and the warrior class have been reduced to serve its interests.

In this Volume 5, we move into the period of contemporary history and explore how American capitalism created the golden age of capitalism and how its influence and military power spread throughout the entire world. We look at the American capitalists' stated plans for empire building since WWII and what their plans are for the future of the American people and the people of the world. We look at how they employ the intellectual and warrior elites, as well as the average American, in service to their vision of global economic dominance.

Why Is History Important To Know?

In our exploration of the history of western civilization, we witnessed the critical events and turning points that gave rise to American thought today. We saw how our attitudes regarding gender, race, class, nationality, and religion took shape and came to express themselves in today's American society. We saw why we think the way we do today.

In this amazing venture, we came to understand that history constitutes nothing less than our collective subconscious programming. It determines our reactions to the present and what we want our future to look like. It is the oceanic wave that pushes us onto the rocky shore of getting out of bed each morning to face the daily grind to which we are becoming increasingly alienated. History provides the raw materials for our thoughts, words, and deeds.

Not knowing our history is very dangerous. If we do not understand what happened in the past, we do not understand why people, including ourselves, think and act the way we do today. We do not understand the long historical process that crystallizes each day in our presence. As such, we are prohibited from making intelligent decisions about what to do next. In our blindness, we are impotent to improve the well-being of our society.

Ignorance of our history does not change its impact on our lives. Rather, our historic programming remains at the subconscious level where it bursts forth on cue when events trigger our instincts, sentiments, and disjointed thoughts. We find ourselves obsessed, attracted, repulsed, or neutral to stimuli without knowing why. We do not know what to believe, so we believe what people tell us. We believe what mainstream media tells us, what the church tells us, what politicians tell us, what our group tells us. People manipulate our feelings and we believe what they say because we do not have a sense of reality to accurately weigh their information. To be manipulated in this way is a normal condition for a child, but it is quite harmful for adults. We become easy prey to others who have an agenda that serves their best interest, but not our own.

No matter our political leanings, if we do not know our history, we are forced to fall back on group sentiments and unfounded prejudices, which cause us to inveigh against those who do not believe as we do. Such irrationality only leads us to repeatedly make the same mistakes over again. Without knowledge of history, we are either reactionaries or utopians, liberals or conservatives, caught up in the ruling elites' strategy of divide and conquer. Just grist for the mill as history turns another cycle.

Without knowing our true history, our ideas about God, human nature, and the natural world are little more than sentimentalized and prejudicial versions of something that got passed down through history to the people who influence our thinking today. And these people, not knowing history either, have just passed to you their myths and stories as if they were the truth. In time, such prejudices become part of the culture of a people. This is how *prejudice* is created. Historians tell us that we are meant to relive the mistakes of the past if we do not know our history. This is what they mean.

The Intention of the Capitalist Elite

The wave of history affects us at every level. At the international and national levels, the elites who rule the world want to intentionally hide our true history from us. They do not want us to know how they got so rich or why we normal people are in the precarious position we find ourselves today. They avert our attention from our history by filling our senses with meaningless ideas and by employing political spokesmen who prey on our sentiments and emotions to turn us against each other. The politicians spread lies and propaganda through the mainstream media. They cover up, ignore, and obfuscate the information from our past that we require as a people if we are to improve our lives and the lives of our children. The capitalists use the media to deify what they want us to believe. We are taught to worship the rich although we know nothing about them. The propaganda of the media holds out an illusory carrot that promises we too can become gods like them if we are willing to work hard enough. All the while, we are working two or three jobs a week to make ends meet. And still the true intentions of the elite, hidden in our history, remain unknown to the general public who plod along, confused and depressed, anxious about what each day will bring. This may be an exaggeration but it is not far from the mark.

Let us clearly understand that the US-based multinational capitalist class, which is comprised of the owners and managers of corporate wealth and power, have a plan. They have always had a plan and it does not include our welfare. It is a plan to dominate the world economically and bring everyone under their control. In the following chapters, we will see how this plan developed and how it is being carried out. The intellectuals, who serve the capitalist elite as participants in their corporate brain trusts or as university professors, government bureaucrats, or politicians, also have a plan. It is to continually reify the illusion that American capitalism is the greatest social system on the planet and that we live in a democracy where political elections really matter. The American military also has a plan. It is also based upon the glorification of the American capitalist model of global dominance. Their job is to destroy any person or any country that stands in the way of the globalist agenda. In this volume, we will also look at the lives of the American people and the crushing problems that we face today as a nation.

Knowing the truth of our history is the first step to empowering ourselves as a people. It will allow us to forsake the debilitating prejudices that we have toward each other and help us make rational decisions going forward. Knowing our history will help us overcome our animosity toward each other, which has been systematically groomed by the elites to keep us divided. It will allow us to open a dialogue across the artificial boundaries that separate us as local communities and help us to build self-reliant communities where people care for each other and where our children are safe.

Because developments in the US since World War II exist within our collective living memory, people of the right and the left both understand that conditions have gotten worse in our society. We are now witnessing the death of the American Dream, the destitution of the poor, the destruction of the working class, the shrinking of the middle class, and the disappearance of millions of jobs that until recently paid a living wage. We have all watched as our moral bearing and the pride we felt in our country got twisted and diminished by economic and political scandals at the highest level of corporate and government power. We have seen our armies and covert operatives bully other countries into giving up their raw materials and we have seen how our military has been used to punish the world's people for showing any sign of resistance. We have felt our tolerance as a nation turn into a grotesque fear of strangers that makes America, which has always been a nation of immigrants, turn against anyone who now wants to live in our land. We have watched this fear translate into the xenophobia, racism, and sexism that now plays out in the mass media as part of the capitalists' divide and conquer strategy.

Divide and conquer has always been the strategy of the ruling class to deflect popular attention from their exploitive practices. It is quite easy to point the finger of blame at a scapegoat and present him, her, or them as the cause of one's problems. Today, the scapegoat internationally is the Muslim people, who just happen to live in the Middle East where the oil exists that the capitalists want to control.

Within the United States itself, the ruling elite has intentionally aggravated the American divide between liberals and conservatives, Democrats and Republicans, the left and the right. It is along these cultural and political lines that it builds our hatred and anger for each other. Among the Left are those who seek social improvement for all Americans by changing the social structures that no longer serve the American people as a whole. Among the Right are those who seek social improvement, but only for their own kind by reversing any progress that has been made toward social inclusiveness. But while the world may applaud the America that stands as a beacon of hope for social inclusion and human unity, the vision of America championed by the left, assuredly, has deadly flaws within it as well. And among these, we must count neo-liberalism, which, in the guise of human service, continues to destroy the people of other countries and exploit their natural resources. So also, we must admit that there are positive values that are offered by the right. Among these, we must include faith in a higher power, pride in family, and community values.

Because this volume on contemporary American history is an attempt to present the American people without a left or right-leaning prejudice, it will be helpful to look at the reasoning behind this approach.

The Impact of Capitalist Plans on the American People

There are certainly positive things that can be said about the American capitalist class, including their ability to efficiently organize the production and delivery of basic needs to billions of people and also provide us with consumer goods never imagined by previous generations. Nonetheless, there has always existed a sociopathic streak in this class that shows itself in their willingness to betray or sacrifice anyone or anything that stands in the way of their ability to optimize their profits. They use everyone and everything as objects for their own self-aggrandizement and then, when they have no further use for us, they are willing to completely destroy our lives as new horizons open to them to make greater profits elsewhere. We can see this in the destruction of the American economy over the last couple of decades.

The majority of Americans have watched the systematic disassembly of American manufacturing, as the corporate elites sent millions of jobs to China, India, Mexico, and other countries where there are no labor unions and where people are forced to work for dirt cheap wages.

The American working class, predominately composed of white people, has watched millions of their jobs disappear. If they were lucky enough to keep their jobs, their wages stagnated and their net worth over the last couple of decades was cut by fifty-three percent. Their lives have been trashed. At the same time, the capitalist class increased its net worth by seventy-five percent. Today, in America, the wealthiest ten percent of the population now own seventy-six percent of all the wealth while fifty percent of the entire country own only one percent. The majority of Americans live on table scraps. These are the poor, the working class, and an ever-expanding percentage of the middle class.[1]

When people lose their jobs, they lose their self-respect. They believe that they have failed their families and they can no longer be trusted or loved. Families as a whole become victim to capitalist exploitation. The situation turns husband against wife and parents against children. We do not know who has our back anymore. We are becoming a frightened and lonely people. Men beat their wives and kids. Women fear their husbands. Kids do not get the security they deserve. Spouses do not believe their partner will stick with them through thick and thin. The divorce rate keeps growing.

We toss and turn each night ridden in guilt and fear of the future and we wake each morning ridden by the same feelings. The only available jobs are the dead end, nonunionized jobs offered by McDonalds or Walmart that do not even allow us to make ends meet. Race relations worsen as the media spreads stories that the minorities are taking white people's jobs.

Consider this. Today 45.3 million Americans, comprising half of US households, live *below the poverty line* on the edge of financial collapse. People suffer from economic PTSD. This is true of people living in the city and in rural areas. Many farmers have had to give up their farms. Since losing their jobs, many men and women have had to work two or three jobs to feed their families. Some keep looking for jobs, but hundreds of thousands, after years of looking, have just given up. Many young millennials have never even had a job. When people quit looking for jobs, they are no longer counted in the unemployment statistics, so it looks like things are okay. The mainstream media tells us that the American economy is getting better, but it is not. Today, a *majority* of Americans still do not have money in their savings accounts to cover an unexpected bill of four hundred dollars.[2] This means, putting off doctor appointments, postponing eyeglasses for the kids, not getting the car repaired, or not having the money to pay a rise in insurance premiums. Many people depend on credit cards to put food on their table and now have to pay exorbitant credit card rates instead of using their meager cash to pay for their basic needs.

The same conditions, which have long existed for single women and racial minorities, have now begun to affect middle class white men. White people in huge numbers are now feeling the sickening dread of living in poverty. Now the right-wing politicians, in the form of the Trump administration, arrive to prey on the trauma of white Americans by blaming the poor, the women, and the racial minorities for taking white men's jobs. They stir the cauldron of hatred and fill us with their poison. By dividing the American people in this way, the intention of the elites is accomplished in two ways. First, this blame game deflects attention from the rich who are responsible in the first place for destroying American jobs. Secondly, it provides the rationale to cut social service programs to all the lazy moochers who are draining the honest taxpayers' wallets. In actuality, the rich do not want to pay for social service programs even after devastating the economy and throwing millions of people out of work. It is ironic that while the right-wing politicians blame women and minorities for using social service programs, more whites depend on these programs than do the minorities.

As it is, the United States has the worst social service system among all industrialized countries. By destroying the unions and the leftist movements within the last twenty years, the social service system, which was created during the Roosevelt years, has been systematically destroyed by the elites. The Republican Party under President Trump looks to finish the job. Health care programs, free higher education, unemployment benefits, health and safety regulations, paid vacations, child care, and benefits for the elderly have now been either eliminated or significantly reduced. This is the situation faced by the unemployed white American working class today. The situation faced by minorities and single mothers is even worse.

The Role of Public Education in Blaming the Victim

The public education system in this country leads people to believe that if they are not making ends meet it is their own fault. Either they are not smart enough, or do not work hard enough, or maybe it is their personality that the bosses do not like. If a person cannot find a job, it is on them. The same lies that put the blame on the individual worker are the same lies that justify the rich getting richer at everyone else's expense. We are told that the rich are successful because they obviously are smarter and more hardworking than everyone else. These same lies justify the unconscionable and immoral wealth disparities between the one percent and the rest of American society.

The American school system was set up to indoctrinate young people into working in the capitalists' system. When John D. Rockefeller set up the first education system in 1906, the Board of Education's first report specified this intention:

> In our dreams...people yield themselves with perfect docility to our molding hands. The present educational conventions [intellectual and character education] fade from our minds, and unhampered by tradition, we work our own good will upon a grateful and responsive folk. The task we set before ourselves is very simple . . . we will organize children . . . and teach them to do in a perfect way the things their fathers and mothers were doing in an imperfect way.[3]

President Woodrow Wilson clearly expressed the class bias inherent in public education. The purpose of public education was never to promote a meritocracy, it was rather to develop a method by which the capitalist ruling class could control the American public and have us submit to its will. As Wilson said: "We want one class to have a liberal education. We want another class, a very much larger class of necessity, to forego the privilege of a liberal education and fit themselves to perform specific difficult manual tasks."[4]

By the first quarter of the twentieth century, the goal of public education was firmly in place. Ellwood Cubberley, the Dean of the Stanford Graduate School of Education and a pioneer in the field of educational administration, wrote in his book, *Public School Administration*:

> Our schools are, in a sense, factories in which the raw products (children) are to be shaped and fashioned into products to meet the various demands of life . . . It is the business of the school to build its pupils according to

the specifications laid down. Every manufacturing establishment that turns out a standard product or series of products of any kind maintains a force of efficiency experts to study methods of procedure and to measure and test the output of its works . . . [Creating such pupils demands] continuous measurement of production to see if it is according to specifications [and] the elimination of waste in manufacture."[5]

So much for platitudes about "health," "learning," "human dignity," "independence," and "creative endeavor." According to the educational elites, these human qualities are little more than convenient sound bites for justifying public education to the American public. In spite of this class bias, certain brave teachers strive against impossible odds to introduce spiritual, social, and environmental values into their designated curricula.

The rote programming demanded by institutional education caused the student movement of the 1960s, as well as progressives up to the present, to condemn public education as "irrelevant" to their needs as human beings. This position however is diluted by the Republican effort to severely cut public education funding and put pubic dollars into private schools, thus robbing the public of even a minimum of subsidized relevant education and the opportunity for socialization.

Today, we see the same process is still at work. Beginning in elementary school, children are faced with mandatory testing to determine if they will fit into the system or not. The tests are based on math and language skills and, while purportedly objective, are class, gender, and racially biased. This narrow skill set completely ignores our human qualities. It entirely dismisses the need for social awareness or awareness of the natural environment. It eliminates any discussion regarding the care of others or any ethical or spiritual considerations. The system simply trains our children to serve the production process and if they cannot or will not do this, they have only themselves to blame. They have flunked the loyalty test and now they will be denied access to elite schools and higher paying jobs. Through such indoctrination, the American people learn to blame themselves for their failure. They confuse being a servant to the system with their self-worth as human beings. In fact, the people have been sold out by the capitalist system. They have been narrowly trained to work in the system and then the jobs were sent overseas, leaving people with nothing.

The Elimination of Social Concerns from Public Education

Prior to WWII, there was a strong reform movement around the world against the exploitive practices of the capitalist class. The working class fought hand-to-hand combat against the bosses' security forces, and the police in order to establish basic human rights. The movement was world-wide and the working men joined unions, socialist movements, and communist movements in an effort to push back the relentless tide of capitalist exploitation. The workers emphasized solidarity with each other and service to humanity. After WWII, however, with the world laid waste by war, everyone pitched in to rebuild society. In this effort, the antagonism between capitalist and worker was lessened, but the underlying tension between exploiter and exploited never went away. Following the war, the capitalist anti-communist propaganda campaign gradually delegitimized this partnership and began to repress any radical left-wing activity. The people who held progressive ideas were purged from the workplace and labor organizers were suppressed. The corporate media portrayed such people as evil communists. In the place of worker solidarity and social welfare, the capitalist deified their own values of selfish exploitation for wealth and power. The media, since the war, has relentlessly pushed these values at the expense of human compassion and ethical principles.

The Role of TV in Capitalist Society

Today, TV's main objective is to promote these same selfish values. Its relentless focus on sex and violence is based on the premise that you either dominate or are dominated. Cooperation is not projected as a value. Reality TV programs, like the Apprentice, Survivor, or the Bachelor send the same message that, in "the real world," you must develop the skills to dominate others or you will be dominated yourself. Popular shows, like House of Cards or the Game of Thrones, are based upon attempts by sleazy people to dominate others. Most TV shows lack any moral fiber. As Rabbi Lerner, a political activist and the founder of Tikkun magazine, tells us, the main characters in today's TV shows consistently "manipulate others to meet their own needs. From these shows, viewers learn that people are more successful when they know how to use other people to achieve their own ends."[6] This leads decent people to believe that their failure stems from the fact that they are not abusing others enough to realize their own desires.

Even though every American worker knows that their bosses are primarily concerned about themselves, even though we know that the products we create are meant to increase corporate profits rather than serve the common good, and even though working men know that they will be considered less manly for having ethical or environmental concerns, the workers still blame themselves if they lose their jobs or cannot find another job in the system. This guilt remains even after the corporations have moved the jobs overseas and there are no longer enough living wage jobs remaining in America to fill the need. This internal contradiction drives many of us crazy and makes us want to strike out at something or someone. We look to our two-faced politicians to solve our problems.

The Role of the Two-Party System

It will be a shock to the American people to learn that neither the Democrats nor the Republicans have the power to solve our problems. There are very few good guys in any party that will come to our rescue. Neither Obama nor Trump could do this.

The capitalist elite supports both the Left and the Right politically and continually uses one side against the other to keep the American people divided and hating each other. The ruling class does not think in terms of conservative or liberal, right or left. They think only in terms of those who will serve them without question and those who will not.[7] In our ignorance, the politicians incite us to blame each other instead of the rich and powerful, even though it is they who are responsible for our misery. The rich have become powerful by profiting from our labor and by confiscating our natural resources and then letting us twist in the wind as they move on to profit from others.

We believe that in our democracy, our vote can make a difference. It does not. As we shall see, once elected, the politicians forget their promises to the people and begin working with the ruling elites to forward their agenda. This is why the American people are so frustrated with both parties. Donald Trump spoke to this frustration and became president of the United States because he was able to articulate it. The people looked at him as a political outsider, someone who could "drain the swamp" that poisons our lives. They soon discovered that, aside from spreading misogyny and racism, Trump, as president, champions the cause of the rich just as surely as the other politicians whom he denounced. Trump after all is a billionaire.

Most politicians betray us on a daily basis. They are not statesmen or stateswomen who seek the welfare of America as a whole. Rather, they are political operatives, intent on building and maintaining their own wealth and power. Both the Republicans and the Democrats fail the American people because they never address the underlying intentions of the elites. They never point their finger at the real cause of our problems. Through their service to the capitalist class, the politicians have themselves become members of the elite. They would have never been elected to office if the rich did not give them the money to run their campaigns. Once in office, they are beholding to their capitalist donors, not the American people.

Politicians are always coming up with new reasons for hating the "other" group of Americans. The politicians fail us because they do not address the psychological depression or the spiritual emptiness we feel as a result of our immersion in a selfish, war-like, anxiety-ridden, consumption-driven society.

Rather, our misery allows the politicians to manipulate our emotions and betray us on behalf of the capitalist overlords. Our purpose here is not to attack any individual politician but to discuss the underlying dynamic, which perpetuates the existing system at the expense of the American people. Let us start with the right-wing politicians, the Republicans and then move to the Democrats.

The Right Wing

The Right became popular among the American poor whites and white working class during the 1960s and 1970s as a reaction to the Cultural Revolution set in motion by the student, women, and civil rights movements at that time. The right-wing politicians countered by manipulating the poor and working class whites into believing that it was because of the hippies, feminists, and racial minority civil rights activists that the lives of God-fearing, hard-working white people were suffering from the pain of social alienation. Rather than pointing to the capitalists as the cause of people's suffering, the right-wing politicians blamed the most vulnerable people in society for destroying the white people's way of life. In standing up for themselves, the most repressed segments of society, the young, the women, and the racial minorities were painted by the politicians and the religious right as being selfish and uncaring people who were only out for themselves.

While the sexist and racist attitudes of the majority of white males of this country go back to the days of the American revolution and even further back in history, the right-wing politicians stimulate these suppressed emotions and use them to manipulate the poor and working class whites for their own political agendas. In their steady drumbeat of hatred against the vulnerable, the Right has nurtured a culture of racism, sexism, homophobia, and xenophobia, which becomes stronger every day. It was by their appeal to the whites' emotions and sentiments, that the right-wing politicians have been able to polarize this country, enrich themselves in the process, and serve the capitalist class strategy of divide and conquer.

Such scapegoat tactics work temporarily because they help to relieve the feeling of self-guilt that the white working class feels for their economic decline. It allows them to blame someone else for their failure. Unfortunately, they blame the victim rather than the true criminal. This is the work of crafty politicians. When a demagogue like Donald Trump comes along and puts people's feelings of alienation and resentment into words, they rally around him. This gives them a feeling of solidarity with "their people." In addition, it fulfills their need for a strong leader. As this process continues, the siege mentality caused by their belief that liberals and minorities are taking over "their country," leads to an ultra-nationalist movement, which will turn into fascism if not relentlessly confronted. In this process of blaming others, the hatred and anger of the whites finds a focus. It's now time for "the others" to suffer.

Punish the women by taking away their inalienable human rights, and their right to control their own bodies, while justifying rape, domestic abuse, harassment, and shaming. As for racial minorities, kill, brutalize, belittle, and terrorize them. Cut any government support for the women and children. Weaponize the police force and build more private prisons. This is what happens when widespread economic insecurity is coupled with the psychological dysfunction and spiritual wasteland of a white capitalist society.

The Left Wing

As for the Left-wing politicians, they express horror and disdain at the hatred of women and minorities in which the Right engages. Yet, either, because of ignorance, or deception, politicians on the Left continue to support policies that lead to the continual suppression of the American people as a whole. While the progressive Occupy movement called attention to the great disparity in the wealth of the one percent compared to the American people, Left-wing politicians intentionally failed to pick up on this issue. They feign concern for people, but do not want to change the system that oppresses the people. Like their right-wing colleagues, they too blame the victim instead of the criminal. While they may castigate the Right for their horrible behavior, they make no attempt to understand the reasons why such hatred and violence resonates with the poor and working-class whites.

The Democrats, including most left-wing activists, fail to acknowledge the need to change the system. Since many of their jobs exist within the service sector, they can remain busy shuffling papers, giving speeches, or organizing events, which are supposed to help the poor but seldom do. The activists get their grant money from corporations and this prevents them from looking too deeply into the problem. They focus on single problems and piecemeal issues, counting their successes in saving one person while five more are added to the ranks of the oppressed each day.

The Left blindly refuses to acknowledge the fact that it is impossible to slow climate change, or save the life support systems of the planet, or to solve the problems of war, social inequality, or economic disparity without getting rid of capitalism. They fail to recognize the hard truth staring them in the face that the very nature of capitalism is built on manipulation and violence, either psychological or physical.

It is impossible to have world peace while the US capitalist empire barges around the world killing and destroying people in order to fulfill its vision of a world capitalist empire. It is impossible to have economic justice without redistributing the wealth that is now hoarded by the capitalists. It is impossible to improve the lifestyle of the American people without empowering ourselves to destroy the very institutions that are responsible for our misery.

The Left keeps itself divided into silos, each group having its own issues and refusing to unite across these issues to change the fundamental conditions that keep the American people in servitude. They lack a master plan. In fact, they will not even consider working on one. To them, it is something that the American people will never go for.

The Left has another tragic flaw that keeps it from speaking for the American people as a whole. It lacks a universal spiritual vision and, as such, is unable to address the psychological and spiritual pain suffered by all Americans today. To the Left, God is a non-starter, a myth that serves to opiate the masses from their pain. By these means, the left continues to perpetrate the capitalist strategy of divide and conquer.

And so, we come to a situation where the poor, working-class whites and a growing number of middle-class whites, as represented by the Republicans, are pitted against the remaining middle class whites and racial minorities, as represented by the Democrats, and both sides are lined up for battle. It is another false flag that will lead us as a society over the cliff.

Common Ground

For the handful of revolutionaries who seek the welfare of Americans as a whole, this is the time to develop a grand strategy that will bring Americans together across the great divide and will set a new course for us to survive and ultimately prosper. These revolutionaries can be found on the left and the right. Books Two and Three of this trilogy, on the topics of Ideology and Revolution, are intended to help us to accomplish this task.

It is a false and dangerous proposition to believe that there is no common ground between liberals and conservatives. We all want the same thing. Self-respect, supportive neighbors, security, our basic needs met, and a better world for our children. We all want to live in a society based on values that support and care for one another. If we look at tragedies like the horrific storm that devastated the Houston area, we see people of all ages, races, and religious beliefs banding together to help each other. It is during these times of crises that we clearly see this commonality. The destruction of Puerto Rico is another matter, however, one in which the white racist administration of Donald Trump refuses aid to the people of Puerto Rico because they are largely a racial minority.

We need to understand more about each other. Regardless of gender, race, class, religion, or nationality, we are all suffering. We are suffering physically and mentally. We are suffering spiritually. Both the left and the right have children and grandchildren to think about. As human beings we all want the same thing.

It is from this perspective that our analysis of American society since WWII is presented. The United States today represents a society that has been molded over a long historical process. In this volume, we will look at how the elite among the capitalists, intellectuals, and military have set the trends in motion, beginning after WWII, that have led to the problems that we face today as a society.

This volume on Contemporary History is divided into two parts. Part One explores the American capitalist ruling class, the one percent, and looks at the behavior of its institutions of power since WWII. Capitalists control all of these institutions, but some are managed by intellectual and warrior elites. Part Two looks at the living conditions of the American people as a whole. It examiness who we are as a people, the forces that mitigate against our well-being, and the struggle that we have in meeting our basic needs in a sustainable manner. Each Part consists of three chapters.

Chapter One looks at the dealings of the capitalist class. It explores the mechanics of the Federal Reserve Bank, the strategy of US-based multi-national banks, and how the World Bank and the International Monetary Fund have been used to promote economic globalization in the decades following WWII. The chapter explores how "undeveloped" countries, the so-called "Third World," became involved in the capitalist economy through the institution of national debt, and how these countries have fought back to maintain the integrity of their citizens and natural resources in an environment of global economic colonization. The chapter goes on to demonstrate who owns the money in today's world and points out the tenuous state of domestic and international finance that has resulted from the unconscionable concentration of wealth within a tiny capitalist class. The chapter explores the destruction of the American productive capacity by the capitalists and looks at how our manufacturing capacity was moved off shore to take advantage of cheaper labor. It looks at the consequences of the loss of millions of living wage jobs that the American people have had to contend with. It looks at the shrinking of the middle class, and the aching divide that has grown between the super rich one percent and the American people who compose ninety-nine percent of the population. Finally, the chapter looks at the grand strategy of the capitalist class and their effort to secure the oil resources of Eurasia as the end game of economic globalization.

Chapter Two looks at the intellectual class in America and shows how the brightest minds of this class are recruited to serve the interest of the capitalist class. It looks at the response of American intellectuals on the Left and the Right to current social and environmental conditions in the United States and how current religious dogmas and secular ideologies laid the foundation for partisan politics. It looks at how this divide is exploited by politicians in the employ of the capitalist class to keep the American people divided and unaware of the true source of the disintegration of their lives. It discusses the origins of the Council on Foreign Relations and the Trilateral Commission and how these think tanks have served to forward the American capitalists' agenda both within the American society and abroad. The chapter discusses the Trilateralist publication, *The Crisis of Democracy*, which speaks about the "democratic distemper" of the 1960's and 1970's as a major threat to the elites and sets the course for the Trilateralists' control of every US presidency since that of Jimmy Carter, including Democratic and Republican presidencies alike. The chapter then takes a look at the ideology of conservatism in America as it was born of the Southern Baptist Churches following the civil war and made its way through American fundamentalism and American evangelicalism to the more current activities by Baptist religious leaders to gain power through such organizations as the Christian Voice, the Moral Majority, and Charismatic Christianity. It takes this development through the formation of the Tea Party and the Presidency of Donald Trump. It looks at the underlying idea of Christian Reconstructionism, which has become the grand strategy for southern white Christian control of the US government and the imposition of biblical law on American jurisprudence.

The chapter proceeds to look at the ideology of American Liberalism. It defines liberal values and looks at the rise of American liberalism out of liberal Christianity during the Age of the Enlightenment. It then looks at the rise of secular liberalism and the groups that have grown to support the values of this worldview, including the Progressives, NeoLiberals, the New Left, the Greens, and the Occupy Movement.

The chapter looks at how the ideologies of the liberal Left and the conservative Right are used by the capitalists and the politicians in their employ to keep the American people divided along ideological lines. It explains how conservative and liberal ideologies lack any capacity to motivate Americans as a whole to work for the common good. In conclusion, the chapter contends that Americans require an entirely new ideology, a new theory and practice and mode of behavior to unify the Left and the Right and salvage the future of the country and the planet.

In Chapter Three, we discuss the role of the warrior class in the United States and its role in empire building since World War II. The chapter begins with definitions of militarism and the American military-industrial complex. It explores the grand military strategy of "Containment" whose intention was to prevent the growth of Communism after WWII. It looks at the wars in Korea and Vietnam as examples of this strategy put into operation. With the fall of the Soviet Union and the end of the "Cold War," the military-industrial complex required a new enemy to justify its existence. In fact, it required an entirely new plan to forward its goal of global conquest. The articulation of such a strategy was first derived from the Trilateralist publication, *The Grand Chessboard*, published in 1997. This Neo-Liberal strategy focused on global dominance through the control of Eurasia, which includes the Near East, Middle East, and India. Shortly thereafter, the Republican Neo-Conservatives came up with a similar strategy. It was the merger of these strategic plans that guided the Bush/Cheney administration and then the Obama administration in their quest to dominate the world through economic imperialism buttressed by military force. Before moving forward with an analysis of American foreign policy, Chapter Three looks at the "domestic" strategy of population control, which authorized the creation of a police state that will increasingly be used to control the American people to the degree that the elites feel is necessary. The final step in the creation of an American police state will be a declaration of a "national emergency" at which time Americans will completely lose all of our civil and human rights. The chapter looks at the Secure Communities program, the Militarization of the Domestic Police, the National Defense Authorization Act, and Executive Order 13603.

The chapter then turns back to the question of foreign policy and the new grand strategy called the "War on Terrorism." It defines the elite's definition of "terror" and examines the current state of western capitalism in the Middle East. Having equated the concept of "terrorism" with anyone who resists their incursion into the Middle East to confiscate oil supplies, the new "enemy" is now identified as "Islamic Fundamentalism." The chapter looks at the development of Islamic Fundamentalism from the period after WWI when the French and English colonized the region. It then looks at 9/11, the event that shook the world and provided the trigger to unleash an international war on terrorism, a war without end or national boundary. It looks at the role of the Bush/Cheney administration in this event. The chapter looks at the rise of Osama bin Laden to Public Enemy #1 and the stultifying dogmatism inherent in Islamic fundamentalism. It discusses the Arab Spring and the wars in Libya, Afghanistan, Kuwait, Iraq, Syria, and Yemen. It looks at the failed US military's attempt at counterinsurgency through the strategy of "nation building." It looks at what it was like to be a soldier fighting a war in the Middle East and how our soldiers were treated by the US government on their return from war. The chapter concludes with an analysis of the military-industrial complex' war profiteering. It looks at how these particular capitalists create chaos through the strategy of divide and conquer abroad, and how they are able to sell arms to both sides in a conflict thereby creating a war without end.

Part Two looks at America from the perspective of the 'average American' living in the middle and lower classes. It looks at the lives of those who comprise the ninety-nine percent. It paints a picture of our lives as we struggle with a pseudo-culture defined by advertising, TV news, and entertainment, that continues to titillate us with sex and violence, as we struggle with credit card debt, and find ourselves more isolated and frightened of each other. The American pseudo-culture is not a culture that brings us together as a people. Rather it is intended to keep us docile, exploitable, and anxious about tomorrow.

Part Two looks at our home life and how many Americans are having to face uncontrollable debt, domestic violence, drug and alcohol addiction, and diet-related diseases. It looks at what it means to make ends meet in America.

Chapter Four, which begins Part Two, looks at who we are as American people. It looks at the characteristics by which we identify ourselves, our age, gender, race, class, religion, and national ancestry and attempts to define us as Americans by an analysis of these variables. Chapter Five looks at the major social forces that impact us as a people today. These include unemployment and debt, political polarization, national security and government spying, immigration, destruction of the environment, and climate change. Chapter Six explores the struggle for many of us in American society to meet our basic needs, which include food, shelter, clothing, health care, and education. The chapter looks at the multinational corporations that produce the goods and services required to meet these needs and demonstrates how they continue to degrade the quality of these goods and services in order to generate greater profits for themselves.

The Conclusion of this book summarizes the tenets of the capitalist master plan for world domination and how it has been put into practice by the intellectual and military elites of this country. It contends that despite their best efforts, things are not necessarily going as planned, neither domestically nor internationally, yet the elite will stick to their plan regardless of its consequences. The conclusion also projects certain consequences that we can expect to occur in the near future as a result of continuing the elite's plan for world conquest. These developments will occur regardless of whether the Democrats or Republicans control the White House or the Senate. Finally, the conclusion sets the stage for the Books 2 and 3 of *History, Ideology, and Revolution*, which focus on Ideology and Revolution. Book 2 on Ideology presents us with a new worldview, which has the power to unify us as a people and move us beyond the divide and conquer tactics of the Left and the Right. It addresses what it means to be a human being from a physical, mental, and spiritual perspective. It informs us how to create the optimum balance between the needs of the individual and the needs of the collective in a new society. Book 3, on Revolution, shows us how to put such a unifying world view into practice. It is based upon the principles of spiritual unity, economic decentralization, and economic democracy. It allows us to work with our neighbors across ideological divides and to take our future as human beings into our own hands.

Chapter One: American Capitalists in the Global Economy

Just pray God the biblical promise is true:
The poor ye shall always have with you.[8]
Organized greed always defeats disorganized democracy.[9]
Economic power implies a choice not to share.[10]

IN OUR HISTORY OF capitalism, we have learned the following. Capitalism is a system controlled by the economically powerful to serve their objective of amassing wealth at the expense of labor and the environment. The system is characterized by: (1) a *social class structure* composed of private owners and workers, (2) *private ownership* of the means of production, (3) the *production of goods and services* for sale, and (4) the organization of capital to facilitate *ever-expanding profit* for the private owners.

The elements required for the success of capitalism are: (1) arrangements made by governments and corporations to insure a dependable supply of wage labor; (2) a division of that labor; (3) a level of production sufficient to permit sustained investment; (4) the organization of the market large enough to consume the goods and services produced; (5) a political process whereby economic power is benefitted by governmental policy; (6) a legal structure that protects private property above meeting social needs; and (7) a certain capacity to tolerate new ways of making a living.[11]

The above elements had existed in the American economy from the time of the Robber Barons and the institution of the Federal Reserve

Bank in 1913. From this point on, American capitalism made three contributions to the growth of global capitalism. The first was the printing of paper money to fund a world war. The second was the invention of the modern multinational central bank and the third was the globalization of the capitalist economy under the American capitalist class.

When World War II ended, the United States was the supreme empire in the world. Its cities were intact, its industrial economy was in full swing, and its banks, under the control of the Federal Reserve Bank, were in a position to reconstruct the world's political economy under their domination. This new system called "Globalization" is the final stage in the development of capitalism as a political economy. We might call it Global State Monopoly Capitalism. We have now entered a period of time that historians call *Pax Americana* (Peace of America). The term is a reference to *Pax Britannica* or *Pax Romana*, the periods of the British and Roman empires. Pax Americana signifies the hegemony of wealth and power controlled by the United States within the period of contemporary history. It refers to the "peace" that has existed between the great powers for the last seventy years, largely because of America's military hegemony.[12] The "peace" does not, of course, mean world peace, but a relative tranquility in which the economies of the western world specifically were allowed to prosper and came to dominate the world's economy.

The American administration, under the auspices of the Council on Foreign Relations, the State Department, and the Office of Strategic Services, (the original name for the CIA), began to prepare for this eventuality as early as 1940. Three priorities were established: (1) reconstruct Europe, (2) contain Communism, and (3) take over the third world colonies to gain access to their cheap labor and natural resources.

Federal Reserve Bank

If we are to understand the political and economic dynamics of the world since the end of WWII, we must first understand how money works. When we understand this, we will understand how the Federal Reserve

Bank operates and how the United States became the global empire that it is today. We will also begin to understand what needs to be done, if we are to develop a viable alternative to the bankers' destruction of the earth and its people. We have discussed aspects of this mechanism in previous chapters but as the capitalist economy evolved and the bankers increased their stranglehold over human society, it is good to have a complete understanding of how they continue to do this. This section will look at the Federal Reserve Bank of the United States, for it is this bank that changed the economics of the global economy in WWI and WWII and set the stage for developing the internationalization of global capital through the mechanisms of the World Bank and the International Monetary Fund (IMF).

As we have discovered, it is not that a handful of our democratically elected leaders have not tried to create a national bank under the control of the people, but the bankers have always overpowered the US government and established their supremacy. They have been able to accomplish this by buying politicians to do their bidding and by using their mass media to befuddle the public. It is also not a coincidence that assassination attempts had been made against the four presidents who had tried to nationalize the bank. These were Andrew Jackson, James A. Garfield, Abraham Lincoln, and John F. Kennedy. Kennedy was the only president to challenge the Bank in the twentieth century.

Contrary to popular belief, the Federal Reserve Bank is not subject to the laws of the nation. Regarding their august status, Alan Greenspan, a former chairman of the Bank, put it simply: "The Federal Reserve is under the administration of no federal authority."[3] Basically, nobody can tell the bankers what to do. The word "federal" in the bank's name is a ruse meant to confuse the common people. There is nothing federal about the Federal Reserve. They can be traitors to America if it benefits them and they can destroy the country in the interest of their own profits. There is nothing the politicians or judges can legally do about it. In plain language, we are all slaves to the bankers. Neither the Republican Party nor the Democratic Party can change that. The only thing that could be done is if Congress and the President abolish the bank and set up a national bank, but they cannot do this because the nation is so deeply indebted to the bankers that it would lead to a cataclysmic global depression if they did so. This is not to say that the bank cannot be defeated but it would require a revolutionary socio-economic strategy, which would entail people cooperating to provide their own basic necessities. This would require a popular revolution to decentralize the economy regarding basic needs.

For those who would free themselves from control of the bankers, we first must know who controls us and by what means they continue to do so. In this struggle against the Bank, we need to understand that the majority of the world's people are in its debt and the American people are no exception.

Who Controls the Bank Today?

To ask "who controls the Federal Reserve Bank?" is to ask "who controls humanity?" The answer to this question has been a well-guarded secret for centuries and is therefore almost impossible to decipher. One of the latest attempts to answer this question was made by author Dean Henderson,[14] but he was denied access to information by bank regulatory agencies on the grounds of "national security." Nonetheless, his research has produced these findings: Ten private banks control all twelve Federal Reserve Bank branches. These are N. M. Rothschild of London,[15] Rothschild Bank of Berlin,[16] Warburg Bank of Hamburg,[17] Warburg Bank of Amsterdam,[18] Lehman Brothers of New York,[19] Lazard Brothers of Paris,[20] Kuhn Loeb Bank of New York (American Express),[21] Israel Moses Seif Bank of Italy,[22] Goldman Sachs of New York [23] and J. P. Morgan Chase Bank of New York."[24] Today some of these banks no longer exist and others have merged.

Nonetheless, Henderson demonstrates that throughout the history of capitalism, eight banking families have come to prevail and it is they who now dominate the US economy and the world economy. These families are the Rothschilds, Warburgs, Lehmans, Lazards, Kuhn Loebs, Sachs, Morgans, and Rockefellers.

The intent of these international banking families today can be witnessed in their creation of a global economy (globalization) under their control. While the super-rich create a media "spin" that globalization is an inevitable course of nature, the bankers continue to hide their identities just as they did when they formed the Federal Reserve Bank in 1913. The mass media, which they own, is quick to label any information that attempts to expose their private central banking cartel as a "conspiracy theory."[25] Yet the facts remain.[26] The Federal Reserve Bank will not reveal its owners. The only thing they will admit is that the Bank is controlled by its private bank shareholders. On the international level, there is also an International Monetary Fund[27] and World Bank[28] set up on a model of the Federal Reserve Bank. Neither of these banks are democratically controlled either.

While the bankers remain silent, their think tanks, specifically the Council on Foreign Relations[29] and the Trilateral Commission[30] have revealed in their in-house publications and through their actions that the international elites act specifically to dominate the world economy. We also have organizations like the Bilderberg Group, which brings the ruling elite together to discuss problems confronting their new world order.[31] Their discussions are never made public.

How Do the Bankers Control the US Government?

In 1913, it was clear to everyone that a "bank of banks" was necessary to act as a referee that could stabilize the country's money supply during panics. This was necessary to promote economic growth and prevent depressions. Before the creation of the Fed, banks throughout the country issued their own bank notes based on their own assets (gold, loan portfolios, etc.). The bank notes served as a medium of exchange because people knew if they accepted a bank note in exchange for goods or services, they could go to the bank and cash in the note for gold. With every bank issuing its own currency, however, travel over distances created a problem. A bank in New York might not accept banknotes from Illinois or California. A central bank, however, could solve this problem. In this system, banks would deposit some of their assets in the Fed and in return they would receive bank notes that served as a national currency, acceptable anywhere. In the beginning, the Fed could not print money at will as it does today; it was limited by the assets that it held from other banks. In essence, the Fed was simply trying to match the supply of money with the demand for money. When the economy was expanding, they would pump in cash (Federal Reserve Notes), and when it was contracting, it would take out cash.[32] Of course, there was the matter of *interest* that banks paid for their Federal Reserve Notes. Money has a price tag called the interest rate.

If this was the case, how did the situation come about where the Fed came to control the US government? Why is the world in debt to the Fed? As we have learned in Volume Four, the bankers control governments by controlling their bonds, i.e., the IOUs of the government. The debt of almost every country in the world today is a result of manipulation by the big banking elites.

The British economist John Maynard Keynes, before World War II, originally proposed the theory that government debt could serve as a driver of economic activity. He argued that business decisions, in contrast to the "invisible hand" theory of Adam Smith, often led to negative economic consequences like panics and depressions. These sometimes are too severe for the economy to self-correct and therefore require action by the central bankers and the government to stabilize the economy.[33] Today, Keynesian economists advocate a mixed economy, which although remaining predominantly controlled by the private sector, also has a role for government intervention in times of economic downturns. This intervention may take the form of bank bailouts or injections of great amounts of currency into the system to kick start a trashed economy (Quantitative Easing).

Keynes justified intervention in the economy on the part of the government. In doing so, he provided the rationale for the ultimate collaboration between the bankers and the federal government. This idea built upon the system of *state monopoly capitalism*, which began with the partnership between J. P. Morgan and Theodore Roosevelt. It is through this system that the bankers were able to completely control the federal government.

The first thing to understand about how Keynesian theory is applied by the Federal Reserve Bank today is that money is not created until the instant it is borrowed by the federal government. The amount of currency in circulation is directly proportional to the debt of the government to the bankers. Paper money (currency) is basically monetized debt, i.e., it is government debt turned into money. We may think that our financial system is based on gold, which actually is real money, but it is not. It is based on Federal Reserve Notes that are issued only after the federal government borrows money from it.

A stockpile of Federal Reserve Notes in a vault is not really money, it is only paper, until it is borrowed. Borrowing creates money and paying off the debt causes money to vanish back into nothing again. This is worth remembering because if the government were to pay off all its debt, there would be no "money" circulating in the economy.

As we continue our description of how the bankers control the government, never take your eyes off this simple fact. The Federal Reserve Bank, which is privately owned, has the legal authority to loan money to the federal government, which it gets by printing money on a printing press, which costs them nothing, and then it sells it to others, including our government for a price. Through this sleight of hand, our country goes deeper and deeper into debt, and so does every other branch of government and the American people as well. Everyone and every organization is indebted to the big bankers.

The result of this trap, according to Ronald Reagan's Grace Commission is that, "one hundred percent of what is collected [in taxes] is absorbed solely by interest on the Federal Debt . . . all individual income tax revenues are gone before one nickel is spent on the services taxpayers expect from government."[34] Our system literally depends on the creation of continuously greater debt loads in perpetuity, and if new borrowers cannot be enticed into taking out loans, the whole economy collapses, leaving the bankers in control of everything (plus interest).

Republican Representative Ron Paul of Texas, who had introduced legislation to Audit the Fed, explained the ramifications of the Fed's control of money. "Due to nearly a century of inflationary monetary policy on the part of the Federal Reserve, the US dollar stands at historically low levels. Investors around the world are shunning the dollar, and millions of Americans see their salaries, savings accounts, and pensions eroded away by rising inflation." He added, "We stand on the precipice of an unprecedented monetary collapse, and as a result many people have begun to look for alternatives to the dollar."[35]

The consequences of monetary central planning on the part of the big bankers led Nobel Prize-winning economist Friedrich A. Hayek to believe that the continuation of civilization itself depended on ending the corrupt process. He mistakenly blamed government instead of the bankers for the problem, however. He wrote in *The Denationalization of Money*, "The only way to avoid being driven by continuing inflation into a controlled and directed economy, and therefore ultimately in order to save civilization, will be to deprive governments of their power over the supply of money."[36] The greatest minds in economics—from Ludwig von Mises to Murray Rothbard—have echoed his concerns.

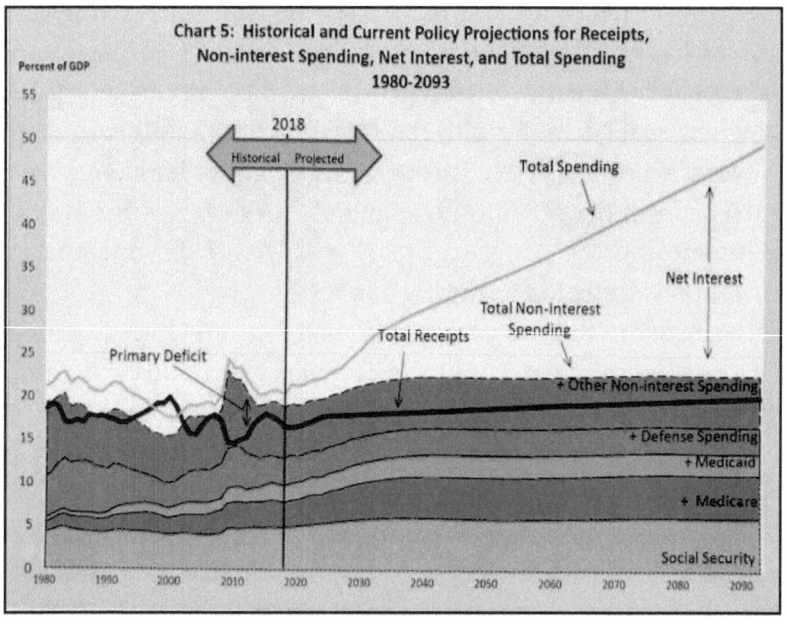

Fig. 5-1: Interest vs Certain Government Programs

Currently the US national debt as a share of the economy is a ravaging seventy-eight percent.[37] As the above chart demonstrates, in 2015, the net interest payment on debt was greater than all the money spent on pollution control, food and nutrition assistance, higher education and unemployment benefits combined. If we had done what Thomas

Jefferson, Andrew Jackson, Abraham Lincoln, and John F. Kennedy wanted to do, we could have used our money for these purposes.

Only the big US-based multinational banks and corporations are the beneficiaries of this system. The Federal Reserve, along with providing the US government with money for its projects, also provides the private monopolies with enough cash to set up the projects they need to expropriate labor and raw materials from the world's people. These big banks and corporations have the first crack at the money supply and thus pay a smaller price for it than we do when we need to borrow it from them. This advantage allows the multinationals to buy the natural resources, machines and other means of production, including our labor, to control the economy and the goods and services produced. Americans, and the world, have become enslaved by this simple process. No wonder the bankers keep it shrouded in mystery and use such a complex, unintelligible, and abstruse language to describe their activities. It is why Henry Ford said, "It is well enough that people of the nation do not understand our banking and monetary system, for if they did, I believe there would be a revolution before tomorrow morning."[38]

Just as the Federal Reserve Bank is a cartel,[39] so it is linked in the larger banking system which is also composed of cartels. Through this network the US and European banks have dominated the world economy for the last several hundred years.

The object of the money game as played by the Federal Reserve Bank is simple. It is to provide the federal government and US-based multinational corporations with the money to support US domination of the world's economy. A second objective is to shift inevitable losses from the bankers to the taxpayers. This is the predatory intention of the richest people in the world. It is how they get rich and how they stay rich. The name of the game is debt creation.

Debt: An Overview

In 1994, a man named G. Edward Griffin wrote a book called *The Creature from Jekyll Island: A Second Look at the Federal Reserve Bank*.[40] It is a testament to Griffin's genius that he was able to figure out the rules by which bankers control money and the dynamics by which they are able to skim money from people.

While economists dedicate themselves at the altar of the "dismal science," creating endless charts and graphs that do nothing but confuse the situation and while the true intentions of the banking cartel is disguised by confused and fragmented news stories in the mainstream media, the underlying truth of capitalist exploitation is discovered by looking at the established rules of the game that the bankers have set for themselves. The rules never change, nor does the banking elite that controls the game. Let's take a look at some of these rules.

The entire function of the Federal Reserve Bank is to convert debt into money. As the US government expands its military and its social programs, it does not have the tax base to pay for these costs. As we have seen, the entire tax receipts are used to pay off the interest on the government debt to the bankers. To get the money they need, therefore, the government has to take out further loans from the Bank. It does this by printing treasury notes, or what are also called government bonds. The bonds are the IOUs issued by the government to the Bank. By issuing bonds, the government is saying, make us a loan and within a specified period of time, we will pay back the amount of the loan along with interest. The Bank then sells these IOUs on behalf of the Treasury Department on the open market to other countries, banks, businesses, individuals, etc. The IOUs, of course, pay a premium above their face value which is the incentive for people to buy the debt paper.

Any bonds that are not bought by the public are then "bought" by the Federal Reserve Bank itself, which takes the bonds and writes a check for them, to the government. There is no actual money to back up this check. Rather the Fed prints money to buy the bonds on the spot. These bonds then become the Bank's "reserves." They are quite special because the Fed can now use them as the base for creating nine additional dollars for every dollar created to pay for the bonds themselves. While the money created by the Fed to buy the bonds, in the first place, is given to the federal government to spend however they like, the money created on top of those bonds (nine additional dollars for every dollar) is the source of all bank loans made to the nation's banks and big businesses.

The bottom line is that Congress and the banking cartel have entered into a partnership in which the cartel has the privilege of collecting interest on money, which it creates out of nothing. Congress, on the other hand, has access to unlimited funding without having to tell the voters their taxes are being raised. This also permits the government to side step the scrutiny of their actions that would come with increased taxes. It is not that the government is not taxing the US citizens through this process. The tax in this instance is called *inflation*. Our money buys less each year. This is the essence of the US monetary system. It allows for unlimited spending and unlimited debt. This limitless spending provides the finance capital by which the multinational banks and corporations are able to control the wealth of other nations and that of the American people. This limitless spending is used for warfare, to fund insurgencies, to destroy the planet, and every possible action to diminish our stature as human beings.

How the Bank Makes the Money

The federal government uses a specially made paper and adds ink to the front and back surfaces and creates impressive designs and calls the paper a *"bond"* or *"Treasury Note."* To convert these IOUs into paper bills and checkbook money is the function of the Federal Reserve Bank. To bring about this transformation, the bond is given to the Fed where it is classified as a reserve, more specifically a "Securities Asset." The bond is considered an asset because it is assumed that the government will keep its promise to pay insofar as it has the ability to tax the American people. So the Fed now has an 'asset' that can be used to offset a liability of equal value. It then creates this liability by adding ink to another piece of paper and giving it to the government in return for the asset. This second piece of paper is called a *"Federal Reserve Note."* It is what we think of as money. Yet there is no money in any account to actually cover this note. It is only based on the government's IOU. For everyone else, writing a check with nothing to back it up would be fraud and result in imprisonment. The Fed, however, has the legal right to commit fraud, simply because the politicians need the money for all their projects without having to raise taxes. On the books everything is "balanced" because the liability of the money is offset by the "asset" of the IOU. In summary, the government prints bonds (IOUs) and sells them to the Fed at an interest rate that needs to be paid at some future date. In response, the Fed prints money (Federal Reserve Notes) that it gives to the government in the amount of the bonds that it buys.

The Federal Reserve Notes received by the government in exchange for its IOUs are then endorsed and sent to one of the Federal Reserve Banks where they now become a "*Government Deposit..* This deposit can now be used to pay government expenses and is thus transformed into "*Government Checks.*" These checks become the first wave of new fiat money to flood the economy. Recipients of these government checks now deposit them into their own bank accounts where they become "*Commercial Bank Deposits.*" Commercial Bank deposits immediately take on a split personality. On the one hand, they are *liabilities* to the bank because they are owed back to the depositors. But as long as they remain in the bank, they are also considered an asset, because they can be used to make money when the bankers loan them out. Therefore, the books are once again balanced—the assets offset the liabilities. But now comes the sweet part for the bankers. Through a mechanism called "*Fractional Reserve Banking,*" the deposits are made to serve an additional purpose. The on-hand deposits in the bank are now "reclassified" in the books and called "*Bank Reserves.*" Having given the name "reserves" to the deposits, the bankers can now use these deposits as a base to materialize even larger amounts of fiat money.

Here is how it works. Through Fractional Reserve Banking, the banks are permitted by the Fed to hold as little as ten percent of their deposits as "reserves." For example, if they receive one million dollars, in the first wave of fiat money from the Fed, they have nine hundred thousand dollars more than they are required to keep on hand (one million dollars less ten percent reserves). This nine hundred thousand dollars is now called "*Excess Reserves.*" As such this money is now available for lending and is converted into "*Bank Loans.*"

You may ask how is it possible to loan out this money when it is still owned by previous depositors who are still free to write checks against it, withdraw cash, etc. The answer is that when the new loans are made, they are not made with the same money. They are made with brand new money created out of thin air again. The nation's money supply just increased by ninety percent of the banks' reserves. The "old" money received from depositors requires the bankers to pay interest and perform services for the privilege of using it. But with the "new" money, the bankers can make loans at an interest rate or they can buy what they want for themselves, buildings, land, labor, etc. This allows the banks to control our labor as well as our natural resources before we even have an opportunity to know what is happening. It does not stop here. As the second wave of fiat money enters the economy through fractional lending, it comes right back into the banking system, just as the first wave did, in the form of more *"Commercial Deposits."*

The process now repeats with ten percent less for loans each time around. If a loan is made on Friday, it becomes a deposit on Monday. The deposit is reclassified as a reserve and ninety percent of that becomes an excess reserve which once again is available to loan. In the first wave one million dollars produces nine hundred thousand dollars; in the second wave it produces eight hundred and ten thousand dollars; in the third wave it produces seven hundred and twenty thousand dollars, etc. It takes about twenty-eight times for the process to play itself out. In this way, government debt underlies the money supply for the economy. The government debt creates a money supply more than twenty-five times the amount of the original government debt.

The Connection between Work and Debt

Now that we know how money is created out of government debt, we must ask ourselves, where does the money to pay the interest to the bankers come from? Let's look at a typical example. If we borrow ten thousand dollars at nine percent we will owe the bank ten thouand nine hundred dollars but the bank does not create the nine hundred dollars out of nothing as it does the principal. Where then does it come from? Basically, the interest payment comes out of human labor. This is the reality of our connection to the bankers' magic trick. This is the part that enslaves us to the system. Here is how it works. Let us assume that you pay back your ten thousand dollar loan at about nine hundred dollars per month, of which eighty dollars is your monthly interest payment. This eighty dollars is profit to the bank that they can spend any way that they want. It is not extinguished, as is the principal on the loan as each payment is made. So, this remains as spendable money for the bank. Let us say the bank decides it wants its floors washed and waxed once a week. You find yourself in a pinch for money so you apply for the job at eighty dollars per month. The result is that you earn the money to pay back the interest through your labor. As long as you perform labor for the bank each month, the same dollars go back into the bank as interest. Then back to you as wages, then back to the bank as interest payment.

In the larger picture, it is not necessary for you to work for the bank. No matter where you earn the money, its origin was a bank and its ultimate destination is a bank. The loop through which the money travels can be large or small, but the fact remains all interest is repaid eventually by human labor.

As G. Edward Griffin explains the process:

> . . . the total of this human effort ultimately is for the benefit of those who create fiat money. It is a form of modern serfdom in which the great mass of society works as indentured servants to a ruling class of financial nobility.[41]

Inflation and Deflation

If the money created out of government debt exceeds that required to meet the exchange of goods and services, prices go up, and the value of money goes down. This is called *inflation*. If the Fed grows the money supply by three percent per year this raises the prices accordingly. But if your wages do not rise along with inflation, your purchasing power is reduced by three perceent. Inflation serves as a hidden tax on the population. While some wages and salaries may rise to adjust for inflation, most do not. Thus, inflation is another means by which the rich get richer and the poor get poorer. The middle class gets squeezed in the middle. As we have seen, since the last bubble bust and bailout, ten percent of the middle class has disappeared and is no longer in the majority. The jobs will not be coming back at the income level once experienced.

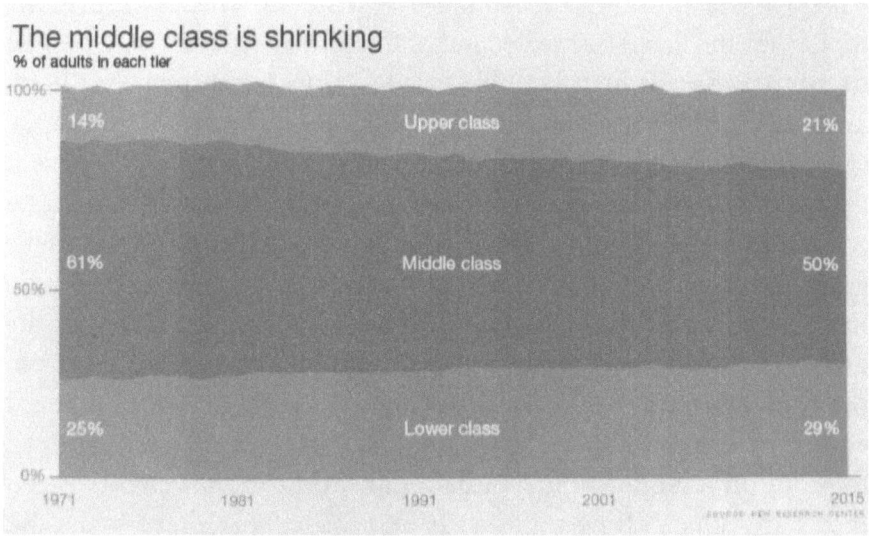

Fig. 5-2: Shrinking Middle Class
(Courtesy of the Pew Research Center)

On the other hand, if the money created out of government debt is not enough to meet the amount required to meet the exchange of goods and services, prices go down and the value of money goes up. This is called *deflation*. Both inflation and deflation have a negative impact on the economy and people's lives.

Bad Debts

The rules of the game have to do with creating money out of government debt and keeping track of what was created through an accounting process. The rules determine how bankers keep score. The exploitation of people by the big banks actually begins when the Federal Reserve Bank allows commercial banks to create checkbook money out of nothing. The banks derive profit from this unearned money, not by spending it, but by lending it to people and collecting interest on the loan.

If a borrower cannot repay the loan the bankers take his assets, for example, his car or house, or garnish his wages. If the borrower has no assets, however, the bank must "write off" the loan. Since the money for the loan was created out of thin air (except for some clerical overhead) there is little tangible loss of value. It is primarily a book keeping entry.

A bookkeeping loss is still bad for the bank, however, because it causes the loan as an asset to be removed from the ledger without a reduction in liabilities. In other words, the bankers must still make good on those cancelled checks that the borrower spent. They can do this in two ways. They can draw upon the capital investment of the owners (stock holders of the bank) or they can deduct the loss from the bank's current profits. In either case, the owners lose an amount equal to the amount of the money not paid back. If the bank is forced to write-off a large amount of bad loans, the amount could exceed the entire value of the bank's equity and the bank is forced to declare bankruptcy and goes out of business. We have seen this happen before, most recently after the housing bubble collapse in 2007, when even the multi-national banks faced bankruptcy.

For smaller banks that are owned locally this is a genuine concern. Because they are more susceptible to bad loans, they are more cautious about making big loans. But for those with an "in" at the Federal Reserve, those big international banks that are owned by Fed members or those in their network, this is not the case. These big banks can loan as much money as their corporate elite desire in order to buy up companies, exploit resources, manipulate the stock market, etc., without consequence of default. This is because they fall under the "Too Big to Fail" category.[42]

At this point, there is no level playing field between the small banks and the big banks. If a small bank fails, a big bank buys its assets for a song. If a big bank fails, the government bails it out. This is another way that wealth is extracted from localities and centralized in the hands of the global banks.

The Bankers' Play Book

Now that we understand the rules, let us look at some of the "plays" the big banks use to bring us under their domination. Griffin discusses six strategies that he calls: (1) the Perpetual Debt Play, (2) the Debt Roll-Over Play, (3) the Up-The-Ante Play, (4) the Rescheduling Play, (5) the Protect the Public Play, and (6) the Guaranteed Payment Play. Let us take a quick look at these six maneuvers that trap the average person, corporation, or government into a debt, which becomes more inescapable as the relationship with the bank unfolds.

The Perpetual Debt Play

One result of the big banks being protected from loss no matter what they do is that they have little reason to be cautious. The larger the loan they can make, the better it is because it will create the most profit for the least amount of effort. A single loan for five hundred million dollars is just as easy to process as a loan of fifty thousand dollars. If the five hundred million is repaid with interest, it is "bonus" time for the bankers. If the recipient defaults on the loan, however, the federal government will ensure that the bank does not go bankrupt. After all, the public must be protected.

It must be remembered that because the banks make their money on interest, they do not want to be quickly repaid. If a loan is paid too quickly, the bank must find another customer. It is therefore much better to have the original customer pay only interest and never make payments on the original loan itself. This is the chief method by which bankers keep us continually in debt. Think about your credit card. Why are interest rates set so high? It is part of the "perpetual debt play" strategy that keeps you making the "minimum monthly payment." Your principle is never repaid because you have to keep paying the high interest rate each month. You keep paying the interest for years. Now think about the federal government. It borrows money but never pays back the debt. It continually borrows and then borrows more to pay the interest on what it owes.

The Debt Roll-Over Play

It is more profitable for the big banks to make large loans even if unsound. When the borrower cannot pay, the banks simply "roll-over the loan." This appears as a concession, but it is actually another step toward the goal of creating perpetual interest. To make the roll-over play, the banks use the money they "created out of nothing" and lend it to the borrower so that he will be able to keep paying the interest on the old loan. Thus, the disaster of customer default is changed into a brilliant play. The old loan is maintained as an asset on the books and has now grown, thereby leading to higher interest payments and greater profit.

The Up-The-Ante Play

After a while the borrower becomes nervous. He is in a situation where he is making interest payments with nothing left for himself. This happens quite often with third world governments. The government realizes that all its tax receipts are only going to the bank so it stops paying the interest. Now the bank's lawyers are called in. The borrower refuses to pay and the banks threaten to black ball the borrower so that he will never again be able to borrow money from any bank. Finally, a "compromise" is worked out. The bank agrees to produce more money out of nothing. This new money allows the borrower to pay the interest, but there is also a kicker in that the borrower receives extra money to use in anyway he chooses. The borrower now has money to pay the interest and continue his own pursuits. The bankers have a larger loan, higher interest payments and more profits. The game is proceeding well. This play can be repeated several times until reality finally dawns on the borrower that it has sunk into a pit of debt with no way out.

The Rescheduling Play

Once this reality dawns on the borrower, the roll-over approach is completely rejected and default on the debt appears inevitable. Again, the lawyers come into the game and a new game-saving play is put into motion. The loan has now been "rescheduled." This means that the interest rate is lowered and the payments are extended out over a longer period of time. This is purely cosmetic, but it creates the feeling in the borrower that the burden is not so heavy and easier to carry. But it also makes the repayment of the loan more unlikely. It postpones the day of reckoning and the loan remains an asset and the interest payments continue. The play is not only pulled on individuals and small businesses, but it is also pulled on third world governments with great success.

The Protect-The-Public Play

Eventually the day of reckoning arrives. The borrower knows he can never pay the debt and refuses to make any more interest payments. If the borrower is an individual or small business, he may declare bankruptcy or insolvency and the banks will take what they can and swallow the loss. In most cases, the interest payments have already exceeded the original outlay of the loan. The borrower has been bled dry and there is nothing more to do. If the borrower is a larger corporation or a government, however, the banks still have a final maneuver. The lawyers and executives from both sides get together under the arbitration of a senior bank or government institution like the IMF to seek a means to continue the game. The reason ostensibly is that it is in "the public interest" to do so. Witness what went on with Greece, Spain, Italy, and Ireland over the last few years. The drama that we watched Greece go through has been played innumerable times with the governments of third world countries. This is the major mechanism by which they have been bled dry. As a consequence, the banks take control of the country's public infrastructure and impose draconian constraints on any government spending. These are called "austerity measures" that the people must now suffer. These austerity measures are "legitimized" by the International Monetary

Fund (IMF). Austerity programs include the termination of public expenditures on children's programs, health care, education, and other social service programs. Instead, this money is now paid to the bankers.

The Big Bailout

After the bubble burst on the real estate market in 2007, as a result of bank corruption, the government rushed in to bail out the big banks. Both the Bush and the Obama administrations were complicit in this bailout. The government and corporate elite went on talk shows and were quoted in the media saying that without a bailout of the big banks, the entire banking system would fail and chaos would ensue. The banks had to be saved at all cost.

The American public was bled for an additional seven hundred billion dollars to bail out the banks.[43] The Bailout of the Big Banks consists of the "Protect-The-Public" standard maneuver in the bankers' playbook. The only difference from the other plays is the scope of the bailout. Instead of only one bank or corporation or third world country facing default, the entire banking elite of the US and Europe faced the end game. While the scope was staggering and forced the world to think in terms of trillions of dollars' worth of debt, instead of tens of billions, the maneuver was basically the same. In this case, the lender bank was the Federal Reserve Bank and the hapless borrowers were the cartel of international bankers themselves who found themselves, through their own greed and lack of due diligence, vastly over-extended in the housing mortgage debacle.

Under these circumstances, Secretary of the Treasury, Henry Paulson, who worked for Goldman Sachs before becoming Secretary, and the other finance officers of the big banks went to Congress (the referee) and told them that the banks had exhausted their ability to absorb the losses they encountered due to housing defaults and that if Congress did not bail out the banks, the entire banking system would collapse and the US, even the entire world economy, would be thrown into a deep depression in which there would be no escape. What is needed, they argued with great passion, was for Congress to provide enough money to the banks either directly or indirectly (through the Fed) to pay for the banks' loses (debts) and have enough money left over to jump start the economy. The members of Congress, deeply beholding to the banks for their jobs, agreed and put the American people in debt to cover the bad loans of the banks. While the banks came out scot-free, suffering no punishment or injury for their corruption, the world was thrown into a worldwide recession/depression in which millions of people lost their jobs, their savings, and their homes, because of the banks' actions. In a final slap in the face to Americans, the percentage of the loan made to the banks that was supposed to jumpstart the economy was never spent on the jump start. The bankers could not see a good reason to invest in the US domestic economy and used the money instead to play the stock market and to buy back their own corporate stock, thus increasing their own wealth at the expense of the people.

The Guaranteed Payment Play

A variation on the play of having the government make direct payments to the banks is to have the government provide credit to them. This means that the government will guarantee future relief to the big banks should the borrowers default on their loans. Once Congress agrees to be a party to this swindle, it becomes a co-signer on the loan and the losses are transferred from the ledgers of the bankers and placed on the backs of the American taxpayer. The American taxpayer has no idea how they have assumed the debt, they just know that since it occurred, the quality of their lives has vastly deteriorated. Jobs have become scarce, small businesses have failed, and government support for human services and education has been severely reduced. There is no money for research in the public interest. Meanwhile the banks are richer than ever and their CEOs are still able to give themselves multi-million dollar bonuses each year.

To shift the blame from themselves, the mass media, owned by the bankers, excoriate the small businessman who raises prices, or the selfish union worker who demands higher wages, or the farmer who wants more money for his crops, or the "welfare queens" for depending on welfare checks, or the blacks and Latinos for taking "American jobs." They also blame the veterans and the sick and elderly who require government services. They blame government departments that protect the environment or provide a safety net for the people. The people, befuddled by these tactics, turn to blaming each other. The Politicians, as is blatantly obvious in the Trump administration, fan the flames of ultra-nationalism, misogyny, and racism to continue the charade. As we tear each other apart, we do not notice that our nation has been diminished through the manipulations of the big bankers and their Federal Reserve System.

Money is the Federal Reserve Banks' IOU

In the section above, we looked at the bankers' playbook. It revealed the system by which government debt is created out of paper and how the debt is extended by virtue of the Federal Reserve Bank's legal right to print money at will. While we must grant the fact that money does not manage itself and that bankers do provide a valuable service to our society, their reward should be commensurate with their service. They should not have the legal permission to print money at will as a strategy to impoverish Americans and the world's people. The granting of this "privilege" by the US politicians has resulted in the enslavement of our government, businesses, and people in a perpetual manner. Such an unregulated banking system has become the means by which the bankers are allowed to destroy our health, our families, our communities, and our natural environment. Americans will never again have a prosperous and secure economy, so long as the Federal Reserve and the big banks continue to exist in an unregulated manner.

The only thing that makes a Federal Reserve Note worth anything is that the government made it *legal tender*, which means that you have no choice but to accept it as a medium of exchange in any business dealing. Dollar bills used to have "silver certificate" or "gold certificate" printed on them when paper money was based on real money. Now it is not. Take a look at any bill in your pocket and you will no longer see silver or gold certificate, instead you will see written across the top of the bill "Federal Reserve Note."

According to a Federal Reserve Bank of Chicago booklet entitled "Modern Money Mechanics" it states:

> In the United States neither paper currency nor deposits have value as commodities. Intrinsically, a dollar bill is just a piece of paper. Deposits are merely book entries. Coins do have some intrinsic value as metal, but generally far less than their face amount.
>
> What, then, makes these instruments—checks, paper money, and coins—acceptable at face value in payment of all debts and for other monetary uses? Mainly, it is the confidence people have that they will be able to exchange such money for other financial assets and real goods and services whenever they choose to do so. This partly is a matter of law; currency has been designated "legal tender" by the government – that is, it must be accepted."[44]

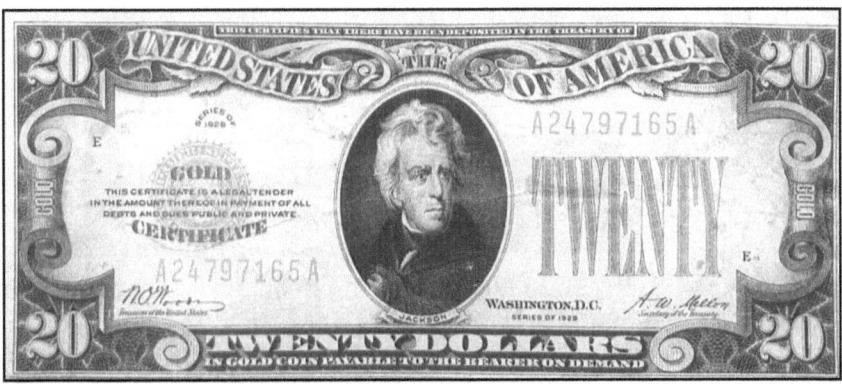

Fig. 5-3: $20 Gold Certificate

While it may be confusing to realize that our total money supply is backed by nothing but debt; it is also mind-boggling to realize that if all debt was paid back, there would be no money left in circulation. The more we pay down the government debt, the less money there will be in the economy.

Robert Hemphill, a past Credit Manager of the Federal Reserve Bank in Atlanta had this to say:

> If all the bank loans were paid, no one could have a bank deposit, and there would not be a dollar of coin or currency in circulation. This is a staggering thought. We are completely dependent on the commercial banks. Someone has to borrow every dollar we have in circulation, cash or credit. If the banks create ample synthetic money we are prosperous; if not, we starve. We are absolutely without a permanent money system. When one gets a complete grasp of the picture, the tragic absurdity of our hopeless situation is almost incredible – but there it is.[45]

This fundamental truth about the Federal Reserve monetary system belies the politicians "demand" for a balanced budget. It belies the Republicans mantra that social services for the people must be cut to balance the budget. There will never be a balanced budget so long as we have a private bank called the Federal Reserve System. The system set up by the bankers will collapse if the government stops borrowing money, and the government must continue to borrow from the Federal Reserve if it wants to add money to the economy. In this way, the government has no other option than to go further into debt.

Is it any wonder that we are continuously encouraged to buy more, even if much of what we buy is junk and lasts only a short time? Is it any wonder why our entire identity as human beings has been reduced to being mere "consumers." We are identified simply as a consumer society. Why? By having a banker-controlled Federal Reserve System, consumerism is the only way to keep the system going. The GDP (Gross Domestic Product), which measures the wealth of a nation in a capitalist system, is composed of four variables: investment, consumption, government spending, and net exports. The US economy is driven by consumption. It makes up seventy-one percent of our GDP. Compare this to China where consumption only makes up thirty-five percent of their GDP.[46]

Consumerism is essential to the strategy of the banks and corporations to continue to profit off the American people. Consumption is also the means by which we pay our taxes. We are taxed on what we buy. While the amount of taxes received by the government from the public is not enough to meet government expenses, the illusion that the government can always pay its debt, because it has the ability to collect taxes, remains the rationale for the entire debt economy that the bankers created. The ability to collect taxes creates the "trust" among the buyers of the national debt. It makes them believe that their investment is solid. While few large investors believe this anymore, they continue to believe that the world economy still revolves around the US dollar and thus everyone is pressured to "trust" its viability. This faith in the dollar as a world currency, however, is quickly slipping away because the debt of the US government is now obviously too large to ever be repaid.

The Ebb and Flow of the Economy is Based on Aggregate Supply and Demand

Under normal conditions, when the total demand for goods and services within an economy is greater than the total supply, the economy will expand to meet the demand. Conversely, when the aggregate supply is greater than the demand, the economy will slow down until the inventory of goods decreases. This is the natural movement of an economy. However, the expansion and contraction of the economy is not left to follow its natural course because the Fed and the government indiscriminately add or withdraw money from the economy as per their own desires, either for profits in the case of the bankers, or for money to run programs as in the case of the government. To a large extent, these programs are predominately related to warfare and include the buying of weaponry and the funding of invasions into other countries to expropriate their resources.

When the central bank provides too little money, the economy contracts. We go into a deflation (recession, depression). Money becomes scarce, jobs are lost, and prices become cheaper. This is because people do not have much money to spend and cannot afford higher prices. If, on the other hand, the central bank provides too much money, inflation occurs. The economy heats up and prices rise to absorb the extra money.

The natural contraction and expansion of the US economy, however, no longer exists. It has not existed since the Federal Reserve started printing money out of the blue to fund WWI. Ever since that time, the economy has continued to be manipulated by those who manage the money supply. Instead of serving the economy, the bank, along with the federal government, have come to manipulate it to suit their own ends. As we have seen, the government wants to spend more money than it receives in taxes so it borrows money from the Fed, which then changes the debt into money. This gives politicians the ability to spend money on anything that they want whenever they want. On the other hand, because the bankers want to derive profits by making loans, they are all too willing to feed the federal government's limitless thirst for more money. This situation makes it possible for the US military to be constantly engaged in colonial wars and for the government to pass seven billion dollar military budgets each year.

The deeper the federal debt, the more money the Bank prints. The more money it prints, the more money it can sell on the open market. By such a manner, the Fed is at the very heart of economic globalization. While this is great for the capitalist class, human society is so much in debt that the ability to pay back that debt becomes more remote each day. In carrying so much debt or in finding themselves unemployed or underemployed, people cannot continue to buy things like they used to. The reason that we are now living through this unending Great Recession is because so many jobs have been lost and those jobs that continue to exist pay so little that people cannot make a living even by working full time or having two jobs. As this is occurring, the national government keeps the economy on life support by increasing public debt to fund wars and certain social service programs, but these programs do not raise recipients above the poverty level. The cycle of unemployment and underemployment continues because the bankers know there are too fewer buyers for their products to start new businesses. This is the big picture. It does not hold true in specific cases, but it holds true, nonetheless, if we look at the aggregate supply and demand of the global economy. In this context, we see that the normal ebb and flow of an economy has been replaced by the boom and bust economy as a result of money manipulation. The housing boom results in the bust of the Great Recession. A boom and bust cycle is characterized by more severe periods of expansion and contraction. It is somewhat like climate change. The more toxic our environment becomes, the more severe the weather patterns.

Pundits have spoken in glowing terms about the Trump economy, but the underlying truth is quite different and we should not be surprised. Trump is a billionaire who takes care of his own. The vast sums of money that he injected into the economy through tax breaks went to the richest of the rich. And now to pay for those tax breaks, he is poised to cut major social service programs, including health care and social security. Meanwhile his tariff wars with other countries are forcing mass layoffs in manufacturing and grain to rot in the fields of desperate farmers.

The Fed has "printed" more than two trillion dollars since the Great Recession began in order to keep the banks afloat and the American people on life support.[47] Because there is poor demand, the US corporations do not want to invest in jobs to create more supply. Consequently, the money just sits in bank accounts. To stimulate the use of money the Fed and other central banks have set the price (interest rate) of money so low that it costs virtually nothing for the banks and corporations to borrow it. What do you do if you have so much money, but there is nowhere to invest it? Well, you can buy other companies that will give you greater dominance over an economic sector or allow you to profit by economizing through mergers. You can buy back shares of your own stock if you are a publicly traded company. But the biggest use of this "surplus money," even as millions of Americans struggle to keep their heads above the poverty line, is to gamble with it in the stock market.

This is the monopoly game whereby bankers, hedge fund managers, and other private "investors" manipulate the value of paper money by buying and selling stocks and bonds, national currencies, debentures, etc. In this game, the biggest payload is gained by creating stock market "bubbles" through pump and dump schemes. These bubbles shorten the boom and bust cycle of the economy, which then requires the Fed to further manipulate the money supply to prevent the economy from crashing on the downside. We will look at this fraudulent money-making technique a little later in this chapter.

A point that needs to be reinforced here is that whether the economy is expanding or contracting, the bankers make money. As we have said, money is nothing more than government debt, which we pay back through taxes, inflation, payments on loans, and the long working hours of our day. When the economy is expanding, the bankers make loans and build up profits through the interest payments on the "loans" they make. If the economy is contracting, and people fail to meet their debt obligations, the banks repossess people's cars or home or business or gouge them with high interest credit cards. The banks can legally garnish wages, foreclose on property, etc. In this way, the bankers always win. We are living in a Monopoly economy where one of the players is the banker and has an unlimited supply of money. There is no way that he can lose. When we run out of money, he keeps us in the game by loaning us money, but this only causes us to fall deeper into debt. Unfortunately, in the real world our very livelihoods, our food, our shelter, and our basic needs are at stake while the bankers keep taking our money off the table. They have gained the legal "privilege" to do this through deception, murder, greed, ruthlessness, and by the aid of corrupt and ignorant politicians whom they buy for a song by making donations to their campaigns.

The Role of Politicians in the Debt Game

We have explained how the Federal Reserve Bank makes money out of nothing by "monetizing the debt" of the US Government and, in so doing, is granted the privilege of enslaving the American people and the people of the world who are now in their debt.

We have mentioned how a handful of past presidents have tried to fight banker control and have been targeted for assassination for their efforts. We have seen in Volume 4 of *The Untold Story of Western Civilization*, how the bankers create busts and booms as means to continue to siphon wealth from the people and how they plunged the country into a depression to teach Andrew Jackson and the American people a lesson about the consequences of crossing them.

We have also seen how Andrew Jackson was able to balance the budget for the last time in US history by getting rid of the Bank.

But there is something else here that we must look at, and that is the motivation of politicians to grant the bankers absolute power. Once in office, we notice that politicians never challenge the rule of the bankers. If we are feeling generous, we might excuse them for not understanding what is going on. After all, they begin as freshmen congressmen, while the banking elite has been around since the revolutionary war. Most politicians never figure out what is going on, nor care to. The Fed is off limits to them and therefore out of their field of vision. Yet, if they wanted to know more, they could certainly find out. For example, in a recent You Tube tape of a Jim Lehrer interview with Alan Greenspan, (former Chairman of the Fed), Lehrer asked Greenspan what should be the proper relationship of the Chairman of the Fed to the President of the United States. Greenspan shrugged off the question as inconsequential but offered this slick explanation:

> The Federal Reserve is an independent agency and that means there is no other agency of government which can overrule the actions that we take. So long as that is in place and there is no evidence that the administration, Congress or anybody else is requesting to do something other, then what the relationship is doesn't frankly matter.[48]

There has never been a clearer statement as to why democracy does not work in our country. At the highest level of government, the American people have absolutely no say in the workings of the American economy. It is important for us to understand this. *Fed bankers do not answer to any federal agency or any law.* This means that they rule us as any master rules his slaves. Any vote that we make for any politician, even the president of the United States, will not alter this reality. This is why *political democracy* is a gross sham without *economic democracy*. Without economic democracy, we are ruled by the bankers and the big corporations, which control our food, housing, health care, education, energy, and consumer goods. Our federal system is not intended to help us improve our lives or help us become better human beings; it is only there to regulate Americans and to train us for specific job slots in the bankers' machine. Such is the system that Alexander Hamilton put in place at the founding of our nation, and why to this day he remains the darling of the capitalist class.

Bretton Woods: The Federal Reserve Note Goes International

Now that we have an understanding of how the Federal Reserve Bank works and how the bankers and the politicians collude to maintain their power over the American people, let us now look at how this US State Monopoly partnership came to rule the world.

After WWII ended, there was a legitimate need to rebuild the world economy. During the war, the bankers had funded both democracy and fascism by supplying goods, services, and weapons to both sides.[49] Now, as the war ended, it was time to continue to profit by loaning money to rebuild the cities and country sides that their money had helped to destroy. To do this, it was necessary to create a monetary system that would allow countries to trade with each other despite the fact that they all had their own currencies. This problem was addressed at the Bretton Woods Conference that was held toward the end of WWII as part of the United Nations effort. The participants at the Bretton Woods Conference established an international monetary system that allowed economic exchange between the US, Canada, Western Europe, Australia, and Japan. The mechanism developed to do this was to make every country adopt a monetary policy that maintained an exchange rate by tying each currency to the universal standard of the American dollar. To facilitate this process, the Conference also created the International Monetary Fund (IMF), to bridge temporary imbalances of payments between trading nations, and created the World Bank, to make development loans to other countries.

"Free trade" required the free convertibility of one national currency to the next. In the nineteenth and early twentieth centuries, gold played the key role in international monetary transactions. The gold standard was used to back all national currencies. The value of a national currency was determined by its fixed relationship to gold. In this way, gold was used to settle international accounts. The gold standard maintained fixed exchange rates that were seen as desirable because they reduced the risk in trading with other countries.

Imbalances in international trade were rectified automatically by the gold standard (unless the country went to war). A country with a trade deficit, for example, would have to deplete its gold reserves by the amount of its deficit and, accordingly, it would also have to reduce its money supply by that amount. With less money, the country could not afford to buy as many imported goods. With less money, domestic prices would also be lowered as would the cost of producing its goods. This would boost exports because they would now be cheaper to buy for the nations with which it traded. On the other hand, any country that inflated its currency beyond that allowed by its gold supply would increase the cost of its goods domestically and in the world market, thereby suffering a loss of demand. This loss of demand would require an adjustment in the country's gold supply because its exports would become less than its imports. This imbalance would require the country to credit its gold to its trading partners and thereby lose gold. This would decrease the amount of money available to spend and thus end the inflation. In an honest system, the gold standard worked perfectly.

The problems with the world economy in the twentieth century had started when the Federal Reserve Bank of the United States secretly began to print money unilaterally without the backing of gold as a means for the country to fund WWI. Having the ability to secretly print money without it being backed by gold, had the effect of turning every nation that traded with the United States into beggars because they were put at an unfair trade advantage with the United States. The US was able to create cheaper goods and more of them than their gold supply would normally allow. As the US sent these cheaper goods to other countries, many of whom were now embroiled in the war, this created a gross imbalance of payments. According to the rules, this imbalance had to be rectified by payment of gold to the United States. This had the effect of making the importing countries have less money in circulation and thus contracting their economies.

The architects of Bretton Woods knew that they had to create a system whereby exchange rates could be stabilized and the actions taken by the United States in World War I would not happen again. Yet there was a problem. Due to the expansion of the global economy after WWII, it was argued by the bankers that it was not possible to use a system of permanently fixed rates that had characterized the classic gold standard of the nineteenth century. The gold supply, it was argued, was no longer sufficient to meet the demands of growing international trade and investment. Further, a sizable share of the world's known gold reserves was located in the Soviet Union, which would later emerge as a Cold War rival to the United States and Western Europe. The biggest obstacle of all, however, was that the American bankers demanded that the dollar serve as the "gold standard" in the new post-war economy.

John Maynard Keynes was an English economist who first proposed that recessions and depressions could be mitigated by government deficit spending, a theory that has guided Federal Reserve Bank policy to this day. At the Bretton Woods conference, Keynes recommended that attendees create a new international currency called Bancor. Bancor would not actually be money so much as it would be a unit of account used to track international flows of assets and liabilities. Gold could be exchanged for Bancors, but countries could not exchange Bancors for gold. Individuals or corporations could not hold or trade in Bancor. Countries with excess Bancor assets or excess Bancor liabilities would be charged to take action to restore their balance of trade.[50] In other words, Bancor, would serve the same purpose as did gold in the days of the gold standard. It would be a universal store of value.

Under heavy pressure from the United States, however, this recommendation was rejected and the idea of Bancor was replaced by the US dollar. In so doing, what would have been a fair system of global trade was replaced by a system, under the control of the Federal Reserve Bank that guaranteed its hegemony over the world economy. The Federal Reserve Bank, in demanding that the US dollar serve as the *reserve currency* of the world, argued that because of the strength of the U.S. economy, the fixed relationship of the dollar to gold (thirty-five dollars an ounce), and the commitment of the US government to convert dollars into gold at that price, made the dollar "as good as gold." In fact, they argued, the dollar was even better than gold because it earned interest and was more flexible than gold as a medium of exchange.

In this way, a new fixed exchange rate in global trade was created that was not pegged to gold or Bancor, but to the dollar. Theoretically, countries could still demand payment in gold from the US if they wanted to exchange their dollars for gold. In practice, this turned out to be a scam. In 1971, President Nixon severed the fixed relationship of the dollar to gold, and other countries no longer could demand gold for the dollars that they held as foreign reserves.

Nonetheless, at the time of Bretton Woods, most people were more open to the United States recommendations. The US, after all, was the only country with the capacity to rebuild Europe and industrialize other countries of the world.

To activate the new system of fixed exchange rates, member states were required to establish a parity of their national currencies in terms of the reserve currency (the dollar).

In other words, they had to "peg" their currency to the dollar at a set rate of exchange. Having done so, they were required to maintain their exchange rates within plus or minus one percent of parity by buying or selling dollars on the international market. In this way, the US dollar took over the role that gold had played under the gold standard and thereby became the new world currency. As the world's key currency, all international transactions became denominated in US dollars.[51]

If member countries wanted to change their par value with the dollar by more than ten percent they required IMF approval. The approval was dependent upon the IMF's determination that a country's balance of payments was in a "fundamental disequilibrium." The formal definition of fundamental disequilibrium was never determined, but it was related to how output fluctuated with a change in the money supply.[52] Any country that unilaterally tried to change its par value without approval, or after being denied, was then penalized by being denied access to the IMF. This would become a significant liability for many third world countries once they became involved in the world of international finance.

The Birth of "Undeveloped" and "Developing" Countries

These terms, as a description of countries, did not always exist. They were created by the power elite after WWII. Some background information is here required. As WWII dragged on, it became obvious to American strategists that the weakened European powers would no longer be able to maintain their exploitation of their third world colonies. This would result in the end of traditional colonial empires. Who better to create a new geopolitical order than the United States?

As these colonies gained political liberation after the war, they became eligible to receive "foreign aid" from the United States. To replace the obsolete term "colonies" the administration came up with new designations: "undeveloped," "underdeveloped," and "developing" nations. These terms were applied to all non-industrialized countries of the world that were non-communist.

As the idea gained steam, the strategy to exploit the resources of these countries became wrapped in idealistic language. These poor countries were not to be exploited as they had been under colonialism, but required compassion and help to develop themselves. Thus, without any discussion with the governments of these countries as to what they perceived to be own needs; without any request on their part for aid, the US strategists coined the idea of "development assistance." This "assistance" became the cornerstone of economic imperialism, as it quickly turned into debt, over-indebtedness, and dependency, the hallmarks of the Federal Reserve Bank's modus operandi.

By having access to an unlimited supply of money through the Federal Reserve Bank and its international network, US-based multinational corporations were able to seize control over raw materials, the production processes, and the markets of smaller and weaker countries around the world. Even during the Cold War, when the American people were traumatized by the possibility of nuclear destruction and our children were taught to crawl under their desks in the case of an air attack, Chase Manhattan Bank (Rockefeller) and others were setting up bank branches in Russia and China.

In time, the process of global imperialism turned into international monopoly capitalism or Globalization. Now the corporate elite no longer needed to reduce their prices in order to secure a larger market. They simply agree on prices and even the specifications of their products. Among the elite, it is considered unsportsmanlike to introduce radically new technology that would cut profits of the other corporations in the club. It is no wonder then why sustainable energy technology has had such a difficult time finding financial support.

Trying to play catch up with the American corporations, Europeans began to fight back. They formed the European Union to coordinate economic expansion. Their mechanism for growth became government-initiated mergers. The governments worked with European-based corporations to concentrate their largest industries. Through bigness they were able to compete with the Americans. This, of course, outraged the US-based corporations who then went crying to the federal government demanding support.

Fred Borch, former chairman of the board of General Electric, told the National Foreign Trade Convention in 1972, that "our government must recognize and accept—as the Japanese and European governments have long ago—that business and its employees are practically the sole source of national income." (This was not true.) He argued that government must now develop a "positive" attitude toward business that would "promote the corporation's ability to grow. . . . Corporate lobbyists demanded that the President and Congress screen every economic proposal in terms of its impact on US international competitiveness."[53]

This heavy hand had the desired effect of silencing critics of corporations within government and created an even tighter coordination between national policy and corporate policy. The unions were silenced. They had no power to keep US-based corporations from setting up plants abroad. Finally, during the 1960s and 1970s, the students of the New Left, who had been critical of the unholy alliance between big business and big government, were also silenced. Having educated themselves about state monopoly capitalism and its penchant to create wars in order to force its will on local people, the students challenged *The Establishment* in any event in which they were involved. Having lost patience with these "hippies," the government decided to shoot their own children dead in the streets at Kent State University. The youth movement was further demoralized by the assassination of its heroes, John Kennedy, Robert Kennedy, and Martin Luther King. The bankers and the corporate CEOs —the ruling capitalist elite—had successfully silenced their domestic critics by the mid-1970s. Who did the bankers consider their internal enemies to be? A Trilateral Commission publication written by its strategists, Michel J. Crozier, Samuel P. Huntington and Joji Watanuki, entitled *The Crisis of Democracy*, declared that the big threats to "democracy" were women, blacks and "value-oriented" intellectuals.[54] These essentially were people who questioned the status quo instead of just doing their jobs. More on this in Chapter Two.

The Third World (Perpetually Undeveloped Countries)

While the Soviet Union and its allies slowed Western capitalist expansion in Eastern Europe and the countries of the Russian steppes, and while China did the same in certain countries in the Far East, the capitalist corporations, nonetheless, had free reign in most of the third world, particularly the countries in Central America, South America, Africa, the Middle East, the islands of the world, and most countries in Asia.

The "third world" was a term originally coined by Mao Tse-tung when describing the economic divisions of the world. To Mao, there were the capitalist countries (first world), the Soviet Union Eastern Bloc (second world) and everyone else (the third world). Mao considered China to be a third world country, as was India. Third world countries contained eighty percent of humanity, but only twenty percent of the world's financial wealth. At the time, these countries were not rich, but they were not impoverished either. Although most had been colonized prior to WWII, they still maintained their own cultures, in which they took pride, and they had their extended families and village life. The majority of people had their basic needs met. This was about to end as the US capitalists' relentless hunt for raw materials was felt around the globe.

Even as the war was drawing to an end, the US was pressuring Britain and France to dismantle their colonial empires so that the whole third world would be opened to American corporations. Understandably, the European's balked at this "suggestion" and this did not make for a smooth transition. The colonial governments did not want to relinquish their administrations and in some countries like Angola, Mozambique, Algeria, and Kenya the local people fought wars of independence. India rebelled in its own way and gained political independence.

Even though the decolonized countries had gained political independence, this did not mean that they would have economic independence. They just had a new master. The new master did not need to establish colonial administrations to get what it wanted.

Through development loans and incurred debt, the third world countries fell one by one to the conditions set by the US imperialists. They would "provide raw materials, investment opportunities, markets, and cheap labor" to the US empire."[55]

The primary threats to the US capitalists in this endeavor were "nationalist regimes" who wanted to keep their natural resources for the improvement of their own people. In most cases, the US characterized these governments as communist terrorists.

The American form of economic imperialism spread across the globe. Some examples include Guatemala, Cuba, the Dominican Republic, Chile, El Salvador, South Korea, Cambodia, Vietnam, Taiwan, etc. More recently we have the examples of Iraq, Afghanistan, and Libya.

However one describes this imperialism, whether the critique comes from the left or the right, the fact remains that the third world countries increasingly became recipients of US military bases, security agreements, investments in raw material extractions, new office buildings for multinational corporations, and foreign-aid programs[56] that favored multinational corporations over local people. Whether we condemn this phenomenon as American imperialism or laud it in pretty words to extol the process by which the US "brought democracy to the world," the fact remains that this expansion was only made possible by US foreign policy, backed up by the CIA and US military, that forced countries to keep their borders open to American corporations, and acquiesce to the exploitation of their resources and forced business deals. There are certainly gentler terms for this economic assault on the world, but "imperialism," by definition, clearly expresses the nature of US actions. The values of nationalism, imperialism, and militarism that had been formed in the cauldron of Europe politics centuries before, had now reached its highest expression in the advent of the United States global empire, Pax Americana.

Making an Example of Chile

Let us take a look at Chile as a specific example of what happened when a country resisted the United States' encroachment. The people of Chile had elected Salvador Allende, a socialist President in 1970. This was due in large part because US corporations like ITT, Kennecott, Anaconda, Purina, Bank of America, and others were ravaging the resources of the country and the people wanted it to end. ITT's director, John McCone, a former head of CIA, invested heavily in an effort to stop Allende from being elected president. After Allende was elected, McCone changed strategies and developed a plan to conduct a coup d'état. The first step was to spread "economic chaos" in the country to soften up the population. As McCone plotted, Allende began his administration by nationalizing the Ananconda and Kennecott's copper mines. The US government under Nixon swung into action. They cut the US Export-Import Bank credits to Chile and pressured the World Bank and IMF (in which they had the dominate voice) to disapprove all further loans to Chile. They also pressured other private banks to cut off credit. During Allende's first year in office, access to capital in international markets dropped from two hundred and twenty million dollars to thirty-five million dollars. The global corporations also joined the campaign by refusing to sell spare parts and machinery even for cash.

The American people had no idea what was going on. Certainly, Chile presented no national security risk to Americans. The people of Chile simply wanted greater freedom to control their own resources and livelihood. On September 11, 1973, the military, citing a call by the Chilean Congress to end his presidency, illegally staged a coup against Allende.

As the armed forces surrounded La Moneda Palace, Allende gave his last speech vowing not to resign, and allegedly committed suicide thereafter. After Allende's ousting, General Augusto Pinochet, who led the coup d'état, was installed in power along with a military *junta* that suppressed all public dissent. The United States government, which had worked to create the conditions for the coup, promptly recognized the junta government and supported its consolidation of power.[57]

In the first months of the fascist takeover, the dead and disappeared numbered in the thousands. In the days immediately following the coup, the Assistant Secretary of State for Inter-American Affairs informed Henry Kissinger, that the National Stadium was being used to hold 5,000 prisoners. Sitting on benches in the hot sun for days, the junta randomly shot and tortured people or grabbed women to rape. Two years later, in 1975, the CIA reported that up to 3,811 prisoners were still being held in the Stadium.[58]

What happened in Chile was the United States capitalists' way of telling the people of the world not to oppose its control over their own resources. While the banks and corporations tightened their grip on the world's people, the US government was telling the American people that our government was fighting to defend democracy and to stop the spread of communism in the world. What they did not tell us was that the "communists" were anyone who voiced any opposition to US imperialism. They included dissidents and leftists, union workers, peasant leaders, priests and nuns, students, teachers, intellectuals, small business people, in short, anyone who loved their country and their freedom as much as we Americans love ours.

Once the military dictatorship was established in Chile, the US corporations took over the economy. The new government cut tariffs on imports, suppressed union power, and "privatized" hundreds of state-controlled industries. Human services were put under the control of private corporations.

Unfortunately, what happened to Chile was nothing new in Latin American where small countries had long been considered to be the private property of US capital. For example, in 1920 a United Fruit (now United Brands and Chiquita) manager wrote to a company lawyer describing the company's true intentions in Honduras:

> We must produce a disembowelment of the incipient economy of the country in order to increase and help our aims. We have to prolong its tragic, tormented, and revolutionary life; the wind must blow only on our sails and the water must only wet our keel.[59]

Ten years later the company was still employing armed bands to intimidate striking workers in Honduras. Company planes were used to kidnap strike leaders and fly them to El Salvador. Other countries in Latin America also experienced their version of US imperialism.

South Africa, on another continent, was a variation of the same theme. While the US government joined a U.N. vote for a resolution condemning apartheid, US corporations were supporting the apartheid government. GM, Ford, and Chrysler made major investments in the country, legitimized the apartheid government, and reinforced its economy.

While third world countries were endowed with abundant natural wealth, a willing labor force, and potential markets, they have remained impoverished for decades. In fact beginning after WWII and existing into the present, many have actually gotten poorer.

The reason for this, according to the US mainstream press, reveals the vile racism that drives the capitalists and their legions of apologists. The press explained that the greatest number of "backward" nations is comprised of brown, black, and yellow people who could never compete in the dynamic white world. It was the same spin made by the former European imperialists who claimed that being exploited by white men was a good thing for "backward" people because it brought white civilization and religion to them. These racist white capitalists conveniently forgot that the so-called "backward" people created the greatest civilizations in history at a time when white people were still living as barbarians.

In their book *Global Reach*, Richard Barnet and Ronald Muller paint a vivid picture of what life is like in a third world country after decades of American imperialism. All these countries share the same symptoms of underdevelopment to a lesser or greater degree.

> The countries are a contradiction of rags and riches. One out of every ten thousand persons lives in a palace with high walls and gardens and a Cadillac in the drive-

way. A few blocks away hundreds are sleeping in the streets, which they share with beggars, chewing-gum hawkers, prostitutes, and shoeshine boys. Around the corner tens of thousands are jammed in huts without electricity or plumbing. Outside the cities, most of the population scratches out a bare subsistence on small plots, many owned by the few who lived behind the high walls. Even where the soil is rich and the climate agreeable most people go to sleep hungry. The stock market is booming, but babies die and children with distended bellies and spindly legs are everywhere. There are luxurious restaurants and stinking open sewers. The capital boasts late-model computers and receives jumbo jets every day, but more than half of the people cannot read. . . .

 Nationalist slogans are prominent, but the basic industries are in the hands of foreigners. The houses behind the walls are filled with imported cameras, TVs, tape recorders, and fine furniture from the United States or Europe, but the major family investment is likely to be a Swiss bank account. There appear to be three groups in the country distinguishable by what they consume. A tiny group live on a scale that would make a Rockefeller squirm. A second group, still relatively small in number, lives much like the affluent middle class in the United States—the same cars, the same Scotch, the same household appliances. The vast majority eat picturesque native foods like black beans, rice and lentil soup—in small quantities. The first two groups are strong believers in individual development for themselves and their family, but they see no solution for the growing plight of the third group. So they fear them, and their walls grow higher. For the third group disease, filth, and sudden death are constant companions, but there is an air of resignation about them. Life has always been full of pain and uncertainty and it always will be. The only development they see is the same journey from cradle to an early grave that their fathers and their grandfathers took."⁶⁰

It is argued by capitalist economists that third world countries lack the infrastructure to create more wealth— roads, communications systems, schools, technology, etc. In other words, they lacked the "capital stock" to develop their economies. The traditional analysis is that the countries never produced the wealth necessary to generate the savings required to invest in their own economic growth. As we have already seen, however, this economic analysis is disingenuous because finance capital, under modern capitalism, has nothing to do with savings. It has to do with the ability to create paper out of thin air—paper that is used to control people everywhere because it poses as a legitimate and legally binding media of exchange and store of value. Of course, this worthless paper is backed by the CIA, Special Forces, and, if necessary, the US army. As far as Africa, South America, and Central America are concerned, we must also remember that the Europeans, and then Americans, decimated the labor force of the continent by enslaving their populations. It was this enslavement that allowed the capitalist countries to develop its capital stock.

If the majority of the countries in the world are poor, even though they are rich in natural resources, it is because the foreign corporations who control the wealth in those countries take immense profits from those countries instead of investing in the local people. The finance capital generated by the natural wealth of these "underdeveloped" countries is not used to develop local factories, schools, and other structures required to meet the local people's basic needs. Rather it is siphoned off to the "developed" world, first as plunder, then in the more respectable form of dividends, interest on loans, stocks, technical fees, etc. In other words, the wealth is used to finance the luxurious amenities of the capitalists and to expand continued opportunities for profits. Today these profits are used for the most part to gamble on the stock market, invest in derivatives, or wager on currency wars. The capital that was left in the countries went to the small class of locals who cooperated with the foreigners in the expropriation of the local people's wealth. Thus, over the years, the wealth of the "undeveloped" countries has been systematically depleted and the people impoverished. This process has gone on regardless of whether a Democrat or Republican administration was in power.

Today most third world countries continue to suffer from three institutional weaknesses. They lack a strong local administration that seeks the welfare of the people. They lack a strong labor movement. And they lack local businesses that are able to compete with the global corporations. This situation creates a subsistence environment in which it's every man for himself. And let us not forget the lesson of Chile. The policeman of the world is always ready to kill local leaders for speaking up and the banks always stand ready to destroy what little economy there is if the people do not remain docile.

The US-Based Multinational Corporation

The US-based multinational corporation became the first institution in human history dedicated to central planning on a world scale. In this sense, it inevitably came into conflict with the governments of nation-states. The president of IBM World Trade Corporation stated:

> For business purposes, the boundaries that separate one nation from another are no more real than the equator. They are merely convenient demarcations of ethnic, linguistic, and cultural entities. They do not define business requirements or consumer trends. Once management understands and accepts this world economy, its view of the marketplace – and its planning – necessarily expand. The world outside the home country is no longer viewed as series of disconnected customers and prospects for its products, but as an extension of a single market.[61]

As early as the 1960s, companies like GM, IBM, Pepsico, GE, Exxon, etc., were making daily business decisions which had more impact on peoples' ability to meet their basic needs than any sovereign government. Where people lived, what they ate, drank, wore, what kind of education they got, what medicine they took, etc., were already largely determined by the global corporations. In the process, the governments of third world countries were coerced into taking out huge loans from the World Bank and other global banks to pay for the infrastructure required by the foreign corporations in order to exploit the local resources. These countries got hooked on the debt game and have had to face the IMF imposed "austerity measures" in which the local people are further impoverished by a diversity of means, all designed to make the bankers and corporations rich at the expense of the people.

In the process of globalization, the US corporations lost all allegiance to the American people. For over four hundred years, human beings had been organized in nation states and under the dominance of national leaders. In many of these countries, the people had a vote in who their leaders would be. Yet, while the people have political freedom, they never possessed economic freedom. They were always under the dominance of the banks and the corporations. As the banks and corporations of the United States began to earn more money by exploiting third world countries, they did not need the US labor force anymore. They simply moved their operations and their jobs overseas. By 1972, over one hundred and twenty of the largest US-based corporations had a higher rate of profits from abroad than from domestic operations. Consequently, US corporations have been shifting more and more of their assets abroad. In the United States, we experienced this exodus of corporations in the destruction of our industrial base. During the 1970s and 1980s, what was once the country's foundry became the countries "rust belt." During the 1990s, forty-seven large corporations moved their headquarters overseas. Last year CNN published a list of American corporations that have either exported American jobs, or have hired foreign workers at a cheaper wage. This list contains seven hundred and ninety-one major American companies.[62] President Trump in his campaign to Make America Great Again attempted, to no avail, to shame the multinational corporations for exporting jobs. Few, if any corporations, complied with his request. Trump was helpless to do any more than talk and soon forgot the whole thing.

International Banks and the Expansion of American Imperialism

Despite the Cold War, the United States has clearly been the world's supreme power since WWII. The government of the United States and US-based banks and corporations have had free reign to exploit the world with its so-called "dollar diplomacy."[63] To realize its ambitions, the US government acted quickly to set up the United Nations, the World Bank, and the International Monetary Fund. Coming out of the war, the four great allied powers were the United States, Britain, the Soviet Union, and China. The US intention behind the United Nations was to prevent another world war between the capitalists and the communists, to rebuild Europe, and to bring the third world countries under US dominance. The stated objectives of the U.N. were to maintain international peace and security, promote human rights, foster social and economic development, protect the environment, and provide humanitarian aid in cases of famine, natural disaster, or armed conflict. Idealistic language has always been the capitalists' velvet glove to hide its iron fist.

Founded in October 1945, the U.N. had representation from fifty-one member states. It now has representatives from one hundred and ninety-three countries. The headquarters of the United Nations is in New York City, built on land donated by the Rockefellers. The UN also has satellite offices in Geneva, Nairobi, and Vienna.

Originally, the U.N. was composed of six major organs. These include the *U.N. Secretariat* that administers the U.N.; *the International Court* which handles legal disputes between nations; the *General Assembly*, which is composed of all member states and serves as a venue for discussion and decision making regarding issues of global concern; the *U.N. Security Council* which is responsible for maintaining international peace; the *U.N. Economic and Social Council* which seeks to create cooperation between member states on economic and social issues. Finally, there was the *U.N. Trusteeship Council*, which was originally designed to manage colonial possessions that were being transferred between countries after WWI. This Council is no longer active.

The U.N. Charter stipulates that each primary organ of the U.N. can establish various specialized agencies to fulfill its duties. Some best-known agencies are the International Atomic Energy Agency, the Food and Agriculture Organization, UNESCO (United Nations Educational, Scientific and Cultural Organization), the World Health Organization (WHO), and the International Labour Organization. There are seventeen such specialized agencies active today. As far as the US banks and multinational corporations are concerned, however, the most significant specialized agencies are the World Bank and the International Monetary Fund. Not surprising, they are not answerable to any U.N. organ, including the Secretariat.

The World Bank and the International Monetary Fund are international institutions set up at Bretton Woods under the requirements of the Federal Reserve Bank to advance the interests of the US economic elites. In other words, these international banks were designed to promote economic globalization according to the designs of the American bankers. The relationship between the Fed and its subordinate international banks still exists today as evidenced by a June, 1916 Conference sponsored by the FED entitled: Joint World Bank/International Monetary Fund/Federal Reserve Board "Conference on Policy Challenges for the Financial Sector." The announcement for this conference contained the following description of its purpose:

> This 3-day program is designed for senior level officials from around the world who hold key positions in the financial sector. These officials generally are governors, deputy governors, heads, or deputy heads of banking supervisory authorities, or high-level staff involved in, or capable of influencing, policy formulation as it concerns the supervision and regulation of banks in their respective countries. Participation in this program is by invitation only.[64]

The specific aim of the conference was to "provide policymakers a forum for identifying, developing, and challenging responses to strategy and policy issues. Debates will encompass major economic, legal, and institutional strategies and policies that are necessary to ensure that appropriate regulatory and prudential safeguards are in place to support sound and sustainable economic growth."

Once the World Bank and International Monetary Fund were established, the US-based multinational corporations were instructed in becoming world managers, tasked by the bankers to integrate the organization, technology, money, and the capitalist ideology of "free trade" into a global world market. By the 1970s, George Ball, former Secretary of State and chairman of Lehman Brothers International exulted: "men are able for the first time to utilize world resources with an efficiency dictated by the objective logic of profit."[65]

The World Bank

The World Bank, based in Washington DC, is actually a group of five international banks that make loans to "developing" countries. These are the International Bank for Reconstruction and Development (IBRD), the International Development Association (IDA), the International Finance Corporation (IFC), the Multilateral Investment Guarantee Agency (MIGA), and the International Centre for Settlement of Investment Disputes (ICSID). The stated purpose of the Bank is to fight poverty and increase prosperity. The reality is that the Bank is one of the main mechanisms responsible for systematically impoverishing third world nations around the world.

The first bank created of the World Bank Group was the International Bank for Reconstruction and Development. This bank was set up as early as 1944 with the expressed purpose of reconstructing the war-ravaged countries of Europe by offering development finance. The bank began lending in 1946, immediately after the war. When the United States realized that there was great profit to be made in this endeavor, it undercut the IBRD by launching the Marshall Plan.[66] When the Marshall Plan diminished the IBRD's mandate, the bank turned its attention to making loans to the third world countries. The other branches of the World Bank were created to maintain bank profitability by rescheduling loans and also to help private investors profit from third world economies. The IDA, for example, was set up in 1960 to provide long term loans that allowed countries to receive new money to pay back old debts in line with the bankers' play book. The IFC encourages multinational companies to invest in the private sector in undeveloped countries. The MIGA's role is to offer private investors technical assistance and insurance against losses incurred because of "non-commercial risks" (problems with the local government or people's insurgencies). Finally, the purpose of the ICSID is to resolve legal disputes between international investors in order to encourage the investment of foreign capital and to mitigate noncommercial risk.[67]

In 2004, John Perkins, a former employee of the World Bank, blew the whistle on the bank's corrupt intentions in his widely-read book, *Confessions of an Economic Hit Man*.[68] The book reveals how World Bank loans to third world increases income inequality by forcing third world countries to accept development loans for large construction projects in which foreign corporations are hired to do the job. This is the method that allows large US companies to exploit cheap labor and destroy local environments. Perkins describes what he calls a system of corporatocracy and greed as the driving force behind the World Bank.

Perkins refers to himself as an "economic hit man" because his job was to convince the political and financial leaders of third countries to accept enormous development loans from the World Bank and private foreign banks. Once saddled with debts these countries were unable to pay, they were forced to acquiesce to political pressure from the United States. In this way, Perkins argues, the third world nations were effectively neutralized politically. At the same time, their domestic economies were crippled as foreign banks and corporations exported profits that should have been used to alleviate domestic poverty. Perkins described the role of an economic hit man as follows:

> Economic hit men (EHMs) are highly paid professionals who cheat countries around the globe out of trillions of dollars. They funnel money from the World

Bank, the US Agency for International Development (USAID), and other foreign "aid" organizations into the coffers of huge corporations and the pockets of a few wealthy families who control the planet's natural resources. Their tools included fraudulent financial reports, rigged elections, payoffs, extortion, sex, and murder. They play a game as old as empire, but one that has taken on new and terrifying dimensions during this time of globalization.[69]

Perkins reveals that it was Kermit Roosevelt Jr., the grandson of Teddy Roosevelt, while active in the CIA, who, in the early 1950s, organized the coup d'état against Iran's democratically elected government. This particular breach of another country's sovereignty was atypical in that it was accomplished without US military intervention. It proved so successful, that the idea of an economic hit man became popular with the US government. The US did not have to worry about a military confrontation with Russia, using such tactics. The only problem was that Kermit was a CIA operative, which would have been embarrassing if he had gotten caught. At that point, the decision was made to use organizations like the CIA and the NSA to recruit potential economic hit men and then send them to work for private consulting companies, engineering firms, construction companies, etc., so that, if they were caught, there would be no connection with the US government.[70]

Perkins was vilified for his revelations by the mainstream press, including the Washington Post, New York Time, Boston Magazine, and the Economist. Even the US State Department felt it necessary to respond to Perkins' charges. The best they could come up with, however, was that he did not provide corroborating testimony that the NSA was involved in hiring economic hit men.

Perkins was not the only whistleblower to "out" the corruption of the World Bank and the US government's involvement in the destruction of third world countries.[71] While the stated purpose of the World Bank and International Monetary Fund is to "alleviate poverty," something does not smell right when hundreds of billions of dollars, which are supposedly loaned to alleviate poverty, only result in greater poverty. To understand this contradiction, we must look at the way the World Bank operates in practice. Steve Berkman, an employee of the Bank from 1983 to 2002, during which time he worked in twenty-one countries and also established the Anti-Corruption and Fraud Investigation Unit in the Bank, tells us that the management of the Bank:

> ... has built a wall of misinformation around its lending operations, creating the illusion that all is well in the world of development. They have created the myth that they are at the "cutting edge" of development, while they hide the appalling number of failures within the Bank's portfolio – failures that enrich the governing elites of the Third World, while creating mountains of debt that cannot be repaid. Singing their own praises, they lead the Bank ever farther from its primary mission, ignoring their professional and fiduciary obligations as they advance their individual careers, while the people they have promised to help continue to live in poverty.[72]

Berkman tells us that whether we are discussing huge multimillion-dollar contracts or simple daily transactions, Bank officials have concocted many ways to embezzle bank funds. They create shell companies, facilitate rigged bids, create fraudulent procurement documents, establish hidden project accounts, authorize payments to themselves, etc. The loss of these funds that should have gone to reduce poverty are multiplied by the loss of economic opportunity by at least a factor of ten.

Berkman believes that of the approximately five hundred billion dollars purported to be loaned to third world countries, at least one hundred billion dollars has been skimmed off by the Bank's management. This theft of money by the bankers has resulted in roads that could not be found, millions paid for rehabilitation of structures that could not be verified, millions to improve social services that were never provided, and millions lost to facilitate better economic policies and better governance. Much of the money, which actually is invested in third world development, is then further skimmed off by local corrupt officials and foreign corporations.

Local people have generally hated the World Bank, and protests and riots against its actions have been held on every continent to express the people's anger. A clear example of World Bank corruption can be seen in the appointment of Paul Wolfowitz by George W. Bush as the president of the World Bank.[73] Wolfowitz was the man who created the Bush Doctrine,[74] which led to the US withdrew from the ABM treaty with the USSR. The purpose of the treaty was to limit the production of anti-ballistic missiles.[75] Wolfowitz also rejected the Kyoto protocol which was an international treaty to limit greenhouse gas emissions that contribute to climate change.[76] The Bush Doctrine holds that the US has the right to attack any other country unilaterally without making its intentions known in advance. As president of the World Bank, the corruption of Wolfowitz was reflected in his giving his girlfriend Shaha Riza an exorbitant salary as an employee of the bank. When the scandal broke, he had to give up his post.[77]

Fig. 5-4: IMF/World Bank Protest Sign

The International Monetary Fund

The International Monetary Fund (IMF), a companion to the World Bank, was originally designed to promote international economic cooperation and provide its member countries with short-term loans so they could trade with other countries and achieve balance of payments. In other words, the IMF loans money to poor countries so they can pay their debts to the rich countries who have initially exploited their natural resources and then sent them products at a much higher cost. This is one of the plays of the bankers that we explored in our section on the Federal Reserve Bank. This system leads to the greater impoverishment of "developing" countries despite the banks publicly stated objective to alleviate poverty. As third world debt expanded, it led to the *debt crisis* of the 1980's.[78] Since then, the IMF has assumed the role of bailing out countries during financial crises by loaning them more money designed as emergency loan packages tied to certain conditions. This is the "Protect the Public" play of the Federal Reserve Bank referred to above. The certain conditions imposed on the debtor nation are referred to as *structural adjustment policies* (SAPs).

According to IMF's structural adjustment policies, a country that is unable to make its debt payments must begin to restructure its economy, sector by sector, and determine how money can be siphoned from them to pay the country's debt. The SAPs are implemented through two kinds of loans. First come the structural adjustment loans (SALs) that have three objectives: (1) keep the country in the debt game by providing another loan to cushion the debt crisis; (2) increase exports by converting the country's natural resources into exportable goods, primarily raw materials; and (3) help multinational corporations establish themselves in countries that are too focused on meeting their own basic needs. Such countries are considered to be too "inward-looking."

The second kind of loan is the *sectoral adjustment loans* (SECALs). These loans are used to transform economic sectors. These loans are flexible to the extent that the government leaders can use the money anyway they want so long as certain conditions are met. These conditions include price deregulation, elimination of minimum wages, currency devaluation, etc., and serve to benefit the foreign corporations' takeover of that sector. These loans are also susceptible to corruption because politicians can skim off any amount of money that they can get away with.[79] These IMF loans force the country into exporting more and spending less on domestic needs. The SAPs usually result in the government having to take the following measures:

> The elimination of customs barriers. This has the effect of eliminating goods produced by the local people who can now no longer compete with international goods that are often used to flood the market and drive out local people. If, for example, Egyptian peasants cannot produce wheat cheaper than American farmers, they are forced to abandon their farms and move to the slums of Cairo looking for work.

Incentives to export. In order to obtain the currency required to pay the debt and balance the budget, countries are forced to "modernize" their export product sectors, normally foods and raw materials. Banks are willing to make additional loans for this and push the country even further into debt.

Deregulation of prices. Countries are forced to deregulate wages, interest rates, and exchange rates and "liberalize" their legislation to increase greater foreign ownership and the ability to take profits out of the country.

Privatization. This entails forcing third world countries to sell their infrastructure to foreign corporations in order to raise money to pay their debts.

Public Spending Cuts. Governments are forced to cut their investment in their own people by reducing funds for education, health, housing, social services, and basic needs.

By manipulating the local economy to export their raw materials and food, instead of concentrating on local needs, the IMF widens the gap between the rich and the poor and puts the people increasingly under the stranglehold of foreign corporations. By forcing countries to institute merciless laws of competition and draconian debt service, the banks reduce the local population to paupers. The local people lose purchasing power, have their wages reduced and are forced to leave their villages and towns to compete with each other in the urban slums. The IMF destroys the standard of living of the local people and each day contributes to their greater impoverishment. Women are especially vulnerable to the IMF's SAPs because they are at the bottom of the foreign-controlled production line. Often this means losing their husbands who are driven to the big cities or to work on big plantations owned by foreign capitalists. By robbing the public sector of funds for social service such as education and health care, these tasks fall on women. They must care for the sick, pay for higher priced foods, and add hours of work to their day. The SAPs cause malnutrition, fatigue, and disease for women, children, and the poor in third world countries.[80] Aside from the toll on local people, the IMFs programs also lessen job creation and reduce economic growth, the opposite of its "idealistic" stated objectives.

The IMF is basically a global loan shark that exerts enormous leverage over more than sixty countries in the world. Once having been manipulated into accepting World Bank and IMF loans, countries fall further into debt from which they cannot escape. The Banks follow their playbook to keep loaning.[81]

The GATT

The mechanism that established the ground rules for "free trade" and allowed the US banking and corporate industry to economically exploit the countries of the world, was a protocol called the General Agreement on Tariffs and Trade (GATT) signed in Geneva in 1947.

This agreement, not surprisingly, did not include third world governments in the drafting of the rules. It was forced upon them. It took until 1994, however, for the heavy hand of US capitalism and its paratner Europe to force the third world countries to acquiesce to capitalist exploitation by signing the Marrakesh Agreement. At the session's end, the representative from Mauritius spoke for his third world colleagues when he said, "We lost everything, but we will put our head on the chopping block with dignity."[82]

The Marrakesh Agreement was eventually institutionalized in the directives of the U.N. World Trade Organization (WTO) in 1995. The WTO's charter contains no social, ecological, or cultural clause that would help establish any semblance of equitable terms of trade between the industrialized countries and the so-called "developing countries." While the terms of the WTO are enforced to keep third world countries from putting up tariff barriers against multinationals, they are ignored when industrialized countries put up trade barriers against third world countries. This can be seen in the textile industry where the third world faces tariffs set up by the US that cost them an estimated fifty billion dollars per year. According to a 1992 study, the total cost for unequal treatment in dealing with the capitalist countries costs third world countries about five hundred billion dollars per year.[83]

The Principle upon Which International Capital Works

It seems like everyone in our country has lost his moral bearing, from the highest government officials and senior corporate leaders all the way down to schoolteachers and local community leaders. The ethos of my fellow Americans seems to have changed from one of personal integrity and responsibility to "getting yours" – the all-out attempt, by any means possible, to get the most amount of benefits with the least amount of work.
Porter Stansberry [84]

Why do the leaders of major institutions within a capitalist system consistently become corrupt? Does the capitalist system automatically lead to corruption, or do imperfect human beings, once given the opportunity to profit at the expense of others, always take the opportunity to do so? I think we can assume that immediately after WWII, most of the seven hundred and thirty delegates from forty-four Allied countries who attended the Bretton Woods conference had good intentions. After living through the greatest hell on earth ever experienced, many actually wanted to create world peace and make the world a better place.[85] However, we also know that there were many others among the bankers and corporation executives of the US, who slavered at the opportunity to exploit the world that now lay at their feet.

John Commons, who lived through WWI and WWII, was an American institutional economist and labor historian.[86] He once wrote that, "Economic power is simply power to withhold from others what they need." What they need may include food, shelter, health care, jobs, or income. Economic power is the driving force of the capitalist system. Economic power implies a choice not to share in order to gain wealth for oneself. This automatically leads to inequality of possession. Every step that capitalism takes in its expansion, therefore increases this inequality. Since those with economic power in a capitalist system are by definition a minority class, the rules of self-aggrandizement require that they protect their wealth and their positions of power from being undermined by the majority. It is the same dynamic of the master-slave relationship. Economic power on a national scale is thus joined to political rule and military protection. The capitalist class will never relinquish power unless forced to do so. They are ever active to consolidate and structure their advantage.

Government rules and regulations in support of those who possess economic power are more easily enforced when the people accept the legitimacy of those who rule over them. In time, people in the US and the world have become more compliant. We now accept our servitude by saying "it's just the way life is." We have got enough problems just getting by day to day. In truth, many of us have no sense of history by which we can judge our current situation. We have few role models to encourage us to throw off the chain of our enslavement to debt. So long as we accept our servitude, the economically powerful have triumphed and are able to continue to amass more profit at our expense.

When economic power exercises its control over the mass media and political institutions, the "law" that supports the interests of the capitalist class is interpreted as being "practical." Slavery was considered practical. The current impoverishment of people to the point that we cannot meet our basic needs is considered practical. The destruction of the earth is considered practical. Power creates practicality. No self-respecting American would dare challenge what is practical.

The people are hindered by the fact that their intellectual leaders on both the Left and the Right avoid the history of economic power. Leftist journals rarely deal with the history of American capitalism. They analyze the contemporary conditions without context. The Left is powerless to neither understand the trend of capitalism nor know how to defeat it. They pull dead babies out of the stream every day and run around stamping our fires, but never think of asking where all the dead bodies come from or who specifically lit the fires. They never look upstream. They never investigate. For this reason, liberal politicians have always been unable to build a movement against the bankers that has any staying power.

On the Right, we have the same problem. While we must applaud those few conservatives who speak against the Federal Reserve Bank, for the most part, like the Left, they conceive of capitalism as something eternal, something blessed by God's own imprimatur, a part of human nature. Since capitalism is eternal, it neither ages nor decays. It is impervious to any attempts to change it. The majority of the Right view any criticism of capitalism as blasphemy. Rather they scapegoat the people themselves for our misery. They target women, blacks, Latinos, Muslims, liberals, gays, and other minorities as the cause of America's demise.

There are undoubtedly politicians on the Left and the Right who profit from their service to the capitalist system. In return for a few bucks in campaign donations and bribes offered, once in office, they serve their masters by befuddling the people and diverting our attention from the real cause of our problems. We can understand this. Who would not prefer an upper middle-class lifestyle to being attacked as a maniac and having their family threatened? This is the same fate of local organizers in other countries that we occasionally read about.

The main stream media in the United States is exclusively devoted to celebrations of capitalism rather than to a critical analysis of its origin and history of exploitation.[87] Thus, despite the best intentions of individuals, the capitalist system advances with little opposition, even as the world crumbles to the ground under its destructive march.

The United Nations and Resistance to International Monopoly Capitalism

When the United Nations was established in New York City just after WWII, the US made sure that they controlled all the important agencies, particularly the Security Council, the International Court of Justice, and the World Bank/IMF. What they did not control was the General Assembly wherein all countries had a voice to speak their mind. This was not so important to the bankers and big business in the United States, however, because no proclamations or resolutions of the General Assembly could over-rule their authority or interfere with their economic exploits. Nor could the General Assembly hold sway over any of the U.N. agencies controlled by the US as mentioned above. Basically, the General Assembly was a harmless institution so far as the capitalists were concerned. However, despite the capitalists' dismissal, it does provide a forum for discussion and a means by which the leaders of the third world were able to speak with each other and eventually reach a consensus regarding the nature of their exploitation by capitalist foreign corporations. The General Assembly did author many publications that documented the process of exploitation experienced by the third world. The bottom line is that the General Assembly helped third world countries to not feel alone. Countries could see that the economic exploitation that was happening in their country was also happening to others. In the General Assembly, third world countries comprised the majority of nations.

During the late 1940s and 1950s, the General Assembly spent its time discussing the universal rights of human beings and developing documents that acknowledged these rights. Among these were the Declaration of the Rights of the Child (1946), the landmark Universal Declaration of Human Rights adopted in 1948, the International Covenant on Civil and Political Rights (1966), and the International Covenant on Economic, Social and Cultural Rights (1966). In practice, however, the General Assembly is unable to take significant action against human rights abuses without a Security Council resolution, which unfortunately is never forthcoming. Nonetheless the General Assembly continues to do substantial work in investigating and reporting abuses.

Secretary-General of the United Nations Ban Ki-moon spoke to the impetus of the General Assembly's endeavor:

> The campaign reminds us that in a world still reeling from the horrors of the Second World War, the Declaration [of Human Rights] was the first global statement of what we now take for granted -- the inherent dignity and equality of all human beings.[88]

During the 1960s, the General Assembly turned its attention to creating education courses, manuals, and other mechanisms to train the new bureaucracies of third world countries that had gained their political independence from the European colonialists. England, France, Spain, Portugal, and other capitalist countries could no longer afford the expenses of having to maintain political bureaucracies in their colonies. Thus, with additional pressure from the US, they withdrew from the political arenas of their former colonies. With the establishment of so many new sovereign states, who were now joining the U.N., there was a lack of administrative functionaries to run the new governments. The General Assembly attempted to address this need.

Relinquishing political control over their third world colonies proved to be a boon for the European capitalists because they could now shunt the cost and responsibility of governance to local people while still keeping them enslaved economically.

During the late 1960s, the third world countries began an on-going dialogue with the capitalist countries to mitigate the negative impact of the "free market" system. The discussions became known as the "North-South Dialogue" with the capitalists referred to as the North and the third world referred to as the South.

During the 1970s, frustrated by the uncooperative nature of the capitalist countries to yield any ground, the third world countries, organized themselves in the U.N. as the *Group of 77*. They drafted their own global economic strategy to contest the capitalist stranglehold over their economies. Called the *Declaration for the Establishment of a New International Economic Order (NIEO)*, it was adopted by the United Nations General Assembly in 1974. Along with the declaration, a *Programme of Action and a Charter of Economic Rights and Duties of States* were also adopted by the

General Assembly. Together these documents made the case for a better use of natural resources and a more equitable distribution of wealth.

The main tenets of these documents were that:

1. Developing countries must be entitled to regulate and control the activities of multinational corporations operating within their territory.
2. They must be free to nationalize or expropriate foreign property on conditions favorable to them.
3. They must be free to set up associations of primary commodities producers similar to OPEC.
4. All other States must recognize this right and refrain from taking economic, military, or political measures calculated to restrict it.
5. International trade should be based on the need to ensure stable, equitable, and remunerative prices for raw materials, generalized non-reciprocal and nondiscriminatory tariff preferences, as well as transfer of technology to developing countries; and should provide economic and technical assistance without any strings attached.

Getting 77 countries to agree on anything was a herculean task. Any change in a word or phrase could unravel consensus at any time. This forced the Group of 77 to be doctrinaire in their dealings with the capitalists. There could be no nuance regarding basic terms. Given that the capitalists were not willing to negotiate any detail that reduced their power over the third world countries, the work behind the NIEO proved fruitless in moving the capitalist countries to take any action whatsoever.

Global Power Blocs

By the early 1980s, there were four main power blocs on the planet: (1) the capitalist countries of the OECD, (2) the Soviet Union, (3) OPEC, and (4) the Group of 77.

The OECD

The *OECD* (Organization for Economic Cooperation and Development) was an outgrowth of the Organization for European Economic Cooperation (OEEC) that was established in 1947 to run the US-financed Marshall Plan for reconstruction of Europe after WWII. The European countries had been making war on each other for centuries but WWII laid waste to the entire continent. By making individual governments recognize the interdependence of their economies, the OEEC fostered a new era of cooperation. Encouraged by its success and the prospect of carrying its work forward on a global stage, Canada and the US joined OEEC members in signing the new OECD Convention on December 14, 1960. The Organization for Economic Co-operation and Development (OECD) was officially born on September 30, 1961, when the Convention entered into force.

Other countries joined the OECD, starting with Japan in 1964. Today, OECD is comprised of twenty-five hundred staff and thirty-four member countries worldwide. The OECD provides the capitalist countries with a large think-tank that develops policies and economic strategies to enhance its members' wealth. Since the creation of the OECD, the US has seen its national wealth almost triple. Other OECD countries have seen similar growth, and in some cases even more spectacular wealth generation.[89]

The Union of Soviet Socialist Republics (USSR)

The *Union of Soviet Socialist Republics, (U.S.S.R.)* also called the Soviet Union existed from 1917 to 1991. In the second half of the twentieth century, it played a formidable role in the economic development of the planet. It consisted of fifteen Soviet Socialist Republics: Armenia, Azerbaijan, Belarus, Estonia, Georgia, Kazakhstan, Kyrgyzstan, Latvia, Lithuania, Moldova, Russia, Tajikistan, Turkmenistan, Ukraine, and Uzbekistan. The capital of the USSR was Moscow.

During the time of its existence, the Union of Soviet Socialist Republics was by area the world's largest power bloc. The majority of its population was made up of East Slavs (Russians, Ukrainians, and Belo-Russians).

These groups together made up more than two-thirds of the total population of the USSR in the late 1980s. While democratic in structure, in actuality, the political system was authoritarian and highly centralized under the control of the Communist Party. This also applied to the economic system. The economy of the entire region was controlled by a series of five-year plans that set targets for all forms of production.

During the late 1960s to the 1980s, the Soviet Union and the United States were in the deep freeze of the Cold War. The USSR also had its hands full maintaining control over its client states in Eastern Europe and trying to assist or control those third world countries, which were trying to keep out of the sphere of the capitalist world. During this time, the USSR lost the good will of many Arab countries when they failed to come to the aid of the Arabs during the 1967 Arab-Israeli War. But the USSR was able to rebuild its influence by arming its Arab client states afterward.

The USSR invaded Czechoslovakia in 1968 and crushed a progressive movement of the local people that it perceived as a threat to its iron fisted control. In 1969, Russia and China had a falling out that resulted in armed conflict along the Ussuri River that divided the two countries. The Soviet Union strengthened its presence along the Chinese border and extended military aid to India, Pakistan, and North Vietnam in an effort to curb Chinese influence.

In 1971, the Soviets replaced Walter Ulbricht, the leader of East Germany with Erich Honecker because they believed the Germans were becoming too self-assertive. Honecker who had built the Berlin Wall and gave the "shoot to kill" order to stop any attempted escapes, ironically, upon taking power, began a program of "consumer socialism" and sought to normalize relations with West Germany. Honecker also led East Germany in becoming a full member of the United Nations.[90]

About this same time, the Soviets, themselves, began looking for a way to establish cordial relations with the West. The policy under Brezhnev in 1969 became known as "détente." In 1970, the USSR signed treaties with West Germany and Poland that recognized the inviolability of existing frontiers. On May 26, 1972, US President Richard M. Nixon and Leonid Brezhnev signed the first SALT (Strategic Arms Limitation Treaty) agreement in Moscow, which recognized that nuclear war was no longer a feasible option. The following year in Washington, D.C., the two signed an agreement designed to avert nuclear war. The Soviets also removed some of their restrictions on Jewish emigration. The number of Jews leaving the Soviet Union rose steadily until it peaked in 1979.

On August 1, 1975, the heads of thirty-three European governments and those of the United States and Canada convened at Helsinki to sign the Final Act of the Conference on Security and Cooperation in Europe. The Helsinki Accords recognized the postwar frontiers in Europe as inviolable. The early 1970s appeared to be a period of considerable success for the Soviets in foreign policy.

In 1975, North Vietnam was victorious over South Vietnam and forced an ignominious US withdrawal. Vietnam, Cambodia, and Laos were now firmly in the communist camp. Pro-Soviet regimes took over in Angola, Mozambique, and other former Portuguese colonies. In the horn of Africa, Ethiopia and South Yemen joined the Soviet camp. In Afghanistan, cooperation resulted in a treaty of friendship with Moscow.

The US reaction to this "expansionism" was severe. President Carter refused to submit SALT II for ratification to the US Senate and imposed an embargo on grain exports. In 1980, Ronald Reagan was elected president. Reagan was determined to increase US defense spending rapidly, partly to strengthen US security. but also to force Moscow to follow suit. He was advised that a sharp rise in the Soviet defense budget would have grave consequences for the domestic Soviet economy. This proved to be correct. The president initiated a space-based anti-ballistic missile system, which he claimed would render nuclear weapons "impotent and obsolete." The administration's effort quickly became dubbed "Star Wars" because of the systems' planned reliance on high-technology laser beam weapons deployed in space. The Russian communist party's attempt to keep up in the arms race, helped set the stage for the fall of the Soviet Union by 1991.[91]

The Soviet Union was a formidable opponent of capitalism for many years. It served to keep the capitalists out of many countries and to broadcast a critical analysis of capitalist exploitation. Unfortunately, in many ways, it was a worse system than capitalism. It was as exploitive as capitalism, but it also allowed less rights to the people under its control. Further it left no room for personal or spiritual growth. As such, it never was, nor will it ever be, a model that can serve us in moving toward a universal human society.

Organization of Petroleum Exporting Countries (OPEC)

OPEC (Organization of Petroleum Exporting Countries) is an intergovernmental organization of twelve oil-producing countries made up of Algeria, Angola, Ecuador, Iran, Iraq, Kuwait, Libya, Nigeria, Qatar, Saudi Arabia, the United Arab Emirates and Venezuela. OPEC was founded during the 1960s and 1970s with the intention to unifying and coordinating its members' petroleum policies. OPEC evolved after a hard struggle by the oil-producing countries to wrest control of their raw material from western corporations. The countries of OPEC experienced the same oppression and exploitation as did other third world countries. Yet, because of the need of the capitalist industrial society for oil and gas, and because oil was such a visible and widely dispersed commodity, by acting in consort, the oil producing countries were able to outmaneuver the capitalists after a difficult struggle. Their example gained the admiration of the third world and became the model for the vision and policies projected in the New International Economic Order (NIEO). The tool OPEC used to gain control over their oil supplies was the passing of laws to nationalize the oil industries within their countries.

Middle Eastern countries including Iraq, Iran, Saudi Arabia, and Kuwait were all poor and underdeveloped before the discovery of oil during the beginning of the twentieth century. They were desert kingdoms that had few natural resources and were without adequate finances to maintain a modern state. Peasants and nomad tribes made up a majority of the population.[92] When oil was discovered, the countries did not have enough knowledge of the oil industry to make use of the newly discovered natural resources. They could not mine or market their petroleum.

The major oil companies understood the value of oil to the industrial process and, having the technology to mine it, negotiated concession agreements with these undeveloped countries. Despite the countries' efforts to create a fair settlement, they were unable to claim any of the oil they mined.[93] As a result, the world's greatest oil supply came to be largely controlled by seven corporations based in the United States and Europe. Five of the companies were American (Chevron, Exxon, Gulf, Mobil, and Texaco), one was British (British Petroleum), and one was Anglo-Dutch (Royal Dutch/Shell). These companies have since merged into four oil companies: Shell, ExxonMobil, Chevron, and British Petroleum (BP)

The movement to nationalize the oil began once the developing countries came to realize that the oil companies were taking extreme advantage of them. Led by Venezuela, the countries joined together as OPEC and gradually they gained control of their own oil supplies rather than allowing the oil companies to control them.

In 1973, the leading OPEC countries, angry at the West's support of Israel in the Yom Kippur War, created an oil embargo and stopped providing oil to the United States and Western Europe. In doing so, the oil prices in the United States went from three dollars a barrel to twelve dollars a barrel, spurring a recession. It is interesting, however, that there were many good things that came out of the embargo in the US. For example, people started purchasing smaller, more fuel-efficient cars, the actual cost of energy began to be looked at in earnest, and the speed limit was reduced to fifty-five miles an hour on highways, resulting in less traffic fatalities and a reduced use of gasoline. People also began setting their thermostats to sixty-five rather than seventy-two degrees.[94]

While the OPEC nations discovered that their oil could be used as political and economic leverage against the capitalist countries, this strategy did not translate in the same way for other third world countries. Their raw materials did not have the same status as oil and they were therefore unsuccessful in employing the OPEC strategy.

The Group of 77

The Group of 77 is the fourth power bloc within human society. It is a loose coalition of developing nations, designed to promote its members' collective economic interests and create a negotiating capacity in the United Nations. While seventy-seven nations founded the organization, the organization had since expanded to one hundred and thirty-threemember countries. The group was founded in June, 1964 by the "Joint Declaration of the Seventy-Seven Countries" issued at the United Nations Conference on Trade and Development (UNCTAD). The group held its first major meeting in Algiers in 1967, where it adopted the *Charter of Algiers* [95] and established the basis for permanent institutional structures.[96]

Following the *Non-Aligned Movement (NAM)*, which was founded in Belgrade in 1961, the third world countries joined together to form the Group of 77. The intention of this movement was to protect third world interests in reference to the OECD and the Soviet Union. Their objective was world peace, which they hoped to achieve by not aligning themselves with either of the superpowers or its surrogates.

The organization was largely conceived by India's first prime minister, Jawaharlal Nehru; Indonesia's first president, Sukarno; Egypt's second president, Gamal Abdel Nasser; Ghana's first president Kwame Nkrumah; and Yugoslavia's president, Josip Broz Tito. All five leaders were prominent advocates of a middle course for the third world, or as they were known by the OECD, the "Developing World."[97]

The Non-Aligned movement was never established as a formal organization, but became the name that referred to the participants of the *Conference of Heads of State or Government of Non-Aligned Countries* first held in 1961. Nehru described the five pillars to be used as a guide for the Non-Aligned Movement. The five principles were:

1. Mutual respect for each other's territorial integrity and sovereignty;
2. Mutual non-aggression;
3. Mutual non-interference in domestic affairs ;
4. Equality and mutual benefit; and
5. Peaceful co-existence

In an opening speech given during the conference that produced the *Havana Declaration of 1979*, Fidel Castro addressed the assembly with these words:

> Let us all join together closely. Let us put together the growing forces of our vigorous movement in the United Nations and in all international forums to demand economic justice for our peoples and to bring an end to domination of our resources and the robbery of our

sweat. Let us join together to demand our right to development, our right to life, our right to the future.[98]

Today, the countries of the Non-Aligned Movement represent nearly two-thirds of the United Nations' members and contain fifty-five percent of the world population.

In 1985, another conference of non-aligned countries was held in Cuba to discuss the debt crisis. One prominent Brazilian politician, Luis Ignacio Silva, who later became president of Brazil, expressed the sentiment of the Third World in these terms:

> Without being radical or overly bold, I will tell you that the Third World War has already started - a silent war, not for that reason any the less sinister. This war is tearing down Brazil, Latin America and practically all the Third World. Instead of soldiers dying there are children, instead of millions of wounded there are millions of unemployed; instead of destruction of bridges there is the tearing down of factories, schools, hospitals, and entire economies . . . It is a war by the United States against the Latin American continent and the Third World. It is a war over the foreign debt, one which has as its main weapon interest, a weapon more deadly than the atom bomb, more shattering than a laser beam.[99]

If a bank or foreign corporation had used its hard-earned money to help these developing nations, then we might sympathize with their insistence that their loans be repaid. But the money used to make the loans was created from fractional reserve banking. The money loaned to the Third World came from the ninety percent the banks allow themselves to loan on the ten percent they actually held. It did not exist, it was created from nothing, and now people are suffering and dying in an effort to pay it back.

This banking strategy of the capitalist class has gone beyond clever financing and is now wholesale murder.[100]

The Brandt Report

In 1980, as the strain between the capitalist countries and the third world countries continued to increase due to economic exploitation, the UN General Assembly created the *Independent Commission on International Development Issues*, as a means to understand the dynamics of the international economy and develop a solution to the great economic divide that separated the rich industrialized countries of the northern hemisphere (The North) and the masses of impoverished people in the undeveloped countries of the southern hemisphere (The South).[101]

The Commission was chaired by Willy Brandt, former Chancellor of West Germany, and included some of the brightest minds representing the four power blocs indicated above. The Commission published what came to be known as The *Brandt Report*. This report provided an understanding of the drastic differences in the economic development of the Northern and Southern hemispheres of the world. Its recommendation on how to bridge this ever-expanding divide received much publicity and wide-ranging acceptance as the best way forward for governments to realistically reduce the growing economic disparity. Notwithstanding their wide acceptance among the world's intellectuals, the governments never adopted the proposals put forward, because the capitalists were not about to share their wealth with those who they were intentionally impoverishing. The means of building capitalist wealth, after all, was the impoverishment of others.

The Report emphasized that "cooperation," not competition was required to facilitate economic development that could lead to "self-fulfillment and the use of a nation's productive forces and its full human potential." The commission argued that human development meant more than economic development; it also meant greater human dignity, security, justice, and equity. The Commission stressed that the world could no longer carry on as if it was business as usual. It appealed to all world leaders and people from every strata of life to participate in shaping a common future for humanity.

While emphasizing the common global economy, it drew a clear distinction between the huge populations of the South living in poverty and the riches of the North, and cited the reason for the difference was economic power, particularly the North's domination of "the international economic system, its rules and regulations, and its international institutions of trade, money, and finance."

To address the great imbalance, the commission advocated a large-scale transfer of resources to the South in order to strike a balance and revive a failing world economy. It rejected the idea that the rich nations' main role in fighting poverty was to supply "development aid." Rather it called outright for a restructuring of the global economy to allow developing countries a chance to participate realistically in meeting their own basic needs and contribute to the world economy. The report concentrated on meeting the basic need for food, health care, housing, and education.[102]

Despite its clear analysis of global economic conditions and its detailed strategies for resolving the economic problems of the world, the capitalist North gave the Brandt Report little more than a yawn and stone walled any attempts to discuss it, much less negotiate. A look at the United Nations General Assembly's 11th Special Session that occurred the same year as the publishing of the Brandt Report confirms the mindsets of the capitalist countries and the third world at the time.

The UN General Assembly 11th Special Session, 1980

When the 11th Special Session of the General Assembly began, the President of the Session opened with a sobering assessment of the condition of the international economy: "We enter the decade of the 1980s in a state of crisis. The international community is experiencing the most serious economic crisis since the great depression of the 1930s." Secretary of State Edmund Muskie of the United States echoed this statement, proclaiming: "We are in the middle of a world economic crisis." Foreign Minister Genscher of West Germany warned, "We are confronted by a world economic and political situation in which the future development of developing countries and hence the peaceful development of the world as a whole are in jeopardy."[103]

The Sweden representative admitted that, "The idea of bringing change in the world economic order in favor of the developing countries has remained empty rhetoric in too many quarters." Of course, speakers from the third world reinforced these statements in even more alarming terms. There was general agreement from all the power blocs concerning the validity of the conclusions of the Brandt report, which was referred to again and again in the opening sessions by the speakers of both the North and the South.

When it came time to analyzing the causes of the current crisis, however, the differences quickly emerged. The capitalist countries blamed OPEC for the crisis saying that their price increases created a global recession. This was, of course, a smokescreen to take the attention off them. They also vigorously defended the behavior of the World Bank/IMF as contributing to global growth that was of benefit to all.

For their part, the third world countries blamed the causes of the economic crisis on the capitalist banks and corporations. Mr. Benyania of Algeria, speaking for his peers, characterized the present order as "having relied on the systematic exploitation of the wealth of other countries, which was a determining factor in the expansion and development of the Western countries, today it ravages the third world, which has been turned into an unwilling shock absorber and a forced stabilizer of the crisis."[104]

OPEC, angry about the assault made by the US and other capitalist countries, was caught in having to defend itself from charges that it was responsible for the current crisis. The representative of the Soviet Union stated that the present international economic system: "has served the interests of imperialist monopolies and has entered into an irreconcilable contradiction with the vital interests of the vast majority of the countries and the general development of the international situation." He said that the capitalist countries had an obligation to assist developing countries based on "compensation for the damage caused by colonial exploitation" or "as compensation for the losses being incurred by the developing countries at the present time as a result of the activities of transnational corporations."[105]

Mr. Li Qiang of China stated: "China belongs to the third world, and it will always stand by the developing countries through thick and thin, and will support each other . . . China has done what it could in extending aid to other developing countries, despite many difficulties in its own economy."[106]

The opening statements of the Special Session revealed the immense gap between the aspirations of the third world for a more equitable playing field and the unwillingness of the capitalist countries, led by the United States, to make any changes to satisfy those aspirations. The North backpedaled, put up smoke screens, defended itself, and criticized OPEC and the "utopian" ideas put forth by the other speakers. The reluctance of the capitalist countries to negotiate stemmed from their reluctance to give up anything of value. They looked at negotiations as an exercise solely to benefit the third world countries. And since the South was far weaker than the North, it knew that the South could not force the North to invest in benefitting the poor countries.

The North had no understanding or appreciation for the idea of cooperation even if, in the long term, it would create a better and more equitable world. This remains the tragic flaw of the capitalist North, and has now begun to have great negative repercussions for the people of America and Europe. Now that the mighty countries of China and India are on the rise, they are taking jobs from the Northern countries and destroying the capitalist economies. Of course, the capitalist banks and corporations are still profiting from this development. Wherever it is possible to make a dollar, be it from war, famine, the destruction of local economies, the exploitation of raw materials, or the destruction of the environment, you will find the big capitalist around the table making their plans.

When the haggling began at the 11th Special Session, no concessions were made. Participants never got past the first agenda item as to which institution would arbitrate the discussions. The North wanted the World Bank/IMF to be the final arbiter of any negotiations, while the South wanted the General Assembly to serve this role. This sticking point prevented any further discussion of any substance.

In the capitalist countries, the people remained ignorant of the life and death process being played out on the world stage. Corporate mainstream media, in fact, went on the attack against the United Nations, minimizing its importance and criticizing its anti-Americanism.

The Brundtland Report (Our Common Future)

The deadlock among the power blocs in the global economy only added to the rising pressure. The exploitation of the third world continued. Poverty and environmental destruction continued. By now, the deteriorating condition of the natural environment due to economic exploitation was becoming a bigger issue within the capitalist countries themselves. Ever since the first Earth Day was held in the United States in 1970, the damage to ecosystems, the loss of bio-diversity, the destruction of the planet's life support systems, and the impact of climate change had been building in the collective consciousness. So also, rapid population growth, particularly in the third world, and its impact on the earth's resources became a concern. Startling environmental data was beginning to emerge that the people of the world were consuming two percent of the earth's forests per year. This meant that within fifty years the forests would be gone, along with the species that lived in them. The weather patterns would be radically changed by drought, etc.

Having little success in creating a dialogue between the North and the South on such vital issues, the Secretary General of the United Nations, Javier Perez de Cuellar did the only thing he could—he appointed another commission to look at the world's problems. Formally known as the *World Commission on Environment and Development (WCED)*, it was informally called the Brundtland Commission, so named after its Chairman Gro Harlem Brundtland, the former Prime Minister of Norway. The Commission was given the following mandate: Propose long-term environmental strategies for achieving sustainable development to the year 2000 and beyond. It began its work after being recognized by the General Assembly in 1984.

The Commission members, similar to the Brandt Commission, were high-level functionaries from all four power blocs. William Doyle Ruckelshaus, who served as the first head of the newly created Environmental Protection Agency (EPA) in 1970 under President Nixon, represented the US. During the shakeup following Nixon's impeachment, Ruckelshaus was appointed acting Director of the Federal Bureau of Investigation, and then Deputy Attorney General of the United States. He had a reputation for integrity within the system and, on his watch at the EPA, was responsible for banning DDT despite great pressure on him.

While the capitalist countries were beginning to look for ways to reduce their environmental impact, the third world countries initially looked at environmental issues as a ruse by the capitalist nations to take attention off economic development. They had bought into the capitalist doctrine that the only way that the third world countries could get out of their plight was through rapid growth. Because of their need for growth, (which was continually exasperated by the fact that profits were drained from their countries by the capitalist corporations), the third world leaders believed that they could not achieve that growth by factoring in environmental consequences. They wanted to use the cheapest methods possible to industrialize. Unfortunately, these often caused the most environmental damage and fostered unethical labor practices.

The United Nations saw the need for the Brundtland Commission to address environmental challenges in relation to the economic and social concerns for which the Third World had been fighting over the last three decades. In other words, the work of the Commission was seen as a response to the intersection between the global economic monopoly of the capitalist countries and the emerging ecological disaster. This meant that it had to develop a solution that would allow continued "growth" without harming the environment.[107]

To accomplish this impossibility, required a paradigm shift. An entirely new vision was required to replace the established capitalist modus operandi known as "business as usual." The new vision became crystallized in the term *Sustainable Development* that appeared in the Commission's report in 1987 called *Our Common Future*. By definition:

> Sustainable development is development that meets the needs of the present without compromising the ability of future generations to meet their own needs." It contains within it two key concepts: the concept of 'needs', in particular the essential needs of the world's poor, to which overriding priority should be given; and the idea of limitations imposed by the state of technology and social organization on the environment's ability to meet present and future needs.[108]

More than any other idea that had emerged to date, the new paradigm presented in *Our Common Future* seized the imagination of the earth's people. To be able to articulate this paradigm, the commissioners spent three years traveling to every continent to speak with people of all levels of society concerning their vision of life and what could be done to improve the world. Given this broad-based participation in the process of defining the new paradigm of sustainable development, two new elements evolved in the historic effort to create a just world. The first was that local networks began in many countries to promote environmental stewardship. Most of these networks linked governments and non-government organizations (NGOs). One such network, for example, was President Clinton's Council on Sustainable Development, which was initiated in 1993 and existed until 1999.[109] In this Council, although long forgotten, government and business leaders came together to share ideas on how to encourage sustainable development.

In 1988, the U.N. established the Intergovernmental Panel on Climate Change (IPCC) to collect, assess, and report on global scientific research concerning climate change.[110] Its first report, published in 1990, alerted humanity that the world's scientific community had overwhelmingly determined that human activities were substantially increasing the atmospheric concentrations of carbon dioxide, methane, and nitrous oxide,[111] which was causing the Earth's atmosphere to warm up. The scientists had calculated that carbon dioxide (CO_2) had been responsible for over half the enhanced greenhouse effect. They predicted that under a "business as usual" scenario, the global mean temperature would continue to rise throughout the twenty-first century. In light of this astounding discovery, the U.N. sponsored the Kyoto Protocol in 1997.

The Kyoto Protocol was an international treaty, which committed national governments to reduce greenhouse gases emissions, based on the premise that: (1) global warming exists and (2) man-made CO_2 emissions have caused it. The Kyoto Protocol was adopted in Kyoto, Japan, on December 11, 1997 and entered into force on February 16, 2005. There are currently 192 parties who have signed the treaty. The United States never signed it.[112]

Another great accomplish of the U.N. in its quest to serve the interests of humanity as a whole, was its sponsorship of a series of global conferences based on the theme of sustainable development. During the 1990s, the U.N. sponsored major worldwide conferences that brought governments and peoples' organizations (NGOs) together to plan the conferences and review official documents. As the governments met, the peoples' organizations held parallel conferences (the NGO Forum) in which groups from around the world met and developed their own statements.

The main conferences were the:

- Earth Summit (UN Conference on Environment and Development), Rio de Janerio, Brazil - 1992
- World Conference on Human Rights, Vienna, Austria - 1993
- International Conference on Population and Development, Cairo, Egypt - 1994
- World Summit for Social Development, Copenhagen, Denmark - March 1995
- Fourth World Conference on Women, Beijing, China - September 1995
- UN Conference on Human Settlements - Habitat II, Istanbul, Turkey - June 1996
- World Food Summit, Rome, Italy - November 1996
- Earth Summit II or RIO+5, UN Headquarters, New York City, USA, 1997

Of these conferences, the one that created the most enthusiasm and optimism was the Earth Summit. The Summit produced several important documents: *Agenda 21*, the *Rio Declaration on Environment and Development*, the *Statement of Forest Principles*, the *United Nations Framework Convention on Climate Change*, and the *United Nations Convention on Biological Diversity*.

In addition, the Summit set the stage for the development of two more important documents. The first was "Caring for the Earth: A Strategy for Sustainable Living" jointly published by the U.N. Environmental Programme, the World Conservation Union, and the World Wide Fund for Nature in 1991. The second was the *Earth Charter*, which has been in the process of development since 1994. Its most recent draft has over two thousand organizations that formally support it. The Earth Charter is now increasingly recognized as a global consensus statement on the meaning of sustainability, the challenge and vision of sustainable development, and the principles by which sustainable development is to be achieved. It is used as a basis for peace negotiations, as a reference document in the development of global standards and codes of ethics, as a resource for governance and legislative processes, as a community development tool, and as an educational framework for sustainable development.[113]

The Earth Summit brought the governments of one hundred and seventy-two nations together and also drew representatives from over twenty-four hundred international organizations to the NGO Forum. The forum was open to the public and visitors numbered seventeen thousand people.[114]

The significance of the worldwide participation by citizens' groups in the U.N. conferences should not be underestimated. Prior to the Earth Summit, most NGOs were only interested in meeting with groups who shared their specific issues. The twelve hundred NGOs that were officially affiliated with the United Nations were divided into interest sectors—education, women, children, environment, development, health care, agriculture, etc. They had neither reason nor interest in having any interaction with NGOs outside their interest group. After the Earth Summit, however, this was no longer the case. NGOs now meet across interests and across national boundaries motivated by the vision of sustainable development as proposed in the Earth Charter, Agenda 21 and other global documents. People are finding that their specific issues and concerns are interconnected and interdependent and are now anchoring their causes to the common theme of sustainable development. This is something new for humanity. It signals not only the birth of a worldwide movement but also the beginning of an intellectual revolution.

An expression of this development was that in the year 2000, the one hundred and ninety-two United Nations member states, along with international NGOS, jointly agreed to achieve eight Millennium Development Goals by 2015.[115] The goals were to:

1. Eradicate extreme poverty and hunger;
2. Achieve universal primary education;
3. Promote gender equality and empower women;
4. Reduce child mortality;
5. Improve maternal health;[116]
6. Combat HIV/AIDS, malaria, and other diseases; and
7. Ensure environmental sustainability.

Despite these progressive intentions, the reality of capitalism, with its accelerating wars and exploitation of human beings and its destruction of nature, made such goals impossible to achieve.

The Domestic Consequences of US Imperialism

In the United States, opposition to capitalist globalization began to grow in the 1970s. The strongest opposition came from organized labor unions. US factories had been cutting their labor force by tens of thousands of jobs and the process was not stopping. The labor unions realized that the corporations were closing their factories in the US, but were rebuilding them in third world countries where labor costs were cheaper than slave labor. At the time, sixty percent of the workers in Hong Kong were working in sweatshops seven days a week for a dollar a day. To minimize the bargaining power of the US workers, many corporations had also set up duplicate production facilities so that they could shift from one site to another in the event of labor disturbances. In time, the only unions in the United States to survive with any power were those that work for the government. However, it remains the goal of many Republican governors to destroy these government unions as well.

In 1996, the Democratic Policy Committee, chaired by Richard Gephardt, received a staff report entitled "Who is Downsizing the American Dream?" The opening paragraph read:

> There is wide agreement among those who study the American electorate that growing voter anger in the United States is closely associated with the decline in wages and job security experienced by a wide segment of the population during the past decade and a half.[117]

The report quoted American voices from across the country:

> "I am no longer a middle class person. They have lowered me to a lower class." (Tacoma, WA)
>
> "Our poor and our very rich are spreading further and further apart. The ones in the middle are almost gone." (San Diego, CA)
>
> "I have three jobs and my husband has three jobs." (San Diego, CA)
>
> "So there is no more job security, there is no more vested pension funds. Those people who have worked for 25 years are nervous. Their families are constantly nervous. I have seen personally the results of big business restructuring and putting people's jobs in jeopardy." (Des Moines, IA)
>
> "I'm concerned about a breakdown in the family as far as values. I don't know whether it's due to families where both husband and wife and maybe a child need to be working outside the home in order to maintain some semblance of a lifestyle – not an extravagant one but just survival." (Raleigh NC)

From 1947 to 1995, Per Capital GDP grew over one hundred and forty percent, demonstrating that the American worker more than doubled productivity in America. Yet, sometime during the late 1970s, American labor stopped sharing in the wealth that they created. The Bureau of Labor statistics reported in 1995 that the "average hourly wage has fallen by eleven percent over the past seventeen years."[118]

The situation has not improved, but has only gotten worse as we struggle through the second decade of the new millennium. According to CNN, the Millennials are the first generation of Americans to ever earn less than their parents' generation. As long as the bankers' policies continue to be supported by both Republicans and Democrats, we can expect that increasing numbers of people will fall deeper into debt and extreme poverty. Today, the present economy only works for thirty percent of the population, while tens of millions have been eliminated from the middle class and greater numbers have sunk below the poverty line.

Currently in the US, there are only enough full-time jobs for fifty percent of the working age population and half of the full-time jobs pay under thirty-five thousand dollars per year.[119] Here is how David DeGraw in his book *The Economics of Revolution*, published in 2014, put it:

> Since 2007, the economy has lost over 14 million full-time jobs while the overall population has grown by 17 million people. In current conditions, it is impossible for 70% of the working-age population to earn enough income to afford basic necessities without taking on ever-increasing levels of debt, which they will never be able to pay back because there are not enough jobs that generate the necessary income to keep up with the cost of living.[120]

From 2007 – 2013, overall wealth increased twenty-six percent while the median household lost a shocking forty-three percent of their wealth. If median wealth continues to decline at this rate, over fifty percent of US households will be bankrupt within the next decade. Mainstream propaganda has temporarily obscured the fact that we are sitting on a ticking economic time bomb. Statistical fraud by the government on poverty, cost of living, and unemployment cannot cover up the fact that the *overwhelming majority* of the population is on a fast track to impoverishment.

The government's policies and actions in dealing with the growing epidemic of poverty are the very definition of tyranny. It could not be more blatant. Just when the economy has reached a point where there are not enough jobs that generate an adequate income to sustain the cost of living for the *majority of the population*, the government is cutting billions of dollars from assistance programs and pouring billions of dollars into the military and prison industry.[121]

How the US-based Multinational Corporations Control Us

The big corporations have seized control over the production of our basic needs and in so doing have destroyed the small towns and rural areas of our country. They have swept small businesses out of existence and have seized control of our food, shelter, clothing, health care, and education. These basic needs are our birthright as human beings. We have fought for these rights and have given our blood, sweat, and tears to build a democracy, which ensures our access to them.

Instead, food in this country is controlled by four big companies, which have the power to starve us out unless the government grants them subsidies and other pay offs. These companies genetically modify the food we eat and spend tens of millions of dollars preventing the labeling of food packaging that reveals this to be the case. The corporations poison our soil, air and water with chemicals while the majority of food created is now derived from genetically modified corn and soybean, including corn syrup. Corporate food causes six of the ten leading killer diseases in America. These are heart disease, obesity, diabetes and cancer, stroke, and chronic liver disease.[122] Corporate food is what we eat when we go to fast food chains like MacDonald's, Arby's Wendy's, Burger King, etc.

Health insurance and the cost of pharmaceuticals are more expensive than the average American can afford. At the same time, the industry suppresses research into generic herbs and medicines that would be affordable to people, but from which the companies cannot profit. The government does not pay for research into these fields and thus the universities must depend upon corporate grants to do research. The public good has been sacrificed for corporate profits.

There is never a discussion in the mass media between the causal link between our processed diet and the health care crisis in America.

Clothing is so cheap because it is produced by enslaved adults and children in third world countries. Domestic companies cannot compete and have been driven out of business.

Housing prices have been manipulated through a pump and dump scheme that have ruined families and added to the homeless on our streets.

Education loans are saddling the young with debt that will take them a lifetime to pay. In the meantime, the value of a college education diminishes because there are far fewer jobs for the young.

Corporations have moved most of the manufacturing jobs out of the country, so that for the most part only hi-tech and service jobs remain. Currently, eighty percent of US private sector employment, or one hundred and thirty-one million jobs, are service jobs.[123] From our experience, we know that most of these jobs are low paying. The manufacturing jobs will not come back to the US because the big banks always go where labor is cheapest. Once they have exploited the labor in China, Mexico, and India, they will look for an even more destitute working force and the same cycle will start all over until there is nothing left of the planet. Unemployment and underemployment will keep growing globally. This is a direct consequence of the capitalists' relentless pursuit of profit.

The government employment and unemployment statistics in the US are a pure fabrication because they do not count the people too discouraged to keep looking for work or those who are underemployed, that is, those working full time but unable to make ends meet because their paycheck is so paltry.

While the military industrial complex keeps growing in order to suppress other countries so that the bankers can steal their resources, this does not mean that the average soldier knows what he is doing. Nor does it mean that he or she earns a living wage or will receive decent medical care if something happens to him or her. In the meantime, on the domestic front, the police departments are becoming militarized by the big banks,[124] the Pentagon,[125] and the Department of Homeland Securing (DHS),[126] so as to contain the American population as pressure builds and protests turn violent. This process of militarization of the domestic police force has resulted in more violence against racial minorities and greater isolation of the police from the general public.

The corporations continue to destroy the natural environment and local people have no say in the matter. When fossil fuels are extracted, for example, and local people come down with cancer and other illnesses, due to the toxins used in the process, their county boards cannot defend them. The decisions to control the corporations are made at the state level, which overrides decisions at the local level. And if the state government chooses to protect the local people, the federal government will override the state decisions in favor of the multinational corporations. In the meantime, the corporations continue to spread lies about climate change and stall any federal government attempts to cut greenhouse gas emissions. Under the Trump administration this atrocity has reached epic proportions.

If this is not enough for the American people to bear, the mass media harangues us with a pseudo-culture that destroys our sense of humanity and our community spirit. It replaces our good will with the urge for relentless consumerism through false advertising, psychological manipulation, and the avoidance of the real issues facing us as a society.

Liberals and progressives are locked into this system. Instead of being leaders, they blame people's ignorance for lack of change. They spread the myth that if only people understood the facts, they would stand up and do something about it. The American people already know what is going on. Here is what Don Hazen, a twenty year editor of Alternet, had to say in his recent article *Apocalypse Now: Seriously, It's Time for a Major Rethink about Liberal and Progressive Politics*.[127]

> Americans are very pessimistic: 76 percent of respondents in a Wall Street Journal poll did not feel confident that their children's generation will have a better life than theirs. That's up from 60 percent in 2007. Optimism for Americans peaked in 2001. The percentage of American adults who believe the country is on the wrong track jumped eight percentage points just this summer, to 71 percent, the WSJ poll found.
>
> And Americans' dark views of the future are rational, as their lives have become so much more difficult and depressing. People are working longer hours, working

far past previous retirement age—if they can retire at all. Many Americans do not take vacations. And many Americans of all ages cannot find good jobs, or can only find low-paying and often part-time work, which causes their lifestyles to plummet. College graduates are burdened with heavy debt.

Younger generations know that the perhaps romantic notion of the American Dream, for most people, lies in the trash bin. Over the past 15 years there was more than a fifty percent increase in people thinking there is a lack of opportunity in America (it is now just about half of all Americans). And fifty-nine percent of Americans believe the American Dream is impossible to achieve for most people.

Today, the liberals have no idea how to secure a sustainable economic system to meet the basic necessities of the American people. The best they can come up with is greater dependency on the government dole. The conservatives repeat their mantra that the economy would bounce back if government would reduce spending on social service programs, cut regulations that hamper big business, and provide greater tax incentives for the rich. Under the Trump administration the conservatives got their wish, but when regulations were cut, the corporations ravaged the natural environmen,t which led to climate change and the consequent environmental disasters live floods, droughts, forest fires, sea-rise, and even new disasters that meteorologists are still trying to come up with names for.

In the meantime, the bankers and large corporations continue to exploit the labor and resources of our country and the countries of the world regardless of what political party is in power. As they continue to amass greater wealth; their stranglehold on the world's people grows greater.

In 2000, US banks and corporations began outsourcing jobs to China. This began as soon as China joined the World Trade Organization. Between 2001 and 2013, Americans lost three million and two hudred thousand jobs to China alone.[128] The label "Made in America" became an anachronism and Walmart stores spread across the land to sell "Made in China" goods at cheap prices, effectively destroying hometown retail stores. The jobs lost to China's cheap labor devastated American employment opportunities and eroded wages.

Of the millions of jobs lost, two-thirds were in the manufacturing sector where wages were at least decent. Now those jobs are gone forever; our industrial cities are destroyed; and the American middle class continues to shrink.

The capitalist-owned mass media blames the Chinese for America's suffering. They editorialize against China's currency manipulation[129] and other trade-distorting practices.[130] They condemn China for suppressing labor rights.[131] Yes, these issues are real, just as they were real when any capitalist country begins its period of free market capitalism. The problem is that the American mass media never protests the fact that the US corporations outsourced millions of American jobs to China and other third world countries and in so doing destroyed the American economy and the American middle class. It is, after all, the blood, sweat, and tears of the American people who had built those corporations and who deserve better. The federal government never came to our rescue nor even stood up for the American people. "It is just the way things are done." The anger of the American people is real, but it is misdirected against ourselves, against our women and minorities. Only a handful of politicians have the guts to point their finger at the real enemy—the slick bankers sitting in their wood paneled boardrooms plotting how to maintain their "sustainable economic growth" as the world goes into spasms.

I'm Forever Blowing Bubbles

To keep the juggernaut on track and prevent a popular uprising, the US government continues to borrow money from the Fed to pay for things like unemployment compensation, welfare, disability payments, etc. But the money barely pays for people's subsistence and unemployment compensation stops after a couple of months. Because small towns and rural areas are the hardest hit by unemployment, it is not unusual for government welfare payments to be greater than the income derived from farming, manufacturing, and retail services combined. The government calls these payments "transfer payments." Transfer payments may keep people alive and passive, but they also lead to depression, suicide, domestic violence, racial hatred, and more. Today, we can see what happens when people are frightened too long by economic insecurity. They develop an economic form of PTSD. They become angry and begin to act out. The society polarizes and becomes more extreme. The conservatives turn into ultra-nationalists and lean toward fascism. The liberals keep stamping out the fires, but are too timid and ill-informed to point their finger at the real culprits causing global scale human misery.

Economic insecurity intensifies when the American consumer can no longer afford to meet their basic needs. This makes bankers and big corporations less willing to invest in the local economy because nobody will buy their stuff. They also do not want to make loans to local small businesses even though these businesses actually create most of the American jobs. The bankers would rather loan to the multi-nationals. This is another reason that American unemployment remains so high.[132]

In time, the US bankers and big corporations who refuse to invest in domestic production, will find themselves in the situation of not being able to invest in third world countries either because the raw materials and cheap products of these countries will no longer have a market in the industrialized countries to justify production.

Under such circumstances, what will the investors, banks, corporations, hedge funds, etc., do to continue to make a profit if there is no production to profit from? Basically, they turn their attention inward by merging with other corporations or by buying back their own stocks and bonds. But mostly they gamble on the value of different paper money. Paper consists of federal bonds, national currencies, corporate bonds, municipal bonds, mortgages, stocks, derivatives, etc. In common parlance, "they play the stock market." This is why the Dow Jones keeps rising as people continue to suffer. This is why "Wall Street" can be on a tear while "Main Street" goes to hell.

The majority of transfer payments generated from federal debt in order to keep the most destitute and vulnerable alive, eventually winds up in the banks and corporation where giant piles of cash sit idle while the American infrastructure decays, the human service network shrinks, and Americans go hungry.

One of the tricks that bankers use to profit from the stock market is to create paper bubbles. It is an old trick. Edwin LeFevre, who wrote the classic *Reminiscences of a Stock Operator* in 1923, tells us that the first rule of manipulating a stock price is to "make a market" for it.[133]

Making a market is at the core of a *pump and dump scheme*.[134] When this scheme is expanded from manipulating a single stock to manipulating an entire industry, making a market becomes making a "bubble."[135] A bubble begins when the stock manipulators begin a rumor to the effect that an industry is set to go sky-high and that the smart investor will invest in that industry's corporations before everyone else learns about it.

Take the dot-com bubble for example. Due to the growth of the internet, venture capitalists, many of whom worked for big banks, saw an opportunity to make fast money by employing their tried and true "pump and dump" scheme. Goldman Sachs, one of the biggest investor banks and the inventor of the "Initial Public Offering (IPO)"[136] has this game down to a science. As Matt Taibbi, tells us in the famous *Rolling Stone's* article "The Great American Bubble Machine:"

> The bank's unprecedented reach and power have enabled it to turn all of America into a giant pump-and-dump scam, manipulating whole economic sectors for years at a time, moving the dice game as this or that market collapses, and all the time gorging itself on the unseen costs that are breaking families everywhere — high gas prices, rising consumer credit rates, half-eaten pension funds, mass layoffs, future taxes to pay off bailouts. All that money that you're losing, it's going somewhere, and in both a literal and a figurative sense, Goldman Sachs is where it's going: The bank is a huge, highly sophisticated engine for converting the useful, deployed wealth of society into the least useful, most wasteful and insoluble substance on Earth — pure profit for rich individuals.[137]

They achieve this using the same playbook over and over again. The formula is relatively simple: Goldman positions itself in the middle of a speculative bubble, selling investments they know are crap. Then they hoover up vast sums from the middle and lower floors of society with the aid of a crippled and corrupt state that allows it to rewrite the rules in exchange for the relative pennies the bank throws at political patronage. Finally, when it all goes bust, leaving millions of ordinary citizens broke and starving, they begin the entire process over again, riding in to rescue us all by lending us back our own money at interest, selling themselves as men above greed, just a bunch of really smart guys keeping the wheels greased.[138]

While Taibbi focused his article on Goldman Sachs, arguably one of the most fraudulent of companies, all the big banks use this technique to bilk the public. The basic pump and dump scheme works like this. During the dot.com bubble, companies that were nothing more than concepts scribbled on the back of paper napkins in a coffee shop were taken public by the big banks like Goldman through I*nitial Public Offerings (IPOs)*. The companies were hyped by the mass media, including the *Wall Street Journal* and the stocks, although practically worthless, were sold to the public through pension funds, mutual funds, institutional endowments, and the purchase of individual stocks by single investors. The banks pumped the stocks and the prices soared beyond any true valuation of a company's worth. The public scampered to get a piece of the action. But when the bankers thought that they could not get any more suckers to buy the stock, they pulled out their cash and made a bundle, while the public was left holding an empty bag as the stock price collapsed.

Although there were rules against such practices, and everyone knew the rules, the banks and the federal government, represented at the time by Robert Rubin, the Secretary of the Treasury and Chair of the Council on Foreign Relations under Bill Clinton, (and also an alumnus of Goldman Sachs), turned a blind eye to the colossal theft and fraud.

Jay Ritter, a professor of finance at the University of Florida who specialized in IPOs, said banks like Goldman knew full well that many of the public offerings they were touting would never make a dime.[139] Goldman Sachs and the bankers were hyping stocks in which they were not even requiring to see profit in the foreseeable future. How was Goldman able to make such extraordinary profits out of defrauding the American people?

The mechanism Goldman Sachs used to drive runaway stock prices in worthless companies was a technique they called "laddering." Laddering is a technique used to manipulate the share price. It works like this. Goldman Sachs finds some people with an interesting idea, for example E-Toys. When the bank approaches them, it is like a recording studio coming to a garage band promising wealth and fame. Goldman prices the shares and determines how many stocks to release in exchange for a substantial fee, typically six percent to seven percent of the money raised. Goldman then promises its best clients the right to buy big chunks of the IPO at a low offering price in exchange for a promise that they will buy more shares later on the open market. That simple demand gives Goldman inside knowledge of the IPO's future, knowledge that is not disclosed to anyone else who is buying or trading the stock. Goldman now knows that certain of its clients who bought X amount of shares at fifteen dollars are also going to buy Y more shares at twenty or twenty-five dollars, virtually guaranteeing that the price is going to go to twenty-five and beyond. In this way, Goldman can artificially jack up the new company's price. A six percent fee on a five hundred million dollar IPO is serious money.

Nicholas Maier, the syndicate manager of Cramer & Co. told the SEC that while working for Cramer between 1996 and 1998, he was repeatedly forced to engage in laddering practices during IPO deals with Goldman:

> Goldman, from what I witnessed, they were the worst perpetrator," Maier said. "They totally fueled the bubble. And it's specifically that kind of behavior that has caused the market crash. They built these stocks upon an illegal foundation — manipulated up — and ultimately, it really was the small person who ended up buying in.[140]

In 2005, Goldman agreed to pay forty million dollars for its laddering violations—a puny penalty relative to the enormous profits it made by blowing up the bubble.[141]

Goldman also depended upon bribery to sell smelly shares. In this case, Goldman offered the idea guys executive positions in the company and "hot" opening shares at low prices in exchange for future underwriting business with them.

According to Taibbi, in one case, Goldman allegedly gave a multimillion-dollar special offering to eBay CEO Meg Whitman, who later joined Goldman's board, in exchange for a future internet banking business. According to a report by the House Financial Services Committee in 2002, Goldman gave special stock offerings to executives in twenty-one companies that it took public, including Yahoo, Tyco, and Enron. Goldman angrily denounced the HFS report as "an egregious distortion of the facts" despite the fact that, shortly before, the bank had to cough up one hundred and ten million dollars to settle an investigation into bribery by New York state regulators. "The spinning of hot IPO shares was not a harmless corporate perk," then-attorney general Eliot Spitzer said. "Instead, it was an integral part of a fraudulent scheme to win new investment-banking business."[142]

Such practices turned the Internet bubble into one of the greatest financial disasters in world history. The stock market crash of 2000-2002 caused some five trillion dollars of wealth to be wiped out on the NASDAQ alone. The middle class was scalped again by the very banks it respected and revered. As for the bankers, they learned again how easy it was to inflate bubbles. Even better, the bank executives, instead of being punished for defrauding the public, received multi-million dollar bonuses. The bigger the mania and irrationality they created, the greater was their reward.

After the dot.com bubble, the bankers went on to create the Housing Bubble and later the Oil Bubble where people saw the price of a gas reach four dollars a gallon.

The crisis caused by the Housing Bubble has had severe, long-lasting consequences for the world economy. It set off a worldwide depression, euphemistically called the Great Recession. Nearly nine million American jobs were lost after the Panic of 2008 when the bubble burst. It is estimated that economic output in our country dropped forty percent from 2007 and that housing prices fell nearly thirty percent, trapping millions of homeowners in homes that were worth less than their monthly mortgage payments. The U.S. stock market fell approximately fifty percent by early 2009. Even today economic growth remains below pre-crisis levels and jobs that offer a living wage are virtually impossible to find. The millennial generation suffers from high unemployment, high student debt, and the inability to even rent or own a home. Consequently, many are forced to continue to live with their parents. The people of Europe also continue to struggle with their own economic crisis, with elevated unemployment and rapidly increased debt.[143] If such devastation has affected the industrialized countries, you can imagine what devastation the third world has experienced.

After the housing bubble, the big banks followed up with another bubble, a money bubble that became known as the *Great Bailout* in which trillions of dollars were transferred to the big banks at the expense of the American economy and the American family. Today, we are still reeling from the reverberations of that transfer. The world capitalist economy has not yet recovered, and in all probability never will.

For years after 2008, when the economy crashed, the Federal Reserve kept their printing presses running full-tilt. Its "quantitative easing" policies, which basically entailed printing trillions of dollars in exchange for receiving government IOUs, were used to keep the people on "bread and water" after millions lost their jobs and the value of their homes collapsed. The Federal Reserve's balance sheet which represents the total amount of currency in circulation or in a central bank's reserves, expanded from $1.1 trillion in 2008 to $4 trillion in 2014.[144] Now that the economy has "recovered" in 2019 and the Bank is able to charge 1.25% on the money it prints, it now wants to get the trillions of dollars of IOUs (Treasury bonds) off its books. As they begin to sell these trillions of dollars in bonds to the public, we will see how this affects the stock market, inflation, and the people's ability to make ends meet.

The most important test of the value of Federal Reserve Notes, i.e., our money supply, is whether it facilitates real economic growth for our families. On this score, the evidence is overwhelmingly negative. Measured in ounces of gold, per-family income in the United States has declined since 1971, retreating back to 1950s levels, despite the advent of two-income families.

Measured another way (using the government's own consumer price index as the measure of annual inflation), real family income remained essentially unchanged since 1971. This stagnancy occurred even as wives went to work along with their husbands. The capitalists now got two laborers for the price of one. Household earnings, in real terms, have fallen thirty to fifty percent since President Nixon abandoned the gold standard in 1971.

Paper money works okay for the rich because they can reduce their exposure to the dollar by investing in other things. They can also access credit at a low rate and purchase huge assets with this cheap paper. But more paper money in the system is horrible for the middle class, whose wages do not keep pace with the cost of living that is caused by the paper inflation. If you want to know why there is so much discrepancy in incomes and wealth in the US, all answers lead back to the Federal Reserve Bank and its economy built on debt.

The big Monopoly game continues to grind to its conclusion and it will most likely end with a bang and not a whimper. It may not be a universal Big Bang but it certainly will be a global Big Bang.

Obviously, it will not be good news. If we follow the "business as usual" trends, the stage is being set for WWIII and it will be even bigger than the last. We can see this develop in the tendency toward domestic polarization and foreign polarization as the US and Russia square off again, and the Trump administration taunts North Korea and Iran. The contest between the ultra-nationalists and socialists on the regional and national stages is now beginning. The ultra-nationalists, composed primarily of Christian white supremacists historically turn against women and racial minorities as economic pressures mount.

Today, the polarization is also complicated by the resumption of conflict between the Christian capitalists and the Muslim people, as millions of refugees flee from the war torn countries of the Middle East.

If we are to stem the tide of polarization that will inevitably lead to war; if we want to minimize disaster and create a better world for our children, it is necessary to understand some fundamental truths about ourselves as human beings. We cannot afford to ignore or dream walk through the coming days. We will need to be sharp and informed and get to know our neighbors. We will have to adopt the highest spiritual teachings of our religions. For Christians, this means loving one's neighbor as one's self. Whether we consider ourselves to be liberals or conservatives, we need to come together at the local level to secure our communities against the collapse of the global system. If we cannot see ourselves as being victims of the same system and overcome our prejudices against each other, we will lose everything we value. If, however, we understand some basic truths about ourselves and about our society and we are willing to take action, we can minimize the disaster. It is the time now for warriors and heroes. And we must succeed for the future welfare of our children. When the Native American tribes sat down to discuss their future, they considered the welfare of seven generations down the road. We need to do the same.

Who Owns the Money Today?

People have been trying to find the answer to this question for as long as there has been capitalism. Because the capitalists are so secretive in their dealings, and no public information has been available, conspiracy theories abound. Recently, however, something new has developed. A system analyst, named James Glattfelder, in applying the scientific principles of his field to the workings of the global economy, has produced a groundbreaking study that reveals how power flows through the global system and how it has become concentrated in the hands of a very small number of people. He revealed his findings in a TED talk called "Who Controls the World?"[145]

It is important to realize that this scientific study is not based on conspiracy theory, hearsay, or political ideology. Rather, Glattfelder designed a scientific experiment based upon a simple premise: "Follow the money." His study employed the mathematics used to model natural systems and applied it to comprehensive corporate data in order to map ownership among the world's multi-national corporations. From a massive database of 37 million companies, Glattfelder pulled out 43,060 multinational corporations that are connected by their shareholders, that is, their owners.

Digging further, he constructed a model that actually displayed just how connected these companies are to one another through ownership of shares and their corresponding operating revenues. In his discovery of "ownership networks," he was able to show how these networks are organized and how powerful they actually are.

Glattfelder further boiled these connections down to 1318 main actors, those who were the most connected.

New Scientist wrote an article about Glattfeld's report and summarized his findings.[146] Each of the 1318 corporate owners had ties to two or more other companies, and on average they were connected to twenty. These people collectively own, through their shares, the majority of the world's large blue chip and manufacturing firms which represent sixty per cent of global revenues. When Glattfelder's team further untangled the web of ownership, it found that the ownership of multinational corporations could be traced back to a tightly knit nucleus of one hundred and forty-seven companies. The ownership of these one hundred and forty-seven giant international banks and corporations, alone controlled two thirds of the wealth of the blue chip and manufacturing firms that, in turn, controlled sixty percent of the global economy. In effect, less than 1 per cent of the companies were able to control forty percent of the entire network.

An analysis of the top shareholders of these one hundred and forty-seven companies revealed that a mere seven hundred and thirty people controlled a whopping eighty percent of the entire revenue of multi-national corporations worldwide. It should come as no surprise that most of these corporations are banks and financial institutions in the United States and England.

Here are the top ten multinational companies that hold the most economic power over the global economy:

1. Barclays plc
2. Capital Group Companies Inc.
3. Fidelity Management and Research Corporation
4. AXA
5. State Street Corporation
6. JPMorgan Chase & Co.
7. Legal & General Group plc
8. Vanguard Group Inc.
9. UBS AG
10. Merrill Lynch & Co Inc.

Morgan Stanley, Credit Suisse, and Goldman Sachs, are in the top twenty-five. Among the fifty richest and most powerful companies in the world, forty-nine are all financial institutions, banks, and insurance companies. Only Walmart crept into the super elite.

These companies essentially push money around to each other as they develop "profit making" opportunities. The Federal Reserve and other central banks feed them money as they need it to buy out businesses, countries, armies, etc. No one can compete with them so they continually suck money out of the global economy to the point that now it is shriveling like a dried fruit.

If you want to know who your enemies are, the directors and major shareholders of these corporations are the people. If you look at the board of directors of these companies, you can actually learn the names of the guys who run the world. These are the men who keep the capitalist juggernaut on track. They destroy societies and the environment. They are unconcerned about your suffering. They do not worry about climate change. They are not answerable to any government. These are our real enemies. They are the enemies of all mankind. They are the enemies of the natural world. And under the legal system of the world we have no legitimate means to stop them. They are above the law. The only way to dethrone them is to bring down the capitalist system. They will not be dislodged by liberal or progressive politicians working in the federal government. They will only be dislodged when the majority of the middle class has nothing left to lose.

Here's the interconnectedness of the top players in this international plunder:

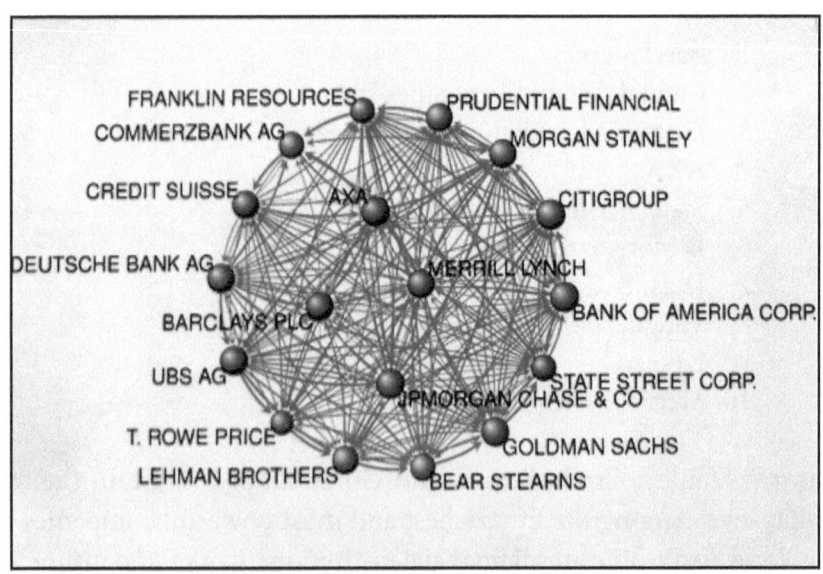

Fig. 5-5: Inter-Connectedness of Largest Companies

Industrialist Henry Ford once said, "It is well enough that people of the nation do not understand our banking and money system, for if they did, I believe there would be a revolution before tomorrow morning."[147]

But now, thanks to James Glattfelder and his team, we do understand our banking and money system. And its like Jimmy Mengel, managing editor of *Outsider Club*, observed: "It's one thing to have suspicions that someone is working behind the scenes to control the world's money supply. It's quite another to have scientific evidence that clearly supports it . . . ."[148]

How Much Money Are We Talking About?

The wealth of the ruling class is staggering. According to the Credit Suisse 2014 Global Wealth Databook.[149] each year since 2008, the year the *housing bubble* popped and the Great Recession began, America's richest one percent have made more than the cost of all US social service programs put together. Depending on the estimate, the one percent take in anywhere from $2.3 trillion to $5.7 trillion per year.

Even the smaller estimate of $2.3 trillion per year is more than the budgets for Social Security ($860 billion), Medicare ($524 billion), Medicaid ($304 billion), and the entire safety net ($286 billion) for SNAP (Supplemental Nutrition Assistance Program), WIC (Supplemental Nutrition Program for Women, Infants, and Children), Child Nutrition, Earned Income Tax Credit, Supplemental Security Income, Temporary Assistance for Needy Families, and Housing.

The multimillionaires and billionaires hold over ninety percent of their assets in low-risk investments (bonds and cash), the stock market, and real estate. They spend less than one percent of their investments in startup businesses. A recent study[150] found that less than one percent of all entrepreneurs came from very rich or very poor backgrounds. They come from the middle class. This proves the misconception of the conservatives that taxing the rich prevents job creation and harms the economy. It is the middle class not the rich who create American jobs.

Rich owners and executives of the multinational corporations, instead of investing in jobs, use their money on *stock buybacks*. In 1981, major corporations were spending less than 3 percent of their combined net income on buybacks, but in recent years they have been spending up to ninety-five percent of their profits on buybacks and dividends.[151]

Oxfam reported that just eighty-five people own as much as half the world. Here in the US, with nearly a third of the world's wealth, just forty-seven individuals, own more than one hundred and sixty million Americans (about sixty million households) who earned below the median wealth level of fifty-three thousand dollars.[152]

The gap between the rich and poor at the global level can be illustrated by the fact that the three wealthiest individuals in the world have assets that exceed those of the poorest ten percent of the world's population. The net worth of the world's billionaires increased from less than one trillion dollars in 2000 to over seven trillion dollars in 2015 so the gap is increasing dramatically.[153] As in the US, the middle class in Europe is also disappearing because of this concentration of wealth.

According to a study reported in *Newsweek*, President Trump's much vaunted Tax Cut and Jobs Act, which was to save the American worker has proven to be little more than a give-away of more public money to the super-rich. Big businesses received nine times more in tax cuts than what they passed on to their workers. The study also found that companies spent thirty-seven times as much on stock buybacks than they did on bonuses and increased wages for workers. It should be no surprise that a billionaire like Trump would pander to his class interests rather than be concerned about the average American.[154]

Are We On The Brink Of Financial Collapse?

This question is difficult to answer. There is certainly a monetary and a fiscal crisis. The value of the US currency and the world's currencies will experience major tremors if the Federal Reserve Bank releases its US Treasuries that are worth trillions of dollars of debt onto the market too quickly. On the other hand, the capitalists may try to keep the economy engaged in wasteful spending by creating more wars and even World War III. While the owners of the world are undoubtedly smart guys, they are not as smart as they think they are or as smart as we give them credit for. In fact, the forty-seven people who dominate the US economy have a mental disease. They are sociopaths. A sociopath is "a person with a personality disorder manifesting itself in extreme antisocial attitudes and behavior and a lack of conscience."[155] Their obsessive greed has led the capitalists to make fundamental errors in their method of wealth extraction based upon the manipulation of the money supply.

As we have just seen, the American capitalists, in lieu of investing in production and infrastructure repair, have chosen to manipulate the economy through the creation of bubbles by which they can exercise pump and dump schemes and walk away with fortunes. The negative impact experienced by society, when they pop their bubble, leaves people without jobs or the income required to keep the economy functioning by purchasing goods and services. People are forced to cut back on buying things and the economy stagnates. Since the Great Recession began in 2007, the economy has grown very little, if at all. In order to keep society from collapsing into a depression, the Federal Reserve Bank has had to flood the country, and the world, with dollars that they have printed based on government debt. They have been doing this same thing since the dot.com bubble began in 1997. In other words, the Fed has printed money in huge quantities after each bubble to keep the misery that would normally be caused during the economic downside from triggering massive public unrest. The consequences of each bubble caused greater economic instability, so that when the housing bubble burst, the Fed had to bail out the big banks themselves. They also had to print enough money for "transfer payments" to keep people from rioting, as had occurred during the Great Depression.

The extra dollars put into the economy after each bubble popping downturn were meant to stimulate the domestic economy and prevent a depression. But it did not work. The reason is that the US has the largest economy in the world and the dollar is still the world currency. When the US economy goes into a recession, the world goes into a recession and when the dollars get printed, they impact not only the US, but the whole world. Even after having printed trillions of dollars to bail out the banks and the US economy through "quantitative easing," we have not experienced inflation because the dollars are dispersed into the global economy as well. This massive economy easily absorbs the dollars, but the amount is still too small to stimulate the domestic economy or the world economy. Consequently, the economy of the entire world is stagnant. This situation resembles the Great Depression, but now on a global scale. The government in the 1930s went into debt to keep the people from rioting, but never spent enough money to restart the economy. Today this same dynamic exists in the US economy.

From our knowledge of the Great Depression, it was only due to the start of WWII that the capitalists began to invest again in the American economy. They did not invest in the economy to get the country out of the Depression. Like today, they sat on the sidelines while the government programs kept the country on life-support.

One of the stipulations of the Bank Bailout was that the bankers invest some of the "bail out" money into the economy, but they reneged on this obligation because they did not see an opportunity to profit from an economy in which people had no money. Instead of investing therefore, they preferred to pile up the cash they received or spend it in other ways. Some of it went overseas to shore up their operations there or to make new acquisitions. Even though the Fed pumped in trillions of dollars and lowered the interest rate on money to zero, this still did not prompt big business to invest in the US economy.

Coupled with the massive loss of jobs to China and other countries, the American consumer base was vitally wounded. This is why the American economy has just been coasting along at a recession pace for the past twenty years.

The government created so much money to stabilize the economy that the national debt now stands at over seventeen trillion dollars. This means that the government owes seventeen trillion dollars to individual investors, US banks, other governments, the Fed, etc., who have bought government bonds. These bonds come due every day and the Treasury pays off these bonds by issuing more bonds and borrowing more money from the Federal Reserve Bank.

If you are a small businessman or householder and you spend more than you earn every month, you must either use up your savings or rack up credit card debt. Because the federal government has no savings, all it can do is continually rack up debt and pay an increasing amount of interest on the debt. How long can they afford to do this until they are bankrupt? Phrased another way, will the bonds of the US government ever reach a stage when nobody wants to buy them because they do not believe they will ever get their money back?

At this point in the game, in 2018, holding federal bonds do not make an investor any money. According to the US Treasury, 10-year bonds, issued on December 31, 2018, pay the holder less than one percent interest over a ten-year term.[156] This is consistent with the rate of inflation, so to put your money into federal bonds is to make no money or literally lose money. The governments of the world are losing billions of dollars each year by having to hold US bonds as dictated by the Bretton Woods agreement. No one is happy about this.

If you were a government losing millions of dollars each year by holding dollars as your foreign reserves, what would you do? Logically, you would begin to diversify your portfolio. You would sell dollars and buy more Euros or rubles or renminbi or any other currency that might hold up better. You would hold more gold. You would set up barter agreements with other countries that allowed you to exchange goods without having to pay for them in dollars. In short, you would do anything you could to protect your savings against the decline of the dollar. This has now been going on for over a decade and a dollar collapse becomes more probable with each passing day.

If this is the case, why do countries keep buying bonds? There are several reasons. The first is that the Bretton Woods agreement requires a country to peg its currency to the value of the dollar and use the dollars to purchase goods in the international market. Without dollars you cannot buy a lot of materials you need for your economy. For example, it is almost impossible to buy oil without paying for it in dollars. The reason that the United States destroyed Qaddafi in Libya was that he announced that he would accept currencies other than the dollar in payment for oil. Qaddafi went so far as to encourage countries in the Middle East and Africa to use a new currency based on gold for internal trade. The second reason to still hold bonds, is that if you are a country, bank, or institutional investor, you understand that even though the US bonds are losing their ability to store value and are worthless when it comes to making a profit, other currencies are no less secure. The US bond for the moment is therefore the least of the evils. People know that if the global economy nose dives into a deeper recession or depression everyone will run to the dollar to preserve their wealth because, other than gold, it is still more trustworthy than other currencies.

Domestic Debt

In the US alone, every state government is in debt. The map below shows the amount of debt owed by each state based on its population. While debt invested in state improvements can be positive, debts used to pay normal expenses or interest are bad. Every state is now billions of dollars in debt not because of infrastructure improvements, but because the money is used for day to day operations or to make interest payments on its borrowing. The states' debt increases every year and the interest payments on the debt eats up more of the money that would otherwise be used to pay for the states' services.

According to the last national census in 2012, the aggregate state debt was about $1.3 trillion dollars. Local governments owed an additional $1.8 trillion dollars. When we add federal, state, and local government debt together, we owe over $20 trillion dollars. This constitutes about twenty percent of the total budgets of all US government agencies, which presently tops one hundred trillion dollars.[157]

American households are also deeply in debt. We owe a total of $13 trillion dollars in mortgage payments. We owe $2.8 trillion in consumer debt. And we owe another $807 billion in credit card debt, which is based on usurious interest payments that keep many people from ever being able to pay the principle. In addition, federal student loans now top $1 trillion. This total debt, which equals $200,000 per family is balanced in the ledger by a mere $7,000 per family savings account. And now laws are being passed to throw debtors into prison.[158]

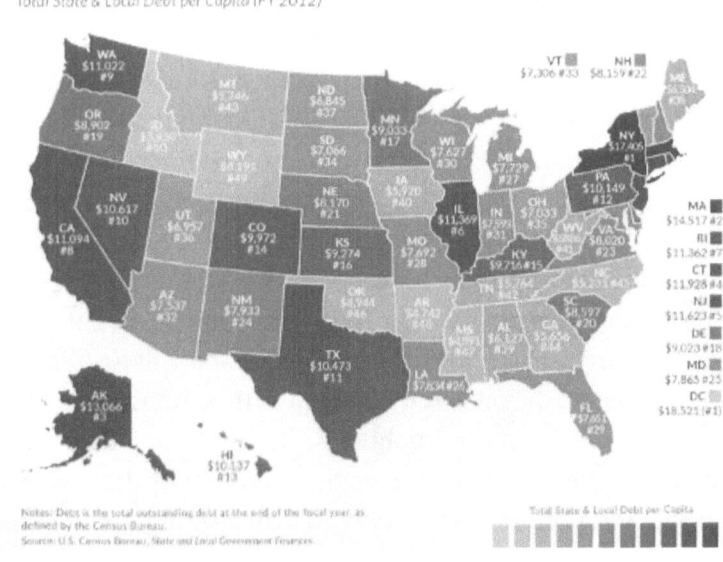

Fig. 5-6: State and Local Debt Per Capita

The situation continues to get worse. The debt will continue to expand, while savings will continue to shrink. This is the end result of having given the bankers control over the money supply. It is inevitable that the American people will continue to go deeper into debt. The American consumer culture will see to this. Listen to any TV or radio newscaster employed by the mass media and you will hear the same message. When consumers spend money, it is good for the economy and when they save money it is bad for the economy. Thus, paying down debt or saving money is bad and unpatriotic.

Consumer spending, we all know, requires consumer borrowing and thus consumer debt. It would be different if we were borrowing money to invest in our future, but we are borrowing it to meet our basic needs. This means that consumer debt is increasing even as our productive capacity continues to increase. Both Bush and Obama, conservative and liberal, encouraged Americans to run up debt as the patriotic thing to do. Thus, America today has too much consumption and too much borrowing. We also have too little production and too little savings. It is not rational to believe that things will get better if we just sit it out.

In order to keep the debt economy from imploding, the federal government has created another bubble. It is a debt bubble. This will be the last of the bubbles. There is nowhere to go after this. There will be no further sector of the economy to exploit, no industry in which to create another bubble. The whole earth has got their money into this final bubble. People, who watch the economy, whether on the left or the right, understand that there is no coming back to normalcy when this debt bubble pops. There will be no safety net and nothing to bail out the banks. At some point in the future, someone, some country, some bank, some institutional investor will cash in a large quantity of their bonds and the game will begin to unravel. Just as the housing bubble began to unravel, so too will the debt bubble. When people panic, they will start cashing in their bonds. Everyone will start running from bonds and nobody will want to buy them. This will cause the bonds to lose value overnight. The value of the dollar, which is tied to the bond on a one-to-one ratio, will also plummet. When the dollar plummets, the value of all the goods and services that are priced in dollars will also plummet. The economy will grind to a halt, factories will close, and bankruptcies will spread across the land.

The Great Recession will turn into the second Great Depression or the Greater Depression. Only this time, the government will have no money to keep social service programs going without causing hyperinflation. Anyone on a fixed income will starve without help from friends or family. Homelessness will become a permanent lifestyle of the poor and even many within the middle class. Price and wage unpredictability will cause chaos and leave big business on the sidelines again. The corporations will fire their workers and sit on their piles of cash unable to make a profit. In order to get people to invest in bonds, the federal government will have to offer higher interest rates, which will further choke off production. If corporations will not invest in an economy when the cost of money is free, how do we expect them to do so when money is more expensive? Even the big banks will be threatened because their profits are dependent upon bonds, stocks, and loans to businesses. Only this time, when the debt bubble pops, there will be no government money to bail them out.

As we shall see in Chapter Three, this is the nightmare scenario that the US military has long anticipated and for which it has long been planning. They will set up large camps to contain the growing millions of jobless and homeless. These refugee camps will hopefully keep our children alive as long as possible but who knows what will happen after that.

The sociopaths, who will have brought down the world's economy by their obsessive greed, will wish they would have listened to the Brandt report and the Brundtland report and the International Panel on Climate Change and the New International Economic Order, or any other voice that predicted an economic and environmental catastrophe based on business-as-usual. Perhaps the sociopaths will not suffer for their actions. Perhaps they will live out their lives behind iron fences and private security forces and spend their enormous wealth on new gadgets that only they will still be able to purchase. It is unlikely, however, that their children will enjoy living in a golden cage any more than ours will enjoy living in refugee camps.

What is the Solution to This Existential Crisis?

We are facing, without doubt, one of the biggest upheavals of social order in the history of western civilization. In fact, we will be witnessing the death throes of western civilization. While the UN has offered suggestions to correct the demise of capitalism, they have been ignored by the bankers, because they will never reverse their course and start giving money back without the ability to profit. This means that domestically, we have three possible strategies to salvage the future. There is the conservative approach, the liberal/progressive approach, and the revolutionary approach.

The traditional approach is simple: tighten the money supply, raise interest rates, and slash government services. While conservatives admit that this will cause a lot of pain in the short term, they justify such an approach in theory because tight money and high interest rates will slow borrowing. People, they believe, will then begin to pay their debts. High interest rates will encourage savings and these savings can eventually be used to invest in new enterprises. A shrinking government will also open up the field to the free market in which investors will put their money into what people need rather than what is politically popular. In the meantime, they insist, we will have to accept a much lower standard of living.[159] The conservative approach, in other words, recommends depression (deflation) as a cure. While there are certain points that are justified within the mechanics of a capitalist system, the tragic flaw in this approach is that it leaves the capitalists with their fortunes intact and places all the pain on the people. It is also unlikely that people will be able to pay their debts because they do not have jobs. As such, we will be unable to recreate a full-blown consumer economy in which the capitalists are willing to invest. And without such an economy, they will continue to hoard their money and sit on the sidelines.

We have learned from the previous Great Depression that even with large amounts of government spending, the economy never gathered momentum. The Great Depression would have continued to be great if it were not for the creation of a war economy. The capitalists invested in this because they could make a profit from supplying the opposing governments with the supplies that they required to destroy each other. It is quite plausible that a second Great Depression may lead to World War III as stress becomes unbearable among the world's people. Therefore, it is also plausible that this might bring capital back into the economy, but it is a price that nobody in their right mind would want to pay. Given the weaponry now available to mankind, World War III would decimate the planet and kill billions of people.

As for the liberal approach, it is equally simple although diametrically opposed to the conservative approach. The liberal/progressives want to spend more government money, keep interest rates low and increase government services. They want to do what FDR did in the Great Depression, only now the government would have to print even more money and go deeper into debt at a time when US bonds are already under stress. The liberal approach recommends inflation as a cure. While there are certain points that make sense in a capitalist economy, the tragic flaw in this strategy is that again the capitalists are left sitting on their piles of cash while the American family circles the drain. Even with more government debt and more government spending, the economy will not speed up because the government, on its own, cannot create sustainable full employment. They cannot do it without investment from the big banks and corporations who will just continue to sit on the sidelines because they cannot make enough profit by investing in production.

The conservative approach will lead to deflation while the liberal approach will lead to inflation. Insofar as neither side will get its way, they will constantly be fighting each other through their political parties. And even if one side triumphs, no matter which side, the social and environmental crises would not be stopped. In the meantime, the American people will become more desperate and afraid. Anger and hate will erupt and people on the left and the right will become more extreme in our behavior. Domestically, the polarization that we experienced between the supporters of Trump and Clinton/Sanders signals this emerging trend. It is only beginning.

In the world, the same polarization will occur. Countries will line up on the left or the right. Conflicts will become more frequent as people become more desperate and this inevitable will lead to World War III unless we figure out a way to stop it.[160]

This leads us to the revolutionary strategy mentioned above. The revolutionary strategy is for the left and the right to band together at the local level and build grassroots economies geared toward meeting our own basic needs. Basic needs are what we need to survive and gain ground. These are nutritious food, energy-efficient housing, adequate clothing, the opportunity to receive a higher education, and good health care. This movement has already begun to gain adherents, but is in an infant stage. Nonetheless, by supporting this course of action, we may be able to stabilize our communities, meet our basic needs, and protect the natural resources on which we depend for survival. It will still be a struggle, but one which can bring us together instead of tearing us apart. It is a battle worth fighting in order to maintain our humanity and the values that we hold most dear. This is a strategy that both conservatives and liberal middle class Americans could get behind.

The End Game Strategy of the Capitalist Countries (Plan A)

"We are grateful to the Washington Post, The New York Times, Time Magazine and other great publications whose directors have attended our meetings and respected their promises of discretion for almost 40 years. It would have been impossible for us to develop our plan for the world if we had been subjected to the lights of publicity during those years. But the world is more sophisticated and prepared to march towards a world government. The supranational sovereignty of an intellectual elite and world bankers is surely preferable to the national auto-determination practiced in past centuries." - David Rockefeller, Bilderberg, 1991[161]

The building blocks of this desired "supranational sovereignty" have been put into place over the last three decades. The institutions are on the ground and policies are being put into place. The latest expression of policy change in support of the supranational sovereignty was the Trans-Pacific Partnership pushed so strenuously by the Obama administration.[162] Although killed by Donald Trump, the policy will surface again under a different name or at a different time. This is inevitable if the handful of capitalists maintain their power. But, as we have said, these "smart guys" are not that bright when it comes to things other than making profit. As the bankers struggle to complete their corporate dominance over the countries of the world, they have created a situation that, in their obsession, they were unable to envision.

Let us take an overview of the big picture. According to the U.N. Population Division, in 1950, there were a little over 2 billion people on the earth. By 2000, there were over 6 billion. This means that in fifty years, the human population more than tripled, adding the equivalent of the populations of China and India. Currently, we are well passed 7 billion people and it is projected there will be 9.1 billion people by 2050, adding another China and India.

This phenomenal growth rate fueled the global economy, which grew seven-fold since 1950, when the population explosion began. As such, we are now consuming more of the earth's resources than the earth is capable of regenerating on its own or that we can put back. As Americans, we consume the lion's share of these resources. In fact, it has been calculated that if every country on earth consumed at the rate of Americans, we would require four earths to sustain us.[163]

Fig. 5-7: Density of World Population in 2019
(The darker the shade the more populace the country)

In 2005, the United Nations and the World Bank sponsored a Millenium Ecosystem Assessment of the Earth's natural capital. The report was prepared by thirteen hundred and sixty experts in ninety-five countries. They stated unequivocally that of the world's twenty-four basic eco-systems, sixty percent (fifteen of twenty-four) had already been degraded and were being used unsustainably.[164]

Industrial civilization now stands in direct opposition to the welfare of the planet. This can be seen in the example of fossil fuel use. Industrial civilization needs fossil fuels to survive. Yet the emissions from burning fossil fuels are destroying the earth's life support systems and the eco-systems on which industrial civilization depends. Demand for this source of energy has not abated. More wars consume more fossil fuels and even though the domestic economies are stagnant, the demand for oil remains high. In regard to domestic economies, eighty percent of the cost of producing food is derived from fossil fuels—farm machinery, pesticides, herbicides, fungicides, crop drying, transportation, packaging, etc. Without oil, modern agriculture is dead.

Food production is a big issue. Human population growth has been made possible by an increased food supply, which in turn has been made possible by an abundance of cheap fossil fuels. These fuels, however, have polluted our air, soil, and water and have heated up the atmosphere. In addition, powerful water pumps used for irrigation have severally drained underground aquifers and our reserves of safe drinking water.

Global food production and the world stock of grains have already begun to decline, diminished by eroding soils, deteriorating rangelands, collapsing fisheries, falling water tables, rising temperatures, and, of course, more mouths to feed. A recent study using state of the art computer simulation has revealed that:

> A warmer world is expected to have severe consequences for global agriculture and food supply, reducing yields of major crops even as population and demand increases. Now, a new analysis combining climate, agricultural, and hydrological models finds that shortages of freshwater used for irrigation could double the detrimental effects of climate change on agriculture.
>
> Given the present trajectory of greenhouse gas emissions, agricultural models estimate that climate change will directly reduce food production from maize, soybeans, wheat and rice by as much as 43 percent by the end of the 21st Century. But hydrological models looking at the effect of warming climate on freshwater supplies project further agricultural losses, due to the reversion of 20 to 60 million hectares of currently irrigated fields back to rain-fed crops.[165]

This startling revelation signals wide spread famine in our future. It portends that we could lose eighty percent of our grain growing capacity by the end of the century at a time when we will have added billions more people.

The Capitalist Plan

"More than at any time in history, mankind faces the crossroads. One path leads to despair and utter hopelessness, the other to total extinction. I pray we have the wisdom to choose wisely." Woody Allen[166]

"The era of the resource war has arrived." General Alexander Haig[167]

"Energy security is a fundamental component of national security. Military force will be an increasingly important prerequisite to safe guard the flow of foreign oil." Former Secretary of Energy Spencer Abraham[168]

"When I have discussed the problem of severe disruption of Gulf oil with government officials in London and Washington the usual reply is that since there is no option other than oil and we must just make the best of things. When I questioned an expert on the US National Security Council about the lack of any 'Plan B' if the existing political strategy in the Gulf (Plan A) failed, he merely explained that America's Plan B was to make sure that Plan A worked". Dan Plesch, British Foreign Policy Centre[169]

Today, the powerful capitalist nation states are circling each other in preparation for the endgame of industrial civilization, as we know it. The unquestioned goal in this final contest will be to control the remaining oil resources on the planet. The United States has moved its armies into Central Asia and the Middle East to take control of the last large remaining oil fields. Russia, China, Iran, and Brazil are forming a counterbalance. China and India especially have been gulping down great quantities of oil to feed their rapidly industrializing economies. Due to peak oil, there is no increased production capacity in the world. In the meantime, the local people in the Middle East feel used and abused by the capitalist countries and have begun to fight back.

The cost of maintaining US forces in Central Asia and the Middle East, since the onset of the so-called *War on Terror* has reached 6 trillion dollars.[170] This expense, of course, is being met by selling US Treasuries. The total US outstanding debt is currently $17.2 trillion, forty percent of which is now owned by foreign nations. China owns $1.3 trillion and Japan owns $1.18 trillion. Currently eighty-five percent of the world's savings is absorbed by US debt.[171]

As long as the US dollar remains the reserve currency in world trade, countries must buy dollars in order to buy oil on the international market.

This monopoly on the money supply, however, is crumbling away, as oil producers are beginning to convert their pricing to rubles and Euros and currency traders watch for opportunities to short the dollar on week days. Now central banks are beginning to sell dollars in exchange for gold and other currencies to protect the value of their reserve holdings. The US borrows over a billion dollars a day to support its military might and protect its consumer economy. The current cost of maintaining the military is approximately seven hundred billion dollars per year. This is equal to the military budgets of the next fourteen countries' combined.[172] The US military cannot survive without fossil fuels.

The United States Department of Defense (DOD) is one of the largest consumers of energy in the world. In 2007, it was responsible for ninety-three percent of all US government fuel consumption (Air Force: fifty-two percent; Navy: thirty-three percent; Army: seven percent. Other DOD: one percent). It uses 4.6 billion gallons of fuel annually, an average of 12.6 million gallons of fuel per day.[173] In 2006, the Department of Defense also used 30,000 gigawatt hours (GWH) of electricity, at a cost of almost $2.2 billion. This is enough electricity to power more than 2.6 million average American homes. It is easy to see why the US army is so strongly committed to gaining access to the remaining oil supply on the planet.

In order to maintain its global industrial base, the capitalists depend upon the US military to confront any opposition. They depend on the US government as a whole to support their industrial base, support the military, and keep the American people from rioting. To do this the US government is going deeper into debt, to the point that its IOUs are becoming a risky asset to hold.

Any country, including Japan, Saudi Arabia, or Russia, or even a small country like South Korea, could push the dollar off the cliff. These countries will not do so without hurting themselves, but as the struggle for resource dominance intensifies, this internal contradiction will quickly play itself out.

To try to take pressure off of the dollar, the Republicans in the US continue to wage war on human services, women, immigrants, racial minorities and people with different sexual identities. Depending on specific opportunities they push to cut food stamps, social security, early education, unemployment compensation, and other human service programs. At the same time, they stump for greater military spending. Under both Republic and Democratic administration the government continues to prepare for homeland population/crowd control in the event of an environmental or financial disaster.

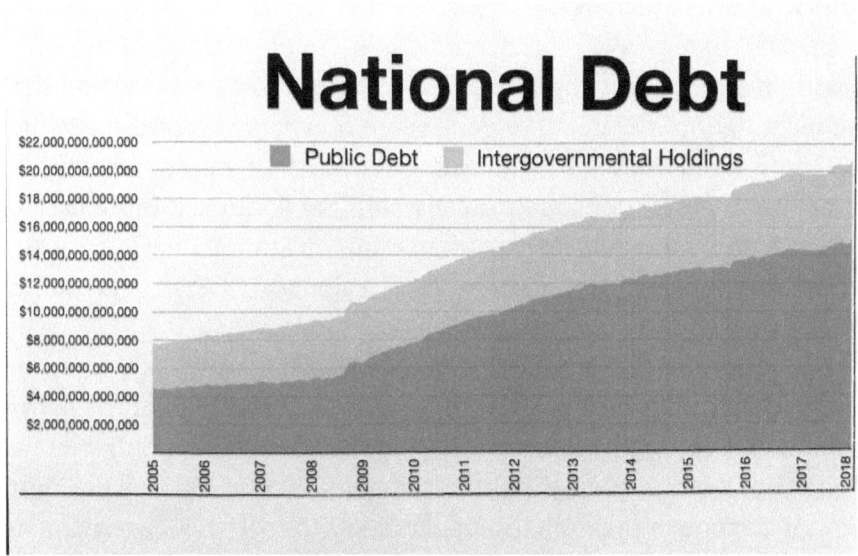

Fig. 5-8: Recent Federal Debt

Empowered by the Patriot Act and similar legislation, the National Security Agency (NSA), Federala Emergency Management Agency (FEMA), and the Department of Homeland Security are setting up the systems to deal with this inevitability.

The trends in macro-finance that speak to the implementation of Plan A being put into practice include the perpetual War on Terror, the use of mass media to craft propaganda instead of support investigative journalism, the gutting of environmental legislation, the reduction of financial resources to state and localities, and the intense development of an infrastructure for population/crowd control. The government also realizes, despite the public posturing of Republicans to the contrary, that climate catastrophe is upon us. As far back as 2004, a Defense Department study predicted that "abrupt climate change" would likely occur within a decade triggering violent storms, mega-droughts, dust storms, and soil loss. Faced with starvation or raiding, the paper concluded that human groups would start to raid each other. Eventually the impact of climate change would lead to the breakdown of the "carrying capacity" of the planet and its ability to sustain the present population.[174]

Plan A is the last ditch effort of the capitalists to maintain their system of global economic colonization. Plan A is also the response of China, Russia, and its partners, who see no other alternative as long as that is the US strategy. Plan A, therefore, is mutually assured destruction based on the premise that there is not enough to go around and that we must fight to the death to get a share of what is left. All the while, we continue to voraciously consume the earth's remaining resources in a "throw-away" consumer society so that we can sell more useless products to raise capital to pay off our all-consuming debt. This is the framework for the end game that has already begun. Plan A is leading us as a species down the road to oblivion.

The question that reasonable people ask themselves is why is the ruling class doing this? Do not they know that the lives of their own children are at stake? Unfortunately, the capitalists would rather let the politicians worry about the future; there is money to be made right now. If any one of the capitalist bankers acts to curb the juggernaut, he becomes non-competitive and will lose the wealth heor she spent years accumulating. The game must go on.

Conclusion

In this chapter, on economic developments in the US since WWII, we have witnessed how European-based colonialism morphed into a US-based economic imperialism. We have watched how the trends set in motion during the English Industrial Revolution grew and quickened in their expression, so that in the last half-century they have reached the apex of their development. Pax Americana represent the Golden Age of modern history as defined by the rise of industrial civilization. But now the system has passed its peak and has begun its path of decline. As the decline continues, the pace of change will quicken. We are already watching changes occur at a pace we never imagined in our lifetimes. We can see it in the pace of social polarization, in the multiplication of war fronts, in the extreme manipulation of money, in the severe changes in climate, and mass migrations. By systematically destroying the natural world and polarizing human society, the bankers have unleashed demons that they themselves never anticipated. They have set the course for their own demise as a ruling class and for the rise of military dictatorships across the planet.

As global monopoly capitalism reached its apogee in the United States, the US-based capitalists, and those in Europe, had come to exercise a control over humanity that was never before witnessed in history. They established the world's first global empire. And yet, the methods that they used to create this empire have now become the very force which undermines it and leads it to its ultimate destruction. In this final phase of capitalism, everyone and everything has become the property of the banks. The middle class is disappearing in Europe and the United States and the ranks of the poor and oppressed are swelling throughout the world. While the transfer of Western jobs to China and India have recently created a larger middle class in those countries, their growth was short lived and it is already beginning to slow down. The extraction of the earth's materials and the processing of these materials into industrial and consumer products has ravaged the earth's eco-systems and destroyed the planetary life-support systems. Arable soil, potable water, breathable air, and protective forests are all in serious decline. Today, we are approaching a global existential crisis in which the very survival of industrial civilization and the very life support systems of the planet are at stake.

There will inevitably be greater polarization and more riots and incarcerations as we are pushed further down this road. We can see this already happening in the split between the conservative ultra-nationalists and the liberal progressives, between Trump and Sanders supporters, between black people and the white racists, between women and the fundamentalist Christians. All the while the capitalist hide behind their divide-and-conquer strategy. Yet even if people were to understand who their real enemies are, this still does not mean there will be a revolution. In order for a revolution to occur there has to be a new vision, a new strategy for change, and a revolutionary leadership to sound the call to action. A revolution will also require a spiritual vision that can sustain people's hope through the chaos that the future promises. In the following chapter, we will look at the existing philosophies of the left and the right within the capitalist system and demonstrate why neither of these philosophies is able to create a revolutionary leadership capable of taking Americans beyond the self-destructive system of capitalism. In Books Two and Three of this Trilogy we will explore a universal revolutionary vision and a specific course of action.

As it stands now, our survival becomes more dependent on a choice—revolution or continued compliance to the status quo. What will it be?

Chapter Two: The American Intellectuals

WHILE THE AMERICAN INTELLECTUALS constitute a distinct social class from the capitalists, many of them directly serve the capitalist class in its efforts to rule the world. Those, who specifically dedicate themselves to this task, are called by the capitalists "policy-oriented intellectuals."[175] These policy-oriented intellectuals exist within both the Republican and Democratic parties. They also existed in international bodies like the League of Nations and today the United Nations.[176]

Policy-Oriented Intellectuals vs Value-Oriented Intellectuals

During the tumultuous decade of the 1960s, a left-wing youth movement created a cultural backlash against the capitalist values of nationalism, militarism, and imperialism that expressed itself as a vociferous attack on the American "Establishment." To counter this "democratic distemper," David Rockefeller, Chair of Chase Manhattan Bank (now JPMorgan Chase) and Director of the Council on Foreign Relations, created the Trilateral Commission in 1973. It immediately became the most influential think tank of the world banking elite. While the Council of Foreign Relations was an Anglo-American assembly of the elite capitalists and their chief intellectuals, the Trilateral Commission brought Japanese, European, and Canadian capitalists to the table. Soon after its formation, the Trilateralists published a book entitled *The Crisis of Democracy*.[177] The book examined the reasons for the popular uprising of the "New Left" and its disdain for the capitalist system in the United States, Europe, and Japan. It recommended ways for the elites to confront this "increased political activity" in order "to restore the prestige and authority of central government institutions." It is enlightening to read this in-house book for several reasons, not the least of which it provides a window into the thinking of the elite who, despite living in democratic nation states, believe they are entitled to rule the world simply because they have the money to do so. Secondly, the book is important because it makes a clear distinction between "policy-oriented intellectuals" who support the values of the capitalist class vs "value-oriented intellectuals" who support the values of democracy.

Let us begin our story by looking at the development of US capitalism after WWII and how it came to shape the thinking of the "policy-oriented intellectuals" in their service to the ruling class today. We have seen in our Volume 4 of *The Untold Story of Western Civilization*, on Modern History, how the partnership between JP Morgan and Teddy Roosevelt gave rise to State Monopoly Capitalism toward the end of the nineteenth century. This partnership between the monopoly capitalists and the government intellectuals continued to flourish through WWI and the Great Depression and paved the way for the domination of US capitalism after WWII.

The way that the capitalists distinguish between intellectuals is different from the way that the American people make that distinction. We distinguish intellectuals based upon their liberal or conservative positions and to which political party they belong. To the capitalists, however, both left-wing and the right-wing intellectuals serve their capitalist masters in the role of policy-oriented intellectuals, while, on the other hand, a minority of both left-wing and right-wing intellectuals also challenge the validity of the capitalist system as value-oriented intellectuals. Thus, for the capitalists, the distinction between the left and the right is a meaningless distinction. Rather, it is only useful insofar as the capitalists can use the rivalry between liberals and conservatives as a mechanism to divide and conquer the American people and keep us from understanding the real cause of our suffering—the capitalist class itself. The capitalists are able to maintain their divide and conquer strategy because they control the mass media and because they control both political parties by providing funding for their candidates to run for office. If the economy is in a contractive phase they throw a few cents at the Republicans, if it is in an expansive phase, they throw a few cents at the Democrats.

The Origins of the Council on Foreign Relations

Ever since the inauguration of George Washington, US presidents have understood that the warfare between European nations from the fifth to the twentieth century was not due to matters of principle or values (they were all Christian nations), but to disputes over territories and the wealth and power that they promised. As for the people of the US, historically, we wanted no part of the European wars.

By the twentieth century, however, the US government had forgotten the isolationist policies of previous administrations and now, being an international power in its own right, sought to play a more dominant role on the world stage. As part of the emerging ideology of state monopoly capitalism, a succession of Presidents, beginning with Woodrow Wilson, sought to expand the role of the government in domestic matters, but also to expand the role of the federal government in promoting US capitalism abroad.

In 1913, the Federal Reserve System was established along with the 16th Amendment that established a Federal Income Tax. In 1914, the Harrison Federal Narcotics Act was passed, granting the federal government vast new police powers over an issue that had previously been successfully dealt with as a medical problem. In the same year, World War I began in Europe. In 1917, America entered World War I on the side of Britain and France, despite Wilson's 1916 campaign slogan for his second term of office, "He Kept Us Out of War."[178]

President Wilson now spoke of a "war to make the world safe for democracy."[179] This was, of course, pure propaganda to entice the American people into war. In actuality, the US capitalists wanted access to the resources of the British and French colonies in Africa and Asia. The American government had never given a second thought to the liberation of these colonies from French and British rule even though our allies were guilty of the most brutal suppression of local democratic movements in their colonies. During the war, Britain, France, and the US government also allied themselves with the communist regime in Russia, which was most certainly not supportive of a democracy at the time.

When WWI ended, everyone was sick of the appalling carnage and destruction of the world. To prevent another catastrophe of this size, the allied powers created the League of Nations. WWI was supposed to be "the war to end all wars." The League of Nations was to serve as a mechanism to ensure collective security. After the war, despite the lust of American capitalists for the Britain and French colonies, our allies retained their colonial empires and, under the League's Trusteeship system, also took control of German colonies in East Africa and South-West Africa.[180]

The United States Senate rejected membership in the League of Nations fearing it would subordinate America to the British Empire. It was in response to this rejection that the American and British elites began a series of "discreet" meetings that resulted in the formation of the *Council on Foreign Relations*.[181] The isolationist philosophy of the American people was still dominant in domestic politics. Americans never trusted the British, but the US capitalists had from the beginning always been in bed with the British capitalists.

The Council on Foreign Relations was incorporated in New York in 1921. Among the founders were John Foster Dulles, later Secretary of State; Allen Dulles, later head of the Office of Strategic Services (OSS) and the Central Intelligence Agency (CIA); Edward Mandell House, a top assistant to President Wilson; and John W. Davis, who became the first President of the Council. Davis was personal attorney for J. P. Morgan, head of Morgan Guaranty Trust, and in 1924 received the Democrat nomination for President, despite never having been elected to any lower office. In the formation of the Council on Foreign Relations, we see the formal process by which intellectual expertise was recruited to forward the advance of Anglo-American nationalism, militarism, and imperialism.

From the beginning, the Council urged the United States government to cooperate with the League of Nations. The Rockefeller family began funding the Council and bought the Harold Pratt House on East 68th Street in New York to serve as its headquarters. Fast forward to the end of WWII and the Rockefellers would also fund the United Nations and donate land on the East River in Manhattan for its headquarters.

The League of Nations obviously did not end war for all time. The onerous war reparations that it exacted from Germany at the end of WWI bankrupted that country and gave rise to Adolf Hitler; his organization, and military build-up generously funded by US capitalists.[182] As other European governments prepared for yet another war to fight Hitler's expansion, the American people remained committed to staying out of war. As late as October 1941, opinion polls showed eighty-eight percent of the American people opposed entering the European war.[183]

Independent of the American people's desires, however, the Council on Foreign Relations, also financed by grants from the Rockefeller Foundation, began doing research for the State Department in 1939. By 1942, after America entered the War, the State Department established an Advisory Committee on Postwar Foreign Policy, which included no less than seven members of the Council on Foreign Relations.

By the end of the war, the US delegation to the organizational meetings of the United Nations contained over forty members of the Council on Foreign Relations. Among the members were Franklin Roosevelt's Secretary of State, Edward R Stettinius, John Foster Dulles, John J McCloy, Nelson Rockefeller, Adlai Stevenson, and Alger Hiss.[184]

The "invisible government" of the Council on Foreign Relations continued to determine US foreign policy for the next twenty-five years. To this day, it still serves to consolidate studies by policy-oriented intellectuals on international relations and publishes their findings that are then read by politicians and other policy-oriented intellectuals around the country and the world. Many of these people hold tenured positions within American academia, but also in the fields of politics, economics, and the mass media. Through the Council on Foreign Relations, the American intellectual class is indoctrinated into the thinking of the capitalist class.

The Trilateral Commission

In 1973, David Rockefeller, who served as the Chairman of the Council on Foreign Relations, decided to create the Trilateral Commission that would bring other European and Japanese capitalists and intellectuals into the fold of the Anglo-American banking cartel. Thus, the term "trilateral' stands for North America, Western Europe, and Japan.

According to their website, the Trilateral Commission would bring together "experienced leaders" within the private sector to discuss issues of global concern at a time when communication and cooperation between Europe, North America, and Asia were lacking."[185]

To quote its founding declaration:

> To be effective in meeting common problems, Japan, Western Europe, and North America will have to consult and cooperate more closely, on the basis of equality, to develop and carry out coordinated policies on matters affecting their common interests . . . refrain from unilateral actions incompatible with their interdependence and from actions detrimental to other regions . . . [and] take advantage of existing international and regional organizations and further enhance their role.

David Rockefeller appointed Zbigniew Brzezinski to be the Chair of the organization. Brzezinski, who had been a consultant to Democratic presidents going back to John Kennedy, had just written his 1970 book, *Between Two Ages: America's Role in the Technetronic Era*. In his book, Brzezinski argued that it was necessary to coordinate policy between the industrialized elites due to the instability caused by increasing economic inequality in the rest of the world.[186] In other words, "we better get ourselves on the same page because the exploited people are beginning to act out."

Other founding members of the Trilateral Commission included:

- Henry D. Owen, foreign policy studies director at the Brookings Institution;
- George S. Franklin, executive director of the Council on Foreign Relations in New York;
- Robert R. Bowie, the Foreign Policy Association and director of the Harvard Center for International Affairs;
- William Scranton, former governor of Pennsylvania;
- Edwin Reischauer, professor at Harvard University and United States Ambassador to Japan, from 1961-1966;
- Max Kohnstamm, European Policy Centre; and
- Tadashi Yamamoto, Japan Center for International Exchange

In short time, the Trilateral Commission recruited members from the largest multinational corporations in the world, the highest levels of government, the cream of mainstream media, and the best policy-oriented brains of academia. The Commission would serve as a think tank to bring the "policy-oriented intellectuals" of the industrialized world together to forward the goals of the international banking elite. Its members from the mainstream media would then promote Trilateralist values to the American people in newspapers, magazines, and television.

Within the US, the Commission quickly came to control the foreign and domestic policy of America by grooming every US president since Jimmy Carter and by filling each president's administrations with Trilateral Commission members. The capitalists' intent was to ensure that the popular uprising against the Establishment that they derisively referred to as a "democratic distemper" would no longer be a problem. It did not matter to the Trilateralists if the administrations were Democratic or Republican. Jimmy Carter, Ronald Reagan, George H. W. Bush, Bill Clinton, George W. Bush, and Barak Obama would all serve on the Trilateral Commission and appoint its members to their administrations.

While Trilateral Commission bylaws exclude persons holding public office from membership, the bylaws are only a legal nicety. The relationships and the network of influence always remains in place and in some cases, politicians remained members even while serving their terms of office.

The Trilateral Commission's ultimate agenda is the formation of a world government under their control. This has raised criticism from the right and the left "value-oriented intellectuals." For example, Republican Barry Goldwater, in his book *With No Apologies*, called the Trilateral Commission "a skillful, coordinated effort to seize control and consolidate the four centers of power: political, monetary, intellectual, and ecclesiastical. . . . [in] the creation of a worldwide economic power superior to the political governments of the nation-states involved."[187] This view represents the thinking of the majority of right wing, "value oriented intellectuals" concerning the Trilateral Commission to this day.

Libertarian Ron Paul, when running for president in 2012, commented on the Trilateralists:

> You referred to who really pulls the strings. For years now, it's been claimed by many, and there's pretty good evidence, that those who are involved in the Trilateral Commission and the Council on Foreign Relations usually end up in positions of power. And I believe this is true. If you look at the Federal Reserve, if you look at key positions at the World Bank or the IMF, they all come from these groups. If you have national television on, you might see a big debate about the Far East crisis, and you have Brzezinski and Kissinger talking about how to do it. One says don't invade today, invade tomorrow. And the other says, invade immediately. That's the only difference you find between the Rockefeller trilateralists.[188]

On the other hand, Noam Chomsky, a renowned spokesperson for the leftist value-oriented intellectuals, described the intentions of the Trilateral Commission this way:

> [The Trilateral Commission] was concerned with trying to induce what they called "more moderation in democracy"—turn people back to passivity and obedience so they don't put so many constraints on state power and so on. In particular they were worried about young people. They were concerned about the institutions responsible for the indoctrination of the young (that's their phrase), meaning schools, universities, church and so on—they're not doing their job, [the young are] not being sufficiently indoctrinated. They're too free to pursue their own initiatives and concerns and you've got to control them better.[189]

There were several reasons that had led David Rockefeller to form the Trilateral Commission. First, Nixon had removed the US dollar from the gold standard established at Bretton Woods and, in doing so, had thrown international trade relations up for grabs. This was very bad for business and disrupted the operations of the international capitalist bankers. Secondly, Rockefeller was also concerned about the cultural upheaval and domestic unrest caused by the younger generation throughout the United States and Europe. Thirdly, the Middle East oil producing countries had managed to nationalize their oil reserves and stop western oil companies from exploiting their oil. They had formed the Organization of Petroleum Exporting Countries (OPEC). Upon gaining control over their own oil, the OPEC countries hiked the price of oil to even the score with the western capitalists (they were especially angered when the Western capitalists consistently defended Israel in its three wars with the Arab countries).[190]

An immediate consequence of the price hike in oil was that many third world countries were unable to pay the higher rate. Because they needed oil to continue to industrialize, they were forced to borrow more money from the banks to pay for the increase. This overextended the banks, which began to worry about the ability of these countries to pay them back. Rockefeller's Chase Manhattan bank alone had loaned over fifty-seven billion dollars to third world countries.

To secure the position of the banks, Rockefeller knew that he would need the cooperation of countries beyond the pale of the Council on

Foreign Relations. He would need the power of the industrialized world as a whole to confront this development. This meant bringing Canada, France, Germany, Italy, and Japan to the table. With this combined power, he could strengthen the power of the World Bank and the IMF to collect the debts of the third world countries on behalf of the bankers.[191]

The Trilateralists were also able to gain a commitment from Saudi Arabia not to accept payment for oil in any other currency beside the US dollar. This secured its position as the world's reserve currency despite the fact that it was no longer based on gold. In addition, the tens of billions of dollars generated by the OPEC oil hike were placed in American and European banks where these "petro-dollars" were then used by the multinational banks and corporations to make loans to countries that allowed them to exploit even more natural resources and labor. The third world countries were in a no-win situation. They had to borrow money from the banks and go more deeply into debt even though it was their money that the bankers were loaning back to them. Having moved to contain the damage of the "Nixon Shocks" and set up a process for getting the third world countries to pay their debts by using the hammer of the World Bank and IMF, Rockefeller turned his attention to the dangers on the US domestic front. In 1973, the US was winding down from its involvement in Vietnam. The Vietnam War had proved to be a costly venture, and the youth movement had turned a majority of the American people against the idea of the Establishment's militarism and imperialism abroad.

The Trilateral Commission and the US Presidency

To silence the youth movement and rebuild the authority of the federal government that had been challenged by the "democratic surge" of the 1960s, the Trilaterial Commission focused its attention on gaining control of the US presidency. They were eminently successful. Since 1977, the Trilateralists have, to a large extent, controlled the administrations of Jimmy Carter, Ronald Reagan, George H. W. Bush, Bill Clinton, George Bush, and Barak Obama. Hillary Clinton would have been the next Trilaterialist president had it not been for the Donald Trump upset. The Democratic presidents were more inclined to Trilateralist values than the Republicans, but they all accepted key Trilateralist strategists into their administration and working with the policy-oriented Trilateral experts on globalization strategies. Trump was somewhat of a wild card, but he would keep the wars going and support fossil fuel production.

The Carter Administration

It all began in 1975 when Jimmy Carter, as a candidate for Governor of Georgia, was burnishing his international credentials by shaking hands with foreign dignitaries in meetings set up by Coca-Cola whose headquarters were in Jimmy's state. Jimmy happened to be in London when David Rockefeller was there to recruit members for the Trilateral Commission. The two met and David recruited Jimmy Carter to be a member of the Trilateral Commission. Having then been given the nod by Rockefeller, Zbigniew Brzezinski, Chair of the Trilateral Commission, began to groom Carter for president of the United States. Jimmy's image was meticulously crafted to address the concerns of the American people as determined by national polls. He was then marketed by the Trilateralist media and finally his administration was staffed by members of the Trilateral Commission.

It appears that Jimmy Carter grew into a compassionate Christian over the years, having had a moving religious experience,[192] but in the late 1960s, in his bid for governor, he was a different man. He was racist and anti-labor, having identified himself with George Wallace, Lester Maddox, and segregationist, Richard Russel. In his campaign for governor, he accused his rival, Governor Carl Sanders for "selling out to big unions" when Sanders wanted to repeal Georgia's reactionary "right to work laws." Why was Carter anti-union? It was because of his connection to Coca-Cola. Robert Woodruff, the chair of Coke and also a member of the Trilateralists, led the charge of big business to take advantage of cheap labor in the "New South." This was at a time when the Democratic Party still ruled in the South as they had for over one hundred years.[193] Once elected to be president in 1977, the Trilateralists took over the

Carter administration. The following members of his administration were members of the Trilateral Commission:

- Zbigniew Brzezinski – National Security Advisor;
- Walter Mondale – Vice-President;
- Cyrus Vance – Secretary of State;
- W. Michael Blumenthal – Secretary of the Treasury;
- Harold Brown – Secretary of Defense;
- Paul Warnke – Director of Arms Control and Disbursement;
- Warren Christopher – Deputy Secretary of State;
- Richard N. Cooper – Undersecretary of State for Economic Affairs;
- C. Fred Bergsten – Assistant Secretary of Treasury for International Economic Affairs;
- Richard Holbrooke – Assistant Secretary for East Asian and Pacific Affairs;
- Anthony Lake – Underassistant Secretary of State for Policy Planning;
- Anthony Solomon – Undersecretary of the Treasury for Monetary Affairs;
- Lucy Wilson Benson – Undersecretary of State for Security Affairs;
- Charles Duncan – Undersecretary of Defense;
- Andrew Young – Ambassador to the United Nations;
- Richard Gardner – Ambassador to Italy; and
- Sol Linowitz – Carter's Representative on the Panama Canal[194]

One of the Carter administration's first acts upon taking office was to give the World Bank a $3.2 billion dollar appropriation. This amounted to a $2.4 billion increase over the 1976 fiscal year appropriation. This appropriation was then used by the World Bank to make loans to third world countries in order to pay their debts to the big private banks. The big bankers now no longer had to worry about third world oil debts even though the "developing" countries went further into debt, all on the tab of the American people.

The Reagan Administration

Eventually David Rockefeller soured on Jimmy Carter. At issue was Carter's proclivity to pressure third world dictators into stopping human rights violations. The Trilateralists considered this politically incorrect because they worried that such an approach would produce revolutions in "friendly countries." In an article by Henry Kissinger, in *Trialogue*, (Fall 1978), he recommended that the US government practice "selectivity" in its international human rights policy and be more lenient towards "authoritarian regimes" as they were more likely to evolve into democracies than were Communist states. America's human rights policy, he said, "must maintain this crucial distinction."[195] It was, of course, an absurd, self-serving proposal because everyone knows that only by revolting against dictators can people establish a democracy. Not surprising, however, Kissinger's argument struck a chord with David, who began to look for a suitable replacement for Carter.

He found an acceptable replacement in Ronald Reagan, who he then assisted to become president in 1980. The only problem with Reagan, according to David, was that in his electoral campaign he had been critical of the *Trilateral Commission*. But this changed soon enough when, according to David, "Reagan ultimately came to understand Trilateral's value and invited the entire membership to a reception at the White House in April 1984".[196]

The Reagan Administration embraced Kissinger's "crucial distinction," by giving strong support to dictators who supported the bankers, while adopting a belligerent posture against the Communist states. David praised Reagan by saying, "It is heartening that the current administration in Washington is dedicated to encouraging the private sector and lessening the role of government."[197] This was banker-speak for the fact that Reagan drastically cut taxes for the rich while at the same time reducing money to social service programs.

The national debt exploded under the Reagan administration. The money was used to fund his Strategic Defense Initiative (SDI) which the mainstream media fondly called "Star Wars." Billions of dollars worth of US bonds were issued to pay for this program.

The Trilateralists in Japan and Germany encouraged their countrymen to buy the bonds. Saudi Arabia also pitched in. This quickened the movement by which international governments came to invest big time in US debt. Today China and Japan have invested over one trillion dollars each in US Treasury bonds.

Reagan was elected by convincing millions of Americans that he would end the domination of the economy by the big banks of the Eastern Establishment. Unfortunately, it was not true. While Reagan, himself, was not a member, of the Council on Foreign Relations or the Trilateral Commission, his vice-president George H. W. Bush was. So also were many members of his administration who included:

- Kenneth M. Duberstein, Chief of Staff;
- Alexander Haig (Secretary of State);
- George Shultz (Secretary of State);
- William J. Crowe Jr. (Chairman, US Joint Chiefs of Staff Nicholas Brady (Secretary of Treasury);
- Donald Regan (Secretary of Treasury);
- John C. Whitehead (Deputy Secretary of State);
- Caspar Weinberger (Secretary of Defense);
- Frank Carlucci (Deputy Secretary of Defense);
- Winston Lord (Ambassador to China);
- Malcolm Baldridge (Secretary of Commerce) ;
- William Brock (Secretary of Labor); and
- Alan Greenspan (Chairman of the Federal Reserve)[198]

The George H. W. Bush Administration

When Reagan retired from office, his Vice President, George H. W. Bush, became President. Bush was a long time Trilateralist as were key members of his administration including, Dick Cheney (Secretary of Defense), Nicholas Brady (Secretary of the Treasury), James Baker (Secretary of State), and Lawrence Eagleburger (Acting Secretary of State).

George H. W. had surrendered his seat on the Council of Foreign Relations and the Trilateral Commission during his election campaign because the Republican voting base began to condemn him for being "too liberal." Bush obviously could not be seen as a supporter of the Eastern Establishment. As a Texan, he owed big dues to the Texas oil barons who had funded his campaign and who had their own twist on international policy. Bush's presidency is remembered for his war on Iraq and for his expansion of executive authority in matters concerning national security and domestic surveillance. During his reign, the Eastern press criticized Bush for his "Imperial Presidency." It was all meaningless language spewed out to confuse the American public and keep our minds off our own misery.

Shortly after taking office, President Bush ended price controls on US oil. This led to a massive increase in US production and declining US dependence on Middle East oil. Prices for oil dropped on the world market.

This act destroyed OPEC's discipline. Some members wanted to pump more oil to try to maintain their income. Others, like Iraq, wanted to cut production to keep prices high. Iraq's Saddam Hussein, in particular, was in a bind. He was short on cash having to reconstruct his country after his war with Iran. His neighbors, Saudi Arabia and Kuwait, were also hounding Hussein to repay his war debt to them even though they had supported his invasion of Iran.

When OPEC oil ministers met in late July of 1990, Hussein vehemently argued that other OPEC members should cut production to drive the price of oil back up. Hussein also wanted Saudi Arabia and Kuwait to cancel Iraq's debt. None of Hussein's demands were met and as tensions grew unbearable, he responded by invading Kuwait, which Iraq had long claimed as its own.

When he was pushed out of that country by the US army, he set fire to Kuwait's oil fields. This was President Bush's opportunity to help create the Trilateralists' "New World Order."[199] Bush had his Secretary of State, James Baker, lobby members of the UN Security Council to support a war against Iraq. This was quite unusual because, according to the US Constitution, he was supposed to go to Congress to get permission to commit US citizens to a foreign war.

The oligarchs, however, rarely supported the rules of democracy despite what their intellectual mouthpieces told the people during election campaigns. President Bush and Secretary of State Baker pushed a series of resolutions through the United Nations Security Council condemning Iraq, demanding Iraq's withdrawal from Kuwait, and authorizing the use of force to eject Iraq from Kuwait.

On the basis of UN resolutions, 661 through 665, President Bush sent four hundred an fifty thousand US troops to Saudi Arabia without authorization from Congress.

The Gulf War, codenamed *Operation Desert Shield*, was a war waged by coalition forces led by the United States against Iraq in response to Iraq's invasion and annexation of Kuwait.[200] US President George H. W. Bush began the war by deploying US forces into Saudi Arabia, and urging other countries to send their own forces to the scene. The great majority of the Coalition's military forces were from the US, Saudi Arabia, Britain, and Egypt in that order. Kuwait and Saudi Arabia paid thirty-two billion dollars of the sixty billion dollar cost of the war.[201]

Bush's imperial actions caused the longtime Democratic Congressman from Texas, Henry B. Gonzalez, who had served as the Chair of the Banking, Finance, and Urban Affairs Committee, to call for an investigation into the Bush administration, charging that Bush had promised seven billion dollars in aid and credits to the Soviet government to secure the support of Soviet President Gorbachev in the U. N. Security Council's vote for the war. Also, according to Gonzalez, Bush promised three million dollars to the communist Chinese government to ensure that China abstain, rather than veto the Security Council's resolution on the use of force against Iraq.

Bush also offered US government aid to Romania and other governments represented on the Security Council at the time of the vote.[202] This, of course, was all in the name of promoting democracy around the world.

Apparently, George H. W. Bush, the son of Prescott Bush, who had helped fund Hitler's war machine, was capable of the same kind of deadly duplicity against the American people as his corrupt father.

Once they had a chance to talk about it, Congress supported the war. Senate Republican Leader Bob Dole, for example, in a bald declaration of the capitalist's right to manipulate other people's governments, argued convincingly that the war would "guarantee access to Persian Gulf oil supplies."[203]

The Bill Clinton Administration

Whereas George H. W. Bush was among the founding members of the Trilateral Commission, retaining his connections even while officially "on leave of absence in government service," Bill Clinton was a latecomer to the organization, being invited to join only before his presidency. He was the third "member" of the Trilateral Commission to be elected President since the Commission was founded in 1973.

President-elect Clinton in late December announced his choices for his Cabinet and top administration positions. Among the Trilateralists who entered his administration were:

- Al Gore - Vice President;
- Lawrence Summers – Secretary of the Treasury;
- Warren M. Christopher - Secretary of State;
- William S. Cohen - Secretary of Defense;
- William J. Perry - Secretary of Defense;
- Anthony Lake - National Security Advisor;
- Ronald H. Brown - Secretary of Commerce;
- Bruce Babbitt - Secretary of Interior;
- William Coleman Jr. – Secretary of Transportation;
- Donna E. Shalala - Secretary of Health and Human Services;
- Alice M. Rivlin - Deputy Budget Director;
- Madeleine Albright - UN Ambassador;
- Peter Tarnoff - Under Secretary of State for International Security of Affairs;
- Henry G. Cisneros - Secretary of Housing and Urban Development;
- Walter Mondale - U.S. Ambassador to Japan;
- William J. Crowe - Chairman of the Foreign Intelligence Advisory Board;
- Joseph Nye - Assistant Secretary for Defense; and
- Lloyd N. Cutler - Counsel to the President.[204]

The Clinton Administration, which contained a greater number of Trilateralists than that of George Bush, had the onerous task of rebuilding the Trilateralist global vision after George Bush's war in the Middle East had put its neoliberal agenda on the back burner.

In terms of his foreign policy, Clinton adopted the recommendations of Trilateralist Paper No. 41, "Global Cooperation after the Cold War" (1991) that was co-authored by Joseph Nye, who became Clinton's Assistant Secretary for Defense.[205]

Anthony Lake, Clinton's National Security Advisor, argued that the "major market democracies" must "act together" to prevent "economic disaster" by "updating international economic institutions" and "striking hard" for global free trade. Such pronouncements were music to the ears of David Rockefeller and would help explain David's reported efforts to protect Clinton from impeachment after the Lewinsky scandal broke in 1998.[206]

The George W. Bush Administration

George W. was also a member of the Trilateral Commission and the following Trilateralists filled important positions in his administration:

- Richard B. Cheney - Vice President;
- Colin L. Powell - Secretary of State
- Donald H. Rumsfeld - Secretary of Defense ;
- Robert B. Zoellick – US Trade Representative, President of the World Bank;
- Brent Scowcroft – National Security Advisor;
- Richard N. Haass - Special Envoy to Northern Ireland and Coordinator for the Future of Afghanistan;
- Stephen J. Friedman - Chairman of the United States President's Foreign Intelligence Advisory Board; and
- Richard N. Perle - Chairman of the Defense Policy Board Advisory Committee.

After the success of George Bush Senior's Operation Desert Storm in 1991, the Pentagon, led by then Defense Secretary Dick Cheney, paid a Halliburton subsidiary (BRS) $8.5 million to study the use of private military forces to work alongside American soldiers in combat zones.

In 1995, Cheney became chairman and CEO of Halliburton. We get a sense of Cheney's character because, under his leadership, Halliburton had been fined millions of dollars by the US government for federal trade violations in Iraq and Libya.

Nonetheless, in 1998, Cheney's Halliburton merged with Dresser Industries, which was a multinational corporation headquartered in Dallas, Texas. Dresser provided a wide range of technology, products, and services used for developing energy and natural resources. Prescott Bush was a director of Dresser Industries and his son, former president George H. W. Bush also worked for Dresser Industries in the early 1950s.[207] Halliburton's headquarters were also in Dallas, Texas. This helps to explain the Bush-Cheney relationship.

This piece of the puzzle also helps explain why the Bush-Cheney administration was so interested in going to war with Iraq. Their interest, in fact, ran much deeper than any softsell, neo-liberal values mouthed by the Trilateralist elite. Cheney and Bush's tendency was to take what they wanted by physical force. Once again, the blatant nationalism, militarism, and imperialism served up by the Bush administration's Neo-Conservative ideology, damaged the Trilateralist's "we're-all-in-this-to-make-a-better-world" marketing and helped to fracture the international consensus that Rockefeller was trying to build. The Trilateral Commission meetings in Washington and Prague in 2002 were marred by angry debates between US supporters and European opponents of Bush's plans to invade Iraq.[208]

Obviously, David's authority stretched only so far and it weakened the closer one got to Texas. We cannot place too much meaning in this political in-fighting, however, because both the Eastern Establishment and the Texas Establishment have always wanted the same thing. They both want to steal the resources of the world and politically dominate the planet. And they had a long history of cooperating to realize their common goal. The only difference between them is their preferred means to accomplish this. As far as the American people are concerned, the conservatives and liberals and their Republican and Democratic political parties are just like Tweedle Dum and Tweedle Dee posturing as rivals:

> Tweedledum and Tweedledee
> Agreed to have a battle;
> For Tweedledum said Tweedledee
> Had spoiled his nice new rattle.
> Just then flew down a monstrous crow,
> As black as a tar-barrel;
> Which frightened both the heroes so,
> They quite forgot their quarrel.[209]

On September 11, 2001, jet planes crashed into the World Trade Towers and, in doing so, shifted the earth on its axis.[210] When the shock wore off, the majority of Americans were looking for a scapegoat to destroy. The obvious culprit would have been Saudi Arabia because the majority of identified terrorists were supplied with passports by the Saudi government. But the Bush administration wanted to go after Iraq even though there was no evidence to tie them to the atrocity.

So, George W. deliberately lied repeatedly to the American people about finding "weapons of mass destruction" in Iraq. Most Americans, looking back, agree that they had been lied to and that the war against Iraq was a catastrophic mistake. They rue the fact that the war destabilized the Middle East and has caused great suffering to the American people and the people of Iraq. Yet, for having caused the deaths of hundreds of thousands of people, neither Bush nor Cheney has ever been brought to judgment or paid for their crimes.

Apparently, there is no easy answer to the question of why Bush lied to the American people. It appears that there were different motives within his administration for wanting war with Iraq. Daniel Luban, who spent many years studying the war, recently wrote an article, "Iraq War Motives, Ten Years Later"[211] in which he dissects the possible motivations for the war.

According to Luban, as far as George W. himself was concerned, there was probably some revenge in his motive to destroy Iraq considering that his papa George H. W. had attacked Hussein, but had failed to crush him. George W., however, lacked the vision and the visceral greed that characterized the main characters in his administration. These men had long been calculating how they could get their hands on Iraq's huge oil supply. They also salivated over the government contracts that would be granted to rebuild Iraq's infrastructure after the war. Others, with a more moderate motive, spoke of the need to "stabilize" Mideast oil supplies. Some members of the Bush/Cheney administration had a vested interest in Israel's security.

Did any members of the Bush/Cheney administration really believe the media propaganda that Americans fought in Iraq in order to "spread democracy" in a heathen land? This was, after all, what the administration told the American people after it failed to prove that Iraq held "weapons of mass destruction."

As a friendly, low-level intellectual, Bush held to the mythic belief that if he could "shock and awe" the Iraqi people into submission, his friends in his administration could have their dreams fulfilled.

The allegation that Iraq was a "war for oil" can mean two different things. The first motivation for an oil war was that the administration wanted to preserve the stability of US oil supplies in the broader Gulf region as a whole. The second meaning is that the Iraq war was primarily intended to allow US oil companies to confiscate Iraqi oil reserves.

The Carter Doctrine was a policy proclaimed by Jimmy Carter in his State of the Union Address on January 23, 1980, which stated that the United States would use military force, if necessary, to defend its national interests in the Persian Gulf.[212]

Zbigniew Brzezinski, President Carter's National Security Adviser, wrote the following part of Carter's speech:

> Let our position be absolutely clear: An attempt by any outside force to gain control of the Persian Gulf region will be regarded as an assault on the vital interests of the United States of America, and such an assault will be repelled by any means necessary, including military force.[213]

The "war for oil" doctrine of Carter was activated by George H. Bush's *Operation Iraqi Freedom* in 1991.

The motivation for George W.'s war on Iraq was not, apparently, to forward democracy. Hussein was not involved in 9/11 even though he was painted in the American press since the days of Bush Sr. as a satanic character. As such, he did make a perfect scapegoat for US aggression after 9/11. Another reason for wanting to destroy Iraq was the Neo-Conservatives desire to protect Israel.

During the 1990s, several neo-conservatives, who later took positions in the Bush administration, prepared a notorious report for Israeli's Prime Minister Netanyahu called "Clean Break." The "Clean Break" report was prepared in 1996, five years before 9/11, by a study group led by Richard Perle, who later became George W.'s Chairman of the Defense Policy Board Advisory Committee. The report presented an aggressive strategy to build Zionism by advocating the removal of Saddam Hussein from power in Iraq by highlighting its possession of "weapons of mass destruction and by containing Syria." The solution was to engage in proxy warfare against these countries. The report recommended the following policies:

1. Rather than pursuing a "comprehensive peace" with the entire Arab world, Israel should work jointly with Jordan and Turkey to "contain, destabilize, and rollback" those entities that are threats to all three.
2. Changing the nature of relations with the Palestinians, specifically reserving the right of "hot pursuit" anywhere within Palestinian territory as well as attempting to promote alternatives to Arafat's leadership.
3. Changing relations with the United States to stress self-reliance and strategic cooperation.

The report also advised that Israel terminate aid to the Palestinians, which the Neo-Conservatives believed prevented economic reform in Israel.[214]

Another motivation for war with Iraq was "Payback" after 9/11. Jonah Goldberg, an American conservative columnist who wrote for *National Review*, put it this way, "Every ten years or so, the United States needs to pick up some small crappy little country and throw it against the wall, just to show the world we mean business." To the neoconservatives, it was necessary that the US make an example out of someone to demonstrate its continued strength. The Taliban was too small and weak to serve this purpose. Saudi Arabia was in bed with the US banking elite. Saddam, however, fit the bill nicely.

But what about the goal of "spreading Democracy"? Was there any validity in this excuse for invading Iraq? In the run-up to war, this was the motive that appealed most to prowar, neo-liberal opinion-makers in the media, and thus received a good amount of attention. Once the Bush administration failed to come up with the vaunted "weapons of mass destruction" argument, it picked up on the democracy propaganda as its main justification for the war. The American military left Iraq a wasteland after destroying its infrastructure and its people while also unleashing a religious war between the Sunni and Shia of that country. Where is the protection of democracy in that?

Daniel Luban's analysis of the Bush administrations motivation for war with Iraq certainly shed light on the subject, but it fails to elucidate the greatest motivation of all.... Money. We must consider the evidence that it was the money that drove the Bush administration and companies like Halliburton, Bechtel, and the big oil companies to lobby for war in Iraq. In fact, this political clique not only desired war, but schemed and planned for it to happen.

Scott Thompson, the British Desk Officer at *Executive Intelligence Review (EIR) News Service*, a longtime political gadfly, adds to our information concerning the Bush administration's motivation for attacking Iraq in his article "Dick Cheney Has Long Planned to Loot Iraqi Oil."[215]

According to Thompson, a conservative foundation, *Judicial Watch*, announced that Cheney's Energy Task Force had developed a map of Iraq dated March 2001, as well as maps of the neighboring United Arab Emirates (U.A.E.) and Saudi Arabia. The map of Iraq showed oilfields, pipelines, tanker terminals, and refineries, and included eight "blocks" for exploration near the border with Saudi Arabia. Iraq had the second-highest amount of oil reserves of any nation in the world, next to Saudi Arabia. And, this was without exploration of the eight blocks near the Saudi border, nearly a third of the country, which could have made Iraq number one in terms of proven reserves.

At the same time that Cheney was deliberating with his secret Energy Task Force (its membership was kept secret from the public), the US Export-Import Bank was circulating a plan that proposed to raise loans from private banks to pay for reconstruction contracts in Iraq, to be repaid by revenues from future Iraqi oil sales. The purpose of the government's

Export-Import bank is to finance business deals that would otherwise not happen because the private banks were either unable or unwilling to accept the political or commercial risks inherent in the deal.[216] In this case, the bank's plan was drafted on behalf of a trade association known as the *Coalition for Employment Through Exports*. Its chief members were Halliburton Oil Co. and Bechtel.

This information shows that Halliburton, Cheney's company, was actively promoting the "securitization" of Iraq's oil. Securitization is the process of taking an illiquid asset (Iraq's oil in the ground) and through financial engineering, transforming it into a tradable financial asset. In simple language, this would give Halliburton, Bechtel, and others, financial control over the oil fields of Iraq. A spokesman for Platt's Energy news calculated that Iraq's oil output, within a few years, would be five million barrels per day, at a significantly lower cost than oil from other sources. This would allow a staggering theft of Iraqi oil and could have given the multinational corporations the ability to dictate terms to the Organization of Petroleum Exporting Countries (OPEC).

The Bechtel Corp. had already been given an estimated five hundred million dollar contract by the Bush administration, which it obtained through a non-competitive, classified, backroom deal, for general reconstruction, a program that could grow exponentially under the Export-Import Bank plan.[217] On the Board of Bechtel at the time was former Secretary of State George Shultz, who ran George W's Presidential Exploratory Committee and hand-picked many of the leading neo-conservative hawks in his administration. These were the people who, after 9/11, urged war upon Iraq, with Cheney and Secretary of Defense Donald Rumsfeld, both Trilateralists, leading the pack.

As for Halliburton, it had been given control of Iraq's South Oil Co., which is the largest potential oil producer to date in Iraq. Moreover, Cheney, who received twenty million dollars from Halliburton when he became Vice President of the United States, knew that he would receive deferred payments of a size to be determined by Halliburton's Board of Directors, based upon how well he performed in political office.

The Export-Import Bank plan was also being pushed by the *Coalition Provisional Authority (CPA)*, headed by former Kissinger Associates executive L. Paul Bremer. The CPA was responsible for restructuring Iraq's debt and reparation obligations. After the war, Iraq had an outstanding debt of one hunred and twenty billion dollars, and under the old UN "oil-for-food" program, some twenty percent from sale of Iraq's oil went to war reparations for oil-rich Kuwait. Under the Export-Import plan, communist countries, which previously held contracts with Iraq, were largely cut out of the settlement.

Basically, the intent of the corporations was to mortgage Iraq's future oil supplies to pay for expensive postwar reconstruction of Iraq's infrastructure, whose destruction the corporations had themselves initiated. The plan would ultimately crush the average Iraqi citizen's standard of living and give rise to ISIS.

The maps discussed above, which were released to Judicial Watch under the Freedom of Information Act, were republished by Veterans for Common Sense, under the title, "Did Cheney's Secret Energy Meeting Set Stage for Attack?" In their introduction, they wrote: "Here is the smoking gun pointing directly to Vice President Richard Cheney's energy company meetings held at the White House in early 2001 . . . Congress and the press should immediately investigate any linkage between the secret White House deals . . . and the US invasion and occupation of Iraq."[218]

Several organizations sued Cheney's Energy Task Force for its secrecy. Through the various lawsuits, information was revealed that thirty-nine top energy and related firms, between 1999-2002, gave $6.3 million in political contributions, of which $4.5 went to Republicans. Other contributors involved in Energy Task Force meetings included: Bechtel, which gave a total of $645,640, of which $469,690 went to Republicans and $176,950 to Democrats; and Halliburton, which made a total of $480,188 in contributions, of which $463,288 went to Republicans and $15,900 to Democrats.

While these contributions appear to be perfectly legal, they were obviously influence-peddling, or more likely, an expense to put their own people in office.[219] There is no conspiracy really, just business as usual, facilitated by policy-oriented intellectuals in the government. And if those donation sums are accurate, considering the amount of money that the bankers and corporations are making, they are buying their intellectual politicians for peanuts. So much for American democracy.

On April 7, 2009, as Rand Paul, a Republican Libertarian, was preparing to announce his senatorial bid, he told student Republicans at Western Kentucky University.

> "We need to be fearful of companies," he said, "that get so big that they can actually be directing policy." Then he mentioned Cheney and Halliburton specifically: "When the Iraq War started, Halliburton got a billion-dollar no-bid contract. Some of the stuff has been so shoddy and so sloppy that our soldiers are over there dying in the shower from electrocution. I mean, it shouldn't be sloppy work; it shouldn't be bad procurement process. But it really shouldn't be that these people are so powerful that they direct even policy."

He continued to speak to the students about the Iraq War and in doing so revealed the real reason for the war on Iraq:

> The day after 9/11, [CIA chief] George Tenet is going in the [White] House and [Pentagon adviser] Richard Perle is coming out of the White House. And George Tenet should know more about intelligence than anybody in the world, and the first thing Richard Perle says to him on the way out is, "We've got it, now we can go into Iraq." And George Tenet, who supposedly knows as much intelligence as anybody in the White House says, "Well, don't we need to know that they have some connection to 9/11?" And, he [Perle] says, "It doesn't matter." [220]

The atrocity on 9/11, in which three thousand Americans died, was co-opted by the Bush administration and reduced to an excuse for going to war against an innocent country that had long been planned by the Neo-Conservatives.[221] Halliburton and Bechtel made a fortune rebuilding Iraq and performing all types of ancillary tasks for the US military. As for the big oil companies, they also made a killing. They raised their prices due to the threat of oil scarcity during the years around the war.

The big bankers also made a killing by creating the "oil bubble" that raked off billions more from the unsuspecting investor.

Finally, the military-industrial complex again came out on top. The Twin Towers catastrophe was used to enroll Americans in a perpetual "War on Terror." Just as the government had enrolled us in WWI by using the sinking of the Lusitania, and in WWII by using the bombing of Pearl Harbor, the Bush administration enrolled Americans in the War on Terror as a means to take control of Middle East oil. In each of the above events, the government had prior knowledge of enemy plans to commit atrocities against the US people and did nothing to stop it. In each case, they needed American boys to go to war for them. A War on Terror is perfect for the capitalist military-industrial complex because it justifies war and the suppression of local people anywhere on the planet without time limit. It is a war that will never end until the last "terrorist" is dead. It is the perfect war of the future. There is big money to be made in the destruction of the earth and its people.

The Barak Obama Administration

Bush's approval ratings had been slowly declining from their high point of almost ninety percent immediately after 9/11, and were barely fifty percent by his reelection in 2004. During his second term, they dropped even further to twenty-five percent as the Iraq War and the federal response to Hurricane Katrina in 2005 soured public perception of his job performance.[222]

Undoubtedly, the Trilateralists were happy to have a Democrat for president again. They were easier to control than the Republicans who tended to be too "nationalistic" and warlike in their orientation.

Obama did not disappoint. Trilateralist Brent Scowcroft had been an unofficial advisor to Obama and was mentor to Defense Secretary Robert Gates. In addition to Brent Scowcroft, a long-term strategist for the elite, other Trilateralists in the Obama administration included:

- Gen. James L. Jones - National Security Advisor;
- Thomas Donilon - Deputy National Security Advisor;
- Tim Geithner - Secretary of Treasury;
- James Steinberg - Deputy Secretary of State;

- Richard Haass - State Department, Special Envoy;
- Dennis Ross - State Department, Special Envoy;
- Richard Holbrooke, State Department, Special Envoy;
- Susan Rice - Ambassador to the United Nations;
- Paul Volker - Chairman, Economic Recovery Committee;
- Admiral Dennis C. Blair - Director of National Intelligence;
- Kurt M. Campbell - Assistant Secretary of State, Asia & Pacific;[223]
- Diana Farrell, Deputy Assistant on Economic Policy; and
- Austan Goolsbee, Chairman, Council of Economic Advisers.

There are also many other links between the Obama administration and the Trilateral Commission. Secretary of State Hillary Clinton is married to Bill Clinton a member of the Commission. Secretary of Treasury Tim Geithner's advisors include E. Gerald Corrigan, Paul Volker, Alan Greenspan, and Peter G. Peterson, all members. In fact, Geithner's first job after college was with Trilateralist Henry Kissinger at Kissinger Associates.

Obama became president at a time when the Housing Bubble had just burst and Bush, in his parting shot, had authorized billions of dollars to bail out the big banks.

The bankers, motivated by greed and corruption, had initiated another economic bubble that had left millions of Americans homeless and jobless. The mainstream media showered Obama with accolades for his five hundred billion dollar bailout of the banks, claiming that using American tax dollars in this manner was a win-win situation. Sharper minds, however, could see this boondoggle for what it was, another colossal rip-off of the American people. The first rip-off was done by the banks and the second by the government, i.e., the Obama administration. When the dust had cleared the Fed had made a whopping $12.3 trillion dollars in no-interest loans to the big banks.[224]

In actuality, the boondoggle was a death blow to the American middle class. With the beginning of the Great Recession, following the bubble bursting, middle class wealth has been decimated. Middle-class incomeincome has not kept pace with inflation, and our faith in the American economy has been shattered.

The American middle class had kept their savings in their homes. When the bubble burst, homeowners lost fifty-five of their housing wealth, more than seven trillion dollars.[225]

Joseph E. Stiglitz, a professor of economics at Columbia University, and a former chairman of the Council of Economic Advisers and winner of the Nobel Prize in economics, called the deal a win-win-lose situation. It was a win for bankers, a win for investors, and a loss for the American people.

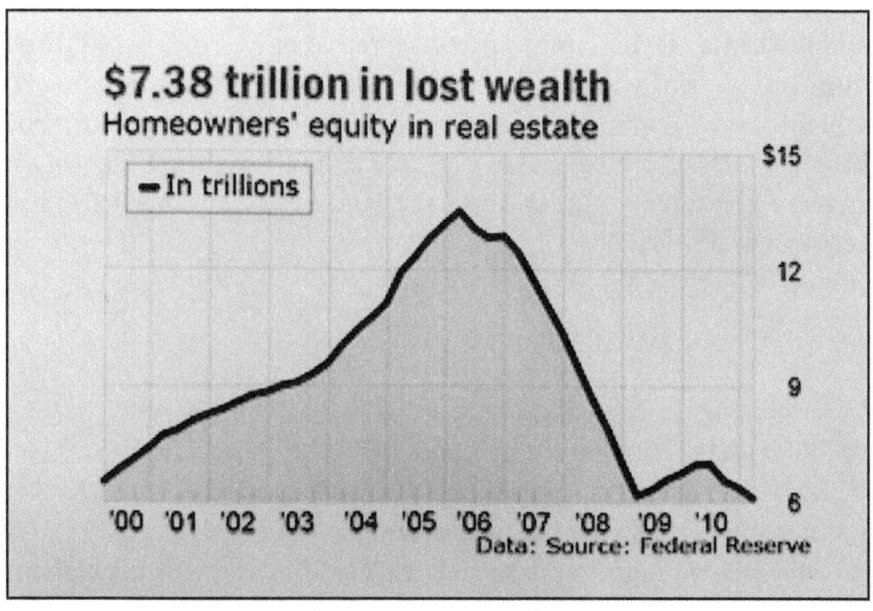

Fig. 5-9: Home Owners Equity in Real Estate: 2000-2010

The reality was that the banks, overcome by greed, consciously kept making bad loans to keep the housing bubble inflated. Only this time it exploded before they had a chance to take their money out. When it exploded, they lost most of the winnings they had gambled. When their bad mortgage loans could not be paid, they lost their capital, and this capital had to be replaced, otherwise they would have to declare bankruptcy.

The best thing that Obama could have done on behalf of the American people at the time would have been to "nationalize" the big banks, as it previously had done with the smaller Continental Illinois and Washington Mutual banks. But this possibility horrified the big bankers, so they went scrambling to the Federal Reserve Bank (FRB), and got the "banker's banker" to persuade Obama to save them by using tax payers' money to keep them from bankruptcy.

The Obama/FRB plan, which was drawn up under Treasury Secretary Timothy Geithner, allowed the bankers to keep their gains while having the public pick up the losses. This brand of American "partnership" is one in which one partner continually robs the other. This is not conspiracy theory, just plain facts.

Without having to go into the actual mechanics of the transaction[226] let us just say that the bankers and the Obama administration colluded in a clever, complex and secretive operation that allowed huge transfers of wealth from the people to the bankers. It allowed Obama to avoid going back to Congress to ask for money to fix our banks, which surely would have created a public outcry. That sleight of hand mortally wounded the American economy, and it has not recovered to this day.

Trans-Pacific Partnership

Regarding the Trans-Pacific Partnership (TPP), Obama said at a meeting of TPP leaders: "This has the potential for being a historic achievement. What we are seeing is momentum building around a Trans-Pacific Partnership that can spur greater economic growth, spur greater jobs growth, and set high standards for trade and investment throughout the Asia Pacific."[227]

Beneath this rhetoric, however, lies the fact that the TPP, while being sold as a trade deal, hardly relates to trade at all. In fact, of the twenty-nine chapters in this document, only five cover traditional trade matters![228]

Lori Wallach, director of Public Citizen, calls the Trans-Pacific Partnership "a corporate coup d'état." The TPP document requires that nations must make their laws and rules conform to TPP's strictures. This would effectively supplant US sovereignty and cancel people's right to be self-governing. Worse, the TPP, if approved, would create permanent corporate rule over nation-states. There is no expiration date on the agreement, and no provision for it to be altered unless all countries agree. Thus, even if Americans voted in a later election to make changes, any other TPP country could overrule us by not agreeing. The corporations in the TPP are referred to as "Investor States." This elevates corporation to the status of statehood and gives them power over nation-states.

In the document that Obama proposed, the corporations would be allowed to create their own court (Investor-State Dispute Resolution) which empowers them to sue governments over environmental, health, consumer, zoning, or any other public policies that the corporations claim are either undermining their TPP "rights" or diminishing their "expected future profits."

The corporate court is not accountable to any national electorate and its decisions are final. There's no appeal to an existing court. If a corporation wins a case, taxpayers of the government being sued suffer an additional loss—they must pony up cash to compensate the corporation for its "loss" of profit.

Since taking office, the Obama administration has spoken out against the sexism, racism, and nationalism of the extreme Right in this country, but at the same time Obama has side stepped the democratic process in his mission to support the global corporate agenda.

Although few liberals would be willing to acknowledge it, the American people have President Trump to thank for stopping the political juggernaut to activate the TPP.

The Trilateralist Media

"We are grateful to the Washington Post, The New York Times, Time Magazine and other great publications whose directors have attended our meetings and respected their promises of discretion for almost 40 years. It would have been impossible for us to develop our plan for the world if we had been subjected to the lights of publicity during those years. But the world is more sophisticated and prepared to march towards a world government. The supranational sovereignty of an intellectual elite and world bankers is surely preferable to the national auto-determination practiced in past centuries." - David Rockefeller, Bilderberg, 1991

Many of the top leaders of mainstream media are and were members of the Trilateral Commission and the Council on Foreign Relations (CFR). Because they share the same values and are linked through these organizations, they are induced to create versions of the news that support the goals of these organizations, whether true or false. More importantly, mainstream media determines what is news and what is not news. They ignore the bankers' ulterior motives while highlighting the threat by local people who rebel against the bankers' oppression and are then called terrorists. The mainstream corporate media keeps us divided by relentless stories that pit race against race, men against women, religion against religion, or nation against nation. They help prevent the development of community consciousness by keeping us enthralled with the scripted scandals of reality TV programs and the squabbles of the Kardashians.

The following is a *small* sampling of members of the media who currently are or once held membership in the CFR or the TC:

- David Bradley, Chairman, Atlantic Media Company;
- Karen Elliot House, former Publisher, the Wall Street Journal;
- Richard Plepler, Co-President, HBO;
- Fareed Zakaria, Editor, Newsweek;
- Mortimer Zuckerman, Chairman, US News & World Reports;
- Michael Bloomberg, Bloomberg LP;
- Andrea Mitchell, Chief Foreign Affairs Correspondent, NBC News;
- Jeffrey Simpson, former National Affairs Columnist, The Globe and Mail;
- Doris Anderson, Editor, Chaterlaine Magazine;
- Emmett Dedmon, Vice President and Editorial Director, Chicago Sun-Times;
- Hedley Donovan, Editor-in-Chief, Time, Inc.;
- Richard Holbrooke, Managing Editor, Foreign Policy Magazine;
- Carl T. Rowan, Syndicated Columnist;
- Laurence A. Tisch, former CEO, CBS;
- Katie Couric, talk show host, CBS, NBC;

- Dan Rather Anchor, CBS Evening News;
- Jane Pfeiffer, former Chair, NBC ;
- Katherine Graham, former publisher of Washington Post;
- Pamela Thompson-Graham, former CEO, CNBC;
- Arthur Sulzberg Jr. former Publisher, New York Times ;
- Michael Elsner, former CEO, The Disney Company;
- Tom Brokaw, Special Correspondent, NBC News;
- David Brinkley, Newscaster, NBC, ABC;
- John Chancellor, Anchor NBC Nightly News;
- Marvin Kalb, Moderator, Meet the Press;
- Herbert Schlosser, former President, NBC;
- Thomas S. Murphy, former CEO, Capital Cities / ABC ;
- Barbara Walters, American Broadcast Journalist, ABC ;
- Diane Sawyer, American Broadcast Journalist, ABC;
- Robert McNeil, Anchor and Journalist, MacNeil/Lehrer Report, PBS;
- Jim Lehrer, Anchor and Journalist, MacNeil/Lehrer Report, PBS;
- Ralph Davidson, former Chair of Time Inc.;
- Henry Grunwald, former managing editor of TIME magazine and editor in chief of Time, Inc.;
- George Will, syndicated newspaper columnist and political commentator;
- Wm. F. Buckley, Jr., founder of National Review; and
- George V. Grune, former CEO, Readers Digest. [229]

Certainly, some of these media intellectuals and capitalists played a larger role than others in the promotion of capitalist values and the disguise and cover-up of their exploitation of the American people, but every one of these people knew who buttered their bread and were grateful for having been invited into the clubhouse of the elite.

The Crisis of Democracy

One of the greatest concerns of the Trilateral Commission during its early days of operation was the rise of the "New Left," "anti-Establishment," or "Hippy Movement" of the 1960s. This movement of the Baby Boomer generation spread across the industrialized world, threatening the capitalist value system and threatening to uncover the exploitive activities of the national and international elites, whom they simply called "The Establishment." The term included the international monopoly capitalists, as well as the national governments of capitalist countries. To uncover the driving force behind the youth movement and make recommendations as to how to contain it, the Trilateralists appointed a committee composed of a representative from each of the three regions, the US, Europe, and Japan. Their findings were published in 1975 in a book entitled *The Crisis of Democracy*.[230]

The bankers and the intellectual elites who supported them were concerned about the youth movement's "major disruptive influence on the world scene."

Let us review the contribution to the *Crisis of Democracy* that was written by Harvard Professor Samuel P. Huntington, who was the American representative on the Trilateralist team that put this study together in 1976. Huntington, at the time, was the director of Harvard's Center for International Affairs. During the Carter administration, he became the White House Coordinator of Security Planning for the powerful National Security Council, which was the president's principal arm for coordinating its policies with various government agencies.

In the *Crisis of Democracy*, Huntington begins by saying that the American youth at the time were the best educated in the world. But while this is a good thing, the American education system also produced a "significant challenge [that] comes from the intellectuals and related groups who assert their disgust with the corruption, materialism, and inefficiency of democracy and with the subservience of democratic government to monopoly capitalism." Huntington contended that the development of this "adversary culture" among intellectuals had affected students, scholars, and the media."[231]

Huntington, having little regard for people who challenged the corruption of the system, quoted Joseph Schumpeter, another Harvard professor, who had written: "Intellectuals are people who wield the power of the spoken and the written word, and one of the touches that distinguish them from other people who do the same is the absence of direct responsibility for practical affairs." This was code for Huntington's belief that the New Left intellectuals were nothing but a bunch of do-nothings who went around shooting their mouths off without taking any responsibility for their actions. Huntington continued:

> In some measure, the advanced industrial societies have spawned a stratum of value-oriented intellectuals who often devote themselves to the derogation of leadership, the challenging of authority, and the unmasking and delegitimization of established institutions, their behavior contrasting with that of the also increasing numbers of technocratic and policy-oriented intellectuals.[232]

Clearly Huntington is disgusted with people who are disgusted with the corruption, materialism, and inefficiency of the capitalist class. We have in this brief paragraph the key to how the bankers and their intellectual proponents look at intellectuals. If you are a "policy-oriented intellectual" you are a good guy. You support the capitalist system and never discuss its corruption, materialism, or inefficiency, which is considered bad taste. The intellectuals, who are members of the Council on Foreign Relations and the Trilateral Commission and serve within the political administrations that we reviewed above, or who are the mass media bosses who promote capitalist ideology and hide the corruption, materialism, and inefficiency from the public, are the "policy-oriented intellectuals." If you are a "value-oriented intellectual", however, you are a bad guy. You are a lazy, irresponsible, subhuman adversary. Not much wiggle room here, definitely not worthy of dialogue. You either support capitalism or you are an enemy.

This distinction between value-oriented and policy-oriented intellectuals, you will notice, is not the same as dividing intellectuals into right wing conservatives and the left-wing liberals. Both left and right-wing intellectuals can be either value-oriented or policy-oriented. As we have seen, it did not matter whether the Trilateralist-dominated presidencies were Democrat or Republican.

Huntington further riffs on the value-oriented intellectuals, whom he calls "adversary intellectuals," by saying that they are only motivated by "private satisfaction, leisure, and the need for belonging and intellectual and esthetic self-fulfillment."

He tells us that these value-oriented intellectuals represent a value system that stands against the traditional values of "materialistic work-oriented, public-spirited values." But now we get to the meat of the matter:

> The rise of this syndrome of values is presumably related to the relative affluence in which most groups in the Trilateral societies came to share during the economic expansion of the 1960s. The new values may not survive recession and resource shortages. But if they do, they pose an additional new problem for democratic government in terms of its ability to mobilize its citizens for the achievement of social and political goals and to impose discipline and sacrifice upon its citizens in order to achieve those goals.[233]

I cannot remember if the American people ever voted for the Trilateral Commission as president or that we gave them our permission to "discipline" us to achieve its goals? Huntington then bemoans the fact that in recent years the operations of "the democratic process seems to have generated a breakdown of traditional means of social control, a delegitimization of political and other forms of authority, and an overload of demands on government, exceeding its capacity to respond." There is too much democracy apparently.

Clearly, the bankers did not view the nation's youth, the New Left hippie culture, as a benign phenomenon. In fact, its emergence had triggered "a crisis of democracy."

It turns out, however, that Huntington is not just disgusted with the hippie value-oriented intellectuals, but also with other segments of society as well. The crisis of democracy can also be blamed on the:

> ... reassertion of the power of Congress and of state and local government, renewed commitment to the idea of equality on the part of intellectuals and other elites, the emergence of "public interest" lobbying groups, increased concern for the rights of and provision of opportunities for minorities and women to participate in the polity and economy, and a pervasive criticism of those who possessed or were even thought to possess excessive power or wealth.[234]

Read that again and let it sink in. Huntington then points to different forms of citizen participation, the marches, demonstrations, protest movements, and "cause" organizations such as Common Cause, Nader groups, and environmental groups as being problematic, creating a "democratic distemper."

This democratic distemper also could be witnessed in the "markedly higher levels of self-consciousness on the part of blacks, Indians, Chicanos, white ethnic groups, students, and women who were beginning to mobilize for greater equality of opportunity."

Huntington tells us that the US government, and the elites who control it, have been most beneficent in that the system had allowed "impressive gains" to be made by minorities and women in their representation in state legislatures and Congress. He crowed about the fact that "in 1974 the voters elected one woman and two Chicano governors."

The overall contention of Huntington, however, confirmed the elites' greatest fears. Things were getting out of hand. And this could be measured in the "reassertion of the primacy of equality as a goal in social, economic, and political life."

American democracy had clearly gone too far. By the first half of the 1970s, the people were demanding more of government while having less respect for it. "The expansion of governmental activities produced doubts about the economic solvency of government while the decrease in governmental authority produced doubts about the political solvency of government."

Huntington completely ignores any discussion of social justice and refuses to mention even in the slightest way, that the people might have a legitimate concern. Instead, he rues the fact that people no longer felt the same compulsion to obey those whom they had previously considered superior to themselves in age, rank, or status. He complained that:

> In the university, students who lacked expertise, came to participate in the decision-making process on many important issues. In the government, organizational hierarchy weakened, and organizational subordinates more readily acted to ignore, to criticize, or to defeat the wishes of their organizational superiors. In politics generally, the authority of wealth was challenged and successful efforts made to introduce reforms to expose and to limit its influence.[235]

The questioning of authority that was set in motion by the value-oriented intellectuals, now pervaded society and this manifested itself in a decline in public trust of political leaders and institutions. Instead people were now looking to guidance from the "adversary" media and "critical" intelligentsia in public affairs.

Huntington then explores the question of who really governs in America. This is particularly enlightening because he completely avoids speaking of the multi-national capitalists. He avoids any discussion of the Federal Reserve Bank, World Bank, IMF, or any of the large multinational corporations that control our food, energy, housing, health care, or education. He delves immediately into an analysis of the US presidency.

He held that presidential power had been diluted by the diffusion of authority in Congress. He also pointed his finger to television. He quotes Walter Cronkite saying that newsmen are not so much dedicated to the government as they are to humanity. He quotes poll results in which people said they thought that television was more influential in creating public opinion that government was. It is interesting that Huntington did not raise the issue of who owned the television stations and what their goals were.

Huntington gives us a deeper insight into how the elites themselves view the presidency. He pointed out that the coalition that the president needed to help him win an election had nothing to do with the coalition that he must assemble in order to rule. This "ruling coalition" depended upon working with powerful politicians in Congress, but also with the corporation heads of the private sector. To look at this revelation a little closer, Huntington is saying that whatever the presidential candidate promises to the people during his campaign has little to do with what he does as president because after he is elected he must concentrate on building relationships with the elites who funded his campaign and who hold the reins of power in the real world.

Huntington dismisses the value of democracy. He quotes Al Smith, a former governor of New York, who said "the only cure for the evils of democracy is more democracy." Huntington disagreed, "Our analysis suggests that applying that cure at the present time could well be adding fuel to the flames. Instead, some of the problems of governance in the United States today stem from an excess of democracy . . . Needed, instead, is a greater degree of moderation in democracy."

After giving examples of instances when democracy does not work, for example, students determining faculty tenure or soldiers voting on battle actions, Huntington makes one of the most outlandish rationales for systemic racism ever recorded. He says that in order for democracy to succeed, some groups, like blacks, should not participate in it:

> [T]he effective operation of a democratic political system usually requires some measure of apathy and noninvolvement on the part of some individuals and groups. In the past, every democratic society has had a marginal population, of greater or lesser size, which has not actively participated in politics.... Marginal social groups, as in the case of the blacks, are now becoming full participants in the political system. Yet the danger of overloading the political system with demands which extend its functions and undermine its authority still remains. Less marginality on the part of some groups thus needs to be replaced by more self-restraint on the part of all groups.[236]

Aside from the blacks, Huntington also blames the middle class for disrupting American society:

> The success of the existing structures of authority in incorporating large elements of the population into the middle class, paradoxically, strengthens precisely those groups which are disposed to challenge the existing structures of authority.[237]

One wonders if this is one of the main reasons that the elite decided to shrink the American middle class. There is no question that in the last two decades, we have seen the cost of education rise, massive student debt, the destruction of millions of American jobs, and massive middle-class debt.

Following his assault on the American people, Huntington baldly states that governance and democracy are warring concepts. An excess of democracy means weak governability while easy governability suggests faulty democracy. Huntington argued that the balance had tilted too far against government. Thus, the US and European governments need to restore a more "equitable relationship between governmental authority and popular control."

Because the bankers owned the American political economy, they acted quickly on Huntington's analysis. The first thing they did, as we have seen, was to take an active role in the grooming of candidates for the presidency. As a testament to their power over the American people, they have directly controlled every presidential candidate, with the exception of President Trump, since Jimmy Carter.

The second thing they did was to conduct a major assault on the black community. The blacks have suffered a disproportionate rate of unemployment since the Trilateralists took control of the economy. Well into the twenty-first century, black people experience the same rate of poverty that they experienced in 1968. In other words, during the absolute reign of the Trilateralists, an entire people have been consistently oppressed economically.[238] During the same time period, social and judicial discrimination has resulted in African Americans having the highest rates of incarceration of any minority group in the country.[239] While only twelve percent of the American population is African-American, of the 2.2 million male inmates, blacks make up forty percent of the incarcerated population. [240]

Under Trilateralist rule, the black community also suffered through a crack epidemic. As early as 1981, crack was appearing in Los Angeles, San Diego, Miami, and Houston.[241] In 1984, the distribution and use of crack exploded to include New York, Philadelphia, Houston, Los Angeles, and Detroit. One dose of crack could be obtained for as little as $2.50.

By the end of 1986, it was available in twenty-eight states and the District of Columbia. According to the 1985–1986 National Narcotics Intelligence Consumers Committee Report, crack also became available in New Orleans, Memphis, San Antonio, Baltimore, Portland, Pittsburgh, Cleveland, Cincinnati, Detroit, Chicago, Minneapolis-Saint Paul, Milwaukee, St. Louis, Atlanta, Oakland, Kansas City, Miami, Newark, Boston, San Francisco, Albany, Buffalo, and Dallas.

By 1986, cocaine-related hospital emergencies rose to 55,200 cases. Some scholars attributed the crack "epidemic" to a "moral panic," noting that the explosion in use and trafficking of the drug actually occurred after the media coverage of the drug portrayed it as an "epidemic." While it is unknown what part the media and government played in creating this epidemic, one thing that we know for sure is that the CIA was involved in drug trafficking to the US. Even though every effort was made to hide this assault on the blacks and American youth, a report by the Reagan administration admitted that the CIA and the Contras of Nicaragua were working together to sell crack to Americans.[242]

Between 1984 and 1989, the homicide rate for black males aged fourteen to twenty-four more than doubled. During this period, the black community also experienced a twenty percent to one hundred percent increase in fetal death rates, low birth-weight babies, weapons arrests, and the number of children in foster care.[243]

To curb the media, which had been complicit in the attack on government and corporate corruption during the 1960s, the bankers also began to reign in 'free speech." The fact is the bankers own the mass media, and therefore can impose any values on American society that they want. Their first attack on free speech was to curtail investigative reporting which often addressed the corruption of government. They replaced it with "value-free journalism." In this type of journalism, there is no right or wrong, no moral compass. There is only relativity. Each side of an argument or situation is viewed with equanimity. Racists have as much legitimacy as blacks, rapist have as much justification for their actions as do their victims. Furthermore, the media was silenced regarding any reporting on the actions of the bankers themselves. Today, the only thing we are told about big banks is the value of their stocks. In the military, journalists are also no longer free to investigate war crimes. Rather, they are now "embedded" into military units where they are essentially told the "truth" to print.

We have taken some time to analyze the *Crisis of Democracy* to demonstrate how the intellectual elite, who are considered "policy-oriented intellectuals," act to serve the banking and corporate elite. We have seen how they classify the intellectual class into the policy-oriented intellectuals and the value-oriented intellectuals.

We have also seen that the distinction between value-oriented and policy-oriented is not the same distinction between right-wing and left- wing intellectuals. Intellectuals on the left or the right may be policy-intellectuals or they may be value-oriented intellectuals. In other words, it is not important to the bankers that an intellectual supports the left or the right because they can use either side to make money and to manipulate the masses. What matters is whether the intellectuals support the bankers' system or not.

In the meantime, the bankers' mass media uses the distinction between the right and the left as a divide and conquer strategy to keep the American people from realizing who their true enemies are. It is like George W. said going into the War in Iraq, "You're either with us or against us." Having said this, the Trilateralist bankers slightly favor the policy-oriented left-wing neoliberals who whole-heartedly support their international agenda as opposed to the conservatives who are more ultra-nationalist in their orientation. So also, as we shall see, the rightwing intellectuals have a more incisive economic critique of American capitalism than the left and tend to raise alarm more often about the workings of the Federal Reserve and the dangers of the debt economy.

Another thing that the Trilaterialists or the Eastern Establishment find uncomfortable with the right wing is that they tend to be more open about their racism and sexism than the left. After all, the bankers do business with people of all races and nationalities and they stand to lose face internationally when the US government appears overtly racist, sexist, or xenophobic. On the other hand, the Trilateralists and other capitalists can depend upon the right wing to support capitalism as a matter of faith. Corporate capitalism for the Right is beyond reproach. Their beef is only with the federal government, not corporate profits.

The Trump Administration

Donald Trump is not a Trilateralist. He lacks the manners and the good graces to fit into their club but, nonetheless, he continues to serve their interests. For example, he perpetuates the "war on terrorism" as his foreign policy.

With his domestic policy, Donald Trump still fills the pockets of the rich by goosing the US economy by ignoring and rescinding environmental protections and ravaging the planet, by strengthening fossil fuel production, by suppressing the communities and families of the poor and people of color, by cutting human services and social service projects, by instituting tax reforms that fatten the bank accounts of the rich, by extorting and bullying other nations, and by feeding the war industry, which includes many politicians among those that benefit from it.[244]

Under the Trump administration, fewer students want to attend college because it costs too much and is not worth it in terms of the availability of good jobs.

Nonetheless, as long as Trump feeds the rich billionaires like himself, the mass media will continue to promote the big lie that his economy is good for the American people. The mainstream news outlets will tell us how GDP has grown and the stock market is soaring.

In reality, under Trump, US life expectancy has fallen because Trump and his associates have worked so hard to make sure millions of Americans lack health insurance. Under Trump the uninsured rate has jumped in two years from 10.9% to 13.7%, while an entire generation suffers from deaths of despair caused by alcohol, drug over doses, and suicide.

The median US household disposable income has not risen under Trump. And the worst part is that the highly touted Trump economy is environmentally toxic and deadly.[245] Economic growth is at the expense of our ravaged natural environment.

Finally, Trump's sense of morality is corrupt. For example, he spends one hundred and fifteen million dollars on golf trips, the equivalent of two hundred and eighty-seven years of presidential salary that he makes the American people pay for. His humanity is equally bankrupt. Trump is one of the most divisive people on the planet as can be seen by his sexism, racist, class bias, national chauvinism, and religious fundamentalism.

Trump appeals to many white Americans because his sexist, racist, nationalist message is conflated with the conservativism that prompts many white people to fear losing their privileged position.

Let us now take a look at the right wing and left wing value-oriented intellectuals in America to determine their differences but also to see if it is possible to overcome the divide and conquer strategy of the ruling elite and build a bridge between the left and the right to address our current crisis.

The Ideology of American Conservatism

According to a recent gallop poll, conservatives in the US are the largest ideological group, at thirty-seven percent. Moderates are close behind at thirty-five percent. Those who identify as liberals remain at twenty-four percent.[246] Conservatism appears to be growing stronger at the state level. The trend is most pronounced among the "least well-off, least educated, most blue collar, most economically hard-hit states."[247]

What is a Conservative?

The word derives from the root to *conserve*—to keep in a sound and safe state. Conservatives want to keep things as they are. They want to protect the status quo from change. In the United States, this entails defending the capitalist system and protecting the American empire with force of arms if necessary. It means keeping the same gender, race, and religious relations that have historically supported the superiority of white Christian males.

A recent article listed the following attributes that people applied to themselves when they called themselves conservatives:

1. An aversion to rapid change; a belief that tradition and prevailing social norms contain handed down wisdom.
2. A desire to preserve traditional morality, as articulated in the Bible, by using cultural norms and the power of the state.
3. A desire to preserve the rules of government articulated in the Declaration of Independence and the US Constitution.
4. An embrace of free-market capitalism.
5. A belief that America is an exceptional nation whose rightful role is leader of the free world.
6. A belief that America should export its brand of democracy through force of arms if necessary.
7. An embrace of localism, community, and family ties, human scale, and a responsibility to the future.
8. A desire to return to the way things once were.
9. An affinity for Republican America's social issues. (For example, gun ownership, father-family homes, country music, disdain for new foods like arugula or fancy mustard).
10. Disdain for American liberalism, multiculturalism, affirmative action, welfare, and, generally, the ideas of the left.
11. A belief that it is a natural right to be left alone by government.
12. The belief that taxes should be lower and government smaller.
13. The belief that the national debt and deficits put America in peril.
14. The belief that whenever possible, government budgets should be balanced.
15. Belief in the sinfulness of man, and the need to be skeptical and humble. [248]

According to George Lakoff, a noted expert on political communications, "the heart of conservatism is strict father morality. . . ."[249] This ancient programming can be traced back to the white Aryan tribes that poured out of the Caucasus and spread to India, the Middle East and Europe, brandishing their new vision of a man's right to ownership of family, goods, and chattel. Lackoff writes that different versions of conservatives are defined by particular domains of interest—individual liberty/self-interest, politics, economics, and social conditions. These domains of interest loosely characterize the Libertarian, Neo-Conservative, Wall Street, and Tea Party conservatives.[250]

Domain of Interest	*Type of Conservative*
Individual liberty	Libertarian
Politics	Neo-Conservative
Economics	Wall Street
Society and Religion	Tea Party

While these various conservative groups share the same "strict father" orientation, they apply it to the different substructures of capitalist society. For example, a focus on unimpeded pursuit of self-interest along with strict limits on state power over the individual defines the libertarian view of right-wing thought. The libertarians by and large represent the largest group of value-oriented intellectuals among the right wing. This is due to their critique of the Federal Reserve Bank and its role in creating a debtor society.

Neo-Conservatives believe in the unbridled use of power (especially military power) to extend the reign of strict father values into every dimension of life, domestic and international. They are concerned with maintaining the global financial and military empire, and the use of police power at home. They sometimes run up against libertarians, who object to the use of governmental power and to global involvements that require the buildup and use of state power. Neo-Conservatives whole-heartedly support US-based capitalism but can become too aggressive for the bankers on occasion as demonstrated by the presidencies of George H. W. and George W. Bush.

Wall Street conservatives are primarily concerned with the acquisition of wealth via the corporate world. These are the capitalists themselves. They include CEOs and upper management of wealthy corporations, investment bankers, venture capitalists, private asset managers, hedge fund managers, etc. These conservatives have many political concerns: tax policy, economic treaties, import-export policy, protection of foreign investments, government contracts, access to minerals on government lands, protection of patents and copyrights, property rights versus environmental rights, energy supplies, control of markets, privatization of public resources, and so on. They tend to work through lobbyists, advertising, and control of the media and public discourse. And most importantly, they pay for the politicians' campaigns. In rare occasions, they will also run for public office.

Finally, there are Tea Party conservatives—social and religious fundamentalists, who act aggressively on every front to dismantle social welfare programs put in place by the liberals and progressives. The tea party conservatives want to keep women and minorities in inferior positions. They fear cultural change. They also provide the Right with value-oriented intellectuals insofar as they challenge the Federal Reserve Bank and the debt economy. They will directly challenge the need for big government, which includes the destruction of the IRS, the EPA, and the NSA.

The Tenets of Conservatism

While the conservatives can be grouped according to their fields of interest, they share the same ideology. The major points of that ideology, according to Lakoff are:

God

Many conservatives view God as the ultimate strict father. This program harkens back to John Calvin and the protestant reformation. God is an all-good and powerful being at the top of a hierarchy. Morality is primarily linked to economic power and is expressed in the capitalist values—frugality, prudence, discipline, patience, etc.

God wants *good* people, i.e., the capitalists, to be in charge. Virtue is rewarded with more power. God therefore wants a hierarchical society in which there are moral authorities who should be obeyed in each domain: individual power, global power, financial power, and social power.

God makes commandments to define right and wrong. One must have *self-discipline* to follow God's commandments. God is punitive. He punishes those who do not follow his commandments, and rewards those who do. Those who are disciplined enough to be moral are disciplined enough to become prosperous and powerful.

Christ, as the son of God, gives sinners a second chance—a chance to be born again and be obedient to God's commandments. He died to save the believers from their sins. Those who do not accept Jesus Christ as their salvation are doomed to eternal damnation.

The Moral Order

Traditional power relations define a natural moral order: God above man, man above nature, adults above children, Western culture above non-Western culture, America above other nations.

The moral order often extends to men above women, whites above nonwhites, Christians above non-Christians, straights above gays.

Morality

Preserving and extending the conservative moral system (strict father morality) is the highest priority. Morality comes in the form of rules and commandments made by a moral authority. To be moral is to be obedient to that authority. It requires internal discipline to control one's natural desires and follow a moral authority. What that authority is depends on your domain of interest: the individual, the Bible, governing institutions—both public and private, Wall Street, or conservative society. Discipline is learned in childhood primarily through punishment for wrongdoing. Morality can be maintained only through a system of rewards and punishments.

The Father Family

While there has always been a strong movement within Catholicism, Judaism, and Islam to keep women in a subservient position, this tendency is also true among the Protestants, especially the Southern Baptists. In order for the strict father-dominated family to remain legitimate in the eyes of society, it is necessary to suppress women. The rationale is as old as the patriarchal values of the Aryan tribes as built upon by the Jewish and Christian mythology of Adam and Eve.

At the Southern Baptist Convention's annual meeting in Kansas City in 1984 the fundamentalists pushed through a resolution barring the ordination of women, "because the man was first in creation and the woman was first in the Edenic fall." With this measure, the fundamentalists closed a perfect loop. Women were not allowed to be "over" men, which means they cannot teach men where religion is concerned, which means they cannot be ordained and serve as pastors, which means they cannot challenge the interpretation of the biblical verses that confine them to a secondary status. Driving the resolution was a fear held in common with their fundamentalist brothers in the Muslim and Jewish worlds—fear of the loss of control of women.[251]

Among the poor religious conservatives, divorce is the highest in the country. According to the latest study,[252] the reason that the divorce rate is highest among conservative religious groups is that their children marry earlier and have their first birth earlier. This fact, along with a lower level of education and a lower level of income, results in higher divorce rates among conservative Protestant youth.

The strict fathers also do not want their daughters to know anything about sex or to help them in any way regarding sexual issues. They want their daughters to be "disciplined" and abstain from sex. Abstinence education might be a good thing if it was taught along with sex education and parenting education and also applied to sons. But this is not the case. Therefore, the children grow up without any guidance or knowledge about their sexuality, and no moral standard regarding parenthood. One of the biggest challenges in any woman's life is giving birth and raising a child and yet no guidance is given to young people to prepare them for it. It is no wonder that teenage sex is on the rise in the poor rural counties where the fundamentalists predominate. And yet these teens do not have the means to raise their children.

Conservatives, at the same time, say that they want to protect children from obscenity and exploitation. In this immoral/amoral world that we live in today, obscenity and exploitation of children is rampant. The fashion industry turns preteen children and even pre-preteen children into sexual objects. TV and the mass media glamorize sex, sex, and more sex. There is a morality in protecting our children from sexual exploitation at an early age. The conservatives get this. The liberal ad men do not seem to.

Another issue that greatly challenges the father-dominated family is women having access to abortion. Conservatives are anti-abortion. In their reasoning, there are only two cases where women want abortions: unmarried teenagers who have been having "illicit" sex, and older women who want to delay child rearing to pursue a career. Both of these fly in the face of the strict father model. Pregnant teenagers have violated the commandments of the strict father. Career women challenge the power and authority of the strict father. Both should be punished by bearing the child; neither should be able to avoid the consequences of their actions, which would violate the strict father model's idea that morality depends on punishment. Since conservative values in general are versions of strict father values, abortion stands as a threat to conservative values and to one's identity as a conservative. Given this position, men are never challenged or held accountable for getting women pregnant.

Conservatives who are "pro-life" are also against prenatal care, postnatal care, and health care for children, all of which can greatly benefit the life of a child. Thus, conservatives are not really "pro-life" in a broader sense of the term. If conservatives are not willing to educate the young about sex and if they are not willing to provide a safety net to support a baby when the mother needs help or is incapable of providing support for her child, their "pro-life" stance becomes greatly diluted. Pro-life then becomes pro-punishment and pro-suffering for both the child and the mother. This approach remains consistent with the necessary punishment of weak daughters and wives who have violated man's rule.

From a larger perspective, a population explosion is currently ravaging the planet's life support systems. Given the capitalist system's profligate waste of resources, there may already be too many of us to live a middle-class lifestyle. Nobody wants to address this issue because few people want to deny themselves the freedom to have their own children. If society will not make a rational decision concerning population growth, then certainly nature will make this choice for us. In the meantime, the question of having a child should remain a mother's choice and not be imposed upon her by dogmatic, micromanaging, religious conservatives who care more about legitimizing their dogma than they do for human life.

There is an argument to be made that if a woman or teenage girl has a baby and cannot support that child there should be consequences. If she did not ask for society's input into her decision to have a child, then why should society have to pick up the cost of that child once she has it? In a case like this, the woman owes a debt to society. We can only hope that society would be magnanimous enough to help support the child out of spiritual concern considering that the conservatives will not allow abortions. Punishment is not a rational response. Nor does it take into account the men's responsibility in creating children.

Along with the control of women, same-sex marriage is another hot button for conservatives. It completely violates the strict father model of the family. A lesbian marriage has no father. A gay marriage has "fathers" who are taken to be less than real men. Since preserving and extending the strict father model is the highest moral value for conservatives, same-sex marriage constitutes an attack on the conservative value system as a whole, and on those whose very identity depends on their having strict father values.

Enomics

Competition for scarce resources also imposes discipline, and hence serves morality. The discipline required to be moral is the same discipline required to win competitions and prosper. The wealthy people tend to be the good people, a natural elite. The poor remain poor because they lack the discipline needed to prosper. The poor, therefore, deserve to be poor and serve the wealthy. The wealthy need and deserve poor people to serve them. The vast and increasing gap between rich and poor is thus seen to be both natural and good.

To the extent that markets are "free," they are a mechanism for the disciplined people to accumulate wealth. Free markets are moral. If everyone pursues his own profit, the profit of all will be maximized. Competition is good; it produces optimal use of resources and disciplined people, and hence serves morality. Regulation is bad; it gets in the way of the free pursuit of profit. Wealthy people serve society by investing and giving jobs to poorer people. This is why conservatives will support the latest wealth divide in which eighty people have a total net worth of $1.9 trillion, equal to the net worth of 3.5 billion people.[253] It does not occur to them that, on a finite planet, the accumulation of wealth by a few exists at the expense of the majority.

Politics

Social programs are immoral. This harkens back to John Calvin. By giving people things they have not earned, social programs remove the incentive to be disciplined, which is necessary for both morality and prosperity. Social programs should be eliminated. Anything that can be done by the private sphere should be done without government interference. The only legitimate role of government is to protect the lives and the private property of Americans, to make profit-seeking as easy as possible for worthy Americans (the disciplined ones), and to promote conservative morality (strict father morality), along with conservative culture and religion. This right-wing dogma gets expressed in comments like that made by Rand Paul in an address to New Hampshire businessmen on January 14, 2015 when he told them that half of the people who receive social security disability benefits are "gaming the system."[254]

Education

Since preserving and extending conservative morality is the highest goal, education should serve that goal. Schools should teach conservative values. Conservatives should gain control of school boards to guarantee this. Teachers should be strict, not nurturing, in the example they set for students and in the content they teach. Education should therefore promote discipline. Undisciplined students should face punishment, including corporal punishment. Intellectually undisciplined students should not be coddled, but should be shamed and punished by not being promoted. Uniform testing should test the level of discipline. There are right and wrong answers for which the students should be tested. Testing defines fairness: Those who pass are rewarded; those not disciplined enough to pass are punished.

Because immoral, undisciplined teachers can lead moral, disciplined children astray, parents should be able to choose to which schools they send their children. Government funding should be taken from public schools and given to parents in the form of vouchers. This will help wealthier (more disciplined and moral) citizens send their children to private or religious schools that teach conservative values and impose appropriate discipline. The vouchers given to poorer (less disciplined and less worthy) people will not be sufficient to allow them to get their children into the better private and religious schools. Schools will thus come to reflect the natural divisions of wealth in society. Of course, students who show exceptional discipline and talent should be given scholarships to the better schools. This will help maintain the social elite as a natural elite.

Health Care

It is the responsibility of parents to take care of their children. To the extent that they cannot, they are not living up to their individual responsibility. No one has the responsibility of doing other people's jobs for them. Thus, prenatal care, postnatal care, health care for children, and care for the aged and infirm are matters of individual responsibility. They are not the responsibility of taxpayers.

The Protestant Religion and the Rise of American Conservatism

The ideology of right-wing intellectuals based upon God, the moral order, discipline, and the sovereign father family can be traced back to the values of the patriarchal Aryan tribes. This crude belief system was acculturated into the West and spread throughout Europe during ancient history and the Middle Ages. In Volume 4 of *The Untold Story of Western Civilization*, on Modern History, we demonstrated how the various religious sects played a key role in the transition of society, especially in the US. During modern times, religion came to America with the Anglican Separatists in the seventeenth century. After coming to the shores of America, this ideology was further codified into the value system of the Right. By now, however, any spiritual essence that it might have held has been crusted over by centuries of dogma, religious platitudes, and self-interest. No one likes to hear their beliefs challenged, especially those with a closed mind, but if we are going to resolve the differences between the left and the right in order to secure our communities and protect the planet going forward, we must put the left and right ideologies under the microscope of a universal ideology, one in which the intention is to seek the welfare of all. In the following section, we will look at how certain religious ideals came to form the core of the political Right.

Evangelicals

The word *evangelical* comes from the Greek word for "gospel" or "good news." During the Reformation, Protestant theologians embraced the label as referring to "gospel truth." When the first European immigrants came to America, they were motivated by two distinct visions of the future. The vision of the "Planting Fathers," who were the Calvinists who separated from the Anglican Church and escaped to America, dreamt of a Christian land and a "City upon a Hill." The "Founding Fathers," on the other hand, dreamt of a land free from religious conflict and a separation of church and state.[255] They chose religious freedom over religious purity.

In the 1730s and 1740s a wave of religious enthusiasm called the "Great Awakening" swept through the American colonies led by an evangelical preacher named Jonathan Edwards who rejected the trappings of organized religion (Anglicans, Catholics, and mainstream Protestant sects) and advocated a personal relationship with God. Edwards, who was a Calvinist theologian and revivalist preacher, laid the ground work for the Evangelical movement that we currently have. Today, the Evangelical statement of faith entails the following:

- The Bible is the inspired, only infallible, authoritative Word of God.
- There is one God, eternally existent in three persons: Father, Son and Holy Spirit.
- The Lord Jesus Christ is the Son of God.
- We believe in His virgin birth, His sinless life, His miracles, His suffering and death in atonement for our sins, His bodily resurrection, His ascension to the right hand of the Father, and His personal return in power and glory.
- Regeneration by the Holy Spirit of lost and sinful people is absolutely essential.
- The Holy Spirit dwells within Christians and enables a godly life.
- We believe in the resurrection of both the saved and the lost; the saved to eternal life and the lost to eternal damnation.
- We believe in the spiritual unity of believers in our Lord Jesus Christ.[256]
- Sharing the gospel through preaching and social action is necessary.

The evangelical movement, inspired in large part by Edwards, gave rise to the Methodist and Baptist religions, which are indigenous to America. A second great wave of evangelicalism swept the colonies between the 1790s and 1840 and greatly energized the emerging Methodist and Baptist sects. The Methodists believed in building loving relationships with their families and neighbors through social service. The Baptists were united in their belief that infant baptisms were not valid because a child could not choose his religion. Baptism, therefore, should be reserved only for consenting adults. Other than this, the Baptists held little dogma in common among themselves. Each church was autonomous and believed whatever it chose to believe.

The Second Great Awakening was responsible for beginning the temperance and abolitionist movements in America and pitted the Congregationalist Church, Presbyterian Church, Dutch Reform Church, and German Reform Church against the establishment Catholic, Anglican, and Lutheran churches.

During the interim period between the first and second "Awakenings," the American Revolution occurred. Being attentively aware of the religious conflict that was growing between the various Christian religions in the colonies and fearing a reprise of the religious wars that had recently ripped apart Europe, the Founding Fathers, in their political deliberations, created a separation of Church and State. While most of them were members of the established Christian Churches or either Deists, they chose an inclusive religious freedom over denominational religious purity. While any religion could have a say in matters of state, none could dominate it. No religion could determine US law or affect US relations with other countries.

Southern Baptists

By the mid-eighteenth century the number of Baptists increased greatly as a result of the Great Awakening inspired by Jonathan Edwards. This was largely a people's movement that gained popularity in the rural South because it rejected the Anglican Church, which was used by the Northern capitalists to dominate people.

From 1624, there had been a law of the land that required white southerners in the Virginia colony to worship in the Anglican Church (Church of England) and support its upkeep with their taxes.[257] Not surprisingly, the English Tories, who comprised the capitalist class at the time, also controlled the Anglican Church and through its edicts were able to control the small planters and middle class people. Yet there had been dissenters from many Protestant sects who had settled in the colony from early on and resented the legal restrictions placed on their own practice of religion. After 1750, evangelical Christians, in the Great Awakening, started a struggle for religious freedom that paralleled the wider struggle for political independence.

The evangelicals took familiar biblical themes and remodeled them into a message of spiritual renewal and a personal God who intervened in human affairs. Slaves in unprecedented numbers were drawn to evangelical Christianity.

After the mid-eighteenth century, evangelical Christians (Baptists, Presbyterians, and Methodists) challenged licensing laws and restrictions on meeting houses. As the Revolution approached, the Baptists soon became active patriots in the Revolutionary War. With their demands for religious liberty, they also included a cry for political liberty. They loyally supported patriots like Patrick Henry, Thomas Jefferson, James Madison, and George Washington, and received the praise from these men in return.

The Baptists in the South played a central role in securing religious liberty from the Anglican Church in Virginia. Like their fellow Baptists in the North, they helped lay the foundations for the national Bill of Rights, which guaranteed religious liberty for all in the new Constitution of the United States.[258] The multiplicity of religious groups in America prohibited the domination of one group that led to the religious persecutions and sectarian warfare that had plagued England and the rest of Europe for centuries. The Baptists, however, proved to be less tolerant of non-Christian faiths namely the traditional religious systems of their black slaves.

In the late 1700s and early 1800s, as the American Revolution began to consolidate its gains, the Baptists also began to organize and expand. They formed missionary societies to spread their Christian beliefs to others. These mission societies led to more expansive organizational structures that would eventually define the denomination of Southern Baptists. By the 1830s, tension began to mount between the Northern and Southern Baptists. One issue that severely divided them was the issue of slavery. Northern Baptists believed that all men were created equal by God and became a powerful force within the abolitionist movement. Southern Baptists, on the other hand, believed that the white race was superior and colored races only existed to serve the whites. Slavery was part of the moral order of things. They argued that it existed in Greece and Rome and was tolerated by the early apostles.[259]

After the Second Great Awakening (1790-1840) any southern Baptist gave up calling for slaves to be freed. They remained neutral on the subject of slavery. Neutrality, however, was not a strong enough stance according to the slave-owning elites who were attracted to the southern Baptist churches. These slave owners now insisted that the Baptist churches condone slavery by allowing slave owners to be missionaries. The Foreign Mission Society, headquartered in New York, held that a person could not be a Baptist missionary and keep his slaves as property. When the Foreign Mission Office refused the request of the slave owners to become missionaries, they were powerful enough to secede and form their own denomination. These southern Baptists met in May of 1845, and broke with the Baptists of the North. They organized the Southern Baptist Convention through which they continued to promote slavery as a tenet of Christianity.[260]

Freed from the censorship of their Northern brethren, the Southern Baptists became strong and vocal advocates for slavery as a Biblical institution. As one leader, Dr. Richard Furman, wrote to the governor of South Carolina, "the right of holding slaves is clearly established in the Holy Scriptures, both by precept and example."[261]

In Reverend Doctor Richard Furman's open letter written in 1838, "Exposition of the Views of the Baptists, Relative to the Coloured Population in the United States in a Communication to the Governor of South Carolina," he presents us with the classic justification for slavery and its support in the Bible. Although well written, it contains not a single quote from Jesus, nor could it. Rather it bases its argument for slavery on references by Paul regarding masters and bondsmen. It is an obvious misrepresentation; however, it assuaged the consciences of the slave owners of the day and provided the ideological justification for slavery in the South. Here is a quote from the letter:

> Had the holding of slaves been a moral evil, it cannot be supposed, that the inspired Apostles, who feared not the faces of men, and were ready to lay down their lives in the cause of their God, would have tolerated it, for a moment, in the Christian Church. If they had done so on a principle of accommodation, in cases where the masters remained heathen, to avoid offences and civil commotion; yet, surely, where both master and servant were Christian, as in the case before us, they would have enforced the law of Christ, and required, that the master should liberate his slave in the first instance. But, instead of this, they let the relationship remain untouched, as being lawful and right, and insist on the relative duties. In proving this subject justifiable

by Scriptural authority, its morality is also proved; for the Divine Law never sanctions immoral actions.²⁶²

The Baptists allowed blacks to attend their services, but only as observers. They could not participate in any way.

Given its overtly racist origins and almost exclusive white membership, the Southern Baptist Convention not only provided the ideological justification for slavery, but it also became one of the driving forces behind Jim Crow laws. The Jim Crow laws were racial segregation laws enacted after the Civil War in the South that continued in force until as late as 1965. They mandated racial segregation in all public facilities in Southern states of the former Confederacy.²⁶³

The Ku Klux Klan became the Southern Baptist Convention's informal paramilitary arm, with many of its leaders also serving as southern Baptist ministers. Founded in 1866, the Ku Klux Klan (KKK), in a very short time, extended into almost every southern state and became a vehicle for white southern resistance to Reconstruction-era policies aimed at establishing political and economic equality for blacks. Its members waged an underground campaign of intimidation and violence directed at white and black Republican leaders. Though the US Congress passed legislation designed to curb Klan terrorism, the organization saw its primary goal, the reestablishment of white supremacy, fulfilled through Democrat victories in state legislatures across the South in the 1870s.²⁶⁴

The Union victory in the Civil War in 1865 may have given over four million slaves their freedom, but the process of rebuilding the South during the Reconstruction period (1865-1877) introduced a new, more virulent strain of racism. Before Lincoln was assassinated in 1865, his vice-president, Andrew Johnson, who hailed from Tennessee, voted against secession and was somewhat of a hero to the North and a traitor to the South. Once Lincoln was dead, however, Johnson returned power to the southern states to continue their racist policies.

The Southern Baptist Convention, which was the heart and soul of the slave owners and white supremacists, used the Democratic Party to regain and maintain power during and after Reconstruction. The Democrats (which was then the party of the conservatives and reactionaries) passed Jim Crow laws to reestablish white supremacy and racial segregation. From 1874, the Ku Klux Klan, as well as other insurgent paramilitary groups such as the White League and Red Shirts, acted to disrupt Republican organizing and intimidate and suppress black voters.[265] The Republican Party at the time was the party of Abraham Lincoln.

Elections from 1868 were accompanied by increasing levels of violence, in which hundreds of blacks were killed.[266] Because the whites controlled all the seats in the Democratic Party and this party represented the majority population of the white South, they had a powerful voting bloc in the national Congress as well. Voting as a bloc within the Democratic Party after they had shrunken the Republican Party by suppressing black voters, they became known as the "Solid South" and had an impact in Washington far in excess of their numbers. Until 1965, the "Solid South"[267] was a one-party system under the Democrats. To be nominated by the Democratic Party in the South meant the same thing as being elected.[268] This held true not only on the national level, but also on the state and local levels.

By adhering to its racist philosophy, southern Christians were put at odds with the overwhelming majority of humanity on the planet. By justifying a status quo, based on racism and slavery in the name of God, they sinned against God and the Creation.

Fundamentalists

In the 1920s and 1930s a controversy arose in the Presbyterian Church in the United States about the role of Christians in modern society and what role they should play. This controversy, referred to as the "Fundamentalist–Modernist Controversy," spread to most major protestant churches in the country.

The movement was triggered by a reaction to liberal theologians who began to take a scientific view of the Bible. The liberal Christians challenged Christian myths and dogma and encouraged men and women to determine whether the Bible was merely a collection of myths, legends, and folklore or whether there was a core of historical truth in it. The "fundamentals," was the term Christian conservatives used in their anti-modernist crusade and a "fundamentalist," was a person who stood for the fundamentals.[269]

The "fundamentals" include: the infallibility of scripture; the virgin birth of Jesus; belief that Christ's death was for the atonement for mankind's sin; the bodily resurrection of Jesus; the historical reality of the miracles of Jesus; and the Second Coming of Christ.[270]

Fundamentalists can be found in all the major denominations of Protestantism in the United States, and they compose the conservative wing within these denominations. They also constitute the main force behind the political right wing in this country.

The split between the fundamentalists and the modernists became characterized as an argument between a "biblical" view of history versus an "evolutionary" view. This contest was given a large impetus by the Scopes Monkey Trial in 1925 when fundamentalists held that there was no support in the Bible for the idea that man derived from lower species. The liberals, on the other hand, promoted the science of evolution and denied that the "myths" in the Bible were based upon historical truth.[271]

Although this schism is called the "Fundamentalist–Modernist Controversy," it triggered a larger reaction to liberal thinking within all the major Christian denominations. In the course of internal tensions between conservative and liberal Christians that lasted for decades, many disgruntled conservatives abandoned their denominations to form their own smaller denominations. In the 1960s, reacting to the "liberal infiltration" of their church, conservative Southern Baptists began a concerted effort to rid their institutions and leadership of liberal leanings. While its initiators called it a Conservative Resurgence, its detractors have labeled it a Fundamentalist Takeover.[272]

The movement was aimed at reorienting and destroying the liberal trajectory and reestablishing an unambiguous affirmation of biblical inerrancy (i.e., The Bible "is without error or fault in all its teaching").[273]

The long confrontation between liberal and conservative Christians resulted in the contemporary division of Protestant America into the so-called mainline Christianity, on the one hand, and evangelical and fundamentalist Christianity on the other. Mainline Christianity includes the Seven Sisters of American Protestantism—the United Methodist Church (UMC), the Evangelical Lutheran Church in America (ELCA), the Presbyterian Church (U.S.A.) (PCUSA), the Episcopal Church (TEC), the American Baptist Churches (ABCUSA), the United Church of Christ (UCC), and the Disciples of Christ—as well as the Quakers, Reformed Church in America (RCA), and other churches.[274]

The fundamentalists are found in all the mainstream religions as the conservative faction, but they are also concentrated in Southern Baptist Churches and among "born-again" evangelicals.

The Christian Voice

The *Christian Voice*, the nation's oldest conservative Christian lobby, was founded by Dr. Robert Grant and Richard Zone in 1978. It brought together several anti-gay and anti-pornography organizations in California.[275] The TV evangelical minister Pat Robertson, who later formed the Christian Coalition, helped provide financial resources for the organization. Paul Weyrich, the leader of the conservative think tank, the Heritage Foundation, and the chief architect of the Christian right movement, which the Christian Voice advocated, agreed to let Grant set up headquarters for his future organization at the headquarters of the Heritage Foundation in Washington DC. Weyrich, a member of the Melkite Greek Catholic Church,[276] then recruited mail king Howard Phillips, a Jew who converted to Evangelical Christianity, and former Nixon administration official, Richard Viguerie, a Roman Catholic who was known for leading crusades to "defund the Left," to help develop The Christian Voice.

The Christian Voice became a lobbying organization, when Grant hired Gary Jarmin, a Washington insider and Republican politico. Jarmin urged Jews, fundamentalists, Roman Catholics, Pentecostals, and charismatics, and others to put aside their differences and work together for common notions of political change. This outreach contrasted with the *Moral Majority*, the *Religious Roundtable*, and the *National Christian Action Coalition*, all of which were more fundamentalist in their ideology and less willing to build political bridges to other religious communities. Insider conflicts, early in the game, resulted in Weyrich, Viguerie, and Phillips abandoning the group after Grant announced that the Christian Voice was "a sham" that was "controlled by three Catholics and a Jew." These men then decided to align themselves with rising televangelist Jerry Falwell and form the Moral Majority.

Despite this loss of leadership, the Christian Voice was successful in its mission. It employed hundreds of political organizers, including Susan Hirschman, Chief of Staff to former House Majority Leader Tom DeLay; Congressman Tom Hagadorn, who chaired the organization for several years; and Tim LaHaye, co-author of the Left Behind series. At one point, US Senators Orrin Hatch (Utah), Roger Jespen (Iowa), and James McClure (Idaho) all served on the organization's board of directors.[277] Many of the techniques used by right wing political campaigns were originally developed by Christian Voice, including the "Political Report Card," which informed conservative voters how their representative voted.

The Christian Voice was the first of the major Christian Right political groups. It was followed in time by the *Christian Coalition, American Coalition for Traditional Values, Concerned Women for America, Moral Majority, Family Research Council*, and other Christian political groups.

At the time of its inception, the Christian Voice sought to counter President Jimmy Carter's influence over the American Christian community. Carter, who considered himself to be a "born-again Christian," was popular among Christian conservatives during his 1976 campaign. After he took office, however, Carter disappointed many Christian conservatives by supporting the Panama Canal Treaty. Most supported Senator Strom Thurmond's position, "The canal is ours, we bought and we paid for it and we should keep it."[278] Many Christian conservatives also considered Carter to be soft on Communism. This perception caused Christian Voice and other Christian right organizations to support Ronald Reagan in 1980. The south had begun to abandon the Democratic Party because of its support for the Civil Rights Act of 1964.

With the influence of Ronald Reagan, many conservative Christian southerners permanently changed their party affiliation from Democrat to Republican, and they have largely remained Republican to this day.

After Reagan's second term began, funding and leadership weakened when Republicans lost control of the US Senate. Many key members of the Christian Voice, including Grant, left to form the *American Freedom Coalition (AFC)*, which was funded by the Unification Church leader Sun Myung Moon.

The AFC represented an attempt to unite political conservatives with conservative religious groups behind a common campaign to preserve and promote what it describes as "traditional values." These included a strong national defense, as well as opposition to abortion, pornography, and communism. Economically, it promoted the right to own property and minimal governmental interference in the marketplace. Religious freedom was promoted to include "moral and religious standards" in government and other social institutions. Robert Grant, who became the AFC president, said it was formed because of the "inability of the 'Christian Right' to achieve its agenda" because of its "fragmentation and its failure to build coalitions with its philosophical allies from other communities. . . ."[279]

The Moral Majority

The Moral Majority had its inception in 1976, when the Southern Baptist TV evangelist Jerry Falwell embarked on a series of "I Love America" rallies across the country to raise awareness of social issues important to Falwell. These rallies promoted Falwell's decision to combat the traditional American principle of separating religion and politics. Through hosting these rallies, Falwell built support for his reforms and positioned himself as a national religious leader. Having already been a part of a well-established network of ministers, within a few years, Falwell was able to launch the *Moral Majority*.[280]

It was Paul Weyrich who coined the term "moral majority."[281] The Moral Majority derived from a struggle to control the *Christian Voice* during 1978 when Robert Grant insulted his co-workers, Paul Weyrich, Terry Dolan, Richard Viguerie, and Howard Phillips who then went to Jerry Falwell and urged him to found the Moral Majority. This was the beginning of the "New Christian Right,"[282] which became a right-wing Christian political faction that is characterized by its strong support of socially conservative policies. Christian conservatives seek to apply their understanding of Christianity to politics in order to influence law and public policy.[283] Among their hot button issues are school prayer, intelligent design (anti-evolution theory), embryonic stem cell research, homosexuality, contraception, abortion, and pornography.[284]

The Moral Majority was founded in June 1979 as a southern-oriented organization although state chapters and political activity soon extended beyond the South. By 1982, Moral Majority surpassed Christian Voice in size and influence.

The Moral Majority's headquarters were in Lynchburg, Virginia, the same city where Falwell was the presiding minister of the nation's largest independent Baptist church, the Thomas Road Baptist Church. Virginia had long been a major center of Christian Right politics. Pat Robertson's Christian Coalition was also headquartered there in 1988.

The organizational bodies of the Moral Majority consisted of a lobbying division, an education component to train ministers in their issues and conduct voter registration drives, and a legal defense fund used to sue the American Civil Liberties Union and oppose secular humanist issues in court. Finally, it had a political action committee that supported candidates who reflected their values.

The Moral Majority was organized into political action committees that campaigned on issues necessary to maintaining their conception of Christian moral law, which they believed also represented the opinions of the majority of Americans. Some issues for which the Moral Majority campaigned included:

- Enforcement of a traditional vision of the father family;
- Opposition to the Equal Rights Amendment (for women);
- Opposition to state recognition and acceptance of homosexual acts, as well as the civil rights of gays and lesbians;
- Outlawing abortion, even in cases involving incest, rape, or in pregnancies where the life of the mother is at stake;
- Support for mandated Christian prayers in schools;
- Targeting Jews and other non-Christians for conversion to conservative Christianity; and
- Opposition to the Strategic Arms Limitation Talks

With a membership of millions, the *Moral Majority* was one of the largest conservative lobby groups in the United States. At its height, the Moral Majority claimed over four million members and over two million donors. These members were spread out over twenty state organizations, of which Washington State became the largest. By 1987, Falwell retired as the formal head of the Moral Majority, although he maintained an active and visible role within the organization. Although the Moral Majority existed for only a decade, it made a significant impact on American politics. It was well funded from the beginning; it delivered consistent messages from the center to the state groups; it had experienced leaders; and its constituents were amenable to the issues that the Moral Majority emphasized. [285]

The Moral Majority's initial political actions were aimed at supporting Jesse Helms' proposed legislation on school prayer. Before long, the Moral Majority became heavily involved in national politics; although at the state level, branches of the Moral Majority continued to pursue specific issues. Leaders within the Moral Majority encouraged ministers to give their congregants political direction, reminding congregants when to vote, who to vote for, and why the Moral Majority held particular positions on issues.

The Moral Majority is probably best known for its involvement in the election of Ronald Reagan. Falwell announced the organization's endorsement of Reagan while attending the Republican convention. According to Jimmy Carter, "that autumn [1980] a group headed by Jerry Falwell purchased ten million dollars in commercials on southern radio and TV to brand me as a traitor to the South and no longer a Christian."[286] Falwell announced Reagan's success was directly due to the Moral Majority and others registering and encouraging churchgoers to vote who had never before been politically active.

Reagan's administration closely followed the agenda of the Moral Majority and the Christian Right. His presidency was termed the "Reagan Revolution," in recognition of the political realignment that occurred in favor of conservative policies. Domestically, the administration favored reducing government social programs, promoting law and order and using states' rights as an argument to cut federal social programs. Once in office, the Reagan administration introduced several tax cuts, which largely benefitted the rich and the corporations. The economic policies enacted in 1981, known as "Reaganomics," basically supported state monopoly capitalism. Called "supply-side economics" the Reagan administration lowered government regulations to production and investment.[287] Regarding foreign policy, Reagan accelerated the massive buildup of the military and the introduction of missile defense systems. The "Reagan Doctrine" granted aid to paramilitary forces seeking to overthrow communist or leftist governments, particularly in war-torn Central America and Afghanistan. Despite the so-called "Revolution" it was just more business-as-usual in service to the capitalist ruling class. It would be more accurate to call it a counter-revolution.

The Moral Majority was still an active organization in the 1988 elections, but with Reagan having reached his two-term limit, the Republican nomination was open to a variety of primary contenders. The evangelical minister and televangelist Reverend Pat Robertson sought the Republican nomination and would have been a natural choice for the Moral Majority's support. Falwell, however, gave his organization's endorsement to contender George H. W. Bush instead. This decision highlighted the rivalry between Falwell and Robertson as televangelists, but also revealed the deep-seated tension that still persisted between competing evangelical traditions. Falwell's fundamentalist tradition was at odds with Robertson's charismatic tradition.

By the end of Ronald Reagan's presidential administration in 1989, the Moral Majority and other Christian Right organizations were in decline. After Reagan's two terms in office, donations had decreased. Apparently, donors did not perceive the nation to be in the same state of moral peril as it had been when Reagan first took office. Without funds, the Moral Majority's disbanded as an organization. Falwell gave it a positive spin announcing that "Our goal has been achieved ... The religious right is solidly in place and ... religious conservatives in America are now in for the duration."[288]

Charismatic Christianity

Charismatic Christianity (Renewalism) is diverse. It is not defined by acceptance of any particular doctrines, practices, or denominational structure. Rather, renewalists share a religious belief where miracles, signs and wonders, and other supernatural events such as prophecy and healing are expected to be present in the lives of believers. While similar in many respects, renewalists differ among themselves in important ways. These differences have led to Charismatic Christianity being categorized into three main groups: Pentecostalism, the charismatic movement, and neo-charismatic movement.

In 1988, following a well-funded, but failed bid for the US presidency, Pat Robertson, a leading Charismatic preacher, TV evangelist, and host of the 700 Club, used the remainder of his campaign resources to form the *Christian Coalition*. During his campaign, Robertson had accumulated a mailing list of several million conservative Christians interested in politics and this mailing list now formed the foundation for the new organization.[289]

In 1990, the national Christian Coalition, Inc. began to produce partisan voter guides which it distributed to conservative Christian churches. After a while, complaints that the voter guides were partisan led to the denial by the IRS of the Christian Coalition, Inc.'s tax-exempt status in 1999. Later that same year, the Coalition prevailed in its five-year defense of a lawsuit brought by the Federal Election Commission.[290]

Ralph Reed, whom Robertson had met when the younger man was working as a waiter at an inaugural dinner for George H. W. Bush in January 1989, became the founding executive director of the Christian Coalition. He remained in the post until August 1997 when he left to enter political consulting, founding his new firm, Century Strategies, based near Atlanta, Georgia.

Robertson served as the Christian Coalition's president from its founding until June 1997, when President Reagan's Secretary of the Interior, Donald P. Hodel, was named president of the Christian Coalition of America (CCA), and former U S Representative Randy Tate (R-WA) was named executive director. After a disagreement with Robertson, Hodel left in January 1999 and Tate soon followed. Robertson re-assumed the presidency, and later turned it and the chairmanship over to the group's Executive Vice President and former State Chairman of South Carolina, Roberta Combs, when he officially left the Coalition in late 2001.

Thereafter, the organization remained embroiled in divisive in-house politics and was also sued by its African American employees for racial discrimination.[291] The District Court issued an injunction against the Christian Coalition and the case was later settled with money paid to the African-American plaintiffs.

From 2002, several vendors sued the Coalition for nonpayment of services rendered. It watched its revenue drop from $26.5 million in 1996 to $1.3 million in 2004.

The Tea Party

The origins of the current Tea Party movement can be traced back to when Republican Congressman Ron Paul in his GOP presidential campaign received a twenty-four hour, record breaking, "money bomb" on December 16, 2007. It was the two hundred and thirty-fourth anniversary of the Boston Tea Party. This event directly contributed to creating a libertarian revival.

The Tea Party movement rejuvenated the Republican Party in the 2010 midterm election and helped the GOP take control of the House and make gains in the Senate. According to exit polls, Tea Party supporters made up forty-one percent of the electorate on November 2, and eighty-six percent of them voted for Republican House candidates. A more recent analysis by the Pew Foundation's Forum on Religion & Public Life found that Tea Party supporters tend to have conservative opinions not just about economic matters, but also about social issues such as abortion and same-sex marriage. In addition, they are more likely than registered voters as a whole to say that their religion is the most important factor in determining their opinions on these social issues. Furthermore, they draw disproportionate support from the ranks of white evangelical Protestants.[292]

The *Tea Party* website that provides news on social issues is www.teaparty.org/. Its articles are predominantly anti-liberal, anti-progressive, anti-Obama, anti-Republican old guard, anti-big government, anti-social service, and anti-immigration.

The Tea Party does not have a uniform agenda. The decentralized character of the Tea Party, with its lack of formal structure, allows each autonomous group to set its own priorities and goals. Goals may conflict and priorities differ between groups, but Tea Party organizers see this as a strength, rather than a weakness, because decentralization helps to immunize the Tea Party against co-opting by outside entities and corruption from within.[293]

National Tea Party organizations, such as the Tea Party Patriots and FreedomWorks, have sought to focus their efforts on economic and limited government issues. They espouse a significant reduction in the size and scope of the government and advocate for a national economy operating without government oversight. They want to limit the size of the federal government, reduce government spending, lower the national debt, and oppose tax increases.

According to the *Tea Party* Patriots website,[294] they are the largest grassroots Tea Party organization in the country, having thousands of grass root organizations as members. Founded in 2009, this group espouses Personal Freedom, Economic Freedom, and A Debt Free Future. From the website:

> The right to be free is endowed by our Creator and is the premise of our Constitution, Bill of Rights, and the American way of life. The Constitution is a timeless document that guarantees our basic freedoms. We support personal freedom so all Americans can live life the way they want as long as it does not harm others, or infringe on another's rights.
>
> We stand for economic freedom which means a growing economy with reduced tax rates and reduced government spending so we all have a chance to earn more money and businesses can hire more people. We support policies that allow you to keep more of your own money to do with as you see fit and policies that will provide for and enable opportunities to find good jobs or create and grow businesses. Likewise, we support policies that will present the best chances for the United States to grow and maintain its position as the world leader for economic opportunity.
>
> We support a debt free future because it is only fair and right to pay the debt we have incurred so our children

and grandchildren are not stuck with our bills. When the government speaks about "raising the debt ceiling," they are simply saying they need to borrow more money they won't ever pay back. Continually increasing the debt of the United States puts an undue and unfair burden on future generations of Americans. It is fair and just to unburden our children from the national debt.

The core issues espoused by the Tea Party Patriots are:

- Reduction of the $17 trillion national debt;
- Freedom to choose one's own healthcare;
- Personal tax reform (they would rather reduce their taxes and have less social programs);
- Reduce big government (especially the IRS and the NSA which reduce personal freedom and spy on Americans); and
- Immigration (they support legal immigration but oppose illegal immigration because it threatens the US job market).[295]

Many other Tea Party groups like Glenn Beck's 9/12 Tea Parties, TeaParty.org, the Iowa Tea Party, and Delaware Patriot Organizations are more concerned with social issues than economic ones. These include abortion, gun control, prayer in schools, and illegal immigration. As one Tea Party Patriot put it:

> It doesn't matter who we vote for, we will become more of a collectivist welfare state. "A republic, if you can keep it," Ben Franklin said. We lost it. And we can't find our way back. It's there though; waiting for us. Freedom and self-reliance.
>
> No governmental control of the economy or redistribution of wealth. No governmental worker unions, no welfare, affirmative action, forced busing, food stamps, social services, Social Security, Medicare, Obamacare, rent control, housing "discrimination," utility subsidies,

foreign wars for Israel, corporate bailouts, utility of currency without gold backing, IRS, HUD, HHS, Dept.'s of Education and Labor, etc. Every free citizen provides for himself and his family.²⁹⁶

Yet, despite its revolutionary fervor for opposing big government and big business, its range of issues contracted significantly. By late 2014, according to the New York Times, the movement had narrowed its focus away from government spending and Obamacare to Obama's immigration policies:

> What started five years ago as a groundswell of conservatives committed to curtailing the reach of the federal government, cutting the deficit, and countering the Wall Street wing of the Republican Party has become a movement largely against immigration overhaul. The politicians, intellectual leaders, and activists who consider themselves part of the Tea Party have redirected their energy from fiscal austerity and small government to stopping any changes that would legitimize people who are here illegally, either through granting them citizenship or legal status.²⁹⁷

When surveying participants of the Tea Party movement, polls have shown that they are primarily registered Republicans, and have an unfavorable opinion of the Democratic Party. The Bloomberg National Poll of adults eighteen and over showed that 40% of Tea Party supporters are fifty-five or older, compared with 32% of all poll respondents; 79% are white (compared with 75%), 61%t are men (compared with 48,5%) and 45% percent identify as "born-again Christians" (as compared to 34% percent for the general population). Thus, the leading demographic for Tea Party members is a white male over fifty-five who is a born again Christian.²⁹⁸

Leaders of the Tea Party movement have included David Koch, Michelle Bachman, Sarah Palin, Ben Carson, Ted Cruz, Rand Paul, and Lt Colonel Allen West.²⁹⁹

Even though the Tea Party is ostensibly more secular in appearance, replacing theocratic language with American Constitution and Bill of

Rights language, it still projects the religious fundamentals of conservatism. These include support for economic individual freedom (capitalism), oppression of the poor (discipline), and support of traditional values (fundamental Christianity.) As such the Tea Party is just the latest iteration of religious conservatism that originated with capitalism and has supported it all along.

Despite the various religious manifestations of this conservative ideology, including Calvinism, Puritanism, fundamentalism, evangelicalism, etc., the underlying ideology for this movement is Dominion Theology, which is derived from the Christian Reconstructionist movement.

Christian Dominionism

Christian Reconstructionism is a fundamentalist movement founded by Rousas John Rushdoony. Based upon Mosaic Law, it has come to have an important influence on the Christian Right in the United States.[300] Writing in *The Institutes of Biblical Law* (the founding document of reconstructionism), Rushdoony holds to the Calvinist view that Old Testament social law should be applied to modern society. He advocates the reinstatement of the Mosaic Law's penal sanctions. Under such a system, the list of civil crimes which carry a death sentence would include homosexuality, adultery, incest, lying about one's virginity, bestiality, witchcraft, idolatry or apostasy, public blasphemy, false prophesying, kidnapping, rape, and bearing false witness in a capital case.[301]

A part of the Christian Reconstructionist belief system is the idea that Christians are the chosen people to rule the world. This has become known as *Dominionism*.[302] In a September 1994 plenary speech to the Christian Coalition national convention, Reverend D. James Kennedy said that "true Christian citizenship" involves an active engagement in society to "take dominion over all things as vice-regents of God."

More than anyone else, it was Sara Diamond[303] who popularized the term "dominionism." She used it to describe the growing political tendency in the Christian Right. Dominionism is a position held among Protestant Christian evangelical and fundamentalist leaders that encourages them to not only be active political participants in civic society, but also to dominate the political process as part of a mandate from God. The idea is based on the Bible's text in Genesis 1:26:

> And God said, Let us make man in our image, after our likeness: and let them have dominion over the fish of the sea, and over the fowl of the air, and over the cattle, and over all the earth, and over every creeping thing that creepeth upon the earth (King James Version).

The vast majority of Christians read this text and conclude that God has appointed them stewards and caretakers of Earth. However, some Christians read this text and believe "that Christians alone are Biblically mandated to occupy all secular institutions until Christ returns." This is the idea of "dominionism."[304]

While most Christians do not want a theocracy as proposed by dominionism, several church leaders have led them in this direction. These include Jerry Falwell, Pat Robertson, and D. James Kennedy who have all endorsed Reconstructionist views.[305] Because the idea is so genuinely radical, most leaders of the Religious Right are careful to distance themselves from it. At the same time, it clearly holds some appeal for many of them. One minister undoubtedly spoke for others when he confessed, 'Though we hide their books under the bed, we read them just the same.' "[306]

Diamond explained that "the primary importance of the Christian Reconstructionist ideology is its role as a catalyst for what is loosely called 'dominion theology.'" Through the impact of Rushdoony and other dominionist writers, the concept that Christians are Biblically mandated to rule over all secular institutions has become the central unifying ideology for the Christian Right."[307]

As such, many in the Christian Right have adopted the idea of taking dominion over the secular institutions of the United States as the "central unifying ideology" of their social movement. And the manner by which to accomplish this is to gain political power through the Republican Party.

Chip Berlet, Senior Analyst, with Political Research Associates tells us it is best to reserve the term ""dominion theology" to describe specific theological currents, while using the term "dominionism" to discuss a tendency toward aggressive political activism by Christians who claim they are mandated by God to take over society. Having said this, Berlet holds that there are two schools of thought among the Dominionists. There are the Christian nationalists, who believe that Biblically-defined immorality and sin breed chaos and anarchy. They fear that liberal secular humanists, feminists, and homosexuals have undermined America's greatness, as God's chosen land. Their vision has elements of theocracy, but they stop short of calling for supplanting the Constitution and Bill of Rights. Even though, this clearly is their intention.

There are, however, the hard-core Dominionists who want the United States to be a Christian theocracy. They see the Constitution and Bill of Rights as mere addendums to Old Testament Biblical law. Like its Calvinist core, they claim that Christian men with specific theological beliefs are ordained by God to run society. Christians and others who do not accept their theological beliefs are second-class citizens. This group has a growing number of adherents in the leadership of the Christian Right.[308]

Under the Bush administrations, the Dominionists were very close to controlling all three branches of the federal government from which they could impose their narrow interpretation of scripture on the rest of society. These people have not gone away, but continue to influence national politics through the Republican Party.

Prominent adherents of Dominionism can be found in the ideologues of Calvinist Christian Reconstructionism, Roman Catholic Integralism, Charismatic/Pentecostal Kingdom Now theology, New Apostolic Reformation, and others. Most of the contemporary movements labeled Dominionist arose in the 1970s from religious movements reasserting aspects of Christian ultra-nationalism.[309]

The Dominionists have had to stretch to support Donald Trump when he became the Republican candidate for President. Even though Trump was a racist, sexist, and ultranationalist, which matched with their ideology, he was definitely not a Christian. Nonetheless, when push came to shove, Christian values took second place to their more primal social sentiments. Jerry Faldwell Jr. spoke in support of Trump during the Republican convention even though Trump owns gambling casinos and is on his third wife. Falwell, the son of the late Moral Majority founder, on the other hand, is president of Liberty University, an evangelical school in Virginia with a dry campus and a student conduct code that deems hand-holding "the only appropriate form of personal contact."

Falwell had even provided Trump with a critical endorsement ahead of the Iowa caucuses because he believed that Islamic terrorism had shoved social issues to the back burner for this presidential cycle. [310]

> "If you look at the polls of evangelicals, in years past, in past elections, the issues that they thought were most important were the social issues," he said. "Now with all the turmoil in the world, when you look at the list of what evangelicals think is important, there's no difference between them and other conservatives and even blue-collar Democrats. The social issues come at the bottom of the list after saving our country. After securing our borders. After stopping terrorism. After . . . getting the debt under control and saving our economy. And so, evangelicals and Christians, they're voting as Americans this time. And maybe in the future when things aren't so chaotic, maybe they will vote more on the social issues again. But it's a different day. We've got to save the country first, and we'll fight about all those other things later."

Actually, Trump and the Religious Right see eye to eye on many issues including rejection of same-sex marriages, gun ownership, Wall St. regulations, abortion, pornography, transgender access to bathrooms, and of course climate denial.[311]

When you stop to think about it, for all the hoopla about the Christian religion, it does not seem to be the first concern of the Christian Right after all. Being Right is more important than being Christian. Regardless of one's Christianity, a conservative is a conservative.

Lessons Learned

In our review of the rise of protestant denominations in western history, we have seen that Calvinism played the dominant force in moving protestant Christians to support capitalism as a God-made political economy. We have seen how Calvinism gave rise to the model of a protestant Christian nation-state that provided the incentive for protestant Christians to engage in political activity. From this perspective, the capitalist is viewed as the ideal man whose ethical qualities (thrift, prudence, sobriety, etc.). Those qualities, which he uses to make money, are the same qualities necessary to enter the kingdom of heaven. The capitalists are the chosen, the *elect* of God. The capitalists are never held responsible for their actions, even if they destroy society or the environment. They are certainly not responsible to care for the poor. Charity is actually a sin against the poor because it robs them of self-discipline. This is the underlying link between Protestantism and capitalism.

While Methodists and Baptists changed this paradigm somewhat by developing a stance that even the poor can enter heaven, strong Calvinist-conservative elements remain in these denominations as well. The last century was witness to a battle between the conservatives, who tenaciously believed in the myths of Christ's virgin birth, resurrection, and status as the only Son of God, and those liberals, who dismissed the mythological Christ and by taking a scientific approach to the Bible placed Christ in a larger spiritual context. The effect of this struggle was a resurgence of the conservative-Calvinistic view that manifested in the rise of the "Christian Right" in American politics.

What conservatives fear most is *change*. To have "an aversion to change," is a serious liability if their goal is to maintain the United States empire status in the industrialized world. Change is inevitable and as the system declines, it gathers speed. Their aversion to change clarifies why the Republican conservatives are so angry, hateful, frightened, and reactive and why they are now embracing an ultra-nationalist vision, which historically has led to fascism. Demagogues like Trump appeal to their racism and to their fears. He offers the promise of the strict father figure who is required to maintain the status quo. The conservatives, even the poor among them, feel that they are losing control of their way of life and they are now fighting tooth and nail to return to the days of former white privilege. Many have greatly suffered as their jobs have been exported and there is a legitimate reason for their fear and anger.

This drives conservatives to oppose anyone who advocates change, the liberals, progressives, greens, women, and minorities.

The conservatives' desire for the US to remain a world empire makes them schizophrenic. While they support a non-interventionist foreign policy, at the same time, they believe that the US should spread democracy by the force of the gun if necessary. Conservatives live in denial about American capitalist exploitation and their oppression of other countries. Consequently, they cannot understand why US troops suffer aggression and hatred from the people in the nations they occupy. If any nation or organization retaliates against the US use of force, the conservatives advocate greater force to contain "the communists or terrorists," who are now seen as the enemies of freedom and democracy. Today, the fear of terrorists (all non-whites) coming to American shores is the greatest conservative fear of all.

While the conservatives support a government that bristles with weaponry both abroad and at home, they want to destroy government-funded domestic social programs. This stems from the Calvinist position that if people do not work, they do not deserve to eat. This heartless doctrine contradicts Christ's teachings, but it is always used as a cover to mask the conservatives' selfishness and self-centeredness.

In economic terms, conservatives refuse to admit that the concentration of wealth in a few hands means poverty for those who have had their wealth taken from them. They refuse to admit that the concentration of wealth actually destroys natural resources and causes climate catastrophe. Capitalists exploit, for their own profit, either labor or natural resources, which cannot then be used by people to meet their own basic needs on the local level. The rich and the Republican leadership know this to be true but they do not want their constituents to know this because it would challenge the legitimacy of the entire capitalist system. Therefore, their tactic has always been to confuse and deny.

It is always easier to blame the victim rather than the perpetrator, especially when the perpetrator is yourself. Blame the blacks and minorities for not being white. Blame the poor for their poverty. Blame the women for being raped. Blame other nations for being weak. Blame other religions for being false. Conservative fundamentalists use religion to justify their superiority complex while condemning their victims to hell. This "blind spot" among the conservative electorate supports a sociopathic system that can no longer be sustained.

In regard to family values, the conservatives believe in a "traditional family" mythology, a "Leave it to Beaver" middle-class family living in suburbia or a small town, with a breadwinner father and a homemaker mother, raising their two biological children. Any deviation from this family model is considered a "nontraditional family." Nontraditional families do not garner conservative support despite the fact that they make up the majority of American households.[312] Support of the traditional family is often another sign of the conservatives' refusal to change.

The conservative white male needs to keep a tight control over women, people of other races, and gays because they are threatened by them. They oppose sex outside of marriage, legally induced abortion, gay civil unions, and gay adoptions. The Republican Party's traditionally accepted role for women is in the kitchen and behind her man. They support abstinence education in regard to sex and support the protection of children from obscenity and exploitation.

Despite their blind adherence to such a narrow socio-sentiment, there is a positive aspect to conservatism. There are some things in society that we want to protect, not because they reflect the system, but because they reflect truths about our humanity. Conservatives have always held *faith* in a higher position than *reason*, just as liberals have always held reason in a position higher than faith. There is a positive aspect to having faith in a higher power. A church or religion can provide its members with a feeling of community and give them a sense of purpose. It can foster a spiritual discipline in day-to-day-life. It can honor good behavior and provide moral strength. A church can provide regular religious services and offer the guidance of a well-intentioned clergyman. It can provide people with a sense of belonging and a shelter from the storm in a hurtful world. A church also acknowledges a person's spiritual being. All these aspects create strength in people. This is why there are a lot of conservatives who are down to earth, good people.

On the other hand, people whose worldview is based on faith instead of reason often do not use their rationality. They remain filled with hate and fear because they do not understand the forces going on in the world that do not fit within their limited worldview. Without the use of rationality, a faith that is based on sentiment is easily and often led astray. Faith needs rationality to bear fruit; otherwise it gets mired in myths and dogmas. Without reason it is too easy for ignorant or deceitful people to lead the believer astray by taking random quotes from the Bible and justifying any action based on them. It does not matter if that action leads to the destruction of the planet, or other people, or other cultures. By following leaders blindly, the conservative believers risk being controlled by dogmas that actually separate them from God and creation, even while they believe they are doing God's will. There is only one way to do God's will and that is to dedicate one's life to merging with Divine Consciousness and to be willing to lay down one's life for the benefit of His/Her creation. If someone tells you that your religion is superior or inferior to another, be very cautious. If someone tells you that you are inferior or superior to another human being, do not believe them. While there may be disagreements among people's definition of God or how God is personified, religions are not doing their job if they divide human beings from one another and from the natural world. As someone once said, divisive religions only use God as an excuse to kill one another.

Having said this, there is also no excuse for denying the spiritual nature of human beings that liberals are wont to do. Because human beings have a physical, mental, and spiritual nature, it is a sign of mental imbalance when liberals will talk about God in a social context because it is too embarrassing to do so. It was not always this way, as we shall see in the next section.

The Ideology of American Liberalism

Liberalism emerged during the Protestant Reformation when Christians were fighting to gain their liberation from the Catholic Church. At that time, there was no distinction between Protestant liberals and conservatives. In the eyes of the Catholic Church, all Protestants were liberal radicals. The split that gave rise to liberalism and conservatism, as we understand these terms today, originated later, during the Enlightenment period which followed the Reformation. It was at this time that a split in thinking occurred between those who dogmatically (faithfully) followed the Bible without question and those who sought to discover the truth of the Bible from a historical or rational perspective. These so-called "free thinkers" asked penetrating questions like who really wrote the Bible? When was it written? What were the motivations of the writers? Were their other gospels that did not make it into the Bible, and if so, why not? These "liberal" thinkers wanted to discover whether all the fantastic stories of miracles in the Bible were truthful or simply myths told by priests to gain control of the populace in their day. This was, after all, how all priest classes had arisen in the ancient world. The split in religious thinking created the conservatives who continued to support the authority of the Bible without question and the liberals who wanted to understand what was true and what was myth within the Bible. This split further heightened, when intellectuals who were actually free to think without threat of death, began to completely reject the significance of the Bible in contemporary life. This led to the emergence of secular thought, and with it the birth of science and the method of scientific inquiry. We now had an intellectual split between faith and reason and between religion and science.

The new rational/scientific worldview began to emerge during the late Renaissance (the late sixteenth and early seventeenth century) with men like Sir Frances Bacon who developed a scientific method to test one's opinions. This approach further alienated the religious conservatives who found it impossible to synthesize this new rational approach within the confines of their Biblical worldview. To use a simple example, the scientific discovery that the world was round clashed with the Bible's description of "the four corners of the earth."

As scientific knowledge evolved, the contradictions between faith and reason became more complex. The scientific explanation of the evolution of species completely contradicted the Biblical explanation of how life evolved found in Genesis. Scientific explanations did not imply that liberal intellectuals did not personally believe in God, or even the divinity of Jesus, but these secular thinkers did tend to reject the supernaturalism of the Bible, meaning those things that could not be proven by reason. In time, however, many who applied the scientific method to reality began to doubt the value of the Bible as a source of verifiable information about reality. They began to question the usefulness of the Bible in bringing peace and justice to the world, considering all the evil that had been and continues to be perpetrated in its name.

Insofar as Protestantism emerged at the same time as did the rise of the capitalist class, which was itself involved in a revolution against the Catholic Church and the aristocratic nobility, both conservative and liberal Protestant churches supported the rise of capitalism and continue to do so today. We have explored in depth, how the capitalist ruling class defines intellectuals as either policy-oriented or value-oriented intellectuals. We have said that these terms do not correlate with the definition of right-wing and leftwing intellectuals which is held by the masses of people.

If we ever hope to achieve a worldwide human society, we will have to overcome the division between conservatives and liberals that has so long kept both sides from seeing reality as a whole. To do this we will have to explore how the value-oriented intellectuals on the right and the left can cooperate to create a more universal value system. This entails recognizing that human beings are simultaneously physical, mental, and spiritual beings and that there is both a scientific and spiritual link to this fundamental reality. But first we must understand the difference between the right and the left. We have explored the relationship of conservatism to capitalism. Now we will explore the relationship of liberalism to capitalism.

What is a Liberal?

The word "liberal" derives from the Latin "liber" (meaning "free" or "not a slave"). It held special meaning in the classical world when a person's freedom stood in marked contrast to being a slave. But the word did not gain popular currency until the Reformation when multitudes of people sought the freedom to think for themselves and were willing to take a stand against the coercive state administration of the Catholic Church and the national monarchies. This confrontation was inspired by the virtues of fairness, tolerance, and democracy. These became more important to secular thinkers than did religious doctrines.

Liberals believe that one should treat others as one would like to be treated in return. "Do unto others as you would have them do unto you." This altruistic sentiment is seen in many religions and cultures. It can also be viewed from the perspectives of psychology, philosophy, sociology, and economics. Psychologically, it involves a person empathizing with others. Philosophically, it involves a person perceiving their neighbor also as "I" or "self." Sociologically, 'love your neighbor as yourself' is applicable between individuals, between groups, and also between individuals and groups. In economics, it entails practices of fair trade abroad and non-exploitation domestically.

Contemporary American liberals, like their conservative brothers and sisters, have been conditioned by the coercion and indoctrination of the capitalist nation state. This means that, for the most part, their sense of morality and fair play only extends to those within the boundaries of their country. Many liberals have jobs within the social service system and are consequently more likely to defend the welfare state against attack by the Right. When politicians acting on behalf of the Trilateralist bankers, seek support from liberals for their foreign exploitation, they know they must couch their propaganda in a nurturing, philanthropic spirit if they want the liberals' support.

As we have seen, Bush promoted the War in Iraq as an effort to bring freedom and democracy to that country. Liberals also feel a desire to protect those who cannot defend themselves. They were willing to destroy Saddam Hussein when they were told that he oppressed his people. On the personal level, liberals believe in being "all that they can be." They want to live their ideals and to accomplish their dreams. Unlike the conservatives, they relish change because only by creating change can things improve. In this way, liberals are more progressive than conservatives.

Liberals are also motivated by taking care of themselves physically. They are not averse to trying new foods or anything new that will help them achieve better health.[313] Liberals also, as a rule, are better educated than conservatives.[314]

Like conservatives, liberals believe that society should be organized in accordance with certain unchangeable and inviolable human rights, especially the rights to life, liberty, property, and the pursuit of happiness.

Unlike conservatives, however, they do not believe that traditions, including religious traditions, hold any inherent value. Rather everything ought to be continuously adjusted for the greater benefit of the group(s) to which they identify. These groups can be based on many factors. They may include only liberals, or Americans, but they may also include all of humanity. For a liberal, neither established religions, hereditary status, nor any traditional assumptions should take precedence over the greater good of the group.

Liberals will therefore oppose any form of authoritarianism, whether in the form of Communism or Fascism. The more radical liberals, those whose ranks include progressives, social democrats, Greens, the New Left, the Occupy movement, etc. have added Capitalism as a system to their list of authoritarian regimes that must be opposed.

Essentially, mainstream liberals want to change what is negative about the status quo. They are not revolutionaries who seek a new system; rather they believe that they can reform capitalism to make it a more humane system. As such, while they will support US exploits abroad and will not shy away from using force of arms against another nation, domestically, they want to change gender and race relations to be more equitable and also oppose religious bigotry that fosters inequality.

Despite their differences with American conservatives, American liberals share the following values with them:

1. A desire to preserve the rules of government articulated in the Declaration of Independence and the U.S. Constitution;
2. An embrace of free-market capitalism;
3. A belief that America is an exceptional nation whose rightful role is leader of the free world;
4. A belief that America should export its brand of democracy through force of arms if necessary;
5. An embrace of localism, community and family ties, human scale, and a responsibility to the future; and
6. A belief that it is a natural right to be left alone by government.

This shows that conservatives and liberals share a lot in common. Where they differ are in the following points:

1. While conservatives are averse to rapid change and believe that tradition and prevailing social norms contain handed down wisdom, liberals embrace change. They do not believe anything in the past is sacrosanct in itself. If it has value, it is because it forwards a better life for their identified group.
2. While conservatives want to preserve traditional morality, as articulated in the Bible, by using cultural norms and the power of the state, liberals want a separation of Church and State. They do not believe the Bible should have any supremacy over any other religious beliefs.
3. Whereas conservatives desire to return to the way things once were, liberals want a new world that is better than the past.
4. Where conservatives have an affinity for Republican social issues, liberals favor the social issues of the Democrats.
5. While conservatives disdain American liberalism, multiculturalism, affirmative action, welfare, and generally the ideas of the left, the liberals disdain American conservatism, the hegemony of the white race, suppression of women's rights, and generally the ideas of the right.
6. While conservatives believe that taxes should be lower and government made smaller, liberals believe that taxes on the rich should be higher and government social programs larger.
7. While conservatives believe that the national debt and deficits put America in peril, liberals hold to Keynesian economics and the unlimited printing of money to fund social service programs.
8. While conservatives believe that whenever possible, government budgets should be balanced, the liberals are content to raise the budget ceiling as per necessity.

9. While conservatives believe in the sinfulness of man and the need to be skeptical and humble, liberals believe in the goodness of man and the need to be tolerant, fair, and nurturing.

For the most part, liberals reject the conservative strict model of the father family. They observe that human beings live in many different family structures and as such they value families based on the love and affinity that family members have for each other.

Just as conservatives are defined by particular domains of interest, such as personal liberty/self-interest, politics, economics, and social conditions, so also can liberals be defined.

Liberal Groups

The above characterization of liberal groups should not be taken as absolute. It is a gross generalization not meant to characterize individuals, but only the tendency of the liberal mindset as a whole. As with conservatives, most liberals will identify with more than one domain of interest. Even so, it is useful to distinguish certain traits that are found among the liberals or the left-wing of society as they pertain to the trends that define the movement of society.

While various liberal groups share the same moral principles, they apply them differently to the different substructures of capitalist society. For example, progressives tend to focus on political activism. Generally, they will try to pressure government to prevent or limit corporate behavior that they see as being destructive of the environment or as exploitive of people. Their role is to try to keep the wolf at bay. They will hold petition drives, marches, demonstrations, lobby, etc., to fight large corporate interests when it impinges on the welfare of the American people.

Domain Of Interest	*Type of Liberal*
Politics	Progressives
Economics	Neo-Liberals
Environment	Greens

| Social Issues | New Left, Occupy, Social Democrats |

Neo-Liberals, on the other hand, support unhindered US laissez faire capitalism. They are the equivalent of the conservative Wall Streeters. In terms of reforms, they support a balanced budget, a reduction of government spending, reducing government programs, a bipartisan fiscal committee, budget transparency, etc. They also support the unhindered exploitation of other countries' resources and labor as long as it is not too obvious.

Greens focus on environmental issues, local self-reliance, social justice, economic justice, and democracy. They share much in common with progressives, but speak out more strongly against climate change and for the rights of local people. They advocate local self-reliance through decentralized economies that are bolstered by sustainable agriculture and gardening.

The New Left, Occupy, and Social Democrats focus on a wide range of social issues including civil rights, gay rights, health care, education, abortion, gender roles, anti-war, and environmental issues. The New Left, which was the radical left among the baby boom generation that so unsettled the Trilateral Commission, differed from previous radical leftist movements (Marxist) that focused more on labor unionization and class issues. The Occupy movement, which was advanced by the millennial generation, was criticized for focusing on too many issues at once. The New Left and the Occupy movement were populist left-wing movements that brought attention to issues of social injustice, but lacked the desire or the capacity to build a political organization. Nonetheless, the critique of capitalism that movement leaders offered placed them squarely in the "value-oriented intellectual" group.

The New Left had a role in turning the American public against the War in Vietnam and the Occupy movement created a message that one percent of the population were systematically exploiting the other ninety-nine percent of the population. But such mass movements did not prove of much value, because they were not followed up by creating concrete alternatives. To simply call attention to the sins and crimes of the capitalists does not serve much purpose. Rather, they only allow the capitalists to know what the people are concerned about and thereby determine how to weaken their movement. The protests of the New Left and the Occupy movement allowed the capitalists to make minor adjustments in the system but these changes did not lead to a loss of power by the elites.

The liberals want change. They are not comfortable with social oppression or economic exploitation. But they do not want to move too fast, nor act in an extreme manner. Liberals tend to be middle class and educated and understandably they do not want to threaten their own jobs or lifestyle. When it comes to creating a revolution, liberals are not any more helpful than the conservatives. While the juggernaut of capitalist exploitation is leading to financial and environmental collapse, by not standing tall, liberals have become part of the problem. They contribute to the inertia that prevents revolutionary change from occurring and this quickens our trend toward climate crash and the inevitable social chaos that it will produce.

As an example of liberal ineptitude, while conservatives flat out deny climate change, liberals are willing to acknowledge that it is a problem, but will not organize against it in any significant numbers. They certainly will not sound the alarm even though the house is already on fire.

Climate change is already responsible for mass migrations on the planet. These numbers will continue to increase as we move into the months and years ahead.

According to research by Zillow, a large real estate corporation, by the year 2100, almost three hundred US cities will lose at least half their homes, and thirty-six US cities will be completely lost. Rising sea levels, and the resulting flooding, could inundate millions of US homes worth hundreds of billions of dollars.[315] We have already witnessed the utter destruction of large sections of New Orleans, Houston, Florida, North Carolina, Puerto Rico, and other islands in the Caribbean Sea in only a few months' time. We have witnessed the destruction of large parts of Northern California from forest fires, droughts, and mud slides.

The loss of American homes and jobs will continue to swell as we enter each new year. What will we do when hundreds, then thousands, and then millions of American homes on the east and west coast begin to be destroyed by high seas and extreme weather? Where will the refugees go? How will they be assimilated into an economy that is already being deconstructed by the capitalist elite?

The tendency of liberals to prefer reason above faith leaves them morally ambivalent concerning revolutionary social and environmental change. They may know what needs to be done, but they often lack the inspiration to do it. Many Liberals put too much stress on personal comfort instead of struggle.

When personal troubles confront them, they use their troubles as an excuse to blame God or society. They convince themselves that their troubles are the reason they never believed in God. By not exploring their spiritual nature, secular liberals go up and down on the waves of life never making any progress because they have no goal to achieve the greatness that lies outside their comfort zone.

The Tenets of Liberalism

God

Liberals were the first ones to revolt against the Catholic Church and the monarchies of Europe. They were the warrior Protestants who fought the good fight against the oppression of the intellectual ruling class ensconced in the Catholic Church. With the coming of the Enlightenment, the liberals split into two camps, those who maintained the importance of Christianity and those who preferred scientific reason. For those liberal intellectuals who continued to support Christianity, they created the Protestant religions that still exist today. Within these Protestant religions, however, another split occurred between the conservative Christians who blindly supported the rituals and myths of Christianity and the liberal Christians who sought a reason to believe in God. The liberal Christians could not reasonably accept the Bible as a matter of blind faith. This split in the Protestant religions continues to this day. Liberal churches made a large contribution to the Progressive Era and to the fight against slavery, but over time they have watched their membership decline.

For the secular intellectuals who rejected religion, they took the responsibility for right action upon themselves. They replaced an abstract idea of God, as an absolute authority, with moral values based upon a universal humanism. Values of tolerance, acceptance, social equality, economic justice, etc., still determine liberal thought and practice today.

Moral Order

Liberals, whether religious or secular, share a concept of moral order even though it is different from that of conservative Christians. Liberal Christians do not look at the Bible and see rules that one must abide by or go to hell. Rather they look at the Bible and see guidelines for how to think about morality and justice. Right and wrong are not necessarily determined by the Bible. Rather, God's morality is determined by truths that may or may not be addressed in the Bible. Liberals believe that as the conditions of life change, God inspires people to change with it and to move beyond the limits of the past. Liberal Christians may also find guidance from other religions and spiritual paths.

For the most part, liberal morality and conservative morality come to the same conclusions about right and wrong, but their routes to those conclusions are different and the moral issues that they prioritize are different. They also differ in their approach to get people to act in a moral manner. Conservatives see the rules in the Bible and the laws of traditional society as the basis for their morality. As such they expect the church and the state to enforce these rules. Liberals, on the other hand, use their reason to determine if something should be a rule or not. For example, a conservative may want to punish a drug pusher because he disobeyed the law, while a liberal may want to punish a drug pusher because research has shown that drugs destroy people's lives and legal steps must be taken to prevent people from having access to dangerous drugs.

Just because the conservatives depend upon the institutional authorities of church and state to define their morality, it does not mean that liberals are any less moral. For example, a recent study from the University of Illinois-Chicago[316] that analyzed twenty-one separate studies of left and right morality, found that overall, liberals showed just as much moral conviction as conservatives, although, they prioritize different issues. Of forty-one separate issues studied, conservatives held the highest moral conviction regarding immigration, abortion, states' rights, gun control, physician-assisted suicide, the deficit, and the federal budget. Liberals, on the other hand, expressed greater moral conviction concerning climate change, the environment, gender and racial equality, income inequality, healthcare reform, and education.[317]

While liberals and conservatives become morally self-righteous about different social issues, they are equally likely to zealously engage in overt political action based upon their moral convictions. The moral convictions of liberals derive from the secular intellectuals of the Enlightenment like Kant or Mill or from the application of their own reason. Jewish intellectuals have also had a strong impact on liberal thought, including Paul Krugman, Joseph Pulitzer, Milton Friedman, Henri Bergson, Benoit Mandelbrot, Albert Einstein, Saul Kripke, Noam Chomsky, and others.

The New Left found its most ardent leaders in Jerry Rubin and Abbie Hoffman and in political theorists like Herbert Marcuse. The Greens found its leaders in Bill Mollison and David Holmgren. The Occupy Movement was strongly influenced by the ideas of Gene Sharp. Again, the problem is that the morality felt by both groups only relates to their chosen group. Neither conservative nor liberal morality is a universal morality, one that seeks the welfare of the world as a whole.

The Nurturant Parent Model

Research by George Lakoff and Jonathan Haidt also demonstrates that the rules that motivate conservatives are based upon the identification of a man within the strict father family arrangement. Liberals, however, are more inspired by a "nurturant parent" morality and this applies to different family arrangements.[318] Liberals feel strongly about issues involving harmfulness and fairness, whereas conservatives are more concerned about whether an issue is based on authority, the values of one's group, or even whether it conjures emotions of disgust.

The nurturant parenting style treats women and men as equal partners who cooperate in raising their children. In this model, children are given more freedom to explore their surroundings under the protection of their parents. Liberals tend to believe that true discipline is not solely a matter of strict obedience to rules and laws but of respect and compassion for others, which can only be taught by example. Basic tenets of this model include:

- Trust in their children's fairness and good judgment;
- Respect of their children's autonomy, thoughts and feelings;
- Support for their children's interests and goals;
- Enjoyment of their children's company;
- Protection of their children from doing injury to self or others, not by establishing rules but by communicating values and discussing their children's behavior with them; and
- Being models of self-control, sensitivity and the values they believe their children will need.[319]

Both conservatives and liberals bring their parenting model to their expectations of government. While conservatives tend to be belligerent and punitive, supporting a strong military and weak social services, liberals want the government to ensure that the citizens are protected and assisted to achieve their potential.

Liberals are also more open to participating in and supporting family structures other than the nuclear father family. These other types include adoption, alloparenting (children raised by other family members), extended family, co-parenting (separate parents), foster care, communes, LGBT (Lesbian, Gay, Bisexual, and Transgender) families, and others.

While the nurturant model is more inclusive, it also has its problems. Whereas the conservative model risks becoming too strict and dogmatic, the liberal model risks raising children without required discipline or respect for boundaries. While children need freedom and support in their exploration of their environment, they also need structure. Liberals are prone to let their children take advantage of them and also to disrespect authority. What is needed is an integration of necessary boundaries with plenty of love. Toward this goal, liberals and conservatives can learn from each other.

Economics

Aside from the neo-liberals who whole-heartedly support State Monopoly Capitalism, progressive liberals believe that the economy should play a role in supporting the general welfare of society. Rather than strict competition, they support a degree of socialism for the good of the people as a whole. This ideal is the basis of the so-called Mixed Economies.

While conservatives believe that competition for scarce resources imposes discipline and thereby serves morality, liberals believe that competition for scarce resources leads to a no-win situation that results in war and devastation. They agree with conservatives that competition is good because it can produce the optimal use of resources and disciplined people, but they disagree with conservatives that there should be competition for the scarce resources themselves. Rather resources should be shared and competition should be directed to optimizing their utility.

Progressive liberals tend to support a strong regulation of the capitalist class, because capitalists ignore fair competition and exploit others through a range of methods including slavery, swindles, scams, stock and currency manipulation, and outright violence against their competitors or those whom the capitalists want to dominate for their labor or resources. They do not believe that the rich have a right to exploit the poor, nor that the poor should serve the wealthy. The gap between the rich and poor is not natural and good, rather it is exploitive and bad. Liberals believe that the rich are extravagant in their expropriation of labor and resources but meager in what they give back. In this respect, the wealthy are not the good people, the religiously sanctioned elite that the conservatives claim, rather they are leading society to a future dystopia characterized by social chaos and environmental collapse.

Progressive liberals tend to be well read and believe that "free markets" is a euphemism for the right of the rich and powerful to exploit the poor without fear of retribution. They understand what the multinational corporations are doing in third world countries. Consequently, these liberals favor regulations on corporations and higher taxes on the rich. Unlike the conservatives who accept the wealth divide as natural and moral, liberals are appalled by the latest wealth divide in which eighty billionaires in the world have a total net worth of $1.9 trillion, equal to the net worth of 3.5 billion people.[320]

Politics

While conservatives believe social programs are immoral, liberals believe that they are the only way to create a harmonious and just society. They do not believe that social programs remove the incentive to be disciplined, rather they reflect a more humane society and prevent social unrest. Because many liberals work within the human service system, they have a stake in maintaining their jobs, but they also better understand the problems that the poor face and the social and economic oppression to which they are subjected, regardless of their personal sense of discipline. The money allotted by the government for social programs is insufficient to teach the poor necessary job skills or provide them with the resources to pull themselves out of poverty. Rather it strings them along, regulating them so they do not become a revolutionary threat.

While the conservatives believe that the only legitimate role of government is to protect the lives and the private property of Americans disciplined enough to have private property, the liberals believe that, at this stage of human evolution, everyone should have an opportunity to meet their basic needs through their own effort (equal rights). Those who are weak or infirm and cannot fight for themselves require assistance from society.

Thus, it is the government's role to ensure these rights and freedoms for all. Consequently, liberals support social equality and egalitarianism, often in opposition to class hierarchy and social injustice.

Education

While conservatives believe that education should serve the goal of preserving and teaching their morality, liberals believe that education should empower individuals and prepare them to deal with complexity, diversity, and social change.[321] It should provide students with a broad knowledge of the world, including science, the humanities, and social studies, along with an in-depth study in a specific area of interest. It should inspire a sense of social responsibility and strong intellectual and practical skills. It should foster competency in communication, analytical, and problem-solving skills, and teach students to apply their knowledge and skills in real-world settings. Teachers need not necessarily be strict so long as they encourage students to develop the necessary skills and knowledge. Education need not promote discipline. Corporal punishment is forbidden. Students should neither be coddled nor shamed. Uniform testing does not necessarily determine right and wrong answers because they are based on the culture of the test designers.

While conservatives support private schools and charter schools, liberals support the public school system. The government should put its money into public schools not vouchers for charter schools. While both conservatives and liberals believe that those individuals with exceptional discipline and talent deserve scholarships to better schools, they differ in their reasons to do so. Conservatives believe this will help maintain the social elite as a natural elite. Liberals believe scholarships to the deserving reflect equal opportunity for all.

Health Care

While it is the primary responsibility of parents to take care of their children, liberals believe that society also has a role to play in ensuring public health. If parents cannot provide for their children, society should take on the responsibility. While prenatal care, postnatal care, health care for children, and care for the aged and infirm are matters of individual responsibility for conservatives, for the liberals, they can be matters of social responsibility if families are unable to care for children or the elderly. Liberals tend to support social security, Medicare, or disability benefits for society's poor, aged, or infirm. As individuals, liberals also tend to be more suspicious of the drug culture of modern medicine and put greater emphasis on alternative medicines and proper nutrition to keep themselves healthy.

The Rise of American Liberalism

At the time of the formation of liberal ideology, the Catholic Church and the landed aristocracy were the conservatives. In this section we will explore the path that liberalism took from the time of the Protestant Reformation until the present day in the United States.

Liberal Christians

It was during the time of the Enlightenment that liberal theology as a movement came into being. The German theologian Friedrich Schleiermacher, (1768 –1834)[322] attempted to reconcile the secular Enlightenment thinkers with Protestant Christianity. He is often called the "Father of Modern Liberal Theology." Schleiermacher held that the religious impetus is due to the feeling of absolute dependence that we feel inside of us. In this way, the development of self-consciousness leads to God-consciousness. The Christian is brought into a deeper reflection of human nature through the man Jesus, in whom God-consciousness has been perfected. The church is a fellowship of believers in God-consciousness and Jesus Christ.[323]

From the mid-nineteenth century through the 1920s, liberal intellectuals began to grapple with the idea of historical time and the notion of progress. This development was stimulated by the Industrial Revolution and the publication of Charles Darwin's *Origin of Species* (1859). The worldview that came out of this exploration became known as "Modernism." Modernist thinking required liberal theologians to make another adjustment in order to bring their religious beliefs into accord with the advancement of knowledge and the issues of modern culture. This caused liberals to weigh the impact of Christian doctrine on personal religious experience as well as on religious institutions and customs. It also promoted a philosophical inquiry into religious knowledge and values. Among important figures during this period were Thomas Huxley and Herbert Spencer in England; William James, John Dewey, Shailer Mathews, and Harry Emerson Fosdick in the United States; and Ernst Troeltsch in Germany.[324]

Liberal theologians differ from conservative theologians in that they do not claim to discover eternal truths, but rather create religious models and concepts that reflect the class, gender, social, and political contexts from which they emerge. They do not regard the Bible as inerrant, but believe Scripture to be "inspired."

As liberal Christians grappled with new social developments, conservative Christians, represented by the Catholic Church and Calvinist-oriented Protestants, reacted and began to push back. Several Catholic churches, for example, threatened to withhold the sacraments from parishioners who cast votes for liberal political candidates. Other priests preached that to vote for liberal candidates was a mortal sin.[325]

Liberal Christians remained undeterred, however, and sought to elevate the teachings of Jesus Christ as the universal standard instead of the rituals and supernatural dogma of the conservatives.[326] The debate over whether to believe or not believe in miracles, as a precondition for accepting the divinity of Jesus Christ, created a crisis within the nineteenth century church.

A belief in the authenticity of miracles was one of five tests established in 1910 by the Presbyterian Church to distinguish true believers from the "educated, 'liberal' Christians."[327] While not all liberals rejected the possibility of miracles, they rejected the dogmatic and hostile response of the conservative Christians. Many liberal Christians began to reject historical interpretations of the Bible, preferring instead to read Jesus' miracles as metaphorical narratives for understanding the power of God.

As the religious struggle continued into the late nineteenth century, liberal Christians began to align themselves with the secular "Progressive Movement" in Western culture and politics. In doing so, they came to equate the Left-wing as the embodiment of God's revelation in history.[328]

Liberal Christianity was most influential within mainstream Protestant churches in the early 20th Century. Some church leaders went so far as to identify Christianity with Marxist doctrine. The American Baptist, Walther Rauschenbusch, identified four institutionalized spiritual evils in American culture. They were individualism, capitalism, nationalism, and militarism. These "evils," in actuality constituted the very foundation of American capitalism. According to Christian Socialist doctrine, these evils were to be replaced by collectivism, socialism, internationalism, and pacifism.

Liberal theology, by putting its emphasis on science and socialist values in a relative world, failed to establish absolute ethical norms outside the Bible for the general population to follow. This led to a moral ambiguity that has plagued liberalism to this day and has been the reason that the liberal churches have watched their membership decline.

The loss of membership led liberal churches in the early 1970s to hire Dean M. Kelley, a liberal sociologist, to study the problem. Writing in *Why Conservative Churches are Growing*,[329] Kelley concluded that conservative churches concentrated more on spiritual needs, while liberal churches concentrated more on political causes. As such, Kelley predicted that the liberal churches would see an on-going decline.[330]

The decline has indeed been significant. Liberal Christianity in America has experienced a decline from forty percent of the American Christian population to twelve percent between 1930 and 2010. Conversely, the evangelical denominations have grown greatly in size, and even the Catholic Church has seen modest gains.[331]

Kelley's argument requires some tweaking. It is not that the conservatives concentrate on spiritual issues to the neglect of political issues. The conservative churches at present control the Republican Party, while the liberal churches remain on the political sidelines. Thus, the truth is that the conservative churches were able to bridge the gap between "religion" and politics while the liberal churches could not. They were unable to bridge this gap because they were unable to distinguish between spirituality and religion.

The problem has yet to be resolved. Fundamentalists, for all their irrationality and divisiveness, understand that the traditional vision of God addresses people's need for hope and salvation. Even at a primitive level, it provides an answer to the human thirst for limitlessness. The emotionally barren rationality of the liberal Christians cannot compete with this deep sentiment within the common people. Thus, the Democrats, who embody the left in US politics, have no language to articulate the role of God in human society, nor is it able to address the spiritual needs of the people. As such, Americans are forced to choose between an irrational divisive religion on the right or a rational argument that lacks spiritual weight and is unable to address the deeper feelings of people on the left. This problem will be addressed in Book II on the tenets of a universal ideology.

Secular Liberals

Secular liberalism has its roots in the humanist movement, which challenged the Catholic Church during the time of the Renaissance in Europe. It affected the seventeenth and eighteenth century British and French Enlightenment thinkers and later the Americans who fought against being colonized by the British.

John Locke, in 1689, established two fundamental liberal principles—economic liberty and intellectual liberty. Locke believed that life, liberty, and property constituted "natural rights." The belief in these rights played a key role in the Glorious Revolution in Britain and provided the justification for the American and French revolutions. It also gave root to the modern liberal concept of "human rights."

In France, Montesquieu spoke out against the monarchy's use of force and the religious tradition of the Church. Instead, he advocated a set of laws that would govern social behavior, including the king's behavior. At this time the French physiocrats, who believed that wealth came from the soil and not from pirated gold, introduced the idea of "laissez faire" to stop the king's interference in trade. Later, Voltaire, a French philosopher, would call for a constitutional monarchy, in which the king would be held accountable by a body of his peers. Rousseau, another philosopher, introduced the idea of a "social contract" in which the people would give up some of their rights in order to have a government that protected social order. At the same time, he asserted that people have the capacity for self-determination and can exist without the church and aristocracy.

David Hume added to the evolution of liberal thought by theorizing that human nature was such that it would eventually revolt against any government attempts to restrict or regulate it in an oppressive manner.

Adam Smith believed that individuals could create a moral and economic life without direction from the state. In applying this principle to economics, he argued in his *Wealth of Nations* that the market could naturally regulate itself and did not require the heavy restrictions of government that were normal at the time.

American intellectuals like Thomas Paine, Thomas Jefferson, and Sam Adams, who were engaged in the American revolutionary war with Britain, built on Locke's principles and called for revolution in the name of "life, liberty, and the pursuit of happiness." They too fought for a democratic government and individual liberty.

The French Revolution, inspired by the American Revolution, also attempted to enshrine liberal ideals, although their transition was much more difficult. The fight of the revolutionary forces against the king, led to the government of Robespierre, who, supported by the ruthless Jacobins, created a central government that eliminated all democratic principles, and instituted the "Reign of Terror." Even so, the French would later surpass the Americans in establishing liberal values such as universal male suffrage, national citizenship, and the "Declaration of the Rights of Man and Citizen." This Declaration was drafted by the Marquis de Lafayette and introduced to the French people the day after the people stormed the Bastille on July 14, 1789. The Declaration, influenced by Thomas Jefferson as well as his own experience fighting for American liberties during the American Revolution, led Lafayette to believe that the natural rights of man are universal, valid at all times and in every place, and pertain to human nature itself. His Declaration became the basis for a nation of free individuals protected equally by law.[332]

John Stuart Mill would ground liberal values by taking a pragmatic approach to creating political institutions. In his *On Liberty*, he maintained that the moral worth of an economic system was determined by its contribution to the overall happiness of the people acting within that system. Gradually the idea of liberal democracy and its system of political parties came to influence the western world.

Neo-Liberals

Classical liberalism in the United States (also called *neo-liberalism*) is the belief that a free market economy is the most productive. If the government just gives the capitalists a free rein they will create a better world for all. Classical liberalism was the original ideology developed by the early merchants to free themselves from the authority of Church and King. Classical liberals in the United States believe that if the economy is left to the natural forces of supply and demand, free of government intervention, the result is the most abundant satisfaction of human wants.

Modern classical liberals, so-called neo-liberals, share many of the same values as conservatives, especially libertarians. They also oppose government intervention to promote social justice, collective bargaining, income redistribution, social service programs, or any regulation of the economy for the common good. Neo-liberals are composed of the capitalists themselves or "policy-oriented intellectuals" who support and promote the existing capitalist state or who attempt to roll back any government programs that seek the general welfare of the people.

Politically, the neo-liberals mainly focus on fiscal reform. They want to limit government spending and make sure that the government does not spend money "beyond its means." They want to cut social programs that "don't work." Basically, their program is for the government to reduce the deficit, balance the budget, eliminate waste, fraud, and abuse, and be more transparent. Essentially, neo-liberals want the government to support unfettered capitalism and to discipline the citizenry to be compliant to its workings.[333] Unfortunately, their fiscal conservatism does not pertain to the corruption and waste in the military-industrial complex.

The Progressives

Toward the end of the nineteenth century, especially in America, some liberal intellectuals began to support a progressive movement to stop the exploitive practices of the monopoly capitalists and the stock manipulators who had created a series of financial panics that had thrown the country into a depression. At this time, the liberals split between those who accepted government intervention in the economy and those who became anti-government and adopted Anarchism. Anarchism is the political philosophy, which rejects compulsory government and believes that government is both harmful and unnecessary.

Anarchists contend that the State lacks moral legitimacy, that there is no obligation or duty to obey the State and, conversely, that the State has no right to command individuals. Anarchists do not advocate the overthrow of the state, but rather a gradual change to free individuals from the oppressive laws and social constraints of the modern state. Anarchists have a lot in common with Libertarians who advocate maximizing individual rights and minimizing the role of the state.

As capitalism continued to drain human and natural resources from the economy and created a severe income gap between the impoverished masses and the elite capitalist class, a theory of modern liberalism developed, called *Progressivism*, which advocated government intervention in the economy to protect individual liberties while at the same time avoiding socialism.

The Progressive Movement began as an attempt to modify the injustices of laissez faire capitalism in America at the time when monopoly capitalists, like Vanderbilt, Rockefeller, Carnegie, and Morgan had seized control of the economic infrastructure of America. We have discussed in Volume IV how the deal was struck between J. P. Morgan and Teddy Roosevelt to put in place the new system of State Monopoly Capitalism in which the federal government would protect the right of the capitalists to continue to exploit labor and resources, if they would provide, in some measure, social services for the poor who were rising up in rebellion against capitalist exploitation.

These efforts to mollify the assault of capitalism on society in the late nineteenth century were not completely new. Even before the Civil War, an effort had begun among liberal activists to reform working conditions and to humanize the treatment of the mentally ill and those in prisons.

Some radical liberals even attempted to drop out of capitalist society and establish utopian communities in which participants lived according to liberal values. These included Brook Farm, Fruitlands, New Harmony, Oneida, and the Shaker communities.[334] Another focal point of the early reform movement was abolitionism, the drive to end the trafficking and enslavement of fellow human beings.

After the Civil War, leading up to WWI, the progressives expanded their focus to include women's rights and the temperance movement. A farm movement also emerged to restore rural life at a time when the cities of America were growing. The progressives challenged the capitalist ideology of Social Darwinism and held that it was possible to improve the lot of everyone in society by working together.

The progressives also rejected religion as a driving force for change. They encouraged the people to improve their own lot in life. Specific goals included: (1) the removal of corrupt government officials and political machines, (2) the increase of voters through universal suffrage, and (3) the applying of pressure on government to play a larger role in solving social problems and establishing fairness in economic matters.

The progressives were able to influence the public through investigative journalism. These brave journalists, whom the rich called "muckrakers," detailed the "horrors of poverty, urban slums, dangerous factory conditions, and child labor, among a host of other ills."[335]

The progressives were able to push through legislation that benefitted the American people as a whole. Among such legislation were the Interstate Commerce Act (1887) and the Sherman Antitrust Act (1890). The progressives were also involved in pushing through new amendments to the Constitution, including the abolition of slavery, prohibition, and the women's right to vote. Other issues on the progressive agenda included conservation, fair railroad rates, and food and drug laws.

At the same time, many progressives began to work in social service agencies that were being established to improve the prospects of the poor. As the liberals fought to protect children from exploitation and harsh working conditions, the capitalists thwarted their efforts through the court system.

In establishing their social programs, the progressives worked almost exclusively with poor whites. They failed to address the needs of the African American and Native American minorities. This was a major shortcoming of the progressive movement at the time.

Liberalism and Progressivism are based upon the premise that human beings have the right to education, human development, and security. To guarantee these rights, liberals have supported a bigger social and economic role for the state. But by supporting this increased power of the state, they demand that it be counterbalanced by guarantees of civil liberties and a stronger system of checks and balances anchored in a free press and pluralistic society.[336]

Teddy Roosevelt

The first great progressive reformer was President Teddy Roosevelt. His "Square Deal" included regulation of railroad rates and pure foods and drugs. He generally supported labor unions and voiced his belief that the courts were biased against the unions. Roosevelt even negotiated a settlement to the great Coal Strike of 1902.

Teddy had a love of nature and he promoted the conservation movement. At a time of seemingly endless resources and tremendous waste, he emphasized the efficient use of natural resources. He dramatically expanded the system of national parks and national forests. [337]

Roosevelt was opposed by the conservatives and classical liberals who believed that social problems would solve themselves if left to the *free market* and the choices of individual corporations. The progressives pointed to the relentless crises faced by the public when big business had no legal oversight. They argued, and still argue today, that by taking a hands-off approach to monopoly capitalism, it only creates more economic inequality, more monopolistic corporations, and thus more oppression of the working people of America. Teddy was not a revolutionary, nor are the progressives. They do not want to end capitalism; they merely want to reform it. Basically, the only thing they succeed in doing is to slow down the rate of exploitation and decline.

Franklin D. Roosevelt

Liberals like John Dewey (education), John Maynard Keynes (economics), Franklin D. Roosevelt (politics), and John Kenneth Galbraith (history) carried the progressives' banner into the twentieth century. Other liberals, who included Friedrich Hayek, Milton Friedman, and Ludwig von Mises, however, argued that the Great Depression of the 1930s and the rise of totalitarian dictatorships were not a result of "laissez-faire" capitalism at all, but a result of too much government intervention and regulation of the market.[338] This contradiction in thinking created the split between the progressive liberals and neo-liberals that continues to this day.

President Franklin D. Roosevelt (1882 – 1945), a progressive, came to office in 1933 amid the economic devastation of the "Great Depression," which was once again caused by capitalist manipulation of the stock market. Franklin offered the nation a "New Deal" that was intended to alleviate economic want and unemployment, provide greater opportunities, and restore prosperity. His presidency from 1933 to 1945, the longest in US history, was marked by a further increase in the role of the Federal government in addressing the nation's economic and social problems. As a progressive, Franklin created work relief programs to provide jobs and also large-scale projects like the Tennessee Valley

Authority. He created the Social Security system to care for the sick and elderly. Despite the New Deal programs, the depression dragged on because the capitalists were unwilling to put their money into the American economy because there were too few consumers for their goods and thus too little potential profit. Such is the situation today as we have struggled for over a decade during the "Great Recession," which was kicked off once more by the big banks' manipulation of stocks and mortgages.

During the Great Depression, the blacks suffered more than whites because of racial discrimination. While Franklin's administration did little for them, he at least did more than previous administrations. His Works Progress Administration, Civilian Conservation Corps, and the Fair Employment Practices Commission opened millions of new jobs to minorities and forbade discrimination in companies with government contracts. The 1.5 million black veterans in 1945 were fully entitled to veteran benefits from the GI Bill on the same basis as everyone else.[339]

The New Deal programs consisted of three goals, "Relief, Recovery, and Reform." Relief was the immediate effort to help the one-third of the population that was hardest hit by the depression. *Recovery* was the goal of restoring the economy to pre-depression levels. It involved "pump priming" (deficit spending), and efforts to re-inflate farm prices that were too low, while increasing foreign trade. *Reform* was based on the assumption that the depression was caused by the inherent instability of the market and that government intervention was necessary to rationalize and stabilize the economy and to balance the interests of farmers, business, and labor. Reform measures included the National Industrial Recovery Act, the regulation of Wall Street by the Securities Exchange Act, the Agricultural Adjustment Act for farm programs, the Federal Deposit Insurance Corporation to insure bank deposits, and the National Labor Relations Act to deal with labor-management relations. Roosevelt, however, refused to legalize any anti-trust programs, leaving the monopolies intact. Except for the Tennessee Valley Authority (TVA), that involved government ownership of the means of production, Roosevelt staunchly opposed socialism and communism.

The Cold War

The essential tenets of Cold War liberalism were Roosevelt's Four Freedoms proposed in 1941. These were freedom of speech and religion and freedom from fear and want. Of these, freedom of speech and freedom of religion were classic liberal freedoms, as was "freedom from fear" (freedom from tyrannical government). "Freedom from want," however, was another matter. Roosevelt proposed a notion of freedom that went beyond government non-interference in private lives. "Freedom from want" justified positive government action to meet economic needs.

In the 1950s and 1960s, both major US political parties included liberal and conservative factions, unlike today where liberals compose the Democratic Party and Conservatives compose the Republican Party. At that time, the Democratic Party had two wings: the Northern and Western liberals, on one hand, and the conservative Southern whites on the other.

The Republican Party was divided into the liberal Wall Street crowd (monopoly capitalists) and the conservative Main Street faction (small business people). The cold war liberals opposed conservatives, but they also opposed socialists and communists, even though they called for government spending for education, science, and infrastructure, notably the expansion of NASA, and the construction of the Interstate Highway System. Both of these systems were promoted for their military value. In large part, the Cold War liberals continued their support for the progressive ideas of Teddy and Franklin Roosevelt. Their issues were:

- A domestic economy built on a balance of power between labor unions and management of large corporations;
- A foreign policy focused on containing the Soviet Union and its allies;
- The continuation of New Deal social welfare programs; and

- An embrace of Keynesian economics which authorized the integration of the federal government and the monopoly bankers through the institution and policies of the Federal Reserve Bank.

Cold War liberalism remained the dominant paradigm in US politics throughout the 1950s. It opposed the communist witch hunts of Senator Joe McCarthy that were supported by John Wayne and other Hollywood reactionaries. Harry S. Truman, who authorized the nuclear attack on Japan, and Hubert Humphrey were both liberals.

Beginning with *To Secure These Rights*, an official report issued by the Truman White House in 1947, liberals increasingly embraced the civil rights movement. In 1948, Truman desegregated the armed forces and the Democrats inserted a strong civil rights plank in the party platform, even though delegates from the Deep South walked out, and nominated a third-party ticket headed by Strom Thurmond.

Cold War liberalism peaked with the landslide victory of Lyndon B. Johnson over Barry Goldwater in the 1964 presidential election. Lyndon Johnson had been a New Deal Democrat in the 1930s and by the 1950s had decided that the Democratic Party had to break from its segregationist past and endorse racial liberalism as well as economic liberalism.

By the 1960s, however, relations between white liberal politicians and the civil rights movement had become increasingly strained. Black leaders accused the liberal politicians of temporizing and procrastinating on civil rights issues. This was an accurate charge because many white liberals believed the grassroots movement for black civil rights only angered many Southern whites and made it more difficult to pass civil rights laws through Congress. In response to this stalemate, civil rights leader Martin Luther King, Jr. agreed to tone down the militancy of the movement to allow the movement's white liberal allies in the government to gain some traction. President Kennedy finally endorsed the movement's March on Washington, and proposed the Civil Rights Act, but he could not get it passed. Lyndon Johnson, who took office in November 1963, after Kennedy's assassination, used Kennedy's murder to mobilize northern support of the black leadership community and to pass major civil rights legislation, the Civil Rights Act of 1964 and the Voting Rights Act of 1965. The result was an end to legalized segregation and a nominal end to restrictions on black voting.

In the impoverished and oppressive inner cities of America, however, this political victory hardly made any difference in the miserable lives of black people. During the 1960s, their pent-up anger exploded into major riots all across the country. Fires burned in Rochester, Harlem, Philadelphia, Watts, Cleveland, Omaha, Newark, Plainfield, Detroit, Minnesota, Chicago, Washington DC, and Baltimore. The causes of these riots were the same problems that blacks face today—police brutality and police shooting of teenagers, poverty, racial discrimination, lack of economic opportunity, inadequate housing, unemployment, exclusion of blacks in politics, the decay of inner-city housing, etc.

The riots served no strategic purpose. There were no local organizers to channel the people's anger. The only result of the riots was to alienate the white working class that had comprised the labor union element in the civil rights coalition.

After the riots, the civil rights movement fractured. Malcolm X, a black militant, tried to organize a black nationalist organization to "heighten the political consciousness" of African Americans.[340] In 1966, a Black Power movement emerged and accused white liberals of trying to control the civil rights agenda. Proponents of Black Power wanted blacks to follow an "ethnic model" for obtaining power. This was the model used by Daley to build his Democratic political machines in Chicago. This strategy, however, put the fledgling Black Power movement on a collision course with the existing urban machine politicians. The radical wing of the Black Power movement was composed of racial separatists who wanted to forsake integration altogether. These radicals, who always got more media attention than their actual numbers might have warranted, contributed to a conservative "white backlash" against liberals and civil rights activists. This backlash began with Barry Goldwater and eventually led to the election of Ronald Reagan. White Democrats in the South moved *en masse* to the Republican Party to vote for Reagan while the religious right, which had aligned with white racists through the KKK and other movements,[341] began their campaign to take over the Republican Party and bend it to its religious agenda.

After Reagan, while the country was still firmly in the grips of a conservative mentality, Democratic president Bill Clinton worked with the conservatives, against strong liberal opposition, to reduce some of the main welfare programs and to implement NAFTA, linking the economies of the US, Canada, and Mexico. This began the drain of American working class jobs to other countries. Union jobs were now replaced by Mexican women, who worked for $3 per hour.

Clinton also tried to push health care reform and environmental protection as liberal agenda items. After Clinton, the next liberal president was Barak Obama. Obama maintained a strong progressive identity in his language and in his protection of social welfare programs, but he promoted the Trilateralist Trans Pacific Partnership, which is also intended to eliminate American jobs and give the multinational corporations supreme authority over national governments and national laws. Obama, also, in a very secretive manner, through the use of executive orders, set up the framework for a police state whenever the government decides to declare a State of Emergency.

The New Left

As we have seen above, the capitalist elite's reaction to the activities of the New Left in the 1960s and early 1970s inspired the formation of the Trilateral Commission and the publication of *The Crisis of Democracy*.

The New Left was a term used mainly in the United States and Europe in reference to the students, activists, educators, agitators, and others who sought to implement a broad range of social reforms in regard to imperialist wars, the rights of women and minorities, gay rights, and the use of drugs. The New Left opposed State Monopoly Capitalism as characterized by the intimate relationship between multinational corporations and the federal government. They referred to this unholy alliance as "The Establishment."

In contrast to earlier leftist or Marxist movements, the New Left did not focus on labor unions or the issues of social class and class struggle that had preoccupied previous socialist thinkers and activists. Rather, in the US, the "New Left" was associated with the Hippie movement, the anti-war student movement, the women's movement, and the Black liberation movement. While initially formed in opposition to the "Old Left" within the Democratic Party, which was composed of pro-war neo-liberals, and moderate Democrats, the groups composing the New Left gradually became more involved in national politics themselves, supporting the presidential candidacies of Eugene McCarthy and George McGovern.

In the 1968 presidential election, McCarthy challenged the incumbent Lyndon B. Johnson for the Democratic presidential nomination, running on an anti-Vietnam War platform. McCarthy's strong success in the New Hampshire primary and his strong polling in the upcoming Wisconsin primary contributed to Johnson's decision to withdraw from the race and lured Robert F. Kennedy and Hubert Humphrey into the contest.

George Stanley McGovern, who was also staunchly anti-Vietnam War, declined the offer from supporters to run for president. However, he did run in the 1972 presidential election.

The New Left began as a student movement that rejected the values of the capitalist culture. It sought liberation through "sex, drugs, and rock and roll." Like the early socialists, they also created a "back to the land" movement and lived collectively on farms referred to as "Hippie Communes." During their college years, the federal government had initiated a draft to fill the ranks of the army fighting in Vietnam. This created an anti-war, anti-draft movement that swept the country. As the administration and the conservatives reacted to these "dirty, ungrateful middle-class brats," the students' rebelliousness only increased. They called out the hypocrisy of the military, the capitalists, and the bureaucratic elites who responded with an escalation of political repression. The image of the Chicago police beating and gassing student protestors in Lincoln Park during the Democratic Convention in 1968 was indelibly marked on the minds of Americans.

The New Left movement died on the campus of Kent State University in May 1970, when the Ohio National Guard fired live ammunition into a student protest against President Nixon's invasion of Cambodia. The guardsmen killed four students and wounding nine others, one of whom suffered permanent paralysis.[342] It was comparable to the Boston Massacre that ignited the American Revolution but, in this case, no revolution followed.

The shootings, however, did cause a strike of four million students on campuses across the country, which in turn caused hundreds of universities, colleges, and high schools to shut down and not reopen for the rest of the semester. While these events helped turn the American people against the Vietnam War, it also signaled the end of the New Left movement. The students went home to the suburbs and any capacity for further organizing completely dissipated.

During the late 1960s, however, student protests and events helped to foster an environment of activism against many social injustices. This was the time that capitalists referred to as a period of "democratic distemper." This period also marked a turning point for the Civil Rights movement in the United States by producing revolutionary movements like the Black Panther Party and the Organization of Afro-American Unity. Black leaders like Malcolm X, Stokely Charmichael, Eldridge Cleaver, Angela Davis, and Erika Huggins helped to empower a "Black is Beautiful" movement that stirred the people of America. This movement also gave rise to the prominent civil rights leader Martin Luther King Jr. who organized the "Poor People's Campaign" to address issues of economic justice.

Today, this legacy is represented by the "Black Lives Matter" movement which has conducted large-scale protests against police brutality and police killings of unarmed black teenagers and young black men. The movement began in the protests and riots in Ferguson, Missouri[343] after the fatal shooting of Michael Brown by the white police officer Darren Wilson in 2014. The unrest sparked a national debate about the relationship between law enforcement officers and blacks and also about the militarization of the police and the Use of Force policy nationwide. Continued activism has expanded to include the struggle against modern-day debtors' prisons, for-profit policing, and school segregation.

The Greens

The Green party is a formally organized political party based on the principles of ecological wisdom, social justice, participatory democracy, nonviolence, sustainability, and respect for diversity. Green party platforms typically embrace social-democratic economic policies.[344]

Green parties exist in nearly ninety countries around the world; many are members of Global Greens an international network of

Green parties. The Global Greens Charter was adopted by consensus at the first Global Greens Congress in Canberra, Australia in 2001. The document sets out the principles that bind together Greens from around the world. It also contains a 'political action' plan covering some of the most pressing problems facing the world.[345] Greens believe that these issues are inherently related to one another as a foundation for world peace.

The map below shows the Global Green parties in national and local governments throughout the world.

The Green Party of the United States (GPUS) is arguably the most progressive party in the country and the fourth-largest party by membership. It promotes environmentalism, nonviolence, social justice, grassroots democracy, gender equality, LGBT rights, and anti-racism. In 2016, the party officially described itself as an "eco-socialist" party.[346]

The Greens track their origin back to the Green Committees of Correspondence (CoC) which were founded in the summer of 1984 with the goals of organizing local Green groups, providing a clearinghouse and newsletter, and working toward the founding of a Green political organization in the United States. The local groups organized themselves into regional confederations. Representatives from these regional confederations also formed an Interregional Committee, which met three times a year to exchange information and coordinate activities between the self-defined regions. This existed until the organization restructured in 1991. The original structure reflected the organization's roots in the bioregional movement, which rejected political boundaries in favor of boundaries indicated by natural phenomena such as watersheds, flora, and fauna, and in the municipal cooperation between local organizers and ecologists, who viewed state and federal governments as illegitimate.

In accordance with the Green principle of grassroots democracy, the Green Committees of Correspondence was a bottoms-up organization.[347] About the only requirement for local groups was that they advocate and adhere to the Ten Key Values. A more explicit explanation of these "Ten Key Values" can be found in Appendix 1

The "Ten Key Values" of the Green movement are:

1.

1. Grassroots democracy
2. Social justice
3. Ecological wisdom
4. Nonviolence
5. Decentralization
6. Community-based economics
7. Women's rights
8. Respect for diversity
9. Global responsibility
10. Future focus[348]

In supporting these values, each group was free to decide on its own purpose, structure, process, and actions. The activities of Green local parties varied widely, from electoral politics (running candidates for local, county, and state office) to alternative institutions (setting up direct farmer-to-consumer marketing and a bank for low-income communities), public education (organizing conferences, forums, and lecture series), media (a Green radio show) and publications, citizen watchdog groups (on water quality and on biotechnology), demonstrations, and support of efforts of other environmentalist and progressive groups.[349]

The Green Committees of Correspondence split into two factions in 1984 because of a contentious argument between those who wanted to concentrate on electoral politics and those who wanted to stay focused on mobilizing at the grass roots level. Those who went ahead to engage in electoral politics became the Green Party of the United States (GPUS), and those who continued to mobilize locally became the Greens/Green Party USA (G/GPUSA).

The Green Party of the United States gained widespread public attention during the 2000 presidential election, when the ticket, composed of Ralph Nader and Winona LaDuke, won 2.7% of the popular vote. Many Democrats and even some Greens vilified Nadar and accused him of spoiling the election for Al Gore, the Democratic candidate.

The GPUS has had several members elected in state legislatures, including those of California, Maine, and Arkansas. A number of Greens also hold positions on the municipal level, including on school boards, city councils, and as mayors.

The Green Party does not accept donations from corporations, political action committees (PACs), 527(c) organizations, or soft money. The party's platforms and rhetoric harshly criticize any corporate influence and control over government, media, and society at large. This is a great handicap in a political system run on capitalist money and a sure formula for being dismissed by the mainstream press, but it is a policy that supports the party's values and integrity.

In the United States, there are Green accredited parties in every state except North Dakota, South Dakota, Vermont, and Utah. As of July 2016, there were "over 100" elected Greens across the United States.[350] Positions held varied greatly, from mayor to city council, school board, to sanitation district.

There is much to be said for having a progressive party like the Greens. Certainly, the party will grow in numbers and public support as people grow increasingly frustrated in their support for the collaborators within the Democratic Party who refuse to confront the main crises that affect the lives of the people.

The Occupy Movement

The Occupy Movement was a response to the suppression of democracy and the social injustices that had occurred around the world due to the strangle hold of American imperialism and the international banking elite beginning after WWII.[351] The Left had fomented the protests of the 1970s and helped foster the rise of the Sustainable Development movement, both of which had been international movements opposed to the globalization of the economy and the destruction of natural resources.

The Occupy movement began in New York City's Zuccotti Park on September 17, 2011 as a protest against the exploitation and corruption of people at the hands of the Wall Street bankers.[352] The *Declaration of the Occupation of New York City* can be found in Appendix 2. By October, the event had fired the imagination of disgruntled people around the country and the world. There were protests in over six hundred US communities and in over nine hundred and fifty cities internationally that were spread across eighty-two countries. Protests were held on every continent except Antarctica.[353]

While local groups often had different focuses, the common grievance was against the global banking elite's suppression of democracy and their exploitation of local people and the environment. In the US, the protestors voiced their anger at the decimation of the American middle class while the tiny capitalist elite grew filthy rich.

The Occupy movement in the US was partly inspired by the 2009 California university tuition hike protests, but also by the anti-austerity protests throughout Europe and even the democratic surge of the Arab Spring, and the 2009 democratic Green Movement in Iran.

The US movement used the slogan "We are the 99%" and organized by using the #Occupy hashtag and websites such as *Occupy Together*. According to the mainstream press, America was going through another "democratic awakening."

Micah White, editor of Adbusters, an anti-consumerism, pro-environment organization that describes itself as "a global network of artists, activists, writers, pranksters, students, educators, and entrepreneurs who want to advance the new social activist movement of the information age," was the one who designed the original Occupy Wall Street concept. He had traveled to California for the tuition protests and had taken part in the occupation of Wheeler Hall. He wrote enthusiastically about the "revolutionary potential of [the students] struggle."[354]

The Spanish Indignados movement preceded the Occupy Wall Street movement by a few months. While beginning in mid-May 2011, there were already hundreds of camps around Spain and across the world by the end of the month. It was the Indignados who called for a worldwide protest against the international banks on October 15. According to Micah White, "[we] basically floated the idea in mid-July into our [email list] and it was spontaneously taken up by all the people of the world, it just kind of snowballed from there."[355]

During the early weeks, the movement was frequently criticized by the news media for having no clearly defined goals, but organizers responded that this absence of particular goals allowed the movement against capitalist exploitation to grow. However, by late October, organizers were trying to rally support for "a Robin Hood tax." This spontaneous effort, while raising consciousness about the need for a tax on Wall Street profits, proved to be ineffective. Decided in the spare of the moment, and on the fly, the particulars of the tax could never be finalized. In late November, the London contingent of the Occupy movement released their first statement on corporations, in which they called for measures to end tax evasion by wealthy firms. The global movement has been called the reinvention of politics, revolution, and utopia in the twenty-first century,[356] but this is an overstatement and does not present a correct picture of the accomplishments of the Occupy movement.

While the movement expressed an over-all commitment to participatory democracy, its organizers lacked a strategic plan or the staying power to follow through on what they had started. The leaders raised up the masses and then left them hanging without direction. Even so, new tactics were tried with some positive results. Much of the movement's participatory democratic process occurred in "working groups," where any protester was able to have his or her say. The groups operated with discussion facilitators rather than leaders. Precedents for this approach were the democracy movement in ancient Greece, the Quaker movement, and the anti-globalization movement of 1999. At general assemblies, working group proposals were made to the meeting participants, who commented upon them using a process called a *stack*; a queue of speakers that anyone could join. In New York City, Occupy Wall Street used what is called a *progressive stack*, in which people from marginalized groups were often allowed to speak before people from dominant groups. Facilitators, or *stack-keepers*, urged speakers to "step forward, or step back" based on which group they belonged to. Women and minorities were allowed to move to the head of the line, while white males waited for a turn to speak.

Non-Violence

The occupy movement began with a commitment to nonviolence, inspired by the writings of Dr. Gene Sharp whose writings had already influenced nonviolent movements in Burma, Serbia, and in Middle Eastern countries during the Arab Spring. Sharp's work was justifiably heralded by the US Occupy leaders who organized study groups across the Occupy camps to discuss his manual for nonviolent revolution entitled *From Dictatorship to Democracy*. The study groups gave particular attention to Sharp's 198 methods of nonviolent action listed in an appendix of the book. A subsequent film about Dr. Sharp's work entitled *How to Start a Revolution*[357] by Ruaridh Arrow, premiered in Boston on September 18, 2011 and was subsequently screened in Occupy camps across the US and Europe.

The main tenets of Sharp's generic strategy for starting a revolution are:

- Develop a strategy for winning freedom and a vision of the society you want.
- Overcome fear by small acts of resistance.
- Use colors and symbols to demonstrate unity of resistance.
- Learn from historical examples of the successes of non-violent movements
- Use non-violent "weapons."
- Identify the dictatorship's pillars of support and develop a strategy to undermine each.
- Use oppressive or brutal acts by the regime as a recruiting tool for your movement.
- Isolate or remove from the movement people who use or advocate violence.[358]

While those with a warrior spirit may not resonate with his last point, Sharp's message to would-be-revolutionaries has always been, "By placing confidence in violent means, one has chosen the very type of struggle with which the oppressors nearly always have superiority."[359] His central message is that the power of dictatorships comes from the willing obedience of the people they govern and if the people can develop techniques of withholding their consent, a regime will crumble.

Sharp's list of 198 "non-violent weapons," ranged from mass demonstrations, to the use of colors and symbols, to mock funerals, and boycotts. Designed to be the direct equivalent of military weapons, they are techniques assembled from a study of defiance against tyranny throughout history. Sharp organized his non-violent weapons methods into three categories: (1) protest and persuasion, (2) noncooperation, and (3) intervention.

His most important work, *From Dictatorship to Democracy*, was written for the Burmese democratic movement in 1993, after the imprisonment of Aung San Suu Kyi. The book caught on like wild fire. From Burma word of mouth spread through Thailand to Indonesia, where it was used against the military dictatorship there. Its success in helping to bring down Milosevic in Serbia in 2000 propelled it into use across Eastern Europe, South America, and the Middle East where it inspired the Egyptian revolution against the dictator Hosni Mubarak. When it reached Russia, however, the government's intelligence services raided the printer and those shops caught selling the book were mysteriously burned to the ground.[360]

Regarding the Occupy movement in the United States, Sharp himself warned that the tactics the movement employed would not be effective because the movement lacked a clear strategic plan and vision. In an Al Jazeera interview, he said, "The [Occupy] protesters don't have a clear objective, something they can actually achieve. If they think they will change the economic system by simply staying in a particular location, then they are likely to be very disappointed. Protest alone accomplishes very little."[361] Sharp pinpointed the major flaw in the Occupy movement. Not only did the leadership lack a concrete set of goals, but they lacked a clear vision and strategy for seizing power.

728As it was, not all Occupiers were committed to nonviolence. By November, the media began to report an increase in violence including incidents of violence against the police. By January of 2012, the movement's commitment to nonviolence was questioned after clashes with the police that saw four hundred arrests in the US city of Oakland.[362] By not channeling the energy of the militants, the leadership allowed their anger and frustration to turn into random acts of violence and riots. This was a flaw within the Occupy movement as well as within the nonviolent movement advocated by Dr. Sharp, although his warning against the use of violence merits strong reflection.

Failings of the Occupy Movement

The lack of a strategy on the part of the organizers resulted in a situation where after seven weeks into the movement, the public was still unsure what the protesters wanted. The movement splintered into too many issues and internal confrontations. For example, the goal of social equality degenerated into endless discussions as to which issue should be prioritized—healthcare, corporate greed, student loans, debt repayment, a minimum wage, etc. By getting lost in this process, the protesters never were able to offer remedies to the people.

In contrast to the Occupy movement, the conservative Tea Party movement was more successful because it focused all of its energy on two issues. The first issue was lowering taxes. This movement led the Tea Party to become a household name because of their association with that one issue. Some people even believed that their name is just an acronym for Taxed Enough Already.

The second issue was Obamacare. Across the country, Tea Partiers confronted their local elected officials and expressed their views about the Obama plan for universal healthcare. Whether individuals agreed with their beliefs, the public knew what the Tea Party wanted.

The Tea Party radicals were also successful in influencing national elections. Several Tea Party candidates were elected to state and national offices. The Tea Party garnered support and became organized, setting up something similar to franchises across the country. They pushed Tea Party supporters into positions of power in an effort to change the system from within.

Another major flaw of the Occupy movement was a complete lack of leadership. When it was founded, that lack of leadership was considered to be a good thing because it created more participatory democracy. However, this proved to be a recipe for no one taking responsibility for the direction of the movement. Organizers could not agree on how to distribute donations or how to communicate with the police. The park became overrun with drug addicts, freeloaders, and trouble-makers who ate the free food and caused trouble. There became no way to tell who was an active protester and who was a run-of-the-mill crack addict. As some organizers complained about this development, others accused them of hypocrisy because they were not even willing to help the homeless.[363]

While the Occupy movement may have forwarded the cause of democracy in a limited way due to its experiment with methods of participatory democracy, it has to be regarded as a failure if its goal was to stop capitalist exploitation in this country and the world.

It is of interest that a small group of activists who identified themselves as "veteran grassroots organizers of Occupy Wall Street" launched a "People for Bernie Sanders" campaign. "Our goal is to establish a government that carries out the will of the people, rather than one that serves to increase the profits of the wealthiest one percent at the expense of the rest of us," they said in a statement. "To that end, we support Bernie Sanders in his bid to become the presidential nominee of the Democratic Party."[364] While Bernie Sanders is a progressive politician, he lost his bid for president in 2016 because the organizers still lacked a strategic plan to mobilize the people for a revolution that would be required to challenge the authority of the one percent.

Conclusion

As we have examined the development of the left and right ideologies, we come to understand the sad truth that neither Conservatism, Liberalism, nor Progressivism has the scope to address the social and environmental crises that are relentlessly destroying our society. These piecemeal ideologies are unable to unite us as human beings at a time when it is imperative that we act in a collective manner. We share a global problem and we need a response by all of humanity. Our old ideas are based on misinformation, false premises, myths, and dogmas that no longer enlighten us as to a course of action. As religion was the opium of the people in Marx's day, so too it remains to this day, only now we must also add the current secular philosophies that support the status quo. They numb our senses and leave us mumbling to ourselves about the idiocy and incompetence all around us. They provide no ground for progress or social synthesis.

We have observed that most people base their actions on sentiment rather than rationality when it comes to living in society. These sentiments are not a product of today's world, rather they result from a programming that was set in place as far back as the beginning of human society, especially the dawn of patriarchal society. These decrepit ideas have been carried across decades and centuries from one generation to the next. When we look at the person in front of us, we are looking at someone who contains in his or her DNA, in his or her karma, a set of values that was established millennia ago. Our programming is a recording of the past that we attempt to use today to solve problems that never even occurred in the past. We walk around unconscious to this fact, unable to throw off the shackles that bind us and prevent us from moving forward as a human society.

Unless we are able to consciously question the validity of our programming and to decide which ideas make sense in light of the challenges we face today, our programming will continually obstruct our ability to make constructive change. It leads to spouting meaningless words and defending meaningless ideas in a war with people who have equally meaningless ideas, all of which have no bearing on the ravaging inferno that is manifesting before our eyes. Intellectuals, on both the left and the right, need to consider the fact that neither of these camps is helping us solve our common crisis. Rather, the opposition of the left and the right has merely become a strategy of divide and conquer mouthed by politicians and the mainstream media according to the dictates of the ruling elite. Whether left or right, if our programming is not consistent with universal values that seek the welfare of all, such ideas are unproductive in today's world. They only perpetuate social stagnancy when the time demands we act quickly and decisively. The platitudes and criticisms of each other that fill our minds can no longer go unchallenged. The destruction of industrial civilization and the planet itself cannot be addressed with simple sound bites from yesterday's minds. Our rage and frustration are a clear sign that we need a bigger dream, a dream of unity and Oneness.

Chapter Three: The American Warriors: Nation as Empire

WHEN THIS CAPITALIST AGE comes to an end, a warrior age will follow.[365] We can see this process unfolding as the Bush and Obama policies initiated a worldwide preemptive strike policy called the "war on terrorism." This war without end shows no sign of abating and continues to create more battlefronts as it sucks more nations into the fight. On the domestic front, the institutionalization of a "national emergency" policy has led to the militarization of the police across the country. These developments, along with the decline of the global economy, are setting the stage for the transformation of power from the capitalist to the warrior class.

As the capitalist economy and the natural environment become increasingly unstable, the people of the world undergo increasing stress and suffering. The world is already being forced to respond to millions of refugees as a result of current wars and environmental catastrophes. The social stress from mass migrations causes fear and anger among the people. Human society becomes more polarized as the political left and right become ever more dismissive and hateful of each other. The tendency toward ultra-nationalism and fascism builds.

In the industrialized West, the long dominant white male finds himself unable to control the rapid pace of change. He is turning inward and becoming more resentful of the social demands made by women, racial minorities, and foreigners. The loss of living wage jobs has exacerbated his deep-seated prejudices. The liberals, reacting to what they see as misogyny, racism, and xenophobia, become more strident regarding the inflexibility of the right concerning this assault on humanity. The conservatives, seeking to maintain the status quo, damn the liberals for their disrespect of tradition and existing power structures. On both sides, the use of physical force becomes more of an option.

As the warrior psychology grows, the existing military institutions and national security forces play a larger role in society. By looking at the history of the American military-industrial complex since WWII, and by examining their current policies and grand strategy, we will better understand what we can expect down the road.

In this chapter, we will examine the principles of the Cold War policy in the wake of WWII and the growth of the Military Industrial Complex. We will look at America's involvement in the wars in Korea and Vietnam to contain communism and the impact of the fall of the USSR on America's military. We will examine how the elites conceptualized a new strategy of global dominance that required the conquest of Eurasia and how this strategy gave rise to the perpetual War on Terrorism and the legalization of a police state on American soil in anticipation of a National Emergency. We will look at the growth of Islamic Fundamentalism and the role of American intelligence in initiating and perpetuating this movement and why this occurred. We will look at what happened on 9/11 and the wars in the Middle East that followed, including the complexities of these wars and the cost in human life and human suffering. We will examine what it is like to be a soldier in the Middle East and how the government responds to the needs of our young men and women as they return home from the war in need of physical and mental treatment. Finally, we will look at the billions of dollars made from this perpetual war by the arms manufacturers and other corporations that benefit from constant violence and war.

What is Militarism?

Let us begin our exploration of the role of the military in the United States by defining what militarism is. Militarism is the belief that the government of a country should maintain a strong military capability and be prepared to use it aggressively to defend or promote national interests. Examples of militarist states include the United States, England, Germany, France, Israel, Turkey, and Russia. Militarism also includes the glorification of the military and the ideals of a professional military class. It often includes the "predominance of the armed forces in the administration or policy of the state."

Today, the ideology of the United States government is predominantly capitalist, although militarism has been a significant element in the imperialist expansion of the US empire.[366] It is poised to gain increasing strength as global tensions and domestic unrest continue to grow.

US Militarism is based on the precedent set by Western European countries when they created standing armies during the eighteenth and nineteenth centuries. At the time, powerful kingdoms were becoming permanent nation-states. These nation-states expanded their power base by the practice of imperialism or what was then called colonialism. The roots of German militarism, for example, can be found in the nineteenth century when the country was unified under Prussian leadership.

After Napoleon Bonaparte conquered Prussia in 1806, he demanded that Prussia reduce its army to no more than four hundred and twenty thousand men. The King of Prussia complied with this order, but at the same time, managed to build a powerful standing army using the art of deception. The King drafted into the Prussian army the permitted number of men for one year, then dismissed that group and drafted another of the same size each consecutive year. After ten years, he was able to gather an army of forty-two thousand men who had at least one year of military training. The officers of the army were drawn from the land-owning nobility; the enlisted men from the working classes. In this way the working class became conditioned to implicitly obey the commands of the officers, thereby creating a class-based culture of deference.[367]

The militaristic culture in Germany continued after World War I and even after the fall of the German monarchy. Adolph Hitler's Third Reich, whose colonialist expansion initiated World War II, was the epitome of a military dictatorship. After its fall, in 1945, militarism in the German culture was dramatically reduced as a backlash against the Nazi period.

In parallel with the twentieth century Nazi regime, Japanese militarists also began to dictate Japan's affairs. The precedent of a strong military role in determining state policy went back to the fifteenth century *Age of Warring States*, when powerful samurai warlords (shoguns) controlled large regions of Japan. A nationalist style of militarism developed in 1868 when the emperor Meiji consolidated the political system of that country. This national militarism was reinforced in 1882 by the *Imperial Rescript to Soldiers and Sailors*,[368] which called for all members of the armed forces to demonstrate absolute loyalty to the Emperor.

During the 1920s, legislation was enacted that gave the Japanese military a veto power over the formation of any Cabinet in a country that operated under a parliamentary system. In the 1930s, the Great Depression withered Japan's economy and gave radical elements within the Japanese military the chance to realize their ambitions of conquering all of Asia. In 1931, the Japanese army invaded Manchuria. Six years later they invaded China. In 1940, Japan entered into an alliance with Nazi Germany and Fascist Italy, two similarly militaristic states in Europe, and advanced out of China and into Southeast Asia.

The alliance of Germany and Japan initiated the involvement of the United States military in WWII. The US banned the sale and transport of petroleum to Japan. This embargo led to the Attack on Pearl Harbor and the entry of the US into World War II.

In the United States, the creation of a standing army came early as the Hamiltonians gained an advantage over the Jeffersonians by creating a strong central government whose military served the American leaders' intention to become a major capitalist country. The army's purpose, at the time, was to pursue an imperialist policy in the Pacific and the Caribbean and to help build the US economy abroad through conquest.

By the time of the Civil War, the Union Army was composed of six hundred thousand men, but as the war ended, the national army fell into disrepair. Reformers in the national government quickly acted to bring the army once again under strict control of the central government. The army was trained in preparation for future economic conflicts and a new command and support structure was built. These reforms led to the development of professional military strategists and the creation of the US Army whose evolution we witness today.

The US Army expanded during the Spanish–American War, which began in 1898. When Spain was defeated, the size of the army was again expanded to occupy and control the new colonies acquired from Spain in its defeat, including Guam, the Philippines, Puerto Rico, and Cuba.

US forces were increased again as we entered World War I in 1917. Over 4.7 million men and women served in the regular US forces, National Guard units, and draft units.[369]

In the period between WWI and WWII, the US Marine Corp was used as a private army to protect US corporations and prop up local military dictators during Latin America's so-called Banana Wars.[370] This experience led the Marines to develop the *USMC Small Wars Manual*, which continues to be a training manual for interventions in small third world countries today.[371]

The purpose of the Marine incursions into small countries is expressly stated in Section II on Strategy:

> Diplomatic agencies usually conduct negotiations with a view to arriving at a peaceful solution to the problem on a basis compatible with both national honor and treaty stipulations. Although the outcome of such negotiations often results in a friendly settlement, the military forces should be prepared for a possibility of an unfavorable termination of the proceedings. *The mobilization of armed forces constitutes a highly effective weapon for forcing the opponent to accede to national demands* without resort to war.[372] When a time limit for peaceful settlement is proscribed by ultimatum the military-naval forces must be prepared to initiate operations upon expiration of the time limit.[373]

It was also during this time that the popular Retired Major General Smedley Butler, who had been a General in WWI, briefed Congress on a "Business Plot" to overthrow Franklin D. Roosevelt's presidency by a military coup.[374] General Smedley testified before a congressional committee that he had been approached by representatives of the New York-based corporate elite with their plan to rid the country of Roosevelt.

A Congressional Committee heard General Butler's testimony, but the capitalist-controlled mainstream media discredited the General and the politicians did not have the stomach to take on Wall Street.

During WWII, the military expanded each year of the war. By 1945, there were 12.2 million Americans in uniform. Sixty one percent were draftees who served an average of thirty-three months. After World War II, the tension between the capitalist countries and the communist countries created the Cold War, which led to a large-scale permanent military and the threat of nuclear war.

The Military-Industrial Complex

When World War II ended with a victory for the US and its allies over the Axis Powers, much of the credit went to Dwight D. "Ike" Eisenhower, who was a five-star general in the United States Army. Ike had served as Supreme Commander of the Allied Forces in Europe. He was responsible for planning and supervising the invasions of North Africa, France, and Germany. In 1951, he became the first Supreme Commander of NATO. At the time, Ike was a genuine American hero and, even today, is considered by many, both on the Left and the Right, to be one of the greatest Americans to ever live.

After the war, Eisenhower entered the 1952 presidential race as a Republican to counter the growing non-interventionist movement initiated by Senator Robert A. Taft. Ike campaigned against "communism, Korea, and corruption" and won in a landslide. This was a sound defeat of the New Deal Coalition led by the Democrats.

Eisenhower's national security policy became known as "The New Look" and reflected his concern for balancing the Cold War military commitments of the United States with paying down the national debt from WWII. His policy included the use of "strategic nuclear weapons" to deter potential threats from the Eastern Bloc and the USSR.[375] Eisenhower also ordered coups in Iran and Guatemala and supported France with aid in its war against the people of North Vietnam. In 1955, the *Formosa Resolution,* drafted by the US Congress, obliged the US to militarily support the pro-Western Republic of China in Taiwan and to continue the isolation of the People's Republic of China.[376]

After the Soviet Union launched Sputnik 1, the first artificial Earth satellite, in 1957, Eisenhower authorized the establishment of NASA, which then led to the "space race." Despite his strong militaristic history, in his 1961 farewell address to the nation, Eisenhower spoke out about the dangers of deficit spending as a means to fund a massive military. He singled out the danger of giving large contracts to private military manufacturers. In this speech, he coined the term "military–industrial complex"[377] and cautioned Americans about its threat to our ideals:

> A vital element in keeping the peace is our military establishment. Our arms must be mighty, ready for instant action, so that no potential aggressor may be tempted to risk his own destruction. . . .
>
> This conjunction of an immense military establishment and a large arms industry is new in the American experience. The total influence—economic, political, even spiritual—is felt in every city, every statehouse, every office of the federal government. We recognize the imperative need for this development. Yet we must not fail to comprehend its grave implications. Our toil, resources and livelihood are all involved; so is the very structure of our society. In the councils of government, we must guard against the acquisition of unwarranted influence, whether sought or unsought, by the military–industrial complex. The potential for the disastrous rise of misplaced power exists, and will persist. We must never let the weight of this combination endanger our liberties or democratic processes. We should take nothing for granted. Only an alert and knowledgeable citizenry can compel the proper meshing of the huge industrial and military machinery of defense with our peaceful methods and goals so that security and liberty may prosper together.[378]

Unfortunately, Eisenhower's caution went unheard. The military–industrial complex (MIC), to which Eisenhower referred, has continued to grow in wealth and power to this day. As we shall see, the alliance between the United States military and the defense industry, which supplies it with weaponry and other goods and services, is so powerful that they command US public policy regardless of whether a Republican or Democrat sits in the president's office. The relationship between the military-industrial complex and the US Congress consists of an entire network of contracts and flows of money and resources among individuals as well as corporations and institutions of the defense contractors, the Pentagon, Congress, and the Executive Branch.

An open door exists in which industry executives become government operatives and government operatives are employed by the arms industry. Essentially, they have become the same people. This "iron triangle" (military, industry, and Congress) has all the hallmarks of *fascism* which Daniel Guerin in his book "Fascism and Big Business" published in 1936 defined as "an informal and changing coalition of groups with vested psychological, moral, and material interests in the continuous development and maintenance of high levels of weaponry, in preservation of colonial markets and in military-strategic conceptions of internal affairs."[379] The series of wars that have been lobbied for by the US weapons merchants has presently reached a crescendo in the so-called "War on Terrorism," a war of all against all, without time limit or territorial boundary, for as long as the United States elites continue their quest of global conquest. Let us look at how the stream of wars, engaged in since WWII, has led to this situation.

The Korean War

The Korean War or the "Fatherland Liberation War" was fought between 1950 and 1953. It was the first military contest between the capitalist and communist countries after WWII. The war began when North Koreans, with assistance from China and the Soviet Union invaded South Korea, which was supported by the US and the United Nations. The war arose from the partition of Korea at the end of World War II.

Japan had ruled Korea from 1910 until the closing days of World War II. Toward the end of the war, the Soviet Union formally declared war on Japan and liberated Korea north of the 38th parallel. U.S. forces subsequently moved into the south. By 1948, as a result of the Cold War between the Soviet Union and the United States, Korea was split into two regions, with separate governments. Both governments claimed to be the legitimate government of Korea, but the Korean people did not accept the border as permanent.

An open war began when North Korean forces moved into the south to unite the country. The United Nations' Security Council declared this act an invasion and called for an immediate ceasefire. The Security Council was made up of permanent representatives from the US, England, France, Russia, and China. At the time of the Security Council vote, however, Russia was absent due to its boycott of the Council because the Council had chosen Taiwan to represent the Chinese people instead of the People's Republic of China.[380] Without opposition, therefore, the Security Council called on its member states to fight the North Koreans' act of aggression. Twenty-one countries of the United Nations eventually contributed to the defense of South Korea, but in actuality, the United States provided eighty-eight percent of UN fighting forces.

After two months of conflict, the South Korean forces were facing defeat, but an amphibious UN counter-offensive at Inchon cut off many of the North Korean troops and forced them back across the border of China. At this point, in October 1950, Chinese forces entered the war. This caused the UN forces to retreat. In the give and take of the war, Seoul, the capitol of South Korea, changed hands four times. The last two years of conflict became a war of attrition, with the front line close to the 38th parallel. In the air, however, the war raged on. Jet fighters confronted each other in air-to-air combat for the first time in history, and Soviet pilots covertly flew in resources for their communist allies. North Korea was subjected to a massive bombing campaign by the United States.

The fighting ended on July 27, 1953 when an armistice was signed. The agreement created the Korean Demilitarized Zone to separate North and South Korea, and allowed the return of prisoners. No peace treaty, however, was signed, and the two Koreas are technically still at war. Periodic clashes, many of which are deadly, have continued to the present.[381]

The Vietnam War

The Vietnam War or the "Resistance War Against America" was a war that occurred in Vietnam, Laos, and Cambodia from November 1, 1955 to the fall of Saigon on April 30, 1975. It was officially fought between North Vietnam and the government of South Vietnam. Similar to the Korean War, the North Vietnamese army was supported by the Soviet Union, China, and other communist allies, while the South Vietnamese army was supported by the United States, Philippines, and other anti-communist allies. Like Korea, the war was considered a Cold War proxy fight.

The Viet Cong was a South Vietnamese communist coalition aided by the North that fought a guerrilla war against the capitalist forces in the south. The People's Army of Vietnam, from the North, engaged in more conventional warfare and at times committed large units to battle. As the war advanced, the military actions of the Viet Cong decreased and the engagement of the conventional army grew. The South Vietnamese and US forces used their air superiority and overwhelming firepower to conduct "search and destroy" operations, involving ground forces, artillery, and airstrikes. The US conducted a large-scale strategic bombing campaign against North Vietnam.

The goal of the North Vietnamese government and the Viet Cong was to reunify Vietnam. They viewed the conflict as a colonial war and a continuation of their fight against France and later the US. The US government viewed its involvement in the war as a way to prevent a Communist takeover of South Vietnam. This was part of the wider Cold War containment policy with the stated aim of stopping the spread of communism.

Beginning in 1950, at the start of the Korean War, American military advisors arrived in Vietnam, which at the time was called French Indochina. US involvement escalated in the early 1960s, with troop size tripling in 1961 and again in 1962. US involvement escalated further following the 1964 Gulf of Tonkin incident, in which a US destroyer allegedly clashed with three North Vietnamese fast attack craft.[382] This incident led to the US Congress passing the Gulf of Tonkin Resolution that gave the President authority to deploy regular combat units to Vietnam in 1965.[383]

Operations soon spilled into the bordering areas of Laos and Cambodia, which were heavily bombed by US forces as American involvement increased and peaked in 1968. This was the year that North Vietnam launched the Tet Offensive. The Tet Offensive, named for the Vietnamese New Year (Tet), was a campaign of surprise attacks against military and civilian command and control centers throughout South Vietnam. The offensive was countrywide and well-coordinated. More than eighty thousand North Vietnamese troops struck more than one hundred towns and cities, including the southern capital of Saigon. The offensive was the largest military operation conducted by either side up to that point in the war.[384]

The Tet Offensive failed in its goal of overthrowing the South Vietnamese government, but it persuaded a large segment of the US population that the government's claims of progress toward winning the war were illusory despite many years of massive US military aid to South Vietnam. In the US and the Western world, this led to a large anti-Vietnam War movement developed as part of the larger counter-culture movement.

Direct US military involvement finally ended on August 15, 1973. The capture of Saigon by the North Vietnamese Army in April marked the end of the war, and North and South Vietnam were reunified the following year. The war exacted a huge human cost in terms of fatalities.[385] Estimates of the number of Vietnamese soldiers and civilians killed vary from 800,000 to 3.1 million. Between 200,000 to 300,000 Cambodians, 20,000 to 200,000 Laotians, and 58,220 Americans also died in the conflict, with a further 1,626 missing in action.[386]

The End of the Cold War

The war in Vietnam changed the military dynamics between the capitalist and communist countries. Proxy wars were becoming too costly and too destabilizing for both the East and the West.

In 1977, following the Vietnam War, President Jimmy Carter began his presidency determined to break from America's militarized past. The

Trilateralists, who had conducted Carter's campaign, now had domestic problems to contend with and the oil embargo had greatly interfered with business as usual. The 1973 Oil Embargo had acutely strained a US economy that had grown increasingly dependent on foreign oil.378

Samuel Huntington, a Trilateralist, had written in the *Crisis of Democracy* in 1975 that:

> The structure of governmental activity in the United States — in terms of both its size and its content — went through two major changes during the quarter-century after World War II. The first change, the Defense Shift, was a response to the external Soviet threat of the 1940s; the second change, the Welfare Shift, was a response to the internal democratic surge of the 1960s. The former was primarily the product of elite leadership; the latter was primarily the result of popular expectations and group demands.[387]

Simply put, the US elites favored militarism as a means to spread capitalism under the guise of containing communism. Militarism was the means by which they promoted their imperial agenda. During the same time that the US military was fighting in Vietnam, it was also selling weapons to Israel, returning troops to Korea, providing logistical support to the French in Zaire, and conducting operations in Cambodia, Cyprus, and Lebanon. The US military provided the stick by which the capitalists were able to punish, threaten, or kill anyone in any other country that opposed their exploitation of labor and resources.

The use of the military in this manner, however, was not the reason given to the American public by the mass media. Rather, the newspapers, magazines, radio, and TV spoke only about "national defense." The military was needed to fight the godless and evil empire of Communism. It was needed to protect Americans from Communists in Korea, Vietnam, Laos, Cambodia, and other third world countries. Understandably, this rationale resonated with the parents of the Baby Boom generation. Many of this generation had fought in WWII or had friends who had died or who were traumatized for life by fighting Adolph Hitler's war machine. The need for national defense was etched in their bones. As such, this was not a generation to contest the massive military-industrial complex that had emerged from the backroom deals between the elite in New York and the Washington politicians and agency bureaucrats.

The younger Americans, called the Baby Boomers, on the other hand, favored social programs. They wanted the government to take care of Americans, our own women and children, our own minorities, students, and disabled. In 1960, during the days of the Vietnam War, the US government spent more than two and a half times more on "national defense" than it did for education. It spent four and a half times more on the military than social security and ten times more than on social welfare. By now, the military-industrial complex was firmly established in the federal government system. As the armed forces expanded to support US-based imperialism abroad, the domestic economy sputtered dismally and the American people became more disgruntled. This unhappiness with the system eventually catalyzed the American youth movement who had now either fought in Vietnam or knew friends who did. The young began to see through the establishment propaganda and to organize against US imperialism. They began to speak out against the injustices of the system, which included the maltreatment of the poor, minorities, and women.

The surge of the New Left caused the Trilateralists to fear that their cover was blown. Huntington defined three major issue clusters of the youth movement: (1) social issues, such as use of drugs, civil liberties, and the role of women; (2) racial issues, involving integration, busing, government aid to minority groups, and urban riots; and (3) military issues, involving the war in Vietnam, the draft, military spending, military aid programs, and the role of the military-industrial complex in general.

As the New Left became more powerful, it sparked a conservative backlash in the country. The left and the right split along party lines as all three sets of issues came to correlate with people's political ideology. To predict the position of an individual on any of these issues, for example, the legalization of marijuana or school integration or the war in Vietnam, one would simply ask people whether they considered themselves to be a Republican or Democrat. This polarization of the left and the right according to political parties did not exist before. Both the Republicans and the Democrats had previously had a left wing and a right wing within their parties.

The Fall of the Union of Soviet Socialist Republics (USSR)

As the United States and European elites recoiled under the domestic pressure for social change, Russia also went through a social revolution that led to the dismantling of its empire, the Soviet Union.

The Soviet Union, which had existed from 1922 until 1991, was a union of Soviet republics governed by the Communist Party, with its headquarters in Moscow. It had its roots in the October Revolution of 1917, when the Bolsheviks, headed by Vladimir Lenin, overthrew the provisional government that had replaced the Czar. Lenin established the Russian Socialist Federative Soviet Republic in 1936. This set off a civil war in which the revolutionary "Reds" fought the counter-revolutionary "Whites."

The Red Army entered several territories of the former Russian Empire and helped local Communists take power through soviets, which were locally elected bodies that nominally acted on behalf of workers and peasants. In 1922, the Communists were victorious against the Whites and formed the Soviet Union by unifying Russia with the Transcaucasus Republic, Ukraine, and Byelorussia.

When Lenin died in 1924, Joseph Stalin came to power. Stalin was primarily a military dictator. Ideologically, he introduced the philosophy that became known as Marxism-Leninism. Basically, this ideology espoused the idea of a revolutionary party, a one-party state, state dominance over the economy and opposition to capitalism. It was the official ideology of the Eastern Bloc countries during the Cold War and remains today the official ideology of China, Cuba, Laos, and Vietnam.[388]

The goal of Marxism–Leninism is to develop socialism through the leadership of a revolutionary vanguard, which is the part of the working class which gains a class-consciousness as a result of its oppression by the capitalist class. The socialist state represents the dominance of the working people as opposed to the capitalist state that represents the dominance of the capitalist class. Theoretically, socialism would eventually lead to communism, which was envisioned as a classless society with common ownership of the economy and full social equality of all members of society. The utopian vision of this ideology was squashed, however, by the reality of Stalin's heavy fist and by the perceived need to fight the capitalist countries that had formed into the North Atlantic Treaty Organization (NATO) during the Cold War.

Stalin suppressed all political opposition to his rule by fomenting political paranoia. He conducted the Great Purge to remove his opponents from the Communist Party using mass arbitrary arrests. He also starved millions of people for non-cooperation with his Five-Year plans. Many of his enemies, who numbered in the tens of millions,[389] were sent to correctional labor camps or sentenced to death. The stunning resilience of the Russian people can be seen in the fact that after decades of brutal punishment by their own government, they went on to defeat the vast Nazi war machine in the East and then occupy the countries of Eastern Europe as well as East Germany.

Following Stalin's death in 1953, a period of political and economic liberalization, known as "de-Stalinization", occurred under the leadership of Nikita Khrushchev. The country quickly developed its industry as millions of peasants were moved into the cities. In the 1970s, there was a brief *détente* in relations with the United States, but tensions resumed when the Soviet Union deployed troops in Afghanistan in 1979. The war drained economic resources and was matched by an escalation of American military aid to Mujahedeen fighters who would later become members of the Taliban and al-Qaeda.

In the mid-1980s, Mikhail Gorbachev, the last General Secretary of the USSR, sought to further liberalize the economy through his policies of *glasnost* and *perestroika*. Glasnost means "political openness." Gorbachev tried to eliminate all traces of Communist Party repression of the people. He eliminated the omnipresent secret police, prohibited the banning of books, released political prisoners, and allowed newspapers to criticize the government. For the first time, other political parties could participate in elections. He gave many new freedoms to the people.

The second set of reforms was known as *perestroika*, which means, "economic restructuring." Gorbachev tried to loosen the government's grip on the economy. Seeing how the capitalist economies flourished, he believed that private initiative would lead to innovation. Individuals and cooperatives were allowed to own businesses for the first time since the 1920s. Workers were given the right to strike for better wages and Gorbachev also encouraged foreign investment in Soviet enterprises.

Unfortunately, while the people exulted in their new-found freedoms, the economic reforms were slow to bear fruit. Perestroika had killed the "command economy" that had kept the Soviet state afloat, but the market economy required additional time to come online. People had no experience of how to start and run a business. In his farewell address, Gorbachev summed up the problem: "The old system collapsed before the new one had time to begin working."

Rationing, shortages, and endless lines for scarce goods seemed to be the only results of Gorbachev's policies. As a result, people grew more and more frustrated with his government.

As this was occurring in Russia, President Reagan, intent on crippling the Soviet Union, launched a massive military buildup called "Star Wars" and condemned the USSR by referring to it as the "Evil Empire." Gorbachev did not take the bait and vowed to bow out of the arms race. He announced that he would withdraw Soviet troops from Afghanistan and began to reduce the Soviet military presence in Eastern Europe.

This effectively destroyed Russia's Eastern European alliances and set these countries up for revolution. The first revolution of 1989 took place in Poland, where the non-Communist trade unionists in the *Solidarity* movement bargained with the Communist government for freer elections and enjoyed great success. This, in turn, sparked peaceful revolutions across Eastern Europe. The Berlin Wall fell in November. That same month, the "velvet revolution" in Czechoslovakia overthrew that country's Communist government. In December, the Romanian people overthrew the brutal dictator Nicolae Ceaucescu and executed him by firing squad. In 1991, as the Russian military was staging a coup against Gorbachev, the Baltic States, Estonia, Lithuania, and Latvia, declared their independence from Moscow. In early December, the Republic of Belarus and Ukraine broke away from the USSR. Weeks later, they were followed by eight of the nine remaining republics.

In 1988, *Time* magazine selected Mikhail Gorbachev to be its "Man of the Year" for his work toward ending the Cold War. The next year, it named him its "Man of the Decade." In 1990, Gorbachev won the Nobel Peace Prize.[390]

With the Russian economy weakened by the destruction of the soviet empire, domestic and foreign capitalists moved in to take advantage of the situation. Raw materials were gobbled up and pirated. The almost complete absence of central authority left no one in charge to control domestic resources. Consequently, the Russian mafia, Russian oligarchs, and foreign companies made deals with local magistrates to ransack the wealth of Russia while the people struggled to survive.

In 1991, the deterioration in Russia caused military hard-liners to stage a coup to overthrow Mikhail Gorbachev and reestablish military control of the country and the Communist Party. In this attempted coup, Boris Yeltsin, the president of Russia rallied the people of Moscow to take back the government and the military coup collapsed.

Nonetheless, the situation remained tenuous. The old rules no longer applied while new rules had yet to be established. The situation required a strong leader to prevent the country from spiraling into chaos. Vladimir Putin was that man. A former KGB agent, he knew all about establishing law and order and exerting power by any means necessary.

On August 9, 1999, Vladimir Putin was appointed acting Prime Minister of the Government of Russia by President Yeltsin. Yeltsin also announced that he wanted to see Putin as his successor. A week later, the State Duma approved Putin's appointment as Prime Minister. He was Russia's fifth Prime Minister in fewer than eighteen months and few people expected him to last any longer than his predecessors.

Yeltsin's main opponents and would-be successors were already campaigning to replace the ailing President, and they fought to prevent Putin's emergence as a potential successor. But Putin's law-and-order image and his unrelenting support for the second war against Chechen rebels combined to raise Putin's popularity and allowed him to win the election.

In December 1999, Yeltsin resigned his presidency due to poor health and, according to the Constitution of Russia, Putin became Acting President of Russia (The Russian Federation). While his opponents had been preparing for an election in June 2000, Yeltsin's resignation resulted in the Presidential elections being held early. In March 2000, Putin won the Presidency with fifty-three percent of the vote.

Between 2000 and 2004, Putin worked to restore the Russian economy. He won the power-struggle with the Russian oligarchs by striking what some called a "grand bargain" that allowed the oligarchs to keep their wealth in exchange for their explicit support of Putin's government.

In 2003, a referendum was held in Chechnya that adopted a new constitution, which declared that the Republic of Chechnya was part of Russia. On the other hand, the region itself acquired autonomy. Chechnya has since been gradually stabilized with the establishment of Parliamentary elections and a Regional Government.

It was also in 2003, that Putin arrested Mikhail Khodorkovsky, Russia's richest man, on charges of fraud and tax evasion. At the time, Khodorkovsky was the wealthiest man in Russia with a fortune estimated to be worth fifteen billion dollars. He was ranked sixteenth on *Forbes* list of billionaires.[391] He had worked his way up the All-Union Leninist Young Communist League (Komsomol) during the Soviet years, and started several businesses during the period of *glasnost* and *perestroika* in the late 1980s. After the dissolution of the Soviet Union, he obtained control of a series of Siberian oil fields, which he unified under the name Yukos, one of the major companies to emerge from the rigged privatization of state assets during the 1990s.

The capitalist press wrote that Putin's charges against Khodorkovsky were in retaliation for Khodorkovsky's donations to both liberal and communist opponents of Putin. Putin's government argued, however, that Khodorkovsky was "corrupting" a large segment of the Duma by trying to prevent changes to the tax code that favored the new oligarchs at the expense of the Russian people. In any case, Khodorkovsky was arrested and his company, *Yukos*, was bankrupted and its assets were auctioned at below-market value, with the largest share acquired by the state oil company *Rosneft*. At the time, Yukos had become one of the biggest and most successful Russian companies, producing twenty percent of Russia's oil output, as much as Libya or Iraq. The capitalist media interpreted the fate of Yukos as a sign that Russia was shifting back to a system of state capitalism. Ten years later, in 2014, the Permanent Arbitration Court in The Hague awarded fifty billion dollars in compensation to Yukos shareholders.[392]

In 2004, Putin was elected to the presidency for a second term, receiving seventy-one percent of the vote. The next year, he launched the National Priority Projects in which he increased funding to Russia's health care, education, housing, and agriculture sectors.

By 2007, however, many Russian people, who had enjoyed the taste of political and economic freedom and who wanted more of it, were becoming tired of Putin's autocratic rule. A series of "Dissenters' Marches" were organized by an umbrella group composed of left and right-wing opponents to Putin's party prior to the 2008 elections. The demonstrations brought tens of thousands of people to the streets. While the demonstrations were legal, they were met with police resistance.

In September 2007, Putin, fearing a popular uprising, dissolved the government upon the "request" of his Prime Minister Mikhail Fradkov. Fradkov told the press that it was necessary to give the President a "free hand" in the run-up to the parliamentary election.

In December 2007, *United Russia*, Putin's party, won 64.24% of the popular vote in their run for State Duma. This was seen by many as an indication of strong popular support of the Putin government. Others saw it as vote fraud.

Because of constitutionally mandated term limits, Putin was ineligible to run for a third consecutive presidential term in 2008. Instead, Dmitry Medvedev won the 2008 presidential election and then appointed Putin as his Prime Minister. In September 2011, after presidential terms were extended from four to six years, Putin announced he would seek a third term as president.

In the months leading up to the presidential election in 2012, tens of thousands of Russians engaged in protests against what they said were the electoral fraud practices of the ruling party during the interim elections. Protesters criticized Putin and United Russia and demanded an annulment of the election results. The protests sparked a fear in the ruling elite that the Russian people were engaged in a strategy of non-violent revolution such as had been successfully carried out against dictators in other countries. In retaliation, Putin allegedly organized a number of paramilitary groups loyal to himself and to the United Russia party to break up any protests. On March 4, 2012, Putin won the 2012 Russian presidential elections with 63.6% of the vote amidst widespread accusations of vote rigging. Anti-Putin protests took place during and directly after the presidential campaign. The most notorious protest was the Pussy Riot on February 21 inspired by a women's rock band, which voiced support for women's and LGBT rights and against the anti-authoritarian regimes of the Putin administration and the Russian

Orthodox Church. Two of the group's leaders were arrested and sent to prison on the charge of "hooliganism."

This protest was followed by another large protest in which twenty thousand people gathered in Moscow on May 6th. Eighty people were injured in confrontations with police, and four hundred and fifty were arrested, with another one hundred and twenty arrests taking place the following day. A counter-protest of so-called Putin supporters numbering around one hundred and thirty thousand people was held at Russia's largest stadium. Afterwards, some of the attendees stated that they had been paid to come, were forced to come by their employers, or were misled into believing that they were going to attend a folk festival instead. The event took the steam out of the liberal movement.

Putin continues to have an adversarial relationship with many of the Russian people. Certainly, some of his actions are justified in his attempt to keep the capitalists from ravaging Russian resources as is their wont. But there is also evidence of dictatorial rule, government corruption, including amassing of his own personal wealth, and a lack of concern for the people's rights and general welfare. It is unlikely that we can look to Putin's Russia for leadership in addressing our worldwide human problems.

The End of the US Cold War Containment Strategy

When the Soviet Union fell, the Cold War ended. The entire world breathed a deep sigh of relief. The fear of nuclear war subsided and people the world over were in a celebratory mood. One would think that the US military would have breathed easier as well, but it did not. Instead the loss of their ardent Soviet foe merely filled them with dread and confusion. They went through an identity crisis. They thought they might now be perceived as inconsequential in determining the course of American history. For the gigantic weapons industry, the end of the Cold War meant that billions of dollars would no longer flow into their coffers. Who would buy their weapons now?

The Berlin Wall was the last symbol of the Cold War and when the German people destroyed it in 1989, the grand strategy of Soviet containment also came tumbling down. Without an overriding strategy, the US military was set adrift and remained so through the decade of the 1990s. During this time, military exploits were relegated to stamping out brush fires in small third world countries. They intervened in the Caribbean, Africa, the Balkans, Central Asia, etc., in an effort to force recalcitrant countries to adapt to the dictates of capitalist globalization. Military strategists referred to these incursions as "military operations other than war."[393]

Despite the initial concerns of the US military, their budget has only increased since the end of the Cold War. The rationale for this increase in funding has resulted from the US military strategists and intelligence agencies quickly identifying a rising new "threat" to American globalization. The grand strategy of "containment" that had governed the Cold War was now replaced by the new grand strategy of "preemptive war" against Arab terrorists, which became popularly known as the "War on Terror."

But how is it that Islamic Fundamentalists became our supreme rival without their having any standing armies or nuclear weapons? How did they come to rival the great Soviet Union as our greatest plague? As far back as 1980, President Carter had stated in his State of the Union Address that the United States would use military force, if necessary, to defend its national interests in the Persian Gulf.[394]

Zbigniew Brzezinski, who had groomed Carter to be President on behalf of the Trilateral Commission and who served as President Carter's National Security Adviser, wrote the following part of the *Carter Doctrine*, which was a policy proclaimed by the President in his State of the Union Address on January 23, 1980:

> Let our position be absolutely clear: An attempt by any outside force to gain control of the Persian Gulf region will be regarded as an assault on the vital interests of the United States of America, and such an assault will be repelled by any means necessary, including military force.[395]

Peak Oil

"Our hands are tied in many cases because we need something that others have. We need their oil." Air Force General Chuck Wald[396]

Despite the fact that the "terrorists" were not "outside forces" but indigenous people who lived in the countries in which the US sought to plunder oil, access to this oil was an issue that both Republicans and Democrats could agree upon. The fate of the American empire, with its vast military-industrial complex was completely dependent upon oil for its existence. Without an adequate supply of oil, America, as we know it, would cease to exist. Thus, when industry scientists raised the alarm about "peak oil," panic struck at the heart of the corporate elites and their military-industrial complex.

As far back as 1956, a geophysicist, M. King Hubbert, who was then working at the Shell research lab in Houston, predicted that US oil production would peak in the early 1970s. Although oil experts and economists roundly criticized his projections at the time as "utter nonsense," Hubbert's words came true in 1971.[397]

"Peak oil" is the point in time when the maximum rate of petroleum extraction is reached, after which time, it enters a terminal decline. Peak oil does not mean oil depletion, rather it means the point of maximum production. It also means that all the easy oil and gas in the world has largely been found. What would follow was the much more difficult work of finding and producing oil and gas from more challenging environments and work areas.

While there has been little to no discussion of peak oil during the last ten years, in large part due to the discovery of the toxic gas extraction method called "fracking," this problem has not gone away. In 2013, a study of seven hundred and thirty-three giant oil fields revealed that only thirty-two percent of the ultimately recoverable oil, condensate, and gas remained.[398]

Ghawar, which is the largest oil field in the world and responsible for approximately half of Saudi Arabia's oil production over the last fifty years, was in decline before 2009.[399] The world's second largest oil field, the Burgan Field in Kuwait, entered decline in November 2005.[400]

For people like the Trilateralists, who, needless to say, think in terms of the big picture, peak oil meant that the planetary expansion of western civilization itself would grind to a halt and thereafter begin to decline. Everything would be downhill from there. Oil was so essential to modern society that peak oil would impact food production, housing, medicine, energy, consumer goods, transportation, culture, in fact, the very economic stability of the country and the industrialized world. In short, the need to control the remaining oil supply became the reason for war throughout the Middle East. Given the capitalist mode of production and the elites' refusal to diversify into alternative energy sources, without access to oil, global famine will be inevitable, leading to global chaos and the destruction of the US empire.

Hubbert had also predicted that world oil production would peak at a rate of 12.5 billion barrels per year, around the year 2000. This prediction proved incorrect, but now industry leaders and analysts believe that world oil production will peak between 2015 and 2030. Natural gas from fracking and a stagnant economy may push these estimates back, perhaps a decade, but the handwriting is still on the wall.

The panic over peak oil was exacerbated by the struggle for oil in the Caspian Sea. Five countries border this inland body of water including Russia, Kazakhstan, Turkmenistan, Azerbaijan, and Iran. Oil exploited by Azerbaijan and Turkmenistan was being shipped via the strategic Southern Corridor route to Europe as a way to counter Russia's energy grip on the continent. But opposition from Russia hindered such moves by objecting to projects like the Trans-Caspian natural gas pipeline. This created increased political tension in the region, with the Caspian Sea serving as an important area of competition between Russia and the West. The standoff between Russia and the Ukraine only increased the importance of the Caspian Sea in this regard.[401]

To guide the American elite's response to peak oil, Zbigniew Brzezinski, the Director of the Trilateral Commission and counsel to every American president since Jimmy Carter, wrote a book in 1997 entitled *The Grand Chessboard: American Primacy and its Geostrategic Imperatives*.[402] The Grand Chessboard has been accused of being a blueprint for world dictatorship. It is, in fact, the playbook of the capitalist class to achieve total economic dominance over the planet. The premise for the Grand Chessboard strategy is that since the Soviet Union collapsed, America is now the supreme power in the world, and America needs to control the remaining oil reserves.

In his book, Brzezinski laid out a plan for seizing control of the Middle East, including the oil rich area around the Caspian Sea. The book begins with a history of the issues faced by great empires of the past and the reason why America deserves to be the supreme world empire today. It argues that America should begin to act like a world empire and expand its global hegemony by controlling the oil of the Middle East and the lands to the north that surrounded the Caspian Sea, as well as land eastward into India. This was the landmass that Brzezinski identified as "Eurasia."

Brzezinski argued that, "Ever since the continents started interacting politically, some five hundred years ago, Eurasia has been the center of world power," thus it was imperative that America, like empires that preceded it, develop an "integrated Eurasian geo-strategy."[403]

About seventy-five percent of the world's people live in Eurasia and the land accounts for about three quarters of the world's known energy resources (oil and gas). Any power that dominated Eurasia would control two of the world's three most advanced and economically productive regions. Control over Eurasia would also imply Africa's subordination, rendering the Western Hemisphere and Australia geopolitically peripheral to the world's central continent.

According to Brzezinski, "The momentum of Asia's economic development is already generating massive pressures for the exploration and exploitation of new sources of energy and the Central Asian region and the Caspian Sea basin are known to contain reserves of natural gas and oil that dwarf those of Kuwait, the Gulf of Mexico, or the North Sea."[404]

As Brzezinski exulted over the idea of America being the first global empire the world has ever known, he also cautioned that there would be repercussions: "In the long run, global politics were bound to become increasingly uncongenial to the concentration of hegemonic power in the hands of a single state." Hence, it was important to act decisively and quickly. Brzezinski laid down the two basic steps required to control Eurasia:

> First, to identify the geo-strategically dynamic Eurasian states that have the power to cause a potentially import-

ant shift in the international distribution of power and to decipher the central external goals of their respective political elites and the likely consequences of their seeking to attain them; and to pinpoint the geopolitically critical Eurasian states whose location and/or existence have catalytic effects either on the more active geostrategic players or on regional conditions.

Second, to formulate specific U.S. policies to offset, co-opt, and/or control the above, so as to preserve and promote vital U.S. interests, and to conceptualize a more comprehensive geo-strategy that establishes on a global scale the interconnection between the more specific U.S. policies.[405]

In other words, given the fall of the Soviet Union and the grim reality of "peak oil," the US needed a new grand strategy to control the world's oil and gas. The key to this strategy was the control of Eurasia.

There was a problem, however, that Brzezinski said needed to be addressed in order to fulfill the Trilateralist dream of global conquest. The problem was the mindset of the American people. Brzezinski lamented that:

It is also a fact that America is too democratic at home to be autocratic abroad. This limits the use of America's power, especially its capacity for military intimidation. Never before has a populist democracy attained international supremacy. But the pursuit of power is not a goal that commands popular passion, except in conditions of a sudden threat or challenge to the public's sense of domestic well-being. The economic self-denial (that is, defense spending) and the human sacrifice (casualties even among professional soldiers) required in the effort are uncongenial to democratic instincts. Democracy is inimical to imperial mobilization.[406]

But Brzezinski had a solution to this dilemma. He knew how to get the American public to buy into the need for an all-out war that the creation of a single global empire would require. His specific words were:

> Moreover, as America becomes an increasingly multi-cultural society, it may find it more difficult to fashion a consensus on foreign policy issues, except in the circumstances of a truly massive and widely perceived direct threat.[407]

Simply put, if the elites wanted to realize their dreams of world dominance, they would have to create a "truly massive and widely perceived direct threat." The planning to create such a direct threat began under the Clinton administration and would result in the destruction of the World Trade Center in New York City on Sept. 11, 2001, under the administration of George W. Bush.

Enter the Neo-Cons

Brzezinski's *The Grand Chessboard* was published in 1997 as a means to guide the strategy of the neo-liberal Trilateralists. In that same year, the neo-conservatives founded an organization called the *Project for the New American Century* whose goal was also to promote an American empire that would dominate the world. They too wanted to engineer a global empire, but they were especially focused on controlling the known global oil reserves and in the process to become filthy rich.

As soon as their offices were set up, the Neo-Cons immediately began writing their blueprint for making this happen. Their report is called "Rebuilding America's Defenses: Strategy, Forces and Resources for a New Century."[408] The report, building on Brzezinski's concept of global empire, became the grand strategic plan of the George W. Bush administration. In essence, it is an aggressive military plan in support of US economic globalization for thetwenty-first century.

The report was initially drawn up at the request of Dick Cheney (Bush's vice-president), Donald Rumsfeld (senior Trilateralist and defense secretary), and Paul Wolfowitz (Rumsfeld's deputy). The strategic plan outlined how Bush's future cabinet intended to take military control of the Gulf region. Their global vision was not as expansive as Brzezinski's, but it focused more intently on controlling the mother lode of the world's known oil and gas reserves in the Middle East. The report states:

> The United States has for decades sought to play a more permanent role in Gulf regional security. While the unresolved conflict with Iraq provides the immediate justification, the need for a substantial American force presence in the Gulf transcends the issue of the regime of Saddam Hussein.[409]

According to the Neo-Cons, the attack on Saddam Hussein's Iraq would only be the first step by which America would take control of the Middle East's oil. They contended that their "American grand strategy" must be advanced "as far into the future as possible." It called for the US to "fight and decisively win multiple, simultaneous major theatre wars" as a "core mission."

Fast-forward to American troops being mired in wars in Afghanistan, Iraq, Libya, Kuwait, Syria, and Yemen.

The report describes the American armed forces destined to be sent abroad as "the cavalry on the new American frontier." While the neo-cons expected blowback from other countries in reaction to being dominated by the US, the Neo-Con solution was simply that the US must "discourage advanced industrial nations from challenging our leadership or even aspiring to a larger regional or global role." This threat was specifically directed at Russia.

And so, it has come to pass. The assault on Iraq and the destabilization of the Middle East had nothing to do with "spreading democracy around the world" as the American people are repeatedly told by the mass media. This was simply a strategic lie to gain our support for their plan. In reality, the wars in Kuwait, Libya, Afghanistan, Iraq, Syria, and Yemen were just part of the human sacrifice required in service to the welfare and profit of the elite.

In the 2000 presidential election, Dick Cheney and the Neo-Cons came to power. To put their plan into effect, they needed a trigger, what Brzezinski called a "truly massive and widely perceived direct threat." to set the stage for the implementation of global war. At this point, they were benefitted by the plan that was already being developed under the Clinton administration by the Trilateralists. As Brzezinski had pointed out, the American people had always been against war. Most of us do not aspire for empire, and prefer to get along with other people. The only reason that the American people got involved in WWII was the shock effect of the Japanese attack on Pearl Harbor. According to the plan of the elites, they needed another shock attack to launch the global war. That event was the bombing of the World Trade Center that occurred on September 11, 2001 and the mass murder of three thousand Americans.

Just prior to the presidential election in 2000, as mentioned above, the elites were beginning to understand that peak oil was even worse than anticipated. The CIA had reported decades ago that oil production peaked in the US during the 1970s and that peak oil hit Russia in 1977.[410] Highly confidential drilling reports from the Caspian Sea conducted by companies like ExxonMobil, where Bush's Secretary of State, Condoleeza Rice, was a member of the board, concluded that its oil reserves were much smaller than expected. Upon hearing this news, the elites began to panic. Large investors and companies began to bail out of the stock market. Between 2000 and 2002, $7.7 trillion dollars were removed from the market.[411]

It was under such conditions that the plan for the "direct threat" was put into play. The first step was to determine how much time the elites had before the economy collapsed due to high oil prices and dwindling supply. How much oil was actually there? Where was it? And who owned it? To answer these questions, Dick Cheney convened the *National Energy Policy Development Group*.[412]

The group's officially stated objective was to "develop a national energy policy designed to help the private sector, and, as necessary and appropriate, State and local governments, promote dependable, affordable, and environmentally sound production and distribution of energy for the future."[413] In actuality, the secret task force was a confab of Neo-Cons and senior executives of the major US oil corporations brought together for the purpose of developing a grand strategy to confiscate the oil of Iraq and then the Middle East. It would provide the Bush administration with specific information of the amounts and location of the major oil reserves in Iraq and other Middle East countries.

The Task Force was composed of Vice President Dick Cheney and the Secretaries of State, Treasury, Interior, Agriculture, Commerce, Transportation, and Energy, as well as other cabinet and senior administration-level officials. According to the Government Accountability Office, these members held ten meetings over the course of three and a half months with petroleum, coal, nuclear, natural gas, and electricity industry representatives and lobbyists. None of the meetings were open to the public. On May 16, 2001, four months before 9/11, the Cheney Group released its final report.

The activities of the Energy Task Force were never disclosed to the public, even though Freedom of Information Act (FOIA) requests (since 19 April 2001) had sought to gain access to its materials. Organizations like Judicial Watch and Sierra Club even launched a lawsuit to gain access to the task force's materials. After several years of legal wrangling, in May 2005 an appeals court permitted the Energy Task Force's records to remain secret.

Two years later, on July 18, 2007, *The Washington Post* reported that the Bush/Cheney administration finally met with environmental organizations and told them the names of those involved in the Task Force. Among the private sector attendees were James J. Rouse, then vice president of Exxon Mobil and a major donor to the Bush inauguration; Kenneth L. Lay, then head of Enron Corp.; Jack N. Gerard, then with the National Mining Association; Red Cavaney, president of the American Petroleum Institute; and Eli Bebout, an old friend of Cheney's from Wyoming, who served in the state Senate and owned an oil and drilling company.[414]

Having garnered the participation and collusion of the main energy producers, the next step was to focus on the needed catastrophic event as proposed by Brzezinski and the neo-con strategists that would win over the American people for the all-out war to control the world's remaining energy resources and achieve global military dominance. As an expert on 9/11 put it, such an event would "provide a pretext for massive sequential military intervention to secure the energy supplies of the Middle East and the lesser (but terribly important) oil-bearing regions including West Africa, Venezuela, Columbia, certain portions of the Southwest Pacific, and any other region with smaller but more readily accessible reserves. The essential thing would be that terrorists or their "allies" must conveniently turn up in each needed area, on schedule."[415]

Domestic Policy: Eavesdropping and the Militarization of Local Law Enforcement

Before we launch into the complexity of the effort to control "Eurasia," let us briefly look at the Trilateralist/Neo-Con's grand strategy as it applied to the American people. Ever since the "democratic distemper" of the 1960s and 1970s, the Trilateralists had been on-guard to prevent the American people's love of democracy from interfering with theTrilateralist plans for world domination. They also worried that their destruction of the American economy in order to take advantage of cheap labor in China and India would cause a backlash. Ever since, the *Crisis of Democracy* exposed this "internal threat" to the American elites, they had been developing plans to deal with domestic unrest should it occur. Both the Bush and the Obama administrations implemented these plans through Executive Orders.

The mainstream media had always painted Barack Obama as a progressive politician, a man of stature similar to the likes of Franklin Roosevelt or John Kennedy. And there was some truth to this portrayal. Obama has certainly spoken out against sexism, racism, ultra-nationalism, and the denial of climate change in this country. He had also, to his credit, taken steps to stop climate change. But at the same time, Obama, in response to the capitalist elite, also set in place new domestic orders to curb civil unrest. These laws were put in place as a result of Executive Orders 13688 and 13603 and the National Defense Authorization, and Patriots Acts.

Secure Communities

Homeland Security established the "Secure Communities" program in 2008, under the Bush administration to share fingerprinting across state and local boundaries on people for "deportation" purposes. This deportation program created a partnership between federal, state, and local law enforcement agencies, the US Immigration and Customs Enforcement agency (ICE), and the Department of Homeland Security (DHS) which acts as the program manager.

The goals of the program are to "identify criminal aliens; prioritize enforcement actions to ensure apprehension and removal of dangerous criminal aliens; and transform criminal alien enforcement processes and systems to achieve lasting results."[416]

The program was created by law under the Bush administration, but it was greatly expanded under the Obama administration in 2009. Under the administration of George W. Bush, ICE recruited a total of fourteen law enforcement jurisdictions. By March 2011, under President Barack Obama, the program was expanded to over twelve hundred and ten participating jurisdictions.[417]

The program has been challenged, however, for lack of clarity as to the definition of who exactly is "a dangerous criminal alien" and what exactly is expected of law enforcement partners in dealing with such people. Without such clarity, the program can be used to cast a wide net over the American people and punish someone for crimes they did not know that they had even committed. Although we are programmed to think that our government would never use this type of orders against the American people, the NSA's use of eavesdropping has defied that belief.

According to the first independent, empirical analysis of the program, using five years of data obtained through the Freedom of Information Act, the program's effect on crime has been zero. The report's conclusion stated, "Secure Communities led to no meaningful reductions in the FBI index crime rate. Nor has it reduced rates of violent crime—homicide, rape, robbery, or aggravated assault." The program, in other words, "has not served its central objective of making communities safer."[418]

Instead, this program permitted mass immigration checks and has turned every local cop and sheriff's deputy into an immigration agent. As we have seen, under the Trump administration, this has harmed the security of noncitizens, who are members of the community, but also any minorities. It threatens the safety of neighborhoods where residents fear the police, knowing that any brush with the law can ruin a life and destroy a family.[419] Sheriff Joe Arpaio's torturous tent city in Maricopa County in Arizona has provided an extreme example of the misuse of this program.

In fiscal year 2016, under Obama, ICE removed 240,255 people from the US, a rate of more than 20,000 people per month. In Trump's first year, he has only deported an average of 16,900 people per month. Trump however has arrested more Latino and Mexican immigrants than Obama by a rate of thirty-eight percnt. Presently, there is a backlog of more than 610,000 cases in the immigration courts according to the Transactional Records Access Clearinghouse at Syracuse University.[420]

Under the Trump administration, the Secure Communities program has been utilized to criminalize hundreds of thousands of Mexican and Latino residents in the US. The criminalization of the immigrant population has coincided with the rise of hate crimes on the part of white racists in the country. It has also caused political paralysis.

Conservatives want to deport undocumented immigrants and build a wall to keep them out. Progressives, on the other hand, want to see a program that would allow the undocumented population to come forward and become legalized and less vulnerable to being criminalized. Progressives would also like to keep issues concerning immigration out of the hands of local police. This would allow the police to focus on fighting real threats, not illusions. Nonetheless, Secure Communities remains in effect as is.

It is not just immigrants that face risk from the US governments war on terrorism. Blacks and other minorities are also put at risk. Here are the signs of a growing police presence:

- Police are killing more people every year.
- Unlawful harassment is becoming the norm.
- Even children are seen as potential criminals.
- Stop and search actions are becoming more common and more invasive.
- New York City's "Stop and Frisk" program is racial profiling.
- Non-criminals are beings arrested for ridiculous things.[421]
- You can now face jail time for not paying your rent.[422]
- The NSA is monitoring every cell phone call and email of every US citizen and storing this data.

- More people are being sentenced to life in prison without parole for nonviolent offenses.[423]
- Police officers don't face the same punishments as civilians.
- America's incarceration rate is the highest in the world.
- Peaceful protesters are being met with violence.
- The government is discrediting and hunting down whistle blowers.
- The FBI can legally monitor your behavior for no reason at all.[424]
- Prisons are being privatized and profits are being made from incarcerations and forced labor.

Americans are paying taxes to support such actions. Policies and technologies that are supposed to protect citizens, are actually more dangerous than the "security threats" that they are designed to stop. Our only option is to understand what is going on and take a stand.

The Militarization of the Domestic Police

A succession of US Supreme Court rulings beginning in the mid-1960s have expanded police power to serve warrants without warning, thereby curtailing the protections against unreasonable search and seizure under the Fourth Amendment.[425]

After the collapse of the World Trade Center in 2001, federal and state governments began to spend seventy-five billion dollars to fight "domestic terrorists." An entirely new market opened up for the military-industrial complex to sell an array of military weapons and products to police departments across the country, including high-tech motion sensors and fully outfitted emergency operations trailers. The market for such products approached thirty-one billion dollars by 2014.

Like the military-industrial complex that became a permanent fixture in the American landscape during the Cold War, the vast network of Homeland Security spyware, concrete barricades, SWAT teams, and high-tech identity screening is now part of the domestic landscape.

The Department of Homeland Security is a collection of agencies ranging from border control to airport security that was sewn together after September 11. It is now the third-largest Cabinet department. Given that no lawmaker is willing to render the US less prepared for a terrorist attack, Homeland Security can depend upon an ample budget into the foreseeable future.[426]

As we have seen in our look at the Secure Communities program, the reason for this militarization of the police is not really about domestic terrorists because our chance of being killed by an immigrant terrorist in America is 3,600,000,000 to 1.[427] The truth of the matter is that terrorists have never been a threat great enough to spend one hundred billion dollars a year. Rather, the perceived threat to the ruling elites is potential civil unrest against their authoritarian policies.

The process of militarization of the police began in earnest after 9/11. The Patriot Act gave law enforcement officers permission to search a home or business without the owner's or the occupant's consent or knowledge, amongst other provisions, if "terrorist activities" were suspected.[428] Obama's Executive Order 13688 permitted the following weapons to be used by police in domestic situations:

- Manned Aircraft, Fixed Wing;
- Manned Aircraft, Rotary Wing;
- Unmanned Aerial Vehicles;
- Armored Vehicles, Wheeled;
- Tactical Vehicles, Wheeled;
- Command and Control Vehicles;
- Specialized Firearms and Ammunition Under .50 Caliber ;
- Breaching Apparatus (a battering ram), ballistic (slugs), or explosive;
- Riot Batons;
- Riot Helmets; and
- Riot Shields

The only military equipment currently prohibited to police is: Tanks, Weaponized Vehicles of Any Kind, Firearms of .50 Caliber or Higher, Ammunition of .50 Caliber or Higher, and Grenade Launchers.[429]

In a 2007 paper on "The Blurring Distinctions Between the Police and Military Institutions and Between War and Law Enforcement," criminal justice professor Peter Kraska defined "police militarization" as "the process whereby civilian police increasingly draw from, and pattern themselves around, the tenets of militarism and the military model."[430]

In June 2014, the American Civil Liberties Union published a report entitled "War Comes Home: The Excessive Militarization of American Policing." Its central point is that "the United States today has become excessively militarized, mainly through federal programs that create incentives for state and local police to use unnecessarily aggressive weapons and tactics designed for the battlefield."[431]

By 2007, more than eighty percent of police departments in towns having a population between twenty-five and fifty thousand had SWAT teams. As the number of teams expanded, the number of SWAT raids has likewise jumped. In 1981, SWAT teams made three thousand "no-knock" raids. By 2005, the number had jumped to fifty thousand.[432] A "no-knock" raid means that police can force entry without announcing themselves.

SWAT teams, a concept created and implemented by former Los Angeles Police Department Chief, Daryl Gates, were originally intended to face violent civil unrest and barricaded gunmen. Now police departments are using them more often than not for nonviolent offenders, and in some circumstances, routine enforcement.

The Dallas SWAT team was even used to break up poker games. In Maricopa County, Arizona, a SWAT team employed a tank in a raid to investigate an allegation of illegal cockfighting. SWAT commandos were deployed to a New Haven, Connecticut bar in 2010 suspected of serving underage drinkers. In 2010, they raided Orlando barbershops looking for guns and drugs, but in the end their only charge was "barbering without a license."[433]

When the militarization of local police departments is enhanced by police racism, people are being killed for just being racial minorities. As the nation witnessed in Ferguson, MO, militarized racism degrades the police force by subjecting targeted communities to brutality and unaccountable abuse. As the ACLU report summarized: "excessive militarism in policing, particularly through the use of paramilitary policing teams, escalates the risk of violence, threatens individual liberties, and unfairly impacts people of color."[434] Police militarization also poses grave and direct dangers to basic civil liberties, including rights of free speech, press, and assembly.

A reporter described his coverage of the police presence in St. Paul during the 2008 GOP convention. He said, "It was the most militarized I have ever seen an American city be, even more so than Manhattan in the week of 9/11—with troops of federal, state and local law enforcement agents marching around with riot gear, machine guns, and tear gas canisters, shouting military chants and marching in military formations. Humvees and law enforcement officers with rifles were posted on various buildings and balconies. Numerous protesters and observers were tear-gassed and injured."[435]

Look what happened with the Occupy Wall Street protests in 2011. The police response was so excessive, and so clearly modeled after battlefield tactics, that there was no doubt that domestic dissent has become one of the primary aims of police militarization.

Police militarization is increasingly aimed at stifling journalism as well. When the police rough up and arrest journalists, it creates an environment where police think they can disregard the law. They tell reporters to stop filming, despite their legal right to do so, or they fire tear gas directly at them to prevent them from doing their job. And if the rights of journalists are being trampled on, you can almost guarantee it is even worse for those who do not have a voice.

The government and police know that protests will become more inevitable given the economic tumult and suffering the US has seen over the last decade and will continue to see into the foreseeable future. Their response has always been to use overwhelming physical force. This tactic, when used on the American people, results in an increase of suspicion and violence against the police themselves and puts them in danger as well. Witness the killing of five police officers by a sniper in Dallas in July 2016.[436]

The police are intentionally being alienated from the people by the steady drumbeat of the war on terrorism and the Homeland Security's seventy-five billion dollar slush fund that allows local cops access to military weapons and equipment. The American people are becoming the enemies in the eyes of the police. And it does not require much investigation to prove that people of color are their first targets.

Police militarization is overwhelmingly and disproportionately directed at minorities and poor communities, but police activity in these neighborhoods is largely kept in the dark. Its only when the people begin to throw rocks at the police that the news media takes notice. If anything positive came from the Ferguson travesty, it is that the excessive process of police militarization had been brought to light.[437] The people of Ferguson are champions that deserve our undying respect for standing up to police violence. Black Lives Matter is a reaction to such violence.

Having said this, we can assume that the majority of police officers are decent human beings dedicated to serving the people in their precincts. Such people deserve our undying respect for the risks that they take on our behalf. Many white officers are caught between racist fellow officers and black communities who hate and mistrust them for being white. The American people should stand with any police officer who questions racism or the militarization of his or her police department. Militarization is not what many officers signed up for. It is unrelated to the police motto—"to serve and protect" our American communities.

The psychology of the police as warriors is to pay more attention to the past than to what is right in front of them. The police, for the most part, do not see that they are being manipulated by the capitalist government. They do not see that the reward they will receive for being "the good guys" by oppressing their neighbors will be nothing but a paycheck. They do not understand that it is better to put their trust in their neighbors who are the nurses, restaurant owners, farmers, park custodians, local ministers, soup kitchen workers, etc., than to surrender it to the men wearing silk suits, sitting in skyscraper board rooms in New York City.

Do our police officers really think they will fare any better than the Iraq War veterans fared? Do they know that more Iraq veterans committed suicide last year than active-duty troops who died in combat.[438] Do they know that the capitalists did not care about them when they came back home with war injuries? Do they remember that the Veterans

Administration had a backlog of six hundred thousand applications for treatment from veterans and that the VA destroyed thousands of medical records of soldiers so as not to take responsibility for them? Do the police officers remember that the whistleblowers who brought this information to light suffered harassment and retaliation from their superiors for their concern about American soldiers.[439] Do our police officers remember how our government dumped the body parts of soldiers in landfills to get rid of them and did not notify the soldiers' families?[440] Do they know that over forty thousand veterans are homeless in America? Do the police think that they will fare much better in their service to the capitalist government? We will need police on the side of the people during the hard times ahead.

A report issued in June, 2014 by the office of Senator Tom Coburn stated that more than 1,000 veterans may have died in the last decade because of malpractice or lack of care from Department of Veterans Affairs medical centers.[441] A total of 4,424 US service members were killed in Iraq between 2003 and 2016.[442] This means that during the same time period, VA hospitals in America killed twenty-three percent as many American soldiers as were killed in battle.

According to P. R. Sarkar's theory of the Social Cycle, which we discuss in Book II on Ideology, the capitalist age will, in turn, give way to another warrior age.[443] The transformation of the domestic police force into military units is a clear sign of how this transformation will occur within the United States. The question for the warriors, who are directly employed by the capitalists, is "whose side will you be on when all hell breaks loose. Will you side with the people or with those who own the system?" As we move down the road, the warriors will have some deep soul-searching to do.

The Patriot Act

Before he was elected president, Obama expressed concern regarding the provisions of the Patriot Act. He expressed worry that it would "allow government fishing expeditions targeting innocent Americans.

We believe the government should be required to convince a judge that the records they are seeking have some connection to a suspected terrorist or spy." 444 However, just minutes before a midnight deadline, President Barack Obama signed into law a four-year extension of Patriot Act measures that allowed the government to spy on any individual on American soil.

While much of the Patriot Act remains permanent law, certain provisions must be renewed periodically because of concerns that they could be used to violate privacy rights. Men of conscience on the left and the right have criticized the Patriot Act for trampling on individual liberties. Ron Paul a Libertarian tried to stall the legislation asking whether the nation "should have some rules that say before they come into your house, before they go into your banking records, that a judge should be asked for permission, that there should be judicial review? Do we want a lawless land?"

Senator Dick Durbin (D-Ill) said he "soon realized it [the Patriot Act] gave too much power to government without enough judicial and congressional oversight."445 Laura Murphy, director of the ACLU Washington legislative office said that, "The Patriot Act has been used improperly again and again by the National Security Administration (NSA) to invade Americans' privacy and violate their constitutional rights."

Those in power are telling the American people that we simply need to trust them to do the right thing and stop asking questions. The American people took the government at its word until Edward Snowden revealed the truth to us. Yet he was hunted down like a dangerous criminal for his heroic efforts on behalf of American freedom.

National Defense Authorization Act (NDAA)

The NDAA is a national security act that was supposed to close Gitmo the infamous US prison that held Iraqi suspects who were imprisoned and tortured without any public scrutiny. The imprisoned men had absolutely no rights. In his campaign speeches Obama promised to close Gitmo. When he became president, he did not.

Obama also left a provision in the NDAA that he first signed into law in 2012 that permits the military to detain American individuals indefinitely without trial.[446] Efforts to squash the provision failed having been fiercely defended by his administration. Chris Hedges, Noam Chomsky, and Daniel Ellsberg filed a lawsuit against this provision, but were "aggressively fought at every turn by the president's attorneys."[447]

Even Senator Ted Cruz voted against the NDAA saying, "Although this legislation does contain several positive provisions that I support, it does not ensure our most basic rights as American citizens are protected."[448]

Top legal experts point out that the NDAA also gives the government the right to assassinate American citizens on US soil without any charges, trial, or other constitutional protection.

Regarding torturing of Americans, however, the government can do that, but they must send American citizens to other countries to be tortured. The government still cannot legally torture Americans on US soil.[449]

Under NDAA 2014 Sec. 1061(g)(1), an overly vague definition of "captured records" gives the government power and guarantees its right to conduct indefinite surveillance on any American citizen. Naomi Klein, a well-known author, social critic, and political activist speaks to the irony of Congress signing this law into practice because, in doing so, they have relinquished their control over the military and subjected themselves to the same surveillance that they consigned to the American people.[450]

Finally, the 2014 NDAA also includes a new provision under Section 1071(a) that authorizes the Defense Department to "establish a 'Conflict Records Research Center' to facilitate research and analysis of records captured from countries, organizations, and individuals, now or once hostile to the United States." If someone sees you protesting the Government's violation of your rights, this is where the government will keep a record on you.

Executive Order 13603

When presidents have an agenda item that they do not want to bring to light through congressional debate, they create an Executive Order.

Executive Order 13603, signed by Obama, concerns "National Defense Resources Preparedness."

Even *Forbes Magazine*, which prides itself on being "The Capitalist Tool" and has a penchant for publishing articles that support the ruling elite as unbiased reporting, had trouble with this one. It states: "This 10-page document is a blueprint for a federal takeover of the economy that would dwarf the looming Obamacare takeover of the health insurance business. Specifically, Obama's plan involves seizing control of:

- All commodities and products that are capable of being ingested by either human beings or animals" (food);
- All forms of energy;
- All forms of civil transportation;
- All usable water from all sources; and
- All health resources—drugs, biological products, medical devices, materials, facilities, health supplies, services, and equipment."[451]

Forced labor (or "induction" as the executive order delicately refers to military conscription) would also be required of prisoners.

Moreover, federal officials would "issue regulations to prioritize and allocate resources." In this process, each government bureaucracy "shall act as necessary and appropriate."

While acknowledging that similar language had appeared in national security executive orders before, the *Forbes* journalist complained that:

> Obama's 13603 seems to describe a potentially totalitarian regime obsessed with control over everything. Obama's executive order makes no effort to justify the destruction of liberty, no effort to explain how amassing totalitarian control would enable government to deal effectively with cyber sabotage, suicide bombings, chemical warfare, nuclear missiles or other possible threats. It's quite likely there would be greater difficulty

responding to threats, since totalitarian regimes suffer from economic chaos, colossal waste, massive corruption and bureaucratic infighting that are inevitable consequences of extreme centralization. Such problems plagued fascist Italy, Nazi Germany, the Soviet Union, communist China and other regimes. Totalitarian control would probably trigger resistance movements and underground networks like those that developed in Western Europe during the Nazi occupation. Totalitarian control could provoke more political turmoil than there was in the Vietnam War era of the 1960s. There would probably be a serious brain drain as talented people with critical skills escaped to freedom wherever that might be. Canada? There's nothing in executive order 13603 about upholding the Constitution or protecting civil liberties.[452]

Despite the outcry, Obama's emergency plan is now national law and ready-to-go, waiting the right moment for its implementation.

The majority of the presidents, senators, and representatives at the federal level are millionaires who want to protect what they have. Both the Republicans and Democrats were willing to pass these laws. At the same time, the American people, whether they vote for the Democrats or Republicans, whether they consider themselves liberals or conservatives, are all becoming alarmed by big government. What the people do not understand yet is that the ruling class is not a conspiracy, it is a political economic class; it is the ruling class and they are willing to do anything to protect their plans of dominance no matter who it negatively impacts. They have exploited the people of the world. They are not patriots. They are doing the same to Americans as to anybody else in this world. The Occupy protesters had correctly identified the enemy, the 1%.

We the people are victims of a divide and conquer strategy that causes us to despise each other for being conservatives or liberals. The ruling elite fans the flames of our conflict and thereby remains hidden from view. Nonetheless we are all beginning to see the truth. The capitalist government as an institution has lost its credibility as a representative of our interests. It is no longer an institution of the people, by the people, and certainly not for the people. Under such conditions, electoral politics at the federal level have become a farce. In the last presidential campaign between Bernie Sanders, Hillary Clinton, and Donald Trump, the options of the American people can be seen. Bernie Sanders appealed to the young and the progressives, but the real battle was between the established order represented by Hillary Clinton and the ultra-nationalist, racist rebellion of the suffering American white people represented by President Trump. Most Americans did not like either of these candidates, but they had no choice in the matter.

The 2014 midterm elections were a clear indication of the progressives failed strategy. In an article for *Truthout* entitled "Who Needs Republicans?"[453] William Rivers Pitt summed up Obama's activities immediately following the annihilation of the Democrats at the voting booth:

> The election was a week ago Tuesday. 72 hours after the last ballots were cast, President Obama was on a plane to Asia, bound and determined to reinvigorate the stalled negotiations over the Trans-Pacific Partnership (TPP) "trade" deal. The TPP has been negotiated by nations and corporations largely in secret, though several chapters of the proposed deal have been leaked to the public.
>
> The TPP, according to all available information, actually has very little to do with trade deals. Instead, it provides direct incentives for countries and corporations to send jobs offshore to low-wage nations. It puts a number of controls on open internet access that leaves our current "net neutrality" debate in deep shade, despite the president's recent rhetoric to the contrary. A wide swath of local and federal laws would be required to comply with TPP policies. Perhaps worst of all, the TPP would elevate multinational corporations to the status of sovereign nations, a level of power those corporations have sought for more than a generation.[454]

In addition to Obama's policies increasing the militarization of local police forces, his foreign policy has been no better than that of the Republican administrations that preceded and followed him. They have all kept the fires burning in the "War on Terrorism." Despite Obama's promise about "no boots on the ground," after the midterm elections, the Obama administration announced that fifteen hundred more US troops would be deployed to Iraq as "advisers." The White House also requested and received an additional $1.6 billion for an "Iraq Train and Equip Fund." We had already spent hundreds of billions of dollars on this project to utterly no avail. Nonetheless, the insider weapons contractors and consultants were happy as hogs at the trough.

In 2015, An ISIS leader named Yousef al-Salafi in Pakistan admitted that ISIS was being funded by the Obama administration in the USA as part of the "Iraq Train and Equip Fund." This statement was forwarded to the US government after the Pakistani government had interrogated Yousef. He revealed that he was getting funding, routed through America, to run the organization in Pakistan and recruit young people to fight in Syria. The man confessed that he and an imam ally were getting paid by the US to recruit youths to join ISIS for six hundred dollars per recruit. At the time, the US was also continuing to fund and train jihadists in Syria to overthrow the Assad regime.[455]

The US also refused to back Egypt's attempt to destroy ISIS, and is more comfortable working with Turkey, which is one of the main backers of ISIS. Perhaps this explains why the Obama government had been so slow to respond to the savagery of ISIS despite the negative press the organization has received. President Trump, who was the first president since President Jimmy Carter not to be directly controlling by the Trilateralists, however, was not hesitant in the least to destroy ISIS until he pulled American troops from northern Syria to protect the oil reserves in the south.

Obama had pontificated in his first year in office that: "My administration is committed to creating an unprecedented level of openness in Government. We will work together to ensure the public trust and establish a system of transparency, public participation, and collaboration."[456] Apparently not.

The question is how long will the American people continue to believe that a vote for any president will cause the US government to change its policies? The election of Donald Trump was only the last-ditch effort to "drain the swamp" of sell-out politicians and government bureaucrats. But Trump will not succeed in keeping his promises to the American people. He has already made clear his betrayal of the American people in service to the capitalist elite, of which he himself is a member.

Our lives will not improve. Rather, instead of believing that the Republicans or Democrats will help us, we need to turn off the TV set, get our nose out of our iPhone, and begin to meet our neighbors to build an America of which we all dream. It must be built from the ground up. The role of leadership in this endeavor will fall to the value-oriented conservatives and progressives who, in their quest for a better America and a better world are willing to rally Americans not as Republicans and Democrats, but as local people who are willing to help their neighbors in a crisis. Such people should realize the American people are depending upon them for their vision. At this point, the progressives and the socialists are leading this charge.

While Obama posed as a progressive who spoke for the American people and the environment, and must be supported for this good work, behind the scenes he also enabled the militarization of local police in anticipation of increased civil unrest; a situation the bankers and other capitalist elites have made inevitable by their actions.

Foreign Policy: The War on Terrorism

In his book *The Pentagon's New Map*, military strategist, Thomas P. M. Barnet summarized the key points of the US military's strategy in the Middle East post-WWII. These were: (1) keep the Israelis strong, (2) keep the House of Saud safe, (3) and keep the fundamentalist radicals down.[457] He then ticked off the various incidents in Middle East history that challenged this strategy, namely, (1) the war between Israel and Islam countries and OPECs use of oil as an economic weapon, (2) the fall of the Shah of Iran, (3) the Tehran embassy hostages, (4) the failed Desert One rescue attempt, (5) the bombing of the Marine barracks in Lebanon,

(6) the establishment of the US Central Command in the Middle East, (7) the Iran-Iraq war, (8) Desert Storm, and (9) the "Shock and Awe" preemptive strike on Iraq by George W.'s administration.

Barnett, however, did not attempt to understand the impact of the US strategy on the residents of the Middle East. Rather, according to his simplistic way of thinking, the globalization of American capitalism is good and anyone who does not accept it is bad. We have previously demonstrated how globalization is, in actuality, a process by which the western capitalist bankers and corporations exploit the people and resources of the third world. These are the same countries that Barnett refers to in his book as the "NonIntegrating Gap."

Barnett's approach may be par for the course for an American military nationalist, but it is useless in helping us understanding the problems that face humanity as a whole and how we might actually create solutions for bringing humanity together to face our common problems. Such human problems Barnett never takes into account even though they directly result from the American elite's strategy of global dominance.

All people are human beings and if we are to work together to end war and climate destruction, we must understand each other's issues. To understand the implications of the US War on Terrorism, let us now look at the rise of what the West calls "Muslim Terrorism."

At present, the most dangerous conflict affecting human beings as a whole is the war between the US-based capitalists and the Middle East Islamic fundamentalists. This war, as it continues, involves more countries and is setting the stage for a new war between the people of the US and Russia.

In this conflict, the capitalists are attempting to expand their exploitation in the face of a fundamentalist revolt against Western imperialism, militarism, and ideological oppression.

The Definition of Terror

Under the Bush/Obama/Trump administrations, the new grand strategy of the United States is to paint the enemies of capitalism as "terrorists" and to declare a "War on Terrorism." This war, by definition, will not end until every terrorist or potential terrorist on the planet has been eliminated. Everyone in the world is now considered to be a potential terrorist, even the people of the United States and Europe. In the meantime, the "War on Terrorism" continues to create new terrorists who are outraged by the wanton invasions and preemptive strikes of the US military on their homelands. The US national security strategy has succeeded in making everyone in the country and on the planet feel even less secure and more suspicious of everyone else.

The capitalist mainstream media has us believe that we need our military and intelligence communities to protect our national interests against the latest forces of evil; that is, Islamic fundamentalists. Conversely, the Islamic fundamentalists who are the targets of house to house searches, carpet bombings, ground assaults, and drone strikes, call the United States the "Great Satan" and refer to US actions as "state terrorism." They claim that the US, and indeed western civilization as a whole, is the instigator of terrorist acts against innocent people.

The Greeks and Romans who founded western European civilization fed rebel slaves to the lions. The Catholic Church, when it came to power, devised sadistic torture devices like the rack and the iron maiden to silence its critics. Today, in the defense of the capitalist system, the US army for all its talk of fair play and bringing peace and democracy to the world has murdered millions of people in wars. Is this action humanistic? Mouthing hollow slogans and composing paeans to world peace can never undo the effects of the Post-WWII assault on the people of third world countries, particularly the Middle East.

The United States government will use the "show of force," force of arms, terror, and suppression of freedoms to keep people from challenging the multinational corporations and the local dictators that support them. While freedom of speech in the US is touted as a sacred right of the people, the media itself is controlled by the capitalists. The American rarely hear the story of people being oppressed in their own countries by US corporations. If anyone abroad, in a country controlled by America, dares to speak out for freedom, be they students, minority leaders, political activists, or religious fundamentalists, they can be tortured, imprisoned, or killed. This is a historical fact. Why is this so? In order to exploit labor and resources from other people, the US corporations must be able to control any resistance that may develop. Even so, the risk of resistance remains high because the exploitation of the people has resulted in great suffering for the local people.

The United Nations report on economic development issued in 2014 revealed that more than 2.2 billion people are "either near or living in poverty," More than half of these, survive on the equivalent of $1.25 or less a day, while twelve percent of the world's population (842 million people) suffer from chronic hunger.[458]

These conditions are not due to Islamic Fundamentalists, but to capitalist "state terrorism." The suffering of all these people is not due to a shortage of resources. The world economy produces enough to provide a decent standard of living for every man, woman, and child on the planet. But the distribution of wealth makes this impossible. Today a mere handful of eighty-five capitalists own as much as the 3.5 billion poorest people combined. By this simple arithmetic, it should not come as a surprise that the US war on terror will continue as long as capitalism exists.

What does it mean to be this poor? According to the UN report: Almost 1.5 billion people are "multi-dimensionally poor, with overlapping deprivations in health, education, and living standards."

Income inequality in the developing countries has risen by eleven percent between 1990 and 2010. The steepest decline in living conditions during 2013 occurred in Central African Republic, Libya, and Syria, the three countries targeted by the US and French for military intervention and political subversion.

About forty-five million people in the Middle East were forcibly displaced due to conflict or persecution by the end of 2012, more than fifteen million of them became refugees.

Nearly half of all elderly people, forty-six percent of those aged sixty or older, suffer from one or more physical or intellectual disabilities.

Concerning children, "7 in 100 will not survive beyond 5, 50 will not have their birth registered, 68 will not receive early childhood education, 17 will never enroll in primary school, 30 will be stunted and 25 will live in abject poverty."[459]

In virtually every country, the U.N. found that the ruling elites were slashing public spending and scrapping long-established programs that underpinned the living standards of the masses. Although the words "capitalism" and "imperialism" do not appear in the text of the U.N. document, the development report nonetheless provides ample raw material for the indictment of the profit system.

This is not to say that the savage attacks against women, other Islamic peoples, and ordinary citizens by militant Islamic fundamentalists, in the name of God, is any less execrable as crimes against humanity. The Islamic fundamentalists have reduced women to the point of a sub-human existence. Women are denied the right to an education, employment, freedom of movement, a fair trial, etc. Women are beaten and executed in public displays to spread the Islamic fundamentalists' sick brand of religion. This is not to mention the ceremonial beheadings of both men and women, the cutting off of limbs for petty crimes, the force-fed dogma, the suppression of art and science, and the punishment of critical thought.

Humanity as a whole is terrorized by both combatant camps.

When President Bush, in going to war with Iraq, told the world that we must choose between the terrorists or the US, we were faced with a choice that diminished our humanity. We became losers no matter which side we chose. Terror is caused by the oppression, suppression, and depression of others in order to exploit them for group gain. This is the situation we are faced with. Both camps bent on terrorizing their enemy for group gain.

The Impact of US Imperialism on Exploited People and on the Imperialists Themselves

US-based corporate capitalism represents the highest stage of capitalism. It represents the "globalization" of capitalism and the fulfillment of their values. Today a small ruling class has concentrated enormous material wealth and power into their own hands, causing immense suffering to the rest of humanity. In general terms, only twenty percent of humanity control eighty percent of the planet's material wealth. Yet within the wealthy twenty percent, less than one-half of one percent control fifty percent of the concentrated wealth.[460] The implications of this sinful concentration of wealth is staggering. Even though the capitalists have moved many production facilities to China and India to take advantage of cheap labor, the masses of people in the so-called third world remain perpetually impoverished, their traditional lifestyles destroyed by the juggernaut of capitalist exploitation.

Today, the oppressed masses of people include great numbers of angry and disgruntled warriors and intellectuals who are at the end of their tether. Islamic fundamentalism is the world's fastest growing religion all over the world, not because it is a better religion than others, but because in most countries, people are forced to lead a subhuman existence and have no means to express their suffering or their rage. Islam provides a vehicle to speak against the exploitative practices and dehumanizing materialist values of corporate capitalism.

When people become increasingly engrossed in material pursuit, two ill-effects occur. First, their minds gradually and steadily drift towards crude matter. Secondly, they begin to think in terms of possessing other's material wealth, their labor, and their resources. This is the psychological explanation of imperialism. It is a mental illness. When expressed externally it takes various forms, such as capitalism, state capitalism, communism, nationalism, caste-imperialism, racism, male chauvinism, etc., which are all the same psychic ailment in various forms.

Because of this psychic ailment, a superpower like the United States forces its own selfish national interests on other weaker states to establish its economic, political, cultural, and military superiority. The capitalist government wants to dominate and exploit other socio-politico-economic units so as to continually become rich at the expense of others.

Imperialism is anti-human. It is a negative force, a destructive phenomenon, which generates exploitative and unjust conditions in individual and collective life. The sick activities of imperialism get reflected in all aspects of human society—art, literature, education, trade, commerce, industry, agriculture, morality, and social relations. A psychology based on slavery, inferiority complex, pseudo-culture, psycho-economic exploitation, and ultra-nationalism grows in parallel with the impoverishment of the people.

Those possessed of the capitalist mentality perceive the world through greedy eyes. They do not have the capacity to correctly or fully understand worldly issues. They do not understand anything except the economic value of things. Their commercial outlook is not confined to the material world only. Rich people seek profit, not only by controlling material resources, but also by exploiting the mental and emotional needs of people, including their faith in God.

After earning hundreds of billions of dollars by manipulating people through their business acumen, the capitalists use a small part of their profit to construct houses of worship and promote the arts because they hope to mask their sins in their search for popular approval.

When people use their intellects over a long period of time solely to accumulate material wealth, all they can think about is "How can I accumulate more?" Their social spirit and sense of humanity gradually disappear until eventually they do not retain even the tiniest scrap of humanity.

As their illness increases as a result of their rabid exploitation and the destruction of millions of lives, the capitalists lose even the last vestiges of social consciousness and the need for a people's revolution becomes inevitable.

Capitalism in the Middle East

As human beings, we each have distinct traits, which differentiate one person from another. Just as each human being has his or her own traits, similarly an entire nation living within a particular geographical, historical, and cultural environment will also inherit certain traits which distinguish that particular group from others. These traits are reproduced by shared experiences and become embedded in the culture of the population. They form a particular bent of mind, an attitude towards life and society, and a unique social outlook.

In the Middle East, the social traits of the Arab tribes, have been formed, in large part, by the Prophet Mohammed and the life-style that he introduced. It is more correct to say lifestyle rather than religion because the Prophet addressed social, political, cultural, and economic behavior as well as spiritual practices. As such it is impossible for the

Arab people to separate church and state as has been accomplished in the West. Nor is it easy for the Arab culture to envision business practices apart from religious obligations.

Now, the best way to express enmity against a person or a race is to deprive that person or race of the freedom to express their customs and lifestyle and to prevent them from channeling their human potentiality accordingly.

Capitalism may not be the polar opposite of Islam, but capitalist colonialism is certainly *ultra vires* to the cultural lifestyle of the Muslim Arab people. It has made the people slaves to circumstances beyond their control and has threatened their dignity as a people. In doing so, it has ridden rough shod over centuries of religious/social enculturation. In the Middle East, capitalism has sucked the vital energy of the people by supporting local dictators like the House of Saud, the Shah of Iran, King Faruk, etc. Capitalism in the Middle East is destroying a way of life and reducing a great mass of people to a joyless and fearful condition of abject poverty. As a consequence, it has stoked the flames of rebellion among the people. In the war between the capitalist West and the Islamic fundamentalists, it was, as we shall see, the capitalists who fired the first shot and who continue to commit the gravest injustices.

The western capitalists, originally the British and the French, came to the Middle East on the prowl for new markets as the Ottoman Empire began to weaken and break apart. France had conquered and colonized Algeria in 1830 and without regard for the people's culture or history, the French began to impose their culture on the population in an attempt to turn them into model French citizens.

At the time, the Middle East and North Africa were a part of the Ottoman Empire, which had been held together by the shared belief in Islam. Ottoman law, in fact, was derived from both Islamic law and the edicts of the sultan.

Beginning in 1853, the British seized control over several independent emirates in the Arabian Peninsula, which had been controlled by local princes or emirs. The Arabs were forced to sign an agreement that recognized Britain as the dominant power in the Gulf and gave Britain authority to control the foreign affairs of the emirates. Later these emirates would become the United Arab Emirates.

In 1869, the French built the Suez Canal in Egypt to link transportation between the Mediterranean and Red Seas. The French sold the Canal to the British, who controlled it for eighty-four years before Egypt nationalized it.

In 1881, the French conquered and colonized Tunisia, which remained a colony until 1950 when it became an independent country after a bloody revolution. In 1882, British troops moved in and colonized Egypt.

As the people of the Middle East watched the foreign capitalists seize control over huge swaths of their land and resources, a backlash began to build.[461]

The Wahhabi leader, Abd al-Aziz ibn Saud, captured Riyadh a major city in Saudi Arabia from rival clansmen in 1902 and ignited a thirty-year campaign against foreign and domestic forces to unify the Arabian Peninsula. In 1905, Yemen was divided between the Ottoman controlled North and the British controlled South.

And so it went, the western capitalists persistently seized the land and resources of the Islamic people in the Middle East. In 1908, oil was discovered in Iran (Persia). By WWI, the British government, which owned fifty-one percent of the oil company that was created, was the dominant power in Iran and exploited the country's oil during WWI.

During WWI, the British tricked the Arab leaders into giving their support (remember Lawrence of Arabia?) by promising to give them their independence after the war. They reneged on their formal agreement and made a secret agreement with the French to divide up the Middle East between themselves.[462] The British also betrayed the Arabs by supporting the formation of the state of Israel in Palestine.[463] This is not to deny the need for the Jewish people to have a homeland of their own, but it is a condemnation of the West who savaged the Jews for centuries and then gave them land that had belonged to another people for thousands of years.

The Growth of Islamic Fundamentalism

Islamic fundamentalism was born in the fight of the local people against foreign oppression. It was later enhanced by military training from the

US and England whose intention was to support these "terrorists" in their fight against the Russians.

Today Islamic Fundamentalism is a well-developed political ideology, which aims to *islamize* or re-islamize the law, institutions, and governments of the Muslim world. Strict Islamic fundamentalists want to set up an Islamic state with a constitutional framework and political organization based on *Sharia*, Islamic law, as its sole legal reference. In this way it is similar to the goals of Christian Dominionists in the US and Orthodox Jews in Israel. The fundamentalists of any religion are the most divisive people in their religions. Whoever does not believe as they do, instantly become their enemies.

Islamic fundamentalism appeared at the turn of this century both as a reaction against Britain and France's attempts to westernize the Muslim world and as a resistance movement against colonial empires, particularly the British.[464]

Islamic fundamentalists believe that the West exploited the people of Islam whose power in the world must be restored. They believe that Islam is the true religion, the religion of God, and its truth is manifest in its power. The fundamentalists hold that in the past, when Muslims believed in their religion, they were powerful. But they have since lost their power because they have abandoned Islam and have reverted to the crude materialistic conditions that preceded God's revelation to the Prophet Muhammad. If Muslims return to the original Islam, however, they can preserve and even restore their power as a people.

Like Christian and Jewish fundamentalists, the Islamic fundamentalists believe that a religious state needs to be created under the sovereignty of their "God." All religious fundamentalists believe that their own empowerment is actually God's plan for mankind. As such any means to accomplish this goal is justified, including persuasion, trickery, the use of violence, and killing. Religion has always been about power and not about spirituality.

Just as Christianity evolved over centuries into a religious ideology, so also has Islam. Wherever you find a Christian in the world you will find Christianity and wherever you find a Muslim in the world you will find Islam. Fortunately for the world, not all Christians and Muslims are fundamentalists. If this were so, there would never be any hope of peace among humanity. Whereas Islam dates back to the sixth century, Islamic fundamentalism began in the nineteenh century as a reaction to capitalist exploitation.

Al-Afghani

Sayyid Jamal al-Din "al-Afghani" (1838-1897) was a Muslim intellectual and activist who lived during the nineteenth century expansion of European countries into the heartland of Islam. As the people sought methods to ward off foreign conquest, Afghani began to calculate how Muslims could have more power to face the colonialists.

Afghani was a bright man whose ideas combined an appeal for unity among Muslims with a modern critique of Western imperialism. He was the prototype of the modern fundamentalist. Afghani was widely traveled, visiting Cairo, Istanbul, Tehran, Kabul, Paris, London, and St. Petersburg. In these places he inveighed against capitalism and lobbied for revolutionary change.

Afghani was obsessed with the question of power. As he continued his work, he began to seek personal power as well. He advocated the removal of certain Muslim rulers while ingratiating himself with others. He was not above the use of physical violence to accomplish his vision. Afghani came to believe that killing was the only solution and that "power is never manifested and concrete unless it weakens and subjugates others." In short, Afghani, like his adversaries the capitalists, was capable of anything in the quest for power. He could just as easily have pleaded his case in a court of law or opened fire on a motorcade of government ministers.

Between Afghani and the emergence of full-blown Islamic fundamentalism, there was a period of time when many Arab liberal and secular nationalists gained prominence among the Islamic people in the Middle East. They had been influenced by the European divide and conquer strategy that posited it was language, not religion, which defined nations. During the years after Afghani, Muslim intellectuals preferred to be called Arabs, Turks, or Persians.

Post-World War I in the Middle East

On August 18, 1919, after the third Anglo-Afghan war, the people of Afghanistan declared their independence from Great Britain. The British wanted to manage the affairs of Afghanistan because it shared a border with India, its prized colony, and because the British believed that the Russians might try to attack India through Afghanistan.[465]

In 1920, all former Ottoman-controlled territories in the Middle East were assigned as "mandates" to Allied powers by the League of Nations. In doing so, the western powers ignored the will of the local people who had chosen their own leaders, for example, King Faisal in Syria and King Abdullah in Iraq. Instead Syria and Lebanon were assigned to France while Palestine and Iraq were given to Britain. Riots immediately broke out in Iraq.

In 1921, Transjordan was created in an attempt to reach a peace in the Middle East. King Abdulla was made the king. Transjordan eventually became Jordan.

In the same year, Reza Khan took control of Persia (Iran). In 1925, he appointed himself Shah and his reign lasted until 1941. He resisted the strict laws and archaic customs of the religious mullahs and reduced the influence of the nobles and sheikhs who ruled the nomadic tribes. He renamed the country Iran in 1935.

In 1922: The League of Nations issued a mandate to Britain to establish a national home for the Jewish people in Palestine. Britain was given responsibility to administer Palestine on behalf of both the Jews and Arabs living there.

In 1923, oil was discovered in Iraq. In the same year, the Republic of Turkey was established. Though nearly all of the population practiced Islam, Mustafa Kemal set up a secular government. Under his leadership, the country set up Western-style economic, social, and political institutions.

The Muslim Brotherhood

An angry reaction to being colonized and having their Muslim culture suppressed, however, continued to smolder in the minds and hearts of the Arab people. The League of Nations decisions merely aggravated this anger. In 1929, an Egyptian school teacher named Hasan al-Banna (1906-1949) founded a movement he called the al-Ikhwān al-Muslimūn (the *Muslim Brotherhood*). This organization gained supporters from Sunnis throughout the Arab world and influenced other Islamist groups such as Hamas in Palestine.

The Brotherhood would later play a major role in the overthrow of the dictatorial rule of the Egyptian President Hosni Mubarak in the January Revolution in 2011. At that time, its members formed the majority of the newly elected political party and Mohamed Morsi, a member of the Brotherhood, was elected President of Egypt. However, the Brotherhood immediately began to oppress the people with its religious dogmas and was soon overthrown by the army headed by General Abdel Fattah El-Sisi, who was eventually elected president in 2014. At this writing, the Muslim Brotherhood is considered a terrorist organization by the governments of Bahrain, Egypt, Russia, Syria, Saudi Arabia, and United Arab Emirates.

The Muslim Brotherhood believes that Islam should not simply be a religious observance, but a comprehensive way of life. The organization supplements traditional Islamic education with Tarbiyah training for male students. Tarbiyah is a comprehensive process of developing a student's character and personality, including spiritual, intellectual, moral, social, and physical aspects. At the time, it also included scouting and militia-type activities to resist the British occupation.

The Brotherhood's goal is to impose their interpretation of the Qur'an and Sunnah (examples of behavior from the Prophet's life) on all Muslim individuals, families, communities, and states. Its credo is "Allah is our objective; the Qur'an is our constitution; the prophet is our leader; Jihad is our way; death for the sake of Allah is our wish."[466]

On one hand, the Brotherhood operated openly as a membership organization to promote political awakening. On the other hand, it created a military wing that acquired weapons and trained members in their use. They fought against the Jewish Zionists in Palestine in 1948, and assassinated capitalist-leaning government officials in Egypt. They lost public support when they began to force their moral teachings on the people by intimidation. When Gamal Abdel Nasser became President of Egypt, he ruthlessly put down the Brotherhood, but they continued to plan activities underground and in prison and they flourished in other Arab countries to which they had dispersed.[467]

The Devotees of Islam

At the same time that the Muslim Brotherhood arose in Egypt, a smaller and more secretive movement, known as the Fadā'iyān-e Islam (*Devotees of Islam*) appeared in Iran, under the leadership of a Shi'ite theology student, Navvab Safavi (1923-1956). Safavi sought to purify Islam in Iran by assassinating certain intellectuals and political figures, who were "corrupting" the people. Despite a series of successful killings and the freeing of several of its assassins from punishment due to the help of the group's powerful clerical supporters, the Devotees of Islam were eventually suppressed and Safavi executed by the Iranian government in the mid-1950s. The group, however, survived as supporters of the Ayatollah Khomeini and the Islamic Revolution of Iran.

The Devotees of Islam were part of the growing nationalist mobilization against capitalist domination in the Middle East that grew after World War II. It adhered to a strict fundamentalism that went beyond generalities about following Sharia. It demanded that its members avoid alcohol, tobacco, opium, films, gambling, and wearing Western clothing. It enforced amputation of the hands of thieves, and the elimination from schools of all non-Muslim curricula, including subjects like music.[468]

Safavi also demanded the veiling of women. There is no such commandment in the Quran that women be veiled. They were only instructed to dress modestly. Although women of all religions, going back in history, wore veils, including Roman and Christian women, the Islamic fundamentalists' demand that women be veiled or be subject to beatings and punishment was a new development to secure male superiority in Islam. There are many Muslim women, nonetheless, who now support the wearing of the veil as a sign of personal modesty and a protection from sexual harassment.

The Devotees of Islam never became a political party and eventually were suppressed for their crimes and religious fanaticism. Safavi himself was executed after plotting a failed assassination attempt against a prime minister. But the seed was planted. One of those clerics who protested Safavi's execution was an obscure, middle-aged cleric named Ruhollah Khomeini, who would continue the work of forging Islam into an ideology of power.[469]

Oil was discovered in Saudi Arabia in 1838. Thus, began a deluge of foreign political and economic deal making in the Holy Land of Islam that elevated the dynasty of the House of Saud in exchange for allowing the corporations to have access to the oil.

In 1941, the Iraqi Prime Minister, Rashid Ali, attempted a coup against the monarchy that was put down by British troops.

Jamaat-e-Islami

In 1941, an Islamic theologian and social activist, Abul Ala Maududi, living in British India, strove to restore "true Islam" by destroying the evils of Western secularism, nationalism, and women's emancipation. The only way to do this was for Muslims to become involved in politics, institute Sharia law, and preserve Islamic culture. He founded the *Jamaat-e-Islami*, which became the largest Islamic organization in Asia.

Jamaat-e-Islami was the first Islamic organization to develop an ideology based on a revolutionary Islam.

Maududi created the Jamaat-e-Islami to sway the Muslim leadership in India, who were dominated by the Muslim League. The League sought a separate, independent state for Muslims (to be called Pakistan) after the withdrawal of the British from India. The Muslim League did not want to be dominated by the Hindu majority in India, but in calling for an independent state they expressed no interest in an Islamic state or Sharia law. Maududi used the League to spread his ideas, which included the abolition of interest-charged on loans, the separation of the sexes, the veiling of women, and criminal penalties such as flogging and amputation for alcohol consumption, theft, fornication, and other crimes.[470]

In Maududi's ideal Islamic state, sovereignty would belong to God alone, and would be exercised on his behalf by a just ruler who would be guided by a reading of God's law in its entirety. As an ideological state, it would be administered for God solely by Muslims who adhered to its ideology, and "whose whole life is devoted to the observance and enforcement" of Islamic law. Non-Muslims, who could not share its ideology, and women, who by nature could not devote their entire lives to it, would have no place in high politics. Everything would come under the purview of this Islamic state. Maududi was certain about what the Islamic state would not resemble: it would be "the very antithesis of secular Western democracy."[471]

The group split into separate independent organizations, Jamaat-e-Islami Pakistan and the Jamaat-e-Islami Hind, following the Partition of India in 1947. Maududi and his party supported the creation of the Islamic state in Pakistan and helped General Muhammad Zia-ul-Haq institutionalize Sharia law in that country.

Maududi's Islamic revolution did not come about by a popular uprising, but by winning over society's leaders and by legal means. His vision of revolution would not stop at India or Pakistan. Maududi envisioned a sweeping revolution among all the Muslim people, a revolution aimed to control all aspects of their lives.[472]

Maududi's many writings were translated into every major language spoken by Muslims and thus provided the spadework for the development of an ideology for an Islamic fundamentalist state.[473]

Jamaat-e-Islami developed in Bangladesh, Kashmir, Britain, and Afghanistan and the organization continues to maintain ties internationally with other Muslim groups.

World War II

The outbreak of World War II pitted the Allied powers (Britain, France, Australia, New Zealand, the Soviet Union, and the US) against the Axis powers (Germany, Italy, and Japan). After six years of fighting, the Allies won the war.

Iran declared its neutrality at the start of World War II, but refused to expel all German nationals from the country because leading up to the war, Germany had been Iran's largest trading partner. After Hitler invaded the Soviet Union in 1941, the Allies needed to create a transportation route across Iran and into the Soviet Union. To do so, they simultaneously invaded Iran. On September 16, Iranian resistance collapsed and Reza Shah Pahlevi abdicated the throne to his son, Mohammed Reza Shah Pahlevi. The Shah was exiled to South Africa and died in 1944.

In 1942, Britain forced Egypt's King Faruq to appoint a pro-British prime minister.

In 1944, France granted Lebanon full independence.

In 1945, Egypt, Iraq, Lebanon, Syria, Saudi Arabia, Transjordan, and northern Yemen formed the *Arab League* with assistance from Britain who saw it as a means to win its fight with the Nazis. The affiliation of states promoted unity among the Arab nation,s but opposed the establishment of a Jewish state in Palestine.

Post World War II

Syria gained its hard-fought independence from France in 1946 after the U.N. called on France to evacuate the country.

The State of Israel was established in 1948. Despite their numerical inferiority (1.3 million Arabs to 650,000 Jews), the Jews were better prepared for conflict than the Arabs. They had quickly established a government under David Ben-Gurion and a standing army. Meanwhile, the Palestinian Arabs were still in disarray after the Arab Revolt against the British administration of the Palestine Mandate. Most of their leaders have been exiled. By 1947, mounting violence, including terrorist acts by both Arabs and Jews, led Britain to declare its mandate over Palestine unworkable. Britain made plans for its withdrawal and left open the question of what to do with Palestine to the UN.

In August, the United Nations Special Committee on Palestine (UNSCOP) recommended the creation of independent Jewish and Arab states. The plan divided Palestine into roughly equal halves, with Jerusalem and religiously significant surrounding sites under the control of a separate international authority. The report also called for the Arab and Jewish states to form a united economic bloc. The Jews accepted this plan, but the Palestinian Arabs did not. The partition plan was approved by majority vote of the UN General Assembly on November 29.

Britain completed its withdrawal from Palestine in early May 1948, and on May 14, the State of Israel was declared. Both the United States and the USSR immediately recognized the new state. In support of the Palestinian Arabs, however, neighboring Arab nations Egypt, Iraq, Jordan, Lebanon, and Syria declared war on Israel the next day. The Israelis repelled the Arab attack. The 1948 War, also known as the Israeli War of Independence, ended in July 1949. Israel signed separate cease-fire agreements with Jordan, Syria, and Egypt, who now controlled about forty percent of what had been Mandatory Palestine. Egypt held the Gaza Strip, Jordan annexed the West Bank, and Syria retained the Golan Heights. The remaining sixty percent was controlled by Israel. About seven hundred thousand Palestinians fled or were expelled from their homes in the new Israeli territory.

In 1953, a US-backed coup removed Iranian Prime Minister Mossadeq from power. The British and American intelligence agencies worried that Mossadeq's nationalist aspirations would lead to a "communist takeover." To prevent this, Dwight Eisenhower approved a joint British-American operation to overthrow Mossadeq. After the first day, it appeared the coup had failed, and the Shah fled to Baghdad. Rioting ensued, flamed by the CIA and British intelligence services, and Mossadeq was defeated. Mohammed Reza Shah Pahlevi returned to power, and General Fazlollah Zahedi, the leader of the military coup, was installed as prime minister.

In the same year, the Sudan gained political independence from Egypt and Britain.

In 1954 an eight-year War of Independence was fought in Algeria against the French. More than a half million people died in the conflict.

In 1956, Sultan Mohammed became King of Morocco, ending the French protectorate of Morocco.

Sayyid Qutb

During the 1950s and 1960s, Sayyid Qutb was a leading member of the Muslim Brotherhood in Egypt. He incorporated the ideology of Maududi into its operations. Qutb authored twenty-four books, including novels, works on education, and books on the social and political role of Islam. His *Fi Zilal al-Quran* (*In the Shade of the Qur'an*) is a thirty-volume commentary on the Quran. Qutb was an intellectual giant whose circle of friends consisted of influential politicians, intellectuals, poets, and literary figures. By the mid-1940s, many of his writings were incorporated into the curricula of schools, colleges, and universities in Egypt.[474]

Qutb borrowed heavily from Maududi who argued that a revolution was required to establish an Islamic state. But while Maududi believed that revolution had to be prepared by a long campaign to convert the intellectuals, Qutb, who was an outspoken critic of Abdel Nasser's presidency, had found himself thrown into prison for many years. For Qutb, Islam was under assault, and its redemption could not wait for a bloodless revolution. Qutb urged that a vanguard organize itself, retreat from western society, denounce lax Muslims as unbelievers, and fight to overturn the political order. As Qutb put it, "those who have usurped the power of God on earth and made His worshippers their slaves will not be dispossessed by dint of Word alone."[475] Qutb thus transformed Maududi's ideology into an explicit logic of revolution. He did not have the chance to implement his theory, however, because he spent almost a decade in prison before his final arrest and hanging. Later fundamentalists would return to his writings, however, to justify their own resort to the use of force. Among these groups were al-Qaeda and the Taliban.

Qutb had spent a couple of years in America in the late 1940s and was repelled by what he saw as a disastrous combination of avid materialism and egoistic individualism that was based on the oppression of women and minorities. Qutb also challenged American imperialism, which he called "Crusaderism." He saw it as a strategy to eradicate Islam. Qutb's work would later prove crucial to the fundamentalist rationale that formal independence from the West had to be accompanied by a purging of Islam's own bloodstream from all Western cultural influence.[476]

In 1956, Tunisia gained independence from France.

In 1959, oil was discovered in Libya and transformed the country into a prosperous nation.

One year later, oil was discovered in Abu Dhabi. A small fishing village was transformed into one of the richest of the United Arab Emirates. In the same year, 1960, Iraq, Iran, Kuwait, Saudi Arabia, and Venezuela formed OPEC, a federation of oil-producing nations.

In 1961, Reza Shah Pahlevi dissolved Iran's legislative body and suspended its constitution. Assuming the role of dictator, he instituted a plan for the westernization of the country, which had been opposed by the religious conservatives. The Shah abolished the practice of sharecropping, nationalized dwindling forests, gave women voting rights, and started a massive rural literacy program. On the other hand, he also established *SAVAK* a domestic security and intelligence service, which served as his secret police. SAVAK became known internationally for its infamous torture and execution of opponents of the *Pahlavi* regime.

In 1961 Kuwait also gained independence from the British. Iraq claimed Kuwait as its own territory and threatened to invade. Kuwait sought British military support and Iraq backed down. It never formally withdrew its claim, however, and in 1990 invaded Kuwait and claimed it as an Iraqi province.

In 1962, a civil war erupted in North Yemen when army officers overthrew the new Imam, Muhammad al-Badr and formed the Yemen Arab Republic. The republicans were backed by Egypt and the Soviet Union, while the Imam's supporters were backed by Saudi Arabia and Britain. In 1967, Southern Yemen accepted Soviet economic aid. In a state of economic shambles following the closure of the Suez Canal and the Six-Day War with Israel, it became the first and only Marxist Arab state.

Yasser Arafat was elected chairman of the Palestine Liberation Organization in 1968.

Muammar Qaddafi

In 1969, revolutionary leader Colonel Muammar al-Qaddafi led a military coup in Libya to overthrow the monarchy of King Idris. Qaddafi abolished the monarchy and proclaimed a Republic, albeit one in which he maintained dictatorial control. Ruling by decree, he implemented measures to remove western colonialists from Libya and strengthened ties with other Arab nationalist governments. Qaddafi promoted a version of "Islamic socialism" that was based on *sharia* law and the nationalization of the oil industry. He used the vast oil fortune to bolster the military, implement social programs, and fund revolutionary militants across the world. In 1973, he initiated a "Popular Revolution" with the formation of General People's Committees (GPCs). While designed to be a system of direct democracy, Qaddafi still retained personal control over major decisions.

He outlined his political ideas in *The Green Book* that was distributed in schools and became part of the Libyan education system.

Qaddafi was mercurial in his rule. People never knew what to expect and any criticism of his actions were met with harsh punishment. Other African countries abandoned him for his constant meddling in their affairs.

During the Arab Spring, in 2011, an anti-Qaddafist uprising, eagerly supported by NATO bombings, led to a Libyan Civil War, during which Qaddafi was captured and killed by National Transitional Council (NTC) militants. The U.N. immediately recognized the NTC as the legitimate government of Libya.[477]

Qaddafi, without question, was a controversial world figure. Supporters praised his anti-imperialist stance and his promotion of Pan-Africanism and Pan-Arabism for which he received many awards. The Western press portrayed him as a dictator and autocrat whose authoritarian administration violated the human rights of Libyan citizens.[478] It appears that both arguments contain an element of truth.

Years after the death of Qaddafi, however, the West is still speaking of Libya as being a "failed state," one ravaged by fighting bands of local militias. Many support Islamic fundamentalism while others support western culture. ISIS has now established a headquarters in Sirte, Qaddafi's hometown, and has vowed to send fighters to Europe on the smuggling boats that now leave the country's unpoliced coastline every week.[479]

Fundamentalist forces opposed to the U.N.-backed Libyan government in Tripoli swept through the country's "oil crescent," seizing control of oil terminal headquarters and gaining control over the export of Libya's economic lifeblood.[480]

Six western nations issued a joint appeal in August 2016 urging that oil facilities be freed from the civil war. Oil production in Libya had collapsed from 1.5 million barrels a day under Qaddafi's administration to a mere two hunded thousand barrels.

In 1971, the United Arab Emirates (UAE) was formally recognized as an independent state.

In 1972, Saudi Arabia negotiated for control of twenty-five percent of the Arabian American Oil Company (Aramco). Until then, Aramco was owned by Standard Oil, Texaco and Mobil. Over the next sixteen years, Aramco was converted to a totally Saudi-owned company called Saudi Arabian Oil Company (Saudi Aramco).

In the same year, Iraq became the first Arab country to nationalize a Western oil corporation. Prior to 1972, US and British companies held a three-quarter share in Iraq's oil production, but the Soviets helped Iraq develop its oil industry to end its reliance on Western companies. The Soviets also helped Iraq to nationalize the Iraq Petroleum Company. In the following years, Iraq rapidly increased its oil output, becoming the world's second largest exporter of oil by 1979.

In 1973, Saudi Arabia led an oil boycott against the US and other Western countries. As a supporter of Egypt, Jordan, and Syria in the 1967 Six-Day War against Israel, Saudi Arabia harbored resentment when the Yom Kippur War (October War) erupted. In retaliation for the United States' support of Israel, Saudi Arabia quadrupled the price of oil. While creating long lines at gas stations in the US, this action also dramatically increased the House of Saud's wealth and political influence.

In 1979, the Iranian Revolution, led by Ayatollah Khomeini, broke out and the Shah of Iran was overthrown.

The Ayatollah Khomeini

During the late 1970s, there were large demonstrations against the cruel dictatorship of the Shah of Iran who was supported by the West. During this time, the teachings of the exiled Ayatollah Khomeini, who was the Shiite Muslims Supreme Leader, were widely circulated among the people through tape recordings. These teachings inspired the revolution against the Shah. In 1978, demonstrators held massive strikes, seized government buildings, shut down businesses, and assassinated government officials. In January 1979, the Shah fled Iran for the United States and Khomeini returned from exile to a welcoming crowd of several million people. The Islamic Revolutionary Council was formed and the country was declared the Islamic Republic of Iran on April 1.

Under the Ayatollah Khomeini, laws based on Sharia were introduced in Iran. This ended the Shah's "modernization" policies. Khomeini's strict version of Islamic religious standards became the law of everyday life and many Iranians were upset by the imposition of fundamentalist Islam on their lives. Many people who favored Western culture left Iran, including most Jews and Christians. The strict religious government continues to this day.

Ruhollah Khomeini had engineered the first successful fundamentalist revolution in Islam. Khomeini's only addition to previous fundamentalist ideologues was his addition of the stipulation that only those people who were steeped in Islamic law should rule. Khomeini has said, "Since Islamic government is a government of law, knowledge of the law is necessary for the ruler, as has been laid down in tradition." The ruler "must surpass all others in knowledge," and be "more learned than everyone else."[481] Since no existing state had such a ruler, Khomeini's doctrine constituted an appeal for revolution in every Muslim country to replace every form of government with the rule by Islamic jurists. In Iran, Islamic jurists had maintained their independence from the state, but Khomeini's doctrine transformed them into a ruling priest class whose goal was now to seize and exercise political power. To the surprise of the world, Khomeini's doctrine was implemented in Iran.

Khomeini also rejuvenated the anti-Western and anti-American position of Islamic fundamentalism. America became the "Great Satan" and was thus viewed as the antithesis to Islam historically and ideologically. This posited an absolute conflict between Islam and the West, not just in history, but in eschatology. It was this mindset that drove Iranian students to seize the US Embassy in Tehran during the days of the Carter administration and hold embassy staff prisoners for four hundred and forty-four days. Political conflict with the West was now transformed into a religious conflict with the "enemies of Islam," led by America and represented regionally by the state of Israel.

Islamic leaders did not accept all of Khomeini's ideas. Among the Sunnis, Islamic jurists usually served the state and worked under lay leaders. It was difficult to create support in these countries for a ruling priest class. Likewise, Khomeini's anti-Americanism was diffused by the Soviet invasion of Afghanistan in 1980 and many Sunni movements mobilized to wage a trans-national Islamic jihad against the Soviets. Many were prepared to cooperate with the US to do this.

Nonetheless, Khomeini's rejection of nominal Muslim kings and presidents was widely received by Muslim fundamentalists. Khomeini had also provided a model for revolution. He demonstrated how cultural alienation could be translated into an anti-foreign sentiment and how this could be used to build a broad revolutionary coalition. In fact, the enthusiasm among fundamentalists for Khomeini's revolution was almost unanimous. For the next decade, much of the effort of fundamentalists was directed at replicating Khomeini's success and bringing about Islamic revolution in other states.

Frustrated by the drudgery of winning mass support, as advocated by Maududi, and inspired by Khomeini's success, Sunni fundamentalists of all stripes began to conspire. The next decade saw revolutionary attempts throughout many countries in the Middle East. The Great Mosque in Saudi Arabia was seized in December 1979 and insurgents called for the overthrow the House of Saud. In 1981, the Egyptian President, Anwar Sadat was assassinated, paving the way for the Mubarak presidency. The Muslim Brethren declared a rebellion against the Syrian regime in 1982. Shi`a movements also directed their rage against the existing governments in Iraq, Saudi Arabia, Kuwait, Lebanon, and the smaller Gulf states. A Shi`ite bomber nearly killed the ruler of Kuwait in 1985. Followers of Khomeini journeyed to Mecca as demonstrators to preach revolution to the assembled pilgrims.

This violence was a culmination of the anger and frustration of Muslim fundamentalists from the continued assault by the West and by Western-supported dictators that threatened their Islamic beliefs and life style. For the first time in the twentieth century, the ideology of Islam had been empowered, and it had happened through revolution. Power for Islam was within reach, if only the fundamentalists were bold enough to run the risk.

Yet, while the 1980s were tumultuous and filled with revolutionary acts, the masses of Muslims did not ignite in revolution. The national rulers struck back, employing ruthless force to isolate and stamp out the "terrorists." Their blood flowed in the gutters of Hama in Syria, Mecca in Saudi Arabia, and Najaf in Iraq. Even so, they managed to create many semi-autonomous pockets of resistance. Some of these pockets were distant from urban centers, such as the Bekaa Valley in Lebanon or the governates of Upper Egypt, but the fundamentalists also set up operations in urban quarters and on university campuses. In such places, Islamic dress for women became compulsory and short-cropped beards for men became customary. Islamic fundamentalism offered the people a simple solution to the complex crisis of state and society. It spoke directly to the poor and the young, the overqualified, and the underemployed, whose numbers were increasing faster than their opportunities under capitalism.[482]

In 1979, the same year that the Shah fled Iran, Saddam Hussein became the president of Iraq. One year later, Hussein led Iraq into a bloody war with the new Islamic Republic of Iran that would last for almost a decade. Tensions between the two countries increased rapidly following the Iranian Revolution when the Ayatollah Khomeini, declared that Iraq needed to stage a coup against Hussein and the Baathist party. Numerous border disputes intensified the conflict. From his side, Saddam Hussein wanted to expand his country's power, prestige, and influence. One way of accomplishing this was to attack Iran. If successful, he would gain new oil fields, more land and power, and deal a blow to the Khomeini regime.

The war lasted for eight years and more than five hundred thousand Iraqis and Iranians died, with neither side able to claim victory.[483]

Afghanistan and the Rise of the Taliban

Afghanistan was originally part of the Persian Empire but began to be controlled by local warlords in 1747. Thereafter, as in the Middle Ages in Europe, strong men would declare themselves kings and rule the territory.

By the beginning of WWII, the country was controlled by Zahir Shah and his brother-in-law Daud Kahn who became the Prime Minister. The country remained neutral during the war and Khan was able get both the US and Russia to help in building Afghanistan. Zahir Shah attempted to initiate political reforms by creating a constitutional monarchy. But over the next decade, radicals believed that he was drifting back to royalist behavior. A new constitution in 1977 promoted Daud Khan to the role of president. He, in turn, appointed a cabinet of cronies, including royal family members. This caused a violent coup led by a leftist faction in the army.[484] Upon victory, the military turned over control of the government to the nation's two leftist political parties, the People's Party and the Banner Party, who had cooperated during the coup, but once in office, the leaders of the People's Party seized power under the leadership of Nur Mohammad Taraki and his Prime Minister Hafizullah Amin.

Despite the advice of Russia who feared a reaction from Islamic fundamentalists, Taraki and Amin immediately established radical new programs based on the Soviet model.[485] Women were granted equal rights, land was redistributed, and leaders of the rival party were persecuted and killed. Within months, a Muslim fundamentalist insurrection broke out across the country. In March 1979, a local resistance group declared a *jihad*, or holy war, against the godless regime in Kabul. In the same month, more than one hundred Soviet citizens living in Herat were seized and killed.

During the upheaval, Taraki and Amin fought among themselves and Amin seized power. The Russians were convinced that Amin's secular policies would continue to inflame the people so they decided to play a more active role in matters. In the winter of 1979, Russian troops occupied the Afghan capital of Kabul, which led to war.[486]

Within days of the Soviet invasion, Amin was either killed or committed suicide. The Russians installed Babrak Karmal as their puppet ruler. Ruling Afghanistan by armed forces, however, proved impossible. While the Russian army was able to seize any area that they wanted, as soon as they shifted their focus, the rebels returned to retake the land.

The Soviet–Afghan War lasted for over nine years from December 1979 to February 1989. Insurgent groups called the *Mujahideen* (literally, those engaged in holy war) fought against the Soviet Army and allied Afghan forces. Over one million people died in the fighting and millions of refugees fled to other countries, mostly to Pakistan and Iran.

During the war with the Soviets, Afghani fundamentalists attracted thousands of jihadists from other countries to fight in the Holy War. During this time, and even prior to the Russian invasion, many received invaluable military training from the United States whose intention was to weaken the Soviet Union. The CIA provided the mujahedeen with hundreds of millions of dollars in weaponry and training to fight communism. In doing so, they helped to arm and train some of the most dangerous Islamic groups in the world today. These fighters would later fill the ranks of the Taliban, Al Qaida, and ISIS.

The Soviet-Afghan war devastated and depopulated an already impoverished country. Below is a picture of a park in Kabul before the Soviet invasion and what the park looked like after forty years of civil war and war with Russia.

Fig. 5-11: Afghanistan Before and After

When Mikhai Gorbachev became the General Secretary of the Soviet Union, he replaced Babrak Karmal with a former police chief, Mohammad Najibullah. Najibullah proved equally ineffective in getting the Afghan people to accept a Soviet presence, and, in 1988, Gorbachev announced that Soviet troops would begin a phased withdrawal. The last battalion crossed the Friendship Bridge over the Amu Darya River in February 1989, leaving President Najibullah to try and run a communist Afghan state on his own.

Contrary to expectations, Najibullah was able to remain in power for three years, holding the Mujaheddin at bay. But eventually he fell in 1992 and was given asylum in the U.N. compound in Kabul.

The insurgents immediately declared an Islamic state, but rival guerilla groups led by local warlords continued to fight each other. In 1994, a mullah (Muslim scholar) from Kandahar, Mohammad Omar Akhund (commonly known as Mullah Omar), formed a guerrilla group, which he called Taliban, meaning "students." Compared to the blatant self-interest and corruption of the warlord groups, the Taliban's simple message of Muslim fundamentalism proved greatly attractive to the people.

Omar's recruits came mainly from Islamic religious schools (madrassas) in Afghanistan and from the Afghan refugee camps across the border in Pakistan. The Taliban fought against the rampant corruption that had emerged after the fall of Najibullah. Omar was personally sickened by the abusive raping of children by warlords and decided to do something about it.

In early 1994, he led thirty men armed with sixteen rifles to free two young girls who had been kidnapped and raped by a warlord. They captured him and hung him from a tank gun barrel.[487] Soon appeals flooded in for Omar to intercede in other cases of sexual abuse of children. His movement gained momentum through the year, and he quickly gathered twelve thousand students to his cause. By November of 1994, Mullah Omar's students had managed to capture the entire Kandahar Province. By the spring of 1995 they had already taken control of twelve of the thirty-one provinces in Afghanistan.[488]

The Taliban wanted to create a moral society, which they believed could only come about through Islam. Initially the students had favored Marxist-Leninism, but when the Soviet invaded Afghanistan, they rejected this ideology for Islam. As they established their power, the fundamentalist dogma that they ascribed to, led the Taliban to create an oppressive regime that horrified the world with its spectacles of public executions and the cruel treatment of women.

In October 2001, following the destruction of the World Trade Center, the Americans invaded Afghanistan believing that Osama bin Laden was hiding in that country. In the process, the Americans overthrew the Taliban and during the December 2001 International Conference on Afghanistan in Germany, Hamid Karzai was selected by prominent Afghan political figures to serve a six-month term as Chairman of the Interim Administration. He subsequently won elections that kept him in power until 2014.[489]

Once the new administration was established, President Obama quickly created an Afghan army to prop up the new government and to serve as surrogates for US soldiers. Over three hundred and fifty thousand men in Afghanistan received military training at this time. It was later estimated that as many as twenty-five percent of the US-trained Afghan security forces were Taliban or al Qaeda operatives and sympathizers. This means that in this single training mission, the US military armed and trained an army of some eighty-seven thousand five hundred enemy infiltrators who took their training home to fight against their governments in Egypt, Algeria, Saudi Arabia, Yemen, Jordan, Palestine, and elsewhere.[490]

Osama bin Laden and al-Qaeda

One of the main reasons that the United States attacked Afghanistan was to kill or capture Osama bin Laden, whom they blamed for assaults on US embassies and the horrific attack on the World Trade Center. PBS *Frontline* did a broadcast entitled "Hunting bin Laden." They received much of their information on bin Laden from an anonymous source close to him. The material below is largely taken from this PBS report.[491]

Osama bin Laden was born in 1957, the seventh son of fifty brothers and sisters. His father Mohammed Awad bin Laden immigrated to Saudi Arabia from South Yemen around 1930. He started his life as a very poor laborer and became the owner of the biggest construction company in the kingdom.

During the reign of King Saud, Mohammed became very close to the royal family when he built King Saud's palace in Riyadh much cheaper than the cheapest bid. While he impressed the king with his business acumen, he also established good relations with other members of the royal family, especially Faisal, younger brother and crown prince to King Saud. The two brothers had a rocky relationship and eventually Faisal took control of the government in 1964.[492] It is said that Mohammed bin Laden played a big role in convincing King Saud to step down in favor of Faisal.

The King had been a lavish spender while Faisal was a progressive reformer. After Saud's departure, the treasury was empty and bin Laden, to support Faisal, literally paid the civil servants' wages of the whole kingdom for six months. King Faisal then issued a decree that all construction projects should go to bin Laden. He was also named the Minister of Public Works.

Mohammed bin Laden had a dominant personality and imposed strict religious and social codes on his children. Osama lost his father when he was thirteen, but he grew up as a religiously committed boy. He received his primary, secondary, and university education in Jeddah and achieved a degree in public administration in 1981. His father used to host hundreds of pilgrims from all over the world during Hajj season. Some of these pilgrims were senior Islamic scholars or leaders of Muslim movements. This habit continued even after his father's death through Osama's elder brothers. In this way, Osama was introduced to the elite of Islam, making many good contacts and establishing long term relations.

At his high school and university, he was introduced to high-powered intellectuals who were members of the Muslim Brotherhood. He had two distinguished teachers in Islamic studies. The first was Abdullah Azzam, who was a Palestinian Sunni Islamic scholar and theologian and founding member of al-Qaeda.[493] Azzam helped the Afghan *Mujahedeen* fight the Soviet invaders by raising funds, recruiting, and organizing the international Arab volunteer effort. Because of this, Azzam is considered the "Father of Global Jihad." It was Azzam who persuaded bin Laden to come to Afghanistan and help the *jihad*. When the war with Russia drew to an end, they jointly established al-Qaeda.

Osama's second influential teacher at the university was Mohammed Qutb. Mohammed was the younger brother of the Egyptian Islamist revolutionary thinker Sayyid Qutb, who we previously discussed. Sayyid was the original propounder of Islamic revolution against the West. After Sayyid was executed by the Egyptian government, Muhammad moved to Saudi Arabia where he promoted his older brother's ideas.

Osama made his first trip to Afghanistan a couple of weeks after the Soviets invaded and occupied the capital of Kabul in December 1979. He was taken by his hosts, the Jamaate-Islami, to Peshawar to see the refugees and meet some leaders. The Jamaat-e-Islami was the organization started by Maududi in India who espoused an Islamic revolution that inspired Sayyid Qutb. The trip was exploratory. It is difficult to know whether or not bin Laden knew at the time, that the CIA was already training mujahedeen to fight the Russians.

Osama bin Laden went back to the kingdom and started lobbying his brothers, relatives, and school friends to support the mujahedeen in Afghanistan. He succeeded in collecting a good sum of money and materials as donations to the jihad. He made a second trip to take the materials to Afghanistan and continued to collect money, going on short trips once or twice a year until 1982. In 1982, he brought construction machinery with him and put them at the disposal of the mujahedeen. He started spending more and more time in Afghanistan and his presence encouraged more Saudis to come.

In 1984, he built a guesthouse in Peshawar (Baitul'ansar) that was intended to be the first station for the Arab mujahedeen when they came to Afghanistan. From here they would be sent for training or to the front. In the next couple of years, Osama built more than six camps. Soon, he decided to run his own battles with his own command. He attracted experienced Arab fighters who were ex-military men from Syria and Egypt. The guesthouse and the camps attracted more Arab mujahedeen to come and there was a significant surge in their numbers.

Osama fought more than five major battles against the Soviets and had hundreds of skirmishes. As bin Laden's camps became more organized, records of combatants and their movements were kept and the operation became known as al-Qaeda, "The Base."

After the Soviet withdrawal from Afghanistan in 1989, bin Laden went back to Saudi Arabia and was banned by the kingdom from further travel because they believed that he intended to start another "front" in South Yemen. Bin Laden had been warning people that Iraq was going to attack Saudi Arabia, but at that time, the government was on good terms with Saddam Hussein, and found bin Laden's message to be embarrassing. He was instructed not to give public talks and keep a low profile. Bin Laden proved to be correct in his warning.

In 1990, Iraq accused Kuwait of stealing Iraqi petroleum through slant drilling and invaded the country. Within two days, most of the Kuwait Armed Forces were either overrun by the Iraqi Republican Guard or fell back into Saudi Arabia and Bahrain. Kuwait was annexed and Saddam Hussein announced a few days later that it was the nineteenth province of Iraq.[494] Osama reacted swiftly to the Iraqi invasion. He immediately forwarded a letter to the king suggesting in detail how to protect the country from potentially advancing Iraqi forces. In addition to many military tactics suggested, he volunteered to bring all the Arab mujahedeen to defend the kingdom. That letter was presented in the first few days of the incident, and the regime gave it consideration.

While he waited for a response, bin Laden heard the news that transformed his life. The Americans were sending troops to Saudi Arabia to fight against Iraq. He took this as a direct assault upon the Arab world and the rule of Islam. He looked upon the Saudi government as traitors to Islam and started to lobby religious scholars and Muslim activists. He succeeded in convincing one of the senior scholars to declare a fatwah (a formal legal opinion) that military training and readiness was a religious duty. He immediately circulated that fatwah and convinced people to come to Afghanistan for training. It was estimated that four thousand men went to Afghanistan in response to the fatwah.

In February 1993, a van bomb exploded in the garage of the World Trade Center in New York City. It was allegedly planted by terrorists backed by Osama bin Laden. Six people were killed, and more than one thousand injured. Millions of dollars' worth of damage was done. Six Islamic extremist conspirators were convicted of the crime in 1997 and in 1998, and received prison sentences of two hundred and forty years each.

The Saudi government responded by raiding Osama's home and placing him under house arrest. One of his brothers helped him sneak out of the country and he went to Afghanistan. There he got involved in the local disputes between the warlords, but was unable to broker any peace. He told his followers not to side with any faction. During his stay in Afghanistan, the Saudis tried more than once to kidnap or kill him in collaboration with the Pakistani intelligence, but his friends in the Saudi and Pakistani governments always leaked their plans, which allowed Osama to escape.

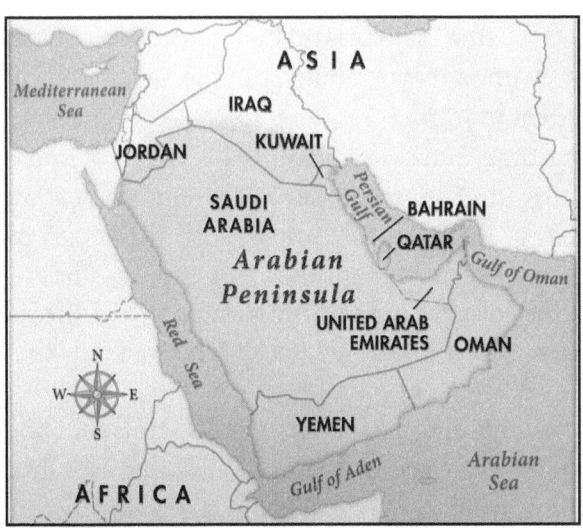

Fig. 5-11: The Arabian Peninsula

Having failed to affect any positive outcome in Afghanistan, bin Laden moved his operation to the Sudan. The move had nothing to do with jihad. He wanted a safe refuge and the new regime in Sudan had raised the banner of Islam. Osama wanted to help the government with construction projects. He gathered construction equipment and started several building projects. He also lobbied Saudi businessmen to invest in Sudan and he met with reasonable success. Many of his brothers and Jeddah merchants still have investments in real estate, farming, and the agricultural industry there.

For the next couple of years, the Saudi government did not express public opposition to bin Laden and his Saudi relatives and friends visited him in Sudan with very little problem. Even though his assets were frozen by the government, it was not publicized. In 1994, however, the Saudi publicized the fact that they had withdrawn his citizenship.

Bin Laden issued a communiqué condemning the Saudi decision and saying that he did not need to be known as a "Saudi" to identify himself. Further, it was not up to al-Saud to admit or expel people from the Arabian Peninsula. He then formed a group of activists in Saudi Arabia called the "Advice and Reform Committee" (ARC). The ARC published letters that harshly criticized the Saudi government using religious rhetoric, but they never contained any appeal to violence against the regime.

In the spring of 1995, a car bomb exploded in the Saudi capital of Riyadh. It was the first major anti-American action in Saudi Arabia. Bin Laden never claimed responsibility, but the Saudi government tried to link the incident to him.

During this time, Sudan underwent a great deal of international pressure for hosting bin Laden and he felt that he had become a burden to his hosts. Early in 1996, he secretly left Sudan with many of his followers for Jalalabad in eastern Afghanistan. This city was under the control of Yunis Khalis, a powerful warlord who later joined the Taliban. While the battle for power still went on among the warlords there, bin Laden was received well by all of them.

Within a few months of his arrival in Afghanistan, bin Laden issued a Declaration of War against the United States. His intention was to expel Americans from the Arabian Peninsula. Like many fundamentalist Muslims, he considered the presence of the evil American infidels in the land of the holy cities of Mecca and Medina to be a great sacrilege.

The Saudi government meanwhile was continually trying to apprehend or kill him during this time. They had offered Yunis Khalis many bribes but he would not betray bin Laden.

In 1996, the Taliban took control of Jalalabad. They sent a delegation to meet bin Laden and he was invited to meet with their leader, Mullah Omar. The Taliban were honored to host and protect a man whom they considered to be a saint who had sacrificed everything for the sake of the Holy War.

From 1996 to 2002, having established its power over Afghanistan, the Taliban severely punished women and restricted their role in society. Under the rule of the Taliban, women were banished from the workforce, forbidden an education, and prohibited to leave their homes unless a close male relative escorted them. In public, they were forced to wear burqas that completely covered the body and left only a small mesh-covered opening through which they could see. Windows of women's houses visible to the public were painted black. Religious minorities and secular individuals also suffered under the Taliban regime. The suppression of women distorted the men's sexuality and many became pedophiles. They were particularly attracted to boys whom they groomed to be seductive dancers.[495]

Mullah Omar, leader of the Taliban, met bin Laden in early 1997 after bin Laden had conducted two TV interviews with Channel 4 and CNN. The Mullah offered respect and admiration to bin Laden, but asked him to keep a low profile while in Afghanistan.

In the same year, the Americans planned an operation with Pakistani intelligence to send Special Forces to Kandahar where bin Laden was residing and kidnap him. The plan was leaked to bin Laden who made it public. The Americans were forced to cancel their plan.

While in Afghanistan, bin Laden nurtured relationships with the Taliban Ulema (religious scholars). He was able to convince forty scholars to issue a fatwah that sanctioned the use of force to expel the American military from the Peninsula. Bin Laden's presence in Afghanistan had again attracted Mujahedeen from many countries to move there. He decided to promote a pan-Islamic jihad instead of just a Saudi or Arabic jihad. In this way, he attracted Kashmiris, Pakistanis, Indians, and Muslims from the Soviet Republics. In February 1998, he formed the *International Front*. The declaration contained two elements, the formation of the front and the fatwah that sanctioned killing Americans and Jews. Apart from two Arabic newspapers, the declaration had minimal coverage by the press.

In August 1998, two bombs exploded in the American embassies of Nairobi, Kenya and Dar es Salaam, Tanzania killing two hundred and twenty-four people. More than five thousand people were wounded. Twelve Americans died in the attack. The US retaliated by launching cruise missiles at suspected al-Qaeda targets in Afghanistan and Sudan. Although there was no proof that bin Laden was involved in the bombings, it was widely suspected that he was. In November, US officials indicted bin Laden on two hundred and twenty-four counts of murder and offered a five-million dollar reward for information leading to his arrest and conviction.

The Americans' launch of cruise missiles shocked the Muslim world. People inside Saudi Arabia and in other Arab countries were filled with rage against America. It became almost shameful to criticize bin Laden. In the mind of average Arabs and Muslims, bin Laden became a man who could drive America so crazy that it started shooting haphazardly at unjustified targets. Those who had turned against bin Laden for the African bombings believed that the arrogance of the American retaliation was much worse than the embassy bombings. They expected more of the Americans than they did of al-Qaeda and bin Laden.

On September 11, 2001, America experienced the deadliest "terrorist attack" in US history. According to mainstream corporate media, nineteen men hijacked four US commercial airliners and crashed them into the World Trade Center in New York, the Pentagon in Washington, DC; and one crashed in Shanksville, Pennsylvania, purportedly on the way to the US Capitol Building. The US government immediately blamed the event on bin Laden and declared a "War on Terrorism." The events of 9/11 provided the trigger required to legitimize the next step in the Trilateralists and the Neo-Cons bid to bring the entire world under their domination. It was also this event that gave rise to what Thomas Barnett, in his book, *The Pentagon's New Map*, declared to be the new grand strategy of the US military, the "Global War on Terrorism."

The War on Terror Unleashed

A number of researchers have accumulated evidence that the Bush Administration knew about these events in advance or may have even been complicit in it; for those interested, a discussion of this research can be found in Appendix 3. Whether you subscribe to the accuracy of this evidence or not, the fact is that there must have been some foreknowledge by the Bush Administration for them to have been able to have launched "Operation Enduring Freedom" in Afghanistan in less than a month after 9/11. Bush immediately declared the new US foreign policy, i.e., the War on Terrorism, and publicly announced that the invasion of Afghanistan was to punish the Taliban for providing safe haven to Osama bin Laden, who the US announced was the mastermind of 9/11. At that time, there was no proof of bin Laden's participation in planning 9/11 and, in fact, he denied participation in the plan. One of the consequences of 9/11, however, was that it silenced the value-oriented intellectuals and kept them from generating any anti-war sentiment among the American people. The Trilateral Commission did not want a reoccurrence of a 1960's anti-war rebellion.

By December, US forces had pushed the Taliban back into the hills and captured the capital city. Osama bin Laden escaped capture. The US facilitated the creation of an interim government under the control of Hamid Karzai. In the 1980s, Karzai, a tribal leader, raised funds for the Afghan Mujahideen who were fighting to expel Soviet Union troops during the Soviet war in Afghanistan (1979-1989).[496] After the Soviet withdrawal, the Islamic State of Afghanistan was established, but then replaced in 1996 when the Taliban came to power and established the Islamic Emirate of Afghanistan.

After the US destroyed the Taliban regime, Germany offered to host a conference in Bonn for Afghan leaders who were favorable to the West. At this International Conference on Afghanistan, Karzai was selected to serve a six-month term as Chairman of the Interim Administration. Afterward, he became President of the Islamic Republic of Afghanistan and remained in power until 2014.

With Afghanistan apparently under control, the Bush administration turned its eyes to the prize it had long been plotting to conquer. Bush stated in an interview with Newsweek that Iraqi President Saddam Hussein was "evil."

Meanwhile, Bush refused to grant *prisoner of war* protection to detainees who were sent to Gitmo, the US detention facility at Guantanamo Bay, Cuba.

In January, Bush, in his State of the Union address, described Iraq, Iran, and North Korea as the "axis of evil."

In March, the Bush administration began its campaign to demonstrate that Saddam Hussein possessed "weapons of mass destruction." By August, in a speech in Nashville, TN, Vice President Dick Cheney declared, "there is no doubt that Saddam Hussein now has weapons of mass destruction."[497]

In September, President Bush declared, "You can't distinguish between al-Qaeda and Saddam Hussein when you talk about the war on terror." Experts questioned this statement and pointed out that a secularist Saddam would be hated and considered an infidel by bin Laden and al-Qaeda.[498]

In October, Jonathan Landay, senior national security and intelligence correspondent for McClatchy Newspapers, who had spent time in Afghanistan and had chronicled ethnic, religious, and political conflicts in Asia, the Middle East, and the Balkans reported that "The White House and the Pentagon . . . are pressuring intelligence analysts to highlight information that supports Bush's Iraq policy and to suppress information and analysis that might undercut congressional, public, or international support for war." [499]

In January 2003, in his State of the Union address, President Bush stated, "the British government has learned that Saddam Hussein recently sought significant quantities of uranium from Africa."[500] This claim had already been proved false by both intelligence agencies and former ambassador Joe Wilson, who had personally investigated it. This indicated that there was a split in the government between those in the Bush administration who were in on the plot and those who were not. This internal conflict played itself out during the following years.

Secretary of State Colin Powell, formerly Chairman of the Joint Chiefs of Staff, certainly was in on the plot because in March, he delivered a speech to the United Nations in which he declared that Saddam had biological weapons and desired to produce nuclear weapons. Powell added that al-Qaeda "continued to have a deep interest in acquiring weapons of mass destruction. Powell's sources for these accusations were Ibn al-Shaykh al-Libi, an al-Qaeda operative captured by American forces, who the Defense Intelligence Agency declared "was intentionally misleading the debriefers."[501] Powell also described mobile chemical weapons labs, based on accounts by Rafid Ahmed Alwan al-Janabi. Eight years later al-Janabi admitted to the Guardian and in a "60 Minutes" interview that he fabricated his story.[502]

In March, Cheney got down to business. Over the course of the war, his company, Halliburton, was awarded multiple no-bid government contracts worth $39.5 billion dollars. No other company was allowed to bid against Halliburton.[503]

On March 18th, the *Washington Post* printed an article by Walter Pincus and Dana Milbank, entitled "Bush Clings to Dubious Allegations about Iraq." The next day, the Bush/Cheney administration invaded Iraq as part of "Operation Iraqi Freedom." Its stated purpose was to disarm Iraq's weapons of mass destruction (WMD), end Saddam Hussein's regime, and free the Iraqi people from a tyrannical dictatorship.

The Center for Public Integrity reported that senior Bush administration officials made "935 false statements" in the two years after September 11, 2001, about the extent of the national security threat posed by Saddam Hussein's Iraq. In retrospect, the center found, the Iraqi regime never possessed WMD and until 2003 did not have any viable ties to al-Qaeda.[504]

On April 27, 2004, CBS' "60 Minutes II" aired a story about US soldiers abusing and torturing Iraqi inmates housed at a prison in Abu Ghraib.[505] A week later, The New Yorker published an article by Seymour Hersh about sadistic and criminal abuses at Abu Ghraib.[506]

US troops were still in Iraq in 2018 even after the country had been torn asunder.

The Pentagon's New Map

It was in 2004 that Thomas P.M. Barnett, a military strategist, wrote his book entitled *The Pentagon's New Map*.[507] Through the use of humor and inside stories, Barnett popularized the Trilateralist/Neo-Con strategy for global imperialism, making it seems as American as mom and apple pie. As a naval intelligence officer, Barnett assumed the posture of a military visionary who articulated the new rules of engagement that became known as the "War on Terrorism" in the wake of 9/11. He softened the language of Brzezinski and the Neo-Cons and made it more palatable for the discerning American audience.

Barnett's career began in 1991, the year that Communist hardliners attempted a coup d'etat against Soviet President Mikhail Gorbachev following six years of his presidency in which he had allowed for a greater freedom of speech through his policy of 'glasnost' and begun a program of economic reform known as 'perestroika', or rebuilding. After three days of massive protest, the coup organizers surrendered, realizing that without the cooperation of the military, they did not have the power to overcome the power of the entire population of the country.

Witnessing this, Barnett recommended to the Pentagon that the US navy make peace with the Russian navy and help them convert their operations to peace-time activity. The old guard comprised of Cold War brass sneered at Barnett's recommendation, but after Yeltsin weathered the attempted coup, diplomatic communication between Russia and the US opened up and paved the way for the acceptance of Barnett's policy brief in which he had advocated peace with the Russians.

With the Cold War grand strategy no longer viable, Barnet later went on to define the course of engagement for the post-Cold War era.

Rules and Their Importance

According to Barnett, the army brass shuffled about directionless for a decade in an environment of "chaos" that followed the fall of the Soviet Union. To enlighten the military brass to the need for a new grand strategy, Barnett argued that globalization was the major trend in human society and that it was being led by the United States of America. As such, it was the requirement of the US armed forces to create a new grand strategy to support this global imperative.

The rule-set of the Cold War was obviously no longer viable and a new rule set was required. While Barnett succeeded in getting the younger officers and commanders to shake their heads in the affirmative concerning this new context, the grand strategy did not crystallize until the fateful day of 9/11 when the twin towers of the World Trade Center, located in the financial district of New York City, came crashing to the ground after purportedly being attacked by Osama bin Laden's *Al Qaeda*.

This tragedy galvanized the American people to action against the "Muslim terrorists" and allowed the Bush/Cheney administration to begin its master plan with a false flag war against Iraq. The threat of global terror, according to the mainstream media, had come home to the shores of America itself and this new reality had to be fought in any place and in any time for as long as it took to eliminate every "terrorist" on the earth. Barnett was the man who popularized this plan and articulated its rationale.

In his power-point presentations to the military elite, Barnet divided up the world into two great camps. There were the industrialize countries that formed the "Functioning Core" and the countries of the "Non-Integrating Gap" that were unwillingly participants in the movement for globalization. The Functioning Core, which began with the US, Canada, Western Europe, and Japan, after WWII, had since been joined by many other countries including Russia, China, Brazil, many countries in Eastern Europe, etc. The countries in the "Non-Integrating Gap," many of who were in the Middle East and Africa, however, had failed to connect with the process of globalization. According to Barnet, this failure to connect spelled danger. Such countries did not share in America's "optimism" for a better world.

Barnett, however, did not view all such countries as "enemies." Rather, he believed that in order to create peace in the world it was necessary to court such countries and make them see the benefit of joining the Functioning Core.

The issue for the armed forces, therefore, was how to encourage this process of integration while at the same time preventing those people who hated America from destroying the globalization process. If the military could find the answer to this question they would be able to articulate its grand strategy for the twenty first century.

Barnett believed that whenever you find a lot of rules governing a system, you also find a lot of people enforcing those rules. Therefore, the clearer the rules, the less enforcement is required because everyone understands the rules and there is less confusion about the correct course of action. People agree with clear rules and are more likely to follow them.

When rules become misaligned across different social sectors, however, the future becomes unstable. The potential for misinterpretation leads to conflicts and a clash of competing rule sets. Thus, the fewer the rules, the less war you have. This is why a grand strategy in support of globalization was essential.

After the Cold War, the US military was involved in fights in Somalia, Haiti, Bosnia, and Kosovo but there was no strategic plan. There were no answers as to "why" they were fighting in these lands. There was only "chaos."

Barnett maintained that a new grand strategy for national security must focus on growing a community of nations that recognized a common set of rules regarding war and peace. Those states that shared the common set of rules would be the "good" states and those that did not would be the "bad" states. Rules for the good states, for example, would be "Don't harbor transnational terrorists within your territory" or "Don't seek weapons of mass destruction." The good states would work collectively to encourage the "bad" states to change their ways, applying military force to persuade them when diplomacy alone could not get the job done.[508]

In his presentations to the army brass, Barnett argued that:

> Enunciating that rule set is the most immediate task in this global war on terrorism, and promoting the global spread of that security rule set through our use of military force overseas (e.g., preemptive war against regimes that openly transgress the rule set) is our most important long-term goal in this struggle.[509]

The brass agreed and, according to Barnett, the military elite lobbied their strategy to the Congress and the president. The military wanted the Republicans and the Democrats to reach a consensus on this new strategy for national security. Apparently, it was not a hard sell considering that both Bush and Obama supported this strategy and worked to institute it. It was a little disingenuous to claim that the military brass, under the wise counsel of Barnett, convinced the Bush administration to adopt his plan. After all, the administration had already articulated its military strategy, believing it to be the perfect tool to justify their invasion of Iraq and to seize control of the Middle East oil. The Bush administration had already organized all the national security agencies in the country under the National Security Administration (NSA), which then began to catalogue and index every phone call from every cell phone throughout the entire world. This created the opportunity for the US intelligence community to spy on every citizen in the world, including the leaders of allied countries and their people. The Bush administration had also created the Patriot Act to monitor US citizens who were now considered to be potential terrorists.

As for Obama, he took his marching order from the Trilateralists who shared the same vision with the Neo-Cons. Obama built on the trajectory established by the Bush administration by ordering drone strikes on suspected "terrorists" anywhere in the world, but mostly throughout the Middle East. His administration also codified the military's grand strategy into constitutional law, bringing the "war on terrorists" into the homes of every American citizen.

American Wars in the Middle East

Despite the horrendous lies and self-aggrandizement of the Bush/Cheney administration, the mass media continued the drum beat about American patriotic troops killing bad guys in Iraq. The American people bought into the Bush administration's propaganda. Bush was re-elected in November 2004, defeating the Democratic nominee, Sen. John Kerry of Massachusetts.

At the end of 2006, Saddam Hussein was executed. The country spun into the chaos of civil war. Bush announced a "troop surge" in Iraq and the deployment of an additional thirty thousand US troops over the opposition of Congress.[510] All the while, reports kept surfacing about the CIA's "black sites" and their use of torture as the "Agency" worked to perfect its interrogation techniques.[511]

In April 2008, David Barstow of *The New York Times* reported that the Pentagon had quietly recruited and was paying retired military officers to be "independent" radio and television analysts. They were secretly coached about how to make the public case for war in Iraq on the air and many of them also had significant, undisclosed financial ties to defense companies that were benefiting from the policies they were "analyzing." Barstow's story was based on eight thousand pages of Department of Defense records obtained under the Freedom of Information Act.[512] For this and other articles on the subject of the Pentagon using media personnel for propaganda won Barstow the Pulitzer Prize.

Barack Obama became the president in 2008. In January, he issued three executive orders: to close the Guantanamo Bay detention facility, to ban torture, and to create an inter-agency task force to review all detention and interrogation procedures. After eight years of his administration none of these orders had been put into practice.

In June 2009, the US handed over control of security in Iraq's urban areas to local Shiite forces, who were then engaged in a civil war against the Sunnis in the country. In Afghanistan, the same kind of breakdown was occurring and Obama ordered an "Afghan Surge," sending thirty thousand more American men and women to fight and die in that country.

In the meantime, the corporations aligned with the Bush/Cheney administration continued to make windfall profits through no-bid contracts with the Pentagon. *Bloomberg News* reported in May that Haliburton had again been awarded a no-bid contract by the Army. The news came on the same day that the Justice Department announced it intended to pursue another lawsuit against the company accusing it of taking kickbacks.[513]

In 2011, the last US combat troops were reported as having withdrawn from Iraq, leaving fifty thousand troops to serve in "advisory roles." US troops remained in Iraq until 2018.

In May 2011, President Obama announced that Osama bin Laden, purported mastermind of the attacks on 9/11, was killed by Navy SEALs during a raid on his compound in Abbottabad, Pakistan.[514]

Public Enemy #1

Osama bin Laden became the poster boy for the Bush/Cheney "War on Terrorism" because of his outspokenness, his wealth, and his social status, having been born into the very elite within Saudi Arabian society. Bin Laden was also not afraid to fight or encourage others to fight against those who would occupy Islamic holy lands and kill its people. His biggest concerns were the occupation of Saudi Arabia by the US army and the massacre of children in Iraq due to US imposed economic sanctions.

The US Army in Saudi Arabia

The US stationed an army in Saudi Arabia during the fight against Saddam Hussein's invasion of Kuwait. After the 1991 Gulf war ended, however, the US did not withdraw its troops from Saudi Arabia. It maintained a presence of five thousand troops whose responsibility was *Operation Southern Watch*. Its mission entailed imposing continued economic sanctions on Iraq by enforcing no-fly zones over that country while also protecting the country's oil exports through the shipping lanes of the Persian Gulf, which were also protected by the US Fifth Fleet based in Bahrain. Since Saudi Arabia housed the holiest sites in Islam (Mecca and Medina), many Muslims were incensed by the permanent US military presence there.

It was the same as if a Muslim army occupied Rome and refused to leave, all the while draining its resources. In 1996, Bin Laden issued a fatwa calling for American troops to get out of Saudi Arabia. In another fatwa, delivered in 1998, he wrote: "for over seven years the United States has been occupying the lands of Islam in the holiest of places, the Arabian Peninsula, plundering its riches, dictating to its rulers, humiliating its people, terrorizing its neighbors, and turning its bases in the Peninsula into a spearhead through which to fight the neighboring Muslim peoples."[515] In an interview conducted in December 1999, bin Laden again talked about the American presence in the Holy Land and stated that it was a provocation to the entire Muslim world.[516]

Economic Sanctions on Iraq

Aside from the American troops being quartered in Saudi Arabia to enforce its expropriation of Iraqi oil, bin Laden and many Muslims were outraged by the continued imposition of economic sanctions on Iraq even as hundreds of thousands of Iraqi children were dying of starvation. In August 1990, soon after Iraq invaded Kuwait, the U.N. Security Council adopted Resolution 661, which imposed economic sanctions on Iraq. But even after the Iraqis withdrew from Kuwait, the sanctions were continued on the fabrication that Saddam Hussein possessed "weapons of mass destruction."

The economic sanctions were still in place eight years later. As a result of these sanctions, five hundred thousand Iraqi children died from starvation and general lack of care, many having been orphaned during the war.[517]

When Republican Madeline Albright, US Secretary of State under Bush, was asked on US television if she thought that the death of half a million Iraqi children from sanctions in Iraq was a price worth paying, Albright replied: "This is a very hard choice, but we think the price is worth it."[518]

In an interview with Bill Richardson, a leader of the Democratic Party, Amy Goodman asked him if he believed that the death of half a million children was worth the economic sanctions the US imposed against Saddam. Richardson replied,"Well, I believe our policy was correct, yes."[519]

At the time, Richardson was one of the most prominent leaders of the Democratic Party, having served as US Ambassador to the United Nations and the Energy Secretary in the Clinton administration. He had also served as a US Congressman and chairman of the 2004 Democratic National Convention, as well as the chairman of the Democratic Governors Association.[520]

A half million innocent children killed as collateral damage in the American "war on terror" and neither the leaders of the right or the left had the human decency to call out this horrendous tragedy. "Collateral damage" on any scale was apparently acceptable to our ruling elite because it is hard to believe that five hundred million children were terrorist operatives. The death of these innocents ranks as one of the greatest crimes against humanity in history. But according to the American mainstream press, it was not a crime, but good policy in an effort to "make the world safe for democracy."

It is understandable that the Muslims of the world would not have seen it this way. In his 1998 fatwa, bin Laden proclaimed the Iraq sanctions a reason to kill Americans:

> "[D]espite the great devastation inflicted on the Iraqi people by the crusader-Zionist alliance, and despite the huge number of those killed, which has exceeded 1 million... despite all this, the Americans are once against trying to repeat the horrific massacres, as though they are not content with the protracted blockade imposed after the ferocious war or the fragmentation and devastation. . . . On that basis, and in compliance with Allah's order, we issue the following fatwa to all Muslims: The ruling to kill the Americans and their allies—civilians and military—is an individual duty for every Muslim. . . ."[521]

In 2004, Osama bin Laden called the sanctions "the greatest mass slaughter of children mankind has ever known."[522] It remains difficult for Muslims to forgive or forget such an "evil" deed. The Great Satan was living up to its name.

He continued by saying, "Your security is not in the hands of Kerry, Bush, or Al Qaeda. Your security is in your own hands. Any state that does not mess with our security, has naturally guaranteed its own security." He concluded, "To the American people, my talk is to you about the best way to avoid another Manhattan," he said. "I tell you: Security is an important element of human life and free people do not give up their security."[523]

Bin Laden made two more TV appearances in 2007.[524] It was in 2008 that President Obama threatened to kill bin Laden.[525] Apparently "the terrorist" had lost his value as a bogeyman because he certainly could have been killed anytime within the previous ten years insofar as the CIA knew of his every move. The government spin that bin

Laden had avoided capture all those years was made to look ridiculous by a UCLA geography class that was given the class assignment to locate bin Laden. Using a probabilistic model they created, they found that there was a 88.9 percent probability that bin Laden was living in a city less than two hundred miles from Tora Bora, his last known location in Afghanistan. The professors and students predicted that he would be located in a large town, not a cave, and that the building would have high ceilings, more than three rooms, cover from trees, a fence, and electricity. Bin Laden's house in Abbottabad, Pakistan, where he was eventually killed, fell completely within the students' projections.[526]

The Second Wave of Islamic Fundamentalism

As is quite obvious, the oil of the Middle East is critical to an industrial economy. First Britain and France, then the US sought to control the oil supply in this region. Rather than making a fair business deal for procuring the oil, they decided to plunder it. The bare-knuckled imperialism of America struck the Muslim population of the Middle East as not only humiliating but also blasphemous. When the US sent troops to the Holy Land in Saudi Arabia, Islamic fundamentalists, not just in the Middle East, but throughout the Muslim world, were inspired to fight the infidels who had come to defile their religion and their sacred lands.

When the Western invasion of the Middle East began, the region was primarily in a preindustrial state, similar to Europe during the Middle Ages. The land was ruled, not by industrial capitalists, but by local warlords and kings and the culture was overseen by the religious Mullahs and Imams of Islam. Islam provided the cultural, political, and to a large extent, the legal structure for the region. Similar to Christians during the Middle Ages, the people were ruled by their religion and lived under a severe patriarchal society that maintained its power by public displays of cruelty and the persecution of women. The religious elites demanded strict obedience to religious law (sharia) under pain of death or mutilation.

Beneath this cultural veneer, the centuries-long conflict between the Shiites and the Sunnis seethed, each accusing the other of blasphemy and of being infidels.[527] Tribal warfare was also rife in the region. When the US landed its troops in Saudi Arabia to fight against Iraq, priests and warlords alike called on the people to fight the unbelievers and infidels. If we want to look at history from a human perspective and not from the limited perspective of current nationalist or religious sentiment, we have to admit that this response is a typical human response. We all react the same way when our land is invaded and we find ourselves bullied and humiliated. It is in our nature as human beings to want to strike back and it is no different for the people in the Middle East. This story, however, becomes more complicated by the fact that the Muslim people as a whole were thrown into a holy war between Shia and Sunni after the American invasion had destroyed the leaders of those lands who had been able to keep the peace between these factions.

The ideology of Jihad against the West had been set in place well before Osama bin Laden came on the scene. Up until WWI, the majority of Middle East territory was a part of the Muslim Ottoman Empire and had been so since the sixteenth century. Thus, the region was one large territory occupied by Muslims under a common law. After WWI, however, the territories of the Ottoman Empire were divided between Britain and France. Specific nation-states were carved out, puppet kings placed on thrones, and the people divided.[528] The people interpreted this foreign occupation primarily as an assault on Islam itself. Being colonized was a sign of Muslim weakness. The only thing to do, therefore, was to eliminate the foreign infidels and rejuvenate Muslim power. Power could be restored either by directly attacking foreigners or by promoting an Islamic awakening.

This was the situation that gave rise to Afghani, the Muslim Brethren, the Devotees of Islam, and other fundamentalist groups. They shared the common desire to redress the imbalance of power between Islam and the Western capitalists.

The religious fundamentalists, who found themselves under the domination of the West, wanted a strong religious leader in a state that was based on Islamic law. What Islamic law (Sharia) actually meant was interpreted differently by different groups, but it was surely not the secular model of constitutional government or multi-party democracy that was the Western model. It might have been different had not hatred for Western imperialism cancelled out any appeal democracy might have had in the minds of the people.

The fundamentalists also rejected nationalism and wanted a return to a pan-Islamic region. They traveled broadly to promote a message of Islamic solidarity.

The first wave Islamist movement was characterized by a vision of an authoritarian Islamic state, a willingness to use violence to fight oppression, and the desire for a panIslamic movement across national boundaries.

The second wave of thinkers, men like Sudan's Hasan al-Turabi, Tunisia's Rashid al-Ghannushi, and Iraq's Sayyid Muhammad Husayn Fadlallah built on the motivations of the first wave thinkers to create a complete ideology that would address the needs of Muslims worldwide.

Using the *Koran* and the traditions of the Prophet Muhammed as the ideological base, they would enforce these teachings by the imposition of an all-encompassing Islamic law, Sharia. Many of the provisions of Sharia had been enforced unevenly over the centuries. Many tenets remained merely intellectual ideals, but now the fundamentalists, faced with the occupation of a foreign, imperialist power, believed that the promise of a consistent Islamic ideology, enforced by the universal law of Sharia, would give the Muslims of the world unimaginable strength as a people.

The fundamentalist activists, therefore, came to insist not only on power, but also on absolute power. It was this insistence that turned many modern Islamists like ISIS into proto-fascists, obsessed with imposing the most draconian and savage cruelties on their own people. As someone commented, ISIS had become obsessed with "dragging their own people kicking and screaming into paradise."

The fundamentalist thinkers could not reject the West in its entirety. Whatever one may think about it, the America's mass culture exercises a magnetic appeal, especially on the world's youth. As Brzezinski pointed out in his book on world dominance, "American television programs and films account for about three-fourths of the global market. American popular music is equally dominant, while American fads, eating habits, and even clothing are increasingly imitated worldwide. The language of the Internet is English and an overwhelming proportion of the global computer chatter also originates from America, influencing the content of global conversation." He also pointed out that people from all over the world come to America for advanced education and that graduates from American universities are to be found in almost every Cabinet on every continent.[529]

The West, despite its apparent crass materialism and moral degeneration, also possessed technologies as well as social and cultural institutions that gave it immense power. To have their own power, the fundamentalists had to use these Western tools or risk being completely overwhelmed. The individual freedoms inherent in the West and the choice of affordable goods also proved attractive to many Muslims, especially the youth. The second generation of thinkers, therefore, was not so much concerned with a strict opposition to the West, but with offering a filter to screen the flow of Western influences. These thinkers all had experience with the West and, as such, had gained credibility for being able to sort the good from the bad of the Western world.

Turabi, for example, received a doctorate in law from the Sorbonne in Paris. He had said, "I was excited by the richness and precision of the French language, the culture, the history of the revolution, the relations between church and state, and the study of the different constitutions. I was not focused exclusively on my law studies. I went to the national library, I visited museums."[530] His partnership with the military regime in Sudan, since 1989, put him in the best position of any contemporary fundamentalist to implement an Islamic state.

Ghannushi, who was a leader in the Tunisian fundamentalist movement, had also studied philosophy at the Sorbonne, and was a student there during the 1968 student uprising. Ghannushi not only read the works of Islamic philosophers, but also Descartes, Bacon, Kant, Hegel, Schopenhauer, and Althusser. But on his return to Tunisia, he concentrated on teaching the ideas of Maududi, Banna, and Qutb to the emerging fundamentalist movement. Ghannushi is now a political refugee in Britain, where he serves as the foremost defender of Islamism in the West.

Fadlallah, an Iraqi Shiite, also studied western philosophy. He traveled to Lebanon in 1966 at the time when Beirut considered itself to be a second Paris. In this melting pot of ideologies, Fadlallah learned to package Islam in a new way. In the course of the 1980s, Fadlallah became the oracle and mentor of Hezbollah, a Shiite military group based in Lebanon.

Turabi, Ghannushi, and Fadlallah did not change the fundamental ideas of the Islamic state developed by Maududi, Qutb, and Khomeini. They simply repackaged it. They played down the themes of "Crusaderism" and the "Great Satan," and substituted the rhetoric of Third World anti-imperialism. Their arguments for the inevitable triumph of Islam drew upon the West's own thinkers who wrote about the decline of western civilization under the crushing dictatorship of capitalism.

Without sacrificing any element of ideological principle, the second wave thinkers worked to present the Islamic fundamentalist movements as an equivalent to the "reform" movements of the former communist bloc. With the Soviet Union gone, the fundamentalists of Islam claimed to pose the last ideological challenge to the United States, the last capitalist superpower. Ahmad Khomeini, son of the Ayatollah Khomeini, said, "After the fall of Marxism, Islam replaced it, and as long as Islam exists, US hostility exists, and as long as US hostility exists, the struggle exists."[531] Islamism, forged by a century of thought, has now claimed the status of a world ideology. Unfortunately, for the fundamentalists, the proof of its validity is not based upon spiritual principles, but once again on the empowerment of the propounders of religious dogma.

The Dogmatism of Islamic Fundamentalism

Though the West has a well-established tradition of separating state and religion, this is not the case in much of the Muslim world. The Islamic fundamentalists want to contest this trend of dividing life into the secular and religious, especially at the local level. Historically, Muslims have viewed Islam as a comprehensive way of life, affecting not only spiritual matters, but also social, economic, and political life as well. Thus, the idea of separating faith from society is inconceivable to a pious Muslim. Rather, they want their religious principles, as revealed in the *Koran* and the traditions of the Prophet, to be put into common practice by a common religious law, Sharia. So far so good. The problem arises, however, when different thinkers and different organizations define Sharia according to different standards, motivations, and beliefs.

Islamic fundamentalism is not a spiritual or God-centered ideology. It does not represent Islam in a universal fashion. Rather, it divides Muslims into believers and apostates (religious traitors) and further divides Muslims from the larger humanity into believers and unbelievers (infidels). Like Jewish and Christian fundamentalists, the Islamists have more love for their ideas and their religiously motivated laws than they have for human beings.

Islamic fundamentalism has demonstrated that it is riddled with negative dogma through the following actions:

- Declaring that anyone who does not follow the tenets of Islam is an infidel and therefore an enemy.
- Suppressing and oppressing women by the male priest class and male fundamentalists as a whole.
- Declaring that any man who dies fighting the infidels will be rewarded in the afterlife with beautiful virgins. (Apparently they had not thought this through.)
- Engaging in a virulent form of anti-homosexuality.
- Using brutal punishments for small offenses, including cutting off the hands of a thief and executing women in public forums.
- Persecuting followers of other religions.
- Massacring women and children and other Muslims who bridle at being saddled with a perverse interpretation of Islamic law.
- Selling "jihad" as a half-truth. Jihad, in the Quran, primarily refers to the internal spiritual process of self-improvement.

The concept of *jihad* simply means to struggle. Islamic guerrillas use it freely to describe their revolutionary struggles. The fighter who fights a

Jihad —a Mujahid—is believed to go straight to paradise if he dies and his enemy will go straight to hell. This is pure dogma.

While the term can mean a holy war, jihad primarily means a struggle, which has spiritual significance. In Islamic theology, the struggle to achieve the Divinity within is termed "the greater jihad" and the struggle with outside forces, such as state power or tyrannical armies is called "the lesser jihad." Islamic fundamentalists have made the lesser jihad the primary jihad and have used their definition to legitimize any kind of behavior, including the massacre of Muslims on holy days.[532]

The dogmatic oppression of women is well documented. According to a dogmatic interpretation of Sharia the crime of rape (zina-bil-jabr) is rarely proven because four adult Muslim males of good reputation must appear as witness to the act. If the charge fails, then the woman who has brought it, can be punished for false accusation (qazf) or, more commonly, for adultery (zina), because through her charge of rape she has admitted to participating in an illicit sexual act. In 1991, two-thirds of the women imprisoned in Pakistan were being held on such charges. This treatment, of course, has a very chilling effect on women who are raped, and allows rape to be perpetrated as a matter of course.

Sharia laws passed in the 1980s give a victim's heirs the right to inflict an equivalent harm. At the same time, however, wealthy Pakistanis can avoid punishment by paying money to the victim's family. Under the law, only half of the amount must be paid if the victim is female.

The most extreme fundamentalists, like the Taliban, deny women the right to work, the right to an education, the right to drive a car, the right to speak or be seen in public, and the right to meet their own basic needs. Women are beaten and oppressed in every way simply for being women. This is their religious dogma. It has nothing to do with spirituality. The male fundamentalists oppress the weakest of Islam, the women and children.

The Arab Spring

Beginning in December 2010, the Middle East went up for grabs. The common people rose up in protest against their oppression. What became known as the *Arab Spring* was a revolutionary wave consisting of demonstrations, protests, riots, and even civil wars across the Arab world. It began in Tunisia with the Tunisian Revolution and then spread to Egypt, Libya, Algeria, Morocco, Iraq, Jordan, Lebanon, Yemen, Bahrain, Oman, and even Saudi Arabia. Its most lasting effect are the civil wars in Syria and Yemen which are still ongoing.

The Arab Spring is widely believed to have been instigated by the youth and workers' unions who were dissatisfied with the oppressive and corrupt rule of national governments. Added pressures included the loss of jobs because of the Great Recession.

Some observers also blamed the US for fomenting revolution, specifically through the National Endowment for Democracy, which received its funds from the Bush administration.[533]

Other analysts say that al-Qaeda played a role in engineering protests against West-leaning governments. It is more than likely that several things can be blamed for triggering the riots. Certainly, many people were sick of being preyed on by oppressive dictators and being subjected to political corruption and human rights violations. Economic decline and extreme poverty served to further humiliate the people. The revolution in Tunisia was triggered by a street vendor, Mohamed Bouazizi, who immolated himself in protest against police corruption and ill-treatment.[534]

Many of the young protesters looked to the Turkish model as an ideal government because of its peaceful elections, fast-growing liberal economy, and secular constitution, even though it was governed by Islamists.

The Arab Spring demonstrations gained a few concessions by the governments, but when the people continued to protest, they were met with violent responses from the authorities. They were faced with attacks from pro-government militias and violent counter-demonstrators. As of 2018, only the uprising in Tunisia resulted in a transition to a constitutional, democratic government.

The Arab Spring contradicted the Western media propaganda that Islamist groups were violent by nature. The facts indicated that most preferred to work within the system as a means to create change. Many had attempted to work from the bottom up, developing their support among the population as a whole, and then work within the political system as legitimate opposition groups.

The Islamic Salvation Front (FIS), for example, was a Sunni Islamist political party in Algeria. It appealed to the pious small businessmen as well as to the unemployed youth. Less than a year after it was recognized as a political party, FIS received more than half of the votes cast by Algerians in the 1990 local government elections. When it appeared to be winning the general election in January 1992, a military coup dismantled the party interning thousands of its officials in the Sahara Desert. It was officially banned two months later.[535]

So too, the Muslim Brotherhood in Egypt worked their way up the political ladder in the neighborhoods of the people. Once they got into power, however, they destroyed their appeal with the people by systematically filling the majority of positions of authority with members of their own organization, while falsely vocalizing their support for democracy. The Muslim Brotherhood destroyed itself by trying to impose its archaic dogmatic values and rules on a people that wanted greater freedom and less dogma.

It is unlikely the Muslim Brotherhood and groups like it would have ever been legal except for the fact that many governments, notably in Egypt, Jordan, and Syria, used Islamists to successfully counter the appeal of Communism. Once these threats had receded, however, it was usually only a short time until the Islamists were again outlawed.

Once the option of operating as an opposition party within the political system was closed to Islamists, they only had two options left. One was to retreat to the mosque and continue to surreptitiously recruit followers and agitate peacefully for change. The other option was to join the ranks of the more radical Islamist groups and resort to violence and so-called terrorism.

The very concept of jihad included the struggle of a good Muslim to protect the Islamic community. To fight for one's people and one's family, was considered a human right, just as it is in America. The self-centered capitalist media, however, cynically called these freedom fighters "terrorists" because they lacked a mechanized army like the capitalists themselves or like the authoritarian dictators who ruled over them. On the same note, you will never hear the capitalist media ever speak of "state terrorism," which is daily perpetrated on civilian populations in countries all over the world to prop up capitalism and/or dictatorial rule.

When governments outlaw or attempt to destroy Islamist organizations, the result is to radicalize their ranks, leading to the escalation of violence. Few governments have been completely successful in eliminating Islamist violence, and many have made their situations worse by causing further radicalization. Violence will inevitably continue to be a problem as long as exploitation exists and other means of expression are closed off.

The Civil War in Syria

The utter failure of the Trilateralist and Neo-Con master plan for world dominance and the unbearable simple-mindedness of the US military's new "grand strategy" as articulated by Thomas Barnett in his book, *The Pentagon's New Map*, can be witnessed in the bloody upheaval of the Middle East that has unfolded over the last sixteen years. Brzezinski's glib rationalization for the US to dominate Eurasia and the world reveals a narcissist's vision of grandeur that gets dwarfed by the massive flood of pain, blood, and infinite complexities that has been unleashed on the people by the American empire's attempt to conquer the Middle East.

The Trilateralist and Neo-Con vision of world dominance gave rise to the infinite complexities involved in the US wars in Afghanistan, Iraq, and Syria. The toll can be counted in millions of dead and even more millions of displaced people. Let us look at the Civil War in Syria to demonstrate just how myopic the rulers of the US Empire actually are.

It is important to understand that in the civil war in Syria, President Assad is a Shiite and is supported by other Shiites and other Shiite regimes. All the opposition forces are Sunni Islamists, like those who fought against his father. These Sunni Islamists are not fighting to create a democratic government or free markets. They are not pro-capitalist or pro-West. They are fighting to oust a Shiite dictator who rules a country whose population is largely Sunni. The opposition forces are composed of members of the armed forces who abandoned the regime to fight against it (FSA). It is buttressed by different militia groups and Sunni Islamist jihadists. In the beginning, the United States attempted to arm only the "moderate" forces of the opposition, but as the war continued, the rebel forces, composed for the most part of various Sunni militia groups, united against Assad. Saudi Arabia, Turkey, and Qatar, all dominated by Sunnis, also want Assad gone. They would have gladly played a more active role in arming the rebels, but the Obama administration held them back. Then Russia took the side of the Assad government and its air force began bombing ISIS held territories.

When the riots and rebellions of the Arab Spring broke out across Muslim countries in December, 2010, the western press exulted that the people of the Middle East had finally grown weary of being dominated by autocratic dictators and were fighting to create democracies within their countries. The Arab Spring was spun as just another sign that the US, by its invasion of Afghanistan and Iraq, were indeed helping to spread democracy around the world. Again, this was just more propaganda to justify the capitalist and militarist elites grand strategy for world conquest.

Here is an account of what has been going on in Syria since 2010 when civil war broke out in that country. Crimes against humanity have been committed by the Syrian government as well as the opposition forces. Sunnis and Shiites have slaughtered each other. In these, and other crimes, the United States also stands accountable.

The wave of Arab uprisings, that began with the Tunisian revolution in January, 2011, reached Syria in mid-March when residents of the small southern town of Dara'a took to the streets to protest the torture of students who had been caught by the police while putting up anti-government graffiti. The protestors demanded that the governor be removed. The national government under Assad responded favorably by firing the governor.

Despite the governor's dismissal, according to an activists report, "Around one thousand protesters gathered in and around the Omari mosque shouting anti-regime slogans, amid a heavy security and army presence."[536]

Meanwhile, video footage posted on the Internet showed new anti-government protests in a suburb of the capital, Damascus, and a village in southern Syria. One clip on YouTube showed several hundred villagers in Sanamein chanting "Freedom!" while another showed dozens gathered in the Hajar Aswad neighborhood of the capital.

As the protests led by the Sunni population spread, Assad made an effort to appease the people. After firing the governor, he now dismissed the Syrian government's thirty-two member cabinet. In actuality, the cabinet held little power in Syria because power was concentrated in the hands of Assad, his family, and his Shiite security forces.[537] In further attempts to appease the people, Assad declared that the State of Emergency law, put in effect in 1963, that allowed the government to suspend constitutional rights, would also be repealed. In addition, he promised to release men held in detention and to revise laws to allow opposition political parties to be formed.[538] These were certainly large steps to democratize the country, but after years of oppression and having the successful examples of Tunisia and Egypt as models for revolution, the Syrian dissidents saw Assad's reforms as too little too late. Now they wanted him to step down. The protests continued. Assad countered by launching a nationwide crackdown that included sending tanks and snipers into cities where protests were being held. Security forces opened fire on the Sunni demonstrators. Water and electricity were shut off and food was confiscated in those cities. By October, estimates for the death toll ranged above twenty-nine hundred, and human rights groups said that over ten thousand people had been arrested. Syrian dissidents formally established the Syrian National Council, which included the Syrian Muslim Brotherhood, other Islamic groups, banned political parties, NGOs, a Kurdish faction, etc.

As the brutal crackdowns continued the violence escalated. Pro-Assad militia from the Assad's Aliwat tribe began to hold counter demonstrations and to beat protestors in the street. This brutality caused large numbers of defections from the Syrian army who then formed the Free Syrian Army and thereafter a full-scale civil war between Shiite and Sunni developed.

Assad's Strategy

Assad's father Hafez al-Assad, who had been the previous ruler of Syria, had survived a series of armed revolts by Sunni Islamists, mainly members of the Muslim Brotherhood, from 1976 until 1982. Like his father,

Assad interpreted the uprising he was now facing as an attempt by Sunnis, who constituted the majority in his country, to overthrow his regime. Hafez had built his counterinsurgency campaign on three strategies for employing his military force. First, he carefully selected and deployed the most trusted military units. Secondly, he raised pro-regime militias, and thirdly, he used those forces to clear insurgents out of major urban areas and then hold those cities with heavy garrisons of troops. Bashar al-Assad attempted to employ the same strategy in 2011-2012, but failed miserably.

By limiting his dependency on a small core of trusted military units, he limited his ability to control all of Syria. Defections and attrition also exacerbated the regime's attempt to confront the opposition. While these developments reduced the numbers of the Syrian Army, it also honed it into a dedicated army in support of Assad.

In addition to the conventional army, pro-Assad militias were also developed as a source of armed reinforcement for the Syrian Army. The mostly-Alawite *shabiha* (mafias) are led by extended members of the Assad family and have been responsible for some of the worst brutality against the Syrian opposition. Local Popular Committees drawn from religious minorities have also armed themselves to protect their communities against opposition fighters. Both types of militia coordinate closely with the regime and receive direct support from the government as well as from Iran's Islamic Revolutionary Guards (IRGC) and Lebanese Hezbollah which are also Shia organizations.

Combatant Groups

The Free Syrian Army (FSA)

As Assad's suppression of protesters increased, hundreds of people were massacred. Seven Syrian officers defected and formed the Free Syrian Army (FSA). They released a video calling on all soldiers to defend civilian protestors and to bring down the Assad regime. Their first action was to seize control of the area surrounding the city of Aleppo and parts of southern Syria.

The Syrian Democratic Forces (SDF)

Faced with the loss of Aleppo and parts of southern Syria, Assad withdrew his troops stationed in the north to fight the Free Syrian Army. This allowed the Kurds, who lived in the north to secure their territory and claim de facto autonomy. In 2015, the Kurd forces joined with some Arab, Assyrian, Armenian, and some Turkmen groups to form the Syrian Democratic Forces. Most Turkmen groups, however, continued to fight under the banner of the Free Syrian Army. The SDF has concentrated its strength against ISIS Sunnis and has driven them from important strategic areas.[539]

The Southern Front

The Southern Front is a loose coalition of fifty-four rebel groups, ranging from secularist to moderately religious. Although they lack a central command, they coordinate activities and have controlled about seventy percent of the Daraa Governorate in the southwest corner of the country. The fighting groups agreed on the name 'Southern Front' to receive funding and weapons from international forces, which opposed the Assad government. Members of the FSA are a part of this coalition and it is said that the groups within the Southern Front receive support from the US.[540]

Jabhat Fateh al-Sham

The al-Nusra front was formed at the end of 2011 when the al-Qaeda leader in Iraq, Abu Bakr al-Baghdadi, ordered Abu Muhammed al-Julani, the al-Qaeda leader in Syria, to organize jihadist groups in the region. The alliance of these groups became known as the al-Nusra Front. In July 2016, the al-Nusra Front changed its name to Jabhat Fateh al-Sham which means the "Front for the Conquest of Syria/the Levant." When al-Baghdadi announced that the Jabhat Fateh al-Sham was to become part of ISIS, the group refused to pledge allegiance to ISIS and continued to affiliate itself with al-Qaeda instead. Since then, clashes between the two groups have deprived al-Qaeda of control of oil fields in east Syria, which provided them with significant income.[541]

Harakat Ahrar al-Sham al-Islamiyya

The "Islamic Movement of the Free Men of the Levant," is a coalition of Islamist and Salafist units that coalesced into a single brigade in order to fight against the Syrian Government.[542] Like the Islamists, who advocate an Islamic state governed by Sharia law, the Salafists are also fundamentalist Muslims. They are perhaps the most strict and severe of the fundamentalists. Often associated with Wahhabism, they assume a literalist, strict and puritanical approach to Islam.[543] They are the second most powerful fighting force against al-Assad, after the Free Syrian Army. The group aims to create an Islamic state under Sharia law, and is openly allied with Jabhat Fateh al-Sham with which it carries out joint operations.

ISIS

The *Islamic State of Iraq and Greater Syria* (*ISIS*), formed as a result of the American invasion of Iraq. When the Americans overthrew Saddam Hussein, his army, along with the existing government structure, was destroyed. This caused the fragile balance between the Shiite and Sunni factions to become undone. During the US occupation they failed to establish an effective Iraqi army and police force to fill the newly created security vacuum. In the meantime, the Americans were trying to establish a democratic national Shi'ite regime, but the regime alienated the Sunni population. While only about twenty-two percent of the population of Iraq are Sunnis, they had previously controlled the country under Hussein. When the Americans attempted to install the Shiites in a position of leadership, the Sunnis fought back.

Al-Qaeda, composed of fundamentalist Sunnis, rapidly expanded their organization by appealing to the Sunni's desire for revenge after their loss of power and current state of alienation. The al-Qaeda's ranks immediately swelled with officers and soldiers who had once served in Saddam's government. As al-Qaeda gained power under the leadership of Abu Musab al-Zarqawi, it waged a guerilla war against the American occupation and against the Shiite population now allied with the Americans. In 2006, Zarqawi was killed by an American drone attack.

As the guerilla war continued, the Sunni fighting force under al-Qaeda took the name *Islamic State of Iraq (ISI)*. ISI served as an umbrella group for several jihadi organizations that continued to fight against the Americans and Shiites.

When the American army withdrew from Iraq, ISI became stronger and when the civil war began in Syria, ISI established a branch in Syria called the al-Nusra Front. After some time, dissention between ISI and al-Nusra occurred, leading to a rift between ISI and al-Qaeda in Iraq. This led to ISI establishing itself in Syria as ISIS, the *Islamic State of Iraq and Greater Syria*.

Beginning in 2014, ISIS achieved significant military victories, the most prominent being the takeover of Mosul, the second largest city in Iraq. It also took control of eastern Syria where it set up its capital city in al-Raqqah. As a result of its success, ISIS declared the establishment of an Islamic State (Caliphate) headed by Abu Bakr al-Baghdadi. In September 2014, the United States declared a comprehensive campaign against ISIS and waged a fierce struggle with it on several fronts. ISIS found itself fighting Americans, Russians, Turks, the Syrian government, and the Syrian Democratic Forces (Kurds, Assyrians, etc.) in Syria and also its enemies back in Iraq.[544]

Shiite/Sunni Conflict in Syria

President Bashar al-Assad, a Shiite, had used his military to attack populations in opposition strongholds by employing artillery, jet bombers, bulldozers, massacres, and even ballistic missiles to force Syrian civilians out of insurgent held areas. Therefore, even when the rebels took over towns and neighborhoods, they lost the population. But the Syrian government is not the only combatant to create brutal and despicable crimes against humanity. ISIS and other Sunni militia organizations have also terrorized and tortured civilians and have gone so far as to force thousands of women and children into sex slavery. It is little wonder that half the Syrian population, almost six million people, left the country, preferring to risk starvation, pain, and death as refugees than to stay in their homeland.

Fears of the Sunni opposition forces resulted in a broad, ultra-nationalist Shiite fighting force, which waged a fierce war against any opposition-led Sunni forces in Syria. Today, even if the Assad regime collapses, Iran and Lebanese Hezbollah are likely to continue to arm these forces in order to preserve their interest in maintaining Shiite control of the country.

At the height of the conflict in 2016, the Assad regime has concentrated its conventional forces in Damascus and Homs. The relatively small forces deployed to the east and north, while achieving some success in curtailing opposition advances, were isolated units that were easily overrun.

Foreign Intervention

The United States

During the first months of the Syrian Civil War, the United States began to supply the Free Syrian Army (FSA) with supplies, including food and pickup trucks. Soon, they were providing training, cash, and intelligence.[545]

On September 10, 2014, President Barack Obama gave a speech at the White House indicating his intent to "degrade and ultimately destroy" the *Islamic State of Iraq and the Levant* (*ISIS*), saying, "I have made it clear that we will hunt down terrorists who threaten our country, wherever they are. That means I will not hesitate to take action against ISIL in Syria, as well as Iraq."[546]

Within two weeks, the United States, Bahrain, Jordan, Qatar, Saudi Arabia, and the United Arab Emirates began air strikes against ISIS and al-Nusra inside Syria.[547] Other countries also began to conduct airstrikes against ISIS including Australia, Canada, France, the Netherlands, England, and Turkey.[548] Turkey, having different motivations, has primarily intervened against Kurdish forces in Syria and Iraq, during which they coordinate activities with ISIS. According to an assessment carried out by the Defense Intelligence Agency (DIA) and the Joint Chiefs of Staff, in 2013, Turkey had effectively subverted the secret US arms supply to moderate rebels (FSA) into a program that provides technical and logistical support to all elements of the opposition, including Jabhat al-Nusra and Islamic State.[549]

This was made possible because, by the end of 2013, the Free Syrian Army had already begun to disintegrate. Its weapon supplies from the

US were being captured by other Islamist groups and its soldiers were defecting to join these groups. FSA headquarters was in shambles.[550]

In 2013, the US was on the verge of conducting military strikes against the Assad government in retaliation for his use of chemical weapons in the Ghouta, the countryside around Damascus. President Obama had previously declared that if Assad used chemical weapons, he would cross a "red line" and the US would retaliate. While the US military was on alert to strike, Obama failed to live up to his own commitment to enforce the "red line." Later, in 2015, with the help of Russia, Assad gave up his chemical weapon stockpile. Obama's critics in 2013 castigated him for failing to attack Assad, claiming that his lack of resolve did lasting damage to America's standing in the world. In 2015, Obama was able to say:

> My commitment was to make sure that Syria was not using chemical weapons and mobilizing the international community to assure that that would not happen. And, in fact, we positioned ourselves to be willing to take military action. The reason we did not was because Assad gave up his chemical weapons. That's not speculation on our part. That, in fact, has been confirmed by the organization internationally that is charged with eliminating chemical weapons.[551]

In the same year, shortly after the Russian military intervened in Syria on behalf of Assad's government, Obama authorized five hundred million dollars to train and supply an additional thirty thousand Syrian Kurds and opposition fighters, emphasizing that the US would continue to supply new fighters because Russia had joined the conflict.[552]

Within a few months, however, the US officially announced the end of its program to train and equip Syrian rebels, calling the program a failure because too few men reported for training. Instead, the administration announced it would use the money to provide ammunition and weapons for groups already engaged in the battle.[553]

In December 2015, the US reportedly shipped hundreds of thousands of small arms, including anti-tank missiles, assault rifles, heavy machine guns, and hand held machine guns through Bulgaria to the opposition fighters. It also sent one hundred and fifty American soldiers to train and gather intelligence for the Kurdish militia.

Turkey

In July 2016, the Syrian army and its allies succeeded in cutting off the last supply road into rebel-held east Aleppo, and laid siege to large areas of the city. The fate of three hundred thoussand people hung in the balance. Airstrikes on residential areas and medical facilities by Syrian and Russian aircraft increased the misery of a city after suffering years of war and deprivation. The Turkish government denounced the siege.

In early August, a coalition of Syrian rebels and Islamist groups in Aleppo, supported by Turkey, staged a last-ditch operation to break the siege. By August 8, the rebels announced that it had driven the government troops out of the Al-Ramouseh district, in southern Aleppo, effectively lifting the siege.

Ahrar al-Sham, the conservative Islamist group composed of Salafist units, was one of the major factions involved in the operation. A spokesperson for the group said that the cooperation between the various rebel groups had allowed them to break the siege. He also added that, "the battles in Aleppo will not stop until we put an end to the regime's existence."[554]

The rebel coalition also included Jabhat Fath al-Sham, the Syrian al Qaeda fighting force. While rebel groups said they had no plans to besiege the government-held west Aleppo, analysts believe that a battle for control of the entire city would be forthcoming.

Aleppo, prior to the civil war, was Syria's largest city and economic hub. Its northern countryside was of vital interest to Turkey because the Kurds had already declared it as part of its de facto independent state. If the Kurds were able to establish independence in Syria, it would destabilize the Kurdish population within Turkey, just across the border and allow them to form a unified state of their own.

For hundreds of years, Aleppo was a territory of the Ottoman Empire, ruled from Istanbul, Turkey. Following World War I and the

Turkish War of Independence, the city of Aleppo was cut off from Turkish control and placed within the newly created state of Syria, while much of the city's rural area to the north remained within the border of Turkey. For Turkish nationalists, therefore, the Assad government's assault against Aleppo seemed almost like an attack on their own country.

Because of Turkey's historical ties to Aleppo, it did not want to see the city returned to Syrian control. It wanted to install its own forces, which could play a more vital role in Syrian politics. Ostensibly, Turkey claimed that its intervention in Aleppo was to drive out ISIS, but the Kurds in the city, believe that they were the main target of Turkey's intervention. The Kurds had been receiving US backing and had been making gains against ISIS.

The Kurdish factions view the intervention of Turkey in Aleppo as a means to prevent the Kurds from uniting their government jurisdictions in the north. According to Wladimir van Wilgenburg, a Middle East expert, "ISIS has controlled large parts of the Syrian-Turkish border and Turkey did nothing. It was only when the Kurdish-led forces threatened to unite their administrations that Turkey intervened."[555]

Turkey's intervention into Syria did take territory away from the Islamic State, but its intention had always been to engage in direct conflict with the Kurdish-led forces in the country. Turkish leaders held high-profile meetings with officials from Russia and Iran, key allies of the Syrian government.

Turkey's military intervention and the gains made by its allied rebel groups in Aleppo suggested an increasingly forceful role by Turkey in Syria's civil war. The intervention however, complicated the grand strategy of the US elites because the Americans now found themselves backing multiple hostile sides in an increasingly convoluted conflict. Determining the good guys and bad guys was not so simple as Thomas P. M. Barnett thought when he wrote his book *The Pentagon's New Map*, which articulated the western capitalist elite's new "War on Terrorism." The rebel forces became more confident in Turkey's help and became more forceful in the way they fought on other fronts.

Russia

Russia and Syria had been allies for a long time and Putin did not wish to lose one of the few remaining countries in the region with which Russia has a good working relationship. Putin claimed that he desires order and stability, and thus the "legitimate" government of Mr. Assad should be supported and strengthened. Mr. Putin pointed to Iraq and Libya as evidence of the chaos that was caused when the US tried to remove leaders from power.

Russia entered Syria's civil war on September 30, 2016 with airstrikes against the rebel forces battling the Assad government. By October 7, it had launched cruise missiles from hundreds of miles away in the Caspian Sea. Russia claimed that the missile strikes were part of a campaign to combat "terrorism," but they were aimed at opposition groups other than ISIS. The Russian air strikes had supported ground attacks by the Assad regime, particularly around the cities of Idlib and Homs.

Opposition forces at the time literally consisted of thousands of fighting groups who moved freely about, sometimes working in coalitions, and sometimes fighting on their own. It was impossible, therefore, for air strikes alone to defeat the rebels. The only thing the air strikes did was to drive more civilians, including women and children, out of the country.

Many rebel groups, with the exception of ISIS, had coordinated strategies despite their differences. In March 2016, Jaysh al-Fatah (the Army of Conquest), a coalition of northern rebel groups including Jabhat al-Nusra and Ahrar al-Sham, took Idlib city. South of Damascus, the Southern Front, also gained strength.

The rebel groups, however, would have faced greater danger if Russia had decided to send ground troops into Syria. Russia had become increasingly aggressive in defending Syria's embattled Bashar Assad. In early November, 2016, Russian government officials went so far as to warn the US not to interfere in Syria or American aircraft would be shot down by advanced Russian air defense systems. The Russians had moved its advanced S-300 missile system into position in Syria after an agreement between the US and Russia failed to stabilize Syria. Former head of the Soviet Union, Mikhail Gorbachev considered the situation between Russia and the United States the most dangerous it had been in decades, similar to the Cuban Missile Crisis. Russia had more nuclear weapons than any country in the world, 7,300 comared to the American's 6,970. It also had an operationally advanced military.[556]

But even without assistance from Russia, there were reports that Iran, Assad's other ally, was already funneling more Shia militiamen into the country, under the direction of its own commanders. Hezbollah, Iran's client militia in Lebanon, had long been fighting for Mr. Assad, as had other Shia militias.

In December 2016, Assad's forces recaptured all of rebel-held parts of Aleppo, ending the four-year battle in the city. On December 29, Vladimir Putin announced a new ceasefire deal had been reached between the Syrian Government and opposition groups (excluding U.N.-designated terrorist groups such as ISIL and Jabhat Fateh al-Sham), with Russia and Turkey acting as guarantors and Iran as a signatory.

By February 14, 2017, however, the ceasefire between Assad forces and rebels had collapsed throughout the country, leading to renewed clashes in various locations and a fresh rebel offensive in Dara'a.

On April 4, 2017, the Syrian government conducted an airstrike on the town of Khan Shaykhun in the Idlib Governorate of Syria. The airstrike was followed by massive civilian chemical poisoning. The release of a toxic gas, killed at least seventy-four people and injured more than five hundred and fifty-seven, according to the opposition Idlib health authority. The chemicals used indicated that the gas originated from the government's chemical stockpile. The attack was the deadliest use of chemical weapons in the Syrian civil war since the Ghouta chemical attack in 2013.

The governments of the United States, United Kingdom, Turkey, Saudi Arabia, France, and Israel, as well as Human Rights Watch attributed the attack to the Syrian forces of President Assad. The Syrian government said the attack was a "fabrication." The Russian government claimed that the incident was staged.

On April 7, the United States launched fifty-nine cruise missiles at Shayrat Air Base, which US intelligence claimed was the source of the attack.

On July 7, 2017, the US, Russia, and Jordan agreed to a ceasefire in part of southwestern Syria, with Russia giving assurances that Assad would abide by the agreement. On July 19, it was reported that the US had decided to halt the CIA program that equipped and trained anti-government rebel groups, a move sought by Russia.

On September 5, a government offensive broke the three-year ISIS siege of Deir ez-Zor, with active participation of the Russian air force and navy. This was followed shortly thereafter by the lifting of the siege of the city's airport.

On October 17, after four months of fierce fighting and the US-led bombardment, the Kurdish-dominated SDF announced they had established full control of the city of Raqqa in northern Syria. At the end of October, the government of Syria said that it still considered Raqqa to be an occupied city that can "only be considered liberated when the Syrian Arab Army enter[ed] it." [557]

On December 6, Russia declared Syria to have been "completely liberated" from ISIS; on December 11, President Putin visited the Russian base in Syria, where he announced that he had ordered the partial withdrawal of the forces deployed to Syria. On December 26, Russian defense minister Sergey Shoigu said that Russia had set about "forming a permanent grouping" at its naval facility at Tartus and Hmeymim airbase. Two days later, Russian foreign minister Sergey Lavrov said that Russia believed that the US forces must leave Syrian territory completely once remnants of the terrorists were completely eliminated.

On January 20, 2018, the Turkish military began a cross-border operation in the Kurdish majority Afrin Canton and the Tel Rifaat Area of Shahba Canton in Northern Syria, against the Kurdish-led Democratic Union Party in Syria (PYD), its armed wing People's Protection Units (YPG), and Syrian Democratic Forces (SDF) positions.

On March 18, on the fifty-eighth day of the Turkish military operation in Afrin, the Turkish-backed Free Syrian Army (TFSA or FSA), Turkish Armed Forces, and disparate rebel groups captured Afrin from the Kurds, displacing up to two hundred thousand people. Shortly after the capture, the attacking army looted parts of the city and solidified control by raising Turkish flags and banners over the city. Turkey's relationship with the US was stretched to breaking point by the Afrin operation, which pitted the two NATO allies and their Syrian proxies against one another.

On April 7, 2018, a chemical attack was made in the city of Douma, with seventy people killed and five hundred injured. On-site medics stated the cause of deaths was exposure to chlorine and sarin gas. The Syrian government denied any use of chemical weapons. Following the incident, Syrian government forces entered and established control over the city of Douma, ending the five-year Siege of Ghouta.

On April 14, the US, UK, and France launched missile strikes on multiple government targets in Syria in response to the chemical attack in Douma.

On May 1, the US government announced "operations to liberate the final ISIS strongholds in Syria,"[558] which would ensure that "populations liberated from ISIS are not exploited by the Assad regime or its Iranian supporters".

On September 17th, Israel hit multiple targets in western Syria. While trying to strike the Israeli planes, Syrian forces shot down a Russian plane, causing the deaths of fifteen Russians. The strikes occurred a few hours after a Russo-Turkish agreement, to create a demilitarized zone around Idlib Governorate, was achieved, which postponed an imminent offensive operation by Syrian government forces and its allies. Russia blamed Israel for the incident claiming that the Israeli military was the sole culprit of the accident.

In the aftermath of the strikes, on September 24, 2018, the Russian defense minister confirmed that the Syrian army would receive S-300 air-defense missile systems to strengthen Syria's combat air defense capabilities. He added that the previous cancellation of the contract for S-300 delivery in 2013 had been due to Israel's request, but following the downing of the Russian aircraft in Syria the situation had changed. The S300 had modern IFF systems which would prevent the missiles from targeting Russian aircraft.

On December 12, the Turkish government announced it would begin operations against Rojava, the Democratic Federation of Northern Syria, which was predominantly a Kurdish area. This was a rebuke of the US which was allied with the Kurds. In response, the Pentagon said that any unilateral military action taken in northern Syria where US forces were operating would be "unacceptable." However, President Trump abruptly announced on December 19, 2018 the withdrawal of all troops from Syria, after which Turkey postponed the planned attack.

On January 5, 2019, a Kurdish fighter was killed and two British special forces troops were seriously injured by an ISIS attack near the town of Deir al-Zour. The injured men were evacuated by US forces.

On January 6, 2019, US National Security Adviser John Bolton said, on a trip to Israel and Turkey, that the withdrawal of US troops from Syria depends on certain conditions, including the assurance that the remnants of ISIS forces are defeated and Kurds in northern Syria were safe from Turkish forces. However, Turkey's President Recep Tayyip Erdogan rejected the call to protect Kurdish troops, whom he regarded as terrorist groups.

On January 10, 2019, US Secretary of State, Mike Pompeo, said at a joint news conference with his Egyptian counterpart Sameh Shoukry in Cairo that the US would withdraw its troops from Syria while continuing the battle against ISIS, but warned that there would be no US reconstruction aid for areas controlled by Syrian President Bashar al-Assad until Iran and its proxies had left.[559]

The Trilateralist, master plan to conquer Eurasia and keep Russian from becoming a regional power had failed miserably. The US master plan had only served to unleash chaos, depravity, and death across the Middle East. The US troops careened from one country to the next, setting them on fire. US attempts to destabilize Syria had only served to aggravate tensions with Turkey and Russia and bring them into the theatre of war. We can add this to the list of failed missions not the least of which is the creation of millions of refugees flooding to tent cities around the world where they still live in subhuman conditions because western country's refuse them entry.

In the meantime, both sides in the civil war, which by now has also become a proxy war for the US and Russia, accuse each other of spreading terrorism, depravity, and crimes against humanity. Both sides are correct. With the region in chaos and thousands of splinter groups and warring countries fighting for self-interest, it appears that Syria is in for another period of escalating violence.[560] In the meantime, more people are leaving Syria as refugees to suffer and dying while carrying the distant hope that they will be welcomed by well-intentioned strangers around the world.

Refugee Migration

The violence in Syria caused millions of people to flee their homes. As early as March 2015, Al-Jazeera estimated that 10.9 million Syrians, or almost half the population, had been displaced.[561] Of these, 3.8 million have become refugees. Approximately one of three of these Syrian refugees (about 667,000 people) sought safety in Lebanon, which is a small country with a population of only 4.8 million people. Other Syrians, of which half are women and children, had also fled to Jordan, Turkey, and Iraq. By 2015, Turkey had accepted about 3 million Syrian refugees, half of whom were spread around cities and a dozen camps under the direct authority of the Turkish Government.

The hosting of large refugee populations takes its toll on a country. Differences between ethnicity, language, culture, and other identity lines cause fear and anxiety among all people involved. Turkey has faced repeated destabilizations in hosting refugees fleeing violence, including those from Bulgaria and Iraq.

For almost seventy years, Jordan has been accepting generations of refugees from the Palestinian territories, Iraq, and Syria. The United Nations High Commissioner for Refugees (UNHCR) indicates that 638,000 Syrian refugees live in Jordan while official Jordanian statistics put the number at 1.3 million.[562] Jordanians do not use the same xenophobic rhetoric against refugees that we find in Europe, Australia, and the United States, but they feel the pressure in terms of a decline in their standard of living as the refugee burden distorts the economy with rising costs. They also feel the pressure in their crowded schools, streets, and hospitals.

The real refugee crisis is in the Middle East, not in Europe or the United States where the backlash is more severe and where the "refugee crisis" is polarizing the Western nations.

Since the start of the Syrian conflict in 2011, 2.5 million Syrians have entered Jordan, according to Jordan's Refugee Affairs Coordination Office. 1.3 million Syrians have now settled in Jordan. Approximately 150,000 have returned to Syria. Over one million have traveled to Turkey or North Africa in search of a route to Europe.

Meanwhile, the western governments behave as if Jordan and Turkey are responsible for taking in the refugees. Because the West throws money at the problem, they act like they do not have to contend with it. Rather, they expect the Middle East countries to accept all the refugees. In addition, the US and NATO countries also claim the right to determine who goes and comes into those countries and when. This insulting attitude is not lost on the local countries. A government spokesman for Jordan, in response to this attitude said, "Jordan is a sovereign state. We have legitimate security concerns."[563]

When the Syrian refugees started arriving in the West, reactionaries began to scream and moan about terrorism coming to their shores. While the US and NATO elites were largely responsible for creating the problem in the first place, the citizens of Western countries, particularly those in the US, after being conditioned by a steady drumbeat of hatred against terrorists, now feared that those same terrorists are coming to their countries to harm them. The government heightened this fear by declaring yellow and orange alerts.

The fear that terrorists may be hiding among the refugees is reasonable. Adequate protections must be put into place, but the fear is vastly overblown by the steady drumbeat of War on Terror propaganda perpetrated by the mass media. The great master plan of the capitalist elites did not consider the possibility of millions of refugees spilling out of the Middle East as a result of their plan. They did not account for the resurgence of ultra-nationalism throughout Europe and America that would result from such a mass migration of people. A recent Pew study links the rise of ultra-nationalism in Europe and the US directly to fears of increasing refugee populations, terrorism, and Western resistance to cultural diversity.[564]

The people of Europe were totally unprepared for the mass exodus of people out of the Middle East. They could not envision the multitudes that would come knocking on their door begging for sanctuary. Because it is impossible to vet such a great number of people or to accommodate them within the domestic economies, the people of Europe have legitimate concerns about terrorism, but also about economic hardship, crime, and the presence of a large body of immigrants whom they do not see as being able to assimilate into their western culture.

Immigration is now the most contentious issue in American and British politics, driving a wedge between liberal and conservative tendencies. One of the primary reasons that the majority of the English voted to leave the European Union was their strong anti-immigration sentiment.⁵⁶⁵ While the media blamed Brexit on the fact that ordinary Britons were bearing an unacceptable economic cost from immigration, this was, in fact, not true. Rather, data showed that Britain was not suffering harmful economic effects from too many new migrants; it was suffering from too much xenophobia, i.e., bigotry against people of different cultural origins.⁵⁶⁶

In the United States, the rise of Donald Trump and the ultra-nationalist backlash to the neo-liberal agenda is largely attributable to the Obama administration's immigration stance. Trump, speaking to cheering crowds, thundered that the only way to make America great again was to stop immigration.⁵⁶⁷ Adding credibility to his demagoguery, were the occasional "lone wolf" attacks by so-called terrorists in the US. There is a visceral fear, not without justification, that ISIS sleeper cells will make their way into the US disguised as refugees. This fear is validated by the wave of attacks that hit Germany, France, and Belgium during the summer of 2016.

On July 18, near Wuerzburg in Bavaria, a seventeen year-old refugee believed to be from Pakistan or Afghanistan wounded five people with an axe before police shot him dead. A twenty-seven year-old Syrian, with an alleged allegiance to ISIS, blew himself up in Ansbach, southern Germany on July 24.

On Bastille Day, an attack in Nice shook Europe as a terrorist took a truck on a rampage and killed eighty-four people. A further ISIS-inspired attack in Normandy, killed Father Jacques Hamel, a Catholic priest, while he was conducting a mass on July 26.⁵⁶⁸ In truth, such terrorist attacks may result from refugees or from Western citizens who are inspired by ISIS because it is willing to take a stand against the grand strategy of the capitalist ruling elite.

As a result of these terrorist attacks, conservatives now view every refugee, even the women and children, as potential Islamic State terrorists. This fear is heightened by the idea that Muslims will ot acculturate into Western societies because they do not accept Western values. More troubling to Europeans, however, is the fear of economic burden and an increase in crime. The above findings correlate highly with whether one believes that a diverse society is a good thing. Only a minority of Europeans believe diversity is good. The majority, who tend to be conservative in their worldview, believe that diversity is a bad thing. Thus, the resurgence of ultra-nationalism is characterized by a growth in racism, sexism, and xenophobia.

The correlation between acceptance of Muslims and a positive view of the value of diversity in Europe differs remarkably from the American view of diversity, in which only seven percent say that a diverse society makes life worse.[569] Thus, Americans, do not mind diversity, but a sizeable minority are equally virulent in their opposition to Muslims entering their country. This opposition to Muslims seems to be a direct result of the constant War on Terror propaganda that Americans are subjected to in their daily lives.

The United States has only committed to accept ten thousand refugees, a dismal amount by any account. Thirty-two countries have taken in more refugees than the US, including Austria, Denmark, Singapore, Switzerland, France, Brazil, and Spain. Insofar as the United States is the wealthiest and most powerful nation in the world and insofar as it is largely responsible for turning the Middle East into a brutal civil war zone in the first place, it is unjust, immoral, and just plain venal for the US government to turn its back on the innocent people who now are the victims of its own grand strategy of conquest.

In the meantime, the people in the refugee camps are becoming more desperate. Many are being exploited by con men and traffickers. For example, almost nine thousand unaccompanied refugee children were officially missing in Germany, as of November 2016. These children, aged thirteen or younger, are believed to have been targeted by organized trafficking gangs.

Children are often smuggled into the country by traffickers and then told they have to pay off debts of as much as fifty-five thousand dollars for their travel. Save the Children found girls as young as thirteen from Nigeria and Romania forced into prostitution after being promised jobs as hairdressers or babysitters. Boys are being forced into child labor or drug dealing to pay their debts.[570]

Unaccompanied women are preyed upon and raped. Many are trafficked into forced labor and prostitution.[571]

It is anyone's guess, how many more terrorists will be created due to the suffering of the people in these camps. In short, the capitalist elites and the military leadership have created a "monster" that they can no longer control. As for the refugees themselves, they had gone through hell just trying to stay alive. They came as families who left behind their homes and possessions; they came as women alone with children, or children by themselves, orphaned by the war. About one in ten refugees are pregnant women.[572] Fifty percent are children. As their situation deteriorates, more terrorists will be created and the fear of terrorists will continue to grow among Western citizens. What is the solution to this problem? It is certainly not international capitalism.

Yemen

The "Empty Quarter" is a vast desert that extends for over a thousand miles. It is located within Northern Yemen and southeastern Saudi Arabia. As a consequence, a clear borderline between the two countries has never been established. In the mid-1980s, however, oil reserves were discovered in the Empty Quarter and set off a conflict between Yemen and Saudi Arabia as to which country owned the oil.

Yemen, as a country did not exist until 1990. Previous to unification, the territory in the south was controlled by Sunni Marxists, while the north was controlled by tribes of Shiite origin. Saudi Arabia had established relations with the northern tribes who lived in and around the Empty Quarter ever since King Saud established Saudi Arabia in 1932. In 1934, Saud's forces fought a brief war with these tribes that resulted in a treaty that, for the first time, formally demarcated part of the border between the two countries. In the process several Yemeni tribes became incorporated into Saudi Arabia. However, because of kinship ties and the grazing patterns of their animals, the border proved difficult to control. One of the stipulations of the treaty was that Yemenis had unrestricted entry to the kingdom.

When the oil boom began in the 1960s, almost two million Yemenis went to Saudi Arabia for jobs where they had certain privileges not available to other immigrant workers. In the short term, this employment brought tremendous benefits to north Yemen, but in the longer term, it also led to negative consequences. For example, it tied the northern Yemen's economy to Saudi Arabia, thus making it vulnerable to changes in political relations with the Saudis. Secondly, the influx of wealth from the workers in Saudi Arabia ruined the domestic economy in northern Yemen by causing inflation, wealth disparity, and the decline of its agricultural base. Villages were left in disrepair.

Within Saudi Arabia, there were also tensions. The Saudi elite feared the large number of Yemenis might foment opposition to their monarchy, while the Yemenis felt unappreciated even though they had shouldered the heavy burden of building the cities and projects across the country.

Civil War in the North

In 1913, shortly before World War I, the Ottoman Empire was forced to cede some autonomy to highland Zaydis, who were Shiite in origin. In 1918, following the collapse of the Ottoman Empire, Imam Yahya Muhammad of the al-Qasimi dynasty declared northern Yemen an independent sovereign state. In 1926, he proclaimed the establishment of the Mutawakkilite Kingdom of Yemen, becoming both a temporal king as well as a (Zaydi) religious leader. Yahya had expanded his power in the north, but collided with the Saudi king Abdul Aziz ibn Saud, which resulted in the treaty between Yemen and Saudi Arabia mentioned above.[573]

A rebellion by the Yemen Arab Republic (YAR) against the Mutawakkilite kingdom led to a protracted civil war in northern Yemen. The YAR was a country from 1962 to 1990 in the northwestern part of what is now Yemen. It united with the Marxist People's Democratic Republic of Yemen, commonly known as South Yemen, in 1990, to form the current Republic of Yemen. In this civil war, Saudi Arabia intervened in support of the Mutawakkilite Kingdom, equipping royalist tribes, and hired hundreds of foreign mercenaries while Britain provided covert support. The Shah of Iran also helped with financial support since the Zaydis' Imam, like today's Houthis, was a Shia Muslim.

Abdul Nasser of Egypt backed the republican side, sending seventy thousand troops and weapons. This proved a military debacle, which has been described as Egypt's Vietnam.

Saudi Arabia pulled out of the conflict in 1965 and Egypt recalled its troops in 1967. The civil war ended with northern Yemen becoming a republic.

Yemeni Unification, 1990

In 1990, northern Yemen (the Yemen Arab Republic) and the southern Marxist-ruled People's Democratic Republic of Yemen united to form a single state, the Republic of Yemen. The unification created a new state with a population of around fifteen million citizens. This was a large population for the area. Yemenis greatly outnumbered Kuwaitis, Omanis, Qataris, Bahrainis, and Emiratis. They also equaled or possibly outnumbered Saudi citizens.

In a region where states are generally run along the autocratic lines of a medieval monarchy, multi-party democracy was as much of a shock to the Arabs as the American revolution was to Europeans at the time. First, there were fears that democratization in Yemen would upset the stability of the Saudi monarchy. Second, there was the fear that Saudi opposition groups might look to Yemen for support, just as the Saudis had interfered in the politics of Yemen.

This fear and hostility on the part of the Saudi monarchy was exasperated by the discovery of oil in the Empty Quarter starting in the mid-1980s.

Impact of the Gulf War, 1990-91

The unification of Yemen also came at a time when Saddam Hussein of Iraq, after the war with Iran, was adopting an increasingly belligerent stance towards Kuwait and Saudi Arabia. Having fought Iran in part to keep the Iranian Shia in check, he was now seeking compensation from them. Yemen itself had long-standing relations with Iraq and Yemeni troops had fought alongside Iraqis in the war with Iran.

The formation of the *Arab Co-operation Council* in 1989, consisting of Iraq, Yemen, Egypt, and Jordan was seen by many Arabs as the birth of a new alliance which might one day challenge the *Cooperation Council for the Arab States of the Gulf*, a regional intergovernmental political and economic union consisting of all Arab monarchies of the Persian Gulf. Its member states include Bahrain, Kuwait, Oman, Qatar, Saudi Arabia, and the United Arab Emirates. Had the Arab Co-operation Council become a success and also developed into a military alliance, the Saudis would have had good reason to be alarmed. As it turned out, however, the Iraqi invasion of Kuwait (and the American response to it) weakened both Iraq and Yemen.

Coming only three months after Yemeni unification, Saddam Hussein's invasion of Kuwait presented Yemen with a stark dilemma. It had long-standing links with Iraq; at the same time, it depended on remittances from Yemeni workers in Saudi Arabia and the other Gulf states.

Whatever side Yemen decided to take, it was bound to suffer. Opting for what it saw as a middle course, Yemen simultaneously condemned the invasion of Kuwait and opposed Western military intervention, arguing instead for a regional Arab solution. But when Yemen, which was a member of the UN Security Council at the time, opposed the Council's decisions that called for invasion and economic sanctions against Iraq, the Saudis interpreted this as a sign of treason.

Consequently, Yemen got the worst of all worlds, suffering more from the war than any other non-combatant country. UN sanctions prohibited its trade with Iraq and the US cut off its aid.

Saudi Arabia ended all economic assistance to Yemen and deployed troops in the Empty Quarter. It also announced that Yemenis working in the kingdom had to leave the country. Within a few weeks, some seven hundred and fifty thousand people were shoved back over the border into Yemen, many of them having to leave behind their homes and possessions.

Thus, Yemen was faced with a sudden loss of income while also having to absorb three quarters of a million people who were now jobless and homeless. Unemployment skyrocketed. For months, several hundred thousand people were camped out on the hot and humid Tihama plain. The numbers dwindled gradually, aided by outbreaks of cholera, which at one point was killing fifty to sixty children every week.

The result of the expulsions hardened attitudes on both sides. A further wave of mass expulsions came in 2013 when the Saudi authorities began a crackdown on undocumented migrant workers. Millions of foreigners living or working in the kingdom were ordered to take steps to legalize their status or leave the country. Once again, this included large numbers of Yemenis who were peremptorily herded across the border.

The Oil Factor

Yemeni oil had just begun to come on line shortly before unification in 1990. By 1989, the northern fields were producing two hundred thousand barrels a day and proven reserves were estimated at four billion barrels. Yemen, for the first time in its history, had an independent source of wealth. This new found economic independence held out the prospect of greater political independence from Saudi Arabia.

Another important effect of oil was the need to settle the border issue in the Empty Quarter. The issue had little practical purpose before the discovery of oil, but shortly after its discovery, Saudi Arabia began to assert territorial claims in oil concession areas allocated to Yemen. Because the amount of oil discovered was a pittance compared to Saudi Arabia's reserves, this suggests that Saudi Arabia was less interested in the oil as it was in limiting Yemen's economic development and independence.

With the outbreak of war in Kuwait, Yemeni oil became vital to assist the repatriation of its people from Saudi Arabia. Now Yemen began to consume its own oil rather than exporting it.

As far as the border issue was concerned, it was a difficult question involving complex and highly technical issues. Both sides had wildly divergent views as to where the border should lie. The relations of the countries resulting from the Gulf war made talks on the border issue impossible during 1990 and 1991. They started in July 1992 and continued half-heartedly for almost two years. They were broken off in April 1994, just as the political crisis in Yemen was turning to war. It was not until 2000 that the Treaty of Jeddah finally settled the issue. Despite the agreement, the border has remained difficult to police. There remains a good deal of unauthorized movement across it, including smuggling.

In 1994, a war broke out between the north and the south in Yemen. Tensions between leaders and the failure to unite their armies triggered a war between them. Within a couple of weeks, the northern forces defeated the southern fighters and imposed unity by force.

The Houthi Rebellion

From 2004 onwards, the Yemeni government has fought a series of wars aimed at crushing the Shia rebels, popularly known as the Houthis, in the far north of the country, adjacent to the Saudi border. The Houthis are officially known as Ansar Allah ("The Supporters of God"). They belong to the Zaydi sect of the Shia. They are believed to account for thirty-five to forty percent of the country's population. The movement is named after its first leader, Hussain Badreddin al-Houthi.

The Houthis began to attract attention through a movement called al-Shabab al-Mu'min ("Believing Youth") whose teenage members disrupted mosques by chanting "Death to America, Death to Israel" after Friday prayers. The Believing Youth had begun as a local effort to defend Zaydi rights, but became increasingly political in its opposition to the Yemeni government's Ali Abdullah Saleh, who was perceived to be pro-American.

Although Yemen had once been ruled by Zaydi imams and President Saleh was also a Zaydi, the Zaydis of the Saada governate had become a marginalized group. Left largely to their own devices, they had become extremely self-reliant, organizing their own affairs and constructing much of the rudimentary local infrastructure themselves in the absence of government help.

In addition to that, they felt their religious tradition was threatened by Saudi influence as an increasing number of their men were converting to the extreme Salafi or Wahhabi version of Sunni Islam. Converts included men of the lower class who bitterly resented their social disadvantage and were attracted to the Salafi financial resources that came from Saudi Arabia.

The Salafis increasingly mocked the beliefs and rituals of the Zaydi majority, threatening them in mosques and accusing them of wanting to destroy the republic in favor of bringing back the religious state of the Imams. As a result of this religious bullying the Zaydi began to strike back. In 2004, armed conflict broke out in the northern governate of Saada, and the Yemen government denounced Hussain al-Houthi for "harming Yemen's stability and interests" and offered a reward of fifty-five thousand dollars for his capture. Shortly afterwards, Hussain al-Houthi was killed, apparently by security forces during an attempt at a mediated peace settlement.

Between 2004 and 2010 the Houthis and the government fought a series of six intermittent wars. The most serious of these began in August 2009 when the government launched "Operation Scorched Earth" against the rebels. The scale of casualties is unknown, but hundreds of thousands of people fled their homes, resulting in a serious humanitarian crisis.[574]

In 2014, Houthi rebels over-ran Sanaa, the capital of Yemen and President Abd Rabbuh Mansur Hadi, Saleh's successor, was forced to flee to Saudi Arabia. The Houthi rapidly extended their control to other parts of the country.

In 2015, the Saudis began a highly destructive aerial bombing campaign against the Houthi, supported by mercenary ground forces. The Saudi elites were worried that the Houthi conflict would spill over into their own southern provinces. To prevent this, they forcibly removed thousands of their own citizens from some four hundred villages and transferred them to makeshift camps. During the same time, Saudi Arabia was fighting to expel al-Qaeda from the kingdom and this drove many militants into Yemen, further exacerbating the problems there. The Houthis and al-Qaeda are sworn enemies.[575]

A Yemeni Civil War broke out between the Houthi and the forces loyal to the President who was living in exile in Saudi Arabia. Al-Qaeda and ISIS also carried out attacks against the Houthi. The United States provided intelligence and logistical support for the Saudi campaign.

As of November 2016, thousands of civilians had been killed and millions had been forced from their homes. According to Oxfam America, eighty percent of the population was in immediate need of aid to prevent a massive famine in the country. It was estimated that one in three of the Saudi air strikes hit civilian sites, including schools, hospitals, markets, and funeral homes. These airstrikes were directly supported by the United States and Britain. The United States also directly fired cruise missiles on rebel-held territory in retaliation for a purported unsuccessful attack on its warship off the coast of Yemen. The Houthi denied firing on the US ship.

The US arms merchants again are profiting from the carnage caused by US foreign policy across the Middle East that continually leads to more carnage and more need for weapons and munitions. The US, in November 2016, approved an additional of $1.29 billion worth of bombs to Saudi Arabia, as its military carries out air strikes in Yemen.[576] This is a small part of a sixty billion dollar arms deal with Saudi Arabia "in a move designed to shore up a region overshadowed by Iran."[577]

The vision of world dominance dreamt by the Trilateralists and the Neo-Cons, continues to play itself out in the Middle East. The entire region is in chaos, millions have died and more millions made homeless.

US Counterinsurgency in Iraq

When the Bush/Cheney administration began its War on Terrorism, the American soldiers were dismally unprepared. The act of conducting war in villages, towns, and cities filled with civilians, women, and children was not the conventional war they had been trained to fight. They were like the British Red Coats marching down the roads of Massachusetts only to be picked off one by one by sharp shooters in the trees. The lessons of guerilla warfare in Vietnam had been intentionally forgotten because they only reminded the military brass of their own failure to win that war. Former Vice Chief of Staff of the Army General Jack Keane speaking on the Jim Lehrer News Hour in April 2006, stated:

> We put an Army on the battlefield that I had been a part of for thirty-seven years. It doesn't have any doctrine, nor was it educated and trained to deal with an insurgency... After the Vietnam War, we purged ourselves of everything that had to do with irregular warfare or insurgency because it had to do with how we lost that war. In hindsight, that was a bad decision.[578]

Thus, the soldiers had nothing to guide their actions. The "rule sets," as Thomas Barnett called policy decisions, did not even exist for the soldiers. No manual on counterinsurgency had been published for more than twenty years. Not having rules for warfare, the army also lacked the equipment to protect the soldiers against urban traps, roadside bombs, etc. The Bush administration sent the soldiers to war without any body armor or bullet-proof vests. Many soldiers or their families were forced to buy body armor for their sons and daughters.[579]

In 2003, David Petraeus was a Major General who saw combat for the first time when he commanded the 101st Airborne Division during the US invasion of Iraq. Petraeus led his division through fierce fighting south of Baghdad, Karbala, Hilla, and Najaf. Following the fall of Baghdad, the division moved north to the ancient Assyrian governate of Nineveh where it spent much of 2003.

Despite Bush's grandstanding "Mission Accomplished" speech on the aircraft carrier *USS Abraham Lincoln* on May 1, 2003,[580] Petraeus knew that great difficulties would follow the fall of Baghdad. The rise of a committed insurgency movement, led by al-Qaeda and populated with thousands of officers and soldiers from Hussein's deposed army, proved this to be true.

The largest city in the Nineveh governate is Mosul, a city of nearly two million people. It was up to Petraeus to stabilize this city. Petraeus had been steeped in "nation-building" strategies during his previous tours in Bosnia and Haiti and thus approached nation-building as a central military mission. He believed it was the key to counterinsurgency and winning over the hearts and minds of the Arab people. He was prepared to act while the civilian authority in Baghdad was still getting organized.

General Petraeus had to engage insurgents and simultaneously jump start the economy by rebuilding local police units, reinvigorating the political process through organizing elections, and also overseeing the repair and upgrade of water and sewage treatment plants, electricity production, and the rebuilding of hospitals, schools, housing, and transportation systems.

One of the General's major accomplishments was the restoration and re-opening of the University of Mosul.[581] The methods used by Gen. Petraeus to accomplish these feats were eventually incorporated into the US Army Counterinsurgency Field Manual.[582]

The Field Manual

The US Army Counterinsurgency Field Manual is arguably the most "idealistic" document that the army has ever produced. It is filled with hope concerning the army's ability to both destroy a country and then rebuild it in the image of a western capitalist society.

The premise of the manual is that to achieve victory over insurgents, the US army must have intelligence on the location and the insurgent enemy and that such information could best be gotten from a population that supported the United States intervention. Thus, the focus of intelligence now shifted from the traditional analysis of conventional enemy units to concentrate on the network of leaders among the insurgents.

This counterinsurgency strategy, however, was not based on helping the local people become self-reliant. Rather it took its cue from the foreign policy initiatives put in place to support the elite's strategy of a US global empire. The Manual spoke of the "Long War" and "Global Counterinsurgency," but it had a liberal bias. As such, to conduct a successful counterinsurgency required, first of all, protection of the people, but it also required "economic development, good governance, and the provision of essential services" all coordinated by good communication that improved over time.[583]

Thus, theoretically, the new counterinsurgency strategy was based on a "population-centered approach" rather than one based exclusively on the insurgents. In order for such an approach to succeed, the army had to figure out a way to separate the people from the insurgents, in other words, to "deny the insurgent 'fish' the cover of the civilian 'sea.'" The army understood that the people would not immediately trust the invading US army, but had to be convinced over time that the army was less a threat than the insurgents. This required a concerted effort to protect the people. Killing of civilians could no longer be dismissed as collateral damage. Every civilian death created an extended family of enemies who would then become insurgents and erode support for the new government. As the manual states: "An operation that kills five insurgents is counterproductive if collateral damage leads to the recruitment of fifty more insurgents."[584]

The army understood that such an approach meant greater risk. They were, after all, faced with an enemy whose forces were citizens of the country that the US had invaded and it was only logical that the civilian population would be "infiltrated" by the enemy. But the army saw this short-term risk as an "operational necessity."

The exit strategy of the counterinsurgency campaign was to be able to leave the country in the sound hands of the new government and the organizations of civil society. Thus, the army viewed its job as including significant and ongoing involvement with civilians at every stage and level of development. This approach was the keystone to the work of "nation-building."

The mindset that supported this approach was that the army was engaged in a "just war" against dictators and "terrorists" who were killing and abusing the local population. While, there was an element of truth to this viewpoint, the over-riding fact was that the US army was invading countries wherein the majority of the citizens of those countries did not believe that the war was a just war, but rather an invasion by an empire with different cultural and religious values who came to take their resources by brute force. Secondly, the US army seemed totally ignorant of the fact that their intervention would destabilize the fragile peace between Shiites and Sunnis which, in fact, erupted into a vicious religious civil war in whatever country the US army destroyed the existing power structure. This was true in Afghanistan, Iraq, Syria, and Yemen. This huge miscalculation, or intentional deception on the part of the military-industrial complex, misled the American soldiers into believing that they were doing a good deed for the civilian populations of the countries they invaded. Therefore, the soldiers could not understand why they were not well received as heroes. Rather they found themselves in an environment fraught with constant danger, unable to trust anyone or to determine who was the "good guy" or the "bad guy," as Barnett had so naively put it in his book.

Nation-Building

The March 2003 invasion of Iraq by the US trashed Iraq's water supply, sewerage, and electrical supply systems leaving the people unable to use their kitchens, bathrooms, or any electrical devices. In the chaos, thieves stripped treatment plants, pumping stations, and generating stations of their equipment, supplies, and electrical wiring. The once-capable workforce of engineers and operating technicians were scattered or left the country.[585]

While reconstruction efforts did have some successes, problems also arose with the implementation process. These problems included inadequate security, pervasive corruption, insufficient funding, and poor coordination between international agencies and local communities. There was also the great cultural gulf and the poor understanding of the Iraqi people by the international community.

Another shortcoming of the nation-building approach, as suggested in the Counterinsurgency Manual, was that the army had no jurisdiction over the intentions of the US Special Forces, the CIA, other intelligence agencies, or the private contractors like Halliburton who had their own agendas and who often acted in contradiction to the army's stated goal of stabilizing the newly occupied territories.

American soldiers in Iraq under General Petraeus began to immediately suffer the consequences of having to adjust to these other actors, as well as the imperatives of the Trilateralist/Neo-Con policies, which were more concerned with global dominance than nation-building and democracy. So also, the soldiers were faced with their own ignorance of the long-inbred socio-religious politics between the Shia and Sunni Muslims, the two main branches of Islam. The root of this hostility went back to the death of the Prophet Muhammed and the question of who was to be his legitimate successor.

The Shia are descendants of those who supported the Prophet's family, particularly his grandsons who were treacherously murdered by the Sunni Muslim warlords at the battle of Karbala in Iraq. The hatred between the two sects, which has lasted for centuries, has always existed just below the surface and was kept in check only by the brutal use of force by the region's kings and dictators. Over time, the conflict of these sects was intensified by geopolitics, as each side fought for control of different areas and states in the region. The US invasion of Iraq set off an internal holy war between the Shia and Sunni sects, reminiscent of the Christian holy wars between Catholics and Protestants during the Middle Ages. There were other local forces in play, as well; for example, the various tribes and armies of warlords who sought to increase their standing amidst the chaos that was set off because of the US bombings and invasion.

Iraq is the heartland of the global Shia community. For a long time, the Shia Muslims of Iraq, who constituted a majority of the population, were discriminated against by Saddam Hussein's Sunni-dominated regime. After the 2003 war and the fall of Saddam Hussein, Shia Muslims seized power across the country, setting up death squads and torturing Sunni Muslims. Sunnis responded with suicide attacks and bombings and by joining the forces of al-Qaeda. The war in Iraq has not diminished the long-standing hatred between the two sects and has only amplified the tensions between the two.

General David Petraeus had created peace with the local Sunni tribes in order to stabilize Mosul. However, the CIA had allied itself almost exclusively with the Kurds who were enemies of the Sunnis and who were seeking to create an autonomous region in the north of Iraq along the Syrian Turkey border.

Because of the CIAs alliance with the Kurds, the local Sunni people came to see the US as just another ally of the Kurds. This perception helped to fill the ranks of al-Qaeda as local Sunni supporters joined their fellow Sunni jihadis. The example of this lack of coordination on the part of US government in Mosul was seen again and again as the years of warfare in the Middle East unfolded.

Any effort to create democracy in these countries, through attempts at nation-building, was therefore undermined, not only by insurgents, but by US government agencies as well. The lack of a common game plan and uncoordinated approach resulted in a gross failure across the region and served only to put American troops in greater harm's way.

Let us take a closer look at the city of Mosul. In 2004, less than a year after General Patraeus' 101st Airborne Division attempted to stabilize Mosul, it was subject to a large counter-attack led by al-Qaeda/Sunni forces and other foreign jihadist groups.

Mosul is located in an area where various ethnic, religious, sectarian, and tribal groups intersect. The distribution of the city is approximately seventy percent Sunni Arab, twenty-five percent Kurd, and the remaining five percent a mixture of Shia, Turkmen, Yazidis, and Christians.

Before the Iraq War, Mosul was home to a large Ba'ath Party headquarters loyal to Saddam Hussein and was also an important military center. Mosul and the surrounding areas contributed over three hundred thousand residents to the military, security, and intelligence services of Hussein's government. This demonstrates why Mosul has served as a major recruiting ground and sanctuary for al-Qaeda insurgents.

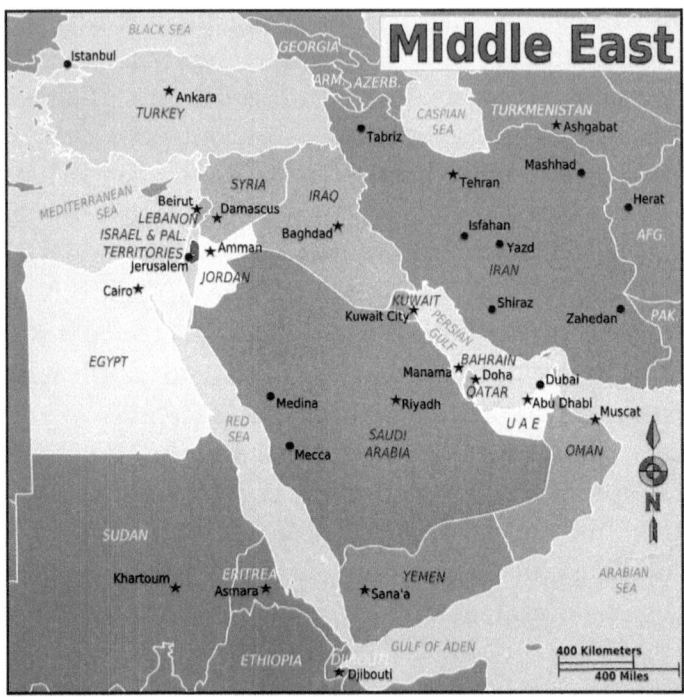

Fig. 5-12: Map of the Middle East

In the initial chaos of the war, before the occupation of Mosul by the 101st Airborne Division, Kurdish political parties and their militias moved to establish a greater presence in the city, while the Sunni Arabs loyal to Hussein began to organize themselves into an insurgent (revolutionary) force.

Petraeus entered the city in 2003 and tried to establish a counter-insurgency campaign by helping to rebuild the city. During 2004, however, internal conflict between Arab Sunnis and Kurds immediately flared up when a smaller force replaced the 101st. The Sunni Arab nationalists came to control the west side of the city, whereas the Kurds controlled the east side.

In November 2004, Mosul's police force collapsed in the face of an insurgent assault. After several weeks of fighting, however, the US-led coalition forces retook the city with the help of a large number of Kurdish forces. This, however, did nothing to change the balance of power or the stalemate between Arabs and Kurds. The Arabs still controlled the west side of the city and the Kurds the east side. The only thing that did change was that the Arab Sunnis, who had identified with the old regime, now identified themselves as al-Qaeda forces. In this way, Mosul developed into a hub of al-Qaeda forces, which later changed their name to ISIS.

By 2007, any attempts at "nation-building" in Mosul was scuttled as the US military initiated a "troop surge" of an additional thirty thousand soldiers to clear Mosul of the so-called terrorists. The surge was partially successful in driving some al-Qaeda troops out of the city, but it only resulted in pushing the insurgents further north where they regrouped.

Other insurgents remained to fight the US troops and their Shia Security Forces. In early 2008, Mosul was considered to be the last urban stronghold of al-Qaeda. There were an estimated two thousand insurgents entrenched across the city.[586]

As of November 2016, al-Qaeda Sunnis, now called ISIS, still remained in control of Mosul. The fight for Mosul, led by the Iraqi Shia Security Forces and Iranian Shiites did not solve anything.

As the US-led coalition worked to coordinate the Iraqi Shia's Security Forces' attack on Mosul, the policy analysts scrambled to determine what the next steps would be when ISIS was forced out of the city. In other words, they had no plan to secure a lasting peace in Iraq. The country would still be home to well-armed militia groups who wanted to kill each other. This was aggravated by the fact that the Shi'ites, who constitute a population majority, would again be relegated to second-class citizens in their own country.

There is also the regional power politics to consider between Shia and Sunni nations in the Middle East, particularly in Iran, Turkey, and Saudi Arabia. Saudi Arabia wanted Iraq to remain in the hands of the Sunni, who were friendly to them. Iran, on the other hand wants Iraq to be in the hands of the Shia, who had long been the majority population in Iraq and who comprised the majority of the Iraqi Security Forces. Meanwhile, Turkey wanted to ensure that the Kurds in northern Iraq were not able to foment tension on their southern border by establishing their own autonomous region along the shared borders of Iraq, Syria, and Turkey where they also constituted large populations.

Finally, the global competition between the US/NATO forces and Russia had also to be considered in order to create peace in Iraq.

Currently, the competition between the old global rivals was again heating up. While the two combatants shared a common interest in driving ISIS out of Mosul in Iraq, they were waging a diplomatic war in Syria, where the Russians have provided armed support to the Assad government, while the US/NATO forces wanted to destroy him and set up their own puppet government. At the time that General Petraeus was attempting to realize his "nation-building strategy in Iraq, Russia was conducting air strikes over the city of Aleppo in Syria as Assad's army sought to drive ISIS out of the city, which was their stronghold in Syria. Russia had also dispatched its northern fleet, including the aircraft carrier, Admiral Kuznetsov, to Syria and had warned the US that if it violated its no-fly zone over Syria, it would target US planes for destruction.

For the first time in decades, the nuclear option was back on the table for both combatants. Russia had deployed nuclear-capable missiles to its territories in the Baltic Sea. It had modernized its short-range weapons in recent years and had about two thousand of these. Such weapons could be used to take out targets of war, including villages, cities, warships, army basis, airfields, etc.

This aggressiveness had provoked the policy analysts in Washington, both on the left and the right, to call for a US no-fly zone over Syria that would take down any Russian planes that violated it.

As far as the goal of nation-building and defending democracy around the world goes, even the most idealistic soldier has now become cynical. Whether the army's initial idealism was real or not, the policy of "nation-building" no longer had the support of the troops or the officers. According to a Military Times–Syracuse University survey published in October 2016, fifty-five percent of the armed forces opposed further nation-building in the Middle East or North Africa. Sixty-one percent wanted less foreign aid. Seventy-four percent of service-members supported either Donald Trump or Gary Johnson for president because they advocated a less militant foreign policy than Barack Obama or Hillary Clinton. A plurality of officers even supported Johnson the Libertarian Party nominee for President because he was the least interventionist candidate in the race.[587]

Welcome Home!

There are 22.6 million veterans in the United States. Of these, more than 2.6 million soldiers served in the Middle East since 2001. As of late 2015, nearly seven thousand had died and another nine hundred thousand were injured.[588] While these are appalling numbers, they did not compare to the deaths experienced by "the enemy" since the war began. It is estimated that four million Muslims had died since the war on terrorism began.[589]

This ranks as the greatest death rate in any war on the planet going back to the American Civil War with the exception of WWI and WWII. By comparison, the Korean War and the Vietnam War led to the death of 3 million each. Russia's war in Afghanistan witnessed the death of 1.3 million people.[590] The American war on terrorism has been going on for sixteen years with no end in sight.

It is difficult to imagine how the incredible death toll affected the people of the Middle East. They lost their spouses, their children, their homes, their neighbors, and their towns. They witnessed horrors unimaginable to the average American. These horrors, however, did not go unnoticed by the American soldiers who had perpetrated this death and destruction, or who lost friends or members of their own families in the War on Terrorism.

The American soldiers in the Middle East wars were not a bunch of heartless, mindless killers. In fact, they were by and large intelligent people. Of those over twenty-five, only twelve percent had less than a high school education, forty-two percent have a high school diploma, twenty-seven percent have some college and twenty percent have a college degree. The army, which is comprised of volunteers, including the National Guard, consisted primarily of white men. Of those deployed, ninety percent were white, eight percent were black, and only two percent were of another race. Also, ninety-five were men and only five percent were women.[591]

Of the 2.6 million soldiers dispatched to Iraq and Afghanistan, more than half return home faced with overwhelming physical and mental disabilities. The soldiers came home disconnected from civilian life, not knowing how to relate to their families or other people's expectations of them. They held the government responsible for not helping them when they return damaged from their war experience. One in two said they knew a fellow soldier who has attempted or committed suicide, and more than one million suffered from problems with their spouses and children and experienced outbursts of anger. These are the two key indicators of post-traumatic stress disorder (PTSD).

What was it Like to Be an American Soldier in Iraq?

Returning soldiers from Iraq, despite their pain and suffering, felt pride in the fact that they had done their job. They believed that they had helped the people by removing a dictator from power. They felt that their lives had been more disciplined in the army and that they had contributed to something bigger and more important than themselves. Most said they did not regret having fought in the war. On the other hand, the hostile environment in which they were dropped unprepared changed their lives forever. In Iraq and Afghanistan, it was impossible to tell the good guy from the bad guy. Something the armchair intellectuals of the Trilateralist/Neo-Cons, who determine American policy, assumed they would be able to do.

Due to a lack of training, the soldiers were ill prepared to understand anything about the environment in which they were ensconced. They found themselves immersed in a violent, foreign culture, unable to speak Arabic, not knowing Muslim culture or the religious/political dynamics at play. Any person they passed on the street was a possible killer. Theirs was an environment of chaos filled with dead bodies and gruesome scenes that they could not get out of their heads despite their bravado and posturing. At any moment they could be shot at, attacked or ambushed, or have a rocket, bomb or mortar shell blow off their face. It was an environment where you killed other people in split second decisions, and likewise saw your friends and comrades die in the same way. It was a torturous environment that, after days, weeks, months, and years of soldiering, distorted their psyches and made them into something they were not. It took away their humanity.

Such an environment made it impossible for the soldiers to sympathize with their victims. That is until they returned home and the guilt and horror of war came flooding into their minds as they sat with their families across the dinner table. Of the 2.6 million American soldiers who fought in Iraq and Afghanistan, over 1.3 million, or more than half of those deployed, returned home with physical and mental problems.[592]

Following are a few statements made by soldiers being treated for PTSD after returning from Iraq.

Specialist Jeff Englehart, twenty-six, of Grand Junction, Colorado served as a Specialist with the Third Brigade, First Infantry Division, in Baquba, about thirty-five miles northeast of Baghdad, for a year beginning in February 2004. "I guess while I was there, the general attitude was, 'A dead Iraqi is just another dead Iraqi. You know, so what? The soldiers honestly thought we were trying to help the people and they were mad because it was almost like a betrayal. Like here we are trying to help you, here I am, you know, thousands of miles away from home and my family, and I have to be here for a year and work every day on these missions. Well, we're trying to help you and you just turn around and try to kill us."[593]

Like many soldiers, Englehart, felt that it was the Iraqi people who had betrayed him. He did not understand that it was the army who had pushed him into war completely unprepared, and that it was the narcissistic grand strategists of global empire and the weapons manufacturers who kept the war going by selling weapons to all sides who had betrayed him. We cannot blame Englehart for hating the Iraqi people, he did not know any better and as far as the elite were concerned this was just as well.

The hatred the American soldiers felt for the Muslim people who had assumedly betrayed them quickly turned into a crude racism, just as it does at home in America where the average white American does not understand the political and economic dynamics at work behind the scenes.

American troops in Iraq not only lacked the training necessary to understand Muslim culture but they also lacked the support to communicate with or even understand Iraqi civilians. Few spoke or read Arabic and translators were either in short supply or unqualified. Any stereotypes about Islam and Arabs that the soldiers and marines carried with them quickly solidified into racist hatred. Specialist Josh Middleton, twenty-three, of New York City, who served in Baghdad and Mosul with the Second Battalion, Eighty-Second Airborne Division in 2004-2005 put it bluntly, "a lot of guys really supported that whole concept that, you know, if they don't speak English and they have darker skin, they're not as human as us, so we can do what we want."

Middleton explained why this racist attitude came so easily to the young soldiers. It began by having to face the constant humiliation of training, "… getting yelled at every day if you have a dirty weapon…" and then finding yourself on the streets of Iraq where "its like life and death. And forty-year-old Iraqi men look at us with fear and we can—do you know what I mean?—we have this power that you can't have. That's really liberating. Life is just knocked down to the primal level."[594]

But it is not just the guilt of their own inhumanity that plagues returning soldiers, it is also the horror of war itself. Specialist Michael Harmon, twenty-four, a medic from Brooklyn who had served a thirteen-month tour beginning in April 2003 with the 167th Armor Regiment, Fourth Infantry Division, in Al-Rashidiya, a small town near Baghdad, said "I'll tell you the point where I really turned. I go out to the scene and [there was] this little, you know, pudgy little two year-old child with the cute little pudgy legs, and I look and she has a bullet through her leg. An IED [improvised explosive device] went off, the gun-happy soldiers just started shooting anywhere and the baby got hit. And this baby looked at me, wasn't crying, wasn't anything, it just looked at me like -- I know she couldn't speak. It might sound crazy, but she was like asking me why. You know, Why do I have a bullet in my leg? I was just like, This is—this is it. This is ridiculous."[595] Often the frustration felt by the soldiers due to their inability to get back at those who were attacking them led to behaviors that were simply meant to punish the local population who they saw as supporting their attackers.

Specialist Philip Chrystal, twenty-three, of Reno, described a scene that was typical of the raids made by American soldiers on civilian homes. Chrystal said he raided between twenty and thirty Iraqi homes during an eleven-month tour in Kirkuk and Hawija that ended in October 2005. He had served with the Third Battalion, 116th Cavalry Brigade. "It starts with the psy-ops vehicles out there, you know, with the big speakers playing a message in Arabic or Farsi or Kurdish or whatever they happen to be, saying, basically, saying, Put your weapons, if you have them, next to the front door in your house. Please come outside, blah, blah, blah, blah, blah. And we had Apaches flying over for security, if they're needed, and it's also a good show of force. And we're running around, and they—we'd done a few houses by this point, and I was with my platoon leader, my squad leader and maybe a couple other people.

"And we were approaching this one house in this farming area, they're, like, built up into little courtyards. So they have, like, the main house, common area. They have, like, a kitchen and then they have a storage shed-type deal. And we're approaching, and they had a family dog. And it was barking ferociously, 'cause it's doing its job. And my squad leader, just out of nowhere, just shoots it. And he didn't—motherfucker—he shot it and it went in the jaw and exited out. So I see this dog—I'm a huge animal lover; I love animals—and this dog has, like, these eyes on it and he's running around spraying blood all over the place. And like, you know, what the hell is going on? The family is sitting right there, with three little children and a mom and a dad, horrified. And I'm at a loss for words. And so, I yell at him. I'm, like, what the fuck are you doing? And so the dog's yelping. It's crying out without a jaw. And I'm looking at the family, and they're just, you know, dead scared. And so I told them, I was like, Fucking shoot it, you know? At least kill it, because that can't be fixed.

"And—I actually get tears from just saying this right now, but—and I had tears then, too—and I'm looking at the kids and they are so scared. So I got the interpreter over with me and, you know, I get my wallet out and I gave them twenty bucks, because that's what I had. And, you know, I had him give it to them and told them that I'm so sorry that asshole did that.

"Was a report ever filed about it?" he asked. "Was anything ever done? Any punishment ever dished out? No, absolutely not." Chrystal said such incidents were very common. "I can tell you hundreds of stories about things like that and they would all pretty much be like the one I just told you. Just a different family, a different time, a different circumstance."

Far more common were stories in which soldiers assaulted a home as part of raids. In their futile search for weapons they left terrorized civilians struggling to repair the damage to their homes or face the long torment of trying to find family members who were hauled away as suspected terrorists.

Sergeant John Bruhns, twenty-nine, of Philadelphia, who estimated that he took part in raids of nearly one thousand Iraqi homes, served in Baghdad with the Third Brigade, First Armor Division, First Battalion, for one year beginning in April 2003. According to Bruhns, raids normally took place between midnight and 5 am. "You want to catch them off guard. You want to catch them in their sleep." Typically, ten soldiers were involved in each raid, with five stationed outside and the rest searching the home.

Once in front of the home, troops, some wearing Kevlar helmets and flak vests with grenade launchers mounted on their weapons, kicked the door in. Bruhns then described the procedure, "You run in. And if there's lights, you turn them on—if the lights are working. If not, you've got flashlights. You leave one rifle team outside while one rifle team goes inside. Each rifle team leader has a headset on with an earpiece and a microphone where he can communicate with the other rifle team leader that's outside.

"You go up the stairs. You grab the man of the house. You rip him out of bed in front of his wife. You put him up against the wall. You have junior-level troops, PFCs [privates first class], specialists will run into the other rooms and grab the family, and you'll group them all together. Then you go into a room and you tear the room to shreds and you make sure there's no weapons or anything that they can use to attack us.

"You get the interpreter and you get the man of the home, and you have him at gunpoint, and you'll ask the interpreter to ask him: 'Do you have any weapons? Do you have any anti-US propaganda, anything at all —anything—anything in here that would lead us to believe that you are somehow involved in insurgent activity or anti-coalition forces activity?'

"Normally they'll say no, because that's normally the truth. So what you'll do is you'll take his sofa cushions and you'll dump them. If he has a couch, you'll turn the couch upside down. You'll go into the fridge, if he has a fridge, and you'll throw everything on the floor, and you'll take his drawers and you'll dump them. You'll open up his closet and you'll throw all the clothes on the floor and basically leave his house looking like a hurricane just hit it.

"And if you find something, then you'll detain him. If not, you'll say, 'Sorry to disturb you. Have a nice evening.' So you've just humiliated this man in front of his entire family and terrorized his entire family and you've destroyed his home. And then you go right next door and you do the same thing in a hundred homes."

This is how America spreads democracy around the world. This is how we make our young men proud to be Americans. Staff Sergeant Timothy John Westphal, thirty-one, of Denver, who served on the outskirts of Tikrit, Iraq, with the Eighteenth Infantry Brigade, First Infantry Division, in 2004, was also involved in raiding homes and he described situations similar to that described by Sergeant Bruhns. Eventually he had a turning point. "I just remember thinking to myself, I just brought terror to someone else under the American flag, and that's just not what I joined the Army to do."[596]

Of course, there is also the horror of seeing their friends and comrades killed. These are the only people a soldier can trust in war. Michael Goss, twenty-nine, served two tours in Iraq. He struggles with severe PTSD and is awaiting treatment from the Veterans Administration. He has been waiting for over a year. Michael relates a story: "One night they said to me, "Sergeant Goss, gather your best guys." I say, "Where we going?" They say, "Don't worry about it, just come on." So we get in the car and go. We drive three blocks away, and there's six dead soldiers on the ground. They say, "You're casualty collecting tonight." I'm not prepared for that. I wasn't taught how to do that. But you're there. So you pick them up, and you put them in a body bag, pieces by pieces, and you go back to your unit, and you stand inside your room. And they're like, "You're going on a patrol, come on." You're like, "Hang on a minute. Let me think about what I just did here." I just put six American guys in damn body bags. Nobody's prepared for that. Nobody's prepared for that thing to blow up on the side of the road. You're talking, and you're driving, and then something blows up, and the next thing you know, two of your guys are missing their faces. They just want you to get up the next day and go, go, let's do it again, you're a soldier."

"It gets to the point where they numb you. They numb you to death. They numb you to anything. You come back, and it starts coming back to you slowly. Now you gotta figure out a way to deal with it. In Iraq you had a way to deal with it, because they kept pushing you back out there. Keep pushing you back out into the streets. Go, go, go."

"We'll fix it when we get back. That's basically what they're telling you. We'll fix it all when we get back. We'll get your head right and everything when we get back to the States. I'm sorry, it's not like that. It's not supposed to be like that. All the soldiers have post-traumatic stress disorder, and they're like, "Hey, you're good. You went to counseling four times, you can go back to Iraq. It's OK." No. It doesn't work that way."

Michael remembers the moment when things went sideways for him. "I have PTSD. I know when I got it—the night I killed an eight year-old girl. Her family was trying to cross a checkpoint. We'd just shot three guys who'd tried to run a checkpoint. And during that mess, they were just trying to get through to get away from it all. And we ended up shooting all them, too. It was a family of six. The only one that survived was a thirteen month-old and her mother. And the worst part about it all was that where I shot my bullets, when I went to see what I'd shot at, there was an 8-year-old girl there. I tried my best to bring her back to life, but there was no use. But that's what triggered my depression."

"When I got out of the Army, I had ten days to get off base. There was no reintegration counseling. As soon as I got back, nobody gave a fuck about anything except that piece of paper that said I got everything out of my room. I got out of the Army, and everything went to shit from there."[597]

The "primal" existence forced upon our young men and women in the Middle East by the old men in New York and Washington inexorably takes its toll, not only on the millions of Iraqi and Afghani people who have died, or who have been wounded or who have lost their families, but it also takes its toll on the millions of American soldiers and their families.

The Department of Veteran Affairs (VA)

The soldiers who return from the War on Terrorism, who are broken, believe that the Department of Veteran Affairs is not meeting their needs. "When I raised my right hand and said, 'I will support and defend the Constitution of the United States of America,' when I gave them everything I could, I expect the same in return," said Christopher Steavens, a former Army staff sergeant. He was serving in Kuwait when a construction accident disabled him. Upon leaving the Army last summer, he filed a claim with the VA, seeking medical care and financial compensation. After seven months, he had not received a response.

While many soldiers have returned to American life and have adjusted, more have returned to find themselves fighting for benefits, struggling to land a job, wrestling with the psychological demons unleashed by combat, or coping with shattered families.[598]

The army calls this condition Post-Traumatic Stress Disorder (PTSD). PTSD is described as a condition that arises when an individual finds adjustment back to a "normal" way of life difficult, given the psychological impact of the catalyzing event. The varying causes and symptoms of PTSD make the condition difficult to predict and identify. Almost twenty-five percent of the returning soldiers with PTSD have multiple conditions that lead to suicide attempts, alcohol abuse, and violent behavior. Such conditions are difficult to treat. The sheer client load of hundreds of thousands of young men and women returning to the US with PTSD overwhelmed the Veterans Administration, which is charged with serving them. They often did not know how to treat the soldiers. Secondly, they lacked the resources to handle the caseload.[599]

Veterans Administration data showed that from 2002 to 2009, one million troops left active duty in Iraq or Afghanistan and became eligible for VA care. Of those troops, forty-six percent came in for VA services. Of those Veterans who used VA care, forty-eight perecnt were diagnosed with a mental health problem.

It is unknown if the VA engaged in a cover up or if they notified the White House and Congress and were ignored, but one thing is clear, the same government that put our soldiers in harm's way is also the same government that threw our soldiers under the bus when they returned from fighting its wars.

For years there was a cover-up regarding the VA's inability to serve the troops returning from Afghanistan and Iraq. By 2014, the VA was embroiled in a scandal as revelations emerged that the waiting list for appointments at the Phoenix VA Medical Center was so long that patients had languished for months and, in some cases, years awaiting treatment. Some of them died before receiving care. As late as April 2016, Fox News reported that the US Department of Veterans Affairs had been systematically shredding thousands of documents related to veterans' claims.[600] Instead of treating our young men and women, they destroyed evidence that proved they needed assistance.

After coming under scrutiny, the VA began to process initial claims more quickly, but in order to reduce its workload, it denied many claims for service. This caused the soldiers to have to appeal the VA's decision to reject their claim. According to the *Washington Times*, more than half of new applications were rejected and required an appeal. Often, multiple appeals are required. The *Times* reported that "More than half of all VA disability appeal cases are sent back for another review … and must be addressed before new cases are opened, leading some veterans to wait years for a final decision." At the time of the article, three hundred thousand veterans were currently waiting for an appeal decision and the average wait time was more than twelve hundred days, or well over three years.[601]

Although the Congress and federal government doubled the budget of the Veterans Administration since the beginning of the Iraq war, the agency still cannot satisfactorily process the influx of patients. As of November 2018, the VA refused to repay underpaid soldiers their due benefits thus depriving millions of soldiers the money they needed to pay their rent. The reason the VA gave for breaking the law was that they would have to process too many claims.[602] It is unfair to blame the people working in the Veterans Administration who are attempting to deal with veterans suffering from PTSD. It is a management problem and the ineptitude of the managers can be traced to the Bush, Obama, and Trump administrations and the bankers and warlords who control their decisions. We are all victims of this heartless group that cares nothing for the citizens of the Middle East or America.

A study by Brown University places the cost of war at $5.9 trillion dollars effective November 2018.[603] As of October 2016, the US people were committed to paying one trillion dollars in lifetime disability compensation that has been awarded to nine hundred and sixty thousand returned veterans. No one believes that this money will be paid in full even as the war continues. How can the US government afford to pay a trillion dollars to returned veterans when even a billion dollars put in the VA budget causes a storm of political wrangling. Meanwhile the arms dealers and the military-industrial elite are making hundreds of billions of dollars creating more chaos, death, and destruction.

This situation should tell us something as Americans? It tells us to be suspicious of all the fighting, death and dying, and the mental illness and trashed families faced by our young people? We are now in the seventeenth year of fighting in the Middle East. It is the longest war Americans have ever fought in and there is no end in sight. Who is it, after all, who benefits from this endless war on terror? The American people have not benefitted. Our sons and daughters have not benefitted. The people in the Middle East have not benefitted. The people of the world have not benefitted. Let us take a look at the people who do benefit.

Despite the Chaos, the "Good Guys" Are Winning

War against a foreign country only happens when the moneyed classes think they are going to profit from it. George Orwell

War is never economically beneficial except for those in positions to profit from war expenditures. Ron Paul

Short of changing human nature…the only way to achieve a practical, livable peace in a world of competing nations is to take the profit out of war. Richard Nixon

I spent 33 years and 4 months in active military service and during that period I spent most of my time as a high class muscle man for Big Business, for Wall Street and the bankers. In short, I was a racketeer, a gangster for capitalism. General Smedley Butler.

Just as the Trilaterialists/Neo-Cons developed their grand strategy of world conquest and the army followed with their own complimentary strategy, the war profiteers also have their own version of the grand strategy, but it never really changes. Their job is to start wars and keep them going as long as possible. This was their strategy in Libya, Afghanistan, Iraq, Syria, and Yemen.

It does not even matter which army that they are supplying. It is even better when they can fund both sides in a conflict. Internal tensions are aggravated into internecine wars in order to make vast new profits from the sale of weaponry and munitions, reconstruction, price inflation, government contracts, and the looting of public resources and finances, which are easier to do in an environment of chaos.

As an example, in 2011, after a decade of war, the Center for Public Integrity took an in-depth look at the billions of dollars spent on Pentagon military contracts that were not competitively bid. The contracts had tripled in size since 9/11, from fifty billion dollars in 2001 to one hundred and forty billion dollars in 2011.[604] In order to pay these billions of dollars to the owners and investors in the US military-industrial complex, the federal government has had to go into debt for the full amount. Our taxes have not been raised to pay for the war because the money is just printed on a printing press so we do not immediately feel the economic consequences. Nonetheless, this money gets siphoned from the funds that could have been used to create American jobs, increase the budgets for education, health care, public infrastructure, and support our troops when they returned home. It could be used to prevent wars in the first place. The big players in the US military industrial complex do not care about the troops, however. Their goal is simple—create wars and make a fortune from the suffering and chaos. It is sickening but this is not an exaggeration.

Let us take a specific example of war profiteering, so that we can begin to understand how the game works. *Seventy American companies* received eight billion dollars in contracts for work in postwar Iraq and Afghanistan between 2009 and 2011. Those companies donated more money to the presidential campaigns of George W. Bush than to any other politician over the previous decade.

Halliburton, which Vice President Dick Cheney led prior to being chosen as Bush's running mate in August 2000, was the top recipient of federal contracts for the two countries, with more than similarly high-ranking ties, was secong at around $1.03 billion. The second company was the international Oil Trading Co. with contracts worth $2.1 billion.[605]

Nearly everyone of the ten largest contracts awarded for work in Iraq and Afghanistan went to companies that employed high-ranking governmnet officials or individuals with close ties to those agencies or Congress. In addition, those top ten contractors were established political donors, contributing nearly eleven million dollars to national political parties, candidates, and political action committees since 1990, according to an analysis of campaign financ records.

Of the seventy companies, nearly sixty percent had employees or board members who were either in or had close ties to the executive branch Republican and Democratic administrations for members for Congress of both parties, or at the highest levels of the military since 1990.[606]

Subterfuge

The Center for Public Integrity's findings are largely based on seventy-three Freedom of Information Act requests and appeals to USAID, the Pentagon, its various uniformed services, and the State Department, as well as an analysis of the General Services Administration database of contracts from 1990 through fiscal year 2002, more than seven million federal contract actions, in all.

Requests for information through the Center's FOIA (Freedom Of Information Act) appeals process were strongly resisted by the military-industrial war profiteers. In fact, it required a lawsuit against the State Department and the Pentagon to release the public information. Because of inconsistencies and scarce information, the total value of contracts awarded for reconstruction work in Iraq and Afghanistan is probably much greater than what was ascertained.

For example, in a list of contracts initially provided to the Center under FOIA, both USAID and the Pentagon *omitted* information about the contracts that they had awarded in Iraq to Bechtel and to Halliburton. Also omitted from the Pentagon's list were other major defense contractors like Fluor, Washington Group International, and Perini Corporation, each of which stood to earn billions for their Pentagon work in Iraq, Afghanistan, and other countries. Combined, these three companies and their subsidiaries had won more than eleven billion dollars in US government contracts from 1990 through fiscal year 2002. It is unknown how much they have earned since then, now eighteen years later.

In their effort to discover the truth about these "under the table" contract deals worth billions of dollars, the Center for Public Integrity had to wade through contradictory information, disputes and subterfuge regarding total amounts of the value of contracts, disagreements between information provided by companies compared to information on their websites, as well as multiple excuses for not coming up with requested information. Often information requests from FOIA were redacted or blacked out. Phone calls went unanswered.

Revolving Doors

In many ways, Science Applications International Corporation (SAIC) is typical of the kinds of American contractors working in Iraq and Afghanistan. SAIC was the third-largest recipient of US government contracts between 2001 and 2011. The company, its employees, and PAC contributed $4.7 million to national political campaigns. When you think about it, it is amazing how cheap it is to buy off politicians in exchange for tens of billions of dollars for war contracts.

SAIC's largest customer is the US government, which accounts for sixty-nine percent of its business, and its company roster is a revolving door of government-corporate influences.

David Kay, the former U.N. weapons inspector, who was hired by the CIA to track down weapons of mass destruction in Iraq, is a former vice president of SAIC. Kay left SAIC to oversee homeland security and counterterrorism for the US government in October 2002.

Christopher "Ryan" Henry, Vice President for Strategic Assessment and Development, left SAIC in February 2003 to become principal Deputy Undersecretary of Defense for policy in George W's administration. Henry now works for the office overseeing his former employer, the Undersecretary of Defense for Policy.

SAIC's Duane P. Andrews, Executive Vice President for Federal Business and Director, served as Assistant Defense Secretary from 1989 to 1993, when he joined SAIC.

Board member W. A. Downing served as Deputy Assistant Director for International Counter-Terrorism initiatives on the National Security Council and joined SAIC after retiring as an Army general in 1996.

Bobby Ray Inman, a board member until October 2003, was a retired US Navy admiral, who once directed the National Security Agency and served as deputy director of central intelligence. Inman is also a member of the board of directors of Fluor, another contractor in Iraq and Afghanistan.

Other companies, like Chemonics International, Perini Corporation, and Sullivan Haave Associates Inc. all have executives who served in high-level positions of the US federal government, including the Bush and Obama administrations.

The Center's investigation also found that many contractors had close working relationships with one another, using each other's expertise through subcontracts. In addition to the war machine contractors, companies like ChevronTexaco, JPMorgan, and MCI/WorldCom also got in on the action.

ChevronTexaco joined five other international oil companies selected by the Iraqi State Oil Marketing Organization to market Iraqi oil. The expected revenue of three hundred million dollars from the sale of oil will be controlled by the US government for "use in rebuilding Iraq."

JPMorgan, the nation's largest bank, had been contracted by the Coalition Provisional Authority to run a consortium of thirteen banks from thirteen countries that would constitute the Trade Bank of Iraq. Bank consortium members were not expected to earn much revenue initially, but banking publications reported that the real windfalls would come once Iraq's oil production resumed full capacity and anticipated billions of dollars would flow through the Trade Bank for financing large development projects.

MCI, formerly WorldCom, was hired by the Pentagon to build a wireless phone network for officials and aid workers in the Baghdad area of Iraq. MCI's reconstruction activities in Iraq were not disclosed in documents the Defense Department provided to the Center under a Freedom of Information Act request. However, an MCI spokesperson said the Pentagon-led Coalition Provisional Authority awarded the contract to MCI in late May 2003. The contract was part of a short-term communications plan costing the Pentagon approximately forty-five million dollars.[607]

Leverage

In addition to the closed contracts and revolving door politics of the military industrial insiders, they also use each crisis they foment as a leverage to convince Congress that the situation is spinning out of control and that the US and its allies require more weapons and soldiers to bring the situation in hand. Their goal is always to lift the caps on the Pentagon's base budget that exists under current law. When they are successful, as they usually are, it means hundreds of billions of new business for Pentagon contractors over the next decade.[608]

It is worth remembering that the War on Terrorism initiated by the Bush administration has only been intensified under the Obama and Trump administrations. While Bush took Americans into Kuwait, Libya, Afghanistan, and Iraq, Obama has kept those fires burning while also involving the US military in Syria, Yemen, and Saudi Arabia. Trump, for his part, is back in Iraq, picking a fight with Iran, and selling weapons for the war in Yemen. The rationale for these wars is always the same, to prevent terrorism and to make the world safe for democracy. Ironically, through their good work, Americans are more frightened of terrorists than they have ever been.

Making Money

Since 9/11 and the onset of the War on Terrorism, the people of the United States have been paying $32.08 million dollars to war profiteers *every hour* of the day since 2001.[609] If this amount was dedicated to human services in the United States, we would have the highest quality of life in the world and unemployment would be a thing of the past. In fact, we could end world hunger ($30 billion per year),[610] or bring the entire world out of poverty ($29.39 billion per year).[611] We could end homelessness in the United States ($20 billion a year)[612] It would cost only $5 billion per year for twenty years to eliminate illiteracy in the entire world.[613] It seems that if Americans were to eliminate hunger, homelessness, and illiteracy in the world this would be a greater contribution to national security and world peace than spending two and a half times that amount for war in the Middle East.

The symbol of the United States Marines is the globe with an American eagle perched on top of it, with wings outspread in protection. If the Marines really want to protect the world, they need to change their grand strategy.

The chart below indicates the money that the American federal government spent on warfare in 2016 compared to to other countries' military expenditures.[614]

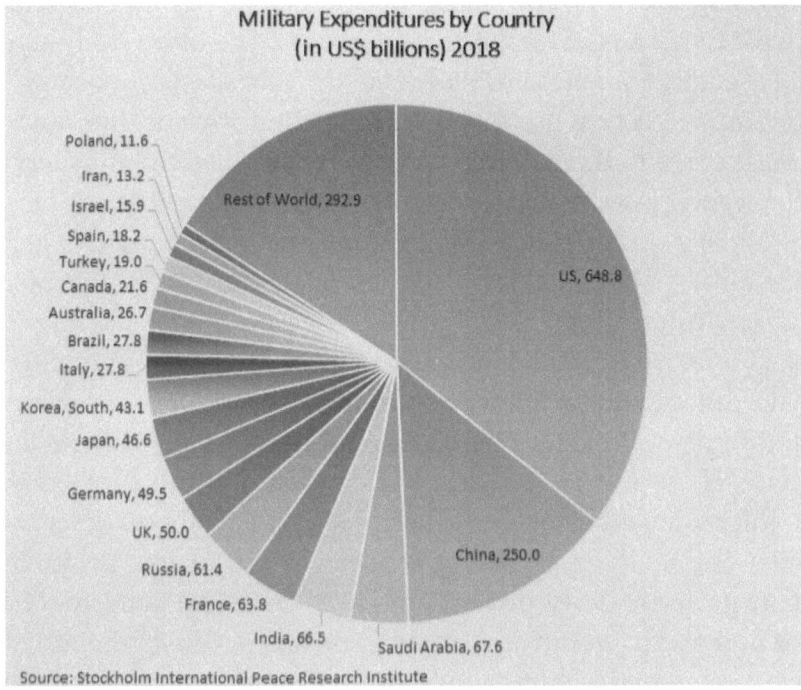

Fig. 5-13: US Warfare Expenditures vs Other Countries

Bad Strategy, Bad Tactics

We can conclude from the above information that if the point of the War on Terror is to protect American security and spread democracy around the world, it has been a failure. But if the strategy all along has been to profit the military-industrial elite by spreading death, destruction, and chaos, it has been a smashing success.

Of the countries that have been invaded by the US army or its surrogates, none have been secured and all remain in a state of chaos lacking a basic infrastructure, economic self-reliance, security forces, or political stability. The deaths of millions of innocent bystanders have not pacified the Islamic fundamentalists of the Middle East or encouraged them to embrace democracy, rather it has only added to the chaos.

The military counter-insurgency strategy based on "nation-building" was a non-starter, while the household raids, random killings, drone strikes, prison torture, and bombings of innocent civilians only served to create thousands of local insurgent groups who move freely across borders and cannot be controlled. Like the Taliban, they move where they want and if driven out of an area by the US army, they leave to fight elsewhere or go into hiding only to return when the army leaves.

The economic sanctions against Iraq, which went on for years, caused the deaths of a million people, half of whom were children. It was not lost on the world that our political leaders expressed absolutely no remorse for this monstrous act.

Not the least of the problems created by the so-called War on Terror, was the dislocation of millions of human beings who now are camped on the borders of the world's nations wanting to get in. These millions of homeless have led to an ultra-right backlash, which suspects that the refugees are infiltrated with "terrorists," who will now enter their country and do them harm. The refugees have polarized the politics and the people of developed nations to the point that both sides look at the other with disdain and hatred in their eyes. This promises even greater profits for the military-industrial complex, who have now begun to militarize the domestic police.

The Flawed Vision of Global Dominance

It seemed so simple when the Trilateralists sat down to map out their conquest of Eurasia and thus the world. It seemed so simple when Dick Cheney and the Neo Cons sat around the table studying the maps of Iraq, envisioning their ownership of all that oil while making a fortune rebuilding the country. It seemed so simple when the military strategists drew up their new grand strategy and told the American people about the necessity of the "War on Terrorism" and how we could identify our new enemies and how the long war on terrorism would not end until every "terrorist" in the entire world was dead or neutralized.

Now, consider the fact that the documents that contain the thinking of the elites are in the public domain and can be found online. Anyone can download the *Crisis of Democracy*, the *Grand Chess Board*, or the Neo-Cons *Rebuilding America's Defenses: Strategies, Forces, and Resources for a*

New Century. If such documents, as well as many other revealing sources of information, can be found by the authors of this book, we can be sure that the intelligence agencies of every country in the world, including Russia, Iran, Turkey, Syria, or any government or "terrorist" organization in the Middle East have also accessed them. The government strategists of these countries would quickly understand the intentions of the United State in its relationship to their government. In short, they would quickly see that it is the US government's intention to dominate them and control their people and national resources. In all honesty, what would you do if you were faced with this information? The American revolutionaries took up arms against British imperialism with much less knowledge of their intentions. Can we expect other human beings to willingly do less?

Here is what Bashar Hafez al-Assad, the current President of Syria, whom the US government is attempting to overthrow, had to say in an interview with the Tehran Foreign Policy Studies Quarterly in October, 2016. "The United States builds its position on hegemony over other states and it has been the case since they took advantage of the USSR collapse and established unilateral control over this world up to this day." Assad said that the real motive for the US military interventions into foreign countries is to coerce them to submit to American authority. This is, in fact, right out of Brzezinski's game plan that was presented to the Trilaterialists.

Assad continued, "Today, the United States are waging wars with the only goal to cement its project of total control by launching attack on everyone, who opposes its dominance." Washington "rejects" and "refuses to acknowledge" the balance of powers in the world affairs and the rise of other states.

Is there any doubt that Assad, and his allies, as well as any other group fighting against US global ambitions, do not understand the American vision of global dominance? Because of the failure of the US to dominate the Middle East, much less Eurasia, Assad believes that the US has been losing its grip, and cannot accept the fact it is not in charge of global affairs. As such it continues in a fruitless attempt to control the world.

Assad believes "What is happening in Syria is an attempt to save what is left from the American and western hegemony in the world." In conclusion, he states, "the only one thing the Americans have succeeded in is creating problems and destroying states, no more than that."[615]

Perhaps now we can understand the reaction of Iran, Russia, and Turkey to the US. Perhaps, the terrorists would not be terrorists if we had not trained them and turned them against us. Granted we have brought down tyrants like Qadaffi and Hussein, but we did so without accounting for the political dynamics at play within those countries. On the other hand, the US government supports other tyrants like those in Saudi Arabia. It is not so much that the US elites oppose tyrants, as it is that they oppose tyrants who will not bow to the elite's vision of global dominance.

Our Idea of American Greatness Is Too Small

It goes without saying that most Americans on the left and the right are becoming sick of the way our American society is deteriorating. Yet, we have no plan to get us out of this endless mess. We have let the elites control our government and our media for too long without protest and now we find ourselves completely at their mercy. As American people, we have for too long rested on our laurels and have allowed the bankers and mercenaries to ravage the world, in our good name. Consequently, our vision of our country is now too small, our idea of God's righteousness is too constricted, our neighborliness is all but extinct, and our knowledge of the upper class and its military-industrial backroom deals too much ignored. The Left thinks that climate change is the greatest danger to our existence while the Right thinks that it's the refugees and terrorists. Few realize that, in the bigger picture, these problems have the same root, the control of oil as a step to world dominance on the part of the elite.

If our energy sources were renewable, the climate would improve and there would be no reason to covet our neighbors' goods. The need for foreign oil would diminish and we would no longer need to terrorize other people to get it. The US War on Terrorism is a hoax invented by the elites for global dominance. It has been a hoax from day one. If the people who are fighting for freedom in their own lands are a threat to us, it is only because we have made them so.

As Americans we have our own problems. We no longer take care of each other. Our infrastructure, economy, social service systems, our education, and health care systems are in disarray. Our political system is based on legal corruption and spite. We have forgotten how to be neighbors to each other. Our society, in fact, is caught up in a downward spiral. The poor people near the vortex feel it more than those on the periphery, but the vortex will inexorably bring all of us down unless we wake up and alter the course of our nation.

In the second part of this volume we will look closely at who we are as Americans as well as the consequences that we face by letting the elites rule us without challenge and plunder the world in our name. We will look at the current issues that confront the American people as a whole. If we can see these problems for what they are and uncover the source of these problems, we can begin to have a larger vision of our society and solutions may become clearer. As American people, we will see why we need a larger vision of ourselves, but also of the world and its people. Here is a small example of what this means.

Our elites have turned the Middle East into chaos for the same reason that it is destroying American society, for a profit. In the Middle East the potential of the people is exhausted. Even if all American troops were pulled out of the Middle East today, the people will still be faced with a filthy, bombed out environment with no infrastructure and rapidly diminished oil reserves. Their source of income will have plummeted and they will be unable to feed themselves. If other countries do not help them, tens of millions additional people will become refugees and the entire world will become 'primal.'

In the Middle East, there is a shortage of drinkable water and the land is semi-desert. The only solution is to do what the Israelis have done. Improve the soil conditions and invest in agriculture. Agriculture can also provide the base for pre-agriculture industries (seeds, humus, tools, etc.) and post-agriculture industries (food processing, manufacturing of building materials, and consumer items from plants and animals). With this base, other industries can gradually be developed. This will also improve the climate conditions.

The same thing can be done in our country if we can get beyond the divide and conquer strategy of the elites and come together as local communities. This is to say, that there is always a way out of a mess, if we think it through. If we believed that there is only One God, then we must all be children of that One God and we therefore have a family relationship with each other. Let us look

Part Two:
The American People

Introduction

IN PART ONE, WE revealed the thinking and behavior of the capitalist elite in America, as well as the intellectual and the military elites who support them. We have examined their goal of world dominance and the mechanisms by which they keep the rest of us oppressed, divided, and ever fearful of each other. The majority of the American people stand against this imperialism and support our democracy, even though we are constantly being undermined by the dominant forces at play. By being subjected to the dictates of the elite's grand strategy, our optimism is rapidly diminished, our liberties are eroded, and the clarity of our mind is muddled by conflicting stories that prevent us from knowing where to put the blame for the decline in our standard of living.

Part Two of this volume begins by looking at who we are as an American people. Except for Native Americans, we are a nation of immigrants and refugees from all over the world. In many ways, the American people represent the world's people because we have all become Americans and have added our neighborhoods, shops and restaurants, fashions, and intellectual acumen to the rich and varied culture of America. Nonetheless, we will try to define ourselves as a unique people by exploring certain key characteristics based upon our age, gender, race, class, religion, and national origin.

After exploring the question of who we are as Americans, we will look at the major social forces in play that diminish our life style and divide us as a people. These debilitating forces include wide-scale unemployment and underemployment, a worsening political polarization, increased police surveillance, endless foreign wars, fear of immigrants, and the impact of pollution and climate change on our environment. Each of these problems directly result from the ruling elite's quest for global dominance.

The major concern of any family is to secure its basic needs. We will end this section with a look at the increasing struggle we as Americans must go through to meet our needs which include food, shelter, clothing, health care and education. We will look at the industries and institutions that provide the goods and services to meet these needs and reveal how their profit motive has resulted in the production of goods and services that diminish in quality while rising in price.

Today, we earn less money for our labor while paying higher prices for inferior goods and services. This process continually transfers our limited wealth to the elites. This has a direct effect on our sense of self-worth and our sense of human dignity.

While it may be demoralizing to look these issues in the face, it is necessary to understand our current condition so that, in moving forward, we may be inspired to work together as Americans, to take control of our own lives, to restore our hard-fought freedoms, and to create a better world for our children. This can be done and will be done and, though it may sound intimidating, we will come to agree that a profound revolution in every sphere of our lives is our only option to avoid a cataclysmic social and environmental crash. As Ben Franklin, on the eve of the first American Revolution so aptly put it, "By failing to prepare, you are preparing to fail."

The ruling elites today have declared war on the American people as assuredly as the British Empire declared war on its American colony one hundred and fifty years ago. The second American revolution has already begun to unfold and for the people to succeed in this fight, we must learn to depend upon our spiritual nature as human beings. Without a universal morality to guide us, we will simply rise and fall on the waves of this psycho-physical reality as directionless as a rudderless boat on an open sea. Like so many empires in the past, ours has begun to leak and we are taking on more water. We are bound to go down with the ship if we do not unite as a people to build another ship that can take us where we want to go.

Such an accomplishment, while difficult, is not only possible but probable as we shall learn in Book Two on Ideology and Book Three on Revolution. The future of humanity is indeed very bright but we must take deliberate steps to bring it about. It is on each of us to support a new way. The first step on this new path is to understand who we are as an American people. It is the intention of chapter four to provide this information.

Chapter 4: The American People

Who We Are

As Americans, we are probably the most diverse nation of people on the planet. We are essentially a country of immigrants who have arrived here from every corner of the world. This is one of our greatest strengths and yet it is one of our greatest burdens because as new people arrive, they elicit nativist prejudices, bigotry, and hatred for "the other" that stews just beneath the surface of American life. Our nation was built on slavery and on the suppression of women and we have not yet come to terms with the impact that these spiritual injustices have on our American psyche. Neither have we fully contemplated how the corporate elites and their chief servants have continually manipulated us for their own profit. Therefore, even though we share a common culture, our differences are continually exploited for someone else's personal gain. The elites' divide and conquer strategy weaken us as American people.

We have discussed above how the elites divide us according to those who support them and those who do not. This simple division is obscured by the policy-oriented politicians and the corporate mainstream media, who continue to aggravate the difference between the political Left and Right that now preoccupies our minds as Americans. Yes, these is a legitimate division between the Left and the Right insofar as we have a different orientation in our values and in the issues that we support. Yet, we have also seen that some people on the Left and Right support the capitalist elite and others do not. If we are to escape the end-game of capitalism, which means continual war and environmental destruction, we must begin to build bridges between those on the Left and the Right who stand opposed to the present system.

In order to do this, we need to first develop a shared vision that can help us overcome our differences, both real and perceived. We can begin this process by looking at ourselves as human beings, independent of the labels of Left and Right. For example, let us put aside our political differences for the moment and try to develop a picture of ourselves as generic human beings. This means shedding our preoccupation with the differences that preoccupy our attention. As a diverse people, there are many approaches that we have taken to differentiate ourselves. We distinguish ourselves based upon age, gender, race, class, locality, religion, and ethnic origin. A montage of these perspectives will hopefully give us a general picture of who we are as Americans.

As of January, 2019, the United States had a resident population of 329,093,110 people, making us the third most populous country in the world. Eighty-one percent of Americans live in the cities and suburbs. The New York City metropolitan area is the most populous in the United States with almost twenty million people.

The American population almost quadrupled during the twentieth century at a growth rate of about 1.3% a year, from seventy-six million people in 1900 to two hundred and eighty-one million in 2000. By 2006, we had three hundred million and today we stand at a little over three hundred and twenty-nine million people. The US Census Bureau projects that by 2060, the US population will be around four hundred ands seventeen million people.

Even though the United States has a low fertility rate, US population growth is among the highest in industrialized countries because of increased immigration levels. This is a mixed blessing because, while immigrants add to our economic vitality and cultural experience and expand our awareness of humanity, many Americans, particularly white people who have lost their jobs over the last couple of decades, have become defensive that these new people, the majority of whom are not white, are here to take away scarce jobs and further throw their lives into desperation and poverty. Such a belief has begun to polarize the country, as it has in other countries as well. The Trump Administration has played on this fear of white Americans by promising to halt the immigration of non-whites, particularly people from the Middle East and Latin America. In this manner, Trump uses "race," or the color of our skin, as a distraction from the real culprits behind the loss of American jobs, specifically the Federal Reserve Bank and the multinational corporations.

The distinction between races has deep roots in the United States, particularly since the American ruling elite made its start-up capital by using the slave labor of blacks and native Americans. This was true not only for the Southern plantation owners, many who were Southern Baptist ministers as well as US Presidents, but also for the banks and corporations in the North who funded the slave trade and supplied the plantations with goods and equipment.

When the Civil War freed the slaves, the Confederate states of the South hated the blacks even more and blamed them for ruining the Southern economy. As such they created laws which essentially recreated slavery in the South. For many white Southerners today, who want to go back to the "good old days," they still harbor great hatred for black Americans. They reinforce their mind-set by developing mythologies as to the superiority of the white race and the inferiority of the black race. We will discuss the myth of racial superiority later in our analysis but for now let us take a look at the way sex and gender affects our perception of who we are as Americans.

Sex and Gender

One's sex/gender is perhaps the most nuclear determinate of one's self-identity. Above every other distinction, we primarily see ourselves as male or female. Men and women are not only biologically different, but we also think differently due to our experiences. While one's sex is cut and dried by virtue of one's biology, one's gender is determined either by one's social role or personal identification based on an internal awareness. Therefore, it is necessary to make the distinction between sex and gender.

There were about 165.6 million females in the United States (fifty-one percent) and 159.1 million males (forty-nine percent), but the sexes are not evenly distributed among the states. The map below shows the ratio of men to women in each of the fifty states, based on 2010 US Census data. The darker states have more men than women, and the lighter states have more women than men. The darker the shade, the greater the disparity.

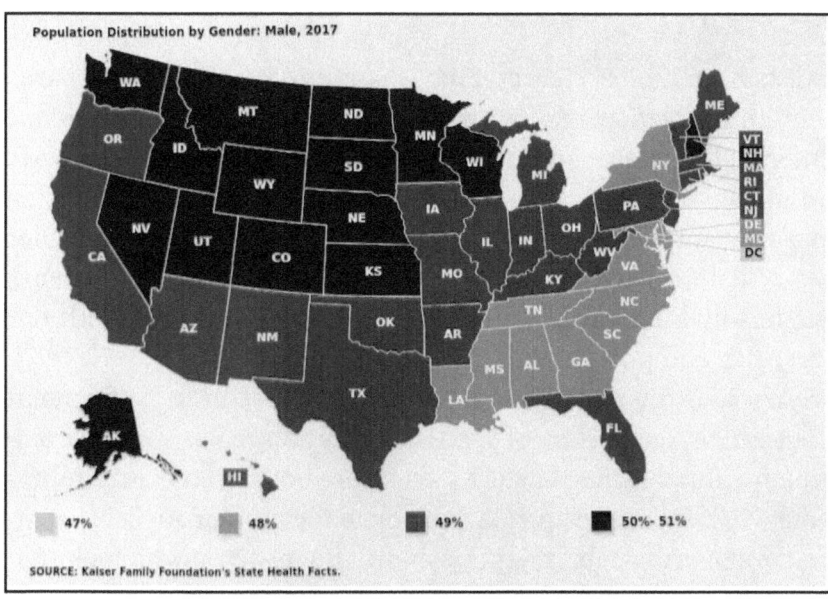

Fig. 5-14: Ratio of Men and Women in the Fifty States

There are only ten states where men outnumber women and among these Alaska has the greatest discrepancy. In Alaska there are 109 men for every 100 women. Washington DC on the other hand has only 90 men for every 100 women. California has 98.8 men for every 100 women. Illinois has 96.2 men for every 100 women and New York has 93.8 men for every 100 women. The primary reasons for the discrepancy are that women live longer than men, but also more men die in battle than women.[616]

While a minority in terms of numbers, men still dominate American society. This results from a long history of patriarchy in Western society. American men feel as threatened by women today as did their counterparts in the Roman Empire when Cato, the elder Roman senator, cautioned the Senate:

> Our fathers have willed that women should be in the power of their fathers, of their brothers, of their husbands. Remember all the laws by which our fathers have bound down the liberty of women, by which they have bent them to the power of men. As soon as they are our equals, they become our superiors.[617]

Sexism is prejudice, stereotyping, shaming, discrimination, harassment and violence against women. Misogyny means a dislike of, contempt for, or an ingrained prejudice against women. Both sexism and misogyny have a long history in the Western world and stems from fear among the men that if women gain equality with them, they will reject their second-class status and soon best them in decision-making and authority and ultimately compete with them for wealth and power.

Sexist and misogynist males today have reason to be frightened because their long history of oppression has only made women stronger and more durable. Fortunately, women are not as petty and vindictive as men. While conservatives, who look to the past for answers, want to keep women in a subservient position, progressives, who look to the future, know full well that there can be no human progress without women playing an equal role in the revolution to come.

The normal distinction between men and women has been blurred in recent years by the introduction of gay rights into the public discourse. It appears that sex and gender are not as simple as we would like to believe. Nonconventional sexual behavior has always been a part of the human experience. Homosexuals exist on every continent and have done so in every age of hisory.

For example, in East Asia, same-sex love has been referred to since the earliest recorded times. Homosexuality in China, known as the *pleasures of the bitten peach, the cut sleeve*, or *the southern custom*, has been recorded since approximately 600 BCE. In Japan, homosexuality, variously known as shudo or nanshoku, has been documented for over one thousand years and had some connections to the Buddhist monastic life and the samurai tradition. This same-sex love culture gave rise to strong traditions of painting and literature documenting and celebrating such relationships.

Similarly, in Thailand, *ladyboys* have been a feature of Thai society for many centuries, and Thai kings had male as well as female lovers.[618]

There is evidence of homosexuality in ancient Africa, including Egypt,[619][620] and throughout the Middle East.[621] Homosexuality and same sex marriages were also widely accepted in Greek and Roman culture.[622]

The Jewish priest class was the first to condemn homosexuality and this was later picked up by the apostle Paul. In the Old Testament (Lev. 18:22, 20:13, Deut. 22:5) and the New Testament (Rom. 1:26) we find words that condemn females who wear male attire, males who wear female attire, and males and females that engaged in homosexual behavior or intercourse.[623]

In the West, however, the full oppression of homosexuals did not begin until the eleventh century when St. Peter Damian, wrote the *Liber Gomorrhianus*, an extended attack on both homosexuality and masturbation.[624] Peter was one of the forerunners of the Gregorian Revolution of the late eleventh century which was marked by the effort to centralize Church governance and raise the status of priests above that of lay Christians. In order to do this, they had to convince the people that priests lived a more moral life than did normal people. The condemnation of masturbation and men having sex with men was part of this process. In order to prevent these practices among the priests, the Church tried to position these sexual acts as a force that undermined morality, religion, and society itself.[625]

It is ironic that the Catholic Church, while ostensibly condemning homosexuality, has given rise to a priest class filled with adulterers and pedophiles.

Because of their oppression at the hand of the Catholic Church, gay people have been forced to live in hiding, or as they say, "in the closet" for centuries. Recently, this oppression has begun to change. Gay people are more accepted in society today as human beings, eligible to receive the same human and civil rights as anyone else.

Despite the desire to simplify reality into good and bad, it is always more complicated than we would like to admit. To understand the fuzzy area between heterosexual men and women and homosexuals, we need to look more closely at the distinction between one's sex and gender. In daily usage, the terms sex and gender are often used interchangeably, but medically speaking these words are not synonymous. Gender comes from the Latin word *genus*, meaning kind or race. It is defined by one's own identification as male, female, or intersex. Gender may also be based on legal status, social interactions, public persona, personal experiences, and psychological disposition.

Sex, on the other hand, comes from the Latin word *sexus*, which means having testicles or ovaries. One's sex is generally assigned at birth by external genital appearance. When an intersex condition is noted in a newborn, i.e., when a child has both male and female sex organs or other sexual characteristics, one sex is often chosen with the intention of simplifying social interactions and rearing.

Simply stated, a person's sex is primarily determined by physical characteristics while a person's gender is primarily determined by one's psychological disposition. Conceptually, professionals state that sex is biologically determined, whereas gender is culturally determined.

Thus, sex and gender are not interchangeable terms. Neither are gender development and sexual development interchangeable. Physiological sexual development progresses through distinct stages from the neonatal period through infancy, childhood, puberty, adolescence, and adulthood. These aspects of physical sexual growth, eroticism, and eventual sexuality, although closely related to gender, should not necessarily be used to draw conclusions about a person's gender definitions.[626]

People who are attracted to others of the same sex are generally called "gays." It is estimated that ten percent of the population is gay.[627] This number has been used since Albert Kinsey did his study of American sexuality in the 1940s. Although recent studies by the National Health Interview Survey and the Williams Institute showed a much lower percentage of the population who specifically identified as gays. When people were asked whether they had engaged in same sex sexual behavior the numbers rose to 8.2 percent of Americans. Additionally, 11 percent reported same-sex attraction. Online surveys tend to yield higher figures than these, which most likely results from a higher degree of anonymity in taking Internet surveys.[628] Gay people often require anonymity because there is still a high penalty for admitting that you are gay in America.

Not all gay people are the same. It is common now to use the rubric "LGBTQ" to characterize the gay community. This acronym stands for Lesbians, Gays, Bisexuals, Transsexuals and Queers. Lesbians are women who have sex with other women. Gays are men who have sex with other men. Bisexuals are men or women who have sex with both sexes. Transsexuals are people who's sexual and gender identities are in conflict. A transsexual feels that he is a man trapped in a woman's body, or that she is a woman trapped in a man's body. Many transsexuals want to permanently transition to the sex to which they identify. It usually requires medical assistance to help align their body with their gender identity. The letter Q can mean either 'questioning' or 'queer.' Either interpretation is accepted. People use the term queer because it is not specific to sexual orientation or to gender identity, but is more of an umbrella term that can encompass a lot of people. Cleo Anderson, a twenty-six year-old intern at GLAAD, a prominent gay rights group, told USA Today that, "Queer means that you are one of those letters (LGBT), but you could be all of those letters and not knowing is OK," she said.[629]

While many religious conservatives consider LGBTQ people to be sinners whose "deviance" can be corrected by a proper indoctrination, this does not seem to be the case. One's gender is core to one's self identity and people should not be condemned because they do not fit the norm. Gays are not an accident of history, or a sin against nature, they are human beings and children of Divinity as are everyone else. If it were not for LGBTQ people, the cultural and artistic legacy of humanity would be greatly diminished.

The Generations

Another way to distinguish ourselves as Americans is by age. It is not only that one's age is important in itself, but each generation has experienced living in America in very distinct ways. This impacts all of our values and our sense of reality.

Sociologists divide Americans into six living generations. These are the GI Generation comprised of four million Americans or one percent of the US population, the Silent Generation comprised of twenty-nine million or nine percent of the population, the Baby Boomers comprised of seventy-five million or twenty-four percent qof the population, Generation X comprised of sixty-six million or twenty-one of the population, Generation Y (The Millenials) comprised of seventy-five million or twenty-three percent of the population, and Generation Z comprised of sixty-nine million or twenty-two percent of the US population.[630] Let us take a brief look at these living generations of Americans.

The GI Generation

The GI Generation was born between 1901-1926. As the children of those who fought in WWI, they also lived through the Great Depression and WWII. They take great pride in the United States as having saved the world by destroying the fascist dictatorship of Adoph Hitler and stemming the advance of godless communism. After WWII they went on to build the *Affluent Society*.

As children, they were looked at as "good kids." New playgrounds, Scouts, vitamins, and child labor laws gave them a sense of security. Most of them went to school and there were more teenagers in school than out of school for the first time.

This generation likes uniformity. It is good and normal for everyone to agree, work the same, and look the same. They like to dress up. Men with suits and ties and women in dresses and hats.

The GI generation is assertive and energetic. They are community-minded, have a strong sense of personal civic duty, and regularly vote. Personal morality is important to them and they carry a strong sense of what is right and wrong. Unfortunately, this morality does not necessarily apply to people outside their group. Consequently, this generation tends toward racism and suppression of women's rights. A woman's place was in the home and behind her man. Even so, this generation married for life. Divorce and having children out of wedlock were not acceptable.

As young people they experienced the "roaring 20s." They introduced jazz, blues, ballads, Ziegfield Follies, Vaudeville, and loved George Gershwin. The radio was introduced at this time and, along with the introduction of air flight, helped develop a national sense of identity.

In the workplace, this generation fought for workers' rights and gave birth to the labor movement.

As far as personal finance goes, they tend to avoid debt, save their money, and buy with cash. They do not waste anything. They can remember living without TV. And in rural areas, many of this generation grew up having no indoor plumbing or electricity.

Because of the epic developments that occurred during their life-time, they are often called the Greatest Generation.

Silent Generation

This generation was born between 1927 and 1945. It was comparatively small because the financial insecurity of the 1930s and the war in the early 1940s caused people to have fewer children.[631]

Economic losses that affected a family's status filled children with an ambitious desire to overcome such losses, leading to a generation with aspirations, goals, and purpose. Children growing up around the time of the Depression experienced a sense of trust in the government due to the efforts of Franklin Delano Roosevelt (1933-1945), whose New Deal programs quickly generated jobs and capital for the American people. Furthermore, this generation came of age during World War II, when patriotism ran high among American citizens. Therefore, this generation is patriotic and trusting of the American government.

As children, this generation went through an era of extreme social conformity, suffocated by the Depression and World War II.

They came of age too late to be war heroes and too early to be youthful free spirits. They married early and came to be known to sociologists as the "Lonely Crowd."[632] They were risk-averse and filled the technical and professional job slots of the post-crisis era. Success was based upon conformity. Many of the more radical members, however, found a voice in early rock 'n roll and social issues. Some became civil-rights advocates. In their midlife, they found themselves trapped between their stolid parents and their passionate children. They could never understand why just "following the rules" no longer worked for their children and grandchildren.[633]

In growing up, their gravest crime in school was passing notes or chewing gum in class. They were expected to be seen, but not heard. As WWII drew to an end, this generation turned to Big Bands and Swing music for release. After the war, they experienced the euphoria of victory and a return to peacetime pursuits. They had peace, jobs, the suburbs, TV, and an environment of expanded opportunities. This gave birth to rock and roll, car mania, fast food drive-ins, Playboy magazine, and the Peace Corp.

This generation is disciplined, self-sacrificing, and cautious. They believe in universal values and near-absolute truths. They are avid readers, especially of newspapers.

This was the generation that fought in the Korean and Vietnam Wars. They also provided the first hopeful signs of civil rights with the founding of the NAACP and cases like Brown vs the Board of Education and Briggs vs Elliott.[634] It was still a time before the feminist revolution, however, and women's roles still remained curtailed. They stayed home to raise children. If they worked, it was only in prescribed jobs like teacher, nurse, or secretary. Like their parents, marriage was for life. Divorce and having children out of wedlock were not acceptable.

In the workplace, men pledged their loyalty to the corporation. Once they got a job, they generally kept it for life. It was a time when everyone shared in corporate profits. Consequently, this generation produced the richest, most free-spending retirees in history.

Baby Boomers

The Baby Boomers were born between 1946 and 1964 and were one of the largest generations in American history with seventy-seven million people. By comparison, their parents' generation was only comprised of fifty million people. The Baby Boomers are so named because of the explosion of births that occurred after World War II, when young men returned home to start their families. The Baby Boomers fall into two broad categories: the save-the-world revolutionaries (Hippies) of the '60s and '70s; and the party-hardy career climbers (Yuppies) of the '70s and '80s.

This was the first generation to attend college en masse. It is also the first generation to grow up in the suburbs. The baby boom and the suburban boom went hand in hand. Prefab "Levittowns" grew up everywhere to accommodate the returning soldiers. Suburban life was the defining lifestyle of the 1950s, as whites abandoned the cities because of higher taxes, racial tensions, and the daily grind. The G.I. Bill had subsidized low-cost mortgages for returning soldiers, which meant that it was often cheaper to buy a suburban house than it was to rent an apartment in the city.[635] By 1960, suburban baby boomers and their parents comprised one-third of the population of the United States.

By the arrival of the 1960s, many of this generation had become disillusioned with suburban consumerism and the mainstream politics of the "Establishment." As the first generation to go to college en masse, they developed a strong sense of themselves as a generation and as a force to be reckoned with. As such, many of them began to fight against the war in Vietnam and for social, economic and political equality for disadvantaged groups. African-American, youth, women, gays and lesbians, American Indians, and Hispanic movements began. Student activists took over college campuses, organized massive demonstrations against the war in Vietnam and occupied parks and other public places. Young people also participated in the wave of uprisings that shook American cities from Newark to Los Angeles in the 1960s.

In her 1963 book, *The Feminine Mystique*, women's-rights advocate Betty Friedan argued that the suburbs were "burying women alive." Being left at home in the suburbs with little stimulation, while their husbands went off to work, was a stultifying experience for many young women. This dissatisfaction, in turn, contributed to the birth of the feminist movement in the 1960s.[636] Even though their mothers were generally housewives whose primary responsibility was child-rearing, women of the baby boom generation began to work outside the home in record numbers, thereby changing the culture of home and the workplace. This was the first generation to have their own children raised in a two-income household where mom was not omnipresent. This was also the first divorce generation, where divorce began to be accepted as a tolerable reality.

The Baby Boomers created a "cultural revolution" in American society. In addition to its political activities, it also challenged American social and cultural expectations. The introduction of marijuana on college campuses and the invention of "the pill" created the conditions for a lifestyle of "sex, drugs, and rock and roll." Mass social gatherings called "Be-ins" and "Loveins" went hand in hand with the introduction of Eastern religions and other esoteric ideas to American society. It was also at this time when white culture and black culture began to merge, thanks in large part to rock and roll music. As they turned away from corporate consumerism, many "Hippies" began to explore their own personal development. Some tried to "drop out" of American life all together by moving to communes as far away from the suburbs as possible.

The writer Tom Wolfe called this generation the "Me" generation, in part because of its pursuit of self-realization as opposed to the traditional values of civic responsibility. But for many others, it was physical pleasure and self-aggrandizement that took precedence. This generation also created the "Yuppies" (young urban professionals) who sought high paying jobs in order to indulge a hedonistic lifestyle that eventually manifested in the Disco culture.[637]

Considered to be self-righteous and self-centered, when the baby boomers want something they want it now. They buy on credit, and have, in large part, been responsible for introducing the consumer credit culture to American society.

The baby-boomers were the first TV generation and, in large part, were responsible for promoting American pop culture around the world. As they were being chased and beaten by Chicago police at the Democratic Party convention in 1968, they chanted to the TV cameras "The whole world is watching. The whole world is watching." They understood how this image would affect the perception of America by the world's people more than the police and the authorities of the previous generations who were now suppressing them.

The Baby Boomers were also the first generation to use the word "retirement" to mean being able to enjoy life after the children have left home. Instead of sitting in a rocking chair, they go skydiving, exercise, and take up hobbies, which increases their longevity.

Generation X

Born between 1965 and 1980, Generation X is a small group "sandwiched" between two larger demographic cohorts, the Baby Boomers and the Millennials. The birth control pill, which was introduced in the early 1960s, was a contributing factor to the declining birth rates seen in this generation. In the United States, however, increased immigration partially offset declining birth rates and contributed to making Generation X an ethnically and culturally diverse generation.[638]

In the US, Generation Xers were among the first children to be bused to attain integration in the public school system. In the 1990's, demographer William Strauss reported Gen Xers were "by any measure the least racist of today's generations".[639]

Children of this generation were born during a time of an increasing divorce rate, which doubled in the mid-1960s, before peaking in 1980. Their Baby Boomer parents had destroyed the long-held values of parents staying together for the sake of the children and had replaced it with a societal value of parental and individual self-actualization.

Generation Xers were the "latch-key kids" who grew up street-smart but isolated, often with divorced or career-driven parents. The higher the educational attainment of the parents, the higher the odds the children of this time would be latchkey children, due to increased maternal participation in the workforce at a time before childcare options outside the home were widely available. The term "latch-key" came from the house key kids wore around their neck, because they would come home from school to an empty house while their parents were still at work. This generation's school problems revolved around drug possession and drug abuse.

They were either raised by the career and money conscious Yuppies or the disillusioned and alienated Hippies amidst societal disappointment over governmental authority and the Vietnam war. Consequently, they pay little attention to government and big business. Rather, they tend to be very individualistic and entrepreneurial. Their social commitment is more focused on helping their neighborhood, than on saving the world.

Having been relatively deprived of their parents' time and attention, they are eager to make marriage work and "be there" for their own children. Even so, Generation X is late to marry (after cohabitation) and, like their parents, quick to divorce. There are many single parents. They are often blamed for not creating enough structure for their children and giving them too much freedom.

Like their parents, this generation also leans toward self-development rather than an organization or specific career. They believe that individual rights prevail over the common good, especially as it applies to minorities.

Gen Xers were children during the crack epidemic, which disproportionately impacted urban areas and especially the African American community. Drug turf battles increased violent crime and crack addiction impacted communities and families. The crack epidemic had a destabilizing impact on families with an increase in the number of children in foster care. In their formative years, AIDS also began to spread. It was the first lethal infectious disease in the history of any culture on earth, which was not subjected to any quarantine. This harsh reality completely chilled any desire for "free love" in which their parents had indulged during their youth. They learned that sex could kill you.

Generation X came of age with MTV and is sometimes called the MTV Generation. They experienced the emergence of music videos, grunge, alternative rock, and hip hop. They were also the first children to have access to computers in their homes and schools.

Once considered to be cynical slackers, this generation grew to gain the support of the country. It proved exceedingly entrepreneurial and hard working. It is credited with helping to create the high-tech industry that fueled the 1990s economic recovery.

Generation Xers average seven career changes in their lifetime and do not think it's normal to work for a company for life, unlike previous generations. At the same time, Gen Xers launched the majority (fifty-five percent) of all new businesses in 2015.

Like their parents, they want what they want and they want it now, but struggle to pay for it. Most live with sizeable credit card debt. They are attracted to labels and brand names.

Generation Y/Millennials.

The Millennials were born between 1981 and 2000. They depart considerably from their parents' generation. Doted on as children, they tend to be optimistic and focused. Crime rates and teen pregnancies fell with this generation. They have been repeatedly told that they are special and they expect the world to treat them that way. They have a sense of themselves as a generation and hold great expectations of the future.

Millennials grew up with the thought that they could be shot and killed at school and learned early that the world was not a safe place. They felt considerable academic pressure and organized themselves through scheduling everything. They prefer to work in teams.

As the first generation to grow up in a digital environment, they stress digital literacy. They have never known a world without computers. A recent survey found that ninetyseven percent of Millennials owned a computer, ninety-four percent owned a mobile phone, and fifty-six percent owned an MP3 player.[640]

They stay in touch with each other through instant messaging and use social networking sites, such as Twitter, Instagram, and Snapchat to create a sense of belonging, make acquaintances, and remain connected with friends. With unlimited access to information they tend to be assertive and hold strong views. To them, the world is open 24/7 and they demand fast and immediate results. A survey also found that students have a closer relationship with their parents than did previous generations. Millennials speak with their parents an average of 1.5 times a day about a wide range of topics.

Only forty percent of Millennials get their news from watching TV, while thirty-four use the Internet to get their news.

Millennials have been hard hit by the transfer of US jobs overseas and by the Great Recession. The youth unemployment rate in the US reached 19.1% in July 2010, which was the highest rate since the statistic started being gathered in 1948. In July 2016, the Department of Labor statistics showed that only 53% of youth ages sixteen to twenty-four were employed.[641]

Underemployment is also a major factor. In the US, economic difficulties have led to dramatic increases in youth poverty, unemployment, and the numbers of young people living with their parents. In April 2012, it was reported that half of all new college graduates in the US were still either unemployed or underemployed, although things have improved somewhat since then.[642]

In 2015, Millennials in New York City were reported to be earning twenty percent less than the generation before them. Despite higher college attendance rates than Generation X, many were stuck in low-paying jobs, with the percentage of degree-educated young adults working in low-wage industries rising from twenty-three percent to thirty-three percent between 2000 and 2014.[643]

While many cannot find jobs despite having college degrees, they find themselves saddled with debt for their education. In 2016, research from the Resolution Foundation in the UK described Millennials as "on course to become the first generation to earn less than the one before."[644]

Understandably, this generation holds wealth in higher esteem than previous generations. Only forty-five percent of Baby Boomers and seventy percent of Generation X considered wealth important, but seventy-five percent of Millennials think it is important. A consequence of this seems to be that they are less interested in political affairs or feel the need to have a "meaningful philosophy of life."[645]

Their economic situation has had a dampening effect on Millennials' rate of marriage, especially for working class members. A 2013 joint study by sociologists at the University of Virginia and Harvard University found that the decline and disappearance of stable full-time jobs with health insurance and pensions has had profound effects on working-class Americans, who now are less likely to marry and have children within marriage than those with college degrees.[646]

Data from a 2014 study of US Millennials revealed over fifty-six percent consider themselves as part of the working class, with only approximately thirty-five percent considering themselves as part of the middle class; this class identity is the lowest polling of any generation.[647]

Research by the Urban Institute conducted in 2014, projected that if current trends continue, Millennials will have the lowest marriage rate compared to previous generations, predicting that by the age forty, 30.7% of millennial women will remain single, approximately twice the share of their single Gen X counterparts. The data showed similar trends for males.[648]

In the United States, Millennials are the least likely to be religious. A study which analyzed data from 11.2 million respondents from four national surveys of US adolescents ages thirteen to eighteen taken between 1966 and 2014 showed that Millennials are less likely to say that religion is important in their lives. While showing less approval for religious organizations, they also report being less spiritual, and spending less time praying or meditating.

The research concluded that the Millennials' lower religious involvement is due to cultural change, not to their being young and unsettled. More of today's adolescents abandon religion before they reach adulthood, with an increasing number not raised with religion at all.

The movement away from religion has been a long trend in the US that has increased since the 1940s. Among the GI Generation, five percent said they were unaffiliated with a religion. This jumped to eight percent with the Silent Generation, thirteen percent with the Baby Boomers, twenty percent with Generation X and twenty-six percent with Millennials.[649]

Millennials tend to be more progressive in their politics. A Pew survey in 2008 held that Millennials are the most likely of any generation to self-identify as liberals and are also more supportive of a progressive domestic social agenda than older generations. This makes Millennials more open to change than older generations.

Millennials tend to be more "politically correct" than their elders. For example, in 2015, a Pew Research study found forty percent of Millennials in the United States supported government restriction of public speech offensive to minority groups. Support for restricting offensive speech was significantly lower among older generations: with twenty-seven of Gen Xers, twenty-four percent of Baby Boomers, and only twelve percent of the Silent Generation supporting such restrictions.[650]

Millennials are also the most educated generation. As of 2008, 39.6% of this generation, between the ages of eighteen to twenty-four were enrolled in college, which was an American record. Along with being educated, Millennials are also very upbeat. Even during tough economic times, they are more optimistic about the future of the US.

Because Millennials are also the most ethnically and racially diverse generation compared to previous generations, it has proven difficult to characterize them as a generation. For example, educators like Fred Bonner, a Samuel DeWitt Proctor Chair in Education at Rutgers University, believe that much of the commentary on the Millennial Generation may be only partially accurate, but overly general and that many of the traits described above apply primarily to white, affluent teenagers and college students whose parents help support them and reassure them that things will be alright.

Bonner interviewed black and Hispanic students who said that some or all of the so-called core traits did not apply to them. For example, they were not raised being doted upon and told that they were special. "It's not that many diverse parents don't want to treat their kids as special,"

Bonner says, "but they often don't have the social and cultural capital, the time and, resources, to do that."[651]

Generation Z

The Center for Generational Kinetics defines this generation as beginning born from 1996 up to the present. Their reasoning is that while 9/11 was the most important defining moment for the Millennials, those born from 1996 onward do not remember it. They conclude that if you do not remember 9/11, you cannot be a Millennial.

There are already over twenty-three million Gen Z children in the United States. Over the next five years they will most likely become the largest generation in American history.

In 2006, there was a population explosion in the US with almost half of the babies born to Hispanic parents. Since the early 1700's the most common last name in the US was Smith, but now it's Rodriguez.

According to Forbes, in 2015, Generation Z already made up twenty-five percent of the US population, making them a larger cohort than the Baby Boomers or Millennials. It is estimated that in the United States, fifty-five percent of Gen Z are non-Hispanic Caucasians, twenty-four percent are Hispanic, fourteen percent are African American, four percnt are Asian, and four percent are multiracial or other.[652] This makes Generational Z the most diverse generation of Americans.

Given that Gen Z are age twenty and under, their defining moments are still happening. Yet, there are certain events that have already had a profound impact on them, including global warming, the Great Recession, continuous war, student loan debt becoming a crisis in America, the Affordable Care Act becoming law, growing up with an African-American US president, gay marriage becoming legal, medical marijuana becoming legal in many states and the fact that there have already been twenty-something entrepreneurs who are billionaires. In addition, social media has always existed for them.

Baby Boomers are their grandparents rather than their parents, and they think Millennials are old. With the advent of computers and web-based learning, children leave behind toys at a younger and younger age. In the 1990s, for example, the average age of a child in Mattel's target market was ten years old, but in 2000 it had dropped to three years old.

As children reach the age of four and five, old enough to play on the computer, they become less interested in toys and begin to desire electronics such as cell phones and video games. Generation Z considers itself to be the first true "digital natives." They are submerged in computer technology from preschool age. Hannah Payne, an eighteen year-old UCLA student and lifestyle blogger says, "I can almost simultaneously create a document, edit it, post a photo on Instagram and talk on the phone, all from the user-friendly interface of my iPhone."

Ninety-eight percent of Generation Z owns a smartphone.[653] Well over half of Gen Z children have televisions in their rooms. thirty-five percent have video games, and fourteen percent have a DVD player. Four million have their own cell phones. While the first electronic device for the Millennials was the iPod, it is an iPhone for Generation Z kids, with seventy-seven percent of twelve to seventeen year olds owning a cellphone in 2015.[654]

Much of this generation has been educated from online applications. For example, in 2015, there were an estimated one hundred and fifty thousand applications, ten percent of these were educational and aimed at children up to college level.[655] Gen Z is already adept at web-based research using such online sources as Wikipedia, YouTube, and Pinterest. They can easily learn how to bake a pie or even make complex upgrades to their computer's operating system by watching videos online. As far as gaining knowledge is concerned, for Gen Z, it is not a matter of having the right information, but how fast you can find the right information. It is astonishing that Gen Z has an attention span of only eight seconds while Millennials have an attention span of twelve seconds.[656]

About three-quarters of thirteen to seventeen years olds use their cell phones daily, more than they watch TV. Over half of surveyed mothers say that their cell phones also influence them in purchasing decisions for toys, apparel, dinner choices, entertainment, TV, mobile devices, and computers.

Gen Z does not remember a time before social media. As a result, they tend to live more of their entire lives on-line. Through their cell phone, they interact with friends and family, make purchases, play games, and also educate themselves. Because technology is such a big part of their lives, it is interesting to see which applications they favor. For example, while Millennials and Gen Z still favor Facebook in terms of total usage,

Gen Z views Facebook as being for "older generations." As Gen Z gain more digital freedom, they appear to prefer more peer-to-peer social media and messaging apps, such as Snapchat, Vine, and Instagram. They might even have an anonymous or fake Instagram account so they can share their experiences without fear of online reputation repercussions. In fact, a recent study showed that nearly twenty-five percent of thirteen to seventeen yearolds left Facebook in 2018! This shows a trend toward apps that are quicker, provide less personal information, and are more visually appealing.[657]

This access to unlimited information forces them to assess at a much earlier age than their parents whether mainstream news and advertising are truthful or not. A 2014 study, which looks at how they see themselves vs their peers, is indicative of this internal conflict. The study *Generation Z Goes to College* found that Generation Z students self-identify as being loyal, compassionate, thoughtful, open-minded, responsible, and determined. How they see their peers is quite different from their own self-identity. They view their peers as competitive, spontaneous, adventuresome, and curious; all characteristics that they do not see readily in themselves.[658]

Gen Z are highly educated. It is likely that a larger percentage of this generation will attend and graduate from college than any previous generation, including the Millennials. According to a Northeastern University Survey, eighty-one percent of Generation Z believe obtaining a college degree is necessary to achieve career goals.[659] As Generation Z enter high school, and they start preparing for college; a primary concern is paying for a college education without acquiring debt. Students report working hard in high school in hopes of earning scholarships and the hope that parents will pay the college costs not covered by scholarships. Students also report interest in ROTC programs as a means of covering college costs.

Corporations are already wrestling with how to incorporate this generation into their work force. Will this highly educated generation be satisfied with lower paying jobs and unemployment? How will they react once they enter the job market? One thing that is known is that teenage summer employment is at historically low rates, even compared to Millennials. "Kids are witnessing start-up companies make it big instantly via social media," said Andrew Schoonover, a fifteen year-old in Olathe, Kan. "We do not want to work at a local fast-food joint for a summer job. We want to make our own business because we see the lucky few who make it big."[660]

The Public Relations Society of America believes that the Great Recession has taught Generation Z to be independent, and has led to an entrepreneurial desire, after seeing their parents and older siblings struggle in the workforce.[661] *Business Insider* describes Generation Z as more conservative, more money-oriented, more entrepreneurial, and pragmatic about money compared to Millennials.[662]

While this may be so, our children are not optimistic about their economic potential. A 2013 survey by Ameritrade found that forty-six percent of Generation Z in the United States between the ages of fourteen and twenty-three were concerned about student debt, while thirty-six percent were worried about being able to afford a college education at all.[663] This generation grew up faced with a growing income gap and a shrinking middle-class, which all have led to increased levels of stress in families.

This increased stress level, which they have experienced their entire lives, has tended to make them more conservative and less experimental than their grandparents' or parents' generations. "I definitely think growing up in a time of hardship, global conflict, and economic troubles has affected my future," said Seimi Park, a seventeen year-old high school senior in Virginia Beach, who always dreamed of a career in fashion, but has recently shifted her sights to law, because it seems safer. "This applies to all my friends," she said. "I think I can speak for my generation when I say that our optimism has long ago been replaced with pragmatism."[664]

Generation Z is also turning to religion for comfort. For example, a 2016 study found that church attendance during young adulthood was forty-one percent among Generation Z, compared with eighteen percent for Millennials at the same age, twenty-one percent of Generation X, and twenty-six percent of Baby Boomers.[665]

Research from the Annie E. Casey Foundation conducted in 2016 also found that Generation Z youth had lower teen pregnancy rates, less substance abuse, and higher on time high school graduation rates compared to Millennials. Looking at teens from 2008 and 2014, researchers found a forty percent drop in teen pregnancy, a thirty-eight percent drop in drug and alcohol abuse, and a twenty-eight percent drop in the percentage of teens who did not graduate on time from high school. Since 2008, the percentage of teen drug and alcohol abuse has also declined by double digits in every state except Louisiana and the District of Columbia. It fell by forty percent or more in eleven states.[666]

Something that bodes well for the future is that Gen Z wants to make a difference in the world. A large portion of them would prefer to have a job that makes a positive impact in some way, and a large portion of them volunteer. Gen Z is also eco-conscious and concerned about humanity's impact on the environment.[667] Their pin-up is Malala Yousafzai, the Pakistani education campaigner, who survived being shot by the Taliban, and who became the world's youngest ever Nobel Prize recipient."[668]

Race

Ever since the sixteenth century, "race" has played a central role in US culture and politics, in large part, due to the institution of black slavery in America. Before the institution of black slavery, plantation owners employed blacks, white, and Native Americans. Many of these workers were bonded to them because of previous debt. A bonded man was essentially a slave who was forced to work off his debt. Once the debt was paid, however, the bonded person was free to leave. This inconsistency made it difficult for the plantation owners to keep enough people in the cotton fields to do the back-breaking labor that was necessary to ensure themselves a profit. This problem was solved by bringing slaves from Africa. Black slavery instantly did away with the plantation owners need to cut down on worker turnover and to secure a steady stream of cheap labor. It also solved the problem of finding runaway indentured servants. Now, any black man not on a plantation was easily recognized as a slave and returned to his slave master for a reward.

By confining the definition of "slave" to blacks, and not whites, it became easier to create a stereotype that easily turned white society against black Americans. They promoted the idea that black slaves were an inferior race, unworthy of respect. Despite the deeply ingrained sense of privilege and racial superiority that white Americans hold when it comes to blacks and people of color, when one begins to actually analyze the question of race, the question of white superiority rapidly breaks down.

According to a United Nations convention on racial discrimination,[669] there is no distinction between the terms "racial" and "ethnic" discrimination. The UN convention further concludes that superiority based on racial differentiation is scientifically false, morally condemnable, socially unjust and dangerous, and there is no justification for racial discrimination, anywhere, in theory or in practice.

Despite the obvious difference in skin tone that we can observe in the people around us, the idea of races based on skin color and the idea of racial superiority or inferiority based on skin color has no basis in scientific fact. Let us start with the fact that the US Census Bureau defines white people as those "having origins in any of the original peoples of Europe, the Middle East, or North Africa." This means that Arabs and Africans are actually white people. In fact, white people, according to the census includes people, not only from Ireland, Germany, England, France, Italian, and Spain, but also people from Poland, Russia, Lebanon, Saudi Arabia, and even Egypt. This is certainly not the definition of white people that Adolph Hitler would have used, nor is it the definition used by white racists in this country, but it is a definition based upon anatomical characteristics.

In the United States, the largest percentage of white people derive from German stock. But these Germans do not all come from Germany. As a matter of fact, German people come to the US from England, Ireland, Alsace, Austria, Belgium, Brazil, Italy Luxembourg, Liechtenstein, Poland, Russia, Denmark, Netherlands, Slovakia, Kazakhstan, Ukraine, Romania, and even from Namibia.[670] In these countries, the German people inter-married with people from other national and racial stocks. In fact, as the world becomes more integrated due to globalization, so does the human race. It's an evolutionary process in which racial divisions lose their significance as human beings begin to share a common culture.

The question of race, from the beginning, had little to do with biology and more to do with politics and culture. What biological differences that do occur have to do with a particular people's adaptation to unique environmental conditions caused by climate, air temperature, the amount of sunlight, etc.

The study of race began with self-serving German intellectuals who wanted to prove that they were more intelligent and more beautiful than other people. As such, they sought a way to distinguish themselves from other people. This idea found converts among other Europeans from England, France, and even the United States who desired to prove that Caucasians, i.e., white people, were superior to people of other "races."

These early western intellectuals grouped "white" people to include some or all of the populations of Europe, North Africa, the Horn of Africa, Western Asia, Central Asia, and South Asia on anatomical features.[671] They used the term Caucasoid to distinguish this group from Mongoloids and Negroids.

The term "Caucasian race" was coined by the German philosopher Christoph Meiners in his *The Outline of History of Mankind* in 1785. Meiners' term was given wider circulation in the 1790s by Johann Friedrich Blumenbach, a German professor of medicine and member of the British Royal Society.[672]

Meiners' treatise was widely read in the German intellectual circles of his day, and taken for truth despite its shoddy scholarship. Meiners originally proposed a taxonomy of human beings based on two races, Caucasians and Mongoloids. He considered Caucasians to be more physically attractive than Mongoloids because they had paler skin. He also claimed that Caucasians were more sensitive and more morally virtuous than Mongoloids. Later, he would make similar distinctions within the Caucasian group, concluding that the Germans were the most attractive and virtuous people among those of the white race.[673]

This racist fantasy was later picked up by Adolph Hitler and the Nazis as a justification for the elimination of German Jews.

The name "Caucasian" derives from the Southern Caucasus/Transcaucasia region (or what are now the countries of Georgia, Azerbaijan, and Armenia) because Meiners considered the people of this region to be the archetype for the grouping. This was, after all, the homeland of the Aryan tribes who spread east into India, south into Iran, and west into northern Europe.

Meiners' classification was not grounded on any scientific criteria but on national and racial prejudice. It was Blumenbach who gave it scientific credibility and a wider audience, by grounding it in the new quantitative method of *craniometry*, i.e., the measurement of the size of the skull.[674] There has been a long attempt by pseudo-scientists to prove that different races have different skull sizes and that Caucasians, having the largest skulls, are therefore the smartest of the races. This theory, much in vogue during the eighteenth and nineteenth centuries, has been largely debunked by today's scientists, who by using more rigorous research have not been able to correlate large skull size with racial intelligence.

A brief history of craniometry reveals the following information. Measurements were first made to compare the skulls of men with those of other animals. This constituted the first use of craniometric studies. A man named Pieter Camper, steeped in the white prejudice of the mid-eighteenth century, began to compare the facial angle of non-whites to those of apes.

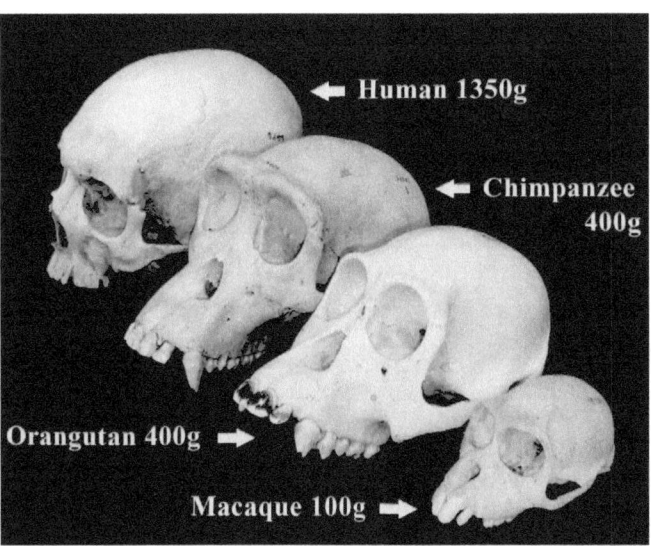

Fig. 5-17: Comparison of Human Skulls to Those of Animals

In the nineteenth century, many scientists contributed to the literature on craniometry, too many to mention. Among those researchers who stood out, however, was Paul Broca (1824–1880), founder of the French Anthropological Society in 1859, who used craniometric methods to compare humans to other animals. There was also T. H. Huxley (1825–1895) of England who, by comparing skeletons of apes to man, developed the "Pithecometra principle," which stated that man and ape were descended from a common ancestor, supporting Charles Darwin's theory of evolution.[675]

Samuel George Morton (1799–1851), influenced by the common white prejudice of his time, believed that he could judge the intellectual capacity of a race by the cranial capacity (the measure of the volume of the interior of the skull). After inspecting three mummies from ancient Egyptian catacombs, Morton concluded that Caucasians and Negroes were already distinct three thousand years ago. Because the bible, however, indicated that Noah's Ark had washed up on Mount Ararat, only a thousand years before this, Morton claimed that Noah's sons could not possibly account for every race on earth. He therefore deduced the theory of *polygenism*, which holds that races have been separate since the start. This view is not held by most scientists today, who believe that all humans derived from a common ancestor in Africa. Christians also rejected Morton's theory because they believe that all people derive from Adam and Eve.

As he continued his studies with the skulls from ancient Egypt, Morton concluded that the ancient Egyptians were not African, but were white. He went on to claim in his treatise Crania Americana that whites had the biggest brains, averaging eight-seven cubic inches, Native Americans were in the middle with an average of eighty-two cubic inches and blacks had the smallest brains with an average of seventy-eight cubic inches.[676] He based this claim on the assumption that bigger skulls meant greater intelligence.

The promotion of an ideology based on the superiority of the white race in America began in earnest with *The Passing of the Great Race* written by Madison Grant in 1916. Grant was an American lawyer known primarily for his work as a eugenicist. He was responsible for the most famous work of "scientific racism."

While Grant's formulation was similar to many nineteenth century racial philosophies which divided the human species into primarily three distinct races: Caucasoids, Negroids, and Mongoloids, he further subdivided Caucasoids into three groups: Nordics (who inhabited Northern Europe and other parts of the continent), Alpines (whose territory included central Europe and parts of Asia), and Mediterraneans (who inhabited Southern Europe, North Africa, and the Middle East).

At the time, Grant was not concerned with proving the superiority of whites over other races, but in proving the superior of Nordic whites over Alpine and Mediterranean whites. According to Grant, too many immigrants from Southern and Eastern Europe were entering the US as opposed to Western and Northern Europeans and, in so doing, were diluting the strength of the country.

Grant promoted the idea of the "Nordic race",[677] a loosely defined biological-cultural grouping rooted in Scandinavia that he claimed was the social group most responsible for human development. In his theory, the Nordics were *Homo europaeus*, the white man *par excellence*.

To prevent the Nordic "race" from being diluted by intermarriage with other lesser whites, Grant advocated the separation, quarantine, and eventual collapse of "undesirable" traits and "worthless race types" from the human gene pool and the promotion, spread, and eventual restoration of desirable traits and "worthwhile race types" conducive to Nordic society. According to Grant:

> A rigid system of selection through the eliminiation of those who are weak or unfit-in other words social failures-would solve the whole question in one hundred years, as well enable us to get rid of the undesirables who crowd our jails, hospitals, and insane asylums.[678]

The individual himself can be nourished, educated, and protected by the community during his lifetime, but the state through sterilization must see to it that his line stops with him, or else future generations will be cursed with an ever-increasing load of misguided sentimentalism. According to Grant, this is a practical, merciful, and inevitable solution of the whole problem, and can be applied to an ever widening circle of social discards, beginning always with the criminal, the diseased, and the insane, and extending gradually to types which may be called weaklings rather than defectives, and perhaps ultimately to worthless race types.[679]

In *The Passing of the Great Race*, Grant further recommends segregating "unfavorable" races in ghettos by installing civil organizations through the public health system to establish quasi-dictatorships in their particular fields. He states the expansion of non-Nordic race types in the Nordic system of freedom would actually mean a slavery to desires, passions, and base behaviors. In turn, this corruption of society would lead to the subjection of the Nordic community to "inferior" races, who would, in turn, long to be dominated and instructed by "superior" ones utilizing authoritarian powers. The result would be the submergence of the indigenous Nordic races under a corrupt and enfeebled system dominated by inferior races, and both, in turn, would be subjected by a new ruling race class.[680]

According to Grant, Nordics were swimming in dangerous waters because they had abandoned their cultural values which in actuality were rooted in religious or superstitious proto-racialism. As such, the Nordics were close to committing "race suicide" by miscegenation and by being outbred by inferior stock taking advantage of the situation.

Grant's book became very popular and went through multiple printings in the United States. It was translated into German in 1925 where the Nordic theory was strongly embraced by the National Socialist (NAZI) movement in the early 1920s and 1930s. Grant's work was the first non-German book ordered to be reprinted by the Nazis when they took power. Adolph Hitler wrote to Grant, "The book is my Bible."[681]

Grant advocated restricted immigration to the United States through limiting immigration from Eastern Europe and Southern Europe, as well as the complete end of immigration from East Asia. He also advocated efforts to purify the American population through selective breeding. If the American people would have accepted Grant's idiotic racist proposals at the time, we would have no Italians, Irish, or even many descendants of Germans living in the United States today. Neither would we have any Poles, Hungarians, Ukranians, Russians, etc.

Acting as an expert on world racial data, Grant provided statistics for the Immigration Act of 1924 to set the quotas on immigrants from certain European countries. He also assisted in the passing and prosecution of several anti-miscegenation laws, which prohibited interracial marriages. Grant helped to develop the Racial Integrity Act of 1924 in the state of Virginia, where he sought to define "colored people" as anyone who contained "one-drop" of sub-Saharan-African ancestry. The Racial Integrity Act required that a racial description of every person be recorded at birth. It divided society into only two classifications: white and colored (essentially all other, which included numerous Native Americans). The law wasn't overturned until 1967 when the United States Supreme Court ruled on *Loving v. Virginia*.

Grant began to fall out of favor in the United States in the 1930s due to the Great Depression which resulted in a backlash against Social Darwinism and to the changing dynamics of racial issues in the United States during the interwar period. The death blow for Grant's ideas came when the Nazis used them at the Nuremberg Trials to defend their crimes against humanity and people could see first-hand the insanity of his theory put into practice.[682]

Getting back to the question of skull size and brain size, subsequent studies indicate that Caucasians do have, on average, bigger brains than people of other races, but this does not have any connection to greater intelligence as white supremacists would have us believe.

For example, many people think that we are superior to animals because we have bigger brains than animals, but whales and elephants have bigger brains than we do. Looked at from another angle, we have the same brain-to-body mass ratio as mice.[683] Einstein was a genius but his brain size was average.

Women have smaller brains than men but they also have more neural complexity in certain areas of the brain than men. For example, while the male brain is larger than the female brain by nine percent, this has nothing to say about a man's mental capacity being greater than a woman's capacity. The cells in a woman's brain are more compact than those of a man's cells. Also, several critical parts of the brain are larger in women than in men, such as the Anterior Cingulate Cortex (ACC), the Prefrontal Cortex (PFC), and the Insula. The ACC is responsible for weighing options and making decisions. Women generally weigh options and make better decisions then men. This is one of the defining traits of acting in a rational manner. The PFC regulates our response to conflict. Women are also cooler under pressure than men. Finally, the Insula controls one's gut feelings. Women are often accused of being "psychic", but in fact the larger Insula in the female brain makes them more equipped to read faces and interpret the tone of voice and the emotions of individuals with whom they are engaged in conversation.[684]

Most scientists today attribute larger skull and brain size to environmental conditions and different genetic traits but the largeness of either skull or brain have nothing to do with intelligence, thus disproving the theory of racial superiority. After almost a century and a half of attempting to prove the superiority of white males, the results are inconclusive and basically worthless.

This has not stopped white men, however, from using this so-called scientific "evidence" of their racial superiority as a reason to belittle people of other races and to justifying their ambitions to dominate others.

In the US, the definition of race has changed over time and the US Census, for example, has struggled with determining a person's race. They have found that the problem with using the word "race" is that many Americans don't know what it means, and how it is different from "origin." Focus groups demonstrate that some people think the words mean the same thing, while others see race as meaning skin color, ancestry, or culture, while origin is the nation or place where they or their parents were born.

US Census forms now have two questions about race and Hispanic origin. The first asks people whether they are of Hispanic, Latino, or Spanish origin, and states that "Hispanic origins are not races." A second question asks, "What is this person's race?" and includes a list of options with checkboxes and write-in spaces. The US government defines Hispanic as an ethnicity, not a race.

In truth, anyone who looks at the question of race at a deeper level, only becomes more confused. Race used to be seen as a fixed physical characteristic but is now more commonly viewed as a fluid product of many influences. The Census Bureau said in a 2013 report "We recognize that race and ethnicity are not quantifiable values. Rather, identity is a complex mix of one's family and social environment, historical or socio-political constructs, personal experience, context, and many other immeasurable factors."[685] In a press release by the US Census Bureau on the question of race in the 2000 Census, it says the "Census Bureau complies with the Office of Management and Budget's standards for maintaining, collecting, and presenting data on race, which were revised in October 1997. They generally reflect a social definition of race recognized in this country. They do not conform to any biological, anthropological, or genetic criteria."[686] It seems certain that as the world becomes more integrated economically, socially, and culturally the question of race will become even more abstract and useless.

→ NOTE: Please answer BOTH Question 8 about Hispanic origin and Question 9 about race. For this census, Hispanic origins are not races.

8. Is Person 1 of Hispanic, Latino, or Spanish origin?
  ☐ No, not of Hispanic, Latino, or Spanish origin
  ☐ Yes, Mexican, Mexican Am., Chicano
  ☐ Yes, Puerto Rican
  ☐ Yes, Cuban
  ☐ Yes, another Hispanic, Latino, or Spanish origin — *Print origin, for example, Argentinean, Colombian, Dominican, Nicaraguan, Salvadoran, Spaniard, and so on.*

9. What is Person 1's race? *Mark* X *one or more boxes.*
  ☐ White
  ☐ Black, African Am., or Negro
  ☐ American Indian or Alaska Native — *Print name of enrolled or principal tribe.*

  ☐ Asian Indian   ☐ Japanese   ☐ Native Hawaiian
  ☐ Chinese   ☐ Korean   ☐ Guamanian or Chamorro
  ☐ Filipino   ☐ Vietnamese   ☐ Samoan
  ☐ Other Asian — *Print race, for example, Hmong, Laotian, Thai, Pakistani, Cambodian, and so on.*   ☐ Other Pacific Islander — *Print race, for example, Fijian, Tongan, and so on.*

  ☐ Some other race — *Print race.*

Fig. 5-16: Questions of Race in the 2000 Census
(Courtesy of Pew Research Center)

In the meantime, however, in the US, White Americans remain the racial majority. Whites, including Hispanics who identify as white, total about 246.7 million people or 77.35% of the population. Non-Hispanic whites total about 197.9 million people or 62.06% of the US population.[687] African Americans are the largest racial minority, accounting for 13.2% or 38.1 million Americans. Asian Americans comprise 19.4 million people or

6.0% of the US population, while Native Americans, make up 0.8% of the population numbering around 2.4 million. These are gross calculations. In reality, it is extremely difficult to pin people down by race. Take Hispanic and Latino Americans for example. They comprise 17% of the population, making up the largest ethnic minority but they are composed of Whites, Blacks, Native Americans, Asians, Pacific Islanders, Mestizos, etc.

While Whites predominate in every region of the country, the majority of African Americans (fifty-five percent) live in the South, while the West is home to forty-two percent of Hispanic and Latino Americans, forty-six percent of Asian Americans, forty-eight percent of American Indians and Alaska Natives, as well as sixty-eight percent of Native Hawaiians and Other Pacific Islanders.

Our simple delineation of American people based upon age, sex and race does not portray the social implications to these distinctions in American society. Existing prejudices against women and minorities are daily cited in the mainstream press and play a great role in determining the perspectives and activities of the political right and left in this country. Today, issues around race have become very divisive, particularly as white men continue to lose jobs or become underemployed in the shrinking US economy.

The US government actually uses census data to set hiring targets. The majority of whites, especially white males, have long been indoctrinated to blame women and minorities for their misfortunes and this ingrained prejudice has given rise to virulent forms of sexism and racism today. This prejudicial and hate-filled mindset has become a debilitating psychic illness that hobbles our intentions to create a better world for ourselves and our children. The misguided attention paid to sex and race in American society also detracts our attention from the class structure in American society, which, in reality, has a greater negative impact on American lives than do age, gender or racial differences.

Class

A stratified society is one marked by inequality, by differences among people that are regarded as being higher or lower... People in similar positions...grow similar in their thinking and lifestyle...they form a pattern, and this pattern creates social class. Dennis Gilbert, The American Class Structure, 1998

It is impossible to understand people's behavior...without the concept of social stratification, because class position has a pervasive influence on almost everything...the clothes we wear...the television shows we watch...the colors we paint our homes in and the names we give our pets...Our position in the social hierarchy affects our health, happiness, and even how long we will live. William Thompson, Joseph Hickey, Society in Focus, 2005.

There are three distinct ways to divide Americans by class. There is the typical model based on wealth distribution that is supported by the mass media. This model divides people into the upper, middle, and lower classes. The second model for determining class status is that provided by Marxists and socialists who divide people according to those who own the means of production and those who don't. In other words, between the capitalists and the workers. Thirdly, there is the class structure introduced by P. R. Sarkar, which is based upon social psychology. This model identifies class structure according to the way people have power in society. This class analysis is useful in seeing how dominant psychological propensities control different social institutions and how people who embody these psychologies come into power as a class during certain eras of history.

Mr. Sarkar identifies four major classes based upon their psychology. Those who excel at controlling money and wealth are the capitalists. They control the banks, corporations, and most of the financial wealth of the country. Intellectuals, another class, have power by controlling ideas. They dominate in such industries as mass media, educational institutions, government bureaucracies, the arts and sciences, and religious organizations. A third class is the warrior class who exert power by the use of physical force. They dominate in the military, police, corrections, sports, etc. They are our heroes. Finally, there are the common people or the masses of society. They do not dominate by any means but are the workers who carry out the will of the other three classes. The only time they have power is by mass action during times of social upheaval or revolution. Let us look at these ways of differentiating classes in American society. Despite their seemingly different approaches, they all tell a common story.

The Upper, Middle, and Lower Classes

The Upper Class

The American class system is typically divided into three main layers: upper class, middle class, and lower class, which are mostly based on socio-economic conditions.

Individuals who are considered to be members of the upper class are the owners of the means of production and most of the country's private wealth. Many are large business owners, top executives, or high-level government officials, who have a great deal of income and/or wealth. The richest among these are those who own and control the US-based multinational banks and corporations.

To understand why the upper class is so rich we must know the difference between income and wealth. These are two distinct concepts. *Income* is salary and/or other money that is regularly received as a result of one's labor, where wealth is the total value of all assets, minus outstanding debts. Another name for wealth is *capital*. Capital, when invested or simply left alone to appreciate or earn interest, produces additional capital independent of one's labor. To say that one is a capitalist means that he or she has enough wealth to live off its earnings without having to work.

The upper class actually has two layers: the upper-upper class and the lower-upper class. The majority of upper-class members fall into the lower-upper class. These are mostly the 'working rich' or 'new money.' They are usually individuals who still earn their lifestyle instead of inheriting it. Professional athletes, actors, and successful entrepreneurs are all examples. These individuals are still wealthy, but also have a high income. Even so, their wealth is relatively insignificant compared to the capitalist elite.

The upper-upper class, or the capitalist elite, makes up less than one percent of the US population. They make up the small circle of international bankers and corporation owners. In the first chapter, we discovered how this small elite was able to acquire its wealth by creating a debt economy in which everyone owes them money. This money has a price tag and, in many cases, the debtor spends his or her entire life just paying the interest on the debt, never affording to pay the principle. This is the most debilitating form of slavery, one that even destroys people's ability to meet their basic needs of food, shelter, clothing, health care, and education.

We have shown in the first chapter, how in the US, with nearly a third of the world's wealth, just forty-seven individuals own more than the entire one hundred and sixty million people who earn less than fifty-three thousand dollars per year. At the global level, the wealth of the richest one percent amounts to one hundred and ten trillion dollars. This is sixty-five times the total wealth of fifty percent of humanity.[688] The pain and suffering of the American people and the world's people are on the shoulders of the super-rich, not on the shoulders of women or minorities who get blamed for taking white men's jobs.

The Middle Class

The next step down in the social hierarchy of the US class system is the middle class, which includes about half of the US population. Most advertisements are directed towards this audience, and the fictional characters in popular culture shown on TV shows and in movies and books are typically middle-class members. The greatest amount of social mobility occurs at this level, whether it's upward, downward, or horizontal.

Like the upper class, the middle class has several layers: upper-middle, average-middle, and lower-middle. Upper-middles are those who earn above-average salaries, and typically live in fairly expensive houses in nice neighborhoods. Almost all of them are college graduates, and many go on to highly prestigious white-collar jobs—doctors, lawyers, businessmen, local politicians, and so on.

The center layer of the middle class is the average-middle, and the family income at this level is roughly the national average. Members typically work at less prestigious white-collar jobs - managers, teachers, office workers, small businessmen, and so on. Most are college graduates.

The lower-middle class is generally called the working class. They typically hold blue-collar jobs, such as police officers, electricians, truck drivers, plumbers, miners, factory workers, and more. They earn slightly less than the national average. It is this class that was hurt the most when the capitalists transferred American jobs overseas. The working class was able to earn a decent wage because many of them belonged to unions but now the union movement has largely been destroyed in America.

The white working class tends to resent professionals, middle managers, teachers, etc., whom they see as being condescending, smug, and don't know what they are talking about. They admire the rich, however, because they mistakenly believe the rich worked hard and earned their money. This perception has to do with the fact that they have never met the rich but they have to take orders from the middle class who rule over them in school, on the job, and in the human service system. The working class does not dream of becoming upper middle-class, with its different culture, food, and lifestyle. Rather, they dream of living in their own class where they feel comfortable but just have more money. The main thing is to be independent and not have to take orders from anyone else.[689] With the great national job loss during the Great Recession, many people in the middle range of the middle class dropped into the lower middle class, and those in this class dropped down into the lower class and have never been able to recuperate.

The Lower Class

The remainder of the population makes up the lower class. There are two layers to this class. The upper lower class are also called the "working poor". Members of this class typically have a low educational level, hold low-prestige jobs, and earn a pitiable income. They are not highly skilled, and work minimum-wage jobs. They live pay check to pay check and are still unable to meet their basic needs. They have very little job security if any, and are either right at or below the poverty line. Lack of money is a continual stress for these people and the stress never lets up because they are barely able to get by. For the most part, society tends to look down on them, especially those who are single mothers or members of minority groups.

The lowest position in the social class hierarchy is the underclass, the lower-lower class. The underclass is characterized by extreme poverty, joblessness, homelessness, crime, violence, and so on.[690] The combination of lack of education and opportunity, coupled with desperation and a hostile environment make life a living hell for these people. They live in a world of piles of garbage, graffiti, dilapidated buildings, teenage gangs, broken windows, scamming and stealing. These are the "clients" of the human service system. They receive a stipend that is less than they need to meet their basic needs but generally enough to keep them from rioting in the streets.

Marxist Class Analysis

When Marxists or socialists look at class structure in society, they do not base their analysis on income or wealth but rather on a person's role in the production process. In other words, within Marxian class theory, the structure of the production process forms the basis of class structure. Based on this, Marxists define modern society as having three distinct classes: The Capitalists (bourgeoisie) who own the means of production and purchase the labor power of others; the Workers (proletariat) who do not own any means of production or the ability to purchase the labor power of others and who must consequently sell their own labor power to stay alive; and a third class who own their own means of production but who do not purchase other people's labor. This class includes self-employed skilled labor and artisans, small shopkeepers, and many professionals (petty bourgeoisie).

To Marx, these classes are composed of people who possess intrinsic tendencies and interests that differ from each other. There is a fundamental antagonism between the capitalist and the working class because it is in the laborer's best interest to maximize wages and benefits while it is in the capitalist's best interest to keep wages and benefits as small as possible in order to maximize their own profits. In other words, profit is made at the expense of the workers. In his Communist Manifesto, Marx wrote:

> The history of all hitherto existing society is the history of class struggles… Freeman and slave, patrician and plebeian, lord and serf, guild-master and journeyman, in a word, oppressor and oppressed, stood in constant opposition to one another, carried on an uninterrupted, now hidden, now open fight, a fight that each time

> ended, either in a revolutionary reconstruction of society at large, or in the common ruin of the contending classes.... The modern bourgeois society that has sprouted from the ruins of feudal society has not done away with class antagonisms. It has but established new classes, new conditions of oppression, new forms of struggle in place of the old ones. Our epoch, the epoch of the bourgeoisie, possesses, however, this distinctive feature: it has simplified class antagonisms. Society as a whole is more and more splitting up into two great hostile camps, into two great classes directly facing each other: Bourgeoisie and Proletariat.[691]

To Marx, class conflict is the key driving force of history and the main determinant of the trajectory of society. Marx believed that the capitalists had an advantage because they were aware of themselves as a group and supported each other. They had a "class consciousness." This class consciousness allows the capitalist to systematically take advantage of the workers and therefore continue to profit at the workers' expense.

The workers, on the other hand, lack a class consciousness and are thus powerless to confront the capitalist class in a strategic way. In the past, labor unions, were able to help certain sections of the working class to benefit, but these did not extend to the working class as a whole. It is the intention of the capitalist class to keep the working class divided and powerless. They accomplish this through their mass media and by using policy-oriented intellectuals to foment political issues that stigmatize different sections of the working people and keep them divided. As we've seen, the central divide-and-conquer strategy of the capitalists is to aggravate the differences between liberals and conservatives. It is also used to foment hatred among white males against equality-minded women and minority groups.

The state of inequality between the capitalist and the workers is made to look normal by these divide-and-conquer strategies which are reproduced daily through the mainstream media. Through these means, the middle and lower-class working people are forced into a subservient position by the power of capital, which has incrementally stolen the means of production from them. It is only after the working people become conscious of their situation and their power and begin to organize themselves through collective political action, do they develop a class consciousness. Only by developing this class consciousness will they be able to take control of their lives by establishing a new political economy that serves their interests instead of the interests of the capitalist class. This new system, Marx called socialism. It is a system that places people above capital.

We have seen the struggle during the twentieth century to create socialist societies but so far all attempts have failed because of the supreme difficulty of creating a sustainable economy to meet people's basic needs under their own control, and, at the same time, fend off the capitalist forces which are bent on destroying such economies through assassinations, economic boycotts, invasions, etc.

How did people get into this situation? As we have seen in the volume on Modern History and in chapter one of this volume, it all started when the capitalist class had enough capital to begin to buy out the estates of the Church and aristocracy and were able to gain control over the serfs by displacing them and by converting their labor into wage labor. Private farms and manufacturing jobs, in which people were self-employed, were no longer as viable as they were before the industrial revolution, because automation made manufacturing very cheap. Many people who once controlled their own labor-time were converted into wage-workers through industrialization. Today, groups, which in the past subsisted on stipends or private wealth, like doctors, academics or lawyers, now also increasingly work as wage laborers.[692]

Class by Social Psychology

A third method to analyze class, is the one that has been used in this five-volume history of western civilization. It is based upon the socio-economic theory espoused by Prabhat Rainjan Sarkar, in India, and developed during the 1950s. P. R. Sarkar called his theory the *Progressive Utilization Theory*[693] and held that human needs are comprised of physical, mental, and spiritual needs. As such, his class analysis is neither based on income and wealth, nor on the relationship to the means of production. Rather, it takes a psychological approach to human organization. It looks at how the human mind interacts with the natural and social environment in order to establish power over it. Basically, there are four ways to have power in this physical-mental world. A consistent manner of responding to challenges determines one's psychological class. The first group called "Shudras," (the masses) are overwhelmed by the psycho-physical waves of reality. Unable to contend with it, this group spends its energy simply trying to exist. The second group, called Ksattriyas (warriors), commands this psycho-physical reality by physical force. The third group, called Vipras (intellectuals), commands by psychic (mental) force. The fourth group, called Vaesyas (merchant/capitalists), commands by controlling wealth and the means of production.

According to P. R. Sarkar, physical force, mental force and money are the typical ways to have power in this relative world. There is one other way to have power in this world, but it is rarer. This is the spiritual power of the mystic. The mystic has power by virtue of his or her spiritual intuition. Sarkar calls such people "Sadvipras." Well-known sadvipras are Jesus Christ, Shiva, Buddha, Mohammad among others. There are, of course, many other sadvipras who are not so well known that can be found among all people around the world.

In Sanskrit, these groups are called varn´as and constitute the class system of India. Sarkar's interpretation of varn'as, however, is not one of immutable social position in which people are locked into a social hierarchy by birth, but rather, one's varna, according to Sarkar, is determined by his or her main psychological propensity which, in turn, determines the nature of one's mode of thinking and actions.

The first group (the masses or shúdras) displays the characteristics of the undeveloped human mind dominated by the material and social environment and by basic instincts. The shúdra mind lacks vibrancy due to its preoccupation with materiality. There is little original expression of higher ideals or culture. Of course, the shúdra mind of the modern era is obviously more developed than the shúdra mentality of prehistory or the previous ages of history. Hence, according to Sarkar, the varn´as are relative categories. On the individual level, every mind possesses a mixture of and the potential for all the four varn´as - though one psychology tends to be dominant.

Basically, the shúdras as a class are those who have few aspirations and little mental dynamism. They live according to the pressures of material conditions and the dominant trends of the collective psychology, which is the combined psychology of the society as a whole. Shúdra psychology is essentially the mass psychology. It requires the guidance and inspiration of those with more developed minds who actually define the direction and momentum of the collective psychology.

Today, the shudras compose the lower classes who are unable to contend with the forces in society. As the capitalist system continues to squeeze the life out of people, however, more and more intellectuals and warriors are thrown into the lower class. Having more evolved minds, but relegated to the same conditions of poverty, they constitute a disgruntled group who cannot be long suppressed without a volatile reaction.

The second varn´a (warrior or ks´attriya) is constituted by those with the warrior mentality. They have a fighting spirit. They display bravery and embrace challenge and struggle. On a rudimentary level, the warrior mind seeks to establish domination or control over matter through physical force, even valor. On the positive side, warriors live by the social codes of honor, discipline, self-sacrifice, and responsibility. On the negative side, they exhibit blind adherence to authority, ruthlessness, brutality and the need to dominate others. The warriors today, except for the elite, tend to inhabit the lower classes and the working class, although they can exist in any class, including the upper class, as exemplified by talented professional athletes. They are the soldiers, police, athletes and anyone who seeks to dominate matter or people by physical force.

The intellectual class (vipras) constitutes the third varn´a. They have a developed intellect and seek to influence the external or social environment by virtue of their mental faculty. On the positive side, intellectuals seek to serve the common good through scientific and cultural achievements. They keep the focus of society on moral and spiritual values. On the negative side, they exploit the weaknesses of others by their strong intellects, they look down on others, and they easily become cynics and discourage others.

The fourth social class is that of the merchants (vaeshyas). This is the mercantile, entrepreneurial, or capitalist class that excels in the handling and accumulation of money and wealth. Modern history, which blasted off with the Industrial Revolution, continues to be dominated by the psychology of this class. Just as the warriors dominated ancient history and the intellectuals dominated the middle ages, so the merchants dominate the modern and contemporary age.

In history, the warrior age gave way to the intellectual age, which in turn, gave way to the capitalist age. The capitalist age will give way, in turn, to the second warrior age. We can see this transfer of power already beginning to take shape. The beginning of any age is characterized by great dynamism on all levels - politically, culturally, economically, etc., as the new leadership frees the people from the oppressive institutions of the old order. The age peaks in a golden era as the new class overcomes the obstacles of the old order and solidifies its control over society. In time, however, the social system again declines as the dominant class increases its power at the expense of meeting the basic needs of the people as a whole. Social unrest builds as the exploitation becomes more systematized.

In this way, the merchant class brought great dynamism to a society suffering under a corrupt priest class and the feudal system of the Holy Roman Empire. The golden age of modern history is the period of Pax Americana since the end of WWII. Now, however, the era of the capitalist class has begun to exceed its welcome.

As the dominant capitalist class seeks to expand its wealth and power beyond the bounds of human decency, morality and democratic principles, they do so at the expense of greater numbers of people, the majority of whom are losing the capacity to meet their basic survival needs.

The present economy is characterized by greater consolidation and efficiencies within the corporations in the effort to maximize profits. This process entails laying off workers, employing robots, and seeking the cheapest labor in the world market. The employment and purchasing power of the American working people have suffered greatly due to this inevitable process. The environment is also destroyed as consumerism is relentlessly pursued. As money continues to become highly centralized, less of it circulates in the society and purchasing capacity diminishes.

The intellectual or warrior minded are now forced to live in the same economic condition as the shúdras. Under increased pressure, due to market failure and the difficulty to meet their basic necessities, the people under the leadership of these disgruntled intellectuals and warriors will eventually rise up and take economic and social relations into their own hands. This revolution will end the merchant era and signal the beginning of a new warrior era.

If we overlap the three methods of class analysis, we find certain common characteristics between them. Those with the psychology of capitalists today constitute the upper class and control the means of production. Those with the psychology of the intellectuals and warriors constitute the middle class and work for the capitalist system. Those with the psychology of shudras constitute the lower class and suffer from gross exploitation by the elite of the capitalist, intellectual, and warrior classes. These are the masses who Marx called the lumpen proletariat. However, as the masses of the lower class are gradually expanded by intellectuals and warriors who have fallen out of the middle class due to economic forces, these disgruntled people have the capacity to lead the next revolution to a warrior age.[694]

One final distinction needs to be made before we move on. While the capitalists constitute the ruling class, the power elite is also composed of high-powered intellectuals and warriors whose behavior we have witnessed in the earlier chapters. It is the power elite that dominates the collective psychology of American society and, in doing so, dominates the middle and lower classes. [695] Today this power elite operates through organizations like the Council on Foreign Relations, the Trilateral Commission, the Bilderberg Group, the World Economic Forum, the World Bank, the Organization for Economic Co-operation and Development (OECD), etc. A 2002 study of the power elite in the United States under President George W. Bush identified 7,314 institutional positions of power encompassing 5,778 individuals.[696] A later study of US society noted demographic characteristics of this élite group as follows: The power elite administer the banks, corporations, foundations, law firms, universities, military branches, government agencies, and civic organizations. By age, they range from fifty-six to sixty years old. Eighty percent are white Anglo-Saxon men. The remainder is mostly white women with a few minorities. Nearly all the elite have a college education, with almost half graduating with advanced degrees. About fifty-four percent of the big-business leaders and forty-two percent of the government élite graduated from just twelve prestigious universities thereby consolidating their status as the elite. Most also hold exclusive membership in one or more social clubs in major cities like

London, New York, Chicago, Boston, and Washington DC.

Religion

Much has already been said about religion in previous volumes of this *The Untold Story of Western Civilization*. In Volume 3, Chapters 3 through 8, we discussed the rise and reign of the Catholic Church during the Middles Ages. In Volume 4, Chapter 2 on Modern History, we explored the Protestant revolt and the rise of Protestant sects. In Chapter 4, we witnessed the rise of the Baptist, Methodist, and Church of God in Christ sects, which are indigenous to American soil and which laid the foundation for evangelical Christianity in the US. In Chapter 2 of this Volume on Contemporary History we discussed the connection between Evangelical Christians and the rise of American conservatism.

Even though Christianity is the predominant religion in the US, the Founding Fathers, wishing to avoid the religious wars that wracked Christian Europe for centuries, enshrined the tenet of religious freedom in the American Constitution in order to give every American the scope to worship or not worship according to their own beliefs. Today, most Americans belong to one of the following religions:

Christian Faiths 70.6%
Evangelical Protestant 25.4%
Catholic 20.8%
Mainline Protestant 14.7%
Historically Black Protestant 6.5%
Mormon 1.6%
Jehovah's Witness 0.8%
Orthodox Christian 0.5%
Other Christian 0.4%
Metaphysical Family < 0.3%
Others in the "Other Christian" Tradition < 0.3%

Non-Christian Faiths 5.9%
Jewish 1.9%
Muslim 0.9%

Buddhist 0.7%
Hindu 0.7%
Unaffiliated (religious "nones") 22.8%
Atheist 3.1%
Agnostic 4.0%
Nothing in particular 15.8%
Don't know 0.6% [697]

So much has been written about religion in America, but the context of this presentation is to look at the impact that religions have upon the goal of optimizing human unity and protecting our home planet.

The chart below was abstracted from the Pew Research Center's Religious Landscape Study in which they surveyed thirty-five thousand Americans across the fifty states about their religious affiliations, beliefs, and practices, and social and political views.[698]

Main Religions in America and Their Position on Key Social Issues

	Population	Political Party	Education	Belief in God	Source of Morality	Abortion	LGBTQ	Climate	Size of Govt
US	308,745,538								
Evangelical Christians	83,897,000	R 56% D 28% U 16%	High school or less 43%- Some College 35%- College 14% Post-grad 7%	98%	Rel. 60% Common Sense 30%	Legal 33%- Illegal- 63%	Accept 36% Discourage 55%	Pro-Env 45%- Pro-jobs 48%	Smaller 64%- Larger 30%

Catholics	70,180,000	R 37%- D 44%- U 19%	High school or less 46%- Some College 27%- College 16%-Postgrad 10%	91%	Rel 30% Common Sense 48%	Legal 48%- Illigal- 47%	Accept 70% Discourage 23%	Pro-Env 55%- Pro-jobs 39%	Smaller 48%- Larger 47%
Mainline Protestants	36,000,000	R 44% D 40% U 16%	High school or less 37%- Some College 30%- College 19%-Postgrad 14%	91%	Rel 29% Common Sense 51%	Legal 60%- Illigal- 35%	Accept 66% Discourage 26%	Pro-Env 56%- Pro-jobs 38%	Smaller 59%- Larger 34%
Black Protestants	27,600,000	R 10% D 80% U 10%	High school or less 52%- Some College 33%- College 9%-Postgrad 6%	98%	Rel 47% Common Sense 41%	Legal 52%- Illigal- 42%	Accept 51% Discourage 40%	Pro-Env 58%- Pro-jobs 36%	Smaller 23%- Larger 70%
Jews	5,300,000	R 26% D 64% U 9%	High school or less 19%- Some College 22%- College 29%-Postgrad 31%	64%	Rel 17% Common Sense 50%	Legal 83%- Illigal- 15%	Accept 81% Discourage 16%	Pro-Env 71%- Pro-jobs 25%	Smaller 40%- Larger 53%
Muslims	3,300,000	R 17% D 62% U 21%	High school or less 36%- Some College 25%- College 23%-Postgrad 17%	96%	Rel 37% Common Sense 36%	Legal 55%- Illigal- 37%	Accept 45% Discourage 47%	Pro-Env 67%- Pro-jobs 27%	Smaller 23%- Larger 73%

| Athe- ists/ Ag- nos- tics/ None | 70,394,000 | R 23% D 54% U 22% | High school or less 38%- Some College 32%- College 18%-Post- grad 11% | 49% | Rel 7% Com- mon Sense 57% | Legal 73%- Illi- gal- 23% | Ac- cept 83% Dis- cour- age 12% | Pro- Env 68%- Pro- jobs 27% | Small- er 47%- Larger 46% |

By looking at the chart, we can see a high correlation between the strictness of one's belief in the authority of the Bible and a distinct callousness toward women, homosexuals, the poor, as well as the natural world. This callousness is reflected in one's desire to make abortion illegal under any circumstances, to persecute homosexuals, to reduce government services to the poor, and to weaken environmental protections.

Sixty-three percent of Evangelicals believe that abortion should be illegal in all or most cases. The desire to make abortions illegal also correlates highly with the tendency of religious fundamentalists to suppress women in every other way. This includes a higher tolerance for rape of women, the promotion of weak legal restraints on men's violence against women, the fight against reproductive services, the proliferation of anti-abortion laws, the promotion of abstinence education that only applies to women, the support for personhood laws regarding the fetus, the war on birth control and contraception, etc.[699] It includes keeping women in an inferior position within their churches and within society at large.

The evolution of European Christianity was built upon the tenets of patriarchy, which sought to systematically eliminate any expressions of women's authority that was held sacred by European tribes prior to the assault of the Christian Church upon their way of life. The systematic condemnation of women's authority by the Church ultimately resulted in the witch hunts in Europe and even today remains at the root of the misogyny within Christianity, particularly among Catholics and fundamentalist Protestant sects.

Today, The Religious Right's hostility toward LGBTQ Americans is also well known. Among Evangelicals, fifty-five percent believe that homosexuality should be discouraged, while only thirty-six percent believe it should be accepted. Sixty-four percent also oppose same-sex marriage while only twenty-eight percent favor it.

For years, fundamentalist political organizations have denounced LGBTQ people and used the proceeds of their multi-million-dollar operations to pass laws against women and homosexuals, including the outlawing of same-sex marriage and laws that disrespect the needs of transgender individuals.

Rhetoric from people like TV preacher and Christian Coalition founder Pat Robertson and Lou Sheldon of the Traditional Values Coalition link homosexuals with Satan. Robertson once asserted that "Many of those people involved with Adolf Hitler were Satanists, many of them were homosexuals. The two things seem to go together."[700]

Or take the comments of the Catholic Cardinal Robert Sarah who condemned same-sex marriage as a "demonic" attack on the traditional family. The Cardinal said that God "is being eroded, eclipsed, liquidated" by laws "promoting transgender equality." Another Catholic Cardinal Raymond Burke told his flock that Irish people who voted in favor of same-sex marriage were "worse than pagans."[701]

Unfortunately, the Christian fundamentalists' lack of compassion for their fellow human beings does not stop at women and homosexuals. It also includes a disdain for anybody who is not out there making money, regardless of circumstances. The rejection of poor people was certainly not an aspect of the teachings of Jesus Christ, but it became a strong tenet of early Protestantism, especially after John Calvin proclaimed that the rising capitalist class was God's chosen people and the poor were to be damned to eternal hell, having been provided a human form only to serve the capitalists in this world.[702] This view permeated the theology of the emerging Protestant sects throughout Europe and eventually gave rise to what became known as the Protestant Work Ethic in the United States. A corollary of this class-based dogma is that if a person does not work, he does not deserve to eat. Any charity, therefore, is considered to be worthless and even sinful, regardless of people's circumstances. Today fifty-six percent of Evangelicals still believe that government assistance does more harm than good, while only thirty-eight percent believe it genuinely helps people. Comparatively, forty-eight percent of Catholics and fifty-nine percent of Mainline Protestants believe that services to the poor should be reduced. The majority of Buddhists, Hindus, Black Protestants, Jews, and Muslims, on the other hand, believe that services to the poor should be expanded.

After a relentless assault by Christian sects on the poor for generations, the label of "being poor" has developed into a stereotype that has relegated the unemployed, be they welfare recipients, the working poor, teenage mothers, drug addicts, the homeless, and others—to "a single condemned class, feared and despised by this segment of society."[703]

As white Christians become more susceptible to losing their jobs to other countries or to automation, their sense of self-worth suffers greatly because they believe, as their religion has taught them, that it is their fault that they are unemployed and they feel sinful, guilty, and depressed if they have to accept "charity" from the government or any other organization. As a consequence, today, middle-aged white Americans without a college degree are at increasing risk of dying by drug use, alcoholism, suicide, heart disease, and cancer. Angus Deaton, a Nobel Prize-winning Princeton University economist states the obvious when he tells us, "America is not a great place for people with only a high school degree, and I don't think that's going to get better anytime soon"[704]

The fundamentalist Christian sects have become identified with the Republic party because this party is willing to pander to their religious beliefs in order to gain their support for policies that continue to siphon money from people's pockets to the ruling class. For example, the big oil and chemical companies risk losing billions of dollars if Americans become serious about climate change. Therefore, the Republican politicians have convinced religious fundamentalists that climate change is a ruse invented by liberals to destroy their jobs. This has led forty-eight percent of American's polled to want weaker environmental laws while only forty-five percent want stricter laws.

Fundamentalist Christians believe that they are justified in holding their divisive and untenable position on the environment because their ministers, many of whom are themselves driven by the desire for wealth and political power, promote mythical Biblical prophecies about the end of days, in which Jesus will return, destroy all the unbelievers, and whisk the believers up to eternal life in heaven. Given their blind faith in such myths, it makes no sense to concern one's self with the fate of the earth or its deteriorating condition. Further, many fundamentalists have fallen under the sway of *Dominionism,* which is promulgated by certain Evangelical ministers. It is based on an idea derived from the Book of Genesis, in which God tells Adam and Eve to have "dominion" over the Earth and its animals. Today, "Dominionism" has come to mean that Christians have a God-given right to rule over the United States and the natural world and, in fact, are biblically mandated to control all earthly institutions until the second coming of Jesus.[705] Unfortunately, Christian domination does not include the idea of being a caretaker of the natural world or having empathy for non-Christians.

Finally, Christian fundamentalists are more likely to reject the science of evolution. Only eleven percent say that we evolved naturally; twenty-five percent say that we evolved by God's design; while fifty-seven percent reject the science of evolution completely, believing instead that humans have always existed in our present form.[706]

Regarding the above chart, it was difficult to get exact numbers regarding the membership of religious organizations. Statistics are grouped in different ways, and studies vary in their findings. Therefore, the numbers given above for the populations of the different religions should be considered as ballpark calculations. Even so, it tells us a lot about ourselves as Americans. For example, the biggest religious group in the country is Evangelical Christians. A strong majority of this group vote Republican. They form the core of what has become known as the Religious Right. By race, Evangelicals are seventy-six percent White, with eleven percent being Latinos and six percent being Black. This makes Evangelicals the whitest religion in America. They are heavily concentrated in the South, particularly in states like Kentucky, Tennessee, and Alabama. Their ancestors largely originated from Southern England. Later, in the eighteenth century, large groups of Scottish lowlanders, Northern English, and Scots-Irish settled in Appalachia and the Piedmont. Following them were larger numbers of English indentured servants from across the English Midlands and Southern England. There are also pockets of Germans who live in the Edwards Plateau of Texas. They arrived in the region in the 1840s. Much of the population of East Texas, Louisiana, and coastal Mississippi and Alabama traces its primary ancestry to French colonists of the eighteenth century.[707]

Seventy-eight percent of Evangelicals have less than a college education, with forty-three percent having only achieved a high school diploma or less. Only Black Protestants have a lower education rate. Nonetheless, the education rate of Evangelicals is not that much lower than other religions, except, perhaps, the Jews who are the most highly educated group in the US. Not surprisingly, only forty-two percent of Evangelicals earn fifty thousand dollars or more per year. This is lower than all other religions, except for Black Protestants among whom only twenty five percent earn fifty thousand dollars or more.

Ninety-eight percent of Evangelicals believe strongly in God and ninety-six percent believe that religion is important in one's life. Aside from Mormons and Jehovah Witnesses, Evangelicals attend religious services more than any other religious population. Again, except for Mormons and Jehovah Witnesses, the Evangelicals turn to religion more than reason to guide their idea of right or wrong. Sixty percent say their morality is based upon the Bible while only thirty percent say it is based on reason. By contrast, only thirty percent of Catholics and Mainline Protestants say they depend upon the Bible for moral guidance.

Fifty-five percent of Evangelicals believe that the Bible is the word of God and must be taken literally. This is a higher percentage than that of any other religious group, except for Black Protestants among whom fifty-nine percent say the Bible should be taken literally. This compares to only twenty-six percent among Catholics and twenty-four percent among Mainline Protestants who believe this is true.

There is a great problem with believing that the Bible is the Word of God and giving it absolute authority over society. For one thing, as we saw in Volume 2 of The Untold Story of Western Civilization, any close analysis of the Bible, whether from a scientific or philosophical standpoint, reveals that the Bible is a composition written by many priests and scribes over the centuries and contains many myths, contradictions, rewrites, etc.[708] For example, the Society of Biblical Literature published a paper in 2014 entitled "Evidence of Editing: Growth and Change of Texts in the Hebrew Bible", which shows how "successive scribes updated the texts to accord with changed historical and social circumstances and with new religious concepts." The Society found that "editorial reworking of the Hebrew Bible continued unabated for centuries" and that the scribes repeatedly changed the "form, meaning, and content of the texts." The Society found that "editorial modification was the rule rather than the exception, and accordingly signs of editing can be found in all parts of the Hebrew Bible."[709]

The same situation occurs in the New Testament. For example, the earliest Christian texts, including some of Paul's Epistles date to about the middle of the first century. Like the Gospels that followed, they were written by hand, and successors were copied by hand. Mistakes crept in. As the scribes tried to clarify the meaning of Jesus, his mission and stories, the texts themselves often changed from generation to generation.

Most changes were inconsequential, but others were more important and continue to affect people today. For example, the famous tale in John's Gospel in which Jesus challenges a mob about to stone a woman accused of adultery, saying, "Let any one of you who is without sin be the first to throw a stone at her" is a variant that copyists began inserting into John beginning three hundred years after that Gospel first appeared. Or more, remarkable, in the conclusion to Mark, the description of Jesus appearing to various disciples after his resurrection does not appear in the earliest manuscripts, casting considerable doubt on the story of Jesus' bodily resurrection.

In another example from Luke, the crucified Jesus' plea that his executioners be forgiven "for they know not what they are doing" likewise does not appear in the earliest versions of his Gospel.

According to biblical scholars at the Baptist Theological Seminary in Gentilly, "even after the fourth century the Church definitively settled on the books it accepted as divinely inspired accounts of the Christian vision, some of the texts within those books were still subject to slight changes —and some had already seen changes since being first published."[710]

Changes to the Bible are ongoing. The New King James Version (NKJV), for example, is only the latest translation of the Bible. It was published by HarperCollins (a subsidiary of News Corp). The New Testament was published in 1979, the Psalms in 1980, and the full Bible in 1982.[711] Words were changed to make the language more concurrent, but do the new words hold the same meaning as the words they replaced?

Aside from the fact that the text itself is continually changing, Biblical passages are open to many interpretations and have been used to bolster almost any arguments with both good and bad results. Biblical passages can be used to excoriate the poor or humbly ask us to serve them. They are used to send us to war or bid us practice peace. They have encouraged us to love our neighbor and to hate him. The sentiments of people who follow the Bible blindly are easily manipulated by religious and political leaders who have their own agendas. Being guided only by blind faith in a text they do not understand makes them less capable of judging other's interpretations of these same texts in a rational manner for themselves. This blinkered view leads to a belief that morality is black and white; that a woman cannot have an abortion no matter the extenuating circumstances; that homosexuals are an abomination to God's plan; that the environment needs to be dominated rather than protected; and that the science of evolution is fake news perpetrated by liberal scientists to weaken their faith. Such blind sentiments destroy a person's humanity. They serve neither the Creator nor the Creation, but only those demagogues and exploiters who befool the people for their own self-interest and petty hatreds.

All this is to say that the interpretation of selected scriptural passages by certain popular fundamentalist ministers has created an "us versus them" interpretation of reality that is an affront to human unity and the care of the natural world. Once such prejudicial interpretations of the Bible become encoded into religious dogma, any adversarial positions cannot exist, even if, in the future, the dogma is proven wrong. This is the danger of blind faith, not faith in God, but blind faith in a minister, or religious dogma, no matter what the source. Having said this, there does not seem to be a connection between blind faith and morality. There are polls that support the premise that Christians are more tolerant of others and other polls that support the premise that non-religious people are more tolerant of others. This leaves the question to be answered by ourselves. Are we as individuals tolerant of others and concerned about the fate of the natural world, or are we hateful of others and callous about the fate of the planet?

What is certain is that religion, or belief in God, continues to play a positive role in many peoples' lives and there are many religious people who espouse universal values and who provide us with great role models in humility, devotion, and selfless service. The acid test for determining the true value of a religion is its concurrence with universal love and service to those less fortunate. While history has demonstrated that true spiritualists (sadvipras) can use any religion to progress toward the Divine, they are unable to do so by accepting every tenet of their religion on blind faith. As spiritualists, we must rationally determine if what we are being taught promotes the greatest good. If it does not, we must be willing to stand against it.

National Origin

The United States is a nation of immigrants.[712] People of every nationality have had a profound impact on life in America and have contributed to its success.

The wide variety of immigrants to the US and the contributions that they have made to our society indicates the reason that our culture is so rich. Appendix C provides more detail about our population's places of origin. The US has had a checkered past when it comes to accepting immigrants. Often, particular groups of whites have tried to keep out other whites and people of color. Under the Trump administration, America is shutting its doors to immigrants, particularly Latinos and Muslims (Semites) out of fear of terrorism and economic uncertainty. The world sees our nation recoil in fright and many people in other countries are now losing faith in the US as a nation, the first among equals. We were always revered as a model of an inclusive human society. We were the place that people dreamt of, a land where people could go to experience freedom and opportunity. But now things are changing.

We have so far tried to present an overview of the American people by virtue of age, gender, race, class, religion, and country of origin. In doing so, we have attempted to parse the major characteristics of American society in order to get a sense of who we are as a people. Within each distinguishing characteristic, be it age, sex/gender, race, class, religion or national origin, there can be found grounds for contention and opposition. Opinions regarding these characteristics are then packaged into the political platforms of the Right and the Left and are used to keep us divided and at each other's throats.

To remain subjected to these Left and Right agendas is to neutralize ourselves as a people. It is to continue to be manipulated by those who run the political-economic system that enslaves us. In order to free ourselves from political agendas that never seem to improve our economic conditions regardless of which political party is in power, we need to develop a fresh look at our common situation. The best way to do this is to look at the major social forces that now impact us as an American society. It is in reaction to these forces that the American people have chosen to behave the way we do.

Rank	Ancestry	Population	Percent of total population
1	German	46,403,053	14.7%
2	Black or African American (non-Hispanic)	38,785,726	12.3%
3	Mexican	34,640,287	10.9%
4	Irish	33,526,444	10.6%
5	English	24,787,018	7.8%
6	American	22,746,991	7.2%
7	Italian	17,285,619	5.5%
8	French (including French Canadian)	10,332,020	3.3%
9	Polish	9,385,766	3.0%
10	Scottish	5,409,343	1.7%
11	Puerto Rican	5,174,554	1.6%
12	Norwegian	4,445,030	1.4%
13	Dutch	4,289,116	1.4%
14	Swedish	3,933,024	1.2%
15	Chinese	3,852,099	1.2%
16	Asian Indian	3,303,512	1.0%
17	Scotch-Irish	3,046,005	1.0%
18	Russian	2,843,400	0.9%
19	West Indian (non-Hispanic)	2,824,722	0.9%
20	Filipino	2,717,844	0.9%
21	Other	2,717,844	10%

Fig. 5-17: National Ancestry

Chapter Five: Social Forces

IN PREVIOUS CHAPTERS WE have shown how the capitalist ruling class, its policy-oriented intellectuals, and military elite have acted to centralize power in a few hands. Now, we will look at the consequences of these actions on the American people as a whole. As such, we will explore the fears and anger that now consume the American people as a result of unemployment and debt, excessive political polarization, the fear of terrorism, and the construction of a Big Brother national security apparatus. In addition, to these negative social forces, the American people are also faced with an impending environmental crisis due to climate change, pollution, the death of species, and the destruction of the carrying capacity of the planet.

Each of these forces is, in itself, a large life-altering concern, but the confluence of all these forces are creating the perfect storm for the breakdown of American society as we know it. Nonetheless, the authors remain optimistic that we will succeed in mitigating the destruction of our society by the elites and we will be able to create a new society that benefits all Americans regardless of political leaning.

Unemployment and Debt

Today, Americans are very pessimistic. Whether we lean to the left or to the right politically, the great majority of us do not believe that our children's generation will have a better life than ours. Our dark views of the future are rational, as our lives have become more difficult and depressing. We work longer hours, work far past previous retirement age and, for many, retirement is no longer an option. Many Americans have stopped taking vacations. And many Americans of all ages cannot find good jobs, or can only find low-paying and often part-time work, which causes their lifestyles to plummet. College graduates are burdened with heavy debt,[713] as are senior citizens who cannot afford health care.

In Chapter One of this volume on Contemporary History we examined the workings of American capitalism. We saw how the Federal Reserve Bank, composed of private bankers, came to control the money supply of the government of the United States and, in doing so, has been able to charge the American people interest on every dollar that it prints on its printing presses. We learned that, in 2015, the government had to pay two hundred and twenty-three billion dollars in interest on its fourteen trillion dollar debt. This staggering amount was greater than the government's total spending on pollution control (eight billion dollars), Food and Nutrition Assistance (one hundred and seven billion dollars), Higher Education (sixty billion dollars) and Unemployment Benefits (one hundred and forty-two dollars).

Although it is difficult to see the direct impact of this debt on the American family, we all, nonetheless, feel it in our lives. The effects of the national debt on the economy are not abstract. High levels of federal debt cause:

> **Higher costs of living**: Large amounts of debt mean higher interest rates on everything from credit cards to mortgage loans.
>
> **Generational inequality**: By increasing its debt, the government is placing higher debt burdens on our children and threatening their standard of living and retirement.
>
> **Reduced fiscal flexibility**: Our debt levels doubled between 2008 and 2013 from thirty-five percent of GDP to over seventy percent, a result of, and in response to, the banker-created Great Recession. Now, with a debt that ranks in the trillions of dollars, the government has less flexibility to respond to future crises caused by international events or economic downturns.

Fiscal crises: Unchecked debt growth will eventually lead to a fiscal crisis, as recently occurred across Europe. At that point, investors in US debt will demand higher returns, driving up interest payments, and leading to a debt situation spiraling out of control.

Slower wage growth: Perhaps the greatest effect of a staggering national debt on American families is that every dollar an investor spends buying government debt is a dollar not invested in American jobs. High debt "crowds out" more productive investments, leading to slower economic growth and lower wages.

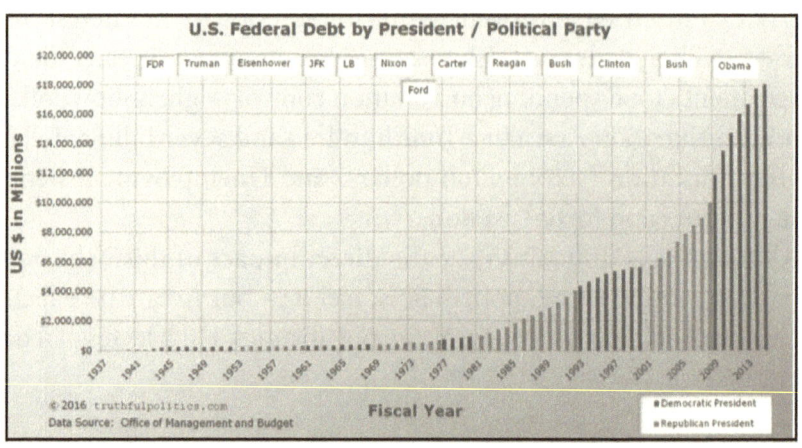

Fig. 5-18: Federal Debt By President & Political Party
(chart from truthfulpolitics.com)

From the above chart, we can also see that when Nixon cut the dollar's tie to gold in 1971, the government was able to borrow money without limitation and the bankers were able to print as many dollars as the government desired.

Every year since 1971, the government, regardless of political party in power, expanded the US debt year to year. What has been the impact of this on the American people? During this time, the middle class shrunk by eleven percent and the lower class grew by four percent. Tens of millions of Americans have had their lives diminished by increased debt and unemployment. This has led to a broad increase in anger, anxiety, and depression, which continues to grow.

The white working class, which has been especially hard hit by these developments, is hoping that President Trump will reverse this trend and bring good paying jobs back to America. This will not happen for reasons we will explain later. At this point, what is important for Americans to understand is that for many international capitalists, it is no longer profitable to invest in American labor.

John Commons, an American institutional economist and labor historian who lived through WWI and WWII, explored in his *Legal Foundations of Capitalism*[714] the principle that "Economic power is simply power to withhold from others what they need." What they need may include food, shelter, health care, jobs, or income. Economic power is the driving force of the capitalist system. Economic power implies a choice not to share in order to gain wealth for oneself. This automatically leads to inequality of possession. Every step that capitalism takes in its expansion, therefore, increases this inequality.

Today, the main problem that American families face is the lack of jobs that pay a living wage. People are hurting and our politicians are not listening to them. Neither the Left nor the Right is willing to point the finger of blame at the capitalist bankers for the ruin of the American economy.

In 2008, the banker's mortgage debacle caused unemployment in the US to shoot up to ten percent and gave rise to what is now called the Great Recession. To keep the big banks from going under as a result of their greed and utter disregard for the lives of the American people, the acquiescent federal government took on billions of dollars in debt in order to save the profligate bankers. According to their agreement with the government, once the banks became financially stable, they were supposed to begin making loans to businesses in order to rebuild the US economy. However, the problem is that big businesses will only invest in production, and thereby provide jobs to workers, when they believe that they can make a profit by doing so. Because the total expenditure on US goods and services had declined due to the economic collapse, the bankers and the big businesses had no incentive to invest in the US economy.[715] They calculated that the American people cannot afford to buy their stuff so why invest in economic recovery.

The Impact on the Family Structure

Faced with job loss and a precipitous decline in their standard of living, the impact of the Great Recession caused American families to go into shock. Because families are so different, it is difficult to generalize in all cases about the impact of the recession on the American family but certain things are beyond question. First, birth rates plummeted. It has been calculated that women who are in their early twenties are projected to have some four hundred thousand fewer lifetime births and an additional 1.5 percent of them will never have a birth.[716]

Another effect of the Great Recession was that the divorce rate dropped. This may sound like a good thing and, most likely, it was in certain cases, but the main reason that the divorce rate dropped was that the costs of divorcing became too expensive. Not just legal fees, but the cost of moving as well as employment disruptions added to the pressures.[717]

During the Great Recession, as unemployment rose so did domestic violence. Particularly, when the recession hit, there was a spike in intimate-partner violence coinciding with the sharp rise in men's unemployment rates. For example, the *New York Times* reported in 2009 that, in New York's recession-year court backlog, "Cases involving charges like assault by family members were up eighteen percent statewide." Philadelphia, in the same year, saw a sixty-seven percent increase in domestic homicides. The violence indicated in the above examples was mirrored nationally. Scientists equate this rise in domestic violence with the Great Recession, in part because domestic violence had been falling in the fifteen years before the recession and only spiked beginning in 2008-2009.[718]

The Great Recession also triggered a surge in child abuse. A study of abusive head trauma in Pittsburgh, Seattle, Columbus (OH), and Cincinnati found strong evidence of an increase in cases since the start of the recession. Using data from the Child Protection Teams at four major hospitals from January 2004 through June 2009, the researchers found a rate of 4.8 cases of abusive head trauma in children before December 2007, which they identified as the start of the recession, and 9.3 per month after that.

The doctors wrote, "Abusive head trauma is the leading cause of death from child abuse. Poverty and stress are risk factors for abuse. During an economic recession, these risks are amplified while social service supports are often decreased."[719]

The Unemployment Rate and the Employment Rate

The federal government is not very forthright when it comes to labor force statistics. They naturally want to put the best spin on the question of employment so as not to provoke the people who suffer in silence believing that it is their own fault that they cannot find a job. We hear about "official unemployment," "adjusted unemployment figures," the "employment rate," "Americans not in the labor force," "labor force participation rate," "applicants for unemployment compensation", etc. How do we make sense of all these different number charts?

As of January 2017, the "unemployment rate" in America was 7.6 million people or 4.8% of the labor force. This caused the Obama democrats to crow about their accomplishment. They said, when Obama took office the unemployment rate was 10%, now it was only 4.8%. "We cut unemployment in half and have the lowest jobless claims since 1973. The economy is strong."

But if things were so rosy, why did Trump inherit the White House by telling people that the country was in the toilet. Why did people respond to this message if it was not true?

Well, simply stated, for many of Americans, what Trump told the American people was true. In fact, it was what they had been saying for years. According to the National Jobs for All Coalition (NJAC) who spend a lot of their time researching employment and unemployment statistics, the government figure of 4.8% unemployment rate hides the true condition of the American people. In addition to the official unemployment figure of 7.6 million people, they identify another 11.5 million workers as the "hidden unemployed." The hidden employed are comprised of 5.8 million workers who are working part-time because they cannot find full-time jobs, and another 5.7 million workers who want jobs, but have become disheartened and are no longer looking for work. Once a person is out of the job market for six months, they are no longer considered in labor statistics.[720]

When we count all Americans who want jobs and cannot find a full time job, the number quickly jumps from 7.6 million workers "officially unemployed" to 19.1 million workers who cannot find full time jobs that cover the cost of their basic needs.[721] That is 11.5% of the workforce. In short, there are 3.5 workers looking for jobs for every job that is available.

But the problem does not end here. Millions more Americans are working full-time, year-round, yet earn less than the official poverty level for a family of four. In 2015, that number was 17.4 million people. This represents 15.7% of full-time, full-year workers.[722] The poverty level in 2015 was $24,257 for a family of four.

While the Obama administration and the mainstream media were crowing that jobless claims in the US had reached their lowest number since 1973, thousands of fast food workers, airport workers, home care workers, and adjunct professors were marching in the streets across the country to protest humiliating labor conditions and demanding a $15 minimum wage. Most of these workers, as we write, make far below $15 per hour. Many make as low as $7.25 per hour, the current federal minimum wage. These people usually lack any kind of benefits. Many adjunct professors, have contingent, temporary jobs, sometimes consisting of only one poorly paid course per year. Many peopled are working two or even three jobs a week in an attempt to cobble together enough income to cover basic needs.

According to the Obama administration, all of these workers were considered "employed." They were viewed as part of the American economy's success story, a big part of which was our five percent unemployment rate. As president Barack Obama boasted in February, 2016: "The United States of America right now has the strongest, most durable economy in the world."[723]

Obama's claims of a strong economy rang hollow for the many millions of workers who said, and continue to say, they cannot make enough to survive. It was the genius of Trump to tap into the frustration of these millions of Americans by promising to put them back to work in living wage jobs.

The vaunted American economy might have looked good on paper, but on the streets of American towns and cities it was a failure. First of all, millions of Americans had been out of work for more than six months and were no longer considered to be looking for work. Secondly, many workers, lost full-time jobs and were turned into temps, contract workers, freelancers, and other "self-employed" categories that paid little and provided no benefits. These people, who comprised 15.8% of the American labor market had no safety net. They spent days trying to get paid for their last job and days trying to get the next one. They had no advocates for them in the workplace, and little bargaining power to improve their lot.[724]

Thirdly, many middle-class workers lost their jobs and were forced to take low-wage service jobs. The five percent unemployment rate, in other words, hid, and continues to hide, the devastating story of underemployment, wage loss, and survival anxiety that defines life for millions of Americans.

Making matters much worse, the Obama administration failed to come up with a plan that adequately supported these people. Donald Trump in his campaign declared: "Don't believe those phony numbers when you hear 4.9% and 5% unemployment. The number's probably 28%, 29%, as high as 35%. In fact, I even heard recently 42%." To be clear, Trump's 42% claim is a lie. But for the millions of Americans working low-wage or temporary jobs or suffering from long-term unemployment, it felt like the truth.[725]

Donald Trump became president because he acknowledged these people's suffering. White people felt like they were finally being listened to, but Donald Trump was, and is, a demagogue. He wants the people's adulation, but he is only really concerned about himself and other billionaires like himself. Instead of addressing the real reason for the unemployment of Americans, he placed the blame for white people's suffering on Mexicans, women, blacks, and Arabs. He divided us as a people by appealing to the lowest common denominator of a confused and anxious white population.

How will the Trump presidency bring back living wage, full-time jobs to America? It is unlikely that he will. Let us take, for example, the question of manufacturing jobs. During the decade beginning in 2000, America lost a catastrophic five million jobs. Robert Reich, President Clinton's Labor Secretary, at the time explained that, "The majority of manufacturing job losses is due to productivity increases." The conservative *National Review's* Kevin Williamson, echoed this "positive" sentiment by flatly stating "the fall in [manufacturing] employment in America and elsewhere should be seen as a good thing."[726]

Others like Robert Atkinson, President of the Information Technology and Innovation Foundation, argued that, "The real reason the US lost 5.7 million manufacturing jobs in the last decade was due to the decline in manufacturing output, which in turn was caused by US manufacturing losing out in global competition."[727] "During the 2000's," he continued, "13 of the 19 aggregate-level U.S. manufacturing sectors, which employed 55% of manufacturing workers in 2000, experienced absolute declines in real output. For example, motor vehicle output decreased 45%, textiles 47%, and apparel 40%. In other words, manufacturing establishments were producing less, and so of course they employed fewer workers."[728]

A recent report issued in February 2017 by John Silvia, chief economist at Wells Fargo Economics, claimed that we're still struggling to recover from the Great Recession and that, in important ways, we'll never really recover.

Silva stated that, "Real disposable incomes are about eleven trillion dollars lower over those nine years, amounting to a loss of more than thirty-five thousand dollars per person. That's the equivalent of everyone in America getting laid off for eleven months."[729]

The loss of tens of millions of jobs, and hundreds of billions of dollars of investment permanently altered the character of the labor market.

Silva said that the older generation (Baby Boomers) took a huge hit to their wealth, which was mostly in housing, but also in their retirement portfolios. Many of these older workers have had to delay retirement. For those between twenty-five and fifty-five, job loss has been the biggest challenge. "About a quarter of them will never make it up because they have a lower earning trajectory."

For Millennials, the Great Recession has forced them to re-evaluate their lives and their place in the economy. They know they will never have a real job unless they have a college credential, so millions are doing what it takes, including taking on massive debt, to get there. Most have downsized their expectations about consumption.[730]

Thus, we see that some experts blame the loss of American jobs on an increase in production and others on a decrease in production. Who is to be believed?

Bernie Sanders and Donald Trump blamed Mexico and China for the loss of American jobs. They claimed that these countries are increasing market share in the same industrial sectors that America has long dominated, through coordinating national efforts and by undercutting us on labor costs. Thus, these politicians fall into the group of experts who blame underproduction for loss of American jobs.

To help clarify the situation, a practical example might serve us better than all the government and expert opinions about why America lost so many jobs.

When the German engineering company Siemens Energy opened a gas turbine production plant in Charlotte, N.C., in 2011, some ten thousand people showed up at a job fair for eight hundred positions. But fewer than fifteen percent of the applicants were able to pass a reading, writing, and math screening test geared toward a ninth-grade education.[731]

The CEO of Siemens USA explained the need for more educated workers. "In our factories, there's a computer about every twenty or thirty feet. People on the plant floor need to be much more skilled than they were in the past. There are no jobs for high school graduates at Siemens today."[732]

Many manufacturing companies are in the same situation. John Deere dealerships, for example, repair million-dollar farming machinery. Each of these machines is filled with dozens of computers. Fixing tractors and grain harvesters now requires advanced math and comprehension skills and the ability to solve problems as they appear. "The toolbox is now a computer," said Andy Winnett,[733] who directs the company's agricultural program at Walla Walla Community College in Washington.

These are the types of good-paying jobs that President Trump has promised to bring back to working-class communities, but what if the working class in America no longer has the skills to fill those job positions. Computers have not only replaced workers, they have also made it more difficult for those applying for new job openings to compete because they do not have the skills to work with computers.

This scenario is worth looking at. According to a recent Ball State University study, nearly nine out of ten jobs that disappeared since 2000 were lost to automation, not to workers in other countries.[734]

The study begins by looking at the question of productivity. The most common measure of productivity is the average product of labor, which is the value of all goods manufactured in the US divided by the number of workers. In 2012, the average product of labor for all manufacturing was $149,299, but ranged from a low of $45,930 for manufacturers of apparel and leather goods to $733,861 for petroleum and coal products manufacturing. From 1998 through 2012, productivity grew in all sectors when adjusted for inflation. That growth was highest in the production of computer and electronic products, with a remarkable 829 percent growth.

Double-digit growth also occurred in automobiles, transportation equipment, miscellaneous products, primary metals machinery, electrical equipment, and food. Much of this productivity increase was due to growth in the use of information technology. However, major declines in production occurred in the manufacturing of minerals, fabricated metals, furniture, textiles, apparel, paper, and plastics.

In general, the output per worker in 2000 was much lower than it is today. And the chief reason for this is automation and information technology advances. The researchers concluded that if the level of productivity in 2000 had been applied to the 2010 level of production, America would have required 20.9 million manufacturing workers. Instead, we employed only 12.1 million.[735]

In short, computers have replaced the need for almost sixty percent of American manufacturing jobs. This means that even if the president could return manufacturing jobs to America, a high school diploma would no longer be good enough to fill them. This is rarely discussed in political debates about the loss of American manufacturing jobs. Unfortunately, the unemployment problem is about to get worse rather than better. This is because new Artificial Intelligence technology is about to replace millions more American workers.

Jane Fraser, CEO of Citigroup's Latin America business, speaking at a Fortune Magazine business summit stated, "We are expecting five hundred billion objects to become connected to the internet and this automation is going to hollow out middle and working-class jobs. Technology is replacing these jobs."[736]

Stephen Hawking, the world-famous physicist, wrote that "the automation of factories has already decimated jobs in traditional manufacturing, and the rise of artificial intelligence is likely to extend this job destruction deep into the middle classes, with only the most caring, creative, or supervisory roles remaining."737

Just as we have witnessed with information technology and computers, artificial intelligence will bring radical increases in productivity, but it will be at the cost of massive unemployment and uncertainty, as human jobs are replaced by intelligent machines.

A report by Citibank in February 2016 predicted that forty-seven percent of US jobs are at risk of automation. In the UK, thirty-five percent are at risk and in China, seventy-seven percent. Across the OECD (Organization for Economic Cooperation and Development), they predicted an average of fifty-seven jobs lost to artificial intelligence technology. This led Stephen Hawking to declare "The development of full artificial intelligence could spell the end of the human race."738

Automation, according to Hawking "will accelerate the already widening economic inequality around the world. The internet and the platforms that it makes possible allow very small groups of individuals to make enormous profits while employing very few people. This is inevitable, it is economic progress, but it is also socially destructive."

Hawkings, as well as others, blame this growing reality for the current level of economic anxiety and the rise in right-wing, populist politics in the West. "We are living in a world of widening, not diminishing, financial inequality, in which many people can see not just their standard of living, but their ability to earn a living at all, disappearing. It is no wonder then that they are searching for a new deal, which Trump and Brexit might have appeared to represent."739

Moshe Vardi, a computer science professor at Rice University in Texas, told the American Association for the Advancement of Science: We are approaching the time when machines will be able to outperform humans at almost any task. Society needs to confront this question before it is upon us: if machines are capable of doing almost any work humans can do, what will humans do?740

Another question is who will be able to buy the products built by artificial intelligent machines, with so many people out of work? If people have no jobs and cannot afford to buy things, such a scenario presents a picture of masses of unemployed people, a stagnant economy, growing frustration and anger, the high risk of greater conflict, rebellion and war, while the bankers sit on their cash with little incentive to invest in the economy. This is checkmate.

Rather than look at the viability of such a scenario coming to pass, the cheerleaders of capitalism say that with more free time we will be free to pursue leisure activities. It has always been a part of the American Dream that as we work hard, we will advance technology, which will allow us more leisure time to do what we want. Unfortunately, under capitalism, current technological advancements are not maintaining an adequate standard of living for everyone. In reality, the increased leisure time that capitalist supporters anticipate will only exist for the unemployed and under-employed. There is a definite solution to this problem, but it is not one that is presently dreamed of by politicians on the Left or the Right or by the American people in general. The solution is for the American people to meet their own basic needs by creating their own local economies using appropriate technology and following the principles of economic decentralization and economic democracy. These local "people's economies" will not be easily achieved, but they are doable and we shall speak of this solution in Book II, *Universal Ideology*.

The Trump Economy

Much noise has been made in the mainstream press about the benefits of the Trump economy. Has Trump's administration actually improved the US economy. Looking at the same calculations that we used to analysis the Obama economy, we find a similar performance. An article in *Fortune* magazine in October 2018 makes the comparison between the two economies, one under a Democrat president, the other under the Republican.

The article demonstrates that: (1) Trump could reach his twenty-five million job growth goal even if the economy continued to grow at the pace under Obama, and (2) the unemployment rate shows pretty much the same progression from Obama to Trump.

For all of Trump's boasting to make America Great Again by cutting population increase and giving the capitalists more money to spend, here is a comparison chart as to the accomplishments of the Obama and Trump administrations. And remember, the false calculations regarding employment and unemployment numbers under Obama continue to exist under Trump.

The following chart makes a monthly comparison between the average employment gains under Obama and Trump. It shows that the average employment gain in Obama's last six years in office (after getting out of the recession's impact) was two hundred and one thousand. And the average for his last five years was two hundred and seven thousand, essentially the same as the two hundred and eight thousand for the first nine months of 2018 under Trump.

Employment Statistics for Obama:
- 2009: Negative 422,000 per month or Lost 5.1 million jobs (teeth of the recession)
- 2010: 88,000 per month or 1.05 million for the year
- 2011: 174,000 per month or 2.09 million
- 2012: 179,000 per month or 2.14 million
- 2013: 192,000 per month or 2.3 million
- 2014: 250,000 per month or 3 million
- 2015: 226,000 per month or 2.7 million
- 2016: 187,000 per month or 2.24 million

Employment Statistics for Trump through September, 2018:
- 2017: 182,000 per month or 2.19 million
- Through September 2018: 208,000 per month or 2.5 million run rate

Unemployment Statistics for Bush, Obama and Trump

The unemployment rate shows pretty much the same progression from President Obama to President Trump. The unemployment rate started to climb the last two years of President Bush's second term and substantially in Obama's first year as the Great Recession, which he had inherited, was having a huge impact.

Bush's last four years in office:
- December 2005: 4.9%
- December 2006: 4.4%, decreased 0.5%

- December 2007: 5.0%, increased 0.6%
- December 2008: 7.3%, increased 2.3%

Obama's time in office
- December 2009: 9.9%, increased 2.6% (teeth of the recession)
- December 2010: 9.3%, decreased 0.6%
- December 2011: 8.5%, decreased 0.8%
- December 2012: 7.9%, decreased 0.6%
- December 2013: 6.7%, decreased 1.2%
- December 2014: 5.6%, decreased 1.1%
- December 2015: 5.0%, decreased 0.6%
- December 2016: 4.7%, decreased 0.3%

Trump's through September:
- December 2017: 4.1%, decreased 0.6%
- September 2018: 3.7%, decreased 0.4%[741]

Considering Trump's failed attempts to get US-based multinational corporations to return jobs to America and considering his slashing of exports because of his trade war, the question is whether he will be able to maintain the economic trajectory that has been established over several presidencies, or will his plans tank the US economy. Whatever the circumstances that affect the US economy in 2019 and 2020, the American people are unlikely to experience any improvement in our standard of living.

In October, 2018, the same month as the above study, an article appeared in *The American Prospect* magazine that looked at the impact of Trump's economy on the average American worker. The article found that while the stock market has boomed since Trump became president, (over eighty percent of the stock market is owned by the richest ten percent of Americans anyway,) most Americans never got much out of Trump's market boom to begin with.[742]

Secondly, Trump's tariffs on imports of steel, aluminum, and some Chinese products have started pushing up prices for many US companies that rely on those items to create final products, forcing many firms to make tough decisions about where to cut costs.

While many large companies have decided to pass on those costs to consumers, which impacts our wallets, many smaller US businesses have been forced to cut labor costs to offset the higher amounts they are paying for parts.

From Wisconsin to South Carolina, small businesses have started to lay off employees, and they are citing Trump's tariffs. Many firms have warned that the worst is yet to come.[743] But it is not just the manufacturing industries that have suffered from the Trump's trade war. Farmers are also hurting. For example, a total of eighty-four farms in the upper Midwest filed for bankruptcy between July 2017 and June 2018, according to the *Minneapolis Star Tribune*. That is more than double the number of bankruptcy filings during the same period in 2013 and 2014 in Wisconsin, Minnesota, North Dakota, South Dakota, and Montana.

Farms that produce corn, soybeans, milk, and beef were already suffering due to low global demand and low prices, and Trump's trade war is making the problem even worse. China has slapped billions of dollars worth of tariffs on US agriculture exports in response to Trump's tariffs on Chinese products. Other countries, including Canada, have also added duties to US agriculture products in response to Trump's tariffs on all imported steel and aluminum.

The problem has gotten so bad that the Trump administration has to launch a **twelve billion dollar** aid package for US farmers having to cope with retaliatory tariffs. In September, 2018, the government wrote **twenty-five million dollars** worth of bailout loan checks to the agriculture industry.

But even the bailout may not be enough to keep farms open. Bankers in the Midwest are worried that too many farmers are falling behind on loan payments. "We're just waiting for a turnaround," one Minnesota banker told the Star Tribune. "We're waiting for the tariff problem to go away."[744]

It does not seem like the Trump administration is going to let that happen anytime soon.[745] Americans are also suffering in other ways under the Trump economy. Trump slashed taxes on the wealthy and promised everyone else a four thousand dollar wage boost. The rich got their tax cut, but the boost never happened. This is why we did not see the Republicans campaigning on their tax cut.[746] Trump also refuses to raise the minimum wage, stuck at $7.25 an hour, while his Labor Department repeals a rule that increased the number of workers entitled to time-and-a-half for overtime.

While the statistics show that unemployment is down to 3.7 percent, jobs are less secure than ever. Contract workers, who are not eligible for family or medical leave, unemployment insurance, the minimum wage, or worker's compensation, are now doing one out of every five jobs in America.

Meanwhile, housing costs are skyrocketing, with Americans now paying a third or more of their paychecks in rent or mortgages. Trump responded by making drastic cuts in low-income housing. His secretary of Housing and Urban Development also wants to triple the rent paid by poor households in subsidized housing.

Health-care costs continue to rise faster than inflation. Trump's response was to undermine the Affordable Care Act. Over the past two years, some four million people have lost health-care coverage.

Pharmaceutical costs are also out of control. And while Trump campaigned on a promise to reign in drug costs, he has allowed the biggest pharmacist, CVS, to merge with one of the biggest health insurers, Aetna to create a behemoth with the power to raise prices even further.

The cost of college also continues to soar.

Climate change is undermining the standard of living of ordinary Americans, as more people are hit with floods, mudslides, tornados, draughts, and wildfires. Even those who have so far avoided direct hits will be paying more for insurance, or having a harder time getting it. People living on flood plains, or in trailers, or without home insurance, are paying the highest price. Trump responded by allowing more carbon into the atmosphere and making climate change even worse. While the Republicans continue to lie to their base that climate change is a fantasy made up by liberals to confuse the American people, ninety-seven of the world's scientists, the great majority of the world's leaders of sovereign governments, the heads of international organizations, as well as the Pentagon and other government agencies acknowledge climate change and are working to confront it.

The Trump administration will never admit to the reality of climate change because much of Trump's vaunted economic progress is based upon destroying environmental safeguards that were put in place by previous administrations to protect the planet and its eco-systems and to mitigate the pollution of our air, water and soil.

Whether you lean to the Left or the Right, ask yourself whether your life really improved under the Obama and Trump administrations.

Family Debt

While millions of Americans struggle to make ends meet, we are sinking more deeply into debt. The Baby Boom generation legitimized the credit card. Easier access to credit helped us buy what many see as the necessities of a middle-class life—a home, a car, an education. Those assets, in turn, gave us the stability and earning power to build personal wealth. Regular mortgage payments acted as a form of saving and made home ownership a form of financial security.

Borrowing now has taken on a very different character. During the housing boom, home equity became a means to compensate for stagnant incomes. After the housing bust, however, we were forced to turn to loans or credit card debt to make ends meet. In doing so, our debt soared.

Consider that those in the bottom thirty percent of the income scale make an average of fourteen thousand dollars a year, which includes the value of many government benefits like food stamps or disability payments. But these people spend more than twenty-five thousand, or one hundred and eighty-two percent, of their annual income mostly on basic needs like housing, food, and transportation.[747] This group includes most senior citizens and students as well as the unemployed and underemployed.

What happens when people do not make enough money to pay for their basic needs? They are forced to make impossible choices as to which bills to pay. Do they make the car payment this month or the rent payment? Do they spend money on food or a doctor bill? Often people turn to payday lenders or credit cards where usurious interest rates push them further into debt from which they are unable to recover.

A recent Federal Reserve Bank survey asked people how they would pay a four hundred dollar emergency bill. Forty-seven percent of respondents said that either they would cover the expense by borrowing or selling something, or they would not be able to come up with the four hundred dollars at all. Respondents were people from the lower class and the middle class. As one middle class man commented on his poverty:

> I know what it is like to have to juggle creditors to make it through a week. I know what it is like to have to swallow my pride and constantly dun people to pay me so that I can pay

> others. I know what it is like to have liens slapped on me and to have my bank account levied by creditors. I know what it is like to be down to my last $5—literally— while I wait for a paycheck to arrive, and I know what it is like to subsist for days on a diet of eggs. I know what it is like to dread going to the mailbox, because there will always be new bills to pay but seldom a check with which to pay them. I know what it is like to have to tell my daughter that I didn't know if I would be able to pay for her wedding; it all depended on whether something good happened. And I know what it is like to have to borrow money from my adult daughters because my wife and I ran out of heating oil.[748]

The man described the shame and humiliation that he faced and why people do not talk about their poverty. Rather they suffer in silence.

Here are some of the biggest financial stressors, particularly for the poor:

> The poor spend nearly three-quarters of their annual income on housing alone. Keeping a roof over one's head is the biggest expense for everyone, but it eats up seventy-two percent of the poor's income. Comparatively, the cost of shelter is thirty percent for the middle class and only nineteen percent for the upper class. It is next to impossible for a full-time, minimum wage worker to find a market-rate, two-bedroom apartment that is affordable anywhere in the country, yet only one-in-four eligible families receive housing assistance. It is one of the federal safety net's most underfunded programs.

> Regarding transportation, spending on cars and public transportation can eat up nearly thirty percent of a poor person's annual income, compared to seventeen percent for the middle class and only ten percent for the upper class. There are no federal subsidies to get poor people to work even though it is often hard for low-income people to get to their jobs, or even to grocery stores or day care centers. Some must take two or three buses—that is, if public trans-

portation is even available. And a car can be costly to buy and maintain.

Many poor families cannot afford to put food on the table every day even though they spend twenty-eight percent of their income on food. Because meat, eggs, fresh fruits and vegetables are particularly pricey, they often buy inexpensive junk food that provides calories but lacks adequate nutrition. The diet-related disease epidemic in this country, which includes obesity, diabetes, heart disease, and certain cancers, testifies to this reality.

Even when accounting for government benefits, like food stamps, food is still a major expense for the poor. Food stamps seldom last the entire month and more families must rely on food banks just to survive.

By contrast, the middle class spends twelve percent of their income on food and the upper class spends seven percent.[749] Things are not much better for the middle class, many of whom were working class people who lost their jobs to automation.

As of 2013, the average debt of middle-class families amounted to one hundred and twenty-two percent of their annual income according to the Federal Reserve.[750]

According to an American Household Credit Card Debt Study, in 2015, the average US household *with debt* owed $130,922. This included credit cards, mortgages, auto loans, student loans, and other forms of debt. Here is a breakdown of the debt of the average American household as of the fourth quarter of 2015.[751]

Type of debt	Average for households with this type of debt	Total U.S. debt of this type	Households with this type of debt	% of American households with this type of debt (approximate)	Overall average household debt
Credit cards	$15,762	$733 billion	46.5 million	35%	$5,517
Mortgages	$168,614	$8.25 trillion	48.9 million	36%	$60,700

Auto loans	$27,141	$1.06 trillion	39.1 million	29%	$7,871
Student loans	$48,172	$1.23 trillion	25.5 million	19%	$9,153
All debt	$130,922	$12.12 trillion	92.6 million	69%	$90,336

This debt burden costs more than sixty-six hundred dollars in interest per year, about nine percent of the average income.[752] Household debt has increased over eleven percent during the last decade. While "don't spend above your means" will always be sound advice, it is no longer an option for most Americans. The household debt increase that we are seeing is not just a case of lifestyle rot. The rapid growth in food, housing, medical care, and education is now dwarfing income growth. This is making it virtually impossible to meet basic needs without leaning on credit cards and loans. These circumstances exist for American people across the board. It does not matter how we vote or whether we consider ourselves liberals or conservatives.

Political Polarization

Another major social force impacting Americans today is the way we are divided politically. We saw in Chapter Two how the ruling elite in this country divide the intellectual class. It is not based upon whether we are conservatives or liberals, or whether we are Republicans or Democrats. These divisions are only for public consumption. The rich, on the other hand, are only concerned whether those conservative and liberal politicians are willing to serve the ruling elite or not. In order to get elected, politicians need campaign financing and this money comes from the ruling elite. Therefore, the politicians, especially those on the federal level, all serve the interests of the rich. The elite call them "policy-oriented" intellectuals. Whether they are Republicans or Democrats is of little concern.

Because the American people do not understand this underlying reality, we believe that our well-being depends upon whether conservatives or liberals or whether Republicans or Democrats are in power. We believe that these politicians actually make decisions that will affect our lives for the better. To a certain extent this is true. After all, the laws passed by Republicans and

Democrats do differ because they are based upon different ideologies that support different segments of the population, but, in actuality, these issues are trivial compared to the continued negative impact on everyone's lives by the ruling elite. All presidents, whether Democrat or Republican support American wars of imperial conquest. All presidents promoted the economic rape and pillage of other nations' labor and resources, particularly in the third world. All presidents have fostered the economic decisions that have decimated the middle class in America. All presidents have contributed to militarizing the police and the establishing a surveillance bureaucracy that intrudes on every family in America. All presidents have consistently lied to the American people in their duty to the elite. Yet, the American people still do not understand this. Why?

It is because the ruling elite, in order to foster their exploitation, have divided the American people by promoting opposing ideologies that are daily trumpeted in the mainstream media. In general terms, the liberals support racial minorities, the poor, women, and those who have been unjustly treated by the system. Conservatives on the other hand support white people, particularly white males, who also see themselves victimized by the system. The liberal strongholds are big cities, the conservative strongholds are the white suburbs and rural America. In Chapter Two, we discussed in detail the ideologies that are supported by the Left and the Right and there is no need to repeat this information here. Rather, at this point, we want to see the impact of the conflicting political parties' ideologies on the American people as they both become more extreme due to the continued trend toward an impoverished America.

The two-party political system in America is failing us. Instead of uniting us to face our common problems, it is dividing us. Instead of bringing us together as a people, it is aggravating our differences and polarizing us as a society. Today, due to political diatribes, in which one party continually harangues the other, people have also become more severe in their positions. Not long ago, it was possible to find liberals and conservatives in both parties. Now, almost all the liberals are in the Democratic party and most of the conservatives are in the Republican party. As someone observed, we were once one nation with two parties, now we are two nations each with one party.

Republicans believe that Democrats are close-minded, immoral, lazy, dishonest, and unintelligent (in that order). Conversely, Democrats think Republicans are close-minded, dishonest, immoral, unintelligent, and lazy (in that order.)[753]

There is a kind of principled political opposition that says, "I disagree with your ideas and will oppose them, but as I oppose them, I will deal with you honestly and fairly and encourage others to do the same." Then there is an opposition that says, "You are bad and dangerous, and I will use any legal (or borderline legal) means to defeat you, including lying, sowing chaos, and encouraging others to do the same." Today, both parties are locked in this position. Statesmen who seek the benefit of Americans as a whole are rare.

In 2014, the Pew Research Center did a comprehensive survey of political attitudes among American politicians. They found that "Republicans and Democrats are more divided along ideological lines—and partisan antipathy is deeper and more extensive—than at any point in the last two decades."[754]

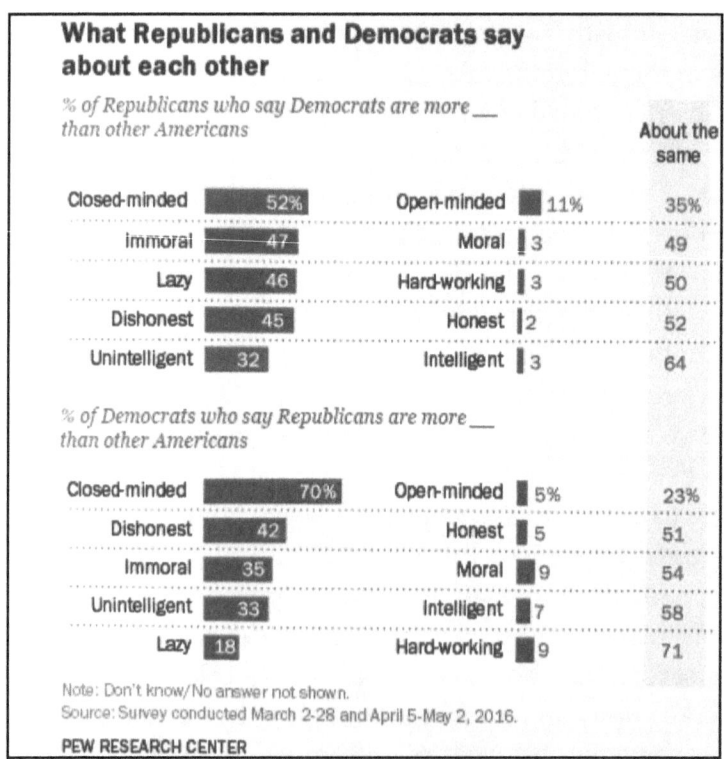

Fig. 5-19: What Republicans and Democrats Say About Each Othe
(Courtesy of Pew Research Center)

Partisan animosity has increased substantially over the same period. In each party, the share with a highly negative view of the opposing party has more than doubled since 1994. Most of the American politicians have gone beyond disliking one another. They have come to believe that the opposing party's policies "are so misguided that they threaten the nation's well-being." In this way, the political parties have been reduced to "Ideological silos" and are dragging the people with them. Fortunately, these sentiments are not yet shared by most Americans. The majority of us do not have uniformly conservative or liberal views. Most of us do not see either party as a threat to the nation. And we still believe our representatives in government should meet halfway to resolve contentious disputes rather than hold out for more of what they want.

Yet, while most of us remain in the center ideologically, the most ideologically oriented and politically rancorous Americans make their voices heard through greater participation in every stage of the political process. This is helping to move Republicans more to the right and Democrats more to the left. Whether primary voting, writing letters to officials, volunteering for or donating to a campaign, the most politically polarized are more actively involved in politics, amplifying the divisive voices least willing to see the parties meet each other halfway. Yet, as Americans, we may not be able to ensure that our own good sense will triumph in the days ahead. Certainly, the campaign of Hillary Clinton and Donald Trump divided us beyond anything we have seen in our lifetime. Politics is becoming much more personal as more people on the Left and the Right say it is important to them to live in a place where most people share their political views. Although still small, a growing number of liberals (twenty-three percent) and conservatives (thirty percent) say that they would be unhappy if an immediate family member married a member of the opposite party.

Most Americans, regardless of their ideological preferences, want to live in communities where they can live close to extended family and high-quality schools. But far more liberals than conservatives think it is important that a community have racial and ethnic diversity (seventy-six percent vs twenty percent). At the same time, conservatives are more likely than liberals to attach importance to living in a place where many people share their religious faith (fifty-seven percent vs seventeen percent of liberals).[755] Also liberals want to live in a community where houses are smaller and closer together with schools, stores, and restaurants within walking distance, while conservatives want larger houses farther apart with schools, stores, and restaurants several miles away. This speaks to the divide that exists between liberal urban dwellers and conservative suburb and rural dwellers. When Americans looked at the political system under President Obama and the Republican Senate leaders, most of us simply wanted them to meet each other halfway in addressing the issues facing the nation.[756] But then something changed.

The 2016 Election

In 2016, Hillary Clinton and Donald Trump were running for president. A Gallup poll conducted in July showed that they were the worst rated candidates of the last seven decades. Thirty-three percent of Americans considered Hillary a "highly unfavorable" candidate, while forty-two percent considered Trump highly unfavorable. The only candidate with a worse rating since the 1950s was Barry Goldwater with a highly unfavorable rating of twenty-six percent. In other words, the American people considered both candidates inferior.[757] People looked at Hillary as a liar and Trump as an egotist. But the situation was worse than this. Only eleven percent of Republicans and forty-five percent of Democrats said they were "satisfied with the way things are going in the United States at this time." People were angry at the economy and frustrated with the political process.

This anger and frustration drove more Americans to political extremes and fueled the general feeling of discontent expressed by many across the country. This shift created the opportunities for more extreme and polarizing candidates.[758]

The rise of Trump and Bernie Sanders during the 2016 primary season testified to this. Another study published in July by the National Bureau of Economic Research analyzed the content of key congressional speeches between 1873 and 2009 and found that rhetorical partisanship "is far greater today than at any point in the past," greater than it was during the last few years of the Reconstruction Era following the US Civil War.

While anger and frustration were at the root of voters' shift toward political extremes, what was the driving force behind that discontent?

Some researchers held that activists have been able to organize more effectively and are more embedded in the parties than they used to be. There is some truth to this. But it is not the entire answer, nor is it the predominant answer for the rise of Donald Trump. The real driving force was the greater wealth inequality, the loss of jobs that provided a living wage, and the noose of debt that was chocking the life out of the middle and lower classes.

Many believe that wealth and income inequality are, at least, partially driving voter frustration and resentment. The fall of the American middle class and simultaneous rise in the percentage of Americans sitting at the very poor and very rich ends of the income spectrum have coincided with academic measures of political polarization over the last few decades.

Former Mississippi Governor, Haley Barbour, who was also a former Republican National Committee chairman, speaking on the topic of Political Polarization in June 2016 at the George W. Bush Presidential Center said that income inequality had progressed to the point that some Americans "can't tell the difference between the recovery and the recession" because "it still feels like a recession."[759]

That financial unevenness, he said, is at the heart of Americans' frustrations, which have boiled over to the point where compromise between Republicans and Democrats is now viewed as a sign of weakness. This is not a stance, he said, that his party, or the broader American political system, was built upon. "I ran the political office in the White House for Ronald Reagan," he said. "Ronald Reagan compromised on everything, because the Democrats had a majority in the House the whole time. He used to say, 'Remember, a fellow that agrees with you eighty percent of the time is a friend and ally. He's not some twenty percent traitor.'"[760]

Enter Trump

As the *National Review*, a conservative publication, said, "No one can reasonably argue that Trump was anything other than a polarizing force in the 2016 election. He relentlessly insulted his opponents, accused them of all manner of monstrous acts, and never, ever backed down.

But was he creating the market for political polarization, or was he merely meeting its existing demands?"[761] Trump insulted women, blacks, Mexicans, Muslims, welfare recipients, and anyone else who found favor with Obama and the Democrat establishment.

Trump's claim that he would bring jobs back to America and that he was a political outsider resonated with the American people, particularly the white working class. According to an exit poll conducted by CNN, men preferred Trump over Clinton fifty-three percent to forty-one percent. Women preferred Clinton to Trump fifty-four percent to forty-two percent. Whites preferred Trump over Clinton fifty-eight percent to thirty-seven percent; blacks preferred Clinton eighty-eight percent to Trump's eight percent. Younger voters (eighteen to forty-four) preferred Clinton over Trump fifty-three percent to thirty-eight percent, while older voters (forty-five to sixty-five and older) preferred Trump over Clinton fifty-two percent to forty-five percent. College grads went for Clinton fifty-two percent versus forty-three percent for Trump, while those without a college degree chose Trump over Clinton by fifty-two percent versus forty-four percent.[762] This divide based upon gender, race, age, and education continues to divide the country.

Because the American public is basically required to vote either Democrat or Republican, they are divided between these two parties, but the division is not as deep as the media suggests. Many people are not comfortable with either party.

How could Trump have won the election? It seems to be because he was able to rouse up the white majority. He blamed women and minorities for all their problems. He blamed Democrats for ignoring their suffering. He promised to bring jobs back to white America. Trump voters believed they finally had a politician that listened to them and identified with them. Having this loud, belligerent leader to follow, Trump voters were finally able to send a defiant message to the political establishment. As political scientist Keith Poole of the University of Georgia said, "The way to understand this election is that it was a 'FY' election. You can't say it, but that means f*** you."[763]

Again, why did they want to send an "FY" message? Because between forty and fifty percent of the lowest-income families in America haven not seen an increase in income for the past forty years and the economic gains of the past eight years have gone mostly to those in the upper-income brackets.

"That's why you keep seeing these polls that say America's on the wrong track," Poole said. In a country divided along economic lines, Trump tapped voters, many rural, who felt left behind. The anger and frustration of the American people did not start with Donald Trump. They had been voting alternately for Republicans and Democrats hoping that something would change but it never did. That is why the white working class, which had been decimated by automation and job loss, felt that they finally had a savior.

How could so many Americans tolerate Trumps sexist and racist remarks? Dr. Peter H. Ditto of the Department of Psychology & Social Behavior School of Social Ecology University of California, Irvine explained it this way. Trump resonated with conservative voters because he spoke to values that political conservatives tend to cherish more than liberals: authority and traditionalism. When Trump made statements that struck liberal voters as unforgivably racist or homophobic, Trump supporters did not necessarily love those statements, either, but they weren't bothered as much as liberals. "When he says racist things, they go, 'Yeah, I don't like that, but it's not a deal-breaker for me; for liberals, it's a deal-breaker.'"[764] On the other hand, while the liberals are outraged by belligerent sexism and racism, conservatives are outraged by the liberals disrespect for patriotism, religion, and the lifestyle of white working class Americans.

This kind of morality schism is hard to overcome. It tends to turn into a self-sustaining cycle of distrust and fighting. Trump gave racists and sexists freedom of speech and it will be difficult to put this back in the closet. On the other hand, liberals are condemning all Trump voters as racists and sexists while this is not true and further aggravates the divide between the people.

Consequences for the People

The deepening divide between liberals and conservatives took a quantum leap with Trump. In Hillary Clinton's concession speech to Donald Trump, the Democratic candidate called America "more deeply divided than we thought."

As soon as he was elected, tens of thousands of anti-Trump protestors took to the streets in almost every big city in the country. Millions of women marched across America and the world protested the election of an admitted sexist. Even in small towns, average Americans found themselves unable to avoid uncomfortable conversations with their friends and neighbors. Josh Klapow, a clinical psychologist at the University of Alabama in Birmingham said, "I know people hanging up the phone on their best friends in the world."

"People are absolutely burning personal bridges, because they're making the decision, consciously, saying, 'I cannot live with you for voting for that person.'" "This is the most socially damaging thing I've ever seen," Klapow concluded.[765]

It looks as if this kind of conflict will continue and probably become worse unless, as Americans, regardless of our political leaning, we take the initiative to prevent our country from ripping apart. Unless we begin to heal our wounds and bridge our differences at the local level, the combination of fewer jobs, less government subsidies, and increased political rancor will quickly turn our neighborhoods into chaos.

If we care about the happiness of the American people, we need to do something about income inequality. Income equality is negatively affecting the lower and middle classes and people are becoming angrier as politicians deliver hollow speeches and lead us to point our finger at each other instead of the real cause of the problem.

Facts to Cool Tempers

The lower and middle classes constitute the overwhelming majority of the American people. We have the same needs whether we are male or female, white, black, brown, yellow, or red, young or old, educated or illiterate, Democrat or Republican. We all want a safe home and a good job. Given the polarization in the two-party system, we have been presented with two different ideologies. The Democrats tend to blame big business for our troubles, while the Republicans blame the government bureaucracy. The truth is that, as the American people, we can no longer depend upon multinational corporations or the federal government to provide us with our basic needs and a supportive environment. If we are to succeed in meeting our basic needs and in creating a better life for our children, we will have to depend upon ourselves and each other to come together and change the political economy from the ground up.

If we can quiet our emotions for a minute and think logically, we can begin to work ourselves out of this desperate situation. To begin with, only 63 million votes were cast for Trump out of America's 250 million adults. There were 73.5 million people who voted against Trump. These include the more than 65.8 million who cast a vote for Hillary Clinton, those who did not have the right to vote, and those who did not exercise that right for various reasons. Still others voted for third-party candidates.[766]

Secondly, Trump's base is not a monolith. There are two types of people who voted for Trump. First, there are those who support Trump primarily because they agree with the authoritarian, white, nationalist order he seeks to establish. These right-wing extremists tend to be racist xenophobes who want to reinforce the supremacy of white people. It is unlikely that these people will ever leave Trump. They represent his die-hard base.

On the other hand, there is a larger body of Trump supporters who voted for him because they believed he embodies a cleansing of those political policies that has decimated white working class and middle-class people forgotten by Republican and Democrat politicians over recent decades.

Those of us who seek unity may never be able to reach the extreme right wing nationalists for whom Trump is the messiah, but we may be able to gain the support of those who are wary of Trump and voted for him out of frustration with the past few decades of political and economic decline.

These people have been switching their votes between Democrats and Republicans over the years, seeking someone who would listen to them. They feel betrayed by the countless politicians who promised to bring decent jobs back to life, but who have consistently failed them. These people have swung back and forth, reacting to the failures of previous candidates to deliver. They are not "Independent" so much as they are just constantly disappointed.[767]

These people voted against Hillary Clinton because, as a longtime member of the Washington establishment, she portended more broken promises. They voted for Trump because he was the first politician in a generation to make a deliberate, authentic pitch for their support.

But now these exasperated people are already wary of President Trump. He is a perpetual liar. He has offended our allies, the media, blacks, Latinos, Muslims, our security forces, other politicians, and anyone else who speaks a word against him. He has appointed men who are misogynists, racists, and climate change deniers and whose goal is to gut environmental regulations. He has filled his administration with business elites who have profited from the foreclosure of American homes and the off-shoring of American businesses.

Most of the exasperated people who voted for Trump are savvy enough to distinguish between his grandstanding about saving a few Carrier factory[768] jobs and the hard reality of changing the economic base of this country to support the people. If Trump provides the wealthy with more tax cuts before raising the federal minimum wage, if Trump takes away Obamacare without replacing it with something better, if Trump fails to deliver on the jobs he promised, they will notice. They have adopted a "wait and see" approach.[769]

Herein lies the hope for Democrats. The party will never satisfy, nor will it seek to satisfy, the alt-right white supremacists, but there will be opportunities to win back the exasperated people. But, even if the Democrats win back these people and a Democrat wins the presidency in 2020 how will that matter to the American people. Obama did little to support the white working class in American who have been devastated by lost jobs.

The fact is that neither the Democrats nor the Republicans can fix the system enough to create full employment in America with jobs that pay a living wage. Those days have passed. Big Business is moving on. Their goal is to replace even more jobs with automation. What will the people do when these additional jobs are lost? The middle class is decimated and the federal government wants to cut any welfare funds to support their families while they are jobless.

Will Joe Biden, Bernie Sanders, or Elizabeth Warren fix the economy? Ever if we grant their sense of humanity and desire to help people, it is unlikely.

What Can Well-Intentioned Americans Do to Begin to Heal the Rift Between Us?

If we are to put America on a straight path, the first thing that we must do is to accept a universal morality. That is to say, we must begin to look at each other as human beings who want the same thing instead of as mortal enemies. Politicians have divided us into two great camps. The white middle and working-class vs those who fight for women's rights, minority rights, the rights of the poor and those who fight for the environment. This is a false divide that has polarized us as a society and created outright hostility among us as a people. There are strong feelings of alarm and moral outrage on both sides of the political divide. Many have reported getting into a fight with a friend or family member over the election.

We are hurting each other by our actions and we must become aware of what we are doing and begin to build bridges. The John Gottman Institute that studies interpersonal communication lists four behaviors that are sure to kill a relationship. These are criticism, contempt, defensiveness, and stonewalling. Of these, contempt is the worse. Examples of contempt are "sarcasm, cynicism, name-calling, eye-rolling, sneering, mockery, and hostile humor." This spirit of contempt has spilled over into how people commonly characterize those on the other side of the political fence.[770]

To reestablish our sense of community, we will need to become conscious of these actions on our part and stop them. It may be that the best policy in speaking to political adversaries is to avoid talk of politics altogether. This setting of healthy boundaries respects differences for the good of the relationship. Talking through these differences is a lot harder, and requires a good deal of moral maturity on the part of both partners. Those who do not possess that maturity, sensitivity, and sophisticated communication skills may need to just keep quiet for the time being.

If you need to speak to someone close to you who has taken a political opposite position, you have to speak in a way that is not condemning, disrespectful, or degrading. The goal is not to get the other to agree with your position, rather it is to learn to speak with each other even though there is strong disagreement between you.

We all know that when we feel anger or anxiety, two strong feelings that this election has brought up, our brains go into alarm-mode, making us cling to our beliefs, doubling-down on them, shutting ourselves off to the other.[771] Emotions speak louder than reason.

Your conversation should not be a debate wherein each side becomes more entrenched and polarized. Acceptance of each other can only happen in an atmosphere where both people feel safe, respected, valued, and understood. This is hard to do, because it means both have to manage their biological reactivity. Scientists have discovered by studying the brain that "When people [are] being challenged, they are less likely to change their minds." Our brains go into defense mode, shutting down any willingness to accept counter arguments. Even people who believed they are open-minded automatically push back on information with which they disagree.

If we are biologically wired to resist opposing political views, is there any prospect for a peaceful future? University of Southern California neuro-scientist, Jonas Kaplan, who studies the brain faced with opposing ideas, said that he found a few brains that slightly showed more openness to change.

He further explained, "Maybe that is a sign of hope, a crack in the door there a little bit. But I do think that is very difficult for us to change our minds about these things that are so important to us and that define us."[772]

While the struggle to be open-minded is inhibited by the hard-wiring in our brain, if our goal is to come together this is the only way to do it. The alternative is to continue a diet of rage, resentment, and contempt fed to us through our favorite liberal or conservative news outlet. The result will be a continued polarization, moving us further away from each other, fostering fear, anger, and alienation.

In attempting to create unity in our communities, we might learn a valuable lesson from Daryl Davis. Davis is a black musician who has successfully convinced Ku Klux Klan members to defect from the organization. He has spoken with hundreds of white supremacists and due to his work, a couple dozen people have left the organization, including at least two prominent figures in senior leadership positions.[773]

If Davis can persuade many klansmen to defect from their hate group, certainly he can help America bridge its political divide.

His belief is that "when you are actively learning about someone else you are passively teaching them about yourself." In listening to his most bitter enemies, Davis heard words and ideas that chilled him to the bone—yet he found that by listening and conversing he could change their minds. Some men even handed over their Klan garb to him.

Davis said that "every racist that I know voted for Donald Trump," However," he added, "that does not mean that everybody who voted for Donald Trump is a racist. There are plenty of people, including good friends of mine, who are not racist, and who voted for Trump. A lot of people wanted a change from what they were accustom to for the last decades … they wanted a change of the status quo, a changing of the guard. And they were willing to overlook his misogyny, his racist or bigoted comments. They just wanted that change. They are not racist people.

He attributes the racism to a campaign focused on fear of outsiders. "They got the most powerful man in the world to say the exact same thing that they've been saying for decades. For over a century," he said. "You know they're going to vote for him."

Here is Davis' advice for talking with those who emotionally oppose your point of view:

The Dos:
- "Gather your information. Be as familiar with the other person's position as you are with your own. You might hear things that frighten you or make you angry or make you sad or hurt you. But these are only words. And you expect that person to have an opposing point of view. That's what you're looking for. To find out why they think that way.
- "Invite them to have a conversation, not to debate. You say, I want to understand why you feel the way you feel. I want you to convince me that I need to change my way of thinking. And I appreciate your sharing your views. That's what people want. They want to be heard. They want to be able to speak their mind freely without fear of retaliation or somebody beating them over the head for their views or ramming their own views down the person's throat. So give them that."

- "Look for commonalities. You can find something in five minutes, even with your worst enemy. And build on those. If the issue is race, change the topic, say 'how do you feel about all these drugs on the street?' Say, 'I think the law needs to crack down on things that people can get addicted to very easily and it's destroying our society.' So you say, 'Well yeah, I agree 100 percent.' So now I see that you want what I want, that drugs are affecting your family the same way they affect my family, so now we're in agreement. So let's focus on that. As we focus more and more and find more things in common, things we have in contrast, such as skin color, matter less and less."

- "When two enemies are talking they're not fighting. They might be yelling and screaming or disagreeing or beating their fists on the table to drive home a point but at least they're talking. It's when the talking ceases that the ground becomes fertile for violence. So you want to keep the conversation going. And the more you keep the conversation going, the more commonalities you will eventually find. When you can't talk to one another you're laying the ground work for trouble."

- "Patience is a virtue. My method worked for me, because I've taken the time and had the patience to learn about the other side. I've read tons of material on the Klan, on the neo-Nazis, on white supremacy, on black supremacy. So I know how the mentality works. And when I go in there I tend to be a little more disarming than someone who does not have that knowledge."

- "I know there comes a point in time when you say, okay, enough time, now things have got to change . . . if you need to legislate something or force something, then fine, you have those tools available. That's why we have lawmakers. But the day the law changed to when black people could ride in the front of the bus, or not have to give up their seat, the day that law changed did not necessarily change the minds of the white riders.

You can legislate behavior but you cannot legislate belief. Patience is what it takes. But patience doesn't mean sitting around on your butt waiting for something to happen. Be proactive. And don't just sit around and talk with your friends who believe the way you do. Invite other people who have differences of opinion."

And the Don'ts:
- "You can become argumentative but don't become condescending. Don't become insulting. You will also hear things that are their opinions that they're going to put out as facts. And you should counter that and correct that. But don't do it in a manner that is insulting or condescending because you know they're wrong, and you're going to beat them over the head for being wrong. Show them the data, or tell them you'll get it, or if they really believe it, say, I know you're wrong, but if you think you're right then bring me the data."
- "Don't explain somebody else's movement. Let them explain it. And then address the points they have defined. There will be key points that you know you can counter and shut down, but let them finish, give them a little more rope. Say, I hear what you're saying but I'm not there yet. I need more clarification from you. You said, blah blah blah. Can you give me more facts on why I should accept that? And they'll come out with these points. Then go to the points that they made. Quote their words and shut down their factual mistakes."[774]

Davis concludes that for Trump opponents, the challenge is not converting the Klansmen who support him. It is helping others see the most toxic elements of his coalition and agenda. Having truth on one's side is an advantage, but only for those who know how to exploit it. The approach Trump opponents used in 2016 failed; perhaps it is time for something new.[775]

For liberals, who believe they are correct in their views one hundred percent of the time and hate Donald Trump, consider this. He has done some good things. For example, he killed the Trans-Pacific Partnership (TPP)[776] and prevented our country from losing its sovereignty to the multinational corporations. Why did not any liberal news outlets thank Donald Trump for this great accomplishment? Ivanka Trump also spoke out against his administration's attack on the LGBTQ community. We did not see anyone thanking her for her intervention.

Of course, the Republicans went bonkers with Trump's proposal. *The New York Daily News* featured a photograph of Trump with the words, "SOAK THE RICH."[777] Conservative experts at the time bashed Trump's plan as economically and politically unviable. The liberals were surprisingly silent.

Many Americans, not understanding the implications of Trump's proposal and being abandoned by the Democrat party on this issue, seemed to think it was a trick of some sort, or a miscalculation that would undermine the favorable effects of trickle-down economics. Many considered it an affront to the American tradition of unfettered economic liberty. Whatever the case, Trump's bid failed to gain traction, resulting in his exploratory committee closing shop after a few months.

In 2011, talk show host George Stephanopoulos asked Trump if he still supported that tax, and Trump said it was no longer viable. "Unfortunately, the world has changed, today you can't do it. Today, and I'm very strongly against tax increases."[778]

Once elected, of course, Trump supported a tax cut for the very elite whom he was willing to tax in his early days. In the meantime, the major political parties in America are crafting their plans to benefit their side at the expense of the other. They do not see that their protracted and intense warfare is moving the country toward a politically unmanageable condition and away from the shared public good. Each side stoops to whatever political maneuvers will damage the reputation or prospects of the other. The growing likelihood is that political legitimacy will continue to erode in this country. In the rising political antipathy, almost anything can happen. What happens when people tire of working together to solve problems?

National Security

One of the greatest examples of how automation and artificial intelligence have infiltrated American life is the vast expansion of the federal intelligence agencies and their commandeering of troves of information on every American citizen. This information was once considered personal and thereby guaranteed against undue search and seizure by the US Constitution.

In Chapter Three, we discussed how the Bush administration's reaction to 9/11 was to create the Homeland Security Administration and empower it with the Patriot Act and the declaration of a "State of National Emergency." After 9/11, we watched as the Bush administration systematically moved to eliminate our rights to privacy in the name of national security. We also saw how the Obama administration forwarded and strengthened this movement to allow the government to spy on American citizens and also created the legal defense for the elimination of all human and civil rights were the government to declare a State of Emergency.

Much of the US public's concern about post-September 11 policies has focused on the government's new surveillance powers, including the ability to track everyone's movement and conversations from our cell phones and emails. The government can now look at our business records, health records, purchases, who are friends are, how we spend our time, where we go, at what times we are home, and other personal data of individual Americans even if there is no suspicion of complicity with terrorism.

While the Bush and Obama administrations argue that the need to wage an all-out "war against terrorism" justifies their conduct, critics raised concerns that civil liberties are being sacrificed for little benefit in national security.

The federal government's actions against the American people and the rule of law are particularly troubling because it is hard to foresee an endpoint to the terrorist danger that the government insists warrants its actions. As the government continues its rampant colonization of other country's labor and resources, it is unlikely that global terrorism will be defeated in the foreseeable future. Does the US government intend to spy on us and hold untried detainees for the rest of our lives?

US anti-terrorism policies directly violate principles woven into our political and legal structure. They also contradict international human rights principles. Human rights law recognizes that individual freedom should not be left to the unfettered whim of rulers. To ensure restraints on the arbitrary or wrongful use of a state's power to detain people, the International Covenant on Civil and Political Rights (ICCPR), to which the United States is a party, requires that the courts—not the executive branch—decide the legality of detention. The ICCPR also establishes specific requirements for court proceedings where a person's liberty is at stake, including that the proceedings be public. Even if there were to be a formally declared state of emergency, restrictions on the right to liberty must be "limited to the extent strictly required by the exigencies of the situation."

Justice cannot exist without respect for human rights. This is true in cases regarding US citizens or prisoners of war. The Bush administration's assault on "Arab terrorists" for 9/11 has had a devastating effect on the psyche of the average American, who now believes that every Arab and every Muslim immigrant is their enemy. Bush and Obama have kept up this charade while protecting the multinational military industrial complex that has fostered the wars in the Middle East, which have led to the emigration of millions of innocent people, only a tiny percentage of whom were allowed in the United States.[779]

The war on justice that began with the Bush anti-terrorism campaign began when the government rounded up over seven hundred individuals from Afghanistan and imprisoned them without rights in a US naval base at Guantanamo Bay in Cuba. Guantanamo was made into a legal no man's land where detainees were initially held first in cages. They were not allowed any communication with the outside world. The Red Cross was allowed to visit the detainees, but were prevented from reporting on their condition. One hundred and twenty detainees had attempted suicide, many after being tortured.[780] The media was not allowed to speak with the detainees nor to even see them except from a distance.

While the Bush administration claimed all those sent to Guantanamo were hardened fighters and terrorists, the "worst of the worst," other US officials told journalists that at least some of those sent to Guantanamo had little or no connection to the US war in Afghanistan. The Guantanamo detainees included very old men and minors, including three children between thirteen and fifteen.

The administration insists that the laws of war gave it unfettered authority to hold combatants as long as the war continued. It argued that the "war" was against terrorism, not the conflict in Afghanistan during which most of the Guantanamo detainees were picked up. In doing so, the Bush administration ignored the Geneva Conventions and the longstanding US military practice which provided that captured combatants be treated as prisoners of war unless and until a "competent tribunal" determines otherwise.

The Bush administration arbitrarily decided that no person apprehended in Afghanistan was entitled to prisoner-of-war status. The United States was thus improperly holding, without charges or trial, soldiers, civilians mistakenly detained, and terrorist suspects arrested outside of Afghanistan who should be prosecuted by civilian courts.

The Bush administration's disregard for judicial review, its use of executive fiat, and its secretive nature made the American people eventually question its legitimacy. Scrutiny by the judiciary, Congress, and the public at large are crucial to prevent the executive branch from warping fundamental rights beyond recognition.[781]

President Obama ran for election on the campaign promise that, if elected, he would close Guantanamo because of its inhumanity and its disregard for American justice. After two terms, Guantanamo continued to exist. Under President Trump, the detention camp for alleged terrorists is now an "enduring mission," and the Pentagon is making plans to keep the center open another twenty-five years.[782]

We saw in Chapter Three how the American government used the War on Terror to continue the business of the military-industrial complex and provide it with a new enemy after the fall of the Soviet Union.[783] We also saw how the Bush and Obama administrations used the War on Terror to set up a comprehensive spy network across the country that centralized data on every American citizen. Our constitutional right to privacy was eliminated. Key to the operation of this spy network was the Bush administration's declaration of the "State of National Emergency" on September 14, 2001.

Combined with the "Authorization for Use of Military Force," this declaration gave the executive branch dictatorial powers, allowed for the invasion and occupation of Iraq (which had nothing to do with 9/11), and bypassed the Geneva Conventions to declare foreign fighters as "enemy combatants," who the administration now tortured and held indefinitely.

The government pumped billions of dollars into new spy centers and gave the FBI "National Security Letters" that allowed them to go after US citizens for any reason, even if there was no suspicion of criminal activity. These "letters" were served on communications service providers like phone companies and ISPs to allow the FBI to secretly demand data about ordinary American citizens' private communications and Internet activity without any meaningful oversight or prior judicial review. Not surprising, those served were subject to a gag order that forbade them from ever revealing the letters' existence to their coworkers, to their friends, or even to their family members, much less the public.[784]

The FBI's systemic abuse of this power has been documented both by a Department of Justice investigation and in documents obtained by the Electronic Frontier Foundation, a consumer watchdog, through a Freedom of Information Act request.[785]

The Department of Justice investigation revealed that the FBI issued almost two hundred thousand national security letters from 2003 through 2006.[786]

Jameel Jaffer, national security director at the American Civil Liberties Union, said that, "The fact that these [National Security Letters] are being used against US citizens and are being used so aggressively, should call into question the claim that these powers are about terrorists and not just about collecting information on all kinds of people."[787] In short, the Bush administration turned the power of the National Security Administration (NSA) against the American people. While the Bush administration claimed that its powers to spy on the American people would only be temporary while the "terrorist threat" was being neutralized, the federal government would never let go of such dictatorial power once it had been gained. It should come as no surprise, therefore, that on September 4, 2016, nearing the end of his second term, Obama extended the 9/11 "Emergency" War on Terror powers, even though Al Qaeda was no longer even a target.[788] The war on terror and the dismantling of human rights has become just another fact of life.[789]

The Trump administration has continued to foster spying on the American people. In July, 2018 the American Civil Liberties Union (ACLU) sued the Trump administration for refusing to make public an important report from the Privacy and Civil Liberties Oversight Board, which was created by Congress to help ensure that national security laws and programs do not infringe on individual rights.

In addition to keeping the report secret, the Trump administration undermined the Privacy and Civil Liberties Oversight Board's proper functioning by refusing to fill vacancies on the Board thus preventing it from doing much of its work to investigate government overreach.[790]

Under Trump, the government had also compelled Apple and Facebook to hand over the personal information of users who were mass arrested at protests against the inauguration of Donald Trump in Washington, DC. The tech giants complied with the data-mining requests, amid mounting concerns over the heavy-handed crackdown against the more than two hundred people detained on January 20, among them journalists, legal observers, and medics.

Evan Greer, the campaign director for Fight for the Future, told AlterNet who released the story, "This trend started long before Trump and seems to be escalating and growing in scale now. This is part of an increasing trend of law enforcement attempting to turn the internet, instead of technology for freedom, into technology for control."[791] More than two hundred of those picked up in the sweep at the anti-fascist, anti-capitalist bloc have been charged with "felony riot," a severe charge which carry penalties of up to ten years in prison and a twenty-five thousand dollar fine. Because the arrests took place in Washington, D.C., the cases are being prosecuted by the US Attorney's Office for the District of Columbia, which is directly accountable to the Department of Justice, at the time overseen by Jeff Sessions.

Mark Goldstone, a National Lawyers Guild-affiliated attorney, who represented numerous defendants in the case, told AlterNet that "several" of his clients have been contacted by Facebook and Apple and informed that their personal information has been requested by law enforcement. In their communication, Apple told the defendants that "Apple will be producing the requested data in a timely manner as required by the legal process."⁷⁹² So now we have reached a stage of government oppression where you cannot legally protest without law enforcement using your on-line records to build a case against you and determining just how punitive that case should be. This situation indicates how ridiculous it is to blame the government or the multinational corporations alone for the problems of the American people. They are simply different hands of the same capitalist class and they work together whenever necessary to control the people.

The "Emergency" powers provided the NSA direct access to your Facebook, email, and Skype accounts and continues to mine your data even as you read this. Both the National Security Agency and the Federal Bureau of Investigation have been secretly mining data directly from the servers of at least nine top US-based technology companies, according to *The Washington Post*.⁷⁹³ These nine technology companies included Microsoft, Yahoo, Google, Facebook, AOL, Skype, YouTube, Apple, and the video chat room community PalTalk. Apparently Dropbox is slated to be the next one added to the list.⁷⁹⁴

Citing a leaked presentation intended for only senior analysts within the NSA's Signals Intelligence Directorate, *The Washington Post* said the agency was spying on American citizens by accessing their on-line data since 2007 under a highly-classified program dubbed "PRISM."⁸⁰⁴

PRISM is an intelligence gathering system between Australia, Canada, New Zealand, the U.K., and the US, which monitors almost anything carried over telephone wires and satellite services, as well as datacenters and cloud services.

The kind of content being extracted from the central servers at these tech companies include audio, video, photos, e-mails, documents, and connection logs. According to the report, the data was extracted to allow the government to track a person's movements and contacts over time. By giving this power to the NSA, the government has permitted an agency whose mission is foreign intelligence, to reach deep inside American companies that host hundreds of millions of American-held accounts on American soil.

The federal government has given itself unlimited power to access what it wants, when it wants, and for whatever reason it wants from the American people in direct opposition to Article 4 of our nation's Bill of Rights, which reads:

> The right of the people to be secure in their persons, houses, papers, and effects, against unreasonable searches and seizures, shall not be violated, and no Warrants shall issue, but upon probable cause, supported by Oath or affirmation, and particularly describing the place to be searched, and the persons or things to be seized.[795]

Thanks to Edward Snowden who leaked the NSA slide presentation to *The Washington Post*, the American people now understand the massive surveillance our government has undertaken against us. The scope of their spying affects every single US citizen and resident while in the country and abroad. While many Americans offhandedly may dismiss concern about their loss of rights, believing they have "nothing to hide" once they think about it, not many would let a complete stranger, who may wish them ill, rifle through their bank statements, emails, photos, and passwords to all their accounts looking for something that they might want to use against them.[796]

As the federal government continues to beat the drum against "Muslim terrorism," their excuse for spying becomes a mantra, which supersedes any other logic or reason. Persistent mass surveillance by the US government on the American people becomes inevitable, creating a culture of fear and a loss of faith in our government. This spying has alienated most Americans, whether on the Left or the Right politically and has made millions of Americans believe that the federal government no longer acts in our best interest. National security has become synonymous with loss of rights and freedoms. It is moving us away from democracy and down the path to totalitarianism.

Corporate Spying on US Citizens

The mass communication network that has been developed from the internet and its link to cell phones and smart appliances has created an environment where not only the government but big business is also spying on the American people.

When someone knows where we are at every moment, how long we stay in a location, who we meet with, who our friends are, what we buy, what our health records say, where we shop, where we work, where we live, where we hang out, where we vacation, how much money we make and how much money we owe, that someone owns us.

The American people are unconscious of what lies ahead. What will the federal government and the multinational corporations do with this information that they are so carefully compiling on us now that they can predict each of our behaviors?

For more than a decade, private investigators have been able to search public and nonpublic records, known addresses, motor vehicle records, marriage licenses, and birth certificates, etc., and condense them into comprehensive reports costing as little as ten dollars. But now they can combine that information with the kinds of things business marketers know about us, such as which politicians we donate to, what we spend on groceries, where we ate last night, who we hang out with, etc., to create an in-depth portrait of us and predict our behavior.

Interactive Data Intelligence (IDI), a year-old company in the so-called data-fusion business, is the first to centralize all that data and build profiles of individuals for corporate clients.[797] Their slogan is "We transform data into intelligence." The company's database service combines public records with purchasing, demographic, and behavioral data. Chief Executive Officer Derek Dubner says the system has built a profile on every American adult, including young people. "We have data on that twenty-one year-old who's living at home with mom and dad," he says.[798]

The company's personal profiles include all known addresses, phone numbers, and e-mail addresses; every piece of property ever bought or sold, plus related mortgages; past and present vehicles owned; criminal citations from speeding tickets on up; voter registration; hunting permits; and names and phone numbers of neighbors. The reports also include photos of cars taken by private companies using automated license plate readers, billions of snapshots tagged with GPS coordinates and time stamps to help corporations survey people.

IDI also runs two coupon websites, allamericansavings.com and samplesandsavings.com, that collect purchasing and behavioral data. The site asks for your e-mail address, birthday, and home address, all of which can be linked to your personal profile. The site also asks if you suffered from arthritis, asthma, diabetes, or depression.

Roger Kay, president of Endpoint Technologies Associates, a consulting company in the industry says, "The cloud never forgets, and imperfect pictures of you composed from your data profile are carefully filled in over time."

Dubner, the CEO of IDI, tells Americans that we have little to fear. His information is used only for good purposes like locating a missing person and nabbing a fraud or terrorism suspect. Hmm. Besides promoting its databases to big-name private investigator firms like Kroll and Control, it also approaches law firms, debt collectors, government agencies, and consumer marketers. Nothing to worry about there. In December, 2016, IDI bought out Fluent, a marketing profiler with one hundred and twenty million profiles of US citizens.

Steve Rambam, the private investigator who hosts *Nowhere to Hide* on the Discovery channel, says, "You may not know what you do on a regular basis, but I know. I know its Thursday, you haven't eaten Chinese food in two weeks, and I know you're due."[799]

But companies like IDI are not the only invaders of our privacy. Take a company like Amazon that most of us use. According to Mike Adams, who runs a popular right-wing website called the Health Ranger, "Amazon isn't just a massive retailer; it's also a dangerous spy machine that collects detailed profiles of your most private thoughts, fetishes, and conversations."[800]

Adams uses the example of Amazon ECHO to prove his point. ECHO, which retails for $179.99, is a hands-free speaker you control with your voice. According to the advertising, ECHO:

- Plays all your music from Amazon Music, Spotify, Pandora, iHeart Radio, Tune In, and more using just your voice;
- Fills the room with immersive, 360° omni-directional audio;
- Allows hands-free convenience with voice-control;
- Hears you from across the room with far-field voice recognition, even while music is playing;
- Answers questions, reads audiobooks and the news,

reports traffic and weather, gives info on local businesses, provides sports scores and schedules, and more using the Alexa Voice Service;
- Controls lights, switches, and thermostats with compatible WeMo, Philips Hue, Samsung SmartThings, Wink, Insteon, Nest, and ecobee smart home devices; and
- Always getting smarter and adding new features, plus thousands of skills like Uber, Domino's, and more.[801]

According to Adams, this device is constantly listening to your most private conversations and processing your voice by uploading segments of audio to Amazon.com servers. He claims that law enforcement agencies have already sought to use audio recordings from ECHO devices to incriminate individuals for words they uttered in their own private homes. He is not the only one to say this. Forbes magazine also wrote an article about police approaching Amazon to use information gained from ECHO.[802]

According to Cris Thomas, a respected security expert and spokesperson for Tenable Network Security, one of the privacy risks of IoT devices is that they are always listening." An IoT device refers to "Internet of Things" devices that allow machines to be hooked up to the internet and used to collect information on you. Such devices range from gas meters to television sets to devices like ECHO. "Owning an Amazon ECHO device, according to Adams, is like planting a law enforcement bug in your own home . . . that YOU pay for!"

The thing that gives Adams' words a reason to consider is that Amazon is collecting information on you from each of its services and combining them to build a profile. Kindle records what books and authors you read, including which text passages you highlight in those books. Amazon FIRE hears your voice and uploads recordings to Amazon servers. They also track and record all your preferences in films, television shows, viewing times, and title ratings. Amazon MUSIC is also used to build your profile.

The Amazon.com website itself builds a psychological profile of your interests and demographics based on your purchase history. We have seen how this information is used to promote "suggested" products but most of us do not know that our psychological profile is being accumulated on Amazon's servers.[803]

Not only are our whereabouts, habits, and physical actions being stored by governments and corporations, but with companies like Amazon, our minds are also being profiled and the information stored. This moves us another giant step away from democracy and into a totalitarian system. A dictator would know immediately who his detractors were and where to round them up. No problem.

Micro Chipping People

Another aspect of the spy culture now developing is called "chipping." In the near future, it may be that chips will be embedded into our bodies and tracked by the internet. Someday we might all be *required* to be implanted with a tiny microchip under our skin so that we can be constantly tracked by government and business. In fact, itvis already happening.

Just recently, State Senator Becky Harris, a Republican representing Las Vegas, presented a bill prohibiting the micro-chipping of human beings on Monday, Feb. 13, 2017 to the Senate Judiciary Committee.[804]

The senator said that the bill is not as far-fetched as it might seem, because it is already happening in some places around the world. She said the sales of "radio frequency identifiers" are escalating around the world. A company in Australia called New Fusion has already sold more than 10,000 implantable chips.[805] These chips each have a unique number, like a social security number, that can read information silently by radio waves.

The Wall Street Journal has reported an estimated thirty thousand to fifty thousand chips have been sold globally.

Harris said the technology is also used by companies in Belgium and Sweden to identify employees. "It's done under the idea to unlock doors or use copy machines or maybe pay for lunch by using your hand," she said.

There are obviously glaring ethical questions about "chipping" people. For example, who owns the chip or the information contained on it and how does someone get "de-chipped" if they are no longer employed by the company that required it. Could the chip be hacked to control someone or stalk them.

Harris said the Nevada bill is modeled after legislation passed by at least ten other states that are concerned about this troublesome development.

Another frightening thing about these chips is that school administrations have begun to use them on school children. At present, they only want to put them on the student ID's to track them, but what happens down the road when an administrator argues that it is less expensive and required less maintenance to put the chip directly into the child.

Dr. Katherine Albrecht, coauthor of the book, "Spychips: How Major Corporations and Government Plan to Track Your Every Purchase and Watch Your Every Move," says, "Schools, of all places, should be teaching children how to participate in a free democratic society, not conditioning them to be tracked like cattle." She warned that school districts, "planning to use RFID should brace themselves for a parent backlash, protests, and lawsuits." [806] Hopefully, she is correct.

Certainly, some legitimate uses of the technology can be identified. People are already putting chips in their pets to find them if they get lost. Those who promote the technology, say the chips could be used to track Alzheimer patients who get lost, or downed pilots during war.[807]

But what happens if and when people become pressured by corporations or the government to be 'chipped.' What if they cannot get a job with a multinational corporation or the federal government without being chipped. Certainly, such a device comes dangerously close to infringing on our personal privacy and democratic liberties.

One's concern about RFID devices gains additional credence when we consider that Adam Savage of Myth Busters had an agreement with the Discovery Channel to investigate the downside of these devices when lawyers from Texas Instruments, along with the chief legal councils for American Express, Visa, Discover, and others, forbade the Discovery Channel from doing such an episode. The Discovery Channel would have lost these companies as advertisers if they disobeyed.[808]

Micro Chipping Clothes

Another invasion of privacy is the effort by clothing manufacturers to put chips in our clothing. While not as invasive as putting chips in our bodies, they serve the same purpose of being able to track our every move and establish information about our daily patterns.

In an article published in 2006, entitled "Spychipped Levi's Brand Jeans Hit the US," it was revealed that Levi Strauss confirmed putting RFID chips in its clothing, but refused to identify the manufacturing location where they were "testing" their new jeans.[809]

At the time, over forty of the world's leading privacy and civil liberties organizations had called for a moratorium on chipping individual consumer items because the technology could be used to track people without their knowledge or consent.

They warned that these chips could be used to track people in public places like shopping malls, sports arenas, libraries, elevators, and even restrooms. By means of these chips, the government or corporations could monitor your every move, from where you do your shopping, which brands you purchase, whether you take your prescribed medication, which schools your children attend, or even right down to what amount of toilet paper you use while in the restroom wearing your RFID-embedded jeans.[810]

Fast forward to 2016 and we have an article in Fashionista entitled, "Why Luxury Brands Are Putting Microchips in Your Clothes and Accessories."[811] Can you guess what reason these manufacturers are using to justify their invasion of privacy? They say it is to help prevent counterfeiting, that is "knock-offs." Each chip contains a unique ID that will allow buyers to scan and authenticate their goods via their smartphones and identify if the branded coat they have just bought is a fake.

Of course, the chips can be deactivated at the point of sale, but for the large brands this would not be in their interests. In Europe, where data privacy laws are stricter, the retailer has to tell the client if they are providing a product with an RFID chip and serial number. In the US, some state laws prohibit the surreptitious scanning of RFID chips in ID cards, but nothing requires a retailer to disclose chips that are embedded in the products they sell.

It is not hard to imagine a day in which everything from our deodorant to the dollar bills in our wallets will be embedded with microchips. And the technology will only get more sophisticated over time. Last year, for example, researchers at Nottingham Trent University in the UK unveiled a prototype for embedding RFID chips into yarns.[812] They have recently launched a company, Advanced E-Textiles Ltd, to bring it to market.

Is this the future that we really want for our children? Are we helpless to prevent it? Are there now too many things going wrong at the same time that we have become immobilized?

Immigrants and Refugees

As the section above on National Origins demonstrates, the United States has always been a country built by immigrants. People from every continent have come to the shores of America and created a new life for themselves and their families. Today, however, the subject of immigration has become one of the most contentious and polarizing issues that we face as a nation. What changed?

Certainly, the immigration issue transcends our national boundary. Both Europe and the Middle East are also reeling from massive influxes of refugees coming out of the seven war-torn countries of that region. Aside from these refugees, the US-led invasion of these Middle Eastern countries also massacred millions of people and destroyed the buildings, infrastructure and the social order of these countries.

The refugee problem in the Middle East is a direct result of US expansionism. As the Middle East turned into hell on earth, six million people left Afghanistan, two million fled Iraq, six hundred thousand fled Kuwait, one million left Libya, and a staggering eleven million refugees have left Syria. Another three hundred thousand people have already fled the conflict in Yemen. These numbers do not include the tens of millions of people who have been displaced within these war-torn countries, but who remained because they do not want to leave their homeland.

As of January 2017, the vast majority of the 4.9 million Syrians who had registered as refugees in another country were in first-asylum countries such as Turkey, Lebanon, Jordan, and Iraq. Only a small fraction were able to find employment and resettle there. Faced with this dim prospect and anxious to establish new lives, nearly 900,000 Syrians headed to Europe and filed asylum claims to enter countries there.

As the hundreds of thousands of refugees poured out of the Middle East, they entered Greece and the countries of Eastern Europe where they received a cold shoulder. Faced with police brutality, fences, and walls, and other signs that they were not welcomed, they tried every tactic to enter the countries of Western Europe, where they initially found a warmer reception, but as their numbers continued to grow and the potential that millions more would come, the people of Western Europe panicked. In the United States, whose armed invasion had caused the mass exodus in the first place, only a few refugees were accepted because the right-wing politicians became apoplectic with the idea that any refugee entering the country was a potential terrorist come to take revenge. As Europe and North American countries came face to face with the consequences of their deeds, the population of these nations split between those who desired to assist the refugees and those who wanted to shut them out at all costs. This process of polarization continues, creating more extreme right wing and left-wing responses even as the conditions of the refugees worsen.

Western Reaction to the Mass Migration

In 2015, Europe opened its arms to over a million Middle East refugees, certainly a huge number but small compared to the countries in the Middle East and Africa that took in the bulk of the people escaping their war-ravaged homelands. As the chart below demonstrates the largest percentage of refugees to Europe came from Syria, Afghanistan, and then Iraq.[813]

Germany, alone processed over 500,000d applications in 2015. But while Germany processed the most asylum applications, it was Hungary that had the highest number in proportion to its population, despite having closed its border with Croatia in an attempt to stop the flow in October. Nearly 1,800 refugees per 100,000 of Hungary's local population claimed asylum in 2015. Sweden followed close behind with 1,667 per 100,000. The figure for Germany was 587 and for the UK it was only 60 applications for every 100,000 residents.[814]

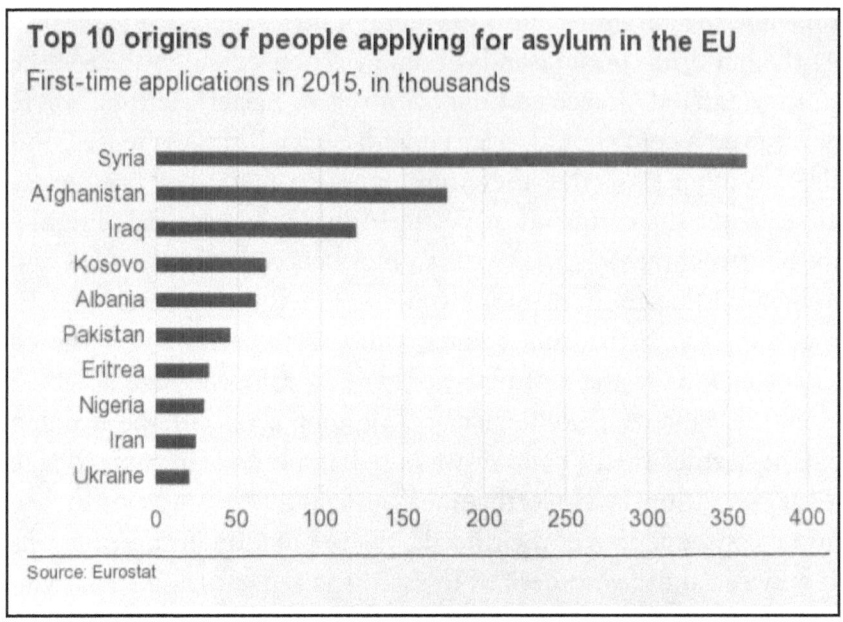

Fig. 5-20: Top Ten Origins of People Applying for Asylum in the EU

As the refugees poured out of the Middle East, moving westward, many were initially stopped in Turkey where the US and Europe had paid this country to establish refugee camps in an effort to stem the flow into their own countries. Faced with a life in refugee camps, many people risked their lives and the lives of their children in dangerous journeys across the Aegean Sea in dinghies to get to Greece or across the Mediterranean to get to Italy and Spain.

Many more attempted to cross by land, but were stopped by the Eastern European countries. The outpouring did not stop in the following year, 2016. At first, the Western Europeans opened their arms to the refugees in a gesture of humanity, realizing that the majority were women and children, but as the flood of people continued, a negative reaction began to boil over in these countries. A right-wing populist movement took to the streets in protest to the influx of refugees and this gave rise to right-wing demagogues who gained popularity in Greece, Germany, Italy, France, and England. As a direct result of the refugee crisis, England withdrew from the European Union and extreme nationalists came close to winning national elections in Germany and France. In the United States, Donald Trump became president by pandering to racist, xenophobic, and Islamophobic sentiments that had already been stimulated during the Obama administration by right wing media outlets like Breitbart and Fox News.

In March 2016, as Europeans began to panic over the endless wave of war refugees coming to its shores, the European Union tried to make a more permanent deal with Turkey. If Turkey would agree to take back all the refugees that were sitting in Greek containment camps, they would give Turkey three billion Euros and agree to "re-energise" talks on admitting Turkey to the European Union. If admitted, this would allow Turks to travel freely and settle in Europe.

The idea behind the EU proposal was that Turkey would become the holding tank for refugees wanting to get into Europe and for every refugee sent back to Turkey from Greece, Turkey would send one refugee to Europe to be processed and accepted. It was called the "One in, one out" plan.[815] The number of refugees that would be accepted back into Europe, however, would be capped at seventy-two thousand per year. Germany would take the lion's share of Syrians, and participation from other EU countries would be on a voluntary basis. At the time there were about forty-five thousand people trapped in Greece alone, including fourteen thousand who were living in squalid conditions near the Greek-Macedonian border at Idomeni where they were barred from travelling to central and northern Europe.

In order for the plan to succeed, it required that the Macedonian border with Greece be sealed to prevent refugees from crossing into Greece over land. In the early 90s, following the collapse of the dictatorship in Albania, at least two hundred and fifty thousand Albanians made the perilous journey over the mountainous border with Greece. Now, twenty-five years later, war refugees have re-opened the smuggling route. There was also the Greek-Bulgarian border, which was crossed by about thirty thousand people in 2015, despite the construction of a fence along parts of its length.[816]

Nonetheless, the European Union plan provided a beacon of hope for some. It would reduce the chaos in the Aegean Sea where thousands of people had already died in dinghies and other boats too heavily laden to make the voyage from Turkey to Greece. The plan would ensure that

Europe lived up to its humanitarian obligations and the refugees from Syria, while being discouraged from trying to get there haphazardly and illegally, could still have a future in Europe. While the European Union bureaucrats were busy drafting their plan to address the resettlement of refugees from Syria, Iraq, Afghanistan, etc., millions of refugees were facing their own desperate problems.

Greece

As 2016 dawned, Greece was Europe's most fragile economy, having been ravaged by six years of World Bank mandated austerity programs and record levels of unemployment. As the refugees poured in, Greece's coping strategies were severely strained. Despite their own suffering, the European Union administration gave Athens a three-month ultimatum to improve the way it processed arrivals and policed its borders, which stretched for nearly eighty-seven hundred miles, the longest in Europe. If it failed to do so, it would face suspension from the European passport-free zone. This would be catastrophic for Greece especially at a time that it was struggling to remain solvent as a nation. If Greece were to go bankrupt, the tens of thousands of refugees trapped in Greece would no longer have any access to even their most rudimentary basic needs.

The Greeks were smarting from the tongue lashing from the EU. Yannis Mouzalas, the minister for migration policy, told the *Observer*, "These flows are not Greece's fault even if, it is true, we have been slow to set up hotspots, and screening was not always what it should have been," he said. "It is Turkey that turns a blind eye to them coming here. It is Turkey that must stop them. Why is Greece guilty? Because it doesn't let them drown?"[817]

Turkey

In 2016, almost three million Syrian refugees were registered in Turkey. Emergency responses have understandably been inadequate. Disjointed policies and emotional political rhetoric did not help the situation. The refugees were faced with innumerable challenges, including learning the language and finding meaningful work, housing, and education. They also had to navigate an unfamiliar and complicated bureaucracy while remaining ever vigilant against exploitation by smugglers, hustlers, and human traffickers. Thousands of children had lost their parents to the wars and were endlessly preyed upon. The refugees' internal struggle was occurring at the same time that Turkey was going through a political upheaval that peaked with the July coup attempt and its aftermath which included mass arrests of thousands of Turks, which only deepened the refugees' sense of insecurity and perilous future.

Some people in Turkey also began to complain that refugees were taking available jobs and receiving social benefits. Right-wing reactionaries raised their voices against the potential for increased crime and terror. Violence against refugees, although isolated, was downplayed in the media. The right-wing populist movement gained momentum when the president said citizenship would be granted to the refugees.

Because the refugees are overwhelmingly Sunni Arabs, internal Muslim politics has also been aggravated. Kurdish nationalists, liberals, secularists, and some Turkish nationalists held that the conservative Justice and Development Party of President Erdogan was using refugees to transform national identity, consolidate power, and reframe Turkey's role in the Middle East as being more Arab, Sunni, and hegemonic. The perception that refugees were a demographic threat and were pawns used by the ruling administration hindered and continues to hinder any constructive debate about the presence and future of the refugees in Turkey.[818]

In mid-March of 2017, the Turkish Deputy Prime Minister Numan Kurtulmus announced that the refugee plan between the European Union and Turkey was dead. The refugees were not responsible for this development. Rather, Turkey's refusal to participate any further in the EU plan had to do with the way that the EU was treating Turkey. The April referendum in which Turks would vote to expand the powers of the president was less than a month away and the president needed to muster his followers by taking a strong stand against Europe.

David Phillips, director of Columbia University's Program on Peacebuilding and Rights and author of *An Uncertain Ally: Turkey Under Erdogan's Dictatorship*, told Foreign Policy magazine that the deal was dead from day one because the EU never intended to implement visa-free travel for the Turks.

"Turkey's candidacy for the EU was never a realistic prospect given European attitudes towards Turkey. The European Parliament suspended negotiations in response to Turkey's egregious human rights abuses after the failed coup of July 15. There is zero chance of this turning around in the near term," Phillips said.[819]

According to Mujtaba Rahman, the head of European analysis at Eurasia Group, a risk consultancy firm, "If Turkey fails to deliver, Europe's next course of action will be to turn Greece into a de facto refugee camp by sealing the border on the Macedonia side."[820]

The Life of Refugees

While the host countries confront the internal and international problems resulting from the tsunami of people pouring out of the war-ravaged countries of the Middle East, the refugees themselves face a hellish life, contained in border camps and subject to every kind of abuse as they face a dangerous and uncertain future.

A natural question to ask is, "How do they meet their basic needs, having left their homes and all their possessions and now find themselves living in tents without employment?" The answer is "With great difficulty."

To begin with, access to medical care is extremely limited. According to Doctors Without Borders, treatment for chronic diseases such as asthma, diabetes, hypertension, and cardiovascular disease are a major concern because the cost of the necessary drugs is out of reach for many. Hospitals are also too expensive.

Most refugees, whether officially registered or not, are housed in substandard structures, which include inadequate collective shelters, farms, garages, unfinished buildings, and old schools that provide little protection against the elements. For those who had enough money to rent houses, they now risk eviction because they cannot afford to pay the rent.

Many refugee camps have no resources that would allow them to send their children to school. It is a terrible experience in itself to see one's children spend their days doing nothing instead of going to school and gaining skills and knowledge. Many refugee children have lost their parents either to the war or to the journey. They are extremely susceptible to exploitation, sexual abuse, and the ever-watchful eye of slave traders.[821]

The refugees find themselves distressed, surrounded by agony and pain with very few provisions. Hopelessness is endemic.

France

In France, the refugees live in a great camp in Calais, which they call "The Jungle." Calais is a port town on the English Channel just a ferry crossing from Dover, England. It is where many refugees had come to seek entrance into the United Kingdom. But the English would have none of it. They chose to withdraw from the European Union rather than take in their share of refugees.

At first the French were sympathetic to the refugees, but as ten thousand came to live in the camp without any access to England, their human sentiment deteriorated. Local authorities began to bulldoze tents without warning. The people's meager belongings, identification papers, and dozens of passports were destroyed and people were forced to sleep outside in the rain. If the youths protested, they were beaten and tear gassed.

With thousands of people living like animals in this squalid camp, the city soon brimmed with anti-migrant, anti-Muslim rage that helped to fuel a budding nationalist movement. Armed groups, on the prowl, began to target migrants in night attacks in Calais and elsewhere in northern France. The stalkers, sometimes masked, would attack at night armed with clubs, brass knuckles, pepper spray, or knives.[822]

Normal conditions in the camp were dehumanizing. Sanitation ranged from appalling to non-existent; and all of the twenty or so mobile lavatories (provided by French government aid) overflowed with feces. Outside of the lavatories, human shit littered every "path" of the camp. Gangrene and dysentery set in.

Food was scarce. The government provides a single service of two thousand hot meals per day, at a time the number of refugees had doubled and continued to grow. The Jungle turned into a living hell that contradicted all sense of humanity.[823]

In October 2016, the French government closed the camp and transported thousands of refugees to processing centers around the country in an attempt to shut down The Jungle once and for all.[824] It did not work. In April 2017, it was reported that the number of refugees in and around Calais was again on the rise, about half of them unaccompanied children. "Eritreans and Sudanese are everywhere along the seafront with no welcome centre," said Amin Trouvé-Baghdouche of Doctors of the World. "They are wandering about, abandoned by the state. Half of them are teenagers of about fifteen to seventeen years old, without their families."[825]

Just as in Greece, where attempts were made to cut off the number of refugees reaching the country, it did not work. This is because millions of people have lost everything. They have nowhere to go. It is a monstrous problem set in motion by the United States ruling elite's vision of world dominance. Certainly, their greed for wealth and power could not imagine the holocaust it set in motion. And still they remain completely callous as to the human misery they have caused.

Time is running out for the refugees in France. Popular support for their welfare has fallen to levels not seen in decades. The government failed to provide enough resources to protect the basic human dignity of the war refugees and even forbade the French people from helping to address these inadequacies.[826]

England

It is a sad irony that for the few thousand refugees who managed to enter England before it shut its borders, life is not much better. Many of these refugees are denied jobs or benefits. Even if they are skilled workers like nurses, accountants, lawyers, etc., and are able to look after themselves, the government does not allow them to work. This makes them totally dependent upon charity from non-profits. This inability to care for themselves fills them with stress, aggression, madness, and depression.

At least 3,373 refugees in the UK have been destitute for months now and the government's plans to remove support payments for families who have been refused asylum, regardless of whether or not they can safely leave the UK, will plunge even more people into poverty.[827]

The United States

In the United States, the country that created the refugee problem,[828] things are not much better. In total, 18,007 Syrian refugees were resettled in the United States between October 1, 2011 and December 31, 2016.[829] By comparison, Canada, a country with fewer resources resettled 40,000 refugees in a shorter time period.[830]

Under the Obama administration, the refugees were resettled to states and localities based on family ties in the United States, health, age, family composition, and language, as well as the cost of living and the availability of jobs, housing, education, and health services in potential placement sites.

The Syrian refugees were placed across the United States, while California, Michigan, and Texas received the most refugees, accounting for thirty percent of the 18,007 total.[831]

After terrorist attacks in Paris in December 2015 and elsewhere in 2016, thirty US governors issued statements opposing the resettlement of Syrian refugees in their states due to fear of terrorism. Of the thirty governors, twenty-nine were Republicans.[832]

As far as the facts are concerned, there was no rational reason to protest against the resettlement of refugees in their states. First of all, most of the refugees were women and children. Secondly, there were already stringent screening measures in place. Thirdly, none of the recent terrorist attacks or mass shootings on American soil were perpetrated by people from the nations that the Republicans wanted to ban. Nonetheless, the Republican hysteria whipped up against the refugees brought Donald Trump to power, a man who had pandered to racist, xenophobic, and Islamophobic sentiments during his presidential campaign and in all likelihood possesses these same sentiments.

In February, one month after Trump's first ban on Muslims, the Associated Press reported that it had obtained a draft homeland security assessment concluding that citizenship was an "unlikely indicator" of a threat. In other words, analysts at the Homeland Security Department's intelligence arm found insufficient evidence that citizens of the countries included in President Donald Trump's travel ban posed a terror threat to the United States.[833]

Later, to cover themselves, the Department said that this finding was taken out of context and that it had three hundred suspects it was investigating. But it gave no proof or was willing to discuss this revision.

It appears that the Republican assault on the refugees is largely based upon racist and xenophobic sentiments. The vast majority of the thirty states opposing Syrian refugee arrivals, for example, had received very few refugees for resettlement. Three states, Alabama, Mississippi, and Wyoming had, in fact, received no Syrian refugees as of the end of 2016. Ten states (Arkansas, Kansas, Louisiana, Maine, New Hampshire, New Mexico, North Dakota, Oklahoma, South Carolina, and South Dakota) had gotten fewer than 100. While nine states (Idaho, Indiana, Iowa, Massachusetts, Nebraska, Nevada, New Jersey, Tennessee, and Wisconsin) were the destination for between 100 and 500 people. Just four states had received more than 1,000 Syrian refugees, with Michigan receiving 1,950, Texas (1,364), Arizona (1,149), and Illinois (1,059). These four states all had strong infrastructures in place to serve these refugees.[834]

Nonetheless, Donald Trump lit a fire under the reactionary sentiments of America by campaigning on a "Ban Muslims" plank. Upon gaining the presidency, he signed an executive order on January 27, 2017 to suspend travel to the United States from the war torn countries in the Middle East. The order left families stranded at airports across the country and immediately caused demonstrations and confusion for thousands of travelers. The order was ultimately blocked by a federal appeals court.

On March 6, 2017, President Trump reissued his Ban Muslim executive order with a few minor changes. The new order continued to impose a ninety-day ban on travelers, but it removed Iraq from the list because Defense Secretary Jim Mattis feared it would hamper cooperation to defeat the Islamic State.[835]

The new order also tempered some of the more outrageous violations of human rights. For example, it now exempted permanent residents and current visa holders from the ban, and dropped language that offered preferential status to refugees who were Christians. It also reversed the indefinite ban on refugees from Syria and replaced it with a one hundred and twenty day freeze that required review and renewal.

Nonetheless, the racist and Islamophobic spirit of the previous executive action was still intact, retaining the original intention to cut the number of refugees admitted to the United States each year to fifty thousand from one hundred and ten thousand. It also left open the possibility of expanding the ban to other countries, and threatened to put Iraq back on the banned list if the country's leaders failed to share intelligence with the US military.

Not surprisingly, the president's revisions did little to stop the criticism from Democrats and immigrant rights advocates, who predicted a renewed fight in the courts.

The Senate Democratic leader, Chuck Schumer of New York, described the new order as a "watered-down ban" that was still "mean-spirited and un-American." Margaret Huang, the executive director of Amnesty International USA, said in a statement that the new order would "cause extreme fear and uncertainty for thousands of families by, once again, putting anti-Muslim hatred into policy."[836]

The president's second attempt at a ban was blocked by federal courts two days later.[837] On June 26, 2018, the Supreme Court upheld Trump's third Muslim Ban, thus refusing to support this country's most basic principles of freedom and equality.

Mexican Immigrants

Aside from refugees from the Middle East, white nationalists are also equally distraught about Mexican and Central American immigrants to the US. For clarification, a refugee is a person who has been forced to leave their country in order to escape war, persecution, or natural disaster. An immigrant, on the other hand, is a person who comes to live permanently in a foreign country.

According to the Department of Homeland Security, in 2012, there were a total of 1,031,631 persons who became legal permanent residents of the United States. However, this number did not include illegal immigrants. Statistics estimate that around 11.7 million illegal immigrants resided in the US in 2015.[838]

To understand the issue of Mexican immigration to the US, it is necessary to understand that it was not always a crime to enter the United States without authorization. For most of American history, immigrants could enter the United States without official permission and not fear criminal prosecution by the federal government. That arrangement only changed in 1929. On the surface, Congress's new prohibition on informal border crossings simply modernized the US immigration system by compelling all immigrants to apply for entry. However, according to Kelly Lytle Hernandez, Associate Professor, History and African-American Studies, University of California, Los Angeles, in her new book *City of Inmates*, says Congress outlawed border crossings with the specific intent of criminalizing, prosecuting, and imprisoning Mexican immigrants.[839]

When US Attorney General Jeff Sessions announced, on April 11, 2017, his plan to step up prosecutions of unlawful entries, saying it is time to "restore a lawful system of immigration,"[840] the law that Sessions had vowed to enforce was designed with racist intent.

The criminalization of informal border crossings came during a large immigration from Mexico. For example, in 1900, only 100,000 Mexican immigrants resided in the United States, but by 1930, nearly 1.5 million Mexican immigrants lived north of the border.

By 1924, Congress had largely adopted a "whites only" immigration system, that also banned all Asian immigration and cut the number of immigrants allowed to enter the United States from anywhere other than northern and western Europe.[841] But whenever Congress tried to cap the number of Mexicans allowed to enter the United States each year, southwestern employers fiercely objected because they had become dependent upon Mexican laborers. In fact, US employers had actually created the era's Mexican immigration boom by recruiting Mexican workers to their southwestern farms, ranches, and railroads, as well as their homes and mines. By the 1920s, western farmers were completely dependent on Mexican workers.

By the close of the 1920s, Mexicans were settling in large numbers across the southwest. They bought homes, started newspapers, churches, and businesses. And many Mexican immigrants in the United States started families, raising a new generation of Mexican American children.

The white supremacists in Congress believed the Mexican people were racially unfit to be US citizens and charged the western employers with setting the stage for racial doom. Amid the escalating conflict between employers in the West and advocates of restriction in Congress, Senator Coleman Bease, from the hills of South Carolina, came up with a compromise. The year was 1929.

According to US immigration officials, Mexicans made nearly one million official border crossings into the United States during the 1920s.

They arrived at a port of entry, paid an entry fee, and submitted to literacy and health tests.

However, many other Mexican immigrants did not register for legal entry because entry fees were prohibitively high for many people and the US authorities subjected the Mexican immigrants to humiliating experiences, in particular, kerosene baths and delousing procedures because they believed Mexican immigrants carried disease and filth on their bodies. Therefore, instead of traveling to a port of entry, many Mexicans informally crossed the border at will, as both US and Mexican citizens had done for centuries.

Blease suggested criminalizing unmonitored entry. According to his bill, anyone "unlawfully entering the country" would commit a misdemeanor, while unlawfully returning to the United States after deportation would commit a felony. The law was particularly designed to impact Mexican immigrants.

Neither the western farmers or businessmen nor the white supremacists objected. Congress passed Blease's bill, and the *Immigration Act of March 4, 1929* dramatically altered the story of crime and punishment in the United States.

White law enforcement went to work caging thousands of Mexican people. By the end of 1930, the US Attorney General reported prosecuting 7,001 cases of unlawful entry. By 1940, U.S. Attorneys had prosecuted more than 44,000 cases.

To accommodate the prisoners, the U.S. Bureau of Prisons built three new prisons in the US-Mexico border region: La Tuna Prison in El Paso, Prison Camp #10 in Tucson, and Terminal Island in Los Angeles.

Only the outbreak of World War II halted the Mexican immigrant prison boom of the 1930s. Mexican workers were now desperately needed north of the border.[842]

After the war, the US returned to its racist stance on Mexican immigration. In 1954, President Dwight Eisenhower launched *Operation Wetback*, a shameful and violent removal of thousands of undocumented Mexican workers. In what has been described as a "quasi-military operation," border patrol agents, along with state and local law enforcement, methodically targeted Mexican-Americans. The result was widespread fear and abuse.[843]

By the end of Operation Wetback, 2.1 million Mexicans who had served America during the war were deported.[844] Under John Kennedy and Lyndon Johnson, the immigration laws were relaxed, with Johnson signing the Immigration Reform Act of 1965. His opponents charged him with letting illegal aliens into the US so that they might all become Democrats.[845]

Richard Nixon believed it was our moral obligation to help developing countries while also maintaining that we had major economic and strategic interests at stake. He recommended increasing the number of visas for Mexicans. Under Gerald Ford, concern increased about the rise in heroin entering the country from Mexico and he ordered more southern border patrols to stop the traffic. Under Jimmy Carter, the issue was raised as to the burden that schools had in educating the children of undocumented workers. His position was that it was the law, as expressed by the Supreme Court, and it would continue to be done.

Under Ronald Reagan, rising levels of illegal immigration led to the Immigration Reform and Control Act of 1986 (IRCA). It provided amnesty for three million illegal immigrants, in return for increased border security and penalties for companies "knowingly" hiring illegal immigrants. The Act also created the H-2A visa for seasonal workers, but did nothing to create new avenues for legal immigration. According to Jeb Bush, the combination of amnesty and inadequate avenues for legal immigration just made the problem worse.[846]

Reagan had said "Latinos are Republicans; they just don't know it yet." He believed that the Republican Party's overriding priority in the years ahead must be to expand and diversify its shrinking demographic base, embracing immigrants generally and Hispanics in particular. According to Rick Perry, then governor of Texas, the Immigration Reform and Control Act of 1986 was supposed to be a comprehensive solution with provisions intended to clamp down on border security, but the provisions were never enforced, and the subsequent explosion in illegal crossings resulted in some 11 million illegal aliens living in the United States. In 2010, an estimated 1.8 million illegal immigrants were residing in Texas, compared with 1.1 million in 2000. In ten years, Perry fumed, that represents an increase of fifty-four percent, or 70,000 persons each year coming to Texas illegally.[847]

During the administration of George H. Bush, the conservatives raised a false flag called *English First*, a movement which advocated a law be passed requiring everyone to speak English if they wanted to be Americans. Bush demonstrated a bit of humanity when he stated in a letter to a colleague that he strongly favored every child learning to speak English, but he did not think we need a federal law to enforce this. He said he worried about prejudice against Hispanics and afraid the "English First" debate would stir up prejudice and curtail linguistic education programs that he thought were essential to teach all Americans to speak English properly.

Mass deportations were renewed under the Clinton administration even though in his speeches he spoke in favor of Hispanics and touted their contribution to the US economy. Nonetheless, during his administration 12.2 million Hispanics, mostly Mexicans, were deported.[848] The mass deportations of Mexicans continued under George W. Bush as an aspect of his War on Terrorism. Bush deported 10.3 million Hispanics.[849] Even so, he remained acutely sensitive to the need of western businessmen for Mexican labor. He spent his administration trying to enforce the southern border, while also trying to design a visa program that would allow workers to come in and go back to Mexico once the need for their labor had ended.[850]

As for Obama, between 2009 and 2016, he deported 5.2 million Hispanics. He tried to address the complexity of the issue of Mexican immigrants by seeking to create a comprehensive reform package. In 2014, he announced a series of executive actions to grant up to five million unauthorized immigrants protection from deportation. In order to benefit from this protection, the immigrants had to have been in the states for five years or have children who were either American citizens or legal residents. They must also register with the government, pass a criminal background check, and pay taxes. His plan did not offer these people citizenship but it did offer to protect them from being deported.[851] Obama's plan also directed law enforcement to prioritize criminals for deportation while allowing high-skilled workers to move or change jobs more easily. He also sought to streamline visas and court procedures, among other things.[852]

Conservatives in Congress immediately accused Obama of abusing his power and pledged to stop his plan through legislative or legal means. Senator John Cornyn, Republican of Texas, speaking for his Republican colleagues, stated "I believe his unilateral action, which is unconstitutional and illegal, will deeply harm our prospects for immigration reform."[853]

At the time of Obama's executive decision, a majority of Americans disapproved of the president acting on the issue without involving Congress. However, half of Americans also said that unauthorized immigrants should be allowed to stay in the United States and eventually apply for citizenship. Thirteen percent said that they should be allowed to legally stay, but not be allowed to apply for citizenship. Only thirty-two percent said they should be required to leave the country.[854]

Nonetheless, the Republicans persisted in taking Obama to court for this decision, charging that he had overstepped his bounds by "unilaterally rewriting congressional laws and circumventing the people's representatives."[855] In January 2016, the Supreme Court decided to hear the case against Obama that was brought by twenty-six states led by Republicans. Obama's plan for immigrants was defeated when the Supreme Court deadlocked in a four to four decision, leaving millions of people, in limbo, fearing for their families and jobs. At the time, prosecutions for unlawful entry and reentry accounted for forty-nine percent of all federal prosecutions and the federal government had spent at least seven billion dollars to lock up unlawful border crossers.

Today, under the Trump administration, the desire to criminalize Mexicans' entry and reentry into the country has gotten much worse. Attorney General Sessions in March 2017 announced his plan to aggressively prosecute unlawful entry in this year and in the years to come. Trump had won over a large constituency by his promise to build a "Big Beautiful Wall" to keep immigrants from Mexico and Central America out of the country.

Under new orders by the Trump administration, nearly all of the United States' eleven million illegal immigrants can now be deported.

Certainly, every country has a right to protect its borders, but in this case, Americans want to use Mexicans for their cheap labor but do not want them to stay in the country. Fear of Mexican "criminals and rapists," as Mr. Trump referred to them, is just another example of America's exploitive and racist temperament. The Republican's inflammatory language against the Mexican people is not based upon any facts or studies.

In fact, the studies show that immigrants are less likely to commit crimes or engage in criminal behavior than native-born Americans.

In fact, sanctuary cities[856] enjoy lower crime and better economies than their non-sanctuary counterparts.[857] This is not to imply that immigrants are not the cause of some crime and violence, but the overall impact is minor compared to the crime and violence committed by US citizens and the violence committed against immigrants.

Even the conservative George W. Bush Institute reported that "Immigration fuels the economy. When immigrants enter the labor force, they increase the productive capacity of the economy and raise GDP. Their incomes rise, but so do those of natives. It is a phenomenon dubbed the "immigration surplus," and while a small share of additional GDP accrues to natives — typically 0.2 to 0.4 percent — it still amounts to thirty-six to seventy-two billion dollars per year."[858]

The Immigrant and Refugee Problem Will Not Go Away.

As the global system breaks down due to the rabid exploitation of the average person by national governments, war profiteers, drug cartels, and multinational corporations, we can only expect the problem of resettling refugees and immigrants to get worse.

Certainly, the mass migrations out of the Middle Eastern countries are born of social upheaval caused by wars, but in addition, we can also expect to see hundreds of thousands and millions of refugees displaced by environmental disasters by the end of the century and this is shaping up to be a much greater challenge for the future of the United States and the world in general.

The projected numbers of environmental refugees who will be forced to leave their country is one billion people by 2050 [859] and two billion by 2100.[860] It is, in fact, impossible to say how many people will be displaced due to climate change, but it can be stated irrefutably that the process has already begun. Whether we are talking about thousands or millions of people being forced to move from their homes, if not their homeland, due to climate changes, we do know, for example, that in the United States, as the sea continues to rise, it is already causing people to abandon their homes in Florida, Louisiana, Puerto Rico and other Caribbean islands. The same problem is predicted to confront cities all along the Atlantic and Pacific where over a hundred million Americans live.

In 2010, 123.3 million people, or thirty-nine percent of the nation's population lived in counties directly on the coastal shorelines and the population is expected to increase by eight percent from 2010 to 2020. Coastal areas are substantially more crowded than the US inland. In fact, the population density of coastal shoreline counties is over six times greater than the corresponding inland counties.[861] A new study projects that as many as 13.1 million people will be driven inland by the rising seas by the end of the century.[862] If this is true, we are talking not just about a coastal catastrophe but a national catastrophe. More people will be displaced in the US than all the people who have become Syrian refugees. It is most likely that the climate refugees will move into inland cities, but will these cities be prepared to handle this great influx of people economically and socially?

Fig. 5-21: New Orleans After Hurricane Katrina

Will people who are forced to move from New York, for example, be considered refugees or immigrants if they move to Indiana or Pennsylvania?

The picture aboveof New Orleans after Hurricane Katrina demonstrates how rising seas can destroy a coastal city. Kevin Trenberth, a noted climate scientist at the National Center for Atmospheric Research, tells us that "Sea-level rise from climate change occurs slowly and gradually, but its effects are profound and manifested when three things or more come together—a storm surge on top of a high tide on top of sea-level rise—so it affects people not as a gradual process, but rather as an episodic, catastrophic one. Hurricane Katrina or Superstorm Sandy are likely poster children for this."[863]

What is the Solution to the Problem of Refugees and Immigrants?

There is a solution, to be sure, but it is a solution that cannot be realized within the current capitalist system. It cannot be realized within a system dependent upon multinational corporations and national governments to solve local problems. Rather, to solve the problem of immigrants and refugees, decisions must be made at the local level and not at the national level. It requires that local people think in terms of their own self-reliance as an answer to fading corporate jobs and the federal dole. Our sense of humanity must begin to override our current left wing, right wing political divide that has been created by national politics. Building local communities based upon the principle of mutual support instead of personal profit must replace national politics in our minds and in our behavior.

If these changes can be made by people at the local level, we can decide for ourselves how many immigrants we want to take into our communities, who will bring money, creativity, skills, and similar values. For their part, the immigrants must make a commitment to throw their support behind the local community. In other words, they must cast their lot, for good or bad, with the economic well-being of the local people and participate in building its self-reliance. Their jobs can be created within the People's Economy,[864] that is, within that part of the local economy that is dedicated to meeting the basic needs of the local people in a sustainable manner. The components of this economy are food, shelter, clothing, health care, education and security.

As Americans, we must begin to realize that the problem of social and environmental upheaval did not arise with the immigrants and refugees who are the victims of the current system, but with the greed of the ruling elite and with our own ignorance and fear. Once we grasp this truth, we will be able to identify our true enemies and begin to fight tooth and nail to survive as a community and as a species on the planet earth.

In order for this to occur, our current political ideology must change. We will need to propagate an anti-exploitation sentiment whether such injustices are based on economics, gender, race, nationality, religion, etc. This is the only way to form a strong nation or community. In addition, we will need to recognize that this world does not belong to any individual or corporation, but is our collective spiritual inheritance. Every living being is the child of the Supreme Being, and all the people of all nations belong to the same family. With such an ideological orientation, we can begin to overcome the sentiments of racism and national superiority that cause nations to continually clash with each other and that allow small elites with imperialist ambitions to destroy our world.

If people, working in their communities in a cooperative manner to meet their own needs, also dedicate themselves to the welfare of the entire human race, every nation will benefit because the world's people will then seek the welfare of our own communities. Along with the theory of spiritual inheritance, the idea that the supreme goal of human existence is the universal Supreme Being will allow us to unify as a human society. Such a spiritual sentiment will keep us united for all time to come. No other theory can save the human race. Within this universal ideology, the question of morality becomes simplified. That which seeks the benefit of the whole is good, and that which seeks to oppress others for self-aggrandizement is bad. Current political and religious ideologies are not based upon this universal sentiment and as such are inadequate to help us face the common problems that currently confront us as human beings.

Destruction of the Environment

As we continue to destroy our natural environment and become more "citified," we lose our understanding and appreciation of the natural world. We forget where we come from. People who still live in rural areas understand this and many are fighting to maintain their natural environment. The trend towards city-living and the impoverishment of rural areas is a dangerous trend because the artificial human environments cannot continue to sustain us as we ravage the natural world. Everything of value begins with the land and water and with the plants and animals that sustain us. In this section, we will look at the impact that Americans are having on other species and the natural environment, and consequently, see what is happening to us as Americans.

Ozone

If you are young, you may not remember the world panic that the discovery of the hole in the ozone layer caused. The ozone layer is a belt of the naturally occurring gas "ozone." It sits 9.3 to 18.6 miles (15 to 30 kilometers) above Earth, and serves as a shield from the harmful ultraviolet B (UVB) radiation emitted by the sun.[865]

Ozone is a highly reactive molecule that contains three oxygen atoms and is constantly being formed and broken down above Earth, in the region called the stratosphere.

During the late 1980s there was widespread concern that the ozone layer was deteriorating due to the release of pollution containing the chemicals chlorine and bromine. Such deterioration allowed large amounts of ultraviolet B rays to reach Earth, which caused and is still causing skin cancer and cataracts in humans and animals as well.

Extra ultraviolet B radiation that reaches the earth, because of the hole in the ozone layer, also inhibits the reproductive cycle of phytoplankton, single-celled organisms such as algae that make up the bottom rung of the food chain. Biologists feared that reductions in phytoplankton populations would lower the populations of other animals. Researchers at the time documented changes in the reproductive rates of young fish, shrimp, and crabs as well as frogs and salamanders exposed to excess ultraviolet B.

It was discovered that chlorofluorocarbons (CFCs), chemicals found mainly in spray aerosols, which had been used by industrialized nations as far back as the 1930s, were the main cause of the destruction of the ozone layer. The hole that was created in the ozone layers allowed massive amounts of ultraviolent rays to enter the earth, causing great harm.

The ozone hole occurred as CFCs reached the upper atmosphere, where they were exposed to ultraviolet rays, which caused them to break down into substances, which included chlorine. The chlorine reacted with the oxygen atoms in the ozone and ripped apart the ozone molecule. Scientists discovered that one atom of chlorine could destroy more than a hundred thousand ozone molecules.

The ozone layer above the Antarctic has been particularly impacted by CFC pollution. The region's cold temperatures sped up the conversion of CFCs to chlorine. In the southern spring and summer, when the sun shines for long periods of the day, chlorine also reacts with ultraviolet rays, and destroys ozone on a massive scale, up to sixty-five percent. In other regions, the ozone layer was deteriorated by about twenty percent.

About ninety percent of the CFCs in the atmosphere were emitted by industrialized countries in the Northern Hemisphere, including the United States and Europe. But thankfully, scientists, the EPA, and a worldwide media campaign, forced these countries to ban CFCs by 1996. Since that time, the amount of chlorine in the atmosphere has continued to fall. Even so, scientists estimate it will take another fifty years for chlorine levels to return to their natural levels.[866]

Air Pollution

While humanity is dodging a bullet by curtailing CFCs, (throw out your hair spray) it has not been as mindful of the toxic chemical pollutants that are continually spewed out into the atmosphere. Air pollution has become a major concern of countries all over the world, but the chemical companies and the fossil fuel industry are fighting for their corporate lives to keep these deadly chemicals in production as long as possible. Air pollution is a main contributor to human and animal sickness and death and is also responsible to a large degree for heating up the atmosphere.

We may cover our mouths in horror at the pollution in cities like Delhi and Beijing where ozone and fine carbon particles from dirty fuels are consistently causing long term lung and heart disease,[867] but an article published in January 2017 reported that London had bypassed Beijing in air pollution. In fact, air pollution has been on the rise throughout Europe.[868] Even Paris, the City of Light, recently had to ban half of its commuters from driving automobiles while making public transportation free. Experts say the smoggy skies are due to emissions from power plants, traffic, and heating; that is, to the burning of fossil fuels.

Pollution is a global problem. Let us break this down a little. Breathing is the most basic function of our bodies. We breathe in oxygen in order to live. This oxygen serves many functions in the human body, including keeping our cells functioning. Without clean air, we die, and quickly. When we breathe in polluted air caused by the burning of fossil fuels, tiny toxic particles enter our lungs that cause permanent lung and heart damage. Andrew Grieve, air quality analyst from King's College in London says, the effect is cumulative, from your first breath to your last breath.[869] Small children, older adults, and people who have respiratory conditions are particularly vulnerable to being exposed to toxins in the air.

But we are not only talking about the most vulnerable. Air pollution affects us all. According to Cornell University, "Water, air, and soil pollution causes forty percent of deaths worldwide." Air pollution alone kills between 5.5 and 6.5 million people every year! [870] Cornell is not the only institution making such an outrageous claim.

Newsweek printed a story about a Global Burden of Disease Study that showed that 5.5 million people across the world die from diseases caused by air pollution.[871] *The New York Times* also reported on a study by the International Energy Agency that echoed the same dire reality: "Study Links 6.5 Million Deaths Each Year to Air Pollution".[872]

In the last fifty years, North America, Western Europe, and Japan have made great strides to combat air pollution by using cleaner fuels, more efficient vehicles, limiting coal burning, and putting restrictions on electric power plants and factories.[873] These "great strides," however, are not great enough to stop or reverse the negative impact of burning fossil fuels. And now, rules that have helped us to breathe better are being systematically eliminated by the Trump administration which is governed by the billionaires who heavily profit from fossil fuels and chemical plants and want to keep them flowing at all costs.

Even before the Trump administration, we were slipping outside the safe zone that was once established to protect us from chemical toxins in the air we breathe. Take New Jersey, for instance. In 2016, it recorded twenty-four days (almost a third of summer days) when the air was unhealthy to breathe. On these days, it failed to meet the national health-quality standard for ground-level ozone or smog. This was four days more than the previous summer.

The New Jersey Chamber of Commerce blamed the problem on too stringent standards and pollution drifting in from other states. They charged that a new state law had changed the acceptable level of pollution from seventy-five ppb to seventy ppb. This was true, but the EPA's own science review suggested that it should be set at sixty ppb to reduce unhealthy levels of smog. In other words, the corporate polluters in New Jersey were still literally getting away with murder. New Jersey has never met the standard for ozone (not to be confused with the ozone in the stratosphere), a pollutant that forms in hot sunny weather when emissions from power plants, businesses, and vehicles "bake" to form smog, which blankets much of the state.

State officials anticipate that climate change will make ozone alert days worse. Of the eleven warmest summers on record in New Jersey since 1895, nine have occurred since 1989.[874]

Another example is Connecticut. Last summer Connecticut's Department of Energy and Environmental Protection predicted unhealthy air quality caused by elevated ground-level ozone pollution. The Commissioner, Robert Klee, took advantage of Father's Day to issue a pollution alert. He urged all dads to "take the weekend off from cutting the lawn" to minimize any health impacts and to avoid contributing additional emissions from their lawn mowers.[875]

Power plants, industrial manufacturing, vehicle exhaust, and burning coal all release small particles into the air that are dangerous to a person's health. Experts believe that the numbers of deaths will continue to increase unless stricter emission standards are enforced.

In the United States, three million tons of toxic chemicals are released into the environment each year. What is the impact of these toxic chemicals on the American people? Generally speaking, they cause cancer, birth defects, immune system defects, and many other serious health problems.[876]

The problem of air pollution is not new. Back in 1962, Rachel Carson, in her famous book *Silent Spring* said, ". . . new chemicals come from our laboratories in an endless stream; almost 500 annually find their way into actual use in the United States alone…500 new chemicals to which the bodies of men and animals are required somehow to adapt each year, chemicals totally outside the limits of biologic experience."[877] Two years after Rachel Carson sounded the above warning, she died of breast cancer.

Now over fifty years later, the pesticide and chemical assault on our health that Rachel Carson exposed in her book has greatly intensified. Despite massive scientific evidence that these chemicals are poisoning us, US regulatory agencies have avoided or delayed taking action on thousands of deadly chemicals, including Monsanto's Roundup (active ingredient glyphosate) and Syngenta's atrazine, the two most heavily sprayed poisons on GMO corn and soybeans, which are America's most planted crops.[878]

US regulatory agencies like the EPA tell us "Don't worry." Now with the EPA gutted by the Trump administration, we will not even have an EPA to tell us not to worry. The poisons will continue to spew and more Americans will die each year.

According to the National Cancer Institute, 1.7 million new cases of cancer will be diagnosed this year. Could this have something to do with the fact that four hundred and twenty known carcinogens or likely carcinogens have been measured in the American people? The exposure to these chemicals are not limited to on-the-job contact with the toxins, but reach us through the air. They also reach us through food packaging, the chemicals in household supplies, cosmetics, and even polluted mother's milk.[879]

Known carcinogens like asbestos, C8, styrene, and bisphenol A, which US regulators have known for years endanger human health and the environment, are allowed to still show up in consumer products because a forty-year-old chemicals law, the Toxic Substances Control Act, keeps regulators from limiting the use of such compounds. For example, the law set such a high burden of scientific proof that the EPA's evidence against asbestos, which kills as many as fifteen thousand Americans a year, was not enough to pass the legal requirements. The law also kept the EPA from studying chemicals in clothing, household cleaning products, furniture, toys, and other products we regularly wear and use. As a result, in the last forty years, the EPA has banned only five of the more than eighty thousand chemicals used in the United States. Only about seven percent of the roughly three thousand high-volume chemicals have been tested for safety.[880]

The Obama administration made a "sweeping overhaul" of this law toward the end of his administration, but the Trump administration, under Scott Pruitt, the head of the EPA, eliminated the environmental safeguards put in place by Obama.[881] This eliminated the government's even meagre authority to hold toxic chemical companies accountable to the American people. Trump has specifically said he will not even consider removing toxic chemicals from the marketplace. While removing scientists from his administration, he has stated that corporate special interests will be free to identify public protections for the Trump administration to repeal.[882]

Who benefits from weak laws and the deaths of Americans? Certainly, the chemical industry, but also the fossil fuel industry, which includes coal, oil, and gas. James Hanson, a climate scientist, who worked for NASA, believes that, "Coal is the single greatest threat to civilization and all life on our planet."[883] What a stunning charge! How could he say such a thing? A report entitled "Europe's Dark Cloud" produced jointly by the Health and Environmental Alliance, Greenpeace, the Climate Action Network, and the World Wildlife Fund sheds light on his pronouncement. For the first time ever, this report analyzed the health impact of all coal-fired power stations in the European Union for which data was available. Scientists analyzed data from two hundred and fifty-seven of the two hundred and eighty plants and found that the emissions from the two and fifty-seven power plants were associated with twenty-two thousand nine hundred deaths in 2013. That is about ninety dead people per year from each power plant.

Their deaths resulted from cardiovascular or respiratory system failure caused by three main pollutants—particulate matter, ground-level ozone, and nitrogen dioxide. The most common causes of death connected to exposure to particulate matter are strokes, heart disease, chronic lung disease, and lung cancer. Around eighty-three percent of the deaths were caused by fine particulate matter.

The particles are formed in the air from the coal plants' sulphur dioxide and nitrogen dioxide emissions. While people living near power plants are particularly vulnerable, the emissions continue to multiply and travel around the globe, impacting the health of people everywhere.[884]

Can you guess what the new EPA's solution to the problem of air pollution is? Stay indoors in an area with filtered air. Avoid activities that make you breathe faster or more deeply. And, if you cannot buy filters for your entire home, create a clean room for sleeping.[885]

As the fossil fuel industries and chemical companies continue to destroy our air, the federal government's only solution to the problem is to make us prisoners in our own homes. What if we need to go outside? Simply wear facemasks and strip and take a shower as soon as you return home. We are looking at our future America, unless we take matters into our own hands, because we can no longer pretend that the federal government and the multinational corporations will address the cause of American deaths due to air pollution.

Fossil Fuel Pollution

In 2015, the US used seven billion barrels of petroleum products. Each barrel released around two hundred and twenty pounds of carbon dioxide equivalent emissions. This adds up to emissions of about seven hundred million metric tons of CO_2e globally, which acts to warm the atmosphere.[886] The graph below shows how many metric tons of pollution are generated each year in the US from burning gasoline, diesel, and jet fuel emissions as well as pollution caused by oil and gas extraction and refining. Regardless of what climate deniers believe, no one can deny that the addition of this massive quantity of CO_2 is contributing to atmospheric temperature rise in a big way.

This discussion of carbon dioxide pollution does not take account of the pollution from methane that is also released in the oil extraction and refining process. Methane is some eighty-four times more potent than carbon dioxide over a twenty year period and anywhere from twenty-eight to thirty-six times more potent over a one hundred year timeframe. Because methane emissions trap heat at a greater degree than carbon dioxide, these emissions are also a big threat to our climate and we produce and emit a lot of methane.

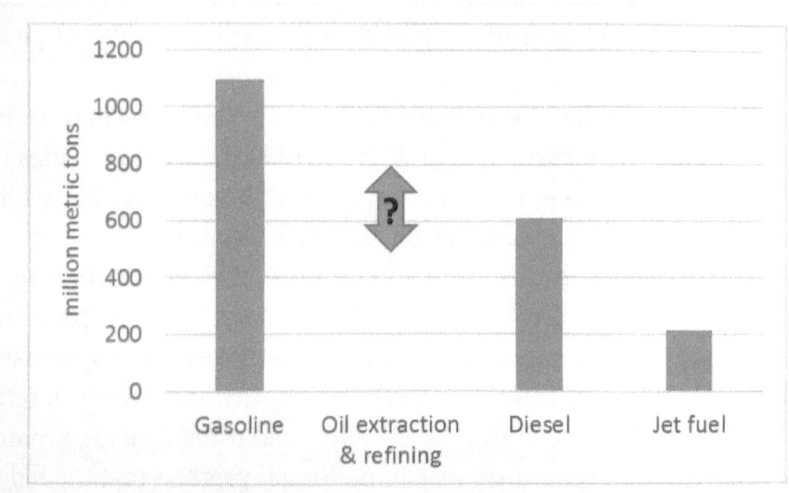

Fig. 5-22: Emissions from Oil Extraction and Refining for Petroleum Products Used in the US (CO2e) Compared to CO2 Emissions from the Use of Major Transportation Fuels in the US. Source: Energy Information Administration and Oil Climate Index.

The three largest methane emitters are the oil and gas sector, the agricultural sector, and the waste management sector. Collectively they discharge the equivalent of another four hundred and fifty and five hundred and fifty million metric tons of CH4 into the atmosphere annually. This is equivalent to the emissions from more than one hundred million cars.

The pollution from the extraction, refinement, and use of fossil fuels is heating our atmosphere to the point of changing our climate and causing devastating results, including droughts, fires, floods, sea level rise, loss of species, etc. In addition, this same pollution is a major cause in the poisoning of the air we breathe.

Many people believe that if we just keep advancing the renewable energy technology, we will be alright. Unfortunately, even if solar and wind capacity continues to grow at breakneck speed, it will not be fast enough to cap global warming under two degrees Celsius, the target set down in the landmark 2015 Paris climate treaty. According to Glen Peters, a researcher at the Center for International Climate and Environmental Research in Oslo, Norway, whose report is covered in *Nature Climate Change*, "The rapid deployment of wind, solar, and electric cars gives some hope, but at this stage, these technologies are not really displacing the growth in fossil fuels or conventional transportation." He said the Earth is overheating mainly due to the burning of oil, gas, and especially coal to power the global economy.[887] We have pointed out above that air pollution causes 5.5 million or twenty-five percent of all deaths in the world each year. We have not considered its impact on the global economy.

According to a recent World Bank report entitled *The Cost of Air Pollution: Strengthening the Economic Case for Action*,[888] job losses caused by health emergencies, long term illnesses, chronic conditions, and deaths caused by air pollution costs the US economy forty-five billion dollars each year. The global economy loses about two hundred and twenty-five billion dollars. If we add in all the welfare costs or the money people are forced to pay in order to receive medical attention, that figure rises to a staggering five trillion dollars per year.[889]

It is little wonder that climate change denial is such a big issue for the giant fossil fuel companies.[890] Their business is at stake. In an effort to slow or prevent legislation that would reduce their profit, they pay millions of dollars each year to "think tanks" to develop arguments that deny the impact of air pollution and climate change. This propaganda, which has been pedaled as truth by the Trump administration and Republicans in Congress, continues to confuse the American people.[891]

As this subterfuge continues, everyone's health continues to decline, including the lives of our children and the yet unborn. On one side, we have the fossil fuel industry and the Trump administration spewing false information and on the other side, we have the world's scientific community and the majority of the world's people.

In order to fight back at this continued assault by the chemical and fossil fuel industries, many non-profits have taken the lead in providing tools for local action. One of these tools is the Oil and Gas Threat Map produced by Earthworks that maps the nation's 1.2 million active oil and gas wells, compressors, and processors.[892] Using the latest peer-reviewed research into the health impacts attributed to oil and gas air pollution, the map conservatively draws a half-mile health threat radius around each facility. Within that total area of 184 thousand square miles of dense pollution, 12.4 million Americans are subject to increased chemical poisoning, including 750,000 children who presently suffer from asthma attacks attributed to ozone smog. In these areas there are 11,543 schools. You can view the map and take action for the sake of your families. For each of the 1,459 counties in the US that host active oil and gas facilities, the interactive map also reports instances of elevated cancer and respiratory risk of the total affected population along with separate counts for Latino & African-Americans.

The searchable map allows users to look up any street address to see if it lies within the health treat radius and also offers infrared videos for hundreds of sites that show the normally invisible pollution.

While the assault on the EPA by the Trump administration will make local work difficult, the well-being of our lives and the lives of our children are now in our own hands. The large-scale, grassroots campaign against fracking that has spread across the country is an example of local people taking charge of their own lives and protecting their neighbors. In this struggle, we cannot count on the media to help us. Since Trump has become president, broadcast news has drastically reduced its coverage of climate change and pollution.[893]

Water Pollution

Considering that two-thirds of the planet is covered with water, we have a tendency to downplay water pollution. This is a big mistake. Only about three percent of the water on the planet is the fresh water that we need for drinking or to use for cooking, hygiene, sanitation, crop irrigation, etc. Of this three percent, only one percent is accessible to humans, the remaining is locked up in ice or moisture in the soil and air. Upon deeper consideration, water is not so plentiful as we have imagined. And yet, we continue to destroy our fresh water supply at a rapid rate.

Today, eighty-five percent of the world population lives in the driest half of the planet. Of these, 783 million people do not have access to clean water and almost 2.5 billion do not have access to adequate sanitation. Six to eight million people die annually from droughts and water-related diseases.[894]

The problems due to lack of fresh water create incredible stress and illness for people. People lose 800,001 babies and toddlers each year to diarrhea due to contaminated water. Another 323 million people face life-threatening diseases due to contaminated water.[895] Add another billion people who are infected by parasites from drinking contaminated water. One of these parasites is the Guinea Worm that grows in the human body and then breaks through the skin like the creature in the Alien. These worms can be near three feet long when they emerge from the human body.[896]

Lack of water is also a direct cause of two of humanity's greatest scourges—war and poverty. Without water, we cannot grow crops, prepare food, manufacture items, etc.

While things are not as bad in the United States as they are in many countries, there is still great cause for concern. There are families all across America who are drinking contaminated water. This is especially true in black and minority neighborhoods. Due to decaying lead pipes in old buildings, over a million children in the US have elevated levels of lead in their blood. Young children are particularly vulnerable to the toxic effects of lead and can suffer profound and permanent adverse effects on the development of their brain and nervous system. Lead in the body is stored in the teeth and bones and distributed to the brain, liver, kidney, and bones over time. Lead, in any quantity is consider unsafe.

At one time, the federal government was a protector of our drinking water and waste water systems. In 1972, the government of Richard Nixon passed the 1972 Clean Water Act that was intended to ensure clean water for swimming and fishing. In 1977, the feds invested almost seventeen billion dollars, but since then, the supply of funding has dried up. In fact, federal funding for our local water utilities has declined eighty-two percent since 1977. Today, the federal government spends a measly $13.68 per American to protect our water supply.[897]

It is clearly not enough, considering that four decades later, our wildlife is dying and bizarre disfigurements of aquatic creatures are becoming commonplace. So also, people are becoming sick and dying from drinking polluted water.[898]

In those cities left behind by technological innovations, cities like Flint, Detroit, Baltimore, and large areas in Philadelphia, water systems are in a state of decay and it is impossible to maintain essential systems without federal assistance. When the cities tried to raise the rates to make repairs, the people, now jobless, could not afford the water bill. In Flint, for example, inadequate funding and outdated infrastructure resulted in cost-cutting that led to a public health crisis.[899]

Actually, the federal Environmental Protection Agency (EPA) knew what was happening and could have intervened in the crisis a full seven months before it finally did. By not taking action to protect the people of Flint, thousands of people, who were mostly black, had to drink months of water tainted with lead.[900]

While the federal government routinely abandons people in their need for fresh water, we must also consider that it is the greatest polluter in the country. The Departments of Energy, Agriculture, Interior, Federal Aviation, Justice, NASA, and multiple other agencies are major polluters.[901]

In citing the federal government, we cannot let corporations off the hook when it comes to water pollution. The Sugar industry and the Beef industry are huge polluters of our rivers and lakes. The scandal[902] in 2016 that occurred when the stench of toxic algae glutted the waterways of southeastern Florida and closed down businesses and beaches during the high tourist season, was caused by run off from sugar plants.[903]

Most Americans have heard of the "Dead Zone" in the Gulf of Mexico that is caused largely by chemical fertilizer run off from farms along the Mississippi river. The run off is loaded with nitrogen that stimulates an overgrowth of algae that sinks, decomposes, and consumes the oxygen needed to support fish and marine life. The Dead Zone in the Gulf is certainly not the only one that humans have created. In fact, there about five hundred and fifty such zones around the world. The Gulf of Mexico dead zone, however, is the second largest in the world, comprising 5,780 square miles.[904]

Perhaps one of the most egregious corporate assaults on our right to fresh water occurs when they take advantage of our most vulnerable communities by buying their municipal water utility and then overcharging them for poor service in order to increase profits from the people's need for water.

Two larger cities, Detroit and Atlanta, have experienced the impact of such water privatization.[905] One step below *egregious* is *demonic*. We can apply this term to a company like Nestlé's that currently controls seventy of the world's bottled water brands in an attempt to monopolize the world's fresh water supply. To be able to sell and make money from water, Nestlé first has to own it.

Whoever owns land or has acquired leasing rights is permitted to pump as much water as he likes from that land. In the rural state of Maine, for example, Nestlé has purchased many such water rights and resources. Every year the company pumps out millions of cubic yards of water and transports it to its huge bottling factories. When the local people find themselves without water for their own use, Nestlé tries to stifle and suppress local opposition to its operations with an army of powerful PR consultants, lawyers, and lobbyists.[906] While advertising their water as superior to tap water, many of these water companies fill their bottles with the same tap water that everyone uses.[907]

It is so disheartening to witness the effects on people from lack of water especially when this problem can be solved by human ingenuity.[908]

The Politics of Water in the US

Why is the federal government so incompetent when it comes to protecting our water supply? It is not so much a situation of incompetence, as it is one of corporate greed and payoffs to politicians. Let us take a closer look at this phenomenon. In 2015, under the Obama administration, the EPA and the Army Corp of Engineers collaborated to create the Clean Water Rule.[909] The rule was intended to protect two million miles of streams and twenty million acres of wetlands that had not been clearly designated under the Clean Water Act. The rule would protect clean water for millions of Americans as one third of Americans get their drinking water from rivers and streams.

In preparation for implementing this rule, the EPA reviewed more than four hundred thousand comments and held outreach events around the country. In these meetings, EPA Administrator Gina McCarthy was clear that the new rule would not affect the "normal farming operations" that were already carved out under the Clean Water Act, nor would new requirements be made for agriculture or forestry.

These industries would retain "all the decades-long exemptions" they currently enjoyed.

A League of Conservation Voters poll found that eighty percent of voters supported the rule as did eighty percent of small businesses, indicating an overwhelming majority of local people supported the new rule.[910]

Yet, immediately, sixteen states filed lawsuits aimed at blocking the Clean Water Rule. Texas, Louisiana, and Mississippi filed a joint lawsuit in a Houston federal court, asserting that the EPA's final rule was "an unconstitutional and impermissible expansion of federal power over the states and their citizens and property owners." Their suit held that Congress had not granted the EPA the power to regulate water and land use.

In self-righteous indignation the sponsors of the lawsuit claimed that "the very structure of the Constitution, and therefore liberty itself, is threatened when administrative agencies attempt to assert independent sovereignty and lawmaking authority that is superior to the states, Congress, and the courts."

In a separate case, Alaska, Arizona, Arkansas, Colorado, Idaho, Missouri, Montana, Nebraska, New Mexico, Nevada, North Dakota, South Dakota, and Wyoming also sought to have the rule overturned. North Dakota Attorney General Wayne Stenehjem called the rule "unnecessary" and "unlawful."[911]

When we look at the state attorneys who filed these lawsuits, we immediately find a common denominator. They are members of the Republican Attorneys General Association (RAGA) which is a Washington, D.C.-based political organization dedicated to electing and re-electing Republicans across the nation to be state attorneys general so as to support their efforts to fight "federal encroachment" and to promote "free markets."[912]

Who funds RAGA? More than $2.4 million, about thirteen percent, came from Koch Industries, Murray Energy, the American Petroleum Institute, Exxon Mobil, the American Coalition for Clean Coal Electricity, and other fossil fuel interests. Another nearly $1.4 million came from the U.S. Chamber of Commerce, which also receives a significant amount of its funds from fossil fuel companies.[913] More money poured into RAGA through Koch-supported non-profits.[914]

This makes one wonder if the Republican Attorney Generals are concerned about the constitution or the need of their funders to keep their pollution options open to the greatest extent.

Despite their efforts, the Clean Water Rule became law. However, one of the first actions of the Trump administration was to issue an Executive Order directing the Environmental Protection Agency (EPA) to abandon the Clean Water Rule. The new Trump directive removed environmental and development protections from most US waterways from which more than one hundred million Americans receives their tap water.[915]

This is why the government no longer protects our water supply.

Land Pollution

People generally have less awareness of land pollution than they have for water pollution, but the consequences of land pollution are equally destructive to life. Land pollution is the degradation of the Earth's surface caused by the misuse of resources and improper disposal of waste. Some examples of land pollution include:

- Illegal dumping in natural habitats;
- Oil spills that happen inland;
- The use of pesticides and other farming chemicals;
- Damage and debris caused from unsustainable mining and logging practices;
- Radiation spills or nuclear accidents;
- Fracking spills; and
- Littering[916]

Deforestation is not so much a pollutant as it is a destroyer of fertile land. Deforested land becomes barren within a couple of years and can never be made fertile again. We see this in the destruction of the rain forest in South America.

As the human population continues to grow, so does the demand for food. Farmers often use highly toxic fertilizers and pesticides to keep insects, fungi, and bacteria away from their crops. The overuse of these chemicals contaminates and also kills the soil, turning it into dirt that no longer contains any life in it.

Extraction and mining activities also pollute the land with toxic chemicals that are left in the soil and carried away in streams. So also, we hear about land cave-ins as a result of mining.

American households are also primary polluters. We produce tons of garbage each year. Consider these statistics:

- Each American, on average, creates 4.4 lbs. of trash every day.
- Collectively, we create 254 million tons of trash each year.
- We throw away 22 billion plastic bottles yearly.
- From our waste paper each years, we can build a 12 foot wall from Los Angeles to New York City.
- All of the paper and plastic cups, forks, and spoons that we dispose of annually would lap the equator 300 times.
- There are over 2,000 active landfills in the country.
- There are thousands of landfills already filled.

There is hope, however. Americans are now recycling 34.3% of our garbage yearly. By recycling and composting, we prevented 87.2 million tons of material from being disposed in 2013, up from 15 million tons in 1980.

Recycling has also prevented one hundred and eighty-six million metric tons of carbon dioxide from being released into the atmosphere, which is the equivalent of thirty-nine million polluting cars. Garbage like aluminum, plastic, paper, cloth, and wood is being collected and sent to local recycling units. Items that cannot be recycled, however, continue to be a cause of land pollution.[917]

Nuclear plants produce huge amount of energy through nuclear fission, but the radioactive waste contains highly toxic chemicals that can affect human health. They are dumped beneath the earth to avoid any casualty. When an event like Fukushima occurs, however, great quantities of radioactive materials also go into the air and water.

Large amounts of solid waste are leftover once sewage from urban centers has been treated. The leftover material is sent to landfill sites, which end up polluting the environment.

The discharge of chemicals on land, puts ecosystems in danger as well. Chemicals are consumed by the animals and plants and thereby make their way into the planet's ecosystems. This process is called bio-magnification and is a serious threat to the ecology. Take for example, the spills of toxic chemicals from fracking operations. There have been thousands of citizen complaints regarding toxic waste spills that have been covered up by the government and oil companies.

A study published in Environmental Science and Technology in February, 2017 revealed that there were 6,648 spills in four states alone —Colorado, New Mexico, North Dakota, and Pennsylvania.[918]

The increasing numbers of barren land plots and the decreasing acres of forests are proceeding at an alarming rate, but something can be done about it:

- Reduce consumption, Recycle materials and Reuse manufactured goods.
- Reduce the use of pesticides and fertilizers in agricultural activities.
- Buy biodegradable products.
- Grow and eat organic food that is grown without the use of pesticides.
- Put policies in place to control waste from industry and the government.

Loss of Species

In the old days, coal miners used to take a caged canary down into the mines with them to warn them of dangerous gases. If the canary keeled over and died, the miners knew that invisible methane gas or carbon dioxide was in the mine and they exited before the poison gases reached a level to kill humans.

Bees

Today, with the drastic degradation of our environment from toxic chemicals, insects serve as our "canary in the coalmine." Today insects are dying in vast numbers as a warning to humanity, but we hardly seem to notice. One species that has garnered some attention is the honeybee. US beekeepers have been reporting annual hive deaths at thirty percent or higher for much of the past ten years, but in the past few years these deaths have risen to forty to fifty percent or more per year.[919]

As always, there are a number of factors contributing to the problem. Experts cite monoculture and the reduction of food supply for bees, as well as pathogens and pesticides. There is not much we can do about fighting pathogens. So also, the switch from monoculture to sustainable agriculture is not likely to occur soon, but there is something we can do about pesticides. When scientists discovered that insecticides containing the neonicotinoid chemicals farmers sprayed on their crops were killing bees, the Europeans banned these insecticides, but in the US, the big chemical companies prevented a ban from happening by spending "hundreds of thousands of dollars" at the federal and state level to lobby against measures to halt the pesticide use.[920]

More than this, a Friends of the Earth report also charged the chemical industry with "infiltrating federal regulatory agencies" by lobbying to get their employees jobs with the US Department of Agriculture and the Environmental Protection Agency. Some of the companies involved include Bayer, Syngenta, and Monsanto, which all profit from pesticide use. The companies are also charged with creating misinformation campaigns against bee-protecting legislation and by "directly funded or influenced science by donating to education initiatives and building strategic alliances with academics."[921]

United Nations scientific research shows that these pesticides are not just harmful to bees but also to humans. Pesticides are responsible for an estimated two hundred thousand acute poisoning deaths each year. Not surprisingly, ninety-nine per cent of fatalities occurred where health, safety, and environmental regulations were weaker. Chronic exposure to pesticides is linked to cancer, Alzheimer's, and Parkinson's diseases, hormone disruption, developmental disorders, and sterility. Those most vulnerable to pesticide poisoning are farmers and agricultural workers, communities living near farms, indigenous communities, and pregnant women and children.[922] If the Trump administration continues to emasculate the Environmental Protection Agency, we can expect more American deaths from chemical toxins in the air, water, and soil.

Monarch butterflies

In my generation, every kid grew up watching monarch butterflies with their black and orange wings, flutter around the neighborhood during warm days. We tried to catch them to look at them up closely. Now, however, a monarch butterfly is a rare sight.

In 2015, the Washington Post published an article entitled, "The Monarch Massacre: Nearly a Billion Butterflies Have Vanished."[923] The butterflies have died off because farmers and homeowners spray herbicides on milkweed plants, which serve as the butterflies' nursery, food source, and home. In the same year, after two decades of destruction, the Fish and Wildlife Service launched a partnership with the National Wildlife Federation and the National Fish and Wildlife Foundation to grow as much milkweed as possible in the hopes of saving the monarchs.

But this is, at best, a Band-Aid approach. In reality, it is Monsanto's Roundup® (Glyphosate), the most widely used herbicide in the world that is wiping out the milkweed that monarch butterflies rely on as the only food for their young. Use of glyphosate has increased dramatically in the past two decades since Monsanto launched its genetically engineered Roundup®-Ready for spraying on corn, soy, canola, and cotton.[924] Today, only thirty million remain. One butterfly for every ten Americans.

Glyphosate remains a mainstream carcinogen. The ways that Monsanto's Roundup cause cancer are: endocrine disruption, free radical formation, and inhibition of free radical-scavenging enzymes, inhibition of certain DNA repairing enzymes, inhibiting the absorption of essential nutrients, renal and pancreatic damage, all which cause cancer. It also destroys gut bacteria and suppresses the immune system.[925] Uh . . . are you sure you want to be spraying that in your backyard?

Birds

Like the canary in the coal mine, birds today are still warning us about toxic dangers in our environment. The news is not good because the birds are in trouble.

Globally, one in eight—more than thirteen hundred species—are threatened with extinction, and the status of most of those is deteriorating, according to BirdLife International. And many others are in worrying decline, from the tropics to the poles. In North America's breadbasket, populations of grassland birds such as meadowlarks are in free fall. Swifts and swallows that snap up insects on the wing are also in widespread decline.[926] As it is, eighty-six of North America's roughly four hundred and fifty breeding species are considered to be "vulnerable," with some populations expected to be cut in half in a matter of decades.[927]

Aside from flying into cars, buildings, power cables, or being caught by feral cats, another big killer of birds is toxic chemicals. A recent report by the American Bird Conservancy concludes that the neonicotinoids found in insecticides like Monsanto's Roundup, are lethal to birds as well as insects. A single corn kernel coated with a neonicotinoid can kill a songbird. Even a tiny grain of wheat or canola treated with the oldest neonicotinoid, imidacloprid, can poison a bird. As little as 1/10th of a corn seed per day during egg-laying season is all that is needed to affect reproduction.

Birds are also affected by these pesticides when they wash off into the streams and rivers that border and run through farmlands. Neonicotinoid contamination levels in surface and groundwater in the US and around the world is strikingly high. It is already beyond the threshold found to kill many aquatic invertebrates.[928]

The American Bird Conservancy report charges that the EPA's risk assessments of neonicotinoids have greatly underestimated their risk by using a scientifically unsound, outdated methodology rather than a rigorous scientific process.[929] Christy Morrissey, an ecotoxicologist at the University of Saskatchewan in Saskatoon and Pierre Mineau, an expert on pesticide ecotoxicology at Carleton University in Ontario, who are researching the impact of the neonicotinoid chemicals in products like Roundup on bird populations, agree about the dangers posed by products like Roundup on insects and birds, as well as human beings.[930] Today, when farmers and home owners have a problem with a pest, they pick up a pesticide at their nearest hardware store. It is that simple. Few understand the consequences to themselves, their families or the wildlife around them.

While corporate propaganda leads us to believe that these deadly chemicals are necessary in order to feed the human population, it is worth remembering that agriculture was successful in feeding people for over twelve thousand years before the manufacturer of toxic chemicals. The Mayan for example, used herbal medicines to combat pests,[931] while the Chinese made their plants so healthy by the use of organic fertilizer that the pests were not attracted to the healthy plants.[932]

We can live without the deadly chemical fertilizers that are killing insects, birds, and ourselves. But more than survival is at stake. As one man put it simply, "I don't want my grandchild to go out in the forest and not hear the songbirds in the spring."[933]

An article printed in *The Hill* entitled, "Trump administration stops probing most bird deaths: report," however, informed us in December, 2019 that the Trump administration had not only stopped looking into bird deaths, but it has discouraged local governments and companies from taking precautionary steps to safeguard the creatures. The reason for this decision was to protect companies responsible for oil spills and chemical contaminations from having to report bird deaths to the Fish and Wildlife Service.[934]

Cats and Dogs

People love their pets, but many of us do not really know how to take care of them. We think we are being conscientious, but we are not. For example, diabetes is on a steep rise among cats and dogs. In England, in the last five years there has been a nine hundred per cent increase in diagnosed cases of the life-threatening condition. According to a study of nine thousand pets by pet insurer Animal Friends, cats are at risk from exploding rates of diabetes—with a 1,161 percent increase in feline claims since 2011. The data also shows cases in dogs have also seen an increase of eight hundred and fifty percent in the same time span.[935]

Weight gain is one of the main reasons diabetes in pets is on the rise and this occurs mainly because owners are feeding human food to their pets.

The same problem exists in the US. The month of November is now recognized as Pet Diabetes Month based on the growing prevalence of diabetes among family pets. Cats, and dogs, like humans, can be diagnosed with type 2 diabetes.⁹³⁶ The main reason that dogs, cats, and people get type 2 diabetes is because they eat junk food.⁹³⁷

While many people also kill dogs and cats for their meat and their fur, this is not a problem in America. Rather, we kill them because there is not enough room in the animal shelters to provide for them. In rural areas, these pets also inadvertently get caught in traps set for wild animals. In towns like Flint, Michigan, pets are also suffering from lead poisoning from drinking polluted water.⁹³⁸

Another cause of death, which has begun to sound alarm bells, is animal vaccinations. The World Small Animal Veterinary Association (WSAVA) has recommended to use vaccines, which help safeguard dogs against a bacterial infection. Consequently, puppies from eight weeks old are being inoculated with vaccines. In Britain, however, in the last three years, the Veterinary Medicines Directorate, which regulates animal drugs, has received two thousand reports of adverse reactions to Nobivac L4, including the suspected deaths of at least one hundred and twenty dogs. The drug manufacturer, MSD Animal Health, denied that Nobivac L4 was harmful to pets and that reports of adverse reactions were "rare."⁹³⁹

And then, of course, every once in a while, we get a news headline like this, "Supplier to Petco and Petsmart captured gassing, freezing, and torturing animals to death on secret video, claims PETA." The U.S. Department of Agriculture released a report on its January inspection of Holmes Chinchilla Ranch in which they found sick and dead animals, inadequate sanitation, untrained employees performing euthanasia and other deficiencies at a Pennsylvania small animal dealer. The facility kept thousands of hamsters, guinea pigs, rabbits, and other species.⁹⁴⁰

Farm Animals

Ninety-four percent of Americans nation-wide agree that it is important to have measures in place to ensure the food coming from farm animals is safe to eat and that animals raised for food on farms deserve to be free from abuse and cruelty. Yet ninety-nine percent of the nearly ten billion farm animals raised each year in the U.S. suffer conditions that would appall people if they saw it. Most of our meat, milk, and eggs come from industrial farms where profit, not animal welfare, is the main concern.[941] Consequently, most farm animals live in highly stressful environments that include such practices as:

- Cages and overcrowding;
- Physical alterations, like teeth-clipping or tail-docking, performed without anesthetic;
- Indoor confinement with poor air quality and unnatural light patterns;
- Inability to engage in natural behaviors;
- Breeding for fast growth or high yields of meat, milk, and eggs that compromises animal welfare;
- Neglect of sick and suffering animals, often due to high ratio of animals to workers; and[942]
- Rough or abusive handling by workers.[943]

Another assault on the cows, pigs, and chickens raised on industrial farms is the massive use of antibiotics to compensate for the unsanitary conditions in which animals are forced to live. The routine "sub-therapeutic" doses of antibiotics for livestock is so common, that even though scientists and government are aware of the risks of using antibiotics in this manner, there is still a long way to go before the practice is fully eliminated. About thirty-two million pounds[944] of antibiotics intended for farm animals are sold every year. While the meat industry claims that this is necessary to help the animals stay healthy and to keep the price of meat low,[945] there is a big problem with this argument. The problem is that continued "sub-therapeutic" dosing of billions of animals is creating disease-resistant superbugs.

For example, over one hundred studies have found that excessive use of antibiotics in livestock is creating drug resistance, not only in animals, but also in humans, putting us at risk of becoming victim to "superbug" bacterial mutations. For example, in a recent experiment with E. coli, the bacteria developed increasing resistance to antibiotics and ultimately survived doses one thousand times higher than they could initially survive, and they did so in a matter of eleven days.[946]

Superbugs currently hospitalize two million people a year in the United States and kill twenty-three thousand according to the CDC.[947] The death toll will continue to rise until or unless the underlying causes are properly addressed.

According to the largest, most thorough review of the drug resistance problem to date, by 2050, antibiotic-resistant disease will claim the lives of ten million people around the world each year. As was noted in The Atlantic:

> The report's language is sober but its numbers are apocalyptic. If antibiotics continue to lose their sting, resistant infections will sap $100 trillion from the world economy between now and 2050, equivalent to $10,000 for every person alive today. . . .[948]

Recently, scientists discovered a bacteria mutation that is resistant to a "last line of defense" antibiotic in the fight against E. coli and pneumonia. In a report published in *The Lancet: Infectious Diseases*, scientists wrote that they had found colistin-resistant bacteria on a Chinese pig farm. Later, they observed this resistant bacteria in raw meat and even humans. Colistin, which has been used for fifty years on animals and humans, is administered only when all other antibiotics have proven ineffective.[949]

According to David Plunkett, senior staff attorney of the Food Safety Program at the Center for Science in the Public Interest, "The number of antibiotics that will be effective in the future keeps getting smaller and smaller as we see antibiotic resistance. When asked about the colistin-resistant bacteria, he replied, "Now, this is the last brick in the wall between us and what the WHO is calling a 'post-antibiotic era.'"[950] Simply put, without antibiotics, we stand naked before severe illnesses and plagues of all sorts.

What is clear is that in order to protect Americans and our natural resources from further destruction, we must create laws to do so. In this effort, however, we are opposed by those corporations who profit by our destruction, and by the politician and the media whom they fund to protect their special interests.

Wild Animals

American Wolves

Wolves have often been painted as evil creatures in children's books and movies, but, in reality, scientists have found they do not live up to their evil reputation. Studies at Yellowstone National Park find that positive effects of wolves are felt throughout the park's ecosystems. Ravens, foxes, wolverines, coyotes, bald eagles, and even bears benefit because they feed on carcasses of animals killed by wolves. Coyotes have declined because wolves view them as competition and keep them out of their territories. Elk change their behavior to avoid wolf predation, which allows willow, aspen, and cottonwood regrowth. This, in turn, provides food for beavers and habitat for songbirds. The ecosystem changes and cascading effects continue and are expected to do so for some time.

Settlers moving westward depleted most populations of bison, deer, elk, and moose that were important prey for wolves. Consequently, wolves then turned to the sheep and cattle raised by the settlers as a replacement for their natural prey. To protect livestock, ranchers and government agencies began an eradication campaign. Bounty programs, initiated in the nineteenth century, continued as late as 1965, offering twenty to fifty dollars per wolf. Wolves were trapped, shot, dug from their dens, and hunted with dogs. Poisoned animal carcasses were left out for wolves, a practice that also killed eagles, ravens, foxes, bears, and other animals that fed on the tainted carrion.

By the time wolves were protected by the Endangered Species Act of 1973, only a few hundred remained in extreme northeastern Minnesota and a small number on Isle Royale, Michigan. Gray wolves were listed as endangered in the contiguous forty-eight States and in Mexico, except in Minnesota where they were listed as threatened. Alaska's wolf population numbers seventy-seven hundred to eleven hundred and twenty and is not endangered or threatened.

The wolf's comeback nationwide is due to its listing under the dangered pecies Act, which provided protection for them from unregulated killing. This resulted in increased scientific research. The Act also created management programs and education efforts that increased public understanding of wolf biology and behavior. Today, about 2,921 wolves live in Minnesota.

In the northern Rocky Mountains, the US Fish and Wildlife Service reintroduced gray wolves into Yellowstone National Park and US Forest Service lands in central Idaho in 1995 and 1996. The reintroduction was successful. By December 2010, there were at least 1,651 wolves in the northern Rocky Mountains of Montana, Idaho, and Wyoming.

Some people consider wolves to be extremely dangerous to humans, but wolf attacks on humans are extremely rare in North America, even in Canada and Alaska where there are consistently large wolf populations. Most documented attacks have been in areas where wolves became habituated to people when they were fed by people or attracted to their garbage.[951]

In January 2017, Representative Collin Peterson, a Democrat from Minnesota proposed a bill entitled the Gray Wolf State Management Act of 2017. This bill led to the removal of the gray wolves in Minnesota, Michigan, Wyoming ,and Yellowstone National Part from the Endangered Species list.[952]

Bears

Black Bears
There are three species of bears in North America, black bears, brown bears, and polar bears, each filling a particular environmental niche. In North America, the black bear (*Ursus americanus*) is the most common species of bear. It is native to the continent and ranges from northern Alaska to Mexico. In fact, the black bear is found in forty-one of the fifty states in the US[953]

Diseases rarely impact black bears. Young or smaller bears are occasionally preyed upon by grizzly bears, wolves, bobcats, and other black bears. Once bears reach maturity at four to eight years of age, however, hunting, trapping, poaching, and vehicle collisions are the main causes of death. Male bears suffer higher vehicle mortality than females because of their larger home ranges, in combination with their habit of crossing and following roadways. Adult male bears are not part of the family unit and therefore lead a solitary existence.

Black bears are highly curious, very intelligent, mobile, and adaptable animals that quickly learn by trial and error, adapting to new stimuli and circumstances.

In many areas of the county, black bear populations have recovered from historic lows. Beginning in the late 1980s through the start of the twenty-first century, black bear numbers increased at a rate of two percent a year continent-wide. Changes benefiting black bears during this time included reforestation of the landscape, black bear reintroduction programs, and regulations on hunting black bears.

Though black bears have not reclaimed all of their original range across America, they have rebounded to populations of an estimated eight hundred thousand bears in thirty-seven states and all Canadian Provinces. At the same time, however, human populations have also expanded and, in some areas, these two expanding populations are intersecting. In overlapping habitats, humans can often coexist with black bears. The challenge is to find a balance between the number of black bears a habitat can support and the number of bears the human community will accept.[954]

In truth, we do not have much to fear: There are only three fatalities a year from black bears even though millions of people hike and camp in the wilderness or live near bear habitat. By comparison, twenty-six people get killed by dogs every year, and ninety people are killed every year by lightning.[955]

Brown Bears

The brown bear is Eurasian in origin, having entered Alaska one hundred thousand years ago, though they did not move south until thirteen thousand years ago.[956] Grizzly bears are a subspecies of brown bear that are still fairly common in the mountainous regions of California, western Canada, and Alaska. In remote western Canada and Alaska there are still about thirty thousand grizzlies, while in California and other western states only about one thousand grizzlies survive.

Brown bears differ in size depending on access to food and water and other ecological considerations. The largest male grizzlies can stand seven feet tall and weigh in at fifteen hundred pounds. They also have one of the largest brains of any extant carnivore relative to their body size and have been known to engage in tool-use.

Adult male bears are particularly aggressive and are avoided by adolescent males both at concentrated feeding opportunities and chance encounters. Female bears with cubs rival adult males in aggression, and are much more intolerant of other bears than single females.

Brown bears usually avoid areas where urbanization has occurred, unlike the smaller, more inoffensive American black bear, which can adapt to areas peripheral to human settlements. However, bears can easily lose their natural cautiousness when attracted to human-created food sources, such as garbage dumps, litterbins, and dumpsters. Brown bears may even venture into human dwellings or barns in search of food as humans encroach on their habitats. Where attractive food and concentrated human settlements overlap, human-bear conflict usually results in a population decline of the bears.

Relocation of the bear has been used to separate bears from the human environment, but it does not address the problem of the bear's newly learned association with humans and our food. Also, placing a bear in another habitat may lead to competition and social conflict with other bears that often results in the injury or death of the less dominant bear. A large proportion of bears that are killed for public safety are female.

In the wild, brown bears seldom attack humans on sight, and usually avoid people. In Russia, it estimated that one in a thousand on-foot encounters with brown bears results in attack.[957] They are, however, unpredictable in temperament, and may attack if they are surprised or feel threatened. Despite the low rate of attack, they appear to be the most dangerous northern carnivore to humans, attacking more people on average annually than American black bears, cougars or gray wolves. Even so, there are on average only two fatal attacks by bears per year in North America.[958]

Polar Bears
The bear species most under assault by human beings is the polar bear. There are estimated to be twenty-two thousand to thirty-one thousand polar bears living across the arctic expanse including Alaska, Canada, Russia, Greenland, and Norway.

Polar bears are the largest land carnivores in the world and sit at the top of the food chain in the biologically rich Arctic. Polar bears feed primarily on the fat of ice-dependent seals but have been known to eat walrus and beluga whales, birds' eggs, and occasional vegetation. The remains of their kills provide food for many other Arctic wildlife species, giving polar bears a vital role in their ecosystem.

Many adaptations make polar bears uniquely suited to life in icy habitats. Their fur is thicker than any other bears' and covers even their feet for warmth and traction on ice. A thick layer of blubber beneath their fur provides buoyancy and insulation. The long neck and narrow skull of the polar bear probably aid in streamlining the animal in the water while warming the air that they breathe, and their front feet are large, flat, and oar-like, making them excellent swimmers.

The most important habitats for polar bears are the edges of pack ice where currents and wind interact, forming a continually melting and refreezing matrix of ice patches and open spaces in the ocean between patches of sea ice. These are the areas where polar bears can find the greatest number of seals.

As the sea ice advances and retreats each season, individual polar bears may travel thousands of miles per year to find food.

Polar bears are generally solitary as adults, except during breeding and cub rearing. They are strong swimmers and individuals have been seen in open Arctic waters as far as two hundred miles from land. Unlike brown bears, polar bears do not hibernate in the winter.[959]

The greatest threat to polar bears is climate change, which is relentlessly destroying their sea ice habitat. Polar bears rely on sea ice to hunt and store energy for the summer and autumn, when food can be scarce. Sea ice now melts earlier in the spring and forms later in the autumn in the bears' southern range, like Hudson Bay and James Bay in Canada. When bears spend longer periods without food, their health declines. For every week earlier the ice breaks up in Hudson Bay, bears come ashore roughly twenty-two pounds lighter and in poorer condition.[960]

Unhealthy bears lead to lower reproduction rates and local extinction. Scientists have found the main cause of death for cubs to be either lack of food or lack of fat on nursing mothers.

Another threat to polar bears is that the oil and gas industry is increasingly moving into the Arctic as more accessible reserves in the south dry up. Contact with oil spills can reduce the insulating effect of the bears' fur. The bear must then use more energy to keep warm, and compensate by increasing its caloric intake, which is, at the same time, becoming more difficult.

Polar bears also ingest oil through grooming and through eating contaminated prey. The ingested oil causes liver and kidney damage and long-term toxicity. Bears can be poisoned by even a limited amount of oil on their fur.

There is currently no effective method for cleaning or controlling an oil spill in icy, arctic waters, where difficult weather conditions are common. Offshore operations pose the greatest risk, because routine emissions, spills, or leaks are discharged directly into the sea or on the sea ice.

As top predators, polar bears are exposed to high levels of pollutants through their food. Bears with high levels of organic pollutants have low levels of vitamin A, thyroid hormones, and some antibodies. These are important for a wide range of biological functions, such as growth, reproduction, and the ability to fight off diseases. These toxins are also causing mutations. For example, females have been found with partially-developed male sexual organs in 1.5 % of the polar bears sampled in recent years. Scientists believe this could be the result of long-range pollutants.

In some areas, the mother bears' milk contains particularly high concentrations of toxic chemicals. The milk can actually poison the cubs, leading to lower survival rates. What are the toxins that are endangering polar bears at this time? They are heat resistant chemicals, like PCBs; industrial by-products such as dioxins and furans, and pesticides like DDT, dieldrin, and lindane.[961]

Loss of Large Mammals Around the World

All around the world, the survival of large mammals is being threatened by human activity and climate change. Lions, tigers, bears, elephants, rhinoceros, great apes—all the exciting and awesome animals that we learned about as children and which provide us with such priceless beauty, fascination, and mystery are now faced with extinction. Extinction does not mean that a bunch of lions are killed, it means that the species is killed off, never to live again.

According to biologists around the world,[962] half of the earth's species could go extinct by 2050, unless we slow our population growth and address man-made climate change. In June 2015, the journal, *Science Advances*, examined the rate at which species were going extinct. It found that the rate of mammal and vertebrate species loss was up to one hundred times higher than past rates, indicating that a mass extinction is already underway.[963]

Science Advances is far from the only study that presents evidence humans are the reason behind the next mass extinction. Pope Francis, a concerned environmentalist, recently convened a world conference entitled, "How to Save the Natural World on Which We Depend." The conference included a workshop on biological extinction, and featured expert speakers. [964]

The conference aimed to highlight biological extinction in a global context and to identify root causes, including hunting, clearing land for agriculture and urban development, the introduction of alien species like weeds, pests, and pathogens, as well as the impact of climate change.

The leading cause of species extinction is habitat destruction, but scientists have found that the distribution of vulnerable species is uneven and highly clumped. There are 'biodiversity hotspots,' habitats which are already disproportionately reduced.

Conservatively, there are almost eight million species of animals, of these about eighty-five percent are terrestrial. According to the most recent studies, scientists now believe that there are:

- 7.77 million species of animals;
- 298,000 species of plants;
- 611,000 species of fungi (moulds, mushrooms);
- 36,400 species of protozoa (single-cell organisms); and
- 27,500 species of chromista (including, eg. brown algae, diatoms, water moulds, etc).[965]

Humanity is rapidly destroying the habitats that are most species-rich. About two-thirds of all species occur in the tropics, largely in the tropical humid forests. These forests originally covered between 5.4 million and 6.9 million square miles, depending on the exact definition, and today only about half of the original area remains. Much of the Amazon rain-forest reduction is recent and clearing has now eliminated three hundred and six thousand square miles of trees since 1970.[966] Burning and selective logging severely damages several times the area that is cleared.[967] The fires that burned Australia's forests in 2019 and 2020 is another example of the destruction of animal habitat that killed thousands of rare species.

Another cause of death for large animals is hunters. According to Dr. McClenachan, an eco-biologist, who discussed her recent study with *The Christian Science Monitor*, "A combination of social and biological factors create an extreme risk of extinction." [968]

Because large animals typically take longer to grow and mature than small creatures, they can be hunted at a faster rate than they can reproduce. And species traded for nonperishable parts, like tusks or dried fins, are in greater danger than species sought healthy and alive.

Also, because nonperishable products can be stockpiled by globally distributed black-market networks, it is far more difficult to monitor poachers and break up their long and diffuse supply chains. This stymies efforts to identify the hunted populations and develop effective conservation strategies.

Conditions are worse for marine mammals because the protections for land animals, as limited as they are, do not hold true in the ocean. Marine animals like whales, sharks, and rays have a greater risk of extinction than do land animals. A recent study published in *Science Magazine* confirms this.[969] As on the land, the larger marine animals are uniquely imperiled right now; e.g. sharks, whales, giant clams, sea turtles, and tuna. According to the authors, the disproportionate threat to larger marine organisms reflects the "unique human propensity to cull the largest members of a population."[970]

What can be done? We must continue trying to preserve natural areas, particularly those areas with topographic features where large animals might have a chance in the face of continued climate change. We can also try to insure sustainable interactions between the people of given areas and their biodiversity. As far as plants are concerned, we can domesticate, cultivate, or put them in seed banks to preserve as many as possible while they are still here. Cryopreservation may also be possible for some of them. All of these methods need to be improved, but they will clearly succeed only when laws and social conditions have been put in place that curtail the destabilizing aggression that we and our ancestors have been practicing for tens of thousands of years. The problem of biological extinction must be viewed within a well-developed social context in which we try to improve our behavior toward the Earth and our fellow species.[971]

Unfortunately, such safeguards are not likely to occur during the Trump administration. The Endangered Species Act, which has prevented ninety-nine percent of the species under its care from vanishing, and is precisely the kind of effective tool we need today, is under attack by the House and Senate. While this act has revived the bald eagle, the American alligator, the California condor, and many others, today's anti-environment interests are proposing to put imperiled wildlife species back on the chopping block.

House Natural Resources Chairman Rob Bishop (R-UT) has said he wants to "repeal and replace" the Endangered Species Act, while, in the meantime, others are supporting legislative proposals that would make it harder for the US Fish and Wildlife Service to resolve Endangered Species Act lawsuits.

Legislative attacks are already being introduced in the current (115th) Congress. Proposed bills would put imperiled species at greater risk by establishing arbitrary land boundaries where species protections would not apply; imposing limitations on the ability of citizens to help enforce the Endangered Species Act; cutting the number of park rangers; undermining the use of science under the Endangered Species Act; declaring open season on individual species, including wolves and sage grouse; and by blocking federal protections or denying existing protections.

As of December 27, 2018, the Center for Biological Diversity reported that the Trump administration is now "on the cusp of finalizing rules drafted by the US Department of the Interior designed to make it harder to protect imperiled wildlife and important habitat." The main reason for wanting to gut the Endangered Species act is to allow further land development and greater profits for the large ranchers and real estate industry.[972]

But this short-sighted approach to making money imperils human beings as well. Biodiversity protects against climate change and helps ensure a stable food supply. And these have economic benefits that dwarf the value of developing land.

Scientists say that while the Endangered Species Act focuses on individual species, it actually helps protect ecosystems that support those species. In turn, healthy ecosystems help keep the air and water clean that people depend on, while also lowering health care costs that result from air, water, and soil pollution.

The greatest economic value of ecosystems is the role they play as greenhouse gas sinks that absorb climate change-causing pollutants like carbon dioxide. By restoring forests, instead of destroying them, they would be able to absorb nearly a third of global carbon emissions. While plants do the actual absorbing of gases, animals, including those protected under the Endangered Species Act, play a key role in keeping those ecosystems intact.[973]

Loss of Plant Species

Plants provide the oxygen we breathe and the food we eat and thereby serve as the foundation of most life on Earth. They also provide the majority of medicines in use today. Of the nearly 300,000 known species of plants, scientists have evaluated only 12,914 species. It appears we still have much to learn. The problem is that many of these species will become extinct before we learn about them. Of the species that we have studied and use, already sixty-eight percent of these plant species are threatened with extinction.[974]

Unlike animals, plants cannot readily move when their habitat is destroyed. Even dominant species in a given ecosystem will disappear over time because they are not able to disperse to new habitat patches. When a plant species in an ecosystem dies out, it also threatens other plant species and insects, etc., that depended upon it.

Although extinction is a natural phenomenon that occurs at a natural rate of about one to five species per year, scientists estimate we are now losing species at one thousand to ten thousand times the natural rate, with literally dozens going extinct every day.[975] At this rate we face a future in which as many as thirty to fifty percent of all species on the planet are headed toward extinction by mid-century.[976]

Unlike past mass extinctions, caused by events like asteroid strikes, volcanic eruptions, and natural climate shifts, the current crisis is almost entirely caused by human beings. In fact, ninety-nine percent of the currently threatened species are at risk from human activities that cause habitat loss, introduce exotic species, or contribute to global warming.[977] Because the rate of change in our biosphere is increasing and because every species' extinction potentially leads to the extinction of others bound to that species in a complex ecological web, numbers of extinctions are likely to snowball in the coming decades as ecosystems unravel.

While conservationists and scientists often justifiably focus their efforts on species-rich ecosystems like rainforests and coral reefs, a comprehensive strategy for saving biodiversity must also include habitat types with fewer species, like grasslands, tundra, and polar seas, for which any loss could be irreversibly devastating.

In the last resolve, biodiversity benefits take place at the local level and it is for the local people to ensure that species survive. This gives us another powerful argument for economic decentralization.

Climate Change

Climate change is one of the most polarizing topics in the US today, not because scientists disagree or because the majority of Americans do not think it is occurring, but because the fossil fuel industry and its financially-supported conservative think tanks continue to pump out misleading information, conduct false ad campaigns, and provide talking points to the Republican party in order to create as much doubt as possible about whether climate change is a real threat or not. These climate-deniers burrow into scientific studies continually questioning their integrity. They tell half-truths and lies. They say there is no consensus among scientists, although ninety-seven percent of climate scientists around the world agree that climate change caused by the burning of fossil fuels is real and catastrophically dangerous to all life on Earth.

Scientific organizations and agencies have warned us innumerable times that we need to act quickly to slow the burning of fossil fuels that emit chemicals that are continually heating the atmosphere if we are to mitigate the making of a hellish planet over the next fifty years. While there may be contradictory findings from time to time, which is a natural result of scientific inquiry, the overall cause of climate change has been agreed upon for decades.

Certainly, climate change due to global warming is a complex issue and when left-wing politicians and non-profits oversimplify it, they open themselves to challenges from climate change deniers. Nonetheless, the majority of the American people believe that climate is changing because we can see and feel the changes all around us—the melting of the ice caps, the violent weather, each year becoming warmer than the last, etc.

The general message of the Left is that "Climate change is global warming caused by too much CO_2 in the atmosphere due to the burning of fossil fuels. We stop climate change by making the transition to renewable energy."[978] This is certainly a key aspect of the story, and we certainly should have begun using more renewable energy twenty years ago, but this is not the whole story and the Left hurts its case by oversimplifying it.

While the burning of fossil fuels and the impact of toxins like nitrous oxide and CFC are heating up our atmosphere, it is also necessary to understand the role that water vapor plays in amplifying the heating of our atmosphere. In fact, water vapor constitutes ninety-five percent of existing greenhouse gases. As the earth heats up, more water evaporates from the oceans and into the atmosphere. The additional water in the atmosphere further heats the surface, leading to even more water evaporating. In effect, water vapor envelops the Earth in a thick, steamy blanket. Warming due to carbon dioxide emissions from fossil fuel combustion evaporates even more water, increasing the thickness of the blanket, which leads to more heating, which leads to more water vapor. The loop is called the water vapor feedback, and it has the potential to be a serious problem.[979]

Climate change deniers often claim that because CO_2 is not as pervasive as water vapor, adding a little more CO_2 to the atmosphere is harmless. What this argument misses is the fact that water vapor creates what scientists call a 'positive feedback loop' in the atmosphere which makes any temperature changes from CO_2 larger than they would be otherwise.

Studies show that water vapor feedback roughly doubles the amount of warming caused by CO2. So, if there is a 1°C change caused by CO2, the water vapor will cause the temperature to go up an additional 1°C. When other feedback loops are included, the total warming from a potential 1°C change caused by CO2 is, in reality, as much as 3°C.

At this point there has been so much attention on the negative impacts of CO2 and other noxious heat trapping gases, that the public has not given enough attention to water vapor's climate warming potential.

We know that water is evaporated from the land and sea and falls as rain or snow all the time. Thus, the amount held in the atmosphere as water vapor varies greatly in just hours and days as a result of the prevailing weather in any location. So even though water vapor is the greatest greenhouse gas, it is relatively short-lived. On the other hand, CO2 is removed from the air by natural geological-scale processes and these take a long time to work. Consequently CO2 stays in our atmosphere for centuries. A small additional amount has a much greater long-term effect.[980]

But how do we mitigate the impact of water vapor in its role in heating our atmosphere? We cannot impact, nor do we want to fool with, the natural hydrological cycle. But there are instances where steam that we create is seen rising into our sky, such as from jet trails and the water cooling towers at power plants. This is man-made water vapor. It gathers in our atmosphere and prevents solar energy from returning to deep space. Instead, it absorbs this thermal energy and heats the atmosphere. The amount of water vapor emissions caused by man is very difficult to quantify, because there are few records at present. Nonetheless, we know that the main culprits are power stations that use huge cooling towers to cool their circulating water and we can see the plumes of steam from miles away. In order to avoid this emission, an alternative method of water cooling can be found, such as using seawater or water from saline aquifers in a closed-circuit system. This would avoid the release of condensation.[981]

We also know that the act of planting trees draws carbon dioxide out of the atmosphere and thereby helps to cool the planet. Large campaigns to plant trees and other vegetation would also mitigate the impact of climate change. This is only to say, that the problem is more complex than is commonly held and that there may be solutions that we have not adequately employed or be aware of simply by concentrating on carbon dioxide.

In any case, the climate change deniers have frittered away so much time already, that even if we could miraculously cut carbon dioxide, methane, and nitrous oxide from the air, we will still be living through increased heat waves and extreme weather that we have already set in motion. It will still take more than a century for the CO_2 levels to drop to three hundred and fifty parts per million (ppm), which is considered by scientists to be the "safe threshold." Today, we stand at four hundred parts per million by volume of the atmosphere.[982]

What do scientists mean by "safe threshold"? They mean that once we exceeded the limit of three hundred and fifty parts per million of CO_2, we opened ourselves to the following climate changes—increasing Earth's average temperature, changes in the patterns and amounts of precipitation, forest fires, reduced ice and snow cover, rising sea levels, increased acidity in the oceans, increased frequency and intensity of extreme weather events, shift in eco-systems, and an increased threat to existing life forms, and the debilitation of human health. Any one of these changes is potentially catastrophic.

We have already begun to experience these changes because we are already fifty ppm over the "safe threshold." As the atmosphere continues to heat up, new threats will emerge, for example, our food supply will be impacted because more land will be too dry to plant. We will then be forced to use more fresh water, which is already in short supply. These problems are projected to cause mass starvation, particularly in the southern hemisphere.

So also, our coastal cities will be lost to rising seas, turning millions of people into environmental refugees, having lost everything they own. What will become of them? Ecosystems will be increasingly jeopardized.[983] The physical and mental wellbeing of our species will be put at unimaginable risk. Because we have already passed the safe threshold, we are already experiencing the above mentioned climate changes regardless of the propaganda of climate change deniers. Some Republican politician deniers, in order to curry favor with their financial backers, will admit to climate change, but will say that it is not caused by human beings, that it is a natural occurring event. Let us examine this.

According to the Environmental Protection Agency website, prior to being gutted by the Trump administration, the "Earth's temperature depends on the balance between energy entering and leaving the planet's system. Simple enough to understand. When incoming energy from the sun is absorbed by the Earth system, Earth warms. When the sun's energy is reflected back into space, Earth avoids warming and cools."[984]

Many factors, both natural and human, can cause changes in Earth's energy balance, including: variations in the sun's energy reaching Earth, changes in the reflectivity of Earth's atmosphere and surface, and changes in the greenhouse effect. All of these changes impact the amount of heat retained by the Earth's atmosphere because when sunlight reaches Earth, it is either reflected or absorbed.

The amount that is reflected or absorbed depends on Earth's surface and atmosphere. Light-colored objects and surfaces, like snow and clouds, reflect most sunlight, while darker objects and surfaces, like the ocean, forests, or soil absorb more sunlight.

These factors have caused Earth's climate to change many times throughout history. In fact, scientists have pieced together a record of Earth's climate, dating back hundreds of thousands of years (and, in some cases, millions or hundreds of millions of years), by analyzing a number of indirect measures of climate such as ice cores, tree rings, glacier lengths, pollen remains, and ocean sediments, and by studying changes in Earth's orbit around the sun.[985]

This demonstrates that the climate system varies naturally over a wide range of time scales. In general, climate changes prior to the Industrial Revolution in the 1700s can be explained by natural causes, such as changes in solar energy, volcanic eruptions, and natural changes in greenhouse gas (GHG) concentrations.

Recent climate changes, however, cannot be explained by natural causes alone. Research indicates that natural causes do not explain most observed warming, especially warming since the mid-twentieth century. Rather, human activities have been the dominant cause of that warming.

Since the Industrial Revolution began around 1750, human activity has contributed substantially to climate change by adding CO_2 and other heat-trapping gases to the atmosphere.

The most important heat-trapping gases directly emitted by humans include carbon dioxide (CO_2), methane (CH_4), nitrous oxide (N_2O), and several other chemicals, which at the moment are lesser threats.

Carbon dioxide is the primary greenhouse gas that is contributing to recent climate change. CO_2 is absorbed and emitted naturally as part of the carbon cycle, through plant and animal respiration, volcanic eruptions, and ocean-atmosphere exchange. However, the human burning of fossil fuels and destruction of ecosystems have released large amounts of CO_2, causing concentrations in the atmosphere to rise.

Atmospheric CO_2 concentrations have increased by more than forty percent since pre-industrial times, from approximately two hundred and eighty parts per million by volume in the eighteenth century to over four hundred today. And recently the monthly average concentration at Mauna Loa, the world's largest volcano, now exceeds four hundred ppm for the first time in human history. The current CO_2 level is higher than it has been in the last eight hundred thousand years.[986]

While volcanic eruptions are responsible for releasing large quantities of CO_2 into the atmosphere, the US Geological Survey (USGS) reports that volcanoes release less than one percent of the carbon dioxide released currently by human activities.[987] In fact, humans are changing climate one hundred and seventy times faster than nature.[988]

This results in over thirty billion tons of CO_2 emitted into the atmosphere every year. Think about that— thirty billion tons per year of CO_2. With these kinds of numbers, it is not difficult to see how we might be warming up the atmosphere and changing the climate.

The graph below produced by the EPA, prior to the Trump administration, shows the increase in greenhouse gas (GHG) concentrations in the atmosphere over the last two thousand years. Increases in concentrations of these gases since 1750 are due to human activities in the industrial era.

Concentration units are parts per million (ppm) or parts per billion (ppb), indicating the number of molecules of the greenhouse gas per million or billion molecules of air.

From reports and from our personal experience of hotter temperatures, melting ice, and rising sea levels, we can already see the impact of global warming. The predictions of what will happen as fossil fuel emissions continue to heat up the planet and the atmosphere include more acidic

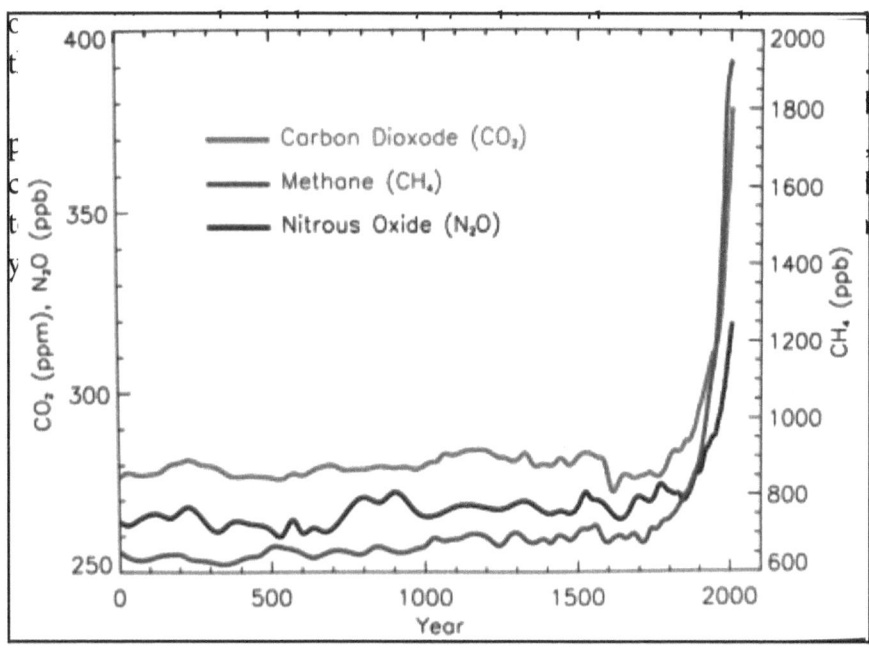

Fig. 5-23: Rise in Greenhouse Gases Over Last Two Thousand Years

Scientists tell us that the start of the Triassic period was a desolate time in Earth's history. It was either the violent volcanoes or a fatal run-in with a comet or asteroid that triggered the extinction of more than ninety percent of Earth's species and ninety-five percent of sea species, all wiped out by high levels of CO_2 in the atmosphere. This caused the climate to be exceedingly dry across the land masses with extremely hot summers and nasty cold winters in the continental interior. Areas near the coast were pummeled by seasonal monsoons. There were no polar ice caps.

Scientists know that climate change has played a role in every mass extinction. And climate change does not occur without a reason.[990] Whereas climate changes occurred in the past due to comet collisions and volcanic eruptions, today it is being caused by humans burning fossil fuels.

According to Aradhna Tripati, a professor at the Institute of the Environment and Sustainability, "It's clear-cut. It's like you're adding drops of poison to a glass of water. You can see it happening."[991]

For the present, the Trump administration and the climate deniers are in office and are doing everything they can to remove the safeguards that have been put in place to curb greenhouse gas emissions caused by the burning of coal, oil, and gas, which create the molecules of carbon dioxide, methane, and nitrous oxide that fill the atmosphere, trapping heat and causing global warming.

Scientists all over the world, having conducted thousands of studies, concur that the atmosphere is warming and the primary cause is human burning of fossil fuels. To them the argument is over. They have moved on to studying how to stop it. It is only ignorance, duplicity, and/or greed that lead the fossil fuel industry and the politicians on their payroll to continually deny the existence of climate change and thereby slow any movement to mitigate its impact on humanity. Even though scientists, medical professionals, religious leaders, world governments, citizens, corporations, the world's scientists, the majority of world leaders, and even the pentagon, say that climate change caused by burning fossil fuels is getting worse, deniers in positions of power continue to turn a deaf ear.

Who are the climate change deniers? Their movement is not "skeptical" scientists as the politicians would have us believe. Rather, the climate change denier movement is led by organizations like the Heritage Foundation, the Cato Institute, and the Ayn Rand Institute which are paid by the Koch Brothers and other fossil fuel industry corporations to develop arguments against the science of climate change. For example, a 2013 study found that seventy-two percent of climate denial books, mostly published since 1990, were linked to right-wing think tanks, a figure that rises to eighty-seven percent if self-published books are excluded.[992]

Naomi Klein, in her groundbreaking book on the politics of climate change, *This Changes Everything*, contends that the climate change deniers are driven by the need to defend global capitalism regardless of cost to the public or the planet. Her research and investigative journalism have caused her to state:

> They know full well that ours is a global economy created by, and fully reliant upon, the burning of fossil fuels and that a dependency on that foundational cannot be changed with a few gentle market mechanisms. It re-

quires heavy-duty interventions: sweeping bans on polluting activities, deep subsides for green alternatives, pricey penalties for violations, new taxes, new public works programs, reversals of privatizations – the list of ideological outrages goes on and on. Everything, in short, that these think tanks – which have always been public proxies for far more powerful corporate interests – have been busily attacking for decades.[993]

The religious right also has a stake in this, according to Klein:

And for many conservatives, particularly religious ones, the challenge goes deeper still, threatening not just faith in markets but core cultural narratives about what humans are doing here on earth. Are we masters, here to subdue and dominate, or are we one species among many, at the mercy of powers more complex and unpredictable than even our most powerful computers can model? As Robert Manne, a professor of politics at La Trobe University in Melbourne, puts it, climate science is for many conservatives 'an affront to their deepest and most cherished basic faith: the capacity and indeed the right of *mankind* to subdue the Earth and all its fruits and to establish a *mastery* over Nature.' For these conservatives, he notes, 'such a thought is not merely mistaken. It is intolerable and deeply offensive. Those preaching this doctrine have to be resisted and indeed denounced.'[994]

Thus, the religious conservative preachers are fervently spitting out their sound bites to their sentimental congregations about how the liberals are perpetrating the biggest hoax on the American people that has ever been attempted.

The battle for the survival of life on earth has begun. The people who see the handwriting on the wall are speaking out, doing research, organizing, marching, holding conferences, planting trees and doing whatever they can to alert the world to the dangers of climate change. On the other side, the fossil fuel and chemical industries and their bought and paid for think tanks and politicians continue to spread lies, intimidate, deny, censor, confuse, and destroy any legislation that has tried to change the capitalist status quo. It is a life and death struggle for humanity and for many species on the planet. A revolution is required to save humanity and the planet. There is no other choice in the matter because the power elite will not change their destructive behavior regardless of reason or common sense. Fortunately, there is a method to create a revolution that has not been widely considered by the average American. This method will be discussed in depth in *Universal Ideology: The Thought of P. R. Sarkar*, and *Nuclear Revolution*, books II and III of this trilogy.

Chapter Six: Meeting Basic Needs

WHILE THE EARTH'S TEMPERATURE continues to rise, species are eliminated and humans become more ill due to pollution and climate change, self-seeking politicians fritter away the hours and days in the countdown to environmental collapse. While the US economy and society drift steadily downward, we the people must still meet our basic needs on a daily basis. This is becoming more difficult because the cost of living keeps rising while the quality of the goods and services required to meet our basic needs continues to worsen. In this section, we will look at the industries that have direct responsibility for providing the American people with our basic necessities of food, shelter, clothing, health care, and education.

What is Right Livelihood?

Before we begin to analyze the systems that provide the American people with their basic necessities, let us assume that in order to create the society of our dreams, everyone would be engaged in *right livelihood*. This is to say that everyone would be working in a job that does not cause harm and is ethically positive. Most of us spend the majority of our waking lives at work, so it is important to assess how our work affects our families and society in general. Given this assumption, let us see if the intention of the corporations that provide our basic needs have our best interest at heart, or are they driven by another motivation.

To begin with, we need to make the distinction between *need* and *desire*. A need is something that one cannot live without. A desire, on the other hand, is something that might give us pleasure or add to the quality of our life, but is not necessary for survival.

Meeting one's basic *needs* is the first priority of every human being and the first priority of every family. It should also be the first goal of human society. In other words, in a democracy, the government and businesses should be primarily motivated to meet the basic needs of the people. This motivation is what legitimizes the existence of government and business. Their role is to foster the health and well-being of its citizens and consumers. When this is not the goal, the health and well-being of the society is diminished and the legitimacy of the government and business is denied.

Without the ability to meet our basic needs, we can neither have the presence of mind, nor the energy and discipline required to make progress, either as individuals or as a society.

This is why American people should stand on the following principle:

> In order to realize the greatest human potential, we must first meet certain basic necessities. It is the birthright of every human being to be guaranteed the opportunity to work for food, clothing, shelter, education, and health care. No one should suffer from lack of, or be denied, these basic necessities due to illness, calamity, fate or greed. It is also the birthright of every human being to receive love and care, and to live in a clean environment, which promotes growth and well-being, without fear.

Given that basic necessities are required for our survival and our all-round health, it is fundamental that these needs are recognized as "human birthrights." In other words, at this state in our evolution as a species, every human being is entitled to their birthright simply by dint of being born. A birthright should be a given and not an exception that is hit or miss due to someone's good or bad fortune.

If people are unable to work due to illness or other environmental factors, the larger society must be structured to support them. Human society has evolved in its capacity to do this and everyone has helped to make it happen. Today, we have systems of communication, finance, and production that are global in scope. Therefore, if we are born into the world today, we deserve to have our basic needs met. There is enough wealth on this planet to be able to do this. What stands in the way of this happening is the ruling elites of national governments and multinational corporations who continually drain wealth from the people due to their relentless greed for more profit. Let us see how this reality plays out in the meeting of people's basic needs.

The Right to Food

As human beings, at this time of history, food is a divine right and a human right. Yet many Americans, in the richest country in the world, go hungry and are malnourished. We need to understand how this happens.

A total of 41,204,000 Americans were food insecure in 2016. This constitutes 12.9 percent of all Americas, or approximately one in eight people. The fear of going hungry varied considerably from state to state, but a staggering 20.1 percent of the people in Mississippi went hungry and 17.2 percent were hungry in Arkansas. These are the two states with the highest rates of food insecurity, although there are people in every county in every state in the country who go hungry sometime during the year.[995]

For households with incomes near or below the federal poverty line, predominately black and Hispanic households and households with children headed by a single parent, the rates of food insecurity were substantially higher than the national average. About fifty-nine percent of these households reported that in the previous month, they had participated in one or more of the three largest Federal nutrition assistance programs: Supplemental Nutrition Assistance Program (SNAP); Special Supplemental Nutritional Program for Women, Infants, and Children (WIC); and National School Lunch Program.

According to the United States Census Bureau, in 2015 there were 43.1 million Americans living in poverty. Race again played a large factor. The 2015 poverty rate for Blacks was 24.1 percent in 2014, for Hispanics

21.4 percent, and for Asians 11.4 percent. For White (non-Hispanic) the poverty rate was 9.1 percent.[996]

One in every five American children, or 14.5 million kids, lived in poverty in 2015. These statistics are all the more painful when we realize that these children are impoverished and hungry because of policies designed by the ruling elite and carried out by the federal government to keep our people weak and in fear.

The elites designed and legislated a food policy that gave rise to an industrialized agriculture sector controlled by a few transnational food corporations together with a small group of mega-retailers. It is a model designed to generate maximum profits for the corporate owners as well as to control the American population. Instead of being dedicated to producing healthy food for all Americans, it focuses on the production of raw materials such as agro-fuels, animal feeds, and the manufacturing of junk foods that has endangered the health of the American people. This corporate food system has decimated rural America, caused an enormous loss of agricultural holdings, and destroyed tens of thousands of farm families. In addition, the junk food it creates has caused widespread cancer, diabetes, heart disease, and obesity.[997]

Industrial Agriculture

Let us begin our discussion of industrialized agriculture with how farmers are represented. Almost all farmers are members of the *American Farm Bureau Federation (AFBF)*, but it is a myth that this organization represents the interests of farmers. Like all large corporations, the AFBF is controlled from the top and its leadership is self-perpetuating by design. The Farm Bureau was not founded by farmers. Actually, it was founded in the early 1900s by the New York Chamber of Commerce and funded by the Rockefellers and the Vanderbilts via the Chicago Board of Trade.[998] It was designed by the elites to counter the nonpartisan, popular farmers' movement that was emerging at the time. The underlying pattern of exploitation of the farmers by the rich has not changed in the ensuing generations. As John Hansen, president of the Nebraska Farmers Union, told *Extra!*:

I've been working on farming concerns for 30 years, and I can't think of a major issue where the Farm Bureau didn't have the same position as the grain and meat processors. It's impossible to represent the interests of food producers [farmers] as well as food processors.... The two groups' economic interests are almost always at odds.⁹⁹⁹

While the mass media positions the American Farm Bureau as a group that promotes farmers' interests, what it basically does is provide workshops and conferences for farmers that promote the sale and use of chemicals.

The Green Revolution

Let us take another example of how the agriculture industry works. In 1958, India experienced a foreign exchange crisis. This was the opportunity that the Rockefellers and other western capitalists had been waiting for to stop once and for all India's socialist leanings and its economic restrictions on foreign capital. The World Bank immediately intervened with its "Aid India Club" and loaned India one billion dollars in aid, which included money for "technical assistance," which meant that farmers would be trained to use the chemicals produced by the Rockefeller-led US agriculture industry. The Ford Foundation also stepped in with a "food crisis" team that pushed agro-chemicals and pharmaceuticals on India, but, not surprisingly, ignored the people's housing and social service needs.

During 1965 and 1966, India experienced a famine. Undersecretary of Commerce Franklin Delano Roosevelt, Jr., led a delegation of executives to New Delhi for the purpose of "persuading the government to adopt policies more attractive to potential investors." Waiting in the wings was Rockefeller's Standard Oil that wanted price and distribution restrictions lifted on their Bombay fertilizer plant. Other petroleum producers lobbied to set up fertilizer plants to utilize naphtha, an otherwise useless petroleum byproduct. Naphtha is a colorless, volatile petroleum distillate, which is an intermediate product between gasoline and benzene, a deadly carcinogen. The Ford and Rockefeller foundations also wanted to expand the use of their new high yield seeds, deliberately bred for large fertilizer and pesticide inputs.[1000] Voila, the Green Revolution was born!

Beginning around 2007, the Rockefeller Foundation and the Gates Foundation together began funding efforts for a "Second Green Revolution," which would feature genetic engineering, and, of course, more insecticides, fungicides, pesticides, chemical fertilizers, and other toxic additives produced from petroleum derivatives. The Rockefeller Foundation pumped in millions of dollars to promote their second assault on indigenous third world farmers, granting almost one hundred and fifty million dollars to Alliance for a Green Revolution in Africa, as well as funding programs of Centro Internacional de Agricultura (CITA), Columbia University, International Fertilizer Development Center, International Water Management Institute, Meridian Institute, and others to promote the Second Green Revolution.[1001]

By such exploits on the part of Big Agriculture, the health of the world's people, as well as the health of their environment, has been compromised and continues to decline, creating even more opportunity for profit.

We have discussed in previous chapters how the ruling elite developed its strategy for global control, and how it emphasized eugenics in order to justify population control, especially in third world countries where they wanted to seize the large quantities of raw materials that existed in those countries. The development of manufactured food and its distribution is an aspect of that plan wherein food can be used as a weapon for population control. Consider that Henry Kissinger, who is a Trilateralist and became one of the key strategists in the Nixon administration, prepared what is known as National Security Study Memo (NSSM#200), in which he elaborated his plan for population reduction. The "Kissinger Plan" specifically stated:

> Whatever may be done to guard against interruptions of supply and to develop domestic alternatives, the U.S. economy will require large and increasing amounts of minerals from abroad, especially from less developed countries. That fact gives the U.S. enhanced interest in the political, economic, and social stability of the supplying countries. Wherever a lessening of population

pressures through reduced birth rates can increase the prospects for such stability, population policy becomes relevant to resource supplies and to the economic interests of the United States.[1002]

While a pretty convoluted sentence, Kissinger was especially concerned that the capitalists' smooth flow of expropriated materials from the third world to the United States would not be interrupted by the local people requiring these same materials for their own needs. Thus, it would require population control of these people.[1003]

In this plan, Kissinger specifically targeted thirteen countries for population control: Bangladesh, Brazil, Colombia, Egypt, Ethiopia, India, Indonesia, Nigeria, Pakistan, Turkey, Thailand, and the Philippines. In short order, Kissinger's call for population control by abortion and birth control was enhanced by the idea of population control by the use of food as a weapon. Kissinger became fond of saying "Control oil, you control nations; control food and you control the people."[1004]

Given Kissinger's anti-human plan to control the populations of third world countries, the corporate elites and their policy-oriented intellectuals went to work putting the plan into action. The Rockefellers took charge of US agriculture policy, using the Council on Foreign Relations and their powerful tax-free foundations worldwide to train an army of young scientists in the hitherto unknown field of microbiology. The name "eugenics" was now renamed "genetics" to make it more acceptable and also to hide its real purpose. Through incremental strategic adjustments made by a handful of chemical, food, and seed corporations and with legal support from selected persons in key departments of the US Government, the giant food corporations were developed that eventually gained the power to rewrite the food regulatory framework in nearly every country of the world, including the United States.[1005]

Today, just five agri-business corporations control the international grain trade. These are Cargill, Bunge, Archer Daniels Midland, Glencore International, and Louis Dreyfus.[1006].

Another five control the global trade in seeds and agricultural chemicals. Monsanto, Syngenta, Bayer, DuPont, and Dow Chemical control genetically engineered seeds and produce the deadly insecticides, herbicides, and pesticides that pollute the landscape and our bodies.

While these powerful oligopolies were being organized, government anti-trust laws were intentionally circumvented to allow them to become monopolies.

In his book, *Seeds of Destruction: The Hidden Agenda of Genetic Manipulation*, F. William Engdahl writes, "It was not surprising that the Pentagon's National Defense University, on the eve of the 2003 Iraq War, issued a paper declaring: "Agribiz is to the United States what oil is to the Middle East." [1007] Agribusiness had become a strategic weapon in the arsenal of the world's only superpower.

The "Green Revolution," sanctified in the press and in universities as the savior of third world people, was part of the Rockefeller agenda to destroy seed diversity and push oil and fossil fuel-based agriculture. While this agenda directly profited the Rockefeller oil companies, the destruction of seed diversity and farmer dependence on proprietary hybrids (GMOs and GE crops) became the first step in food control.

While the Green Revolution technologies led to a spurt in farm productivity, it came at the expense of bio-diversity and farmlands, poisoned aquifers, the suicides of small farmers, and increasingly poor health of the people. This was, after all, the initial purpose of the elites in order to control third world resources.[1008]

GMOs (Genetically Modified Organisms)

The clear strategy of the elites, as put into practice by such companies as Monsanto, Dow, DuPont, with the backing of the federal government, led them to introduce GMO and genetically engineered seeds in every corner of the globe, with their priority being the defenseless third world countries. However, in no time, US and Canadian farmlands also were forced to accept the GMO strategy. Even when it was suspected by scientists that GMO could pose a serious threat to human and animal health and the environment, efforts at independent safety assessment were discontinued. The scientists who carried out honest studies, were vilified. Reputed scientific establishments were silenced or made to toe the line that was supportive of the elite's food control and mass culling agenda. Federal grants to agricultural colleges were cut and agribusiness corporations took over the funding of land grant university research.[1009]

In the US, unlabeled GMO foods were introduced in 1993 and today seventy percent of supermarket foods contain GMOs in varying proportions. The government still refuses to make the large chemical corporations reveal which of their products contain GMOs or engineered "foods." This amounts to the largest biological experiment on human beings that has ever been conducted in the world and nobody knows the impact it will have on our children or future generations. While it is difficult to demonstrate a direct link between corporate "food" and ill-health, what we do know is that diet-related diseases such as heart disease, diabetes, obesity, and certain cancers continue to precipitously rise as more GMO food enters our supermarkets.

There is also a great concern about GMOs reducing genetic diversity in plants and animals.[1010] What will future generations be eating if their diet options are greatly reduced. Will they experience conditions like the great Irish potato famine?

The same funders behind climate-science denial also bankroll PR firms who have built their careers spinning science to deny the health risks of toxic chemicals in the food we eat and products we use every day.[1011]

Today, the rates of childhood cancer are fifty percent higher than when the "war on cancer" began decades ago. All this could be avoided by government policies to limit exposure to cancer-causing chemicals. And yet these policies are never put in place by the Republican or Democratic administrations. It is as Kissinger said, "control food and you control the people."

A predictable cast of characters and groups appear on the scene whenever products like Monsanto's Roundup or other products, composed of toxic chemicals, run into trouble with the latest science research. Requests for public records by US Right to Know, Greenpeace, and Intercept have unearthed thousands of documents that have shed light on this propaganda network.

Key propagandists include Jon Entine, Trevor Butterworth, Henry I. Miller and groups connected with them: STATS, Center for Media and Public Affairs, Genetic Literacy Project, Sense About Science, and the Hoover Institute.

Despite well-documented histories on these PR operatives, Entine, Butterworth, and Miller are still presented as serious science resources by the *Wall Street Journal, New York Times, Los Angeles Times, Newsweek, Philadelphia Enquirer, Harvard Business Review,* and, most often, *Forbes.* These newspapers and magazines publish their propaganda as truth without disclosing their funding sources or their agenda to deregulate the polluting industries that promote them.[1012]

The articles of these propagandists push support for GMOs, pesticides, plastic chemicals, sugar, and sugar substitutes. According to their PR spin, all these products are safe, and anyone who says otherwise is "anti-science."

Whenever the American people try to take a stand against GMOs or the prevalence of deadly chemicals that are making them sick, they are overwhelmed by PR campaigns that spend millions of dollars to sow confusion among the people. Take the recent example of the people of Vermont.

On July 1, 2016, Vermont implemented a law requiring disclosure labels on all food products that contain genetically engineered ingredients (GMOs).[1013] Less than a week after that law went into effect, it was under attack. Monsanto and its bought-and-paid-for politicians in Congress pushed legislation to override Vermont's law. Within two months of the enactment of Vermont's anti-GMO law, President Obama's signed a law that diluted the state law to make it virtually worthless.[1014]

The citizens of Vermont had done their homework on GMOs. The state legislature had spent two years debating the Vermont labeling. They held more than fifty committee hearings and heard testimony from more than one hundred and thirty representatives before passing the bill. Despite the fact that nine of out of ten Americans support laws requiring clear GMO labeling, members of Congress are wedded to helping agricultural giants like Monsanto carry out their population control plan rather than pass a law that keeps the American people safe.

Proponents of genetically modified organisms (GMOs) claim that they are safe to eat. They point to thousands of studies that say that neither animals nor humans show any illnesses or diseases attributable to GMO food. While it is clear that many studies that are purported to be biased are funded by the industry, there are also unbiased findings that support the safety of GMOs. For example, the European Commission has funded one hundred and thirty research projects, carried out by more than five hundred independent teams, on the safety of GM crops. None of those studies found any immediate risks from GMO crops.¹⁰¹⁵

The fact is that the current research on the health risks of GMOs is inconclusive. because of the way the research is framed. Researchers cannot confirm a *direct link* between GMOs and an increased health risks from cancer, heart disease etc. If you are concerned, here are ways to cut your intake of Genetically Modified foods:

- **Know the most commonly modified crops.** Soybeans, corn, cotton (for oil), canola (for oil), squash, zucchini, apples, eggplant, papaya, potato, rice, sugar beets, sugar cane, sweet peppers, tobacco, tomato and wheat are all popular GMOs.¹⁰¹⁶
- **Buy organic foods.** Organic foods are grown from non-GMO seeds.
- **Buy meats from grass-fed animals.** Cows, chickens, pigs and even farmed fish are often on a diet of genetically modified corn or alfalfa. Check that your meat is from animals that are grass-fed or pasture-fed.
- **Read the labels.** The top two genetically modified crops are corn and soy. They are also the most widely used ingredients. Avoid products that contain ingredients like corn syrup and soy lecithin.
- **Buy brands labeled as non-GM or GMO free.** Some products are labeled as non-GM or GMO-free. Meaning, they do not use genetically modified ingredients. GMO-free food sources are listed on the Non-GMO Project website.¹⁰¹⁷
- **Shop at local farmers markets.** Most GM foods come from large industrial farms. Shop at local farmers markets or sign-up for a co-op.¹⁰¹⁸

What is seldom discussed in the debate on GMOs is the fraudulence of the GMO propaganda campaign. We know that the industry is spending millions of dollars to avoid labeling food products that contain GMOs. Why do they do this if GMOs are not a threat to people? The reason or reasons are difficult to pin down, but logically it must be related to their campaign to cover up the wide spread use of toxins that they use in their food production system. We know that these chemicals are causing cancer, heart disease, diabetes, and obesity. While these diseases have not been directly linked to GMOs, they have been linked to the use of pesticides, insecticides, and herbicides used by industrial agriculture to grow their GMO crops.

The industrial agriculture industry has always promoted GMO crops as a scientific breakthrough that increases yields and requires less fertilizers, pesticides, insecticides, and herbicides. They also claim that without GMOs we could not feed the world. This is a patently false claim.[1019]

By creating local food systems based upon organic farming, the people of the world could once again feed themselves as well as free themselves from corporate control. In order to create a local food system, however, requires that local people will support it and work with local farmers to create producer-consumer links.

GMO propaganda about "saving the world" is normally about higher yields and less chemicals, but why would chemical companies want to sell less chemicals? Not surprisingly, an in-depth examination recently published by the *New York Times* found that genetically engineered crops have largely failed to achieve these two claims. Studies have proven that genetically engineered crops have "not accelerated increases in crop yields, nor have they led to an overall reduction in the use of chemical pesticides."[1020]

The *Times* compared crop yields and pesticide use in North America and Europe. While Americans embraced GMOs, the Europeans had always rejected them. The result of the comparison found that the "United States and Canada have gained no discernible advantage in yields, food per acre, when measured against Western Europe. The *Times* study also cited a recent National Academy of Sciences report that found "little evidence that the introduction of GE crops were resulting in more rapid yearly increases in on-farm crop yields in the United States than had been seen prior to the use of GE crops."[1021]

These findings revealed what many scientists, small farmers, and sustainable agriculture experts had always known. Genetically engineered crops have benefitted no one except the corporations selling the chemicals required to grow them. While the industry says that GMO crops reduce the use of chemical toxins, in reality, they have only increased them.

Independent scientific findings also belie the propaganda of Monsanto that the introduction of genetically modified organisms has led to increased yields. Not surprising, the company persists in its false claims. On its website, Monsanto continues to cite statistics reported by PG Economics, a United Kingdom (UK)-based agricultural industry consultancy.[1022] However, that firm has been exposed as a corporate shill by Lobbywatch.org, a UK-based nonprofit that tracks deceptive PR practices.[1023] PG Economics was exposed as having been commissioned to write positive reports on behalf of industry lobby groups whose members include the Big Six agrichemical giants: BASF, Bayer, Dupont, Dow Chemical, Monsanto, and Syngenta.

Even with the introduction of genetically modified seeds, US farmers continue to experience boom-and-bust cycles and today are "generally hurting," regardless of the scale of their farming operations. They remain totally dependent upon GMO seeds and toxic chemicals to grow their crops, predominately wheat, corn, and soybeans. While the farmers have not benefitted, the GMO and GE crops have proven a financial bonanza for the agrichemical industry. The Big Six make tens of billions of dollars in profits by selling their proprietary seeds and toxic chemicals.

According to the *Times* article, "Although some insecticide use has been reduced, overall agrochemical applications have grown exponentially."[1024] Even more telling, French farmers who do not use GE crops have been able to reduce insecticide use by sixty-five percent, while decreasing herbicide use by more than a third.[1025]

According to the Vermont Agency of Agriculture, pesticide use is up thirty-nine percent and new pesticides are being added to the list of toxins used. Climate-threatening nitrogen fertilizers have been up about seventeen percent per year from 2002 to 2012 and their use continues to climb. In the meantime, the toxic chemicals strip the soil of its vitality and require more and more inputs to achieve the same level of production.

The heavy reliance on pesticides and insecticides has also led to the rise of pesticide-resistant superweeds. To combat resistance, farmers are forced to use a chemical cocktail of multiple herbicides while, at the same time, biotech companies are introducing plants to even more powerful and toxic chemicals. It is estimated that there may already be sixty to eighty million acres of farmland in the US with "superweeds" that have built up a resistance to RoundUp.[1026]

Ronnie Cummins, co-founder of Organic Consumers Association says superweed resistance has forced farmers to "use higher and higher amounts of increasingly dangerous poisons" so that "soils are eroded and degraded. Water is polluted. Foods are contaminated." And he asks to what end?[1027] The end, as we have seen above, has always been to limit human population in order to ensure their access to resources for the multinational corporations. The poisoning of Americans is just a byproduct of this corporate goal. Of course, there is also the profit to be made in the death of so many. Over the past fifteen years, the combined market capitalizations of Monsanto and Syngenta have grown more than six-fold.

While the exact toll of genetically engineered agriculture on human and environmental health is hard to calculate, its track record is dismal. We have seen its impact on bees, monarch butterflies, birds, fish, and wildlife. We have noted the increased cancer rates for farm families and those downwind from farms that use chemicals. We have also watched the growth of diet-related diseases from eating foods saturated with toxic chemicals.

The fruit of this chemical feast is not more nutritious food, rather it is the environmental, economic, and cultural decline of America.[1028]

It is not too late to change our food system. Research has shown that agro-ecologically based methods such as organic fertilizers, crop rotation, and cover crops can succeed in meeting our food needs while avoiding the harmful impacts of industrial agriculture.[1029] But, even though healthier and more profitable for farmers,[1030] transitioning from industrial agriculture to organic farming is not easy and exposes growers to financial risk during the transition period, which takes up to three years to reinvigorate the soil. The impetus for change therefore must also require policymakers to develop government policies that support farmers converting to organic and other sustainable systems.[1031] More than this, however, local people must begin to buy real food from local small farmers.

This would be nothing but a revolution, but it is the only way to dislodge corporate control over our food supply and over our lives. To appreciate the value of supporting local farmers who do not grow GMO crops and who strive to use less chemicals and less fossil fuels, we must begin to understand something about food itself.

What Is Food?

The American people have been confused about what constitutes a healthy diet due to relentless fast food and junk food advertising, the proliferation of corporate-funded research, changing government nutritional information, and books promoting fad diets, etc. Let us peel away all the jabber and look at the simple facts. The first thing to understand is that there is a clear distinction between real food and processed food (fast food and junk food). They are not the same. Real food feeds us; processed food destroys us. Everything that we stick in our mouth is not food. Most of the fast food and junk food that we eat today has little to no nutritional value and is relentlessly breaking down our organs and bodily systems. The four major degenerative diseases that Americans suffer from, including cancer, heart disease, diabetes, and obesity are related to a diet of processed food.

What is real food? Real food is food that is produced by nature and not in a chemical lab. Real food is fresh fruits and vegetables, milk, unsweetened yogurt, eggs, cheese, whole grains, certain seafood, locally grown pasture-fed beef, pork, chicken, and turkey, natural fruit and vegetable juices, coffee, tea, and especially water. Real food also contains snacks like dried fruit, seeds, and nuts so long as they contain no chemical additives. Natural sweeteners include honey, maple syrup, and fruit juice concentrates, although these should be used in moderation. This is real food.

In order to stay alive and in good health, our bodies require a source of energy. A unit of energy required by the body is called a calorie. Depending upon the size of a person, how active they are, climatic conditions, etc., the number of calories required differs. However, as a general rule, for a moderately active person, the daily calorie intake should be about twenty-four hundred for boys and men and about two thousand for girls and women. [1032]

Calories come in the form of carbohydrates, proteins, and fats. One gram of carbohydrates or protein is equal to four calories. One gram of fat is equal to eight calories. It takes a little over twenty-eight grams to make an ounce.

The main nutrients your body needs to be healthy are proteins, carbohydrates, fats, vitamins, minerals, and fiber. For a breakdown of the function and source of each of these nutrients, see Appendix D, Function and Source of Nutrients.

Average Calorie Needs		
Age Group	Boys and Men calories per day	Girls and Women calories per day
1 to 3 years	1,000 to 1,400	1,000 to 1,200
4 to 8 years	1,400 to 1,600	1,400 to 1,600
9 to 13 years	1,800 to 2,200	1,600 to 2,000
14 to 18 years	2,400 to 2,800	2,000
19 to 30 years	2,600 to 2,800	2,000 to 2,200
30 to 50 years	2,400 to 2,600	2,000
51 and older	2,200 to 2,400	1,800
Pregnant/Nursing woman		2,500 to 2,900

No nutrient can single-handedly change the way our body or organs work. It is eating a balanced diet of real food that brings it all together. If you eat a diet of fresh fruit and vegetables, whole grains, legumes, and a more moderate consumption of meat, fish, poultry, eggs, and dairy products, you will lose excess weight, stay healthy, and have plenty of energy. You will not have to worry about special diets if you eat protein, fat, and carbohydrates in moderation and you keep away from processed foods.

Processed Food (Fast Food and Junk Food)

What is processed food? By processed food we mean food that has been chemically processed and made primarily from refined ingredients and artificial substances. Fast food and junk food are other names for processed food.

Processed food is what you usually see in convenient stories, gas stations, fast food restaurants, etc. It is what is promoted on TV and in advertising. We are surrounded by it. It usually looks appealing and always tastes good. But do not be fooled. Junk food fills us with calories that have little or no nutritional value. By consuming junk food, we are actually substituting for nutritious food that our bodies really need to be healthy. Have you ever taken time to read the ingredients on processed food packages? It will take you fifteen minutes to read all the names of the chemical additives. Junk foods contain lots of salt, sugar, corn syrup, and fat. These things run down your body instead of strengthening it. Junk food is worse than junk, it is destructive to our body.

If we want to lose weight, have more energy, or make ourselves healthier, we should begin slowly to cut junk food from our diet. Here is a list of junk food items: fish & chips, hamburgers, fish burgers, fried chicken, sausages, hot-dogs, tacos, potato wedges, GMO noodles, white bread, sugary cereals, potato chips, french fries, crisps, popcorn, biscuits, donuts, pancakes, cookies, ice cream, cake, sweet rolls, and candy. You can also add carbonated soda, as well as lemonade, hot chocolate, and milkshakes.[1033]

Basically, this means avoiding all fast food restaurants and anything in a box, bag, can, bottle, or package that has more than five ingredients listed on the label.[1034]

For many of us, this might mean cutting out most of our diet! Research has shown that junk food has increased dramatically in the US, with twenty-five percent of people now consuming predominantly junk food diets.[1035] Remember, we have been indoctrinated for decades to believe that this stuff is food. It is not. Although we are surrounded by it and taught to believe it is harmless, it is literally poisoning us, and slowly breaking down our bodies. It cannot be stated often enough that the four major degenerative diseases in America are caused by eating this stuff. These include obesity, heart disease, cancer, and diabetes.

Let us look more deeply at this serious charge. Junk food is calorie-dense and nutrient poor. Because the calories, which are predominately gotten from corn syrup and white sugar, are not nutritious, they are usually burned off in nervousness or stored in fat cells. They also directly upset our glucagon-insulin balance, which must stay in a certain range in order to fuel our body. When this balance is upset, people get diabetes.

Junk food also has played and continues to play a major role in the obesity epidemic. According to researchers at Harvard University, by the year 2050, forty-two percent of our population is expected to suffer from obesity.[1036] Today, junk food in children's diets accounts for one hundred and eighty-seven extra calories per day, leading to six additional pounds of weight gain per year. Obesity is a major cause of heart disease, stroke, high blood pressure, diabetes, some cancers, gallbladder disease, gallstones, osteoarthritis, gout, asthma, and sleep apnea (when a person stops breathing for short episodes during sleep).[1037]

Junk food is also known to lead to depression in teenagers. This is because hormonal changes at puberty make teens more susceptible to mood and behavioral swings. While a healthy diet plays a role in keeping hormone levels on an even keel, consuming trans fats and the other chemical additives in a junk food diet is associated with a forty-eight percent increase in risk of depression.[1038]

In the manufacturing of junk food, all, or most, nutrients are removed from real food. This means that the vitamins, minerals, and fiber are stripped from what began as real foods and what remains is "empty calories." As a result, people who eat a lot of junk food also develop nutritional deficiencies that result in low energy, mood swings, sleep disturbance, and poor academic achievement.[1039]

Morgan Spurlock, who wrote the documentary *Super Size Me* provided a real -life test of the scientific evidence that junk food caused obesity. He ate at McDonald's restaurants three times per day, eating every item on the chain's menu at least once. He consumed about five thousand calories (the equivalent of 9.26 Big Macs) per day during his experiment. This was twice the caloric intake recommended for a man his size to maintain his weight. As a result, Spurlock, who was thirty-two years old, gained twenty-four pounds, and increased his cholesterol to two hundred and thirty mg/dL. This overconsumption of junk food caused him to experience mood swings, sexual dysfunction, and fat accumulation in his liver. After just four weeks, Spurlock's health had deteriorated to the point that his physician warned him he was putting his life in serious jeopardy if he continued the experiment.

It took Spurlock fourteen months to lose the weight gained from his experiment using a vegan diet.[1040] It does not take a month to experience the bad results of eating junk food. Negative changes to your body begin after just one meal of junk food, according to research published in the *Journal of the American College of Cardiology*.[1041]

When you eat a meal high in sugar, it causes a large spike in your blood-sugar levels called "post-prandial hyperglycemia." In the long term, this can lead to an increased risk of heart attack, but there are short-term effects as well. For example, your tissue becomes inflamed as it does when it gets infected. Your blood vessels constrict and toxic free radicals are generated that damage your cells and tissues. Your blood pressure also rises above normal and your body experiences a surge and then a drop in insulin which leaves you feeling listless, nervous, and hungry soon after your meal. This is what a steady diet of junk food does to your body and why you feel the way you do. The good news is that eating a healthy meal helps your body return to its normal, optimal state, even after just one meal.[1042]

To get an idea of the toll that junk food has taken on the health of Americans, consider that fast food restaurants in America serve fifty million customers per day and much of the commercial baked goods, including buns, as well as fish burgers, hamburgers, and French fries contain trans fats which the Food and Drug Administration have found cause high cholesterol that leads to heart disease.[1043] Today, twelve percent of the diet of American children is junk food.[1044]

As bad, or worse, for you are the so-called soft drinks. Because of the high sugar or high fructose corn syrup, sodium, and caffeine content in soda, the body becomes dehydrated. Over a long period of time this leads to chronic dehydration, which if left untreated can kill you. Dehydration occurs when more water is moving out of our cells and bodies than what we take in through drinking. Another ill effect of drinking soft drinks is bad teeth. Drinking soda regularly destroys the enamel coating on your teeth and causes plaque to build up leading to cavities and gum disease.[1045] According to the American Beverage Association, each American, on average, drinks more than fifty-four gallons of carbonated soft drinks each year.[1046]

Another thing worth knowing is that most soft drinks, as well as most processed foods, contain large quantities of high-fructose corn syrup (HFCS), which is manufactured mostly from genetically modified corn. HFCS is a major contributor to heart disease, obesity, cancer, dementia, liver failure, leaky gut syndrome, and more. Despite its danger to human health, the average American unknowingly consumes an average of fifty grams of HFCS every day.[1047] The average twenty ounce soda contains fifteen teaspoons of sweetener, all of it high fructose corn syrup.[1048]

Aside from excess fat, sodium, sugar, and high-fructose corn syrup, processed food also contains many chemical additives. If you look at the ingredients label for a processed food, you will not have a clue as to what you are putting into your body. Below are the ingredients of a typical protein bar.[1049] What you are looking at is a list of preservatives, colorants, and chemicals that create a particular flavor and texture. This is not real food.

One of the most difficult things for people to do is to change their diets and the agribusiness industry has made this challenge even worse. Junk foods have chemicals built into them that cause us to become addicted to them. If you have ever tried to cut back on junk food, you may have realized that it is not easy to do because we experience "cravings" for them.

Even though our rational, conscious mind may "know" that they are bad for us, we cannot curb our desire for them. Some people think this is just a lack of will power but it is more complicated than this. Junk foods stimulate the reward system in the brain in the same way that drugs like cocaine do.

> WHEY PROTEIN ISOLATE, COCOA POWDER (PROCESSED WITH ALKALI), SOY LECITHIN, ARTIFICIAL FLAVOR, SUCRALOSE, ACESULFAME POTASSIUM], PEANUT BUTTER FLAVORED LAYER [MALTITOL, PALM KERNEL AND PALM OIL, PEANUT BUTTER, PARTIALLY DEFATTED PEANUT FLOUR, NONFAT DRY MILK, WHEY POWDER, PEANUTS, SALT, SOY LECITHIN, ANHYDROUS MILK FAT, COCOA POWDER (PROCESSED WITH ALKALI)], GLYCERIN, PROTEIN BLEND (SOY PROTEIN ISOLATE, WHEY PROTEIN ISOLATE, SODIUM CASEINATE), PEANUTS, HYDROLYZED GELATIN, WATER, POLYDEXTROSE, PEANUT BUTTER (GROUND, ROASTED PEANUTS), CELLULOSE, NATURAL AND ARTIFICIAL FLAVORS, PALM KERNEL OIL, OLIVE OIL, CLARIFIED BUTTER, SOY LECITHIN, GUAR GUM, VITAMIN MINERAL MIX [DICALCIUM PHOSPHATE, MAGNESIUM OXIDE, ASCORBIC ACID (VITAMIN C), SODIUM ASCORBATE, VITAMIN E ACETATE, NIACINAMIDE, ZINC OXIDE, D-CALCIUM PANTOTHENATE, PYRIDOXINE HYDROCHLORIDE (VITAMIN B6), THIAMIN MONONITRATE (VITAMIN B1), RIBOFLAVIN (VITAMIN B2), VITAMIN A PALMITATE, FOLIC ACID, BIOTIN, CHROMIUM AMINO ACID CHELATE, SODIUM SELENITE, PHYLLOQUINONE (VITAMIN K1), CYANOCOBALAMIN (VITAMIN B12)], SALT, MALTODEXTRIN, CITRIC ACID, SUCRALOSE, MONO AND DIGLYCERIDES, DIPOTASSIUM PHOSPHATE.   FR02
> **CONTAINS PEANUTS, SOY AND MILK.**

Fig. 5-24: Ingredients of a Typical Protein Bar

There is a system in our brain that scientists call the *reward system*. The reward system is a group of neural structures responsible for motivation and desire, or craving for a reward. It is also responsible for positive reinforcement, classical conditioning, and positive emotions, particularly ones which involve pleasure as a core component. Primary rewards are those necessary for the survival of one's self and offspring, and include palatable food, sexual contact, and parental investment rewards.

Survival for most animals and humans depends upon maximizing contact with beneficial stimuli and minimizing contact with harmful stimuli. Recognition of rewards serves to increase the likelihood of survival by triggering positive emotions among other things.[1050]

This system was designed to "reward" us when we engage in primal behaviors like eating. The brain knows that when we eat, we are doing something "right," and releases a bunch of chemicals, such as the neurotransmitter dopamine, which make our brains feel pleasure.

Modern junk foods are engineered to cause a reward that is more powerful than anything we were ever exposed to in nature. Whereas eating an apple or a piece of steak might cause a moderate release of dopamine, eating a Ben & Jerry's ice cream is so incredibly rewarding that it releases a massive amount of dopamine.[1051]

Although junk food addiction is something that most people do not know about or talk about, it is a huge problem in society today. It is the main reason why most people just *cannot* stop eating junk foods, no matter how hard they try. Our brain biochemistry has been hijacked by the intense dopamine release that occurs in the brain when we eat junk foods.[1052]

Because most of the vitamins, minerals, and fiber has been removed in processing food, it takes less energy to eat and digest processed foods. We can eat more junk food in a shorter amount of time. That is, we can take in more calories. More than this, junk food requires less calories to digest than real food does. So, we take in more calories and burn less. One study of seventeen healthy men and women compared the difference in energy expenditure after consuming a junk food versus a real food-based meal.[1053] They ate a sandwich, either with multi-grain bread and cheddar cheese (real foods) or with white bread and processed cheese (junk foods). The participants burned twice as many calories digesting the real meal. Another way of saying this is that we only burn half as many calories digesting and metabolizing junk foods compared to whole foods. Where are those unburned calories stored? You guessed it—in new fat cells.

Availability of Real Food

In many areas of the country, real food is not readily available. This is especially true of poor urban neighborhoods and rural areas. These areas are called "food deserts" and they suffer from a lack of grocery stores, farmers' markets, and healthy food providers. This is a big problem because while food deserts are often short on real food, especially fresh fruits and vegetables, they are heavy on local quickie marts that provide a wealth of processed, sugar, and fat laden foods that are known contributors to our nation's obesity epidemic.[1054]

Along with the absence of real food options, poverty and stress also trigger bad dietary choices because stress hormones have the power to not only increase appetite, but also increase cravings for foods that are high in fat and sugar.

A recent study conducted by scientists in China found that people, who merely feel that they are socially inferior, whether or not they actually are, prefer unhealthy food and eat more.[1055] This is another reason while obesity and degenerative diseases are rife among the poor, regardless of race.

As wealth continues to be concentrated in the hands of the rich, which causes wide-scale poverty and joblessness, people's health continues to worsen and junk food is a major cause of this. The 2016 Global Nutrition Report found that one hundred and twenty-nine countries had issues with obesity and malnutrition. Of the one hundred and a twenty-nine, fifty-seven had a serious epidemic. The report states: "We now live in a world where being malnourished is the new normal. It is a world that we must all claim as totally unacceptable."

The report went on to say, "Malnutrition and diet are by far the biggest risk factors for the global burden of disease: every country is facing a serious public health challenge from malnutrition." While every country has some cases of obesity and malnutrition, the United States and Canada show the highest number of overweight and obese people due to living in food deserts, eating junk food, or both. With this scenario has come a slew of health problems that is ruining the health of Americans.[1056]

The situation is more complicated than parents allowing their kids to snack on junk food. When poor parents are forced to find the cheapest food available for their family, it's likely to have more calories and be packed with additives that cause addiction and screws with our health.

This is the predicament that the American people face in trying to meet their basic requirement of food. But if this is true, why do not people know about it? It is because Big Agriculture rarely apologizes or makes amends for its sins against America. Instead, it cuts off the public's ability to discover the truth and learn more about the industry's immoral behavior.

For example, when food activists released a number of videos showing animal abuse on industrial farms and in slaughtering facilities, instead of stating they would improve conditions, the culprits lobbied to enact "Ag Gag" legislation that would punish those who record and distribute images of horrifying conditions at animal agriculture facilities, without the owner's consent.[1057]

Talk about reframing the debate. The law makes concerned citizens the wrongdoers, rather than the animal abusers. You have got to admit, it's pretty ingenious. Not to mention venal and heartless.

False Propaganda

Another tactic is that Big Ag convinced House Republicans to include language in the 2017 House Agricultural Appropriations bill that exempted agricultural commodity groups from Freedom of Information Act (FOIA) requests.[1058] The Freedom of Information Act has been an important tool for journalists and activists to obtain government records when investigating potentially shady activities.

The agro-chemical industry often prevents people from learning the truth about the harmfulness of their products and business practices by threatening the press. An example of this is when a long-time cartoonist at *Farm News* was fired after one of his cartoons offended a big agricultural corporation. The man had worked for the company for twenty-one years and had published over a thousand cartoons.

The cartoon that offended the Big Ag corporations depicts two farmers conversing. One says, "I wish there was more profit in farming." The second replies, "There is. In year 2015 the CEOs of Monsanto, DuPont, Pioneer, and John Deere combined made more money than 2,129 Iowa farmers."[1059]

Covering up the truth is much easier than it is to change one's business practices. What can be done to address this terrible problem? If we are honest with ourselves, the solution does not exist within the capitalist system. The goal of the elites for world dominance and the handful of corporations at the top of the food chain are not concerned in the least with increasing the availability, safety, and healthfulness of food. They have no incentive to do so because it would only mean less profit. Only a revolution in the way people organize themselves at the local level can address this problem. An economic alternative is addressed in more detail in Books Two and Three of this trilogy.

Shelter

Home ownership has always been a big part of the American dream. As the 2000s unfolded, however, this dream turned into a nightmare for many. A housing boom, triggered by cheap loans and fraudulent mortgage "bundles" created a "housing bubble" that burst in late 2007 and sucked the wind out of the entire economy. Millions of people lost their jobs and their homes.

The federal government bailed out the big banks but did little to help the American people who had been victimized by the banks. Almost ten million American families suffered through a foreclosure, were forced to surrender their home to a lender, or sold their home via a distress sale between 2006 and 2014. According to the National Association of Realtors, less than a third of the people who lost their homes are likely to become homeowners again.[1060]

To make matters worse, the Bank of America, Citibank, Aurora, JPMorgan Chase, MetLife Bank, PNC, Sovereign, SunTrust, U.S. Bank, and Wells Fargo, in addition to exploitive loan practices, also used false documents in courtrooms and county offices to take people's homes away from them in foreclosures that never should have happened.[1061] They were able to do this because the chain of title on millions of home mortgages that were bundled together for sale by the banks, often confused the underlying ownership and damaged three hundred and fifty years of functioning property records law. This fraudulent practice by some mortgage companies is still going on in 2020.[1062]

Once again, the American people were forced to bear the brunt of a colossal exploitation on the part of the banking industry and the federal government. All of the losses in capital were put on the backs of the small homeowners, while the banks were bailed out of their losses and went scot free from any punishment. Some, of course, were caught in the act and had to pay back some of the money they stole but the bankers did not go to jail. Even today, there are no laws that say you cannot take a person's home with false evidence.

When people lost their homes, many had to move out of their communities. While nearly all of these families stayed within their same metropolitan areas, the scale of this reshuffling had a profound impact on those cities. In the search for places to live, whites were pitted against blacks for housing and this competition did much to reverse the recent progress in racial integration.

Minorities who lost their homes moved to more distressed neighborhoods, while white homeowners, who had the wherewithal to leave places hit hard by foreclosure, abandoned them.

Because, foreclosure rates, during the housing bust, were highest in the most integrated neighborhoods, the housing crisis reinforced and greatly contributed to a resegregation in neighborhoods.[1063]

The foreclosure migration was deceptively large. Ten million people lost their homes and were forced to move. It was, in fact, the biggest internal migration in American history. By comparison, during the Great Migration, when the South industrialized its agriculture after WWII, 6 million blacks moved North but this movement spanned decades. Again, the number of people that left the Great Plains during the Dust Bowl was only 2.5 million people.[1064]

Among the hardest hit by the Great Recession were Millennials, young people from age twenty-six to thirty-four, who were the prime age group for first-time home buying. Without jobs, there was no way that they could make the leap from renters to homeowners. In fact, many found themselves living back with their parents. Many minorities were also unable to become homeowners again. This was especially true of Hispanic households. The number of Hispanic families who now have to rent is nearly twice the rate of Whites, African Americans, and Asians.

Actually, all Americans have suffered from the housing crisis because the average rent rose 22.3% in the fifty biggest housing markets in the country between 2006 and 2014. The rent increase came at a time when the US median household income had fallen by 4.2%.[1065]

While the housing market has rebounded to some extent, the lives of the mass of Americans caught in the lower-middle and lower-income classes have as yet been unable to stabilize their lives. President Trump promised repeatedly during his campaign that he would "rebuild" the country's inner cities and address their "unacceptable" conditions, but if we look at his actions, his promise was just empty rhetoric. Before Trump became president, the New York public housing administration already had a $17 billion backlog of necessary repairs to its buildings.[1066] But instead of getting help from the new president, Trump's budget called for a $6.2 billion cut to the Department of Housing and Urban Development (HUD), which helps to fund city housing departments like the one in New York.

According to Trump's budget director, Mick Mulvaney, the cuts to HUD "go after waste" and "duplicative programs, programs that simply don't work," eliminating the ones that "can't justify their existence."[1067]

Despite Mulvaney calling this an "America-first budget," much of the country, including New York City, were devastated by these cuts. The cuts significantly reduced the federal money New York City got to operate and repair its public housing at a time when it already did not get the funding it needed to keep its buildings habitable.

One of the serious problems in these housing units is the buildup of harmful mold due to bad roofs leaking rain and snow into the buildings. This health hazard is neglected due to lack of money for repairs. There are other safety issues like hallways that do not have lights; elevators that are broken, and tenants at risk of falling into the shafts.

The residents end up trapped in dangerous housing. Because they have nowhere else to go, they must remain and pay rent for horrible conditions.

Under Trump's 2018 budget, living conditions became unlivable for tenants. When conditions became extremely dangerous, the city was forced to abandon the buildings, throwing more people out on the streets to join the already existing pool of 73,500 people who were homeless in New York City.[1068]

Across the country, poor people who were living in subsidized housing numbered 6.7 million.[1069] Another 1.2 million households were lost during the Great Recession, forcing people to move in with relatives.[1070] Any of these people could find themselves homeless with the least bit of bad luck.

In the meantime, Trump's secretary of the Department of Housing and Urban Development, Ben Carson, had been traveling throughout the US for a number of weeks on a so-called "listening tour," meeting with low-income citizens who relied on the government for assistance.

Carson is a former neurosurgeon with no prior experience in running a federal agency. Instead of responding to the plight of millions of Americans living in the depths of hell, he was more concerned that public housing was too comfortable for people.[1071]

Homelessness

People living in public housing are not in the lowest level of hell. The fallout from the Great Recession created a steep spike in homelessness that is still unmanageable for cities across the country. Over a million and a half Americans were forced to use an emergency shelter or a transitional housing program between October 1, 2008 and September 30, 2009 at the time when the Great Recession hit.

One out of 50—or about 1.5 million—American children were homeless each year, according to a 2009 study by the National Center on Family Homelessness. On any given night, 75,609 veterans were homeless.[1072]

In January 2017, a study by the National Alliance to End Homelessness estimated that [1073]there were over 553,742 homeless in the US on any given night.[1074] Most Americans tend to think of homeless people as burn-outs or those who are mentally ill or addicted to drugs or alcohol, etc. They will be surprised to learn that such people, who are considered to be chronically homeless, only constitute about fifteen percent of the homeless in America. Most of the homeless are families like yours or mine. Families today make up thirty-six percent of the homeless. Typically, families find themselves out on the street due to an unforeseen financial crisis like a medical emergency, a car accident, or a death in the family that prevents them from paying their rent or mortgage.

Homeless families require rent assistance, housing placement services, job assistance, or other short-term, one-time services to help them return to independence and stability.

Another seven percent of the homeless are unaccompanied youth. Young people often become homeless due to family conflict, including divorce, neglect, or abuse. Homeless youth present a particular challenge because they tend to avoid standard homeless assistance programs or government agencies. Beside their fears of the government or the police or their families, most assistant programs cannot even help them. For example, the young are unable to rent an apartment or access public assistance. Our homeless young people, including LGBTQ youth, are especially vulnerable to neglect and abuse. Young people living on the streets in San Francisco have a mortality rate that is more than ten times higher than those who have a home. Cause of death? Suicide or substance abuse.[1075]

Veterans constitute about eight percent of the homeless, about fortthousand people, mostly men. They often become homeless due to war-related disabilities. For a variety of reasons, including physical disability, mental anguish, post-traumatic stress, etc., many veterans are unable to adjust to civilian life. Difficulties in readjusting often give rise to dangerous behaviors, including addiction, abuse, and violence, which, in turn, lead to homelessness. Preventive measures, including job placement services, medical services, housing assistance, and the like, can mitigate the risk of veterans becoming homelessness.

In addition to the above groups of people who are homelessness in the United States, women, who are victims of domestic violence, constitute another large group. According to a survey of the homeless in twenty-five cities, conducted in 2013 by the *US Conference of Mayors*, sixteen percent of the homeless were women who were victims of domestic violence.[1076]

The elderly, unaccompanied children, those who lost everything in a divorce, those lawfully evicted, those with negative cash flow, those who suffer from post-traumatic stress disorder (PTSD), those who were displaced by foreclosure, fire, or natural disasters, those with mental illness, physical disability, no family, substance abuse, lack of needed services, ex-convicts, unemployed or those with low-paying jobs make up the remainder of the homeless in the United States.

Once a person or family loses their home, it is very difficult to find another one due to lack of affordable housing and the stigma that accompanies it. Today even the maximum voucher amount of fifteen hundred dollars a month has failed to keep pace with sky rocketing rents. The low vacancy rate, which tends to hover just below three percent country wide, adds to the difficulty of encouraging landlords to accept vouchers. The great demand for housing creates an opportunity for higher rents. Even with the guaranteed rent from the vouchers, landlords worry about tenants with vouchers not being able to come up with their portion of the rent should the voucher not cover the full amount.

The aforementioned stigma surrounding homelessness creates fear that they will cause problems for other tenants and neighbors. There is also the long approval process, during which the rental remains vacant for inspection and documentation. In response, local governments must offer holding fees while the process goes forward.[1077]

It is not that cities are not trying to address the homeless problem, but why should the responsibility fall on the local people when the problem was created by the multinational bankers and supported by the federal government? Homelessness in the US, like the problem of refugees overseas, is a consequence of present-day capitalism. This is to say, many of the homeless people are victims of larger forces. As Damon Francis, interim medical director of Alameda County Health Care for the Homeless, said "We should be asking, 'what happened to you?' not 'what's wrong with you?'"

But the mainstream media, which is owned by the capitalists, continually spins the issue of homelessness as if it were the fault of the people who have been victimized. Articles on homelessness are littered with words like "riff-raff," "drugs," "drug-addicted," "filth," "feces," and "crime." The recurrent theme is that people who are homeless must have done something wrong with their lives. Where have we heard this before?

Editorials praise government crackdowns and make fun of legislation in support of the homeless as "bad ideas."[1078] Yet, they offer no solutions because there are no solutions within capitalist America. The solution is simple. The people need jobs and homes.

The amount of human suffering that has been caused by the banker's housing crisis is immeasurable. It has torn apart our society. And yet the bankers remain free to continue to exploit the people because we will not rise against them. The millions made homeless by the housing crisis deserve more from the federal government than "I'm sorry you lost your home." Instead, the homeless, who once were our neighbors, our children, our wives and mothers, our brave soldiers will be derided and scapegoated for whatever the federal politicians and the wealthy see fit. After all, who wants to live in a place where dirty street people live? We have turned against our own just as we have so many times before been led to do. At this point, it is up to us alone to change our hearts and to do something about the situation. The solution is not difficult to understand. The homeless need jobs and shelter while a mere eighty-five capitalists hoard as much wealth as half the people on the planet.

Because we have not been thrown out on the streets today, it does not exempt us from a "financial crisis" tomorrow. And remember, while we sit on our hands, refusing to help our neighbors, the seas continue to rise along the coastlines where most of us live.[1079]

Clothing

Clothing has been considered a basic need since the dawn of human existence. We could not have survived the variety of environments that we came to inhabit without clothing. Clothing is both a physical as well as a social requirement. From a physical perspective, clothing provides us with protection, modesty, and safety. From a social perspective it provides us with identity, status, and decoration. Clothing has evolved to be more than just a basic need. Today, it is used to make a statement about who we are. People, within the US, wear different clothing based upon their generation, religions, nationality, class, etc.

In the past, the clothing style that people chose changed slowly. Today, because of technology and communication, styles of clothing change much more frequently. Generally, Americans have three options that determine the type of clothing they wear on a daily basis. The first option is fashion conformity where one selects clothing that is accepted by society or by their sub-group within society. In this case, one dresses for social acceptance and to be liked. The fashions are influenced by popular opinion, trend setters, and popular fads. The second option is *Personal originality*. It occurs when one chooses clothing and accessories to express one's individuality or uniqueness. Rather than conforming to fashion, one dresses to be different or to please oneself. The third option in one's choice of clothing is simply *Classic*. In this case, the fashion transcends frequent changes and is conservative and professional in appearance. Some examples include military uniforms, priest cassocks, or business suits.[1080]

In 1960, an average American household spent over ten percent of its income on clothing and shoes, which is equivalent to roughly four thousand dollars today. The average person bought fewer than twenty-five pieces of clothing each year. About ninety-five percent of those clothes were made in the United States. Each following decade, Americans spent a smaller percentage of their income on clothing yet purchased a greater amount of clothing. During each successive decade, a smaller proportion of those clothes were produced in the US.

Americans and Clothing			
Decade	Annual Amt. Spent on Clothing per Household[1081]	Percent of Family Budget	Percent of Clothing Made in US
1960s	$4,388	10.4%	95%
1970s	$3,603	7.8%	75%
1980s	$2,955	6.0%	70%
1990s	$2,583	5.1%	50%
2000s	$2,263	4.3%	29%
2017	$1,740	3.5%	2%

Today, Americans buy nearly twenty billion dollars articles of clothing a year, close to seventy pieces per person or more than one piece of clothing per week, yet only two percent of this clothing is made in the US.[1082]

In the mid-1970s, large textile mills and factories were built in China and other developing countries in Asia and Latin America where labor and raw materials were cheap. This development allowed US clothing companies to make massive profits while also gaining the ability to quickly manufacture huge orders.

By 1980, even though about seventy percent of the clothing Americans bought was still made domestically, a handful of big retail chains like Gap Inc. and J. C. Penney stopped making their own clothes. Instead, they simply designed and marketed them, but outsourced production to the factories overseas where the work was done at a tiny fraction of the cost of doing it in the US. At the same time, other big companies began to develop vast global supply chains that allowed them to divide up each step of the production process, sending the work to whichever location offered the cheapest, most efficient services. By 2003, Gap was ordering its clothes from more than twelve hundred different factories in forty-two countries.[1083]

A wave of trade liberalization polices in the 1990s, including the North American Free Trade Agreement (NAFTA), effectively wiped out most import restrictions and duties on foreign-made clothing. American clothing outlets increasingly looked to foreign suppliers for all manufacturing needs.

Between 1990 and 2011, almost seven hundred and fifty thousand apparel manufacturing jobs in the US disappeared.[1084] For the one hundred and fifty thousand who still have jobs, they make about thirty-eight times the wage of his or her counterpart in Bangladesh or China.

Today, the clothing industry is a global industry, where designers, manufacturers, merchandisers, and retailers from all over the world collaborate to design, manufacture, and sell clothing, shoes, and accessories. Because clothing has become so inexpensive for the average consumer, the clothing industry today is characterized by short product life cycles, erratic consumer demand, an abundance of product variety, and complex supply chains.[1085]

Within this global industry, the US apparel market is the largest in the world, comprising about twenty-eight percent of the global total. Yet hardly any of this clothing comes with a *Made in the USA* label.[1086]

This development may be good for corporate profits and family budgets in the short term, but is it good for the country? After all, we have lost the ability to manufacture our own clothing and with it three quarter of a million jobs for middle class families. Here we have another instance of good jobs going overseas where technology and cheap labor made Americans superfluous to the job market.

Another problem is that a vast number of people in these other countries who now manufacture American clothing are exploited labor, many of whom live a life similar to slaves. Everyone has heard about *sweatshops*, but what are they and what is going on in them? Here is what you need to know.

A "sweatshop" is defined by the US Department of Labor as a factory that violates two or more labor laws. These may include poor working conditions, unfair wages, unreasonable hours, child labor, and a lack of benefits for workers.

An estimated one hundred and sixty-eight million children ages five to fourteen are forced to work as slaves in garment sweatshops.

The inhumane greed of the clothing industry is revealed by a recent study that showed that doubling the salary of sweatshop workers would only increase the consumer cost of an item by two to six percent. Consumers, on the other hand, would be willing to pay fifteen to twenty-five percent more to know a product did not come from a sweatshop.[1087]

Some people may think that all these garment jobs increased the lifestyle of the people of China, Bangladesh, etc., but sweatshops do not alleviate poverty. The people who work in these jobs, many as slaves or forced labor, must spend the majority of their paycheck on food for their families to survive.

Child labor is especially common in the garment industry. The International Labor Organization (ILO) estimates that one hundred and seventy million children are working in jobs that are detrimental to children and are prohibited by international law. The majority of these child laborers are found in Asia and the Pacific.

A recent report [1088] by the Center for Research on Multinational Corporations (SOMO), and the India Committee of the Netherlands (ICN) revealed that recruiters in southern India convince parents in impoverished rural areas to send their daughters to spinning mills with promises of a well-paid job, comfortable accommodation, three nutritious meals a day, and opportunities for training and schooling, as well as a lump sum payment at the end of three years. The researchers found that "in reality, the children are working under appalling conditions that amount to modern day slavery and the worst forms of child labor".[1089]

Children are seen as "obedient workers" who slip under the radar, making them easy to manage. Sofie Ovaa, global campaign coordinator of Stop Child Labour says: "There is no supervision or social control mechanisms, no unions that can help them to bargain for better working conditions. These are very low-skilled workers without a voice, so they are easy targets."[1090]

Sweatshop factories get away with slave labor and forced labor because the fashion supply chain is so complex and it is hard for the retail chains to control every stage of production. That makes it possible for sweatshops to employ children and forced workers without the big brands easily discovering their actions. Yet, if they really were concerned, they could find this out with some effort.

Because children and women make up eighty-five to ninety percent of sweatshop workers, some employers force them to take birth control and routine pregnancy tests to avoid supporting maternity leave or providing appropriate health benefits. But these impositions are likely the least exploitive of women garment workers. In Bangladesh (the world's second largest exporter of clothes), the minimum wage for garment workers is fifty-three hundred taka or fifty-seven dollars per month, which is far from the eighty-nine hundred taka or ninety-six dollars needed to cover a worker's basic needs, and even further away from a living wage. Many women in the garment industry work between sixty and one hundred and forty hours per week and are then cheated out of their overtime pay. Health and safety are often neglected, workers are denied breaks, and abuses are common.[1091]

A study, made in 2016, found that one in every seven women working in the garment industry in the southern Indian city of Bengaluru had been raped or forced into a sexual act while at work. The report, by the women's rights groups Sisters for Change and Bengaluru-based Munnade, estimated sixty percent of women garment workers faced intimidation and violence in "hostile" workplaces. In addition to economic oppression the women also faced sexual oppression, which included being forced to watch pornography, being punched, choked, and burnt. These crimes were committed in the twelve hundred garment factories in Bengaluru, which supply many global brands.

"We were shocked by the levels of sexual violence (we found) during our survey," said Alison Gordon, executive director of the England-based Sisters for Change. "There is such a permissive environment of abuse in the factory, with the supervisors often being the perpetrators. There is no fear of the existing laws." The women have limited or no legal protection and few formal grievance mechanisms.

Eighty-two percent of the women who responded to the study said they did not report the crimes because they had no faith in the police or senior management to take action.[1092]

Another ethical problem in the garment industry is that virtually all of the models, who represent fashion houses, are forced to remain abnormally thin, in keeping with the perceived aesthetic preferences of the public. This focus on extreme thinness in women has been blamed for eating disorders and poor body image among some women whose bodies do not conform to this idealized image.

Fashions that use real animal fur support the fur industry, which is infamous for its inhumane treatment of animals. Fur is acquired either by trapping wild animals and skinning them or by raising animals domestically for their fur.

Bringing out a new line of clothing every year encourages people to buy new clothes that they do not really need. While some people see this as harmless or as a boon to the economy, others believe that it encourages mindless consumerism and a throw-away culture. Advertising and fashion are closely related, and they both encourage people to consume as much as possible. New fashions are widely advertised as better than whatever came before.

The materials, transportation, and production that are involved in the fashion industry all have an impact on the environment. Many synthetic materials are derived from petroleum, while many more natural materials are grown on land that could be used for food production.

In meeting our basic need for clothing, the American people are forced to subsidize an industry that is built upon human exploitation and slave labor.

A large part of the appeal of expensive, fashionable clothing is that it is exclusive. The vast majority of people cannot afford to buy it, so it grants a level of status and glamour to those who can.

Finally, expensive fashions sometimes use diamonds. "Blood diamonds" are mined under poor conditions, sometimes by violent groups that use the income from the diamonds to fund their activities. While some fashion houses are taking steps to ensure that none of their diamonds come from these sources, this is still a prevalent reality.[1093]

The garment industry today has minimized the functional aspect of clothing and has debased it into a consumer status symbol. Such a development saps our sense of humanity and encourages a shallow mentality and disregard for others. It also diminishes our self-reliance as a people.

Health Care

Health care is a vast, complex subject. As President Trump so aptly put it, "Nobody knew health care could be so complicated."[1094] There are hundreds of articles and news features produced everyday regarding health care in this country. And, of course, they are often contradictory, biased, and piecemeal in their approach. The purpose of this book is to demonstrate, as we have previously demonstrated, that the capitalist elite has shaped the basic needs delivery systems in order to extract immense profits for themselves and that this another reason why the average person finds it so difficult to afford their basic needs on a daily basis.

Given the wear and tear of life, nothing can continue to function without repairs, much less human beings who have such a complex physical and psychic makeup. For example, we can become physically sick due to genetic diseases, diet-related diseases, by assimilating toxic chemicals, getting poisoned by radiation, or by smoking, drinking, or taking prescription drugs. We can become injured in accidents. We can contract viral or bacterial infections or develop stress due to circumstances in our environment. It is a wonder any of us live past childhood considering that we do not come with a three-year warranty. Psychologically, we are also susceptible to many mental diseases that are caused by genetic disposition, internal stress, and environmental conditions.

Despite this, Americans are living longer than ever and this can be attributed to the modern allopathic medical system with its medical research, drugs, devices, surgeries, and insurance premiums. On the other hand, the shortcomings and corruption of this system, in tacit collaboration with the processed food, fossil fuel, and agro-chemical industries, are creating more diseases than have ever been unleashed on humankind. Americans are living longer, but we are sicker than we have ever been. This is the ideal condition for medical industry profits.

State of Health of Americans

Today, the top ten causes of death in America, according to the Mayo Clinic, are:

1. Heart Disease
2. Cancer
3. Stroke
4. Respiratory Diseases
5. Injuries

6. Diabetes
7. Alzheimer's Disease
8. Influenza and Pneumonia
9. Kidney Disease
10. Septicemia[1095]

Heart disease affects 28.4 million Americans and kills about 635,260 people every year.[1096] About 15 million people live with cancer, and 38.4 percent of Americans will be diagnosed with cancer some time in their lives. More than 600,000 people die of cancer each year.[1097] About 795,000 people suffer from stoke every year and about 140,000 people die from it.[1098] There are 8,600,000 Americans diagnosed with chronic bronchitis and 3.4 million with emphysema each year.[1099] And so the beat goes on.

While diet-related diseases and exposure to toxic chemicals continue to kill most of us, the health care industry remains complicit in our deaths because they never, if ever, address the root causes of our diseases. So also, the mass media avoids any discussion of root causes as if they were a closely guarded state secret. Consequently, the American people are kept in the dark about the causes of the diseases that keep popping up in our households each day, week, and month of our lives. Studies have also shown that the stresses of poverty impact the body's ability to cope with sickness and disease. As Jo Marchand describes her reaction to research, she conducted in her book Cure: *A Journey into the Science of Mind over Body*:

> For me, one of the most surprising—and shocking—revelations of the research described in this book was that the stresses of poverty and inequality are sentencing large sections of the population to lifelong chronic disease before they're even out of diapers.[1100]

Today, the mass media speaks about the health care victory of the American people because we smoke fewer cigarettes, but even ten years ago when hundreds of thousands of Americans were dying of lung cancer due to smoking or when the cigarette companies were suing the EPA for stating that second hand smoke was also killing people,[1101] the mass media was silent on the subject. Cigarette smoking also causes coronary heart disease[1102] and is responsible for thirty percent of all deaths caused by fire,[1103] but few people know this because it is not reported in the press.

While the country has made improvements over the last decade by reducing smoking, our health care has also declined due to increasing cases of obesity, and other diet-related diseases, as well as deaths due to prescription and recreational drug use. The bottom line is, when it comes to health care, even though we are threatened each day by multiple diseases, a single visit to the emergency room would wipe out the savings of half of America's families.[1104] And if this is so, it is understandable why half of all American families cannot afford health insurance. While more people were able to afford health insurance under Obama, the Congressional Budget Office projected that approximately twenty-four million people would lose their coverage by 2026, and premiums would rise fifteen to twenty percent in the short term if the Trump/Republican American Health Care Act was passed.[1105]

A Brief History of American Health Care

In 1847, just prior to the Civil War, physicians, who were basically gentlemen who studied philosophy at the university, got together to form the American Medical Association (AMA). Most of them were not particularly wealthy because they had to compete with Native American healers and housewives, not to mention midwives, homeopaths, herbalists, and even chiropractors.

At the AMA's first convention, a report entitled "Healing the Health-Care System," complained that "The very large number of physicians in the United States has frequently been the subject of remark..... No wonder that the merest pittance in the way of remuneration is scantily doled out even to the most industrious in our ranks."[1106]

This group decided that only they were the true practitioners of medicine, while herbalists, midwives, homeopaths, and Native healers were not. Such healers consequently were not eligible to join the AMA. Thereafter, any "regular" member who was caught dealing with a "non-regular" medical practice got tossed out of the organization.

At the time, the medicine practice of AMA doctors consisted of blood-letting, blistering, mercury poisoning, and a lot of other cures that lead us to question their expertise in light of other medical practices. Two years after the AMA was established, it created an advisory board to analyze "quack" remedies and to enlighten the public in regard to the nature and dangerous tendencies of the remedies of other medical practitioners. This practice continues to this day.

Perhaps as a result of this, it was commonplace for visitors from Europe to speak of the remarkable ill health of the average American. Our skin was sallow, our eyes were sunken, we had thin hair, and our teeth and jaws were crooked. Interestingly, these turned out to be the symptoms of mercury poisoning, a common AMA cure all.

As long as there is a profit to be made, there will be profiteers. We can see this on display among the AMA peddlers of prescription drugs that cause seizures, heart failure, or physical deformities,[1107] but we can also see it on display with the diet-pill supplement industry. There are also those doctors who exploit their patients by recommending unnecessary surgeries. "It's a very serious issue, (and) there really hasn't been a movement to address it," says Lucian Leape, a former surgeon and professor at the Harvard School of Public Health. Leape, a renowned patient safety expert began studying unnecessary surgery after a 1974 congressional report estimated there were 2.4 million cases a year, killing nearly twelve thousand patients.[1108]

At the time the AMA came into existence, traveling sideshows offered bottled cures. Most of these early remedies made you feel good because they contained a high percentage of alcohol. When heroin, and its derivative morphine, were introduced to this country, many new patent remedies cropped up. Then came cocaine and opium. Early Coca-Cola contained cocaine. Early 7 Up contained lithium. Everyone got rich selling drugs.

When the Rockefellers monopolized the oil industry, the automobile had not yet been invented. Searching for other uses for his product, William Rockefeller bottled up crude oil, gave it the pretty name "Nujol," and sold it as a cancer cure. Years later when the Rockefellers were informed that they really should not call their Nujol a cancer cure because it was not curing any cancer and, in fact, the only thing that it did was to give one a good case of diarrhea, the Rockefeller's rebranded Nujol as a laxative.

Later, another group of scientists contacted the Rockefellers and warned them that their Nujol was actually doing damage. It seems that it pulled fat-soluble vitamins from those using it. The Rockefellers responded by fortifying Nujol with some vitamin A and released the new improved version of Nujol, which still leached vitamins and most likely caused cancer, but by the time scientists were about to confirm that Nujol was not a substance humans should be ingesting, the Rockefellers had taken control of the pharmaceutical industry and they quietly dropped Nujol from their pharmacopoeia while promoting other remedies that would eventually also fall by the wayside. Even so, these fraudulent drugs, which are all obsolete today, helped the Rockefellers become the richest people on earth.[1109] It is interesting that despite the AMA's search for quackery, they never charged the Rockefellers of being "quacks."

The Flexner Report

According to the current medical establishment, The Flexner Report "is the most important event in the history of American and Canadian medical education. It … gave rise to modern medical education." Abraham Flexner, for whom the report is named, is considered by the medical establishment to be "one of the great educators of the twentieth century. To him, medical education and medicine in North America owe a considerable debt."[1110]

The actual events leading up to the Flexner Report and its aftermath are, in reality, a bit more sordid.

To begin with, Abraham Flexner was not a doctor, nor did he have any experience in the field of health care. Rather, he was a school teacher whose field of inquire was education philosophy. Flexner was hired by John D. Rockefeller, who was the brother of William Rockefeller and co-owner of Standard Oil, to evaluate the effectiveness of therapies being taught by medical colleges and institutions, with the ultimate goal of dominating control of the pharmaceutical industry.

S. D. Wells, in his *25 Amazing (and Disturbing) Facts About the Hidden History of Medicine* tells us:

> With partnerships including Andrew Carnegie and JP Morgan, a new "doorkeeper" would exist to influence legislative bodies on state and federal levels to create regulations and licensing "red tape" that strictly promoted drug medicine while stifling and shutting down

alternative, inexpensive natural remedies. Those medical colleges and institutions that did not submit to this superpower of regulation were crushed and put out of business.[1111]

The Flexner report, which was entitled, *Medical Education in the United States and Canada*, conveniently recognized allopathic doctors as the only legitimate medical practitioners in the country. Flexner advocated that a unique education system administered by the AMA be established which would put the emphasis on rigid schooling, research, and drugs. Due to the Flexner Report, alternative medical schools in the US were cut from one hundred and sixty to eighty in less than fifteen years, and then down below seventy by World War II. This concentrated control of the health care system is the root cause of the majority of problems with American health care today, including its staggering cost and its unavailability to tens of millions of Americans who cannot afford to be treated by such a costly system. The Flexner report, under the controlling hand of the Rockefellers, and other members of the elite, eliminated the idea that health care should be a basic human right, one that had guided medical practitioners since the days of Hippocrates and replaced it with the goal of amassing booming profits for those capitalists who invested in building the new system.

On the positive side, Flexner brought some needed improvements to medical research and to the field experience of medical students through more hands-on learning, but it did so in favor of pharmaceutical drugs and surgery as opposed to preventative medicine, whole-patient care, and the entire range of natural treatment options.

In this way, the stage was set for the programming of the American public, in which we came to understand modern medicine as a system of synthetic prescription drugs, surgery, and high cost insurance.

While it can be appreciated that greater accountability for medical practitioners in North America at the time was helpful, it is highly suspect that it should have been initiated by the oil industry and others who saw the domination of medicine as another way to amass personal fortunes. Some might consider this to be a conflict of interest and a gross violation of moral standards, if not a criminal pursuit. But that is capitalism for you. Money has since become the ultimate determinate of access and availability to medical treatment.[1112]

The evolution of disease over the last one hundred years is no mystery. At the time the Flexner report was written, coronary heart disease barely existed, but by 1930, just one generation later, it was causing three thousand deaths per year. By 1950, it was the leading cause of mortality in the United States, accounting for more than thirty percent of all deaths. Heart failure is the leading cause of death in Western countries today, even though there was not a single case on record in 1910.

Today, every other man will get cancer in his lifetime, and one of every three woman. At that time, only one in one hundred thousand people had diabetes, yet there are nearly thirty million people in the US who are diagnosed with diabetes and another eighty million with pre-diabetics.[1113]

What is the main driver of this drastic change in our health status? Again, the cause is our exposure to toxic chemicals and the intake of pseudo food in our daily diet. In 1910, one out of every three people in the United States lived on a farm and ate home grown food, free of pesticides and other chemicals. Medicine, at the time, was not a profitable industry. Today, however, only one percent of the US population lives on a farm, and only a small number of people eat organic food free from toxins. During the last five generations, the petro-chemical industry and agribusiness have systematically destroyed US soil, food, water, and natural medicines, while the food industry has filled our stomachs with harmful chemicals and so-called "foods" that our bodies can't process.[1114]

A basic question we must ask ourselves in order to improve our health care is, "What lethal ingredients are we consuming regularly that sicken and kill us and what can we do about reducing our intake of these chemicals?" The health care industry will not explore this question simply because it is not profitable to do so.

While many doctors, nurses, and other health care professionals are heartfelt and dedicated to helping their patients, they themselves are often victims of a system that acquiesced to the goal of the Rockefellers and other profiteers, which was to dominate the chemical and pharmaceutical markets. This capitalist imperative became the *raison d'etre* of the modern health care industry and directly contradicts those who take an oath to serve the public good. On February 7, 2020, Fox Business published an article by Megan Henney entitled, "US health care system causing 'moral injury' among doctors, nurses." The article revealed that the crux of moral injury in physicians is their inability to consistently meet patients' needs, because of a health care environment that's increasingly focused on maximizing profit.[1115]

Big Pharma

Beginning with the Flexner Report in the early half of the twentieth century, the petrochemical giants organized a coup within the medical research facilities, hospitals, and universities. The Rockefeller family continued to sponsor drug-related research while donating large sums of money to universities and medical schools, which conducted such research. The universities' role of serving the public good soon dissolved under pressure from the lucrative pharmaceutical industry.

In 1939, a "Drug Trust" was formed by the Rockefeller empire and the German chemical company IG Farben (Bayer). IG Farben was the company that built Auschwitz for Hitler. It also produced Zyklon B, the pesticide repurposed by the SS for the gas chambers. The company came to be the main supplier of chemical products essential to the Nazi war machine.[1116] After the war, the Nuremberg Tribunal convicted twenty-four IG Farben board members and executives on the basis of mass murder, slavery, and other crimes. Most of them had been released by 1951 and continued to do business in the industry. The Nuremberg Tribunal dissolved IG Farben into Bayer, Hoechst, and BASF. Each of these companies today is twenty times larger than IG Farben was in 1944. For almost three decades after WWII, BASF, Bayer, and Hoechst (Aventis) filled their highest position, chairman of the board, with former members of the Nazi regime.

The Rockefellers, by forming a "Drug Trust" with IG Farben spinoffs, gave these companies legitimacy and included them in the burgeoning pharmaceutical and processed food alliance that included General Mills, Kellogg, Nestle, Bristol-Myers Squibb, Proctor and Gamble, and Roche and Hoechst (Sanofi-Aventis). The Rockefeller empire, through its Chase Manhattan Bank, now JP Morgan Chase, owns over half of the pharmaceutical interests in the United States today. It is the largest drug manufacturing combine in the world. Since WWII, the pharmaceutical industry has steadily netted increasing profits to become the world's second largest manufacturing industry, second only to the arms industry.[1117]

Is there any value in prescription drugs? Obviously, there is. I am alive today because of taking prescription drugs that were prescribed to me after suffering through congenital heart failure. So I am immensely thankful that these drugs were developed. Yet, it should be a concern to everyone that each synthetic drug that is created in a laboratory, while they may perform specific beneficial functions, also cause negative side-effects. These side-effects tear down your body. By taking synthetic drugs, we are actually putting foreign substances in our body, which have the ability to harm or kill us. For example, the drugs that I take safeguard my heart, but harm my liver.

If one were to go through one's individual prescription drugs and read the side-effects, it might open our eyes to the down-side of prescription drugs. Consider the fact that prescription drugs are currently responsible for more deaths annually than illegal drugs. According to Tom Frieden, the director of the Center for Disease Control, "it's a big problem, and it's getting worse."[1118]

Out of the almost eight hundred thousand annual deaths from conventional medicine mistakes, approximately one hundred and twenty-eight thousand of these are the result of prescription drug use.[1119] Consider the current crisis of opioid misuse and overdose and opioid use disorder (OUD). While each year more people die of prescription drug overdoses than died in the entirety of the Vietnam War, the Korean War, or any armed conflict since the end of World War II, each day ninety Americans die prematurely from an overdose that involves an opioid, leaving families and friends bereft.[1120] Even if prescription drugs do not literally kill a patient, they slowly destroy their mind and body.

In her book Cure: *A Journey Into the Science of Mind Over Body*, Jo Marchant describes numerous studies where doctors have researched how the mind and the body working together can increase a patients' ability to either mitigate their disease or improve his or her ability to cope with the effects of the disease. Trials have demonstrated that encouraging the patients to use both the power of their minds and bodies can help reduce the amount of prescriptions drugs needed and their negative side effects. As she says in her book:

> This is the point at which I'd love to conclude that thanks to studies and projects like these we are witnessing a revolution in medicine, in which we'll soon fully understand the role of the mind in health and will come to see the human aspects of care not as an add-on luxury, but as a central, guiding principle towards improving patient outcomes. Unfortunately, the odds are stacked against that happening.[1121]

One obstacle is the way in which research is funded: more than three quarters of clinical trials in the US are funded by drug companies, who understandably have no interest in proving the benefit of any approach to care that might reduce their profits.

Ms. Marchant sees this issue as not only the problem of drug companies, but of government research as well. She points out that of the National Institute of Health's (NIH) thirty billion dollar budget, less than two percent goes toward "testing mind-body therapies," [1122] which would give people greater control over their own health.

Government Regulation

The growth of Big Pharma, and its support from federal regulatory agencies is essentially an assault on free trade. By promoting Big Pharma, the federal government took income from local health care providers and concentrated profits into the hands of the giant corporations. The rationale for this is that it is being done in the name of "science" to protect "the little guy" from purveyors of junk medicine. In reality, no one is protecting us from the giant corporations who are profiting from our illness while simultaneously making us sick and, in many instances, legally killing us.

We are told by the Federal Drug Administration, the American Medical Association, and the National Cancer Institute that the medicine we get is based upon science, but, in this case, objectivity and scientific inquiry do not go hand in hand. Rather Big Pharma controls the practice of medicine with their money. The financial giants of business and industry and their corporate-sponsored philanthropies, such as the American Cancer Society, spend and lobby mightily for laws representing their investments.[1123]

When allopathic doctors try to use or promote natural medicines in their private practice, they are immediately susceptible to attack by the medical establishment, either through negative peer reviews or by contrived research to debunk alternative therapies. If that does not dissuade the doctor, the medical establishment is not above resorting to "disinformation, smear campaigns of libel and slander, harassment, unwarranted IRS audits, enticement of patients and family members to sue doctors where there is no reason (even offering financial payment to do so), entrapment by undercover agents posing as sick patients who may persistently beg for alternative treatments, illegal wiretaps, and break-ins, and records theft."[1124]

The AMA also pressures doctors by threatening to destroy their license to practice medicine. The licensing boards engage in investigations and proceedings, which are kept secret even from the doctors. The only recourse for the doctor is to go through the process, and then go to court afterwards to sue the medical boards, which many physicians have done, but only if they can afford the process. As we know, one way of destroying any practice is for the richer of the two combatants to continually file frivolous lawsuits until the poorer one goes broke. The AMA is also not above presenting fabricated evidence to the state board of medical examiners with a request for an official investigation. Such processes often result in prosecution.

The AMA has been dedicated to destroying practitioners of medical systems other than allopathy (drugs and surgery) since its inception. It opposes all forms of medicine that cut into its member's profits, not just non-traditional forms of medicine. They have attacked midwifery, acupuncture, homeopathy, naturopathy, massage therapy, physical therapy, nutrition, optometry, chelation therapy, etc. It should not surprise us that the National Council Against Health Fraud receives funding from the National Pharmaceutical Council and the AMA. Similarly, the American Council on Science and Health (ACSH) is funded by the National Agricultural Chemicals Association, DuPont, Monsanto, Procter and Gamble, Dow Chemical, and many others from the processed food industry, including Frito-Lay, Burger King, Land O'Lakes, Oscar Meyer, and Hershey Foods. Their main job is to counter all claims against pesticides, irradiated foods, genetically engineered foods, antibiotics, hormones, etc.

Mental Health

A lot can be said for the advancements in mental health care in the US by looking at the practices of Dr. Benjamin Rush who is considered to be the Father of American Psychiatry. Dr. Rush was a Founding Father of the United States who attended the Continental Congress and signed the Declaration of Independence. He served as Surgeon General of the Continental Army and became a professor of chemistry, medical theory, and clinical practice at the University of Pennsylvania.

Dr. Rush was a proponent of many reforms in the areas of medicine and education.[1125] At the Constitutional Convention, he argued that the Bill of Rights contain an amendment to legalize Freedom Of Medical Care, or else, he argued, one form of medicine might gather up enough political strength to push aside all other forms. As we have seen, without his amendment being ratified this is exactly what has happened.[1126] Rush also opposed slavery, advocated for free public schools, sought improved education for women and a more enlightened penal system. In his promotion of public health, he advocated for a clean environment and stressed the importance of personal and military hygiene. As a leading physician, he had a major impact on the emerging medical profession.

Rush believed that illness was the result of imbalances in the body's physical system and was caused by malfunctions in the brain. While this belief helped to dispel the popular myth that illness was caused by the devil and mental illness by possession of demons, nonetheless, in his approach to medicine, he inadvertently killed hundreds of patients in his medical career by his favorite "cures" of bleeding patients until they passed out, purging them by making them vomit and blistering them. He also gave them liberal doses of highly toxic mercury to ingest. Many historians feel that during the 1793 Yellow Fever epidemic, Dr Rush killed more people than the disease itself.[1127]

His study of mental disorder made him one of the founders of American psychiatry. His image still appears on the seal of the American Psychiatric Association. When it came to treating the mentally ill, Dr Benjamin Rush did something highly unorthodox. He listened to his patients, took notes, advocated for his patients, recommending that authorities not beat them or lock them up in small, filthy cells.

Notwithstanding this sense of humanity, he also believed that mental illness could be shaken out of a person. To do this, he devised chairs suspended from the ceiling in which attendants swung and spun the mentally ill patient for hours. Then there was the Tranquilizer Chair, which he devised in 1811 that locked a person up tightly and cut off all light so as to deprive the patient of any visual sensations. The chair came with an opening below allowing the patient to evacuate his/her bowels and a caretaker to change the pan without disturbing the patient.[1128]

While off to a rocky start, mental health care in the US continued to advance. In the 1840's, Dorothea Dix, an educator and social reformer, devoted herself to the welfare of the mentally ill. Her lobbying for these outcasts of society, in fact, led to widespread international reforms. After witnessing the dangerous and unhealthy conditions in which many patients lived, she was able to successfully persuade the US Government to fund the building of thirty-two state psychiatric hospitals. It took her over forty years of her life to do so, but she finally succeeded.

The institutional in-patient care model, pioneered by Dorothea Dix, in which patients lived in hospitals and were treated by professional staff, was considered for over a hundred years to be the most effective way to care for the mentally ill. It was also welcomed by families and communities who did not know how to care for people with a chronic mental illness.

Although institutionalized care increased a person's access to mental health services, the state hospitals were often underfunded and understaffed, and, in time, the institutional care system drew harsh criticism for being little better than the filthy cells to which the mentally ill were originally condemned. For example, the Willowbrook State School for children with mental disabilities was designed for four thousand patients, but by 1965 it had a population of six thousand. At the time, it was the biggest state-run institution for people with mental disabilities in the United States. The living conditions of the children prompted Senator Robert Kennedy to call it a "snake pit." The deplorable conditions included overcrowding, inadequate sanitary facilities, and physical and sexual abuse of the children by members of the school's staff. Public outcry led to its closure in 1987,[1129] and to the passage of the Civil Rights of Institutionalized Persons Act (CRIPA) in 1980.[1130]

As early as the mid-1950s, a movement had already begun to deinstitutionalize the mentally ill and treat them on an out-patient basis. This movement gained momentum due to the development of a variety of antipsychotic drugs and the belief that psychiatric patients would have a higher quality of life if treated in their communities rather than in "large, undifferentiated, and isolated mental hospitals".[1131]

The closure of state psychiatric hospitals in the United States was codified by the Community Mental Health Centers Act of 1963, and strict standards were passed so that only individuals "who posed an imminent danger to themselves or someone else" could be committed to state psychiatric hospitals.

By the mid-1960s, in the US, many severely mentally ill people had been moved from psychiatric institutions to local mental health homes or similar facilities. The number of institutionalized mentally ill patients fell from its peak of five hundred and sixty thousand in the 1950s to one hundred and thirty thousand by 1980. By 2000, the number of state psychiatric hospital beds per one hundred thousand people was twenty-two, down from three hundred and thirty-nine in 1955.[1132]

To replace institutionalized care, community-based care was developed to include a range of treatment facilities, from community mental health centers and smaller supervised residential homes to community-based psychiatric teams.

Community mental health also has its detractors, however. Critics of the deinstitutionalization movement point out that many patients have been moved from in-patient psychiatric hospitals to nursing or residential homes, which are not always staffed or equipped to meet the needs of the mentally ill. In many cases, deinstitutionalization has only shifted the burden of care to the families of mentally ill individuals, though they often lack the financial resources and medical knowledge to provide proper care. Another problem is that the mentally ill become homeless. This puts a burden on the criminal justice system to contain such people, without them having the facilities or the staff to address their illnesses.

Though the institutional-deinstitutionalization debate continues, many health professionals, families, and advocates for the mentally ill would like to see a combination of higher-quality community treatment programs (like intensive case management) and increased availability of intermediate and long-term psychiatric inpatient care for patients in need of a more structured care environment.

The hard reality, however, is that more American families are being forced to cope with someone who is mentally ill and do not have the knowledge or the money to cure these illnesses.

Deteriorating social conditions, joblessness, and hopelessness about the future are leading to greater depression and anxiety. According to a recent article published in the journal *Psychiatric Services*, and reviewed by CBS News, more Americans than ever suffer from stress, depression, and anxiety and many are unable to get the help they need.

An estimated 8.3 million American adults currently suffer from serious psychological distress. Mental illness is on the rise as is suicide. And access to care for the mentally ill is getting worse. Judith Weissman, the research manager in the department of medicine at NYU Langone Medical Center in New York City, states that the increase in mental illness is a lasting after-effect of the Great Recession that began in late 2007. Many people psychologically affected by the Great Recession have not been able to get the help they need, either because they cannot afford it or because their condition hampers their ability to seek out treatment, she said.

> The recession seemed to have pushed the mentally ill to the point where they never recovered. This is a very disturbing finding because of the implications of what mental illness can do to a person in terms of their ability to function and their life span.[1133]

Not only are more Americans suffering from mental illness, but health care facilities are becoming less available to them as the government refuses to fund mental health programs. The NYU Langone Medical Center research team estimated that nearly one in ten distressed Americans in 2014 did not have health insurance that would give them access to a psychiatrist or mental health counselor.

One thing is certain. If Trumpcare will ever completely replace Obamacare, mental health services will be even more inaccessible to the American people.[1134] It will allow health insurance companies to refuse needed treatment for people, which they will eagerly do to cut costs and increase corporate profits.

Health Insurance

How did America end up with its present health insurance system? The government was not always involved in health care insurance. At the time the Flexner Report was written, America was a dangerous place to work. So gruesome were factory injuries and the suffering of American workers that "muckraking" became a literary genre of its own.

In one narrative, an explosion at a Butler County steel mill forced "streams of hot metal on the workmen, engulfing and literally cooking some of them." Some accounts were less spectacular, but more ghastly, like arms being jerked from sockets, regular decapitations, and sawmill accidents.

In 1907, writer William B. Hard, studying a U.S. Steel plant in Chicago estimated that more than ten percent of the steel workforce were injured or killed on the job.

The Russell Sage Foundation, around the same time, conducted a survey that found that among those who survived their workplace accidents, around fifty percent received one hundred dollars or less from the employer, while fifty percent received absolutely no share of the inevitable income loss. At the time, the expenses associated with medical care were calculated at twenty-five percent of the cost of wage loss when someone missed work time due to injury.

As insurance companies grew more sophisticated, they began selling "accident" policies that included disability, death, and burial benefits to employers. The policies did not resemble the health coverage we know today, but the precedent of businesses having a stake in the well-being of their employees was established.

In 1910, mail-order retailer Montgomery Ward solicited what is now considered the nation's first multi-employee health insurance policy, through a plan issued by the London Guarantee and Accident Co. of New York. It paid total annual benefits of up to $28.85 to ill or injured employees.[1135]

At the time of this plan, there was no real health care "system." Many surgeries were still being conducted in the home rather than a clinical setting. Even the health care that was available only dealt with infectious diseases and traumatic injuries and these were hit or miss by today's standards.

Even so, the science of medical care was rapidly progressing, and there was much debate over who ought to pay for such care when an injury or sickness was work related. Was health care a right or a privilege? I. M. Rubinow, the head of the American Association for Labor Legislation, advocated for "compulsory" sickness coverage that would pay for medical costs and disease prevention for all workers, modeled after similar plans taking hold in Europe. Economist Irving Fisher believed health insurance was necessary "to tide workers over the grave emergencies [and to] reduce illness itself."[1136]

This proposal never gained much credence among the capitalists. Even today, unpaid medical bills are the number one cause of personal bankruptcies, outpacing credit-card bills or late mortgage payments.

The capitalists argued that compulsory health insurance would be too costly and would amount to a raise for every worker in America, and "would not materially reduce the amount of sickness." Insurance companies and physicians were not on board, either. Doctors worried then, as now, that health insurers would have too much control over prices and practice methods; insurers worried that a system of "compulsory" health insurance would interfere with their lucrative life insurance business.

Then came the Depression. When people do not have a job, they cannot pay for medical care. Presidents Franklin D. Roosevelt and Harry S. Truman attempted to build compulsory health care into the Social Security Act but failed. Without a means to pay for care, hospitals were struggling. More than one hundred went under, while the rest were operating well below capacity. And even then, many patients who showed up were not paying their bills. With hospitals desperate for new revenue streams, a group of fifteen hundred Dallas-area teachers offered to prepay premiums to the Baylor Hospital in exchange for up to twenty-one days of future care. This deal turned out to be the forerunner of Blue Cross.

Soon plans would involve multiple sets of employees, covering multiple hospitals. By 1935, nineteen prototype Blue Cross plans existed in thirteen states. By 1939, prepayment plans were being created for physicians, too, which were the forerunners to the modern Blue Shield. Around this same time, dam workers for the Kaiser Construction Co. were among the first to have voluntary premiums deducted from their paychecks.

Those premiums then went to an insurer that sent money to an on-site Kaiser doctor who treated those who were injured while working on the dams. In short, everyone, insurers as well as doctors, were paid in advance and the program was soon replicated at construction sites up and down the West Coast.

Also, during the 1930s, two drug categories were developing, sulfa antimicrobials, which were the precursor to antibiotics, and, a decade later, penicillin. Infections that would have been deadly in the 1920s were easily curable just two decades later.

If the Depression motivated hospitals to think about new prepayment models, World War II motivated employers and employee unions to get creative about health benefits. In 1940, less than ten percent (twelve million people) of the US population had any kind of health coverage. By 1950, about half of America was covered. By comparison, under Obamacare, nearly ninety percent of Americans were covered by health insurance even though that percentage is projected to drop if Trumpcare passes.

In 1942, as America entered WWII, Congress passed the Stabilization Act to limit wage increases and inflation, which, in the words of the act, "threaten our military effort and our domestic economic structure." While this Act made sense on the macro-level, it put a strain on employers who needed to recruit workers at a time when many able-bodied men were overseas. To get around the problem, employers began to offer more generous health benefits to workers. Health premiums deducted by employers do not count as income, and, as a result, workers do not pay income or payroll taxes on those benefits. Immediately, insurers began adding new types of coverage. "Major medical" evolved in the 1950s, vision care in 1957, and dental benefits in 1959. In this way, health insurance became a cornerstone of our health care system along with drugs, devices, and surgeries.

A major problem with the health insurance system at the time was that by tying health care to employment, two vulnerable groups were left out of the system, those who are unable to work or worked in low-paying jobs without health benefits, and those who were beyond working age. Seniors, for example, found themselves priced out of the market as greater consumption of health care services resulted in health cost inflation. In the late 1950s, most retirees could not afford health care coverage.

President John F. Kennedy advocated "Medical Care for the Aged," a hospital insurance plan for seniors. After Kennedy's assassination, President Lyndon B. Johnson, with Democratic majorities in the US House and Senate, created the Medicare and Medicaid systems in 1965.[1137] In 2015, under Obamacare, the US spent about $3.2 trillion on health care or nearly ten thousand dollars for every person in the country. It accounted for 17.8 percent of GDP.

Under Obama's Affordable Care Act (ACA), the uninsured rate fell to about ten percent, the lowest in US history. There are certainly problems with Obamacare, for example, many people still cannot afford to pay the high insurance premiums for a coverage that does not kick in until a person has already paid thousands of dollars out of their own pockets. Nonetheless, about ten million people have bought insurance through the exchanges created by the health care law, while an additional ten million poor and disabled became covered by Medicaid.[1138] While the number of insured increased under Obamacare, twenty-four million of the people currently insured are projected to lose their coverage when Trumpcare is passed.[1139]

Having said this, in the effort to achieve health care for every American, our focus should not be on the government, but on the large insurance companies. As Americans, we know that our health insurance is going up next year, as it did this year, last year, and most of the years before that. And it is not just that the price is going up; it is rising faster than wages and inflation, eating away at our ability to pay for other household expenses like food, rent, heat, transportation, etc.

According to a Kaiser Family Foundation study, insurance premiums, which reflect spending on medicines, doctor visits, tests, and hospital stays, have climbed two hundred and thirteen percent since 1999. Wages, by comparison, have risen only sixty percent, while inflation is up forty-four percent.[1140]

Rising health insurance rates often keep workers from getting a raise because employers pay into employee health care coverage, leaving them less money to increase salaries when insurance rates rise.

Customers who shopped on the Affordable Care Act's public insurance exchanges found premium hikes of twenty percent or more in many markets because insurers were uncertain about the future of government health care programs under Trump.[1141]

Trump cut the subsidies provided to people to help them afford insurance under Obamacare. By cutting these subsidies, thirty million people left their reduced subsidy on the table because it was not sufficient to allow them to purchase even the least expensive health care policy. This will amount to over six hundred billion dollars in unclaimed subsidies between 2020 and 2026, which will be transferred from the American people to the rich who will benefit by having their tax payments reduced in like amount.[1142]

How long can this insurance system continue? It will inevitably continue until some big change disrupts the system. Perhaps employers will revert to contracting directly with big hospital systems for health care, cutting out the insurance middleman. Maybe something will slow the process of drug and medical device manufacturing and prices will stabilize. Or perhaps, the American people will just get sick of the insurance companies' high premiums and restricted access to health care and begin to refuse to buy health care insurance. We are not there yet, but if the current trend continues, tomorrow promises increased inequality, higher prices, and reduced quality of services from the health care establishment. At that time, the American people may begin to put greater emphasis on local resources to meet their health care needs.

A strong movement has already begun to revive natural medicines in which Americans depend more on caring for themselves instead of depending on doctors and hospitals for everything. This will mean that we will give more attention to our diet, exercise, rest, and to disciplines like mindfulness and yoga that strengthen the body, quiet the mind, and rejuvenate the spiritual dimensions of our being. Medicinally, it may also mean greater reliance on cannabis, natural supplements, herbal medicines, massage techniques, homeopathy, etc., which can often be accessed at the local level. Who knows, perhaps towns will begin to contract directly with local hospitals for traumas and emergency surgeries on the part of their residents. All of these things are possible when people get fed up with the status quo.

Education

Real education is that which leads to liberation. Shrii P. R. Sarkar

The five minimum physical requirements of all human beings are food, shelter, clothing, medical care and education. Of these, education is the most important factor in furthering the future of society. There is a psychic need to know more and more, and this is called 'mental expansion'. Education should link the physical and psychic need of learners with the spiritual need for happiness that will take them to the stage of all-round liberation. Narendra Raj Purohit

What is Education?

To understand what a proper education is, we must acknowledge something about ourselves as human beings. It is the inherent desire of all human beings to expand our physical and mental strength. Not knowing any better, many of us attempt to achieve this by exploiting others. We completely forget the needs and interests of other living beings in our own quest for more.

The only way to overcome this divisive tendency, is to learn how to divert our physical and psychic longings into spiritual aspirations. Book Two of this trilogy on *Universal Ideology* goes deeply into this subject and explains the intuitional science by which this is achieved. For now, however, let us simply note that, unlike other animals, human beings have the scope to become God-conscious beings. Other animals do not have this capacity.

A proper education should entail physical and mental training to avoid exploiting others and getting exploited by others. To do this, we must understand and develop our true nature. Because of the absence of such training today, people lack the necessary balance between their social environment and their inner psychic state. Many, if not most, of our political and corporate leaders, who speak so sincerely about the welfare of others when giving their speeches, lack even an iota of sincerity. This is basically the condition of the modern world. There is no balance between individual and collective existence. For a balance to be achieved, we will require a proper education system.[1143]

Every person has a right to an education and therefore it should be made accessible to all. Because democracy can never be successful without an educated society, education should also be mandatory. To do this, public education is required.

The Important Need for Education

As we have witnessed so many times, without a proper education, people are easily led by religious, political, and corporate leaders who appeal to their baser instincts and sentiments. This appeal to people's ignorance makes a mockery of democracy. Conversely, we have also observed that when people are educated and think rationally, they do not tolerate being oppressed by false leaders who want to exploit them for personal power. A proper education will lead people to fight against such institutional oppression.[1144]

A proper education should enable a person to stand against the negative influences of their social environment while simultaneously awakening the mental urge to attain a higher life. This is the ideological goal of a proper education. Such an education inspires people. As such, we should do our best to impart a proper education to everyone.

While modern scientists have debunked the myth that we use only ten percent of our brains, the fact remains that we use only a very small percentage of our inherent capacity. Generally speaking, we have the capacity to do an infinite number of things but we have neither the aptitude, desire, nor time to do so. Many of us waste half of our lives in idle pursuits and only a small percentage of our time engaged in worthwhile tasks. Billions of people utilize only their physical capacity but totally neglect their mental and spiritual potential.

Why do human beings fail to utilize their capacity for expansion? First, they lack a proper education as to what should be done and what should not be done. Secondly, they are habitually indolent, suffering from psychic and spiritual inertness. It is the purpose of education to encourage people to expand their consciousness and to overcome this psychic and spiritual inertness.

But this is not the intent of today's education system in the US where children are subjected to gender or race bigotry by teachers and classmates and denied educational resources. This certainly depresses our children and blocks the expression of their capabilities. Such oppression makes them think, "I am inferior. I am worthless. I am ugly." Because of this oppression, many brilliant and gifted people never realize their inherent potentialities and society is denied their contribution. This is certainly a matter of regret and shame, but it is also an act of blatant oppression and exploitation. A proper education system must strongly oppose such cultural biases.

The poor and the oppressed commit many petty crimes because they have never been encouraged to expand their minds. When society keeps calling them sinners and criminals, they develop a deep inferiority complex which tells them, "I am a wretch. I have no future." As well-wishers of humanity and especially as educators we should find the good qualities in these oppressed children and begin to praise their performance. This praise will encourage them to concentrate more on their good qualities than on their negative qualities. Even though this may be incredibly difficult to do in light of a child's antisocial behavior, the day will finally come when he or she will be so preoccupied with doing good deeds that they will cease to commit their crimes.

But if our children are neglected or if they continue to be subjected to unreasonable social punishment, their habit of committing crimes will only become stronger. They will stick to the path of vice so tenaciously that they will become an even greater burden on society. This is the trend of education in America today. For lack of concern for our fellow human beings and for lack of understanding of basic human psychology, our society has created an apartheid education system which is creating more criminals and alienating more of our people.

The problem is due to a defective social order and this state of affairs cannot be allowed to continue. The structure of inequality and injustice must be destroyed for the benefit of all. If we continue along the current path, fewer people will be able to meet their basic needs in the future. Society will continue to polarize and the quest for the Supreme will remain an unattainable dream for the majority of people.

In order to help all people to expand their consciousness in a positive manner, a revolution in education is required. Training in universal morality and spiritual practices will need to be added to the curriculum. Every student from prekindergarten to postgraduate work should be encouraged to develop the noble qualities lying dormant within them. This process must begin in the home and be amplified throughout the new school system. It is only by such means that our society will regain its strength and character.

It is to be acknowledged from the beginning that this will be extremely difficult to do because the capitalist elite are not concerned about the welfare of all, nor about an individual's sense of humanity and they will fight us with their money, their propaganda, and with their weapons. Their only concern is to force us to compete for job slots in their economic machine. Those who are unable to compete are nothing more than surplus labor to the capitalists. The ruling elites only concern is to put fear into the working class that there are many others to take their place if they do not obey. This is why a revolution is required and why it must begin at the local level.

The Goal of Education

The goal of a proper education system is to elevate the all-round standard, and especially the intellectual standard of everyone in the US, as well as the entire world. In order to have peace in the world a proper education is required by all. This means that knowledge should increase in different spheres of life and that our sense of morality should be expanded to include every human being and every aspect of our natural environment as well. Moral training is deficient today and is sorely lacking in the present educational system. The teaching of moral behavior in public schools is made difficult by the fact that people identify morality with religion, which is generally divisive and which should not have a place in public schools. Nonetheless, when we will increase our intellectual standard and act according to a universal moral code, we will gain the respect of all, even from those who desire to exploit us. This is the lesson of all spiritual masters and the lesson of those who seek to live by spiritual precepts. An education system, which is guided by universal moral principles and leads to the acquisition of knowledge, will create a peaceful society.[1145]

The History of US Education

In Volume IV, Chapter 5 of *The Untold Story of Western Civilization* it was described in detail how today's public education system was molded so as to turn children into cogs in the capitalist system. As the American industrial revolution began to move into high gear, the elite required a docile and unimaginative workforce who would not question the legitimacy of the status quo. As described earlier, this led the elite to explore the concept of eugenics. Eugenics is a set of beliefs and practices that aims at "improving" the genetic quality of the human population by either promoting higher rates of sexual reproduction for people with desired traits (i.e., the ruling elite and their acquiescent servants) and reducing the rate of sexual reproduction and sterilization of people with less-desired or undesired traits.[1146]

The educational system of the United States was based upon the same principles of eugenics. As it became incumbent upon the corporate elite to have a docile workforce, they began to invest money into a public education system. The intention for such a system was made perfectly clear at the time. In 1901, Edward A Ross, a progressive American sociologist, eugenicist, and major figure of early criminology, wrote in his book, *Social Control*, "Plans are underway to replace community, family, and church with propaganda, education, and mass media."[1147]

In 1906, the first report of an Education Board set up by John D. Rockefeller expressed their goal this way:

> In our dreams . . . people yield themselves with perfect docility to our molding hands. The present educational conventions [intellectual and character education] fade from our minds, and unhampered by tradition we work our own good will upon a grateful and responsive folk.[1148]

President Woodrow Wilson, following the dictates of the capitalist elite, defined the goal of public education this way:

> We want one class to have a liberal education. We want another class, a very much larger class of necessity, to

forego the privilege of a liberal education and fit themselves to perform specific difficult manual tasks.[1149]

By the first quarter of the twentieth century, the goal of public education was firmly established. Ellwood Cubberley, the Dean of the Stanford Graduate School of Education and a pioneer in the field of educational administration, wrote in his book, *Public School Administration*:

> Our schools are, in a sense, factories in which the raw products (children) are to be shaped and fashioned into products to meet the various demands of life. . . . It is the business of the school to build its pupils according to the specifications laid down.[1150]

In the process of public education, individual creativity was crushed because the school system was established quite explicitly to train the American people as cogs to function in the industrial system of the corporations.

As the complexity of the business world increased and white-collar jobs increased, it became necessary, at least at the college and university level to make liberal arts more accessible to the young. Even so, the original intent of the public education system retains its mandate at the primary and secondary levels of public education, particularly in the schools attended by minority children.

As a corollary to this corporate design, the public was taught that to teach one's children themselves was irresponsible. In the same way, when local people organize to meet their needs, independent of corporate grants, their efforts are seen as a form of aggression or subversion.[1151] Take the anti-fracking movement as an example.

It will not serve us to reject the American public school system completely. But, at the same time, we must acknowledge the intention behind its creation and the impact that it continues to have on our public schools. The American education system utterly failed and continues to fail to inculcate a sense of morality, equality, and social justice in the majority of our children. This is why it is necessary to gain control over the system at the local level and mold it to the welfare of the local people. As such, our curriculum should address those principles and subjects that reinforce and strengthen our march along the path of progress.

Morality, spirituality (not religion), humanity, and science should be the foundation of our new education system.

Free education must be provided for all the local people. Any attempt by the government, religions, or corporations to propagate divisive group sentiments through the medium of public education should be viewed as an attack on the welfare of the local people and the propagandists should be exposed for their exploitation. No "ism" except universalism can be tolerated in our revolutionary educational system.

Those who attempt to disturb human unity are motivated by group politics which destroys various attributes of the human mind, including refined taste, simplicity, and the spirit of service to those less fortunate. For such divisive forces, their main objective is not the welfare of the community but to advance self-interest, the church, or party. Such people, without even trying to improve themselves, want to instigate the people to quarrel among themselves while indulging in self-applause for their own oratory. People should remain vigilant of such demagogues.[1152]

Because the American public education system has always attempted to keep religion out of schools, it has not become a direct problem in the public school system. But while public schools may be free of religious influence, they are not free of nationalistic sentiments. When a school is under the dominance of nationalist values, it cannot, simultaneously be motivated by universal values. Nationalism, as well as other sentiments based on gender, race, or geographic superiority are highly detrimental to the minds of children. The purity of their minds is to a large extent sullied by such sentiments.

People should not be segregated by race or by class privilege because the opportunities for mutual contact and understanding between people provide the seeds of collective welfare. In order to create a feeling of genuine collective welfare, the current mainstream sentiments regarding gender, racial, class, religious, and national sentiments will need to be overcome and intelligent people will have to make a tremendous effort to overcome such prejudicial zeal.

The Profit Motive

The higher education system in America is systematically being destroyed by student debt. The generation of Millennials now owe over $1.48 trillion in student loan debt. This is about $620 billion more than the entire US credit card debt. Spread out among forty-four million students, the average college graduate is saddled with a $39,400 debt that will impoverish them for decades to come. This is despite the fact that the job market requires more college graduates today because a high school diploma is virtually worthless to secure most jobs.[1153] Due to massive student debt, forty-five percent of students say that college was not worth the cost. This debt has also affected young people's personal lives. For example, forty-four percent say that they want to know how much student debt a person has before they are willing to have a serious relationship. Twenty-eight percent have had to delay buying a house and twelve percent have delayed getting married due to student debt.[1154]

Decades ago, in a bow to the capitalist banks, the federal government relinquished direct control of the student loan program, allowing banks and corporations, who were more concerned with profits, rather than diplomas, to seize the flow of federal loan dollars by peddling loans that many students could not afford and then collecting fees from the government to hound those students when they defaulted. The student loan industry that sprung up with this privatization of student loans has lobbied Congress to ensure that these loans are virtually the only consumer debt that cannot be discharged by personal bankruptcy.

At the same time, middle-class incomes have stagnated, college costs have soared, and state governments have also drastically cut their historical investment in public universities. The federal government itself, which is paid by tax dollars to look after the peoples' interests, is one of the big winners in the exploitation of students. By the Department of Education's own calculations, the government, in some years, earns an astounding twenty percent on each loan, turning our young people into profit centers rather than supporting them. And yet, the mainstream media continues the propaganda that our education system is meant to cure inequality and contribute to economic justice.

Our young people and their parents were unprepared for what hit them. Young people today talk about how easy it was to borrow to go to college and how no one, not even their parents, warned them about the risk they were assuming. They say that the colleges made it seem safe to borrow by assuring them that everyone had loans. They talk about how they want to pay off their loans but cannot earn enough to do that.

They did not realize how their loan balance would soar if they missed a payment. They speak of the embarrassment of being hounded by debt collectors and they talk about the unrelenting stress of knowing they probably will never be free of debt.[1155]

This predicament of American families is just another example of how even the best of government intentions eventually gets corrupted by corporate greed.

Education Reform

President Lyndon B. Johnson signed the Higher Education Act of 1965 as part of his "Great Society" programs, in an effort to fight poverty and racial injustice. The Act increased federal money to universities, created scholarships, gave low-interest loans for students, created work-study programs and established a National Teachers Corps. The idea behind the Act was to ensure that any student, regardless of gender or race, who wanted to go to college, would be able to do so through federal scholarships and loans. "This nation could never rest," he said, "while the door to knowledge remained closed to any American."

Under President Richard Nixon, Congress expanded the program in 1972 by creating a quasi-governmental agency, the Student Loan Marketing Association, (Sallie Mae) to increase the amount of money available for student loans.

Sallie Mae created a market for federally-backed student loans. When banks loaned to students, Sallie Mae bought the loans from the banks and this increased the pool of money available for loans.

After he was elected in 1992, Bill Clinton pushed through Congress a major revision of the student loan program that made the federal government the direct lender of the loans and not just the insurer. The direct loan program alarmed Sallie Mae and the banks because now they had to compete with a government-run program that could make loans at a lower interest rate because it did not have to turn a profit.

When Republicans won control of Congress in 1994, they moved to kill the direct loan program and privatize Sallie Mae. After a year of bitter infighting, Clinton and congressional Republicans reached a compromise. The loan program was saved, but Clinton agreed to privatize Sallie Mae. Before privatization, Sallie Mae had little flexibility. The US president appointed one-third of its board, and the Departments of the Treasury and Education had to sign off on most major policy decisions. It could not loan money to students because the banks did that.

The compromise freed Sallie Mae of those restrictions. Originally barred from acquiring other loan issuers, back-office operations or collection agencies, it now could buy any company.

Earlier, it lacked the authority to issue federally guaranteed loans; now it could do so. And for the first time, Sallie Mae could make private student loans, ones not guaranteed by the federal government that commanded much higher interest rates and greater profits.

While the Department of Education technically still oversaw student loans, the privatization of Sallie Mae brought the capitalists out of the woodwork. Now the private capitalists instead of the federal government ran the loan program.

Under its CEO, Albert Lord, Sallie Mae grew by leaps and bounds. Free of government control, it emerged as the dominant company in the field.

Lord's chief competition when he took over Sallie Mae was the Education Department's direct loan program created by Clinton. Since its adoption in 1993, the program had gained popularity steadily on college campuses and captured a third of the student loan market by the time Sallie Mae was privatized.

To undermine these federal loans, Sallie Mae paid colleges to drop out of the federal program and make Sallie Mae the campus student loan provider. It paid college financial loan officers to serve as consultants on Sallie Mae advisory boards.[1156] It paid a New Jersey agency fifteen million dollars to steer business to Sallie Mae.

It placed Sallie Mae employees in university call centers to field questions from students who thought they were getting advice from college loan officers. It sponsored trips and cruises for collegiate financial aid officers. It opened the door for other private lenders to use the same tactics. Needless to say, the Department of Education did not have the budget to compete with these underhanded practices.

Faced with industry lobbying and congressional opposition, the Department of Education struggled to maintain Clinton's direct loan program. After President George W. Bush took office in 2001, the program was cut back even more. By 2007, its share of the student loan market had declined by more than forty percent.[1157]

The vast majority of student loans still come through the federal government. The Federal Reserve Bank of New York has estimated that more than ninety percent of the $1.3 trillion in outstanding student loans are in that category. This means that the government either directly issued these loans or, in the great majority of cases, backed them through Sallie Mae or another private company. The remaining ten percent are private student loans made by banks and companies and are not guaranteed by the government. Although small, the loan debt from private loans is estimated at one hundred billion dollars.

Even though government direct loans are cheaper for the student than private loans, college loan officers say many students succumb to the sales pitch of private lenders because they either do not realize that private loans are more expensive or have maxed out their federal loans. In fact, it is very difficult today to pay for college totally through government loans. The money is just not there.

From 1999 to 2004, Lord's compensation topped two million dollars.[1158] From 2010 to 2013, when students began to shoulder more and more debt, Sallie Mae's profits were $3.5 billion. Lord retired in 2013. The following year, Sallie Mae spun off most of its student loan business into a new company, Navient.

After privatization, Sallie Mae spent more than forty-four million dollars lobbying Congress, the president, and the US Department of Education on hundreds of measures, according to the Center for Responsive Politics. Sallie Mae's political action committee and company executives, led by Lord, have pumped about six million dollars into the campaigns of favored politicians, half to Republicans, half to Democrats.

In Congress, the biggest recipient was Ohio Republican John Boehner. From 1995 until his retirement in 2015, Boehner and his Freedom Project PAC received two hundred and sixty-one thousand dollars from Sallie Mae. As Boehner did the bidding of Sallie Mae lobbyists, he put off public criticism by saying that he supported the private student loan industry because it reflected his belief in free enterprise and his skepticism about big government.

Debt Collection

For nearly a generation after passage of the student loan program in 1965, employees in the Department of Education serviced and collected student loans, but in 1981, during the first year of the Reagan presidency, the Department began to contract with private companies to take over debt collection. The department today pays commissions and sometimes bonuses to private companies based largely on the money they recover when former students default. In fiscal year 2016, for example, the Department of Education estimated that these contractors were paid $2.1 billion in commissions. In the same year, the Department announced that it would phase out contracts with some of the collection agencies for what it called "materially inaccurate representations" to struggling borrowers. The contractors were permitted only to provide information to students on the types of loans available and were supposed to guide them through the thicket of choices. Later, however, they gained the authority to send out bills, keep tabs on payments, and call borrowers if they fell behind. But some have violated their contracts by lying to student borrowers about certain benefits they were eligible for and about waivers on collection fees.

Today, there are eleven major contractors, according to the Department of Education, the largest of which is Navient, the Sallie Mae spinoff. Overall, the servicing companies earn nearly one billion dollars a year in fees.[1159]

When Sallie Mae was privatized in 1996, the big banks descended on the field of education loans. Private equity funds controlled by JP Morgan Chase, Bank of America, and Citigroup bought established debt collection agencies, as did a fund led by one of Mitt Romney's former partners at Bain Capital. Some family-owned debt collectors, such as NCO Financial Systems, became hot properties and would be sold to one private equity fund after another.[1160]

In 2015, the Obama administration launched a pilot program to test whether federal employees could effectively take over the job of collecting on defaulted student loans, while being more helpful and less aggressive than private collectors.

According to Deanne Loonin, who monitored student debt for years for the National Consumer Law Center, the Obama experiment focused on one of the biggest problems borrowers face. "We need to eliminate the private collection agencies from this process," she said. "They are incentivized just to collect money, not to work out ways that might be better for the borrowers. We need to see what else might work."[1161]

As of 2019, President Donald Trump and his Education Secretary, Betsy DeVos, have again proposed a budget that eliminates the Public Service Loan Forgiveness program, which will costs student loan borrowers billions of dollars. Further Trump and DeVos want to eliminate over seven hundred million dollars in federal Perkins Loans as well as massively reduce work-study programs.[1162]

The Impact on Student Loan Borrowers

Student loans make up the nation's second largest consumer debt market, which has grown rapidly in the last decade. The total volume of outstanding student loans has more than doubled, rising from less than $600 billion in 2006 to more than $1.4 trillion today. One in four students, or eight million loan borrowers, are currently in default or struggling to stay current on their loans, despite the availability of income-driven repayment options for the vast majority of borrowers. The average debt is thirty-seven thousand dollars.

As millions of young and middle-aged student loan borrowers struggle to repay their loans, many consumers report that the debt collection agencies are failing to provide the basic level of service necessary. Students report problems such as the agencies losing paperwork or misapplying payments. Borrowers say that when errors arise, they find it difficult to have them corrected. Many borrowers experience serious problems accessing affordable repayment options in order to avoid default.[1163]

The stress of being saddled with heavy debt just when students are beginning their adult life is compounded by the unavailability of good paying jobs. Even if borrowers never run into problems with their loans, the mere existence of the debt is a burden that impacts the way student borrowers make important lifestyle decisions. Many with student debt must delay their decisions to buy a home, get married, have children, save for retirement, or enter a desired career field because of their debt. Student loans were created to be an engine for social mobility and economic justice, but they are, in fact, chains that prevent young people from achieving financial success.

In 2013, a study by the American Student Association (ASA) called "Life Delayed: The Impact of Student Debt on the Daily Lives of Young Americans," reported that twenty-seven percent of respondents to the ASA survey said that they found it difficult to buy daily necessities because of their student loans; sixty-three percent said their debt affected their ability to make larger purchases such as a car; seventy-three percent said they have put off saving for retirement or other investments; and seventy-five said that student loan debt affected their decision or ability to purchase a home.[1164]

In addition, forty-seven indicated it was the deciding factor, or had considerable impact, on their decision or ability to start a small business; twenty-nine percent indicated that they have put off marriage as a result of their student loans; and another forty-three percent said that student debt has delayed their decision to start a family.

The privatization of student loans is another example of how the greed of corporate capitalists continues to destroy the American Dream of US citizens while also subverting the purpose of government to assist the people of our democracy. If student loan borrowers continue to be sidelined by debt, the perilous position of the US economy will continue to drag along or decline, rather than prosper with the help of a new generation of well-educated Americans.[1165]

The Primary and Secondary School System

If we are being honest with ourselves, the greedy financial industry is not the only force in society responsible for denying our children a proper education. We all must share in the blame, particularly at the elementary and high school levels where teachers and parents play a larger role in the education of children.

Parents

Parents often blame teachers for their child's faults, but deny their own responsibilities. In many respects, the children's view of the world has already been molded by the influence of their family environment before they start school. No matter what or how much they learn at school, it is extremely difficult for them to free themselves from the influence of their family. Drawing on what they have learned in the family, the immature minds of children begin to learn about the world and understand it, and to receive ideas and master language so that they can express those ideas. Hence, the primary responsibility for acquainting children with the world lies with their parents or guardians. Children will become assets to society in the future to the extent that their parents or guardians discharge their duties properly.[1166]

In America, the capitalist mentality has turned time into money and everyone is racing along at an ever-frenzied pace. Speed, price, and convenience have become the main drivers of society, whether any good is accomplished or not. The slums continue to grow even though every house has a TV and a cell-phone.

This trend makes it difficult for people to think through anything. We go about our daily lives in a mechanical fog, only jolted out of it when we face a family crisis of some kind.

Many parents say they have no energy left at the end of the day to care for their children in a proper way. "How can we care for the mental and emotional needs of our children when we cannot even provide them with proper food and clothing," they ask. Without a loving contact with their children, parents lose the ability to know what their kids are thinking. The children drift away from their parents at an early age. Single parents have even a more difficult time in this matter.

Granting that parents have a point about the negative impact of teachers, they still must accept primary responsibility for the welfare of their children no matter how difficult. In order to impart a positive outlook in their children, parents only require two virtues—self-restraint and good judgment. Good judgment dictates that children are not subjected to threats, lies, or being terrorizing by parents. Such actions will not give children self-confidence or the will to help others. While threats, lies, and intimidation may achieve some temporary gain, the children will never be compensated for the harm done to them. Their pain will be lifelong.

Children learn from their elders to lie, bully, and be obstinate. In some cases, parents have lost their peace of mind due to poverty and take it out on their kids. Naturally the children will lose respect for their parents, further aggravating negative behavior. All this is to say that, even though parents are faced with a harsh reality, it is possible for them to raise optimistic children.

Teachers

How many teachers try to awaken a genuine thirst for knowledge in their students? Some teachers, many of whom are poorly paid and must suffer the negative behavior of abusive children say, "The government is corrupt and uncaring and the education system itself is only to ensure the profits of the rich. What are we supposed to do?" But can teachers escape their responsibilities by such remarks, even if true? Is there no scope for acquiring knowledge in neglected public schools? Must the schools be completely devoid of the touch of welfare? Other teachers complain that the class sizes are too big and the children too unruly to teach. This is also true in many cases.

Yet, having said this, it is the teachers' responsibility to impart knowledge, teach restraint in social life, give instruction about the workings of society, and teach our young the skills to survive and prosper. As with some parents, some teachers also use fear, lies, offensive remarks, and terror to control their students. Instead of trying to rectify the bad habits of their students, they assail their minds with caustic language. They hurt the feelings of students by ridiculing them.

How can this be avoided? The first point is that teachers must be carefully selected. A degree in education does not necessarily confer on a person the right to become a teacher. Teachers must possess such qualities as personal integrity, strength of character, righteousness, a feeling for social service, unselfishness, an inspiring personality, and leadership ability. Because teachers have such an extremely important role to play in society, their professional standards must be very high.

This is not glib talk; this is what society requires of teachers if we are to improve as a people. To create such teachers, however, we must be aware that many public school teachers are plagued by poor pay, long days, and untenable working conditions. Often, they are not supplied with books and school supplies for the children. Under such circumstances, how much social consciousness can we expect from our teachers? The salaries of teachers should be on a par with, if not higher than, the salaries of the highest paid civil servants. As it is, teachers must often strike to get even a measly salary. They are forced to join unions to do this, but the unions, in order to protect their members, will protect even the worst of teachers and prevent their firing no matter how detrimental they are to the students.

This means that simply raising the salaries of teachers, will not, of itself solve the problem. If teachers are to be held responsible for building ideal men and women, they must also be given the right to formulate educational policies, instead of being mere teaching machines. This should not be the job of politicians.

If the people of a state were to enact such legislation, teachers should not try to ingratiate themselves with so-called political benefactors. They should always keep higher ideals before them as they work. Those who are not teachers should not be allowed to interfere in educational matters that come within the jurisdiction of a school.

As it is today, society gains no lasting benefit when teachers force elementary and high school students to swallow meaningless facts like quinine pills instead of awakening in them a thirst for knowledge.

At present the problems that we see in our education system will not be solved by mere exhortations or by lobbying. These actions will have no effect. The problems of lack of school funding, student bullying, police hall monitors, teacher abuse of students, standardized testing, low pay and lack of respect for teachers, sick-outs, segregation, the student loan crisis, the increasing loss of value of art and humanity degrees, etc., cannot be solve by piecemeal attempts to reform the education system. An entirely new education system will have to be organized.

State and Local Control

It is both positive and negative that education policy and funding is primarily a matter of state and local control. The responsibility for K-12 education rests with the states under the Constitution. In fact, federal support for public K-12 education did not begin until 1965 with the enactment of the *Elementary and Secondary Education Act* (*ESEA*).

The *No Child Left Behind Act of 2001* (*NCLB*) was a reauthorization of *ESEA*. The law's express purposes are to raise achievement for all students and to close the achievement gap. But as the majority of teachers will tell you, the requirements of the No Child Left Behind Act disrupted students learning more than it helped it. Furthermore, what little control that teachers had over their curriculum was all but eliminated. The teacher's role was reduced to preparing her children to take the federal government standardized tests. Depending upon the students' performance, the school district was awarded federal funds. While, on average, across the country, the state contributes 46% of education funds, and the locality contributes 37%, the 8.3% from the feds is significant because it provides the perks that schools need. These include grants for elementary and high school programs for low-income children such as library resources, textbooks and other instructional materials; supplemental education centers and services; as well as professional development for teachers.[1167] These funds come not only from the Department of Education, but also from other Federal agencies such as the Department of Health and Human Services (Head Start) and the Department of Agriculture's School Lunch program.[1168]

Thus, while it is the states and communities that are responsible by law to establish schools and colleges, develop curricula, and determine requirements for enrollment and graduation, the federal government was able to undermine local control by the No Child Left Behind legislation. At the same time, it provides money for poorer children whose communities could not raise the appropriate funds for education.

Let us take a closer look at how poverty shapes education in America. This is necessary to understand if we want to create an education system for all that is independent of outside control.

How Public Schools Operate

Public schools are operated at the state level through departments of education, and locally by school districts with publicly elected or appointed school boards.

Approximately fifteen thousand different school districts operate in the United States, and most are run by counties. Curricula in one state can differ from those in other states.

Students generally go to the public school in the district in which they live; however, with the growth of charter and magnet schools, some students are now being offered more options. Public schools generally accept everyone who wants to go there, regardless of their income or skill level.[1169]

In 1954, public schools were racially desegregated because of the famous Supreme Court case, *Brown vs. the Board of Education*. However, segregation remains as virulent as ever, particularly in the northern states because of class distinctions, not race. Thus, while the separation is not legally culpable, it is segregation nonetheless.

Although the Great Recession that began in 2008 has officially ended, fifty million Americans live below the poverty line; this means that twenty-two percent of all American children live in poverty. The US has the second highest child poverty rate among all wealthy nations.

Since 2009, the United States' education ranking among the world's sixty-five most-developed countries, has fallen six rankings in both mathematics and science, and ten rankings in reading proficiency.[1170] To combat this dramatic slide, the federal government created No Child Left Behind, which has done nothing to change the problem. This tells us that the true cause of falling ranks is not low standards but poverty.

Pedro Noguera, the Peter L. Agnew Professor of Education at New York University Noguera, explains that if you were to exclude the twenty-two percent of students who are living below the poverty line when calculating our international standing, America would rise into the top ten performing countries.[1171]

Rather than face this reality, the federal government puts the blame on teachers. Through its mandated standardized testing, the government evaluates teachers based on their students' scores and then uses these scores to browbeat teachers and local administrators by holding back federal funding from the school district.

Because schools in poor districts cannot afford to lose their lunch programs (sometimes this is the only meal a child will receive in a day) or other resources, the pressure to raise scores was tremendous. The teachers abandoned the curriculums that helped their students think creatively and reshaped their curriculums to cover material in the standardized tests. No more art, music, or even recess. This "blame lazy teacher in poor districts" policy of the federal government had little impact on performance, instead it had a detrimental effect on an entire generation of students.

This is because it held the students in resource poor districts to the same standards as their peers in resource rich districts. By refusing to believe that the achievement gap is a manifestation of social inequality, the government failed to acknowledge that in the poor districts the children had less pre-schooling, a lower allotment of funding, and less opportunity to participate in extra-curricular activities like music lessons, team sports, internships, or social organizations like the Boy Scouts and Girl Scouts of America.[1172]

In America, we are led to believe that our worth is determined by our own decisions, but the reality is that the strongest predictor of academic success is family income.

Let us take a closer look at how this apartheid system, based on economic class, works in today's America. In 2013, the Chicago Ridge School District on the south side of Chicago served fifteen hundred children. It spent $9,794 per child according to Education Week. This was significantly below the national average of $11,841. Roughly two-thirds of Ridge's two elementary schools and one middle school come from low-income families, and a third are learning English as a second language.

One nurse commutes between the three schools, and the two elementary schools share an art teacher and a music teacher. They spend the first half of the year at different schools, then, come January, they switch schools.

In another Chicago school district, an hour north of Ridge, in Chicago's affluent suburb of Lake Forest, Rondout School is the only school in Rondout District 72. It has twenty-two teachers and one hundred and forty-five students, and spends $28,639 on each one of them. This is approximately three times the money spent on a child in Ridge school district.

At Rondout, classes are small, and every student has an individualized learning plan. Nearly all teachers have a decade of experience and earn, on average, more than ninety thousand dollars. Kids have at least one daily break for "mindful movement," and lunch is cooked on-site, including a daily vegetarian option.

Why does Rondout have so much and Ridge so little? The answer is that many of Rondout's neighbors are successful businesses. They pay local taxes, and those taxes help pay for local schools. Ridge simply has less to work with. There are fewer businesses and lower property values. It is property taxes that fund the majority of education. Because property taxes for education are not equally distributed across the city, rich, white neighborhoods have more money to spend on their children than do neighborhoods dominated by minorities and poor whites.

This tale of two schools is not specific to Illinois. A 2012 report by the Schott Foundation for Public Education analyzed data on New York City's public school students and found that students in Harlem, the Bronx, and central Brooklyn neighborhoods, which are overwhelmingly black, Hispanic, or low-income, had less educational opportunity than the predominantly white, Asian, or more affluent students living on the Upper West Side and Upper East Side of Manhattan and parts of Queens.

The report referred to these disparities as de facto "redlining" after the banks' discriminatory practice that keeps racial minorities from living in a particular area or accessing resources.[1173]

Seventy-one percent of black and sixty-nine percent of Hispanic New York City students score in the two lowest achievement levels on the eighth grade English Language Arts test. In comparison, sixty percent of Asian and fifty-nine percent of white, non-Hispanic students score in the two highest levels. Black and Hispanic students, regardless of economic background, are also four times more likely than Asian or white students to be enrolled in a low performing high school, where they have only a twenty-nine percent chance of graduating with a diploma.

Low-income students are taught by teachers with less experience in schools having higher rates of teacher turnover. Because teachers with more education and experience are more highly paid, the report found that the New York City Department of Education spends nineteen percent more to educate students living in wealthy communities than it does on poor children.

While "giftedness" is evenly distributed regardless of background, kids coming from poor families are less likely to be tested to see if they qualify for the city's coveted gifted and talented programs. In 2011, twenty-one percent of kindergarteners overall were tested, but in wealthier sections of the city, as many as seventy percent were assessed compared to seven percent in some poor neighborhoods.

John Jackson, president of the Schott Foundation described the New York City apartheid school system as akin to "testing black, brown, and students of any race or ethnicity living in poverty, on their swimming abilities while also knowingly relegating them to pools where the water has been drained." When the children aren't allowed to compete in an equal landscape, they're "stigmatized as failures", their teachers are labeled as ineffective, "and ultimately their community schools are closed rather than being furnished with the necessary resources and supports to flourish."[1174]

Or take the example of Livingston Junior High School in Sumter County, rural western Alabama. Because the county is primarily farm and timberland there is no adequate tax base to pay for the children's education. The principal of the school told NPR, "In the girl's restroom, they may have four or five stalls, but only one works"

One room, no longer a classroom, leaks when it rains. Garbage cans catch some of the water, but the buckled floor and smell of mold indicates it does not catch it all. Around the school, there are broken windows, peeling paint, and cracked floors.[1175]

Alabama does not send extra dollars to districts like Sumter that serve lots of low-income students. In 2011, plaintiffs from Sumter tried to prove that the state's school funding system was not just unfair, but was also racially discriminatory. In addition to being mainly low-income, all of Sumter's students are African-American. A federal judge excoriated Alabama's funding system in an eight hundred page opinion, which was introduced by a diatribe against racism.[1176] However, not surprisingly, he found the plaintiffs were not entitled to relief from the court.

This brief description of how the apartheid system in America works is not to suggest that localities and states cannot take control of their children's education, it is only to state that the odds are stacked against them due to the poverty created by the race and class bias inherent in the American system.

Signs of Hope

Even so, for those who are willing to fight for their children, it is possible to turn the situation around. For example, a ten-year study of education reform in Chicago schools has identified the five most important ingredients required to have a successful education program and none of them is money. Rather, the five factors are a coherent instructional guidance system, (meaning the faculty works together to create cohesive and goal-oriented lesson plans); the development of the professional capacity of its faculty; strong parent-community-school ties; a student-centered learning climate; and leadership that drives change. It is also necessary for parents and teachers to shift the focus from achievement to "engagement." This is the formula for creating life-long learners with a thirst for knowledge.[1177]

Another lesson to be learned is that national politics, including a fight for changes in legislation is not enough. As Paul Street highlights in his book *Segregated Schools* the major battles against desegregation were fought outside the courtroom:

> there was almost no measurable decline in school segregation in the South between the Brown decision and the middle 1960s. Ten years after Brown, just one fiftieth of Southern black children attended integrated schools in the South. And Northern segregation remained essentially unaltered through the mid-1970s. . . . Southern desegregation picked up speed during the mid-1960s and leaped forward at a practically revolutionary pace during the late 1960s and early 1970s.[1178]

It took the active participation of thousands of Americans in the civil rights and Black Power movements to move desegregation forward and to begin to realize the promise of Brown.[1179]

America has an apartheid education system. Who will do something about it? Who will create the revolution to save our children? What is the first step? As the famous education author Jonathan Kozol described our kids in segregated schools:

> They live an apartheid existence and attend apartheid schools. Few of them know white children any longer. No matter how complex the reasons that have brought us to the point at which we stand, we have, it seems, been

traveling a long way to a place of ultimate surrender that does not look very different from the place where some of us began. If we have agreed to give up on the dream for which so many gave their lives, perhaps at least we ought to have the honesty to say so.[1180]

Conclusion

The purpose of these five volumes of *The Untold Story of Western Civilization* is to bear witness to human evolution as experienced within the progression of western civilization. Assuming the vantage point of a "generic" human being, we have tracked gender relations, race relations, class relations, the impact of western religions and the creation of social formations starting approximately ten thousand years ago. In this sweep of history, we must acknowledge that our evolutionary process has been extremely slow. Insofar as every generation continues to ignore the teachings of the world's spiritual masters and remains obsessed with accumulating material wealth and power at the expense of one's neighbors, the tide of history is one in which, instead of making steady progress, we find ourselves moving in circles, repeatedly meeting the same obstacles because we lack the rationality to learn from our mistakes.

Devoid of rational thought, each generation continues to be governed by the subconscious social program of history that manifests itself in our divisive sentiments toward each other. As such, we trudge forward as a human society, burdened by our gender, race, class, religious and national prejudices which are reflected in our behavior with each new day. We remain unable to change our behavior because we are not even conscious of what has been driving us. We take everything for granted. We are content to call the divisiveness in our subconscious programming "common sense" without ever taking the time to question it.

In this fifth volume of our history, we watched this divisive unconscious programming manifest in the ascendency, peak, and now decline of the Pax Americana empire. As the American ruling elite extended its power over the entire planet, it destabilized nations around the world and significantly destroyed, and continues to destroy, the climate and the life support systems of the planet itself. This massive destruction is the culmination of the trend of western history which lies hidden in our DNA and our emotional makeup.

If we are to survive as a species and to prosper, it is vital to understand the implications of the trends of western civilization on our daily lives. Without this understanding, we will remain unable to grasp our common identity as human beings and to solve our common problems.

The key determinant in our struggle to survive is to free ourselves of the global corporate and government spheres of power upon which we are currently dependent for our current survival, but upon which our future is denied. If we are to succeed as a human species it is necessary to join forces with our neighbors at the local level and take control of meeting our own basic needs. Anything that enhances our capacity to accomplish this will benefit each of us. Anything that opposes this movement will hurt us. It will be a great struggle to accomplish this task because we are programmed by our past actions to fight and kill each other because of our differences. As such, we must also become aware of our prejudices and then take steps to correct them.

As an example of why we must pursue an entirely new course of living, let us recap the course of the American empire since World War II. In doing so, we will see that it is just another iteration of a racist patriarchal empire that was set in play thousands of years ago. Like every other ruling class of every other empire in human history, the ruling class of the United States, when given the opportunity, created its master plan to assert American imperialism over the entire world. Its object was to take control of Eurasia, beginning with the Middle East. Control of the Middle East was critical for the current empire builders because it contained the fossil fuels required to maintain industrial civilization and the empire's highly mechanized military. Fossil fuels, however, are a mixed blessing because while they supply our world with energy, the burning of these fuels also wreaks havoc on the earth's climate and life support systems. This has created the conditions for a perfect storm, the more the elite wants to grow their industrial economy, the more they destroy the planetary systems.

But this eventual reality is barely a blip on their radar. Of greater significance to the American ruling elite is to continually persuade the American people that war in the Middle East is vital for our survival. This is accomplished by continually recreating a "War on Terrorism." The terrorists are anyone in the Middle East (Muslims) who oppose US expansionism. The Bush administration was complicit in creating the destruction of the World Trade Center in order to galvanize American compliance with a war against the Muslim countries that controlled the oil supply. It was the same tactic that American leaders had used to rile up the American people to fight in WWI and WWII. In WWI, they surreptitiously allowed the sinking of the Lusitania and in WWII, the bombing of Pearl Harbor.

The War on Terror followed the simplistic outline of divide and conquer that has always been used historically to rouse the masses to war. The message was simple: "We must kill the bad guys who are threatening our way of life." In reality, however, despite the cheerleading of the mass media, the US government was busy training "terrorists," exploiting "terrorists," employing "terrorists," "making deals with "terrorists" "supporting "terrorists," "selling weapons to "terrorists," in addition to killing "terrorists." In real life there is no such thing as a "terrorist." A person only becomes a terrorist if they oppose the intentions of the US elite at a specific time and place. Real life is so much more complicated than "Kill the bad guys," but the message serves the elite's purpose by constantly injecting fear into the hearts of the American people. We are told that there are countless, invisible cells of Muslim terrorists living in our midst ready to strike. Under such conditions, we certainly cannot assert our humanity and accept into our country the families, single women and orphaned children who are immigrants from the devastation of the Middle East because they may also be terrorists.

The "War on Terror" campaign was the ruling elite's ultimate wet dream. It allowed them to commit Americans to the idea of total war with simultaneous wars fought on multiple fronts, beyond the limits of any time or space. The "War on Terror" is a war without end.

The "Shock and Awe" tactics in the bombing of Iraq, according to the American mainstream media, was supposed to drive out dictators, and pacify the people of the Middle East so that we Americans could teach them how to be more democratic.

Beginning with Ronald Reagan through and including Donald Trump, the United States has instigated or participated in war after war in the Middle East, in Lebanon, Libya, Iraq, Afghanistan, Syria, Yemen, and now potentially with Iran. In this storm of war, large swaths of the Middle East have been pounded into rubble and millions of human beings have lost their lives. A wave of tens of millions more have been driven from their homelands, further destabilizing other countries in the Middle East, Africa and the countries in eastern and western Europe.

Whether America's ruling elite knew about it, or just did not care, the Middle East was, at the time when the wars began, by and large, similar to Europe during the Middle Ages. This is to say that most of it was pre-industrial and ruled by religious dogma and local warlords. Islamic fundamentalists were fighting among themselves in religious wars and women were being persecuted. When the US destabilized the region's power structure, it unleashed a civil war between the Shia and the Sunni. Now sect fights sect, tribe fights tribe, and everyone is fighting "infidels" within the other sect and among the foreign invaders.

As the kettle continues to boil over, the tens of millions of people who were forced to leave their homelands joined others in sprawling refugee camps where they have no hope for the future. There are no jobs for the great majority of these people, no homes, no schools, inadequate health care, and all the while they are being preyed upon by human traffickers, thieves and con artists.

The US army, in its simplistic plan of "counter-terrorism," initially tried to rebuild the infrastructure that their bombs had destroyed, but they soon gave up on this idea. Their bombs and their occupation had undoubtedly made them many enemies among the local people and the army could not figure out who they were actually helping by rebuilding or why so many of the local people resented them.

When the refugee problem became too big for western European countries, the local people reacted and began to hate and abuse the refugees. Ultra-nationalist politicians rose to power. England left the European Union rather than submit to refugee quotas.

The impact of the wars in the Middle East, even though the US took in very few refugees, was to polarize the American people. The biggest threat to the conservatives became the refugees themselves, who were viewed as potential terrorists. For the liberals, however, the biggest threat was the continued use of fossil fuels and the change in climate that it caused. The elite continued to back either political party depending upon the predominant sentiment of the American people at any given time.

While the wars raged on, the economy of the US had begun to unravel due to the banker-induced Great Recession and the offshoring of jobs, particularly to India and China. To prop up the domestic economy, money was printed without anything to back it up. The US had "leased" all of its gold to the bullion banks and the taxes that it collected was drastically insufficient to cover the bond issues (IOUs) required to pay for all the wars. The debt of the US government is now so large that it can never be repaid, other than by issuing more paper money as required, which serves only to lessen its value. This inflation of currency has never worked before in history.

As the debt mounts, interest on the debt continues to compound, forcing the government to put less money into infrastructure, and human services. Combined with the loss of jobs, the American families and American society as a whole are in a slow process of disintegration. Our politicians and mass media continue to foment a domestic civil war between the left and the right, which is essentially a false flag that disguises our common enemy, the elite capitalists who are not only destroying American society but countries all over the world.

The disintegrating of American society can be witnessed in the problems faced by the American people as a result of the elite's grand strategy for world domination. These problems were articulated in Part Two of this volume. They include wide-scale unemployment and underemployment, a worsening political polarization, increased police surveillance, endless foreign wars, fear of immigrants, and the impact of pollution and climate change on our environment. They also include our inability to access our basic needs of food, clothing, shelter, health care, and education in a healthy and moral manner.

Because all human beings now live in a global political and economic matrix and share the same endangered planet, our problems have become universal for the first time in human history. What affects Americans, affects all people and there is no other place in which to escape. Given this, there are no solutions within the capitalist or communist ideologies to address our common human problems. Neither provide:

- o Climate change solutions
- o Refugee solutions
- o Debt solutions
- o Ideological solutions
- o Job solutions
- o An end to the war on terrorism or promise of peace
- o Healthy and affordable opportunities to meet basic needs.

The problem is compounded because of the divisiveness that exists among the American people due to our bigotry regarding gender, race, class, nationality, and religion that is daily aggravated by demagogues among our politicians and mainstream media who paint them as unresolvable problems. Our gender bias goes back to the dawn of patriarchy. Our racial bias goes back to the onset of human slavery. The ruling class has always despised the under classes and has empowered itself at the expense of these classes. Nationalism is an invention of the capitalist revolution and colonialism is just another version of empire building. Our religious bias in America goes back to the dawn of Christianity. These bigotries continue to rule over us because we do not approach them in a conscious manner. Rather, we are ruled by the instincts and group sentiments such bigotry creates in us. Under the ether of such sentiments, we are impeded in our effort to grow as human beings. Because it is always the intention of a ruling elite to exaggerate social tensions, they employ divide-and-conquer strategies, which aggravate our divisive biases and thereby keep our ignorance working in their favor.

As the world continues to break apart, the demagogues heat up their calls for us to fight each other, terrorists and immigrants. The growth of ultra-nationalism and its inherent bigotry will inevitably lead to fascist dictators and police states as it did prior to WWI and WWII. As economic conditions continue to decline and people become more hateful of each other, the matrix of "globalization" will become mired in regional and local wars.

Although our situation appears hopeless, it is never so. It only appears overwhelming because in order to solve our problem we need to abandon the ruling elite and take it upon ourselves to change the tide of human history. We are facing a common situation as human beings that we have never faced before—mass migrations due to social and environmental catastrophes, climate change, and diminishing natural resources. These problems affect the entire human race. Yet our programming is too limited in scope because we cannot think outside our national, religious, class, race, and gender biases.

Thus, while there is a solution to our problem, there are no "easy" answers. Rather, it will depend upon each of us becoming conscious of our prejudices and seeing each other as fellow human beings regardless of gender, race, age, nationality, or differences in religious dogma. It will depend upon our willingness to overcome our left and right political leanings and ascribe to a universal morality, a common spiritual vision, and to build local economies at the grassroots level to meet our basic needs. In this process of rebuilding society from the grassroots, whoever identifies with the local people and is willing to work cooperatively for mutual survival and support should be included as a community member regardless of their gender, race, religion, national origin or political bias.

Like the ruling elites, we also, as American people, require a new grand strategy that is not presently being articulated by our politicians. Our strategy needs to focus on the local environment. It needs to unite us within our communities. Such an approach is the only logical way to counter the current trajectory of capitalist globalization and the destabilization that it continues to cause among people and the natural environment. To respect every human being, while building a local economic infrastructure, is the only solution because:

- Climate change is better dealt with at the local level (as cities are proving);.
- Fossil fuels are more easily replaced at the local level by public transportation, renewable energy, and changes in agricultural techniques;
- People's debt can be diminished by the local exchange of goods and services and the creation of local currencies;
- Jobs can be created by the building of local industries;
- The idea that we should act locally but think for the welfare of all will diminish the ideology of imperialism and nationalistic wars; and

- Immigrants can more easily be assimilated into the local economies as workers.

Book Two of this trilogy on *Universal Ideology* is intended to introduce a universal morality, a spiritual vision based upon the teachings of the world's great spiritual leaders, and to map out a general strategy for building local economies at the grassroots level as the means to meet our basic needs. It is intended to help us see ourselves as human beings, living and cooperating within a true human society that is dedicated to solving our common problems. In other words, Book Two will explore what it means to act as a human being independent of our programmed biases based upon gender, age, race, class, nationality or religion. Our humanity can only be grasped by ascribing to a universal morality and by understanding our common potential. It can only be understood by knowing that we share a common spiritual nature independent of religious myths and dogmas.

Book Two will also look at the principles and practices required to create local "People's Economies" to meet basic needs and stabilize our lives. It will address principles, strategies and organizational structures.

Conclusion to The Untold Story of Western Civilization

We hope this journey through history from the days of matriarchy to the present, has helped to shed light on how we got to where we are today and the obstacles we must overcome to make a change. Volume 5 demonstrated that we are at a critical point in our existence and to continue down this same path will spell disaster. Species on this planet have come and gone; there are no guarantees that our species will survive, unless we all come together and do something now to not only preserve ourselves, but other species and the planetary systems as well.

Although we consider ourselves rational beings, which distinguishes us from other animals, we still tend to be governed more by our instincts and sentiments than our rationality. We are defined by how we interpret reality and how we respond to it. As evolution has shaped our minds and created the sentiments that influence our behavior toward each other, we are driven by these subconscious sentiments that influence what we like and what we do not like, or who we like and who we do not like. As such we define ourselves in boxes lacking a universal outlook. We do not see ourselves as human beings first. This would allow us to see others as fellow human beings with the same desires, hopes, and problems that we have; and how we are all inhabitants of a small world struggling to survive. Instead, we identify ourselves with a particular gender, race, nationality, religious affiliation, etc., Which separates us from our fellow human beings and makes anyone outside our particular affiliation as a potential threat to our well-being.

As we will see in Book 2, *Universal Ideology*, we are on an evolutionary path to experience the divine nature in all of us. It is a need in us to move from imperfection to perfection. However, because we are driven more by our instincts and sentiments, instead of our rational and intuitive mind, we have interpreted this need as a desire to gratify ourselves with material things. As a consequence, we are constantly striving for more wealth, more power, and more fame. And our history is a long list of the consequences of this predisposition.

One of the ways this need manifested itself is the way we experienced the concept of a divine being. During the time of matriarchy, when our ancestors were trying to understand their world and their place in it, a divine spirit was manifested in everything, every rock, tree, animal, etc. And the greatest spirit of all was the divine goddess. She held all the secrets to birth, life, and death. During the time of matriarchy, women spent considerable time trying to extract these secrets and understand how it all worked.

However, in ancient history, the mother goddess was superseded by male gods. Instead of being a part of the mystery of creation, human beings began to see the world as stratified. Male gods now existed at the top of the hierarchical structure. Humans were their servants. Sacrifices were made to them; wars were fought in their name; and every element of existence was dependent on them. Gods now had the same characteristics as human beings, the same desires, jealousies, prejudices, etc. The concept of god was an outside force whose nature was unpredictable and unfathomable, which reflected the world around them. By the time of gilgamesh, we saw how the traits of the gods were now manifesting in man himself. Human beings were now becoming the representatives of the gods and as a result stood above everyone else in the social hierarchy.

While the world was inhabited by numerous gods, with each culture having its own particular pantheon, the ability to raise of one's god above another's god by defeating them in war, served also to raise one's group above another's, with the defeated often becoming the slaves of the victors. Gods became a good excuse for war, enslavement, and creating a hierarchical social structure.

Around 600 BC, we then saw how zoroaster introduced the idea of dual gods; one of good and one of evil. With that came freedom of choice. Humans were no longer just subject to the whim of the gods; they could now choose to be on the side of good or evil. On the other hand, because of zoroaster, the idea of duality came to dominate our relationship with god and our world.

Expanding on Zoroaster, the jews introduced the idea of one god, their god became the only god; all other gods were false. The evil god was demoted to a fallen angel, created by the one god. After the death of jesus christ, the one god became a christian god and by the seventh century, he became the god of Islam. We now had three different "one" gods.

By the beginning of the Middle Ages, the intellectuals parlayed this concept into a gold mine. However, to make it work, they had to ensure that all competing gods and competing philosophies had to be done away with. The Church tried its best to stamp out heretical thinking and any remnants of older religious cultures held over by the "barbarian tribes." This morphed into its infamous activities of crusades, the inquisitions, and witch hunts.

Despite the instructions of the great teachers, like Shiva, Buddha, Christ, and Mohammed, and the words of the Hindu, Buddhist, Christian and Sufi mystics, who all told us that supreme being is not something outside of ourselves, but is found within us and thus the divine experience is a personal experience, religious organizations continue to convince us that to experience god, you must surrender yourself to an intermediary who can run interference between you and the divine. As a result, we spend our spiritual energy more on meeting the demands of this intermediary then on our personal spiritual development. Although many spiritual teachers, also advocate having a spiritual teacher, this guide serves not as an intermediary between an individual and the divine, but as a guide to help one keep on his or her path. This is not to say that religion is incompatible with spirituality. There have been many great spiritualists in every faith. We saw this in the lives and teachings of the great sufi and christian mystics and in the earlier desert fathers. Religious faith can provide a positive structure for getting to the divine; however, most preachers are blinded by their own chosen path and condemn anyone who has chosen a different one. We will explore the idea of spirituality vs religion in greater detail in Book 2.

Another major theme we tracked through history was the cycle of the four social psychologies, the peasants/laborers, warriors, intellectuals, and merchants/capitalists. During various phases of history, one of these social psychologies was dominant; the peasants in pre-history; the warriors in ancient history, the intellectuals in the Middle Ages, and the merchants/capitalists in modern and contemporary history. We saw how each of these psychologies rose to domination and then surrendered to the next psychology, with the exception of the capitalists who, although not yet surrendered, are experiencing a gradual transition to the next phase in which the warrior psychology will again dominate.

We saw how the peasants/laborers were as a group generally overwhelmed by the material world and looked for another to be the leader. We watched how the warrior class rose to leadership by attempting to dominate the material world, by building empires, war machines, and by risking their own lives and others to accumulate greater power and wealth. How their prime instinct was to dominate others physically, to attempt to succeed at tough physical challenges, and to see the world as something to be conquered. We saw how the intellectuals, in rising to power, mentally manipulated the warriors and dominated the peasants by creating a mythology and an organizational structure that only they, as priests, could understand and manage. They made themselves indispensable, by intervening themselves between the other classes and their chance for eternal salvation. Finally, we saw how the merchants/capitalists rose to domination by manipulating the main tool for survival in the modern world, the medium of exchange and how they cleverly manipulate the strengths of the other psychologies for its own purposes. The most insidious outcome of this is how we have been ultimately programmed to believe that this hierarchy is inevitable, that we must accept the fact that there will always be some in charge and we just need to find our place in that hierarchy.

We saw how each of these psychologies built the infrastructure needed for its control and survival; the warriors with their physical empires; the intellectuals with their religious organizations; and the merchants with their manipulation of natural resources, political structures, and rules of exchange. The importance of understanding these psychologies is not only knowing the methods they use to manipulate us, but also if we want to build an alternative social structure, how we need to understand the motives behind their actions if we are to succeed in using their strengths for our purpose. Although, history has demonstrated that there is a cycle where the different psychologies take turns dominating, under the right social environment, this domination can be used for the good of society and not for its subjugation. In Book 2, we will also discuss a fifth psychology; one of whose purpose is to provide the check and balance between the other four psychologies.

The third major theme we tracked is men's treatment of women throughout our history. As we look back, we can see how, as men, our predispositions and biases toward women grew out of the transition from a matriarchal to a patriarchal society. How, in order to eliminate the influence of the great goddess, men created their own warrior gods, which demanded the subservience of women. We saw how in creating the great city-states and empires, men reduced women to the status of slaves. From Hammurabi's Code to the Declaration of Independence, women were seen as second-class citizens, without rights or due process to law. We witnessed how myths like the Garden of Eden blamed women for the fall of all mankind and how the male dominated christian religion used this myth and other misguided misrepresentations from the bible to degrade women as the great evil and the tool of the devil. We saw how the church created the Virgin Mary to counter the beliefs in the great goddess and turned Mary Magdalene, one of the Jesus' most respected disciples, into a whore. How this attitude went to the extreme during the middle ages, when the intellectuals, in the role of priests, declared war on "witches" to further stamp out the influence of women in spiritual practices. This included not only denouncing those beliefs and practices held over from the pre-christian era, but also those of the Church's own female mystics. Although we no longer witness "witch hunts" in the Western World, women are still treated as second class citizens by many and still find themselves subservient to their fathers, brothers, or husbands. We see this in every country in the world.

Our male-dominated historians have suppressed what women have accomplished during the time of matriarchy by raising our human species above the level of other species; framing our social norms, social structure, the rudiments of our spiritual beliefs, and introducing the agricultural revolution. Faced today with a society that stands on the brink of disaster, it is extremely illogical that we would not want to utilize these same skills and abilities to help us change this situation. Our survival depends on it. Without merging the right-brain and left-brain strengths of both men and women, our chance to make significant changes are almost impossible. In fact, to continue to suppress the talents that we need to survive is nothing less than suicidal. Flaws in the matriarchal society caused men to rebel and eventually establish a patriarchal society. Unfortunately, flaws in the patriarchal society have brought us to near ruin. To establish an alternative society that will work for everyone, a merger of the strengths of both the matriarch and the patriarch will be needed. But to accomplish this, men will have to stop seeing women as second-class citizens and instead as partners in this endeavor.

From the early expansion of the patriarch society, we have also seen how we have been programmed to believe that other humans are lesser beings and meant to be dominated and manipulated in order to gain more wealth and security for ourselves. Slavery has been a part of our culture since the time of the aryans. As far back as hammurabi's code, we had three classes; the upper class, the lower/labor class, and slaves. Warrior elites and their priests propagated the myth that there was a natural hierarchy in society conceived by the gods; an order propagated to increase the power and wealth of the elite. In the middle ages, the Catholic Church preached the divine right of kingship to continue propagating this myth, but expanded it to the supernatural realm where the intellectual class succeeded the warrior class as the top of the hierarchy. In the nineteenth century, western intellectuals conceived of a pseudo-science that peddled the idea that some races were inferior to other races due to differences in bone structure. This became a justification for colonialism and enslaving those races that were considered more primitive or less intellectually developed. Once slavery was banned in the Western World, however, a new social philosophy emerged in the 1930's to continue the propagation that certain races were inferior. This was the study of eugenics, which the Nazis latched onto to justify their extermination of millions of people. It was no longer the bone structure that determined inferior races but their genetic makeup. In the us, we slaughtered thousands of native americans and fought a civil war as a consequence of this philosophy of believing others to be inferior. It is ironic that many of people in the us, who consider hispanics, blacks, and asians as inferior races, fail to consider that these cultures built very large and sophisticated civilizations hundreds of years before we ever became a country. Although the Western World has banned slavery and abandoned ideas like eugenics, we find that under the dominance of the capitalists, many women, racial minorities, and poor whites are no better off than slaves, and some cases worse off than slaves that lived during our ancient history and during the middle ages. And whether our programming leads us to accept slavery or class discrimination, the results are the same, our inability to see others as humans like ourselves.

In the late Middle Ages, we found ourselves creating a new box in which to define ourselves, that of nationalism. With the growth of nation states we not only limited ourselves by gender and class, but now we saw ourselves as French vs English, German vs Italian, etc. We fought more wars for the glory of our country and the defeat of other nations. In the united states we fought a war to free ourselves from the nation of great britain, only to begin to dominate other nations not as powerful as us. We see how the capitalist have manipulated this nationalist sentiment to invade other countries to further enrich themselves by appropriating thoses people's natural resources. We can kill other people, ruin their lives, and steal their ability to meet their basic needs, but if it is done under the glory of the flag, it is justifiable. From the time of the agricultural revolution we have been programmed to guard our piece of the earth's turf, whether it be our home, our town, or state, or country. As the capitalists have demonstrated, it does not take much to manipulate this programming to fight against those who serve another flag.

Perhaps one of the most divisive boxes our programming has generated is religion. As far back as the early aryan empires, warriors used their gods to justify wars and the confiscation of other's property. However, it was not until the Middle Ages, that religion became the main reason for going to war. From here on religion became a sophisticated organization that had to destroy its opponents to survive and dominate. In the eleventh century, the Catholic Church went to war against the Muslims; a campaign that was, however, not without its desire for economic gain. Thousands died for what amounted to minimal or no change in the religious structure of the Middle East. Not satisfied with warring with the Muslims, the Catholic Church also fought with the Eastern Orthodox Church.

During the Reformation, many more died during the religious wars that ravaged europe. During, and following, the Reformation, even the protestants broke up into numerous sects, all with their own beliefs about how to attain the one god. While the catholics persecuted the protestants, the protestants persecuted each other. Today there is still a lot of antagonism between religious sects. We see this distinctly in islam where the shi'ites and sunni's continually persecute each other for something that occurred over fourteen hundred years ago. Reviewing our history, we learned that religion is not spirituality. Where the former tends to be divisive and preaches the "truth" of one religion over all other religions, the latter sees all creatures as God's creatures and sees the likeness of the Supreme Being in everything. Religion also preaches the domination of humans over all other inhabitants of the earth.

As we look back over our history, we can see how events have programmed us in believing a certain way about women, other races, nationalities, and religious beliefs. And we can see how these beliefs have led us to the crisis we are now faced with. To survive we need to be aware of how this programming is keeping us divided, disabled, and continually manipulated by those who want to rule over us. If we are to change our desperate situation, we need to adapt a universal ideology and begin seeing our fellow creatures as part of our bigger family whose problems and issues are our problems and issues.

We can see what constant competitiveness for the earth's scarce resources has led to, the inability of greater and greater numbers of people unable to meet their basic needs. It is time we begin to cooperate with each other and determine how to best share those resources. Even those organizations that are struggling to improve the life of women, children, and minorities or fighting to protect the planet and its inhabitants or marching for equal rights for everyone find themselves competing for funding to support their causes instead of pooling their resources for the greater good of all. For this to be possible, we need to improve on our communications skills and our consensus building; talents which women can bring to the table.

Following a universal ideology means overcoming the prejudicial programming to which we have been subjected throughout our history. If those who lean toward an intellectual psychology see warriors as only a brute force, and all brawn and no brains, and if those with a merchant psychological disposition see intellectuals as only talking heads and not doers, we will never grasp the understanding that we need all social psychologies to succeed. To build a new community we need planners, doers, and enforcers/protectors. It is also not enough to claim to be non-prejudiced toward women, minorities, non-christians, etc. We need to demonstrate our outrage and the treatment of our fellow human beings at the hands of the elite. We must be ready to help and protect them like we would any other member of our family. Also, we must realize that we are all on the path to divinity and different religious practices are only different ways of attaining divinity. Whether one is a catholic, sunni, baptist, buddhist, hindu, or any other religious denomination, makes no difference. As long as one's religious practice is directed toward a universal welfare, all paths are acceptable.

In addition to working on improving our relationships with others, we need to work on improving ourselves. To be able to fully embrace a universal ideology, we have to start expanding the use of our rational minds and minimize our tendency to submit to our instinctual and sentimental motivations. Above all, we need to learn to develop the intuitive side of our mind through mediation and self-reflection. How to do this will be discussed in Book 2.

In summary, if there is one take away from our exploration of history it is this.

To overcome the problems that confront us as American citizens we will require a new vision and a new strategy. Like the ruling elites, we also, as american people, require a new grand strategy that is not presently being articulated by our politicians. Our strategy needs to focus on the local environment. It needs to unite us within our communities. We will discuss this strategy more in Book 3, *Nuclear Revolution*.

Our new vision will require the help of anyone who is willing to join our cooperative effort, regardless of age, gender, race, nationality, or religion. The key determinant in our struggle to survive is to free ourselves from the global corporate and government spheres of power upon which we are currently dependent for our survival, but upon which our future is denied. Survival is dependent upon joining forces with our neighbors at the local level and taking control of meeting our own basic needs. Anything that enhances our capacity to accomplish this will benefit each of us. Anything that opposes this movement will hurt us. It will be a great struggle to accomplish this task because of our past programming. As such, we must first become aware of our actions and then take steps to correct them.

We are watching a situation unravel on a scale that we have never seen before. Societies are literally breaking up across the world. The planet itself is breaking up, creating unprecedented challenges to our communities. As each day passes, more people are turned into refugees, running from war, chaos, and environmental damage. Yet our programming does not contain the answers to our problems, it only points to a need to radically change the course of our behavior. Our current thinking is too limited in scope because we cannot think outside the boundaries of our nation-state, our combative religions, our racism, sexism, and prejudices against people who are different from us. We are dying of spiritual thirst. From a spiritual perspective, people are *not* different from us even if they *look* different from us. To help us create a society that is geared toward solving problems in a cooperative manner, we must adopt a spiritual perspective. It is essential that we develop a world-view (ideology) that seeks the benefit of all. In other words, we need a bigger dream. We need a Human Dream. To create the human dream, we will be opposed by everyone who clings to their groupist prejudices, both on the left and right. We will be fighting everyone who clings to the past and everyone who mindlessly starts projects without understanding the consequences of their actions. To bring the Human Dream into the real world we will need new heroes, local heroes, men and women heroes, heroes from all races, heroes from across all nationalities and religions, even heroes from all social classes. To create a Human Dream, we will need a universal ideology, which explores what it is to be a human being and what are the most effective means to create a society in service to humanity as a whole.

The only solution to our predicament entails working together as neighbors at the local level, forsaking our pseudo-culture programming and banding together as teams to help each other meet our basic needs.

Appendix A: Ten Key Values of the US Green Party

1. Grassroots Democracy
   Every human being deserves a say in the decisions that affect their lives and not be subject to the will of another. Therefore, we will work to increase public participation at every level of government and to ensure that our public representatives are fully accountable to the people who elect them. We will also work to create new types of political organizations which expand the process of participatory democracy by directly including citizens in the decision-making process.

2. Social Justice and Equal Opportunity
   All persons should have the rights and opportunity to benefit equally from the resources afforded us by society and the environment. We must consciously confront in ourselves, our organizations, and society at large, barriers such as racism and class oppression, sexism and homophobia, ageism and disability, which act to deny fair treatment and equal justice under the law.

3. Ecological Wisdom
   Human societies must operate with the understanding that we are part of nature, not separate from nature. We must maintain an ecological balance and live within the ecological and resource limits of our communities and our planet. We support a sustainable society which utilizes resources in such a way that future generations will benefit and not suffer from the practices of our generation. To this end we must practice agriculture which replenishes the soil; move to an energy efficient economy; and live in ways that respect the integrity of natural systems.

4. Non-Violence
   It is essential that we develop effective alternatives to society's current patterns of violence. We will work to demilitarize, and elim-

inate weapons of mass destruction, without being naive about the intentions of other governments. We recognize the need for self-defense and the defense of others who are in helpless situations. We promote non-violent methods to oppose practices and policies with which we disagree, and will guide our actions toward lasting personal, community and global peace.

5. Decentralization
   Centralization of wealth and power contributes to social and economic injustice, environmental destruction, and militarization. Therefore, we support a restructuring of social, political and economic institutions away from a system which is controlled by and mostly benefits the powerful few, to a democratic, less bureaucratic system. Decision-making should, as much as possible, remain at the individual and local level, while assuring that civil rights are protected for all citizens.

6. Community-Based Economics And Economic Justice
   We recognize it is essential to create a vibrant and sustainable economic system, one that can create jobs and provide a decent standard of living for all people while maintaining a healthy ecological balance. A successful economic system will offer meaningful work with dignity, while paying a "living wage" which reflects the real value of a person's work. Local communities must look to economic development that assures protection of the environment and workers' rights; broad citizen participation in planning; and enhancement of our "quality of life." We support independently owned and operated companies which are socially responsible, as well as co-operatives and public enterprises that distribute resources and control to more people through democratic participation.

7. Feminism And Gender Equity
   We have inherited a social system based on male domination of politics and economics. We call for the replacement of the cultural ethics of domination and control with more cooperative ways of interacting that respect differences of opinion and gender. Human values such as equity between the sexes, interpersonal responsibility, and honesty must be developed with moral conscience. We

should remember that the process that determines our decisions and actions is just as important as achieving the outcome we want.

8. Respect For Diversity
    We believe it is important to value cultural, ethnic, racial, sexual, religious and spiritual diversity, and to promote the development of respectful relationships across these lines. We believe that the many diverse elements of society should be reflected in our organizations and decision-making bodies, and we support the leadership of people who have been traditionally closed out of leadership roles. We acknowledge and encourage respect for other life forms than our own and the preservation of biodiversity.

9. Personal And Global Responsibility
    We encourage individuals to act to improve their personal well-being and, at the same time, to enhance ecological balance and social harmony. We seek to join with people and organizations around the world to foster peace, economic justice, and the health of the planet.

10. Future Focus And Sustainability
    Our actions and policies should be motivated by long-term goals. We seek to protect valuable natural resources, safely disposing of or "unmaking" all waste we create, while developing a sustainable economics that does not depend on continual expansion for survival. We must counterbalance the drive for short-term profits by assuring that economic development, new technologies, and fiscal policies are responsible to future generations who will inherit the results of our actions.

The Ten Key Values of the Green Party were originally ratified at the Green Party convention in Denver, Colorado in June 2000. There is no authoritative version of the Ten Key Values. They are guiding principles that are adapted and defined to fit each state and local chapter.

Appendix B: Declaration of the Occupation of New York City

As we gather together in solidarity to express a feeling of mass injustice, we must not lose sight of what brought us together. We write so that all people who feel wronged by the corporate forces of the world can know that we are your allies.

As one people, united, we acknowledge the reality: that the future of the human race requires the cooperation of its members; that our system must protect our rights, and upon corruption of that system, it is up to the individuals to protect their own rights, and those of their neighbors; that a democratic government derives its just power from the people, but corporations do not seek consent to extract wealth from the people and the Earth; and that no true democracy is attainable when the process is determined by economic power. We come to you at a time when corporations, which place profit over people, self-interest over justice, and oppression over equality, run our governments. We have peaceably assembled here, as is our right, to let these facts be known.

- They have taken our houses through an illegal foreclosure process, despite not having the original mortgage.
- They have taken bailouts from taxpayers with impunity, and continue to give Executives exorbitant bonuses.
- They have perpetuated inequality and discrimination in the workplace based on age, the color of one's skin, sex, gender identity and sexual orientation.
- They have poisoned the food supply through negligence, and undermined the farming system through monopolization.

- They have profited off of the torture, confinement, and cruel treatment of countless nonhuman animals, and actively hide these practices.
- They have continuously sought to strip employees of the right to negotiate for better pay and safer working conditions.
- They have held students hostage with tens of thousands of dollars of debt on education, which is itself a human right.
- They have consistently outsourced labor and used that outsourcing as leverage to cut workers' healthcare and pay.
- They have influenced the courts to achieve the same rights as people, with none of the culpability or responsibility.
- They have spent millions of dollars on legal teams that look for ways to get them out of contracts in regards to health insurance.
- They have sold our privacy as a commodity.
- They have used the military and police force to prevent freedom of the press.
- They have deliberately declined to recall faulty products endangering lives in pursuit of profit.
- They determine economic policy, despite the catastrophic failures their policies have produced and continue to produce.
- They have donated large sums of money to politicians supposed to be regulating them.
- They continue to block alternate forms of energy to keep us dependent on oil.
- They continue to block generic forms of medicine that could save people's lives in order to protect investments that have already turned a substantive profit.
- They have purposely covered up oil spills, accidents, faulty bookkeeping, and inactive ingredients in pursuit of profit.
- They purposefully keep people misinformed and fearful through their control of the media.

- They have accepted private contracts to murder prisoners even when presented with serious doubts about their guilt.
- They have perpetuated colonialism at home and abroad.
- They have participated in the torture and murder of innocent civilians overseas.
- They continue to create weapons of mass destruction in order to receive government contracts.†

To the people of the world,

We, the New York City General Assembly occupying Wall Street in Liberty Square, urge you to assert your power.

Exercise your right to peaceably assemble; occupy public space; create a process to address the problems we face, and generate solutions accessible to everyone.

To all communities that take action and form groups in the spirit of direct democracy, we offer support, documentation, and all of the resources at our disposal.

Join us and make your voices heard!

† These grievances are not all-inclusive.

Appendix C: 9/11/2001, the Day That Shook the World

There has been a lot of controversy surrounding what happened during the events of 9/11 and who had knowledge about it or even participated in it. Following is a discussion of information, events, and speculation on what happened prior to, during, and after the 9/11 event.

According to a Zogby poll released on August 30th in 2004, "Half of New Yorkers Believe US Leaders Had Foreknowledge of Impending 9-11 Attacks and Consciously Failed To Act; sixty-six percent Call For New Probe of Unanswered Questions by Congress or New York's Attorney General"[1181]

This shows that the majority of Americans were suspicious of the Bush administrations involvement in the events of 9/11. Even so, the mainstream press refused to mention this poll and the only article about the poll was by the *Washington Post*. The link to this article no longer exists.

Was the Bush Administration complicit in the events of 9/11? There is a lot of circumstantial evidence that has led many to conclude that it was. Of course, the main stream media dismisses such interest as the stuff of "conspiracy theories." Such theories have emerged concerning 9/11 events, however, not because people love conspiracy theories, but because the mainstream media failed to do its job of in-depth reporting. The Bush/Cheney administration did everything to cover up an investigation of the event and the mainstream media let them get away with it. Under the obfuscation on the part of the government and media, it is only natural for people to believe that something sinister may have occurred; including some criminal complicity on the part of the government. To this day, the government continues to conceal information concerning 9/11. That being said, there is no proof "beyond a shadow of a doubt" that Bush/Cheney organized the event. There is no smoking gun that proves they planned it. There is no signed confession from anyone. There are only pieces of the puzzle, but these pieces point to much more than the ability of Osama Bin Laden and 19 hijackers to orchestrate such a monumental event on their own.

The mainstream media's strategy, as determined by the Trilateralists after the publication of *The Crisis of Democracy*, has been to report the news in bits and pieces, but not to attempt to put the pieces together so that people can understand what actually is happening. The mainstream media no longer asks tough questions nor engages in investigative journalism, at least not about significant matters. The news is now geared to gossip around pop icons like the Kardashians rather than uncovering the cause of an event that killed three thousand Americans in the heart of our major city and sent our country chaotically spinning into a course of total, endless war. And, in a final insult to the American people, the mainstream press portrays those who seek legitimate answers to the reasons for 9/11 as simple-minded "conspiracy theorists."

The mainstream press would have us believe that a handful of terrorists, living in caves in Afghanistan, engineered the most deadly attack on American soil in US history. This quickly becomes a preposterous proposition when we begin to examine the complexity involved in planning and carrying out such an attack. In fact, it becomes reasonable to suspect the cooperation of the US military, several national governments and key players in the mainstream media. Moreover, if the motivations and actions of the Bush administration at the time are also examined, it can be fairly ascertained what happened. Like the sinking of the Lusitania and the bombing of Pearl Harbor, the US administration had word in advance of an attack and let it happen in order to rile up the American people for another major war. This new war, the War on Terrorism, would be a war without time limit or geographic boundary, it would occur in a preemptive manner, and be directed against everyone and anyone who opposed American global domination. Following is some of the existing information.

The Plan

Even before the Soviets occupied Afghanistan in 1979, the CIA had already been in that country grooming and training the Islamic fundamentalists who would later become members of the Taliban and al-Qaeda. These trainees served the American empire in two ways: they would keep the Russians bogged down in a war that was unwinnable, and unbeknownst to the trainees, they would serve as the future enemy that the US government would need to justify its expansionist policies.

In 1995, events quickened, when the government of the Philippines captured purported plans of al-Qaeda activists Ramzi Yousef and Khalid Sheikh Mohammed who were then living in Manila. The plans, entitled *Project Bojinka* outlined a large-scale, three-phase attack to be performed by the men, both of whom would later be indicted for the destruction of the World Trade Center. The Bojinka plans called for the assassination of Pope John Paul II, the blowing up of eleven airliners in flight from Asia to the United States,[1182] and crashing a plane into CIA headquarters in Fairfax County, Virginia.[1183]

The Bojinka plot was fortunately disrupted by Philippine police after a chemical fire broke out in Yousef and Mohammed's apartment. Their plans were confiscated and turned over to the CIA. These plans provided the rough outline for the 9/11 attack on American soil. While the CIA headquarters was an obvious choice for Islamic fundamentalists, it appears that the Bush/Cheney administration needed a target that would have a greater impact on the American people. The World Trade Center was the obvious choice. First, it had been attacked before by Ramzi Yousef and Khalid Sheikh Mohammed, who were also involved in planning the attack on the World Trade Center on 9/11/2001. Secondly, the World Trade Center housed the archives of criminal investigation records by the Security and Exchange Commission against many large banks and corporations. As such, it contained a paper trail of financial crimes, cooked books, inflated profits, and other corporate offenses. Thirdly, there were also large hordes of gold and stocks belonging to foreign central banks that could be secretly removed and later claimed to be destroyed.[1184]

While the attack on the World Trade Center would galvanize popular support for a perpetual war against revolutionaries in the Middle East, a second attack on the Pentagon would certainly seal the deal.

The Collaborators

Aside from the capabilities of al-Qaeda, if the US government were to pull off a plot of such enormity, it is estimated that it would require three to four years of planning and coordination. It is therefore logical to assume that the planning began during the Bill Clinton presidency (1993-2001) with the full knowledge of Clinton and the Trilateralists in his administration. It is also likely that the NATO commander, Wesley Clark, who had trained al-Qaeda operatives in Kosovo was in on the plan and provided terrorist operatives to help carry out the plot. The actual planning was probably done by strategists within the Trilateral Commission and the Council on Foreign Relations, who were not currently holding public office. A plan of such magnitude required the cooperation of many players. Among these players were certainly al-Qaeda operatives who were either unconscious of their role in the attack or were acting as double agents for al-Qaeda and the US government.

This helps to explain why the Clinton administration overlooked so many opportunities to capture or kill bin Laden and Khalid Sheikh Mohammed between 1998 and 2000 even though the CIA at the time knew that they were planning an attack in the US and had been monitoring their every move, including their plans. Osama bin Laden and his al-Qaeda elite were valued assets to the administration. There were many reasons not to kill them at the time. First, bin Laden's family had financial relations with the Bush family, Henry Kissinger's law firm, as well as many others in the American elite and knew too much. Secondly, he was interrelated with the Saudi ruling class who could severely damage the US economy if the US unduly stepped on their toes. Thirdly, bin Laden was needed to serve the role of Public Enemy Number 1 in order to justify the US government's vision for world dominance. Certainly, bin Laden wanted to strike a blow against the Great Satan, but, unbeknownst to him, he was becoming a pawn in a much larger game on Brzezinski's Chessboard.

As for Khalid Sheikh Mohammed, who was the mastermind behind the major terrorist events carried out by al-Qaeda during the 1990s, the CIA knew of him and his behavior for years, including his plans to blow up the CIA headquarters. Khalid Shaikh Mohammed went to college at North Carolina Agricultural and Technical State University in the US from 1983 to 1986. Then, in 1987, he went to Afghanistan to take part in the fight against the Russians. There he served as the secretary for one of the most powerful Mujahideen warlords at the time, Abdul Rasul

Sayyaf, and recruited many Arabs to fight for Sayyaf's faction. At the time, the *Los Angeles Times* called Sayyaf "the favored recipient of money from the Saudi and American governments."[1185] It is likely that the US was grooming Sayyaf to become the next president of Afghanistan after Karzai stepped down.[1186]

While in Afghanistan, Mohammed got to know bin Laden, Ayman al-Zawahiri, and many other future al-Qaeda leaders.

From 1988 to 1995, Mohammed's brother, Zahid worked as the head of the Pakistani branch of the charity Mercy International. A book published in 1999 alleged that this charity, based in the US and Switzerland, was used by the CIA to funnel money to Muslim militants fighting against US enemies in places such as Bosnia and Afghanistan. In the spring of 1993, US investigators raided Zahid's house while searching for Yousef, the nephew of the Mohammed brothers. Documents and pictures found in Zahid's house showed a close friendship between Zahid and Osama bin Laden. Photos and other evidence also showed close links between the brothers and government officials close to Nawaf Sharif, the prime minister of Pakistan at the time. Despite the raid, Zahid kept his job.[1187]

During the next several years, the CIA "bungled" many attempts to capture Mohammed even though they were aware of his travels to several countries and his terrorist plots, including the first bombing of the World Trade Center, the attack on the USS Cole, the Bojinka plot, and the 9/11 plot. Evidence clearly demonstrated that the CIA tracked the whereabouts of the major al-Qaeda leadership, knew of their travels, their strategy meetings and their plotting, yet refused to arrest them. The question is "Why?" Apparently, the CIA, acting on behalf of the capitalist elite and the US government, needed the terrorists to realize their own plans. By monitoring the plans of Mohammed, bin Laden, and other al-Qaeda operatives, the US plotters were able to build their own plans on the back of al-Qaeda's plans. By doing so, they were able to place their own operatives loyal to Bush/Cheney into the al-Qaeda plot and clear the way for their success in the bombing on 9/11.

It was not that difficult to get the Saudi government to go along with the plot. Its oil reserves were deteriorating rapidly and it was beset with many internal problems, including its own war against fundamentalists like bin Laden, who blamed the royal family for collaborating with the

Americans. Also, at the time, the Saudi's intelligence chief, Prince Turki, had been a close associate of bin Laden's, and kept the US informed of his actions. In other words, the governments had a close working relationship when it came to al-Qaeda. Moreover, both countries were now facing the consequences of their support for the Islamic fundamentalists and had reason to collaborate against those groups whom they could no longer control. It is now common knowledge that the Saudi government assisted the 9/11 plot by issuing passports and making donations to the al-Qaeda plotters. While the mass media held that fifteen of the nineteen al-Qaeda terrorists were Saudi citizens, this is, in fact, not true. The terrorists came from all over the Middle East. As such, the interesting fact is that the Saudi government had issued them passports even though they were not Saudi citizens.[1188] This speaks to a high level of cooperation between the US and Saudi Arabia in the 9/11 plot.

For the 9/11 plot to succeed, it would also require the cooperation of key players in the mainstream media. The Bush/Cheney administration could not afford to have thousands of journalists trying to put a picture together after the fact. This might lead to unfortunate investigative journalism. Rather, what was needed was a clear, prefabricated story, something like the Lee Harvey Oswald single shooter myth that the media herd could get behind and repeat verbatim to the American people. This is not to denigrate the many journalists who did the spade work to uncover the truth about the 9/11 plot in the face of impossible pressure. Such people are due our greatest respect.

As the plotting continued, it became necessary to recruit or to deceive operatives into playing the role of hijackers. Certainly, the CIA had its own long-time deep-cover operatives but others, who were more expendable, also needed to be initiated into the game. In this respect, no intelligence agency knew the Middle East more than the Israeli Mossad, and it was probably a full partner in engineering the event.

Meanwhile, the CIA had an ultra-secret military and intelligence operation called "Opposition Force" (OPFOR) that worked with a similar Israeli team. They used Muslim undercover operatives to pose as bad guys in hijack exercises around the world to test airline security especially in the Middle East.[1189] It is most likely that the US/Israeli operatives who were part of the Bush/Cheney 9/11 plot came from the OPFOR teams.

It is also likely that it was the Israeli's who kept the players on the field until the 9/11 attack, while the Americans would have found it difficult to do so because many American law enforcement agencies, at the time, were trying to apprehend Muslim terrorists.

It is likely that "the core" of the nineteen hijackers were US government OPFOR personnel. This would explain why an examination of an operative like Mohammed Atta's life displayed his penchant for strip clubs, liquor, and women. These could easily have been qualities of a US military operative, but certainly not the qualities of a Muslim fundamentalist eager to become a martyr. It is also unlikely that the majority of the US operatives were killed in the 9/11 attack. Most were probably not even on board the airlines, insofar as the flights were remotely controlled and not by pilots or hijackers.

In April 2004, Sibel Edmonds, who worked for the FBI, claimed she had provided information to the Senate Judiciary Committee investigating the September 11 attacks in February of that year. She stated that the FBI knew of a planned attack months away and that the terrorists were in place. She stated, "There was general information about the time-frame, about methods to be used, but not specifically about how they would be used and about people being in place and who was ordering these sorts of terror attacks. There were other cities that were mentioned. Major cities with skyscrapers."[1190] Sibel Edmonds also spoke of "innumerable regular meetings" between US representatives and bin Laden's deputy, Ayman Al-Zawahiri, leading up to September 2001.[1191] Al-Zawahiri would later become the head of Al-Qaeda. According to Edmonds, the FBI code name for the ongoing relations between US intelligence, the Pentagon, and Al Qaeda was "Operation Gladio B".[1192] The codename had been in use since 1997, four years before 9/11.

On May 13, 2004, John Ashcroft, Attorney General in the Bush administration, submitted statements to justify the use of the State secrets privilege against the planned deposition by Edmonds, and on the same day, the FBI retroactively classified as Top Secret all of the material and statements that had been provided to the Senate Judiciary Committee.

In another example of the government cover-up, preceding the 9/11 event, in July of 2001, regular FBI agents who were closing in on the 9/11 plotters were thrown off the case and threatened with prosecution.

Then, when officers arrested Mohammed Khalifa, bin Laden's brother-in-law and known fundraiser for al-Qaeda plots, Secretary of State Colin Powell personally intervened, and had Khalifa immediately deported to Saudi Arabia and released.[1193]

As far as other collaborators were concerned, it is likely that Russia, Germany, and England also had to be informed in advance, although Russia and Germany probably did not know the whole truth. Months later, Russian president Putin threatened to release satellite photos to prove that the World Trade Center destruction was an inside job.[1194] Why he never did so is unknown.

Later, the Saudis would also blame the US government for orchestrating 9/11. In an article published in the London-based Al-Hayat daily, written by Saudi legal expert Katib al-Shammari, it claims that the US planned the attacks on the World Trade Center in order to create a global war on terror. According to al-Shammari:

> September 11 is one of the winning cards in the American archives, because all the wise people in the world who are experts on American policy and who analyze the images and the videos [of 9/11] agree unanimously that what happened in the [Twin] Towers was a purely American action, planned and carried out within the U.S. Proof of this is the sequence of continuous explosions that dramatically ripped through both buildings. … Expert structural engineers demolished them with explosives, while the planes crashing [into them] only gave the green light for the detonation – they were not the reason for the collapse. But the U.S. still spreads blame in all directions.[1195]

Getting back to the operatives who served as "hijackers", nine of these men lived through the event. These included Mohammed Atta, Ahmed Alnami, Saeed Alghamdi, Salim Alhazmi, Waleed Aslhehri, Wail Alshehri, Abdulaziz Alomari, Klalid Almihdhar, and Marwan. Three of these men, Atta, Alomari and Alghamdi are also known to have received military training by the US.[1196]

As for Khalid Sheikh Mohammed, the supposed mastermind of the operation, he was captured and most likely killed by the CIA, although no information regarding captured suspects has ever been verified. Rather, information has only come from press releases issued by the CIA.

Remote control

The purported hijackers who piloted the large commercial airlines into the World Trade Center had no training by which to accomplish such a feat. It was reported in the mainstream press that a few of the men had been taking lessons in the US to learn how to fly single engine airplanes, but this is a far cry from being able to fly a huge multi-engine jumbo jet commercial airline.

Philip Marshall, a veteran airline captain and former government "special activities" contract pilot wrote a book about 9/11, in which he debunked the mainstream propaganda that the pilot/hijackers Mohamed Atta, Hani Hanjour, Ziad Jarrah, and Marwan al-Shehhi had the skills to fly jumbo jets. First of all, flight instructors around the United States, who attempted to train the hijackers, reported that the men had a very difficult time in their basic training even on small, single-engine airplanes. Thus, according to Marshall, it was ludicrous to assume that the men who were training on small four thousand-pound single-engine propeller airplanes could make the leap to flying a three hundred thousand-pound twin-engine jetliner. Marshall said that it took him twenty years, dozens of ground school courses and fifteen thousand hours between his first lesson and taking command of his first commercial airliner. He said that without putting in the hours of experience it takes to understand the momentum of a heavy 767, the hijackers "would be all over the sky and completely out of control."[1197] Footage of the event, however, showed that the airliners were under control, and that they were flown in a manner that would have required above average skills.

On March 8, 2002, a story in the Portugal News entitled, "September 11—US Government Accused," reported that a group of military and civilian US pilots also seriously questioned the hijackers ability to precisely locate a target two hundred miles from point of take-off. The US pilots believed, given the expertise required to fly those planes into the World Trade Center that the hijackers would have required an expert co-pilot sitting next to them. Either that or the planes were controlled by remote control. The US had on several occasions flown unmanned aircraft similar in size to a Boeing 737.[1198]

Bob Ayling, former British Airways boss, in an interview, confirmed it was now possible to control an aircraft in flight from either the ground or in the air. This was confirmed by other experts who stated that airliners could be controlled by electro-magnetic pulse or radio frequency instrumentation from command and control platforms based either in the air or at ground level.

All members of the pilots' inquiry team also agreed that even if guns were held to their heads none of them would fly a plane into a building. Their reaction would be to ditch the plane into a river or a field, thereby safeguarding the lives of those on the ground.

A further question raised by the inquiry was why none of the so-called pilots had alerted ground control about the hijackers because all pilots are trained to punch a four-digit code into the flight controls transponder to warn ground control crews of a hijacking—but this did not happen.

Captain Hill, a retired pilot for the US Air Force maintained that the four airliners must have been controlled by an Airborne Warning and Control System (AWACS). This system is able to engage several aircraft simultaneously by knocking out their on-board flight controls. He said that all the evidence points to the fact that the pilots and their crews had not taken any evasive action to resist the supposed hijackers. They had not attempted any sudden changes in flight path or nose-dive procedures—which led him to believe that they had no control over their aircraft.[1199]

War Games

A further indication of US government involvement in the 9/11 terrorist events is the fact that at the precise time that the attack on the World Trade Center was in process, the military was conducting war games over New York City. This provided the cover for the remote control of the planes. Michael Ruppert, who wrote Crossing the Rubicon, a minutely detailed investigation of 9/11, believes that the apparatus to control the planes was operated from within the New York City's Office of Emergency Management, where it is known that a Secret Service agent was already in place and reporting to Dick Cheney.[1200]

It is worth noting, that after Cheney conducted the secret Energy Group meeting, in May of 2001, Bush placed Cheney in charge of all terrorist attacks. This gave him complete control of the military and the Federal Emergency Management Agency (FEMA), which is charged with disaster mitigation, preparedness, and response.

In June, Cheney ordered the North American Aerospace Defense Command (NORAD) to change their scramble codes even though they had been in effect since 1976. The codes, which allow an operator to separate signals coming simultaneously from many different aircraft, are necessary to control the movements of those aircraft. Cheney had the codes rewritten so that most decision-making authority was taken from the hands of Air Force field commanders and put in the hands of Dick Cheney's operatives. It appears that Cheney was setting the pieces in place for an event of this kind.

Ruppert summed up a reason for Cheney's deliberations:

> Within their own mindset and within the parameters of an economic and governmental system that functioned (as it continues to function) in the mode of organized crime – incapable of transparency, riddled with corruption and cooked books, based upon the destruction of life for the sake of net profits and supremacy – these men, led by Dick Cheney, chose what they thought was their only logical option. I believe it seemed to them the "right" thing to do; after all, it was only a few thousand lives. Other rulers had made similar choices in the past.[1201]

There are many other details that demonstrate US collusion, if not absolute control, of the 9/11 terrorist attack. For example, the absence of any airplane wreckage at the Pentagon, or the unexplained collapse of World Trade Center 7, or the stock market activity leading up to the event, but these "unexplainable" incidents just add more tinder on the fire.

The evidence for the destruction of the World Trade Center does not support the mainstream propaganda that a highly complex aerospace mission, requiring years of planning by the most sophisticated expertise, could have been accomplished alone by a group of fundamentalist terrorists living in caves in Afghanistan, especially when the CIA was aware of their every move.

Rather, the evidence points to an operation carried out by the American elites in an effort to realize their master plan, to establish a global empire by use of economic and military control. The bombing of the World Trade Center and the Pentagon provided the plotters with the trigger to put their grand strategy into operation. As for the hijackers themselves, some were CIA operatives while others probably believed that they were carrying out an al-Qaeda operation. They simply served as pawns in the larger game of empire.

Immediately after September 11, 2001, bin Laden praised the attacks in America, but denied responsibility for them.[1202] Al Jazeera, a Middle East news service, read a message from bin Laden stating: "I stress that I have not carried out this act, which appears to have been carried out by individuals with their own motivation."[1203]

A few days later, on September 28, 2001, bin Laden stated in an interview published in the Pakistani newspaper *Ummat Karachi*, "I have already said that I am not involved in the September 11 attacks in the United States. As a Muslim, I try my best to avoid telling a lie. I had no knowledge of these attacks, nor do I consider the killing of innocent women, children, and other humans as an appreciable act."[1204]

In late October 2001, Al Jazeera[1205] conducted an interview with Osama bin Laden which was videotaped. In the interview, bin Laden addressed the September 11 attacks, saying:

> If inciting people to do that is terrorism, and if killing those who kill our sons is terrorism, then let history be witness that we are terrorists... We will work to continue this battle, God permitting, until victory or until we meet God before that occurs.[1206]

Interestingly, the FBI's "Most Wanted Terrorists" poster never accused bin Laden of being responsible for 9/11. Instead it only stated that, "Bin Laden is a suspect in other terrorist attacks throughout the world."[1207]

David N. Kelley, the former US attorney in New York, who dealt with the terrorism-related cases at the time of bin Laden's indictment for the 1998 bombings, explained that no formal charges had ever been filed against bin Laden for 9/11, thus he was not wanted for this crime.

For several months after the 9/11 attacks, no one, nor any group, claimed responsibility for the attacks, so the primary responsibility fell solely upon the hijackers. The Bush/Cheney administration reported that all the hijackers had either been killed in the plane crashes or had been captured. All information regarding the captives came from government press releases and never independently authenticated. None had ever left a message claiming responsibility for the attack or why they had carried out the attacks. Soon after the attack, however, many news sources, in contrast to government reports, were able to verify that nine of the nineteen hijackers were still alive, including Mohammed Attra, Ahmed Alnami, Saeed Alghamdi, Salem Alhazmi, Waleed Alshehri, Wail Alshehri, Adbulaziz Alomari, Khalid Almihdhar, and Marwan Alshehhi.[1208] While Khalid Sheikh Mohammed was fingered by the FBI as the man who planned the 9/11 attack, the mainstream media continued to finger bin Laden as the master mind. The Bush administration said that Mohammed was killed after being captured, but no one has ever verified this.

It is generally believed by both sides, that Osama Bin Laden, Khalid Sheikh Mohammed, and Mohammed Atef, who was the military chief of al-Qaeda and one of Osama bin Laden's two deputies, were all involved in plotting the attacks after a meeting together in 1999.[1209] It is also believed that Khalid Sheikh Mohammad was the one who actually planned the attacks and that Atef was the one who organized the hijackers. It has never been proven whether these men acted simply as al-Qaeda operatives or whether they also worked for the CIA.

Saudi Arabia has since been implicated in the 9/11 attack for helping to finance al-Qaeda and allowing them to flourish. A court case brought by families of the victims of 9/11 had gotten legislation passed allowing them to sue Saudi Arabia in court for the crimes of 9/11.

The US government has also been charged with complicity in the 9/11 attack for deliberately blocking any investigation of al-Qaeda prior to the attack. In June 2001, three months before the attack, a "high-placed member of a US intelligence agency" told BBC reporter Greg Palast, "After the [2000] elections, the agencies were told to 'back off' investigating the bin Ladens and Saudi royals."[1210] This was at the time when the Bush/Cheney administration would have begun their plot to create a trigger to initiate their War on Terror and take control of the Middle East.

Apparently, the administration did not want other government agents to muck things up by investigating their secret agents or those who would serve as patsies in the event. As it stands, while the Saudi government can now be sued for complicity with 9/11 events, the Bush/Cheney administration has gotten away scot free.

Appendix D: Immigrants to US by Country of Origin

The largest wave of Germans came to America during the middle of the nineteenth century when the impact of the American and French revolution reached German and the area was in turmoil. Today, the majority of German-Americans can be found in the non-coastal states. Famous Americans of German descent include Sandra Bullock, John Steinbeck, Ben Affleck, Jessica Biel, Tom Cruise, Uma Thurman, David Letterman, Walt Disney, Henry J. Heinz, and Oscar Mayer.

Blacks or African Americans, which is our second largest group, derive primarily from the native populations of Sub-Saharan Africa. Most African Americans are the descendants of people from West and Central Africa who were enslaved during the eighteenth and nineteenth centuries. Prominent contemporary African Americans include Barack Obama, Condoleezza Rice, Oprah Winfrey, Michael Jordan, Denzel Washington, Beyoncé Knowles, and Derek Jeter.

A great famine in the 1840's led to a mass exodus from Ireland. Between 1820 and the 1920's, an estimated 4.5 million Irish moved to the United States, many of whom settled in large cities like New York, Boston, Philadelphia, Chicago, and San Francisco. The Irish have since played a large role in American politics. At least twenty-two US presidents have been of Irish descent. Notable Americans of Irish descent include John F. Kennedy, Neil Armstrong, Henry Ford, F. Scott Fitzgerald, Grace Kelly, Conan O'Brien, Johnny Depp, and Bruce Springsteen.

Between 1990 and 2000 the number of people who reported Mexican ancestry nearly doubled in size. According to the 2000 US Census, Mexican is the most commonly reported ancestry along the Southwestern border of the United States and the leading ancestry in Los Angeles, Houston, Phoenix, San Diego, Dallas, and San Antonio. Notable Americans with Mexican ancestry include Tony Romo, Eva Longoria, Salma Hayek, Mario Lopez, Jessica Alba, Joan Baez, Carlos Santana, and Louis C.K.

English Americans are found in large numbers in the Northwest and West, according to the 2000 US Census. The number of people who reported English ancestry decreased by at least twenty million since the 1980 US Census, partly because more citizens of English descent have started to list themselves as "American." Today almost twenty million people declare themselves to be Americans either as a political statement or because their original ancestry is unknown or mixed. Notable Americans with English ancestry include Justin Timberlake, Clint Eastwood, Orson Welles, Seth MacFarlane, George Clooney, Cher, Liza Minnelli, Ernest Hemingway, and Bill Gates.

Between 1880 and 1920, more than four million Italian immigrants arrived in the United States. Immigrants formed "Little Italys" in many large Northeastern cities as well as remote areas in California and Louisiana. As these communities grew and prospered, Italian food, entertainment, and music greatly influenced American life and culture. Another large wave of immigrants arrived after World War II. Famous Americans of Italian descent include Frank Sinatra, Robert De Niro, Francis Ford Coppola, Tony Bennett, Lady Gaga, Quentin Tarantino, and Madonna.

Polish Americans are the largest of the Slavic groups in the United States and represent some of the earliest colonists in the New World. Immigration reached new heights between the mid-nineteenth century and World War I, when an estimated 2.5 million Poles entered the United States. These new arrivals moved to industrial cities like New York, Buffalo, Detroit, Cleveland, Milwaukee, and Chicago in search of a better life. Notable Americans of Polish ancestry include Steve Wozniak, Martha Stewart, Pat Sajak, Kristen Bell, Neil Diamond, Bernie Sanders, Stan Musial, Harvey Keitel, and Gloria Steinem.

Historically, the number of immigrants from France has been smaller than from other European nations. Figures may also be lower since French Americans are more specifically identified as French Canadian, Acadian, or Louisiana Creole by the US Census. States with the largest French communities include California, Louisiana, Massachusetts, Michigan, and New York. Notable Americans of French descent include Paul Revere, Henry David Thoreau, Warren Buffett, Louis Chevrolet, Zooey Deschanel, Ellen DeGeneres, Jack Kerouac, and Oliver Stone.

More than one million Scots left for the United States in the nineteenth century, many in search of work in the shipping industry. California, Florida, Texas, New York, and Michigan have the most Scottish descendants. Notable Americans with Scottish heritage include Reese Witherspoon, Lucille Ball, Robert Downey Jr., Marilyn Monroe, Ronald Reagan, Johnny Cash, Lyndon B. Johnson, Edgar Allen Poe, and Jay Leno.

Between 1717 and 1775, hundreds of thousands of Scotch-Irish immigrated to the United States, mostly coming from the province of Ulster in Northern Ireland. They were originally Scotch Protestants who moved to Ireland to escape religious persecution. Arriving in America, most settled in New England, but many moved westward toward the frontier, settling in Appalachia or even further west. Today Scotch-Irish can be found throughout the country, but still dominate the East Coast. Famous Americans of Scotch-Irish descent include Daniel Boone, Ulysses S. Grant, John Muir, Elvis Presley, and Andrew Jackson. It was the Scotch-Irish poet, Robert Burns, born in January, who gave us the New Year's anthem, "Auld Lang Syne."

Nearly five million Americans identify as Native American or Alaska Native. As of 2012, seventy percent of Native Americans live in urban areas. The largest American Indian tribe is the Cherokee with 284,000 full-blooded individuals. Alaska has the highest Native American population, followed by New Mexico, South Dakota, Oklahoma, and Montana, according to the 2010 Census. Notable Americans with Native American ancestry include Tina Turner, Rita Coolidge, Tecumseh, Jim Thorpe, Chuck Norris, Geronimo, Crazy Horse, Black Elk, Sitting Bull, Red Cloud and Sacagawea.

New York City was originally called New Amsterdam because it was established by Dutch Immigrants in the early seventeenth century. A second wave of Dutchmen came to America following World War II. Today, Dutch Americans are concentrated in several counties in Michigan and Ohio. Many Dutch Americans also live in California, New York, and Pennsylvania. Notable Americans of Dutch ancestry include Thomas Edison, Walt Whitman, Dick Van Dyke, Franklin D. Roosevelt, Theodore Roosevelt, Humphrey Bogart, Jane Fonda, Clint Eastwood, and Kim Kardashian.

Puerto Ricans first began migrating to the States in large numbers after the Jones-Shafroth Act granted all Puerto Ricans US Citizenship in 1917. Since then, Puerto Rican immigration to the continental US has been significant, with numbers spiking since the late '90s. As of the 2010 Census, the highest number of Puerto Ricans could be found in New York, followed by Florida, New Jersey, and Pennsylvania. The annual Puerto Rican Day Parade in Manhattan draws millions of spectators each year and is one of the largest outdoor events in the United States. Thousands of Puerto Ricans migrated to the US after Hurricane Maria devastated the island in 2017. Famous Americans of Puerto Rican descent include Jennifer Lopez, Joaquin Phoenix, Marc Anthony, Ricky Martin, and Geraldo Rivera.

Norwegian immigration reached its peak between the end of the nineteenth century and the first decade of the twentieth century. Between 1880 and 1893, Norwegian immigration was the second largest in Europe behind Ireland. Historically, the majority of Norwegian Americans live in the upper Midwest, especially Minnesota, western Wisconsin, northern Iowa, and the Dakotas. Famous Americans of Norwegian descent include Lance Armstrong, Sally Ride, Michelle Williams, and Renée Zellweger.

From 1851 to 1930, more than 1.2 million Swedes crossed the Atlantic looking to make a new start. They traditionally settled in Midwest homesteads. By the turn of the century, however, more Swedes moved to urban centers in search of industrial jobs. Today, Minnesota has the largest concentration of Swedish descendants in the country. Notable Americans of Swedish descent include Mark Wahlberg, Buzz Aldrin, Matt Damon, Phil Mickelson, Mamie Eisenhower, and Charles Lindbergh.

Chinese immigrants first began arriving on the West Coast in the early 1820's and trickled in slowly up until the Gold Rush began, at which time the Chinese American population grew exponentially. The majority of Chinese Americans today live in California, with notable communities in Hawaii and around New York City, Boston, and Chicago. Notable Americans with Chinese ancestry include Yo-Yo Ma, Lucy Liu, Bruce Lee, Alexander Wang, Derek Lam, Phillip Lim, Ha Jin, Maxine Hong Kingston, Vera Wang, Steve Chen, Michelle Kwan, and Dan Lin.

Alaska was originally settled and controlled by Russians. After the US purchased the land in 1867, many Russians remained in the territory. However, most came to America during the large wave of European immigration that took place during the late nineteenth century. US states with the highest percentage of people who claim some sort of Russian ancestry include Maryland, New York, North Dakota, and South Dakota, according to the 2000 census. Notable Americans with Russian ancestry include Michael Bloomberg, Leonardo DiCaprio, Milla Jovovich, Sean Penn, Natalie Portman, Joan Rivers, and Michelle Trachtenberg.

Asian Indians had been immigrating to the US in small numbers for decades, but starting in 2000, the population has grown rapidly. The Asian Indian population was one of the most rapidly-growing ethnic groups in the US as of 2011. They comprise over sixteen percent of the Asian-American community and are one of the highest-educated groups in the nation. California, New York, New Jersey, Texas, and Illinois were the states with the highest populations of Indian Americans as of the 2000 Census. Notable Americans with Indian ancestry include Amartya Sen, Kavita Ramdas, Nina Davuluri, Kal Penn, Fareed Zakaria, Nora Jones, Zubin Mehta, Deepak Chopra, Mindy Kaling, Kal Penn, Padma Lakshmi, M. Night Shyamalan, Indra Nooyi, and Sanjay Gupta, Aziz Ansari.

West Indians include Americans who self-identified as Bahamian, Barbadian, Belizean, Bermudan, British West Indian, Dutch West Indian, Haitian, Jamaican, Trinidadian and Tobagonian, or US Virgin Islander. 290,828 people also stated that they were simply "West Indian" or "Other West Indian." Many West Indians first came to the United States in search of economic opportunity at the turn of the century and West Indian immigration continued until the onset of the Great Depression. Another wave of West Indian immigrants came to America in the 1950's and 1960s. Notable Americans of West Indian descent include Sidney Poitier, Al Roker, Tee Corinne, Rick Fox, Colin Powell, Notorious B.I.G., Rihanna, Lenny Kravitz, and Tim Duncan.

The 1965 Immigration Act led large numbers of Filipinos to immigrate to the US. More than forty thousand Filipinos have been arriving in the US annually since 1979. California, Hawaii, greater New York, Illinois, and Texas all have large Filipino populations. Notable Americans with Filipino ancestry include Jose Antonio Vargas, Peter Bacho, Bobby Murphy, Geena Rocero, Philip Vera Cruz, Rob Schneider, Bruno Mars, Monique Lhuillier, and Hailee Steinfeld.

French Canadian Americans make up a large and diverse group. Many immigrated to America from Quebec between 1840 and the late 1920s, while others in more Midwestern states had lived there for generations. Many Americans of recent French-Canadian descent speak French at home. French Canadian Americans today are overwhelmingly concentrated in New England, with the state of Maine having the highest population. Notable Americans of French-Canadian descent include Warren Buffet, Ellen DeGeneres, Alec Baldwin, Willem Defoe, Van Heflin, Beyonce, Louis L'Amour, Jack Kerouac, Celine Dion, Angelina Jolie, Justin Theroux, and Chelsea Clinton.

In the late 1600s, Welsh Quakers began coming to America in droves, settling largely in Pennsylvania and later in Ohio. The Welsh language was commonly spoken in many of these intensely-Welsh areas until the 1950's when it began to die out. Today, Welsh Americans can be found around the country, with particularly high numbers in the Midwest. Notable Americans of Welsh descent include Thomas Jefferson, Abraham Lincoln, Hillary Rodham Clinton, J.P. Morgan, Patricia Arquette, Sinclair Lewis, Jack London, Dick Cheney, Frank Lloyd Wright, Bill Evans, and Bob Hope.

Cubans began immigrating to the states in the early 1900s, with large numbers flowing in after the Cuban revolution of 1959. Today, Cuban Americans are major contributors to politics, professional sports, academia, and the entertainment industry. Nearly seventy percent of Cuban Americans live in Florida, but prominent Cuban communities can also be found within New York and New Jersey. Notable Americans with Cuban ancestry include Jorge Posada, Desi Arnaz, Gloria Estefan, Cameron Diaz, Andy Garcia, Eva Mendes, Sammy Davis Jr., and Narciso Rodriguez.

Before 1960, the U.S. was home to fewer than ten thousan Salvadorans, but the Salvadoran Civil War in the 1980s forced hundreds of thousands of people to flee El Salvador. Many of them came to America. California, Texas, New York, Virginia, and Maryland have the highest number of Salvadorans. They also make up the largest Latino group on Long Island, surpassing Puerto Ricans. Notable Americans with Salvadoran ancestry include singer Sabi, Steve Rodriguez, Rosemary Casals, J.D. Pardo, Christy Turlington, T-Bone, John H. Sununu, and boxer Carlos Hernández.

Arab Americans from Egypt, Iraq, Jordan, Lebanon, Morocco, Palestine, and Syria, among other countries, comprise a large and diverse ancestry group that has been settling in the US since the late 1800s. According to the Arab American Institute, nearly ninety-four percent of Arab Americans live in metropolitan areas. The metropolitan areas with the highest concentration of Arab Americans include Los Angeles, Detroit, New York/New Jersey, Chicago, and Washington, D.C. Notable Americans of Arab ancestry include Edward Said, Ralph Nader, Steve Jobs, Hala Gorani, Najeeb Halaby, Gigi Hadid, Danny Thomas, Ameen Rihani, Michael Anthony Monsoor, Shakira, Soraya, and Frank Zappa.

Many Vietnamese immigrants came to America after the Vietnam War, often via boat, to escape extreme poverty or persecution. Today, Vietnamese Americans make up nearly half of all Vietnamese living overseas and are the fourth-largest Asian American group. Notable Americans of Vietnamese descent include Maggie Q, rapper Tyga, Dustin Nguyen, Viet Xuan Luong, Cung Lee, Jacqueline H. Nguyen, and Eugene H. Trinh.

Czech immigrants were known in the nineteenth and twentieth centuries as "Bohemian" since they originally came from the lands that made up what was once the empire of the Bohemian crown. These lands are now presided over in large part by the Czech Republic. The most Czech Americans can be found in Texas, Illinois, Wisconsin, Minnesota, and Nebraska. Famous Americans of Czech descent include Joseph Bulova, Ray Kroc, Ivanka Trump, Theodore Dreiser, Karen Black, Ashton Kutcher, Kim Novak, Madeleine Albright, John Havlicek, George Blanda, Jason Mraz, and Sissy Spacek.

Hungarian Americans comprise one of America's oldest ethnic groups, with records of Hungarians participating in the American Revolution. After the Hungarian Revolution of 1848, even more Hungarians came to the states in search of a better life. Notable Americans of Hungarian descent include Milton Friedman, John Kerry, Estee Lauder, Paul Simon, Paul Newman, Louis CK, Kate Hudson, Steven Spielberg, Drew Barrymore, and Calvin Klein.

The Portuguese also have a long history in the US, with Portuguese soldiers fighting in the American Revolution. A large wave of Portuguese immigrants also came to the US in the mid-to-late twentieth century. Areas with notable Portuguese populations include the Metro Boston area, the Tri-state area, and the San Francisco/Oakland Bay area. Famous

Americans of Portuguese descent include Lyndsy Marie Fonseca, Emeril Lagasse, Tony Coelho, Keanu Reeves, Katy Perry, Tom Hanks, and James Franco.

Korean Americans make up the second-largest Korean diaspora community in the world. The largest is in China. The 1965 Immigration Act allowed large numbers of Koreans to immigrate to the United States, a pattern which has continued to present day. Since 1975, Koreans have ranked among the top five groups of immigrants to the US. Most Koreans live in New York, New Jersey, California, and Illinois, according to the 2000 Census. Famous Americans with Korean ancestry include Dennis Oh, Sung-Hi Lee, Alexandra Chun, Jamie Chung, Nelson Chai, Sandra Oh, and Do Won Chang.

Danes have been living in the US since the late 1600s, but they steadily immigrated to America for much of the 1800's before Danish immigration tapered off. California, Utah, Minnesota, and Wisconsin all have large numbers of Danish Americans. Famous Americans of Danish descent include Mary Kate & Ashley Olsen, Viggo Mortensen, Leslie Nielsen, Scarlet Johansson, Lars Ulrich of Metallica, the Hanson brothers, and Iggy Pop.

After the fall of dictator Rafael Trujillo in 1965, the US occupied the Dominican Republic in order to end a civil war. The US also eased travel restrictions, and as a result, large numbers of Dominicans began immigrating to the US in the late 1960s. The states with the most Dominican Americans are New York, New Jersey, Florida, Massachusetts, and Pennsylvania. Famous Americans of Dominican heritage include Pedro Martinez, Judy Marte, Nicky Jam, Sammy Sosa, Junot Díaz, Oscar De La Renta, Alex Rodriguez, and Zoe Saldana.

Although Greek heritage has been recorded in the US since the 1600s, the most substantial number of Greek immigrants came to the US from the mid-1800s up until Greece's admission to the European Union in 1981. Today the US is home to the largest Greek community outside of Greece. Americans with Greek ancestry include Jennifer Aniston; Susan Sarandon, Tina Fey, John Stamos, Bob Costas; Olympia Dukakis, Tommy Lee, Zach Galifianakis, Jamie Dimon, Elena Ford, Diane von Furstenberg, John Cassavetes, Elia Kazan, and Paul Anka.

Contemporary History: Pax Americana

NUMBER OF IMMIGRANTS BY COUNTRY BY TIMEFRAME

Countries	1996	1820–1996	1981–1990	1971–1980	1961–1970	1951–1960	1941–1950	1820–1940
Europe: Albania[1]	4,007	12,230	479	329	98	59	85	2,040
Austria[2]	554	2,664,728	4,636	9,478	20,621	67,106	24,860	2,534,617
Belgium	651	212,894	5,706	5,329	9,192	18,575	12,189	158,205
Bulgaria[3]	2,066	78,029	2,342	1,188	619	104	375	65,856
Former Czechoslovakia1	1,389	156,848	11,500	6,023	3,273	918	8,347	120,013
Denmark	608	374,287	5,380	4,439	9,201	10,984	5,393	335,025
Estonia[1]	280	2,254	137	91	163	185	212	506
Finland[1]	602	40,315	3,265	2,868	4,192	4,925	2,503	19,593
France	3,079	795,259	23,124	25,069	45,237	51,121	38,809	594,998
Germany2	6,748	7,105,301	70,111	74,414	190,796	477,765	226,578	6,021,951
Greece	1,452	704,679	29,130	92,369	85,969	47,608	8,973	430,608
Hungary[2]	1,183	167,871	9,764	6,550	5,401	36,637	3,469	1,609,158
Ireland	1,731	4,780,891	32,823	11,490	32,966	48,362	14,789	4,580,557
Italy	2,501	5,353,213	32,894	129,368	214,111	185,491	57,661	4,719,223
Latvia1	736	6,603	359	207	510	352	361	1,192
Lithuania[1]	1,080	7,967	482	248	562	242	683	2,201
Luxembourg1	32	3,284	234	307	556	684	820	565
Netherlands	1,423	382,109	11,958	10,492	30,606	52,277	14,860	253,759
Norway[4]	354	756,448	3,901	3,941	15,484	22,935	10,100	697,095
Poland[5]	8,481	743,376	97,390	37,234	53,539	9,985	7,571	414,755

Portugal	3,766	518,753	40,020	101,710	76,065	19,588	7,423	256,044
Romania[6]	5,198	246,657	39,963	12,393	2,531	1,039	1,076	156,945
Spain	1,591	289,611	15,698	39,141	44,659	7,894	2,898	170,123
Sweden[4]	1,098	1,398,578	10,211	6,531	17,116	21,697	10,665	1,325,208
Switzerland	677	362,792	7,076	8,235	18,453	17,675	10,547	295,680
United Kingdom	13,657	5,197,150	142,123	137,374	213,822	202,824	139,306	4,266,561
Former U.S.S.R.[7]	2,588	3,749,777	84,081	38,961	2,465	671	571	3,343,361
Former Yugoslavia[3]	2,011	158,540	19,182	30,540	20,381	8,225	1,576	56,787
Other Europe	3,605	65,875	2,661	4,049	4,904	9,799	3,447	36,060
Total Europe	147,581	36,410,452	705,630	800,368	1,123,492	1,325,727	621,147	32,468,776
Asia: China[8]	25,106	1,232,740	388,686	124,326	34,764	9,657	16,709	382,173
India	44,859	703,339	261,841	164,134	27,189	1,973	1,761	9,873
Israel	3,126	152,473	36,353	37,713	29,602	25,476	476	—
Japan[9]	6,011	498,333	43,248	49,775	39,988	46,250	1,555	277,591
Turkey	3,657	425,601	20,843	13,399	10,142	3,519	798	361,236
Other Asia	207,413	5,010,282	2,042,025	1,198,831	285,957	66,374	15,729	44,053
Total Asia[10]	268,248	8,000,844	2,066,455	1,588,178	427,642	153,249	37,028	1,074,926
America: Canada and Newfoundland[11]	4,348,54	15,825	169,939	413,310	377,952	171,718	3,005,728	119,204
Central America	44,289	1,153,217	458,753	134,640	101,330	44,751	21,665	49,154
Mexico[12]	163,572	5,246,392	1,653,250	640,294	453,937	299,811	60,589	778,255
South America	61,769	1,588,408	455,977	295,741	257,954	91,628	21,831	121,302
West Indies	116,801	3,372,716	892,392	741,126	470,213	123,091	49,725	446,971
Other America[12]	51	117,574	1,352	995	19,630	59,711	29,276	56

Total America	340,540	15,945,081	3,580,928	1,982,735	1,716,374	996,944	354,804	4,401,466
Africa	52,889	561,569	192,212	80,779	28,954	14,092	7,367	26,060
Australia and New Zealand	2,750	160,870	20,169	23,788	19,562	11,506	13,805	54,437
Pacific Islands[13]	—	63,034	21,041	17,454	5,560	1,470	746	11,089
Countries not specified[14]	5	272,254	196	12	93	12,491	142	253,689
Total all countries	605,793	61,207,884	7,338,062	4,493,314	3,321,667	2,515,479	1,035,039	38,290443,

Figures are totals, not annual averages, and were tabulated as follows: 1820–1867, alien passengers arrived; 1868–1891 and 1895–1897, immigrant aliens arrived; 1892–1894 and 1898 to present, immigrant aliens admitted. From 1989 totals include legalized immigrants. (Data before 1906 relate to country from whence aliens came; 1906–1980, to country of last permanent residence; 1981 to present data based on country of birth.)

1. Countries established since beginning of World War I are included with countries to which they originally belonged.
2. Data for Austria-Hungary is not reported until 1861. Austria and Hungary recorded separately after 1905, Austria included with Germany 1938–45.
3. Bulgaria, Serbia, and Montenegro first reported in 1899. Bulgaria reported separately since 1920. In 1920, separate enumeration for Kingdom of Serbs, Croats, Slovenes; since 1922, recorded as Yugoslavia.
4. Norway included with Sweden 1820–68.
5. Included with Austria-Hungary, Germany, and Russia 1899–1919.
6. No record of immigration until 1880.
7. From 1931–63, the U.S.S.R. was broken down into European U.S.S.R. and Asian U.S.S.R. Since 1964, total U.S.S.R. has been reported in Europe.
8. Beginning in 1957, China includes Taiwan.
9. No record of immigration until 1861.
10. From 1934, Asia included Philippines; before 1934, recorded in separate tables as insular travel.

11. Includes all British North American possessions, 1820–98.
12. No record of immigration, 1886–93.
13. Included with "Countries not specified" prior to 1925.
14. Includes 32,897 persons returning in 1906 to their homes in US.
    NOTE: Data are latest available.
    Source: Department of Justice, Immigration and Naturalization Service.

Appendix E: Function and Sources of Nutrients

There are seven main classes of nutrients that the body needs. These are carbohydrates, proteins, fats, vitamins, minerals, fiber, and water. It is important that everyone consumes these seven nutrients on a daily basis to help them build their bodies and maintain their health. Deficiencies, excesses and imbalances in diet can lead to diseases.

Based on the amount of the nutrients that each person needs to consume on a daily basis, these nutrients are categorized into two groups. These are macronutrients, which should be consumed in fairly large amounts, and micronutrients, which are only required in small amounts.

'Macro' means large. As their name suggests these are nutrients which people need to eat regularly and in a fairly large amount. They include **carbohydrates, fats, proteins, fiber, and water**. These substances are needed for the supply of energy and growth, for metabolism and other body functions. Metabolism means the process involved in the generation of energy and all the 'building blocks' required to maintain the body and its functions.

Macronutrients provide a lot of calories, but the number of calories provided varies, depending on the food source. For example, each gram of carbohydrate or protein provides four calories, while fat provides nine calories for each gram.

Carbohydrates provide energy in the form of calories that the body needs to be able to work, and to support other functions. Carbohydrates are needed in large amounts by the body. Indeed, up to sixty-five percent of our energy comes from carbohydrates. They are the body's main source of fuel because they are easily converted into energy. This energy is usually in the form of glucose, which all tissues and cells in our bodies readily use.

For the brain, kidneys, central nervous system, and muscles to function properly, they need carbohydrates. These carbohydrates are usually stored in the muscles and the liver, where they are later used for energy.

The main sources of carbohydrates are bread, wheat, potatoes of all kinds, corn, rice, pasta, macaroni, banana, sweets, sugar cane, sweet fruits, and honey. Other foods like vegetables, beans, nuts, and seeds contain carbohydrates, but in lesser amounts.

Based on the number of sugar units, carbohydrates are classified into three groups; these are monosaccharides, disaccharides and polysaccharides. Monosaccharides and disaccharides are referred to as simple sugars or simple carbohydrates that our body can easily utilize. For this reason, people with diabetes mellitus should not eat too many of these carbohydrates. Examples include sugar, honey, sweet fruits and sugar cane. Polysaccharides are called complex carbohydrates and they need to be broken down into simple sugars to be used by our body. Examples include starch and cellulose.

About ten percent to thirty-five percent of calories should come from protein. Proteins are needed in our diets for growth (especially important for children, teens, and pregnant women) and to improve immune functions. They also play an important role in making essential hormones and enzymes, in tissue repair, preserving lean muscle mass, and supplying energy in times when carbohydrates are not available.

Pregnant women need protein to build their bodies and that of the babies and placentas, to make extra blood and to store fat. Breastfeeding mothers need protein to make breastmilk. The main sources of proteins are meats, chicken, eggs, breastmilk, beans, ground nuts, lentils, fish, cheese and milk. Vegetables like peas, lima beans, chickpeas, and edamame beans also contain protein.

All animal foods contain more protein than plants and are therefore usually better sources of body building foods. However, even though plant proteins are usually not as good for body-building as animal proteins, they can become more effective nutritionally when both are mixed with each other.

Fats and oils are concentrated sources of energy and so are important nutrients for young children who need a lot of energy-rich food. Fats can also make meals more tastier and satisfying. Fat is found in meat, chicken, milk products, butters, creams, avocado, cooking oils and fats, cheese, fish and ground nuts.

Fats are classified into saturated and unsaturated fats. The classification is important because saturated fats are not good for a person's health because they can cause heart and blood vessel problems.

Unsaturated fats are usually liquid at room temperature. These types of fats are healthy fats. Examples include fats from fish, oil seeds (sesame and sunflower), corn oil and ground nut oil, and breastmilk.

As a general rule, plant sources of fats are better for a person's health than the animal sources, because animal fats contain more saturated fats.

People can live without solid food for a few weeks, but we cannot live without water for more than a few days. An adult needs about two to three quarts of water each day. That is why giving drinks are so important when people lose a lot of water, such as when they have diarrhea. Water is essential for life. We need water for a number of reasons:

- For the body to make cells and fluids such as tears, digestive juices, and breastmilk;
- For the body to make sweat for cooling itself;
- For essential body processes—most take place in water;
- For keeping the lining of the mouth, intestine, eyelids, and lungs wet and healthy; and
- For the production of urine, which carries waste from the body.

Fiber is a mixture of different carbohydrates which are not digested like other nutrients, but pass through the gut nearly unchanged. Foods rich in fiber are vegetables like cabbage, carrots, cassava; fruits like banana and avocado; peas and beans; whole-grain cereals like wheat flour and refined corn or sorghum.

Fiber should be included in the diet for the following reasons:

- Fiber makes food bulky or bigger—this can help a person who is overweight to eat less food ;
- Fibre makes the feces soft and bulky; this can help prevent constipation; and
- Fibre slows the absorption of nutrients, so it helps nu-

trients to enter the blood stream slowly. This is esp-
cially important for patients with diabetes mellitus.

As their name indicates ('micro' means small) micronutrients are substances which people need in their diet in only small amounts. These include **vitamins and minerals.**

Vitamins are classified into two groups:

> **Fat soluble vitamins** (vitamins A, D, E and K) are soluble in fats and fat solvents. They are insoluble in water. So these are utilized only if there is enough fat in the body.
>
> **Water soluble vitamins** (vitamins B and C, and folic acid) are soluble in water and so they cannot be stored in the body.

The best sources of micronutrients in our diets are fruits and vegetables. These two food groups contain essential vitamins and minerals. Animal sources of foods are also both good sources of micronutrients. However, an adequate micronutrient intake can only be achieved through sufficient intake of a balanced diet that includes plenty of fruits and vegetables.

Functions and sources of vitamins.

Vitamins	Function	Food sources
Vitamin A	Night vision	Breastmilk, tomatoes, cabbage, lettuce, pumpkins
	Healing epithelial cells	Mangoes, papaya, carrots
	Normal development of teeth and bones	Liver, kidney, egg yolk, milk, butter, cheese cream

B complex	Metabolism of carbohydrates, proteins and fats	Milk, egg yolk, liver, kidney and heart Whole grain cereals, meat, whole bread, fish, bananas
Vitamin C	Prevention of scurvy Aiding wound healing Assisting absorption of iron	Fresh fruits (oranges, banana, mango, grapefruits, lemons, potatoes) and vegetables (cabbage, carrots, pepper, tomatoes) Breastmilk
Vitamin D	Needed for absorption of calcium from small intestines Calcification of the skeleton	Ultra violet light from the sun Eggs, butter, fish Fortified oils, fats and cereals
Vitamin K	For blood clotting	Green leafy vegetables Fruits, cereals, meat, dairy products

Minerals are the substances that people need to ensure the health and correct working of their soft tissues, fluids and their skeleton. Examples of minerals include calcium, iron, iodine, fluorine, phosphorus, potassium, zinc, selenium, and sodium.

Functions and sources of common minerals

Minerals	Function	Food sources
Calcium	Gives bones and teeth rigidity and strength	Milk, cheese and dairy products
		Foods fortified with calcium, e.g. flour, cereals. eggs, fish cabbage
Iron	Formation of hemoglobin	Meat and meat products
		Eggs, bread, green leafy vegetables, pulses, fruits
Iodine	For normal metabolism of cells	Iodized salt, sea vegetables, yogurt, cow's milk, eggs, and cheese
		Fish; plants grown in iodine-rich soil
Magnesium	Protein synthesis, muscle and nerve function, blood glucose control, and blood pressure regulation.	Spinach
		Beans, nuts, seeds, and whole grains
Zinc	For children to grow and develop normally; for wound healing	Maize, fish, breastmilk, meat, beans

Eating a balanced diet means choosing a wide variety of foods and drinks from all the food groups. It also means eating certain things in very small amounts, namely saturated fat, cholesterol, simple sugar, salt and alcohol. The goal is to take in all of the nutrients you need for health at the recommended levels and perhaps restrict those things that are not good for the body.

Endnotes

1   Jeanne Sahadi, "The richest 10% hold 76% of the wealth," CNN Money, Aug. 18, 2016 https://money.cnn.com/2016/08/18/pf/wealth-inequality/index.html.

2   Jon Greenberg, "47% say they lack ready cash to pay a surprise $400 bill," PunditFact, June 9, 2015, http://www.politifact.com/punditfact/statements/2015/jun/09/hunter-schwarz/47-say-they-lack-ready-cashpay-surprise-400-bill/.

3   See Volume IV of *The Untold Story of Western Civilization* on Modern History, "How Does State Monopoly Capitalism Work".

4   Woodrow Wilson, 28th President of the United States, in a speech to businessmen, and from an address to The New York City High School Teachers Association, January 9, 1909, https://www.goodreads.com/quotes/35754-we-want-one-class-of-persons-to-have-a-liberal.

5   Ellwood P. Cubberley, *Public School Administration: A Statement of the Fundamental Principles Underlying the Organization and Administration of Public Education* (Boston: Houghton Mifflin Co., 1916), 338.

6   Michael Lerner, "Psychopathology in the 2016 Elections," Tikkun, November 1, 2016, http://www.tikkun.org/nextgen/psychopathology-in-the-2016-election-2.

7   See discussion of Crisis of Democracy in Chapter 2 of this Volume.

8   Ross Coggins, "The Development Set," How Matters, February 10, 2012, http://www.howmatters.org/2012/02/10/the-development-set/.

9   Matt Taibbi, "The Great American Bubble Machine," Rolling Stone, April, 5, 2010, http://www.rollingstone.com/politics/news/the-great-american-bubble-machine-20100405.

10   Meyer Weinberg, "A Short History of American Capitalism," accessed February 27, 2009, http://www.newhistory.org/CH01.htm.

11   Meyer Weinberg, "A Short History of American Capitalism."

12   Wikipedia, "Pax Americana," last modified November 9, 2018, http://en.wikipedia.org/wiki/Pax_Americana.

13   Wikipedia, "Alan Greenspan," last edited January 13, 2020, https://en.wikipedia.org/wiki/Alan_Greenspan.

14   Dean Henderson is the author of four books: (1) *Big Oil & Their Bankers in the Persian Gulf: Four Horsemen, Eight Families & Their Global Intelligence*; *Narcotics & Terror Network*; (2) *The Grateful Unrich: Revolution in 50 Countries*; (3) *Das Kartell der Federal Reserve*; and (4) *Stickin' it to the Matrix & The Federal Reserve Cartel*.
15   Rothschild and Co., Homepage, accessed February 27, 2020, https://www.rothschildandco.com/.
16   Rothschild and Co., Homepage, accessed February 27, 2020.
17   M. M. Warburg and Co. Bank, Home Page, accesssed February 27, 2020, https://www.mmwarburg.de/en/.
18   M. M. Warburg and Co. Bank, accessed February 27, 2020.
19   Wikipedia, "Lehman Brothers," last modified Nov. 20, 2018, https://en.wikipedia.org/wiki/Lehman_Brothers.
20   Lazard, Homepage,x February 27, 2020 accessed https://www.lazard.com/.
21   Wikipedia, "Kuhn, Loeb & Co.," last modified February 13, 2020, https://en.wikipedia.org/wiki/Kuhn,_Loeb_%26_Co.
22   We could not find any information on this bank.
23   Goldman Sachs, Homepage, accessed February 27, 2020, www.goldmansachs.com/.
24   JPMorgan Chase and Co., Homepage, accessed February 27, 2020, https://www.jpmorganchase.com/.
25   Wikipedia, "New World Order (conspiracy theory)," last modified Nov. 8, 2018, https://en.wikipedia.org/wiki/New_World_Order_%28conspiracy_theory%29.
26   Dean Henderson, "The Federal Reserve Cartel: The Eight Families," Global Research, June 1, 2011, http://www.globalresearch.ca/index.php?context=va&aid=25080.
27   International Monetary Fund, Homepage, accessed February 27, 2020, https://www.imf.org/external/index.htm.
28   World Bank, Homepage, accessed February 27, 2020, www.worldbank.org/.
29   Council on Foreign Relations, Homepage, accessed February 27, 2020, http://www.cfr.org/.
30   The Trilateral Commission, Homepage, accessed February 27, 2020, http://trilateral.org/.
31   Wikipedia, "List of Bilderberg participants," last modified Nov. 20, 2018, https://en.wikipedia.org/wiki/List_of_Bilderberg_participants.

32   Peter D. Schiff, *The Real Crash: How to Save Yourself and Your Country* (New York: St. Martin's Press, 2014), 30-31.
33   Wikipedia, "Keynesian economics," last modified Nov. 3, 2018, https://en.wikipedia.org/wiki/Keynesian_economics.
34   Wikipedia, "The Grace Commission," last modified Aug. 13, 2018, https://en.wikipedia.org/wiki/The_Grace_Commission.
35   Statement by U.S. Rep. Ron Paul, U.S. House of Representatives, Washington, D.C. Thursday, December 13, 2007, http://www.house.gov/paul/congrec/congrec2007/cr121307h.htm, http://www.gata.org/node/5856.
36   Alex Newman, "Fed Manipulations in the Crosshairs," New American, June 9, 2010, http://www.thenewamerican.com/economy/markets/item/4581-fed-manipulations-in-the-crosshairs.
37   "Everything You Need to Know About the National Debt," FixtheDebt, 2020, https://fixthedebt.org/all-about-national-debt.
38   "Banking and Monetary System," WealthDaily, June 10, 2012, https://www.wealthdaily.com/articles/banking-and-monetary-system/3519.
39   A cartel is a group of formally independent producers whose goal is to increase their collective profits by means of price fixing, limiting supply, or other restrictive practices.
40   G. Edward Griffin, *The Creature from Jekyll Island: A Second Look at the Federal Reserve Bank* (Westlake Village, CA: American Media, 1994), Fourth Edition, 2002, 25-39.
41   G. Edward Griffin, *The Creature from Jekyll Island: A Second Look at the Federal Reserve Bank*, 192. 41 Tami Luhby, "Middle Class no longer dominates in the U.S.," CNN Business, December 9, 2015, http://money.cnn.com/2015/12/09/news/economy/middle-class/.
42   Wikipedia, "Too big to fail," last modified November 2, 2018, https://en.wikipedia.org/wiki/Too_big_to_fail.
43   "The true cost of the bank bailout," PBS, September 3, 2010, http://www.pbs.org/wnet/need-toknow/economy/the-true-cost-of-the-bank-bailout/3309/.
44   G. Edward Griffin, *The Creature from Jekyll Island: A Second Look at the Federal Reserve Bank*, 186.
45   G. Edward Griffin, *The Creature from Jekyll Island: A Second Look at the Federal Reserve Bank*, 188.
46   James Rickards, *The Death of Money: The Coming Collapse of the*

International Monetary System (New York: Penguin Group, 2014), 84, 96.
47   Richard Duncan, "When The Fed Prints Money, What Impact Does It Have On You?" Rich Dad, April 1, 2012, http://www.richdad.com/Resources/Rich-Dad-Financial-Education-Blog/April-2012/When-The-FedPrints-Money,-What-Impact-Does-It-Hav.aspx.
48   YouTube "Greenspan Admits The Federal Reserve Is Above The Law & Answers To No One" Apollyon8, Published on Apr 10, 2011.
49   "Nazis and America: The USA's Fascist Past," History Cooperative, 2020, http://historycooperative.org/nazisamerica-the-usas-fascist-past/.
50   Wikipedia, "Bancor," last modified Nov. 6, 2018, https://en.wikipedia.org/wiki/Bancor.
51   Wikipedia, "Bretton Woods system," last modified Nov. 20, 2018, https://en.wikipedia.org/wiki/Bretton_Woods_system.
52   Wikipedia, "Monetary-disequilibrium theory," last modified August 10, 2018, https://en.wikipedia.org/wiki/Monetary-disequilibrium_theory.
53   Richard J. Barnet and Ronald E. Muller, *Global Reach: The Power of the Multinational Corporations* (New York: Simon and Schuster, 1974), 40.
54   Michel J. Crozier, Samuel P. Huntington, Joji Watanuki, *The Crisis of Democracy* (New York, New York: University Press, 1975,) http://trilateral.org/download/doc/crisis_of_democracy.pdf. 55 "The effects of WW2 in Africa," South African History Online, March 22, 2011, http://www.sahistory.org.za/article/effects-ww2-africa-grade-11.
55   Noam Chomsky. "Deterring Democracy." ZNet, 1992, Retrieved online at https://zcomm.org/deterringdemocracy/.
56   "Imperialism – The cold war and its aftermath," American Foreign Relations, accessed March 5, 2020http://www.americanforeignrelations.com/E-N/Imperialism-The-cold-war-and-its-aftermath.html#ixzz4CzhJrsfd.
57   Wikipedia, "1973 Chilean coup d'etat," last edited January 9, 2019, https://en.wikipedia.org/wiki/1973_Chilean_coup_d%27%C3%A9tat.
58   Wikipedia, "Human rights violations in Pinochet's Chile," last modified December 25, 2018, https://en.wikipedia.org/wiki/Human_rights_violations_in_Pinochet%27s_Chile.
59   Barnet and Muller, *Global Reach: The Power of the Multina-*

tional Corporations, p. 87.
60   Barnet and Muller, *Global Reach: The Power of the Multinational Corporations*, 133-134.
61   Barnet and Muller, *Global Reach: The Power of the Multinational Corporations*, 14-15.
62   "Exporting America," CNN, accessed February 27, 2020, http://www.cnn.com/CNN/Programs/lou.dobbs.tonight/popups/exporting.america/frameset.exclude.html.
63   "Dollar Diplomacy, 1909-1913," US Office of the Historian, accessed March 5, 2020, https://history.state.gov/milestones/1899-1913/dollar-diplo.
64   "International Training and Assistance for Bank Supervisors," Board of Governors of the Federal Reserve System, February 2, 2017, https://www.federalreserve.gov/bankinforeg/ita/sem_pcfs.htm.
65   Barnet and Muller, *Global Reach: The Power of the Multinational Corporations*, 13-14.
66   Jacques B Gelinas, *Freedom From Debt: The Reappropriation of Development Through Financial SelfReliance* (London: Zed Books, 1998) 49.
67   Gelinas, *Freedom From Debt: The Reappropriation of Development Through Financial SelfReliance*, 50.
68   Wikipedia, "Confessions of an Economic Hit Man," last modified December 25, 2018, https://en.wikipedia.org/wiki/Confessions_of_an_Economic_Hit_Man.
69   Wikipedia, Confessions of an Economic Hit Man," last modified February 16, 2020, https://en.wikipedia.org/wiki/Confessions_of_an_Economic_Hit_Man.
70   Wikipedia, "Confessions of an Economic Hit Man," last modified December 25, 2018.
71   Steven Haitt, ed. *A Game As Old As Empire: The Secret World of Economic Hit Men and the Web of Global Corruption* (San Francisco: Berrett-Koehler Publishers, Inc., 2007), Available at https://archive.org/stream/AGameAsOldAsEmpireTheSecretWorldOfEconomicHitMenAndTheWebOf/a_g ame_as_old_as_empire_hxforum_org_sophie_djvu.txt.
72   Steven Haitt, ed. *A Game As Old As Empire: The Secret World of Economic Hit Men and the Web of Global Corruption*, 157.
73   Wikipedia, "Paul Wolfowitz," last modified January 11, 2019,

https://en.wikipedia.org/wiki/Paul_Wolfowitz.
74	Wikipedia, "Bush Doctrine," last modified December 26, 2018, https://en.wikipedia.org/wiki/Bush_Doctrine.
75	Wikipedia, "Anti-Ballistic Missile Treaty," last modified December 26, 2018, https://en.wikipedia.org/wiki/Anti-Ballistic_Missile_Treaty.
76	Wikipedia, "Kyoto Protocol," last modified January 10, 2019, https://en.wikipedia.org/wiki/Kyoto_Protocol.
77	Wikipedia, "Paul Wolfowitz," last modified January 11, 2019.
78	Wikipedia, "Latin American debt crisis," last modified November 15, 2018, https://en.wikipedia.org/wiki/Latin_American_debt_crisis.
79	Gelinas, Gelinas, *Freedom From Debt: The Reappropriation of Development Through Financial SelfReliance*, 54.
80	Gelinas, Gelinas, *Freedom From Debt: The Reappropriation of Development Through Financial SelfReliance*, 54-57.
81	"Global Trade and Economic Justice," Global Exchange, accessed February 27, 2020, https://globalexchange.org/campaigns/legacycampaigns/global-econ-101/.
82	Gelinas, Gelinas, *Freedom From Debt: The Reappropriation of Development Through Financial SelfReliance*, 51.
83	Gelinas, Gelinas, *Freedom From Debt: The Reappropriation of Development Through Financial SelfReliance*, 53.
84	Porter Stansberry, "The Corruption of America," December 21, 2011, https://dailyreckoning.com/the-corruption-of-america/.
85	Wikipedia, "Bretton Woods Conference," last modified October 15, 2018, https://en.wikipedia.org/wiki/Bretton_Woods_Conference. 85
86	Wikipedia, "John R. Commons," last modified December 22, 2019, https://en.wikipedia.org/wiki/John_R._Commons.
87	Meyer Weinberg, "A Short History of American Capitalism," accessed February 27, 2020, http://www.newhistory.org/CH01.htm.
88	Secretary-General's message on Human Rights Day, December 10, 2007, United Nations Secretary-General, https://www.un.org/sg/en/content/sg/statement/2007-12-10/secretary-generals-message-human-rights-dat.
89	OECD.org, Homepage, accessed February 27, 2020, http://www.oecd.org.
90	Wikipedia, "Erich Honecker," last modified December 26,

2018, https://en.wikipedia.org/wiki/Erich_Honecker.
91	Daryl G. Kimball, "Looking Back: The Nuclear Arms Control Legacy of Ronald Reagan," July, 2004, https://www.armscontrol.org/act/2004_07-08/Reagan.
92	Wikipedia, "Nationalization of oil supplies," last modified June 5, 2018, https://en.wikipedia.org/wiki/Nationalization_of_oil_supplies.
93	Adam Bird and Malcolm Brown, "The History and Social Consequences of a Nationalized Oil Industry," Stanford University, June, 2005, https://en.wikipedia.org/wiki/Nationalization_of_oil_supplies#cite_noteTHaSCoaNOI-4.
94	Wikipedia, "1973 oil crisis," last modified December 9, 2018, http://en.wikipedia.org/wiki/1973_oil_crisis. 93 Wikipedia, "Group of 77" last modified November 18, 2018, https://en.wikipedia.org/wiki/Group_of_77.
95	First Ministerial Meeting of the Group Of 77: Charter of Algiers, Algiers, 10-25, October 1967, http://www.g77.org/doc/algier~1.htm.
96	"About the Group of 77," G-77 Homepage, accessed February 27, 2020, http://www.g77.org/doc/.
97	Wikipedia, "Non-Aligned Movement," January 10, 2019, https://en.wikipedia.org/wiki/NonAligned_Movement.
98	"Castro Opening Speech," Sixth Summit Conference of the Non-Aligned Countries, September 3, 1979, Wayback Machine, http://lanic.utexas.edu/project/castro/db/1979/19790903.html.
99	Luis Ignacio Silva at the Havana Debt Conference in August 1985, quoted by Susan George, "A Fate Worse Than Death," 238, accessed February 27, 2020, http://www.xat.org/xat/worldbank.html.
100	Luis Ignacio Silva at the Havana Debt Conference in August 1985, quoted by Susan George, "A Fate Worse Than Death," 238, accessed February 27, 2020.
101	"The Brandt Report: A Summary," Share the World's Resources, January, 2006, https://www.sharing.org/information-centre/reports/brandt-report-summary.
102	"The Brandt Report: A Summary," Share the World's Resources, January, 2006.
103	"The 11th Special Session and the Future of Global Negotiations," UNITAR Policy and Efficacy Studies No. 5, John P. Renninger with James Zech. New York, 1981, 7.
104	"The 11th Special Session and the Future of Global Negotia-

tions," 9.
105   "The 11th Special Session and the Future of Global Negotiations," 11.
106   John P. Renniinger, The 11th Special Session and the Future of Global Negotiations, Policy and Efficacy Studies, No.5 United Nations Institute for Training and Research, 11.
107   Wikipedia, "Brundtland Commission," last modified December 5, 2018, http://en.wikipedia.org/wiki/Brundtland_Commission.
108   *The World Commission on Environment and Development, Our Common Future*, (New York: Oxford University Press, 1987), 43.
109   "The President's Council on Sustainable Development: Overview," accessed February 27, 2020, https://clintonwhitehouse2.archives.gov/PCSD/Overview/index.html.
110   Wikipedia, "Intergovernmental Panel on Climate Change," last modified January 12, 2019, https://en.wikipedia.org/wiki/Intergovernmental_Panel_on_Climate_Change.
111   Wikipedia, "Greenhouse gas," last modified January 9, 2019, https://en.wikipedia.org/wiki/Greenhouse_gas.
112   Wikipedia, "Kyoto Protocol," last modified January 10, 2019, https://en.wikipedia.org/wiki/Kyoto_Protocol.
113   "History of the Earth Charter," Earth Charter Initiative, http://www.earthcharterinaction.org/content/pages/History.html.
114   "UN Conference on Environment and Development (1992)," Earth Summit, http://www.un.org/geninfo/bp/enviro.html.
115   "Millennium Development Goals and Beyond 2015," We Can End Poverty, accesssed February 27, 2020, https://www.un.org/millenniumgoals/.
116   Wikipedia, "United Nations," last modified January 3, 2019, https://en.wikipedia.org/wiki/United_Nations.
117   Democratic Policy Committee, "Who is Downsizing the American Dream?" Washington DC. March 11, 1996.
118   Democratic Policy Committee, "Who is Downsizing the American Dream?" 2.
119   David Degraw, "Peak Inequality: The .01% and the Impoverishment of Society," The Economics of Revolution, accesssed February 27, 2020, http://daviddegraw.org/peak-inequality-the-01-and-the-impoverishment-of-society/#jobs.
120   David DeGraw, The Economics of Revolution (New York:

David DeGraw, 2014), 15.

121   David Degraw, "The Coming Revolution: Evolutionary Leap or Descent into Chaos and Violence," AlterNet, Oct. 15, 2014, http://www.alternet.org/economy/coming-revolution-evolutionary-leap-or-descent-chaos-and-violence?paging=off&current_page=1#bookmark.

122   "Diet and Chronic Disease in the United States," Eat for Life: The Food and Nutrition Board's Guide to Reducing Your Risk of Chronic Disease, 1992, accesssed February 27, 2020, https://www.nap.edu/read/1365/chapter/5#58.

123   "The Service Sector: Projections and Current Stats," AFL-CIO Dept. of Professional Employees, 2011, https://dpeaflcio.org/programs-publications/issue-fact-sheets/the-service-sector-projections-and-currentstats/.

124   Yves Smith, "Is JP Morgan Getting a Good Return on $4.6 Million "Gift" to NYC Police? (Like Special Protection from Occupy Wall Street,) Naked Capitalism, October 2, 2011, http://www.nakedcapitalism.com/2011/10/is-jp-morgan-getting-a-good-return-on-4-6-million-gift-to-nycpolice-like-special-protection-from-occupywallstreet.html.

125   Shawn Musgrave, "The Pentagon Finally Details its Weapons-for-Cops Giveaway," The Marshall Project, December 3, 2014, https://www.themarshallproject.org/2014/12/03/the-pentagon-finally-details-itsweapons-for-cops-giveaway.

126   Hanqing Chen, "The Best Reporting on Federal Push to Militarize Local Police," ProPublica, August 19, 2014, https://www.propublica.org/article/the-best-reporting-on-the-federal-push-to-militarize-local-police.

127   Don Hazen, "Apocalypse Now: Seriously, It's Time for a Major Rethink About Liberal and Progressive Politics, Alternet, October 25, 2014, http://www.alternet.org/activism/apocalypse-now-seriously-its-timemajor-rethink-about-liberal-and-progressive-politics.

128   Katherine Peralta, "Outsourcing to China Cost U.S. 3.2 Million Jobs Since 2001," US News and World Report, December 11, 2014, http://www.usnews.com/news/blogs/data-mine/2014/12/11/outsourcing-to-chinacost-us-32-million-jobs-since-2001.

129   "The Curious Case of China's Currency," The Economist, August 11, 2015, http://www.economist.com/blogs/buttonwood/2015/08/markets-and-economics.

130   Derek Scissors, "The Most Important Chinese Trade Barriers," The Heritage Foundation, July 20, 2012, http://www.heritage.org/research/testimony/2012/07/the-most-important-chinese-trade-barriers. 128 "Five Facts About Workers' Rights in China," The Borgen Project, Sept. 30, 2018, https://borgenproject.org/facts-about-workers-rights-in-china/.
131   Javier C. Hernandez, "Workers' Activism Rises as China's Economy Slows. Xi Aims to Rein Them In," February 6, 2019, https://www.nytimes.com/2019/02/06/world/asia/china-workers-protests.html.
132   James Rickards, *The Death of Money: The Coming Collapse of the International Monetary System* (New York: Penguin Group, 2014), 80.
133   Edwin Lefevre, *Reminiscences of a Stock Operator* (New York: John Wiley and Sons, Inc., 1994).
134   Wikipedia, "Pump and dump," last modified November 1, 2018, https://en.wikipedia.org/wiki/Pump_and_dump.
135   Wikipedia, "Stock market bubble," last modified October 18, 2018, https://en.wikipedia.org/wiki/Stock_market_bubble.
136   Will Kenton, Initial Public Offering – IPO," Investopedia, Dcember 7, 2018, http://www.investopedia.com/terms/i/ipo.asp.
137   Matt Taibbi, "The Great American Bubble Machine, Rolling Stone, April 5, 2010, https://www.rollingstone.com/politics-news/the-great-american-bubble-machine-195229/.
138   Matt Taibbi, "The Great American Bubble Machine," Rolling Stone, April 5, 2010, http://www.rollingstone.com/politics/news/the-great-american-bubble-machine-20100405. 135 Wikipedia, "Dotcom bubble," last modified Jan. 10, 2019, https://en.wikipedia.org/wiki/Dotcom_bubble.
139   Matt Taibbi, "The Great American Bubble Machine," Rolling Stone, April 5, 2010.
140   Matt Taibbi, "The Great American Bubble Machine," Rolling Stone, April 5, 2010.
141   Matt Taibbi, "The Great American Bubble Machine," April 5, 2010.
142   Jenny Anderson, "For Anschutz It's $5 M Payback Time," New York Post, May 12, 2003, http://nypost.com/2003/05/12/for-anschutz-its-5m-payback-time/. 138 Wikipedia, "Subprime mortgage crisis," last modified Dec. 30, 2018, https://en.wikipedia.org/wiki/Subprime_mortgage_crisis.

143   Wikipedia, "Subprime mortgage crisis," last modified December 30, 2018, https://en.wikipedia.org/wiki/Subprime_mortgage_crisis.
144   Porter Stansberry, *America 2020: The Survival Blueprint* (Maryland: Stansberry Research, 2015), 13.
145   James B. Glattfelder, "Who Controls the World," TEDxZurich, 2012, https://www.ted.com/talks/james_b_glattfelder_who_controls_the_world?language=en.
146   Andy Coghlan and Debora MacKenzie, "Revealed – the capitalist network that runs the world," NewScientist, October 19, 2011, https://www.newscientist.com/article/mg21228354-500-revealed-the-capitalist-network-that-runs-the-world/.
147   "Henry Ford Quotes," Brainy Quotes, accessed February 27, 2020, https://www.brainyquote.com/quotes/quotes/h/henryford136294.html.
148   Jimmy Mengel, "Special Report: Who Really Controls the World," Outsider Club, accessed February 27, 2020, http://www.outsiderclub.com/report/who-really-controls-the-world/1032.
149   Paul Buchheit, "5 Facts About How America Is Rigged for a Massive Wealth Transfer to the Rich," AlterNet, November 4, 2014, http://www.alternet.org/economy/5-facts-about-how-america-rigged-massive-wealth-transfer-rich.
150   Heather Boushey and Adam S. Hersh, The American Middle Class, Income Inequality, and the Strength of Our Economy: New Evidence in Economics," Center for American Progress, May, 2012, http://cdn.americanprogress.org/wp-content/uploads/issues/2012/05/pdf/middleclass_growth.pdf.
151   Lu Wang and Callie Bost, "S&P 500 Companies Spend Almost All Profits on Buybacks," Bloomberg, October 5, 2014, https://www.bloomberg.com/news/articles/2014-10-06/s-p-500-companies-spend-almost-allprofits-on-buybacks-payouts.
152   "Working for the Few: Political Capture and Economic Inequality," 178 Oxfam Briefing Paper, January 20, 2014, http://www.oxfam.org/sites/www.oxfam.org/files/bp-working-for-few-political-capture-economicinequality-200114-en.pdf.
153   Wikipedia, "Distribution of Wealth," last modified December 31, 2018, https://en.wikipedia.org/wiki/Distribution_of_wealth.
154   Nicole Goodkind, "Trump's Tax Cuts Didn't Benefit U.S. Workers, Made Rich Companies Richer, Analysis Finds," News-

week, January 6, 2019, https://www.newsweek.com/republican-tax-cuts-trump-wageincreases-879800.
155   "Profile of the Sociopath," accessed February 27, 2020, https://www.mcafee.cc/Bin/sb.html.
156   "Ten Year Real Interest Rate," accessed February 27, 2020, http://www.multpl.com/10-year-real-interest-rate/.
157   Peter D. Schiff, *The Real Crash: America's Coming Bankruptcy - How To Save Yourself and Your Country*,(New York: St. Martin's Press, 2014), 10.
158   Whitney Benns and Blake Strode, "Debtors Prison in 21st-Century America," The Atlantic, February 23, 2016, http://www.theatlantic.com/business/archive/2016/02/debtors-prison/462378/.
159   Peter D. Schiff. *The Real Crash: America's Coming Bankruptcy - How To Save Yourself and Your Country*, 27.
160   Books 2 and 3 of this trilogy, *Ideology* and *Revolution*, address the means to stop the cataclysmic crash of western civilization.
161   David Rockefeller denies that he made the above statement but why wouldn't he deny it. His behavior however, in the formation of the Council on Foreign Relations and the Trilateral Commission supports him making such a statement. As we will see in Chapter Two, both these organizations had heads of major publications as members, yet never reported on the organizations' activities.
162   "Trans-Pacific Partnership," Public Citizen, accessed February 27, 2020, http://www.citizen.org/TPP.
163   Charlotte McDonald, "How many Earths do we need?" BBC, June 16, 2015, http://www.bbc.com/news/magazine-33133712.
164   "Guide to the Millennium Assessment Reports," Millennium Ecosystem Assessment, 2005, https://www.millenniumassessment.org/en/index.html.
165   Joshua Elliott, Delphine Deryng, Christoph Müller, et al., "Constraints and potentials of future irrigation water availability on agricultural production under climate change," PNAS December 16, 2013, DOI: .1073/pnas.1222474110 Provided by University of Chicago.
166   "Woody Allen Quotes," Goodreads, accessed February 27, 2020, https://www.goodreads.com/quotes/6166-more-than-any-othertime-in-history-mankind-faces-a.
167   Michael Klare, *Resource Wars: The New Landscape of Global Conflict* (New York: Henry Holt and Co.), 263.

168 Bill Ridley, "China and the Final War for Resources," 321 Energy, February 9, 2005, http://www.321energy.com/editorials/ridley/ridley020905.html.

169 Dan Plesh, Greg Austin and Fiona Grant, "Britain's Energy Future: Securing the Home Front," The Foreign Policy Center, UK, 2005, https://fpc.org.uk/wp-content/uploads/2006/09/575.pdf.

170 Leo Shane III, "Price tag on the 'war on terror' will top $6 trillion soon," Military Times, November 14, 2018, https://www.militarytimes.com/news/pentagon-congress/2018/11/14/price-tag-of-the-war-on-terror-willtop-6-trillion-soon/.

171 Matthew Higgins and Thomas Klitgaard, "Financial Globalization and the U.S. Current Account Deficit," Current Issues in Economics and Finance, Vol 13, No, 11, 2007, https://www.newyorkfed.org/medialibrary/media/research/current_issues/ci13-11.pdf.

172 Wikipedia, "List of countries by military expenditures," last modified January 10, 2019, https://en.wikipedia.org/wiki/List_of_countries_by_military_expenditures.

173 Wikipedia, "Energy usage of the United States military," last modified December 22, 2018, https://en.wikipedia.org/wiki/Energy_usage_of_the_United_States_military.

174 David Stipp, "The Pentagons Weather Nightmare: The climate could change radically and fast. That would be the mother of all national security issues," Fortune Magazine, February 9, 2004.

175 Michel Crozier, Samuel P. Huntington, Joji Watanuki, *The Crisis of Democracy: On the Governability of Democracies* (New York, New York University Press, 1975).

176 Gene Berkman, "The Trilateral Commission and the New World Order," 1993, https://www.antiwar.com/berkman/trilat.html.

177 Michel Crozier, Samuel P. Huntington, Joji Watanuki, *The Crisis of Democracy: On the Governability of Democracies*.

178 Dr. Charles G. Cogan, "He Kept Us Out of War," Huffington Post, September 15, 2013, https://www.huffingtonpost.com/dr-charles-g-cogan/he-kept-us-out-of-war_b_3931495.html.

179 "Making the World 'Safe for Democracy': Woodrow Wilson Asks for War," History Matters, accessed February 27, 2020, http://historymatters.gmu.edu/d/4943/.

180 Wikipedia, "League of Nations," last modified Janury 3, 2019, https://en.wikipedia.org/wiki/League_of_Nations.

181 Wikipedia, "Council on Foreign Relations," last modified December 28, 2019, https://en.wikipedia.org/wiki/Council_on_Foreign_Relations.
182 "Nazis and America: The USA's Fascist Past," History Cooperative, accessed February 27, 2020, http://historycooperative.org/nazisamerica-the-usas-fascist-past/.
183 Gene Berkman, "The Trilateral Commission and the New World Order," 1993.
184 Dan Smoot, "The Invisible Government," (Dallas TX, The Dan Smoot Report, Inc., 1962), http://www.gutenberg.org/files/20224/20224-h/20224-h.htm.
185 The Trilateral Commission, Homepage, accessed February 27, 2020, http://trilateral.org/.
186 Wikipedia, "Zbigniew Brzezinski," last modified January 4, 2019, https://en.wikipedia.org/wiki/Zbigniew_Brzezinski.
187 Barry Goldwater and Stephen Shadegg, *With No Apologies: The Personal and Political Memoirs of United States Senator Barry M. Goldwater* (New York: William Morrow and Company, 1979), 284-285.
188 "Ron Paul Rants of Trilateral Commission Conspiracy Theories," Real Clear Politics Videos, December 23, 2011, http://www.realclearpolitics.com/video/2011/12/23/ron_paul_rants_on_trilateral_commission_conspiracy_theories.html.
189 Wikipedia, "Trilateral Commission," last modified January 14, 2020, https://en.wikipedia.org/wiki/Trilateral_Commission.
190 Wikipedia, "List of wars involving Israel," last modified October 25, 2018, https://en.wikipedia.org/wiki/List_of_wars_involving_Israel..
191 "The Trilateral Commission," Jeremiah Project, accessed February 27, 2020, http://www.jeremiahproject.com/newworldorder/nworder07.html.
192 As president, he prayed several times a day, and professed that Jesus Christ was the driving force in his life. Carter had been greatly influenced by a sermon he had heard as a young man. It asked, "If you were arrested for being a Christian, would there be enough evidence to convict you?" The New York Times noted that Carter had been instrumental in moving evangelical Christianity closer to the American mainstream during and after his presidency. See https://en.wikipedia.org/wiki/Jimmy_Carter#Religion.
193 Steven F. Hayward, *The Real Jimmy Carter* (Washington, DC:

Regnery Publishing Inc., 2004).

194   "Trilateral Commission, IP0092," Congressional Research Service, The Library of Congress, accessed February 27, 2020, https://www.everycrsreport.com/files/19810501_IP0092_2d3ea09e-2c6068af730f41d315f4ea490bc91878.p df.

195   "Trilateralism and the Legacy of David Rockefeller," accessed February 27, 2020, http://www.bibliotecapleyades.net/exopolitica/esp_exopolitics_G_5.htm.

196   David Rockefeller, *Memoirs* Random House Publishing Group, 418

197   "Trilateralism and the Legacy of David Rockefeller," accessed February 27, 2020.

198   "The Trilateral Commission," Modern History Project, accessed February 27, 2020, http://modernhistoryproject.org/mhp?Article=FinalWarning&C=9.1.

199   Wikipedia, "New world order (politics)," last modified January 2, 2019, https://en.wikipedia.org/wiki/New_world_order_(politics).

200   Wikipedia, "Gulf War," last modified January 10, 2019, https://en.wikipedia.org/wiki/Gulf_War.

201   Wikipedia, "Gulf War," last modified January 10, 2019.

202   Gene Berkman, "The Trilateral Commission and the New World Order," 1993.

203   Gene Berkman, "The Trilateral Commission and the New World Order," 1993.

204   Heinz Duthel, "The Trilateral Commission and the New World Order," IAC Society, 2010.

205   "Trilateralism and the Legacy of David Rockefeller," accessed February 27, 2020.

206   "Trilateralism and the Legacy of David Rockefeller," accessed February 27, 2020.

207   Wikipedia, "Halliburton," last modified January 4, 2019, https://en.wikipedia.org/wiki/Halliburton.

208   "Trilateralism and the Legacy of David Rockefeller," accessed February 27, 2020.

209   Wikipedia, "Tweedledum and Tweedledee," last modified January 12, 2019, https://en.wikipedia.org/wiki/Tweedledum_and_Tweedledee.

210   Wikipedia, "September 11 attacks," January 7, 2019, https://en.wikipedia.org/wiki/September_11_attacks.

211 Daniel Luban, "Iraq War Motives, Ten Years Later," Lobe Log, March 19, 2013, https://lobelog.com/iraq-war-motives-ten-years-later/.
212 Wikipedia, "Carter Doctrine," last modified December 7, 2018, https://en.wikipedia.org/wiki/Carter_Doctrine.
213 "Foreign Relations of the United States, 977-1980," Vol. XVIII, Middle East Region; Arabian Peninsula," Department of State, Office of the Historian, Document 45.
214 "A Clean Break: A New Strategy for Securing the Realm," First neocon report calling for Iraq invasion, Delivered to Israel, 1996, Z Facts, https://zfacts.com/p/139.html.
215 Scott Thompson, "Dick Cheney Has Long Planned to Loot Iraqi Oil," Executive Intelligence Review, August 1, 2003, http://www.larouchepub.com/other/2003/3030cheney_oil.html.
216 211 Wikipedia, "Import-Export Bank of the United States," last modified January 9, 2019, https://en.wikipedia.org/wiki/Export%E2%80%93Import_Bank_of_the_United_States.
217 Bechtel: Profiting from Destruction," Collaborative Report, June 5, 2003, https://corpwatch.org/article/bechtel-profiting-destruction.
218 "Bechtel Group: The Cheney Connection," compiled by Dee Finney, Great Dreams, July 7, 2004, http://www.greatdreams.com/political/bechtel.htm.
219 Scott Thompson, "Dick Cheney Has Long Planned to Loot Iraqi Oil," August 1, 2003.
220 David Corn, "Watch Rand Paul Say Dick Cheney Pushed for the Iraq War So Halliburton Would Profit," Mother Jones, April 7, 2014, http://www.motherjones.com/politics/2014/04/rand-paul-dick-cheneyexploited-911-iraq-halliburton.
221 See Appendix C for a deeper look at the Bush administration's involvement in planning 9/11.
222 "Presidential Approval Ratings – George W. Bush," Gallop, 2001-2008, https://news.gallup.com/poll/116500/presidential-approval-ratings-george-bush.aspx.
223 "Obama's Trilateral Commission Team," Project Censored, May 8, 2010, http://projectcensored.org/22obamas-trilateral-commission-team/.
224 Later Americans would come to find out that the FRB doled out 12.3 trillion dollars to keep the big banks from going bankrupt. Thus, putting the rich above the law. See http://pubrecord.org/na-

tion/8622/pentagon-papers-wall-street/.

225   Rex Nutting, "How the Bubble Destroyed the Middle Class," MarketWatch July 8, 2011, http://www.marketwatch.com/story/how-the-bubble-destroyed-the-middle-class-2011-07-08.

226   For a simple explanation of the dynamics of this partnership see Joseph E. Stiglitz, "Obama's Ersatz Capitalism," The New York Times, March 31, 2009, http://www.nytimes.com/2009/04/01/opinion/01stiglitz.html?ref=opinion&_r=0..

227   Josh Gerstein, "Obama Makes Legacy Play on Trade," Politico, November 16, 2014, http://www.politico.com/story/2014/11/barack-obama-trade-legacy-112939.html#ixzz3JREABMHg.

228   Jim Hightower and Phillip Frazer, "The Trans-Pacific Partnership is not about free trade. It's a corporate coup d'etat against us!," Hightower Lowdown, August 2013, http://www.hightowerlowdown.org/node/3402#.VGuirMkkWdw.

229   "Roster of CFR/Trilateral Commission Members," http://www.apfn.org/apfn/cfr-members.htm.

230   "Full Text of 'The Crisis of Democracy –The Trilateral Commission – 1975," accessed March 6, 2020, https://archive.org/stream/TheCrisisOfDemocracy-TrilateralCommission-1975/crisis_of_democracy_djvu.txt.

231   "Full Text of 'The Crisis of Democracy –The Trilateral Commission – 1975," 6.

232   "Full Text of 'The Crisis of Democracy –The Trilateral Commission – 1975," 6.

233   "Full Text of 'The Crisis of Democracy –The Trilateral Commission – 1975," 6-7.

234   "Crisis of Democracy – Unites States (Part I), Trilateral Commission, accessed March 6, 2020, 59-60. https://archive.org/stream/TheCrisisOfDemocracy-TrilateralCommission-1975/crisis_of_democracy_djvu.txt.

235   "US Political Thought, Notes on Samuel P. Huntington, Chapter III: 'The United States,'" accessed February 27, 2020, http://pages.uoregon.edu/jboland/hntngton.html.

236   "Full Text of 'The Crisis of Democracy –The Trilateral Commission – 1975," 114.

237   "US Political Thought, Notes on Samuel P. Huntington, Chapter III: The United States in the Crisis of Democracy, Michel Crozier,

Samuel P. Huntington, and Joji Watnuki, accessed February 27, 2020, https://page.uoregon.edu/boland/hntngton.html.
238   "Social and Economic Issues of the 1980s and 1990s," Amistad, accessed February 27, 2020, http://www.amistadresource.org/the_future_in_the_present/social_and_economic_issues.html.
239   Wikipedia, "Post-civil rights era in African American history," last modified December 13, 2018, https://en.wikipedia.org/wiki/Post%E2%80%93Civil_Rights_era_in_African-American_history
240   Wikipedia, "Incarceration in the United States," January 14, 2019, https://en.wikipedia.org/wiki/Incarceration_in_the_United_States.
241   "Crack Cocaine: A Short History," Foundation for a Drug-Free World, accessed February 27, 2020, https://www.drugfreeworld.org/drugfacts/crackcocaine/a-short-history.html.
242   Ryan Grim, Matt Sledge, and Matt Ferner, "Key Figures in CIA-Crack Cocaine Scandal Begin To Come Forward," Huffpost, October 10, 2014, https://www.huffingtonpost.com/2014/10/10/gary-webb-darkalliance_n_5961748.html.
243   Wikipedia, "Post-civil rights era in African American history," last modified December 13, 2018.
244   See David Moore, "The Members of Congress Who Profit From War," The American Prospect, January 17, 2020, https://prospect.org/power/the-members-of-congress-who-profit-from-war/.
245   See Joseph E. Stiglitz, "The Truth About the Trump Economy," Project Syndicate, January 17. 2020, https://www.project-syndicate.org/commentary/grim-truth-about-trump-economy-by-joseph-e-stiglitz-2020-01.
246   Lydia Saad. "Conservatives Hang On to Ideological Lead by a Thread,"   Gallup, January 11, 2016, http://www.gallup.com/poll/188129/conservatives-hang-ideology-lead-thread.aspx.
247   Richard Florida, "The Conservative States of America," The Atlantic, March 29, 2011, https://www.theatlantic.com/politics/archive/2011/03/the-conservative-states-of-america/71827/.
248   Colon Friedersdorf, What Americans Mean When They Say They're Conservative," The Atlantic, January 27, 2012, http://www.theatlantic.com/politics/archive/2012/01/what-americans-mean-when-they-saytheyre-conservative/252099/.
249   George Lakoff, *Don't Think of an Elephant* (Vermont: Chelsea Green Publications, 2014), Excerpt at http://truth-out.org/progres-

sivepicks/item/27538-the-strict-father-is-at-the-core-of-conservative-ideologyand-values.
250   George Lakoff, "Don't Think of an Elephant," 2014.
251   "At the Root of the Republican Party War Against Women – Primitive Southern Baptists," Down With Tyranny!, October 22, 214, http://downwithtyranny.blogspot.com/2014/10/at-root-of-republican-party-war-against.html.
252   Jennifer Glass, "Red states, blue states, and divorce: Understanding the impact of conservative Protestantism on regional variation in divorce rates," Council on Contemporary Families, January 16, 2014, https://contemporaryfamilies.org/impact-of-conservative-protestantism-on-regional-divorce-rates/.
253   Zoe Szathmary, "Richest 80 people in the world revealed . . . and 35 of them are American citizens," Daily Mail, January 21, 2015, http://www.dailymail.co.uk/news/article-2919540/Oxfam-report-finds-80-world-srichest-billionaires-wealth-bottom-50-percent-global-population-3-5-BILLION-people.html.
254   Jane C. Timm, "Rand Paul: Half of disability recipients are 'gaming the system," MSNBC, January 14, 2015, http://www.msnbc.com/msnbc/rand-paul-half-disability-recipients-are-gaming-the-system#55682.
255   Frank Lambert, *The Founding Fathers and the Place of Religion in America* ((Princeton NJ: Princeton University Press, 2003), https://press.princeton.edu/titles/7500.html.
256   "Statement of Faith," National Association of Evangelicals," accessed March 6, 2020, http://www.nae.net/statement-of-faith.
257   Colonial Williamsburg History, "Religion in Early Virginia," accessed February 27, 2020, http://www.history.org/almanack/life/religion/religionva.cfm.
258   Derek H. Davis, "Baptists," The First Amendment Encyclopedia, accessed March 6, 2020, https://www.mtsu.edu/first-amendment/article/1319/baptists.
259   "Reverend Dr. Richard Furman's EXPOSITION of The Views of the Baptists, RELATIVE TO THE COLOURED POPULATION In the United States IN A COMMUNICATION To the Governor of South-Carolina," 1838, http://eweb.furman.edu/~benson/docs/rcdfmn1.htm.
260   Wikipedia, "Southern Baptist Convention," last modified Febru-

ary 22, 2019, https://rationalwiki.org/wiki/Southern_Baptist_Convention.
261   "Reverend Dr. Richard Furman's EXPOSITION of The Views of the Baptists, RELATIVE TO THE COLOURED POPULATION In the United States IN A COMMUNICATION To the Governor of South-Carolina," 1838.
262   Bill J. Leonard, "Baptists and the Bible, Slavery and the Lost Cause: Inseparable Hermeneutics of Racism," Furman University, April, 2018, https://www.furman.edu/seeking-abraham-project/wp-content/uploads/sites/20/2018/12/Leonard_speech.pdf.
263   Wikipedia, "Jim Crow laws," last modified January 14, 2019, http://en.wikipedia.org/wiki/Jim_Crow_laws.
264   "Ku Klux Klan," History, updated February 21, 2020, https://www.history.com/topics/reconstruction/ku-klux-klan.
265   George C. Rable, *But There Was No Peace: The Role of Violence in the Politics of Reconstruction* (Athens: University of Georgia Press, 1984), 132.
266   "Grant, Reconstruction and the KKK," American Experience, PBS, accessed February 27, 2020, https://www.pbs.org/wgbh/americanexperience/features/grant-kkk/.
267   Wikipedia, "Solid South," last modified January 3, 2019, http://en.wikipedia.org/wiki/Solid_South.
268   Richard H. Pildes, "Democracy, Anti-Democracy, and the Canon", Constitutional Commentary, Vol.17, 2000, 10.
269   Wikipedia, "Fundamentalist-Modernist controversy," last modified December 13, 2018, http://en.wikipedia.org/wiki/Fundamentalist%E2%80%93Modernist_Controversy.
270   Wikipedia, "Fundamentalism," last modified Jan. 9, 2019, https://en.wikipedia.org/wiki/Fundamentalism#Christian.
271   Wikipedia, "Scopes Trial," last modified January 13, 2019, http://en.wikipedia.org/wiki/Scopes_Trial.
272   Wikipedia, "Southern Baptist Convention conservative resurgence," last modified November 2, 2019, https://en.wikipedia.org/wiki/Southern_Baptist_Convention_conservative_resurgence.
273   Wikipedia, "Biblical inerrancy," last modified January 13, 2019, https://en.wikipedia.org/wiki/Biblical_inerrancy.
274   Wikipedia, "Mainline Protestant," last modified December 27, 2018, https://en.wikipedia.org/wiki/Mainline_Protestant.
275   Wikipedia, "Christian Voice (United States)," last modified

Auguust 15, 2017, https://en.wikipedia.org/wiki/Christian_Voice_(United_States).
276   Wikipedia, "Melkite Greek Catholic Church," last modified December 21, 2018, https://en.wikipedia.org/wiki/Melkite_Greek_Catholic_Church.
277   Wikipedia, "Christian Voice (United States)," last modified Auguust 15, 2017.
278   Wikipedia, "Torrijos-Carter Treaties," last modified January 8, 2018, https://en.wikipedia.org/wiki/Torrijos%E2%80%93Carter_Treaties.
279   "American Freedom Coalition," Right Web, last modified February 28, 1989, http://rightweb.irconline.org/american_freedom_coalition/.
280   Wikipedia, "Moral Majority," last modified December 20, 2018, https://en.wikipedia.org/wiki/Moral_Majority.
281   Wikipedia, "Paul Weyrich," last modified December 21, 2018, https://en.wikipedia.org/wiki/Paul_Weyrich.
282   Wikipedia, "Christian Right," last modified January 15, 2019, https://en.wikipedia.org/wiki/Christian_right.
283   Wikipedia, "Christian Right," last modified January 15, 2019.
284   Wikipedia, "Christian Right," last modified January 15, 2019.
285   Robert Liebman and Robert Wuthnow, *The New Christian Right* (New York: Aldine Publishing Company, 1983), 55-57.
286   Jimmy Carter, *White House Diary* (New York: Farrar, Straus and Giroux, 2010), 469.
287   Wikipedia, "Supply-side economics," last modified December 17, 2019, http://en.wikipedia.org/wiki/Supply-side_economics.
288   Wikipedia, "Moral Majority," last modified December 20, 2018.
289   Wikipedia, "Christian Coalition of America," last modified January 14, 2019, https://en.wikipedia.org/wiki/Christian_Coalition_of_America.
290   Joel D. Vaughan, "*The Rise and Fall of the Christian Coalition* (Eugene, OR: Wipf & Stock, 2009) 177.
291   Ted Olsen, "Christian Coalition Sued for Racial Discrimination," Christianity Today, February 1, 2001, https://www.christianitytoday.com/ct/2001/februaryweb-only/2-26-12.0.html.
292   "The Tea Party and Religion," Pew Research Center, February 23, 2011, http://www.pewforum.org/2011/02/23/tea-party-and-religion/.
293   Wikipedia, "Tea Party movement," last modified February 3, 2020, https://en.wikipedia.org/wiki/Tea_Party_movement.

294   Tea Party Patriots, accessed February 27, 2020, https://www.teapartypatriots.org/.
295   "Our Vision: Core Issues," Tea Party Patriots, accessed March 6, 2020, https://www.teapartypatriots.org/.
296   Tea Party Patriots, accessed February 27, 2020, https://www.teapartypatriots.org/discussions/#/discussion/98/the-only-real-fix-for-our-great-country-isto-raise-revenue-by-bringing-back-businesses-and-jobs.
297   Jeremy W. Peters, "After Obama's Immigration Action, a Blast of Energy for the Tea Party," *New York Times* Novsember 25, 2014.
298   Wikipedia, "Tea Party movement," last modified February 3, 2020.
299   Kueren Holloman and Helen Killeen, "Top 20 most influential people in the Tea Party movement," The Telegraph, Oct. 12, 2010, https://www.telegraph.co.uk/news/worldnews/us-politics/8056713/Top-20-mostinfluential-people-in-the-Tea-Party-movement-10-1.html.
300   Wikipedia, "Christian Reconstructionist," last modified Nov.ember 6, 2018, http://en.wikipedia.org/wiki/Christian_Reconstructionism.
301   Wikipedia, "Christian Reconstructionist," last modified Nov.ember 6, 2018.
302   Wikipedia, "Dominion Theology," last modified January 1, 2019, https://en.wikipedia.org/wiki/Dominion_Theology.
303   Wikipedia, "Sara Diamond," last modified August 27, 2018, http://en.wikipedia.org/wiki/Sara_Diamond.
304   Cberlet, "What is Dominionism? Palin, the Christian Right, and Theocracy," The Rise of the Religious Right in the Republican Party September. 5, 2008, http://www.theocracywatch.org/.
305   William Martin, *With God On Our Side: The Rise of the Religious Right* (New York: Broadway Books, 1996), references throughout.
306   Martin E. Marty and R. Scott Appleby, eds., *Fundamentalisms and the State: Remaking Polities, Economies, and Militance* (Chicago: The University of Chicago Press, 1993), 349.
307   Cberlet, "What is Dominionism? Palin, the Christian Right, and Theocracy," September. 5, 2008.
308   Cberlet, "What is Dominionism? Palin, the Christian Right, and Theocracy," September. 5, 2008.
309   Wikipedia, "Dominion Theology," last modified January 1,

2019, https://en.wikipedia.org/wiki/Dominion_Theology.

310   Laura Vozzella, "Falwell on evangelical's support for Trump: 'They're voting as Americans this time'," https://www.washingtonpost.com/news/post-politics/wp/2016/07/20/falwell-on-evangelicals-support-fortrump-theyre-voting-as-americans-this-time/.

311   Will Drabold, "Read the Republican Platform on Same-Sex Marriage, Guns and Wall Street," Time Magazine, July 18, 2016, http://time.com/4411842/republican-platform-same-sex-marriage-abortion-gunswall-street/.

312   Wikipedia, "Family values," last modified January 4, 2019, http://en.wikipedia.org/wiki/Family_values.

313   Jolie O'Dell, "The Eating Habits of Conservatives vs Liberals," Mashable, May 25, 2011, https://mashable.com/2011/05/25/political-eating/#3TGMWtvqNPqH.

314   Neil Gross, "Why Are the Highly Educated So Liberal," New York Times, May 13, 2016, http://www.nytimes.com/2016/05/15/opinion/why-are-the-highly-educated-so-liberal.html?_r=0.

315   Krishna Rao, "Climate Change and Housing: Will a Rising Tide Sink All Homes," Zillow Research, June 2, 2017. http://www.zillow.com/research/climate-change-underwater-homes-12890/.

316   Linda Skitka et al. "Political Orientation and Moral Conviction: A Conservative Advantage or an Equal Opportunity Motivator of Political Engagement?" (Chicago: University of Illinois-Chicago), accessed February 27, 2020, available at http://www.sydneysymposium.unsw.edu.au/2014/chapters/SkitkaSSSP2014.pdf.

317   Chris Mooney, "Surprise: Liberals are Just as Morally Righteous as Conservatives," Mother Jones, February 19, 2014, http://www.motherjones.com/mojo/2014/02/liberals-conservatives-morality-zealconviction.

318   Wikipedia, "Nurturant parent model," last modified June 17, 2018, https://en.wikipedia.org/wiki/Nurturant_parent_model.

319   Kathryn P. Haydon, "The Nurturing Parent and the Nurturing Teacher," The Creative Post, October 8, 2014, http://www.creativitypost.com/education/the_nurturing_parent_and_the_nurturing_teacher.

320   Zoe Szathmary, "Richest 80 people in the world revealed … and 35 of them are American citizens," Daily Mail, Jan. 21, 2015, http://www.dailymail.co.uk/news/article-2919540/Oxfam-report-finds-80-worlds-richest-billionaires-wealth-bottom-50-percent-global-popula-

tion-3-5-BILLION-people.html.
321   "What Is a Liberal Education," Association of American Colleges and Universities, accessed February 27, 2020, https://www.aacu.org/leap/what-is-a-liberal-education.
322   Wikipedia, "Friedrich Schleiermacher," last modified December 31, 2018, http://en.wikipedia.org/wiki/Friedrich_Schleiermacher.
323   Wikipedia, "Friedrich Schleiermacher," last modified December 31, 2018.
324   Encyclopedia Britannica eds., "Theological liberalism," accessed February 27, 2020, http://www.britannica.com/EBchecked/topic/590847/theological-liberalism.
325   Linda Woodhead et al. "Christianity," in *Religions in the Modern World* (New York: Routledge, 2002), 186 and 193.
326   Burton L. Mack, The Lost Gospel: The Book of Q and Christian Origins, (New York, HarperCollins, 1993), 29.
327   Dan P. McAdams, *The Redemptive Self: Stories Americans Live By* (Oxford: Oxford University Press, 2006), 164.
328   Wikipedia, "Liberal Christianity," last modified January 2, 2019, http://en.wikipedia.org/wiki/Liberal_Christianity.
329   Wikipedia, "Dean M. Kelley," last modified September 5, 2018, http://en.wikipedia.org/wiki/Dean_M._Kelley.
330   Wikipedia, Dean M. Kelley, "Why Conservative Churches are Growing," last modified September 5, 2018, http://en.wikipedia.org/wiki/Dean_M._Kelley.
331   Wikipedia, "Liberal Christianity," last modified January 2, 2019.
332   Wikipedia, "Declaration of the Rights of Man and of the Citizen," last modified January 15, 2019, https://en.wikipedia.org/wiki/Declaration_of_the_Rights_of_Man_and_of_the_Citizen.
333   "Rethinking Neoliberalism: Resisting the Disciplinary Regime," edited by Sanford F. Schram and Marianna Pavlovskaya, (New York: Routledge Taylor and Francis Group, 2017), http://urban.hunter.cuny.edu/~schram/neoliberalproofuncorrected.pdf.
334   Elizabeth Dunn, "5 19th-Century Utopian Communities in the United States," History, January 22, 2013, http://www.history.com/news/history-lists/5-19th-century-utopian-communities-in-the-united-states.
335   "The Progressive Movement," United States History, accessed February 27, 2020, http://www.u-s-history.com/pages/h1061.html.

336   Wikipedia, "Liberalism in the United States," last modified January 10, 2019, http://en.wikipedia.org/wiki/Liberalism_in_the_United_States.
337   Wikipedia, "Presidency of Theodore Roosevelt," last modified, January 6, 2019, https://en.wikipedia.org/wiki/Presidency_of_Theodore_Roosevelt.
338   "Liberalism," The Basics of Philosophy, accessed February 27, 2020, http://www.philosophybasics.com/branch_liberalism.html#Types.
339   Wikipedia, "Liberalism in the United States," last modified January 10, 2019.
340   "Malcolm X: From Nation of Islam to Black Power Movement," Aljazeera, February 21, 2018, https://www.aljazeera.com/news/2018/02/malcolm-nation-islam-black-power-movement180221085553908.html.
341   Elizabeth Kiefer, "How the Women of the KKK Helped Architect a Hate Movement," Refinery29, October 2017.
342   Wikipedia, "Kent State shootings," last modified January 16, 2019, https://en.wikipedia.org/wiki/Kent_State_shootings.
343   Wikipedia, "Ferguson unrest," last modified January 9, 2019, https://en.wikipedia.org/wiki/Ferguson_unrest.
344   Wikipedia, "Green party," last modified January 7, 2019, https://en.wikipedia.org/wiki/Green_party.
345   The Green Charter and political action plan is available for download at https://www.globalgreens.org/globalcharter.
346   Wikipedia, "Eco-socialism," last modified January 3, 2019, https://en.wikipedia.org/wiki/Green_Party_of_the_United_States.
347   The term Committees of Correspondence harkens back to the American Revolution when Sam Adams   created committees in each of the 13 colonies to stay in touch regarding England's activities in each colony and to develop a common strategy for resistance.
348   See Appendix A for an explanation of the Ten Values or visit http://www.gp.org/10kv.
349   Jodean Marks, "A Historical Look at Green Structure: 1984-1992," Synthesis/Regeneration 14, Fall, 1997, http://www.greens.org/s-r/14/14-03.html.
350   Wikipedia, "Green Party of the United States," last modified January 16, 2019, https://en.wikipedia.org/wiki/Green_Party_of_the_United_States.

351   See Appendix B for the Declaration of the Occupation of New York City that was approved by the NYC General Assembly.
352   Unknown to most participants, the Park had been the site of New York's first protest against the British Tea Act in 1773.
353   Wikipedia, "List of Occupy movement protest locations," last modified November 21, 2018, https://en.wikipedia.org/wiki/List_of_Occupy_movement_protest_locations.
354   Wikipedia, "Occupy Movement," last modified January 14, 2019, https://en.wikipedia.org/wiki/Occupy_movement.
355   Andrew Fleming, "Adbusters spark Wall Street protest," Vancouver Courier, September 27, 2011, https://www.webcitation.org/6AIbOo25w?url=http://www.vancourier.com/Adbusters+sparks+Wall+Street +protest/5466332/story.html.
356   Jose Pedro Zuquete, "Another World is Possible? Utopia Revisited," New Global Studies, Vol 5, Issue 2, Article 3, 2011, http://repositorio.ul.pt/bitstream/10451/6021/1/ICS_JPZuquete_Another_ARI.pdf.
357   This film is available in full on YouTube.
358   Gene Sharp, *From Dictatorship to Democracy: A Conceptual Framework for Liberation* (New York: The New Press, 2012), http://www.bbc.com/news/world-middle-east-12522848.
359   Gene Sharp, From Dictatorship to Democracy (New York: The New Press, 2012), 6.
360   Ruaridh Arrow, "Gene Sharp: Author of the nonviolent revolution rulebook," BBC News, February 21, 2011, https://www.bbc.com/news/world-middle-east-12522848.
361   "Q and A: Gene Sharp," Aljazeera, December 6, 2011, https://www.aljazeera.com/indepth/opinion/2011/12/201112113179492201.html.
362   Andre Tartar, "400 Occupy Oakland Protesters Arrested After Invading City Hall and Burning a U.S. Flag," Intelligencer, January 29, 2012, http://nymag.com/intelligencer/2012/01/400-occupy-oakland-protestersarrested.html.
363   Michael Billera, "Occupy Wall Street: The Major Problems With the Movement," International Business Times, November 3, 2011, http://www.ibtimes.com/occupy-wall-street-major-problems-movement650997.
364   Jana Kasperkevic, "Occupy Wall Street: four years later," The Guardian, September 16, 2015, http://www.theguardian.com/world/ng-interactive/2015/sep/16/occupy-wall-street-four-years-latertimeline.

365   See Book II on Universal Ideology, Chapter One on Social Psychology.
366   Wikipedia, "Militarism," last modified December 23, 2018, https://en.wikipedia.org/wiki/Militarism.
367   Wikipedia, "Militarism," last modified December 23, 2018.
368   Michio Fujimura, "Yamagata Aritomo," last edited January 28, 2020, http://www.britannica.com/biography/Yamagata-Aritomo#ref57116.
369   "World War I United States Military Records, 1917 to 1918," Family Search, last edited February 25, 2020, https://familysearch.org/wiki/en/World_War_I_United_States_Military_Records,_1917_to_1918.
370   Wikipedia, "Banana Wars," last modified January 14, 2019, https://en.wikipedia.org/wiki/Banana_Wars.
371   "USMC Small Wars Manual (1940)," USMC, https://archive.org/details/UsmcSmallWarsManual1940Reprinted1990.
372   Authors' italics.
373   Small Wars Manual. United States Marine Corps. 1990. Section II, Strategy, p. 11.
374   Wikipedia, "Business Plot," last modified Dec. 9, 2018, https://en.wikipedia.org/wiki/Business_Plot.
375   Wikipedia, "New Look (policy)," last modified December 22, 2018, https://en.wikipedia.org/wiki/New_Look_%28policy%29.
376   Wikipedia, "Formosa Resolution of 1955," last modified December 3, 2018, https://en.wikipedia.org/wiki/Formosa_Resolution_of_1955.
377   "Dwight D. Eisenhower Farewell Address (January 17, 1961)," Wayback Machine, https://web.archive.org/web/20080513222105/http://www.usa-presidents.info/speeches/eisenhowerfarewell.html.
378   Wikipedia, "Military-industrial complex," last modified January16, 2019, https://en.wikipedia.org/wiki/Military%E2%80%93industrial_complex.
379   Daniel Guerin, *Fascism and Big Business* (New York, Pathfinder Press, 1973). https://libcom.org/files/Daniel%20Guerin-Fascism%20and%20Big%20BusinessPathfinder%20Press%20(2000).pdf.
380   Wikipedia, "United Nations Securing Council Resolution 84," last modified December 16, 2018, https://en.wikipedia.org/wiki/United_Nations_Security_Council_Resolution_84.
381   Wikipedia, "Korean War," last modified January 16, 2019.

https://en.wikipedia.org/wiki/Korean_War.
382   Wikipedia, "Gulf of Tonkin incident," last modified, December 27, 2018, https://en.wikipedia.org/wiki/Gulf_of_Tonkin_incident.
383   Wikipedia, "Gulf of Tonkin Resolution," last modified October 21, 2018, https://en.wikipedia.org/wiki/Gulf_of_Tonkin_Resolution.
384   Wikipedia, "Tet Offensive," last modified January 15, 2019, https://en.wikipedia.org/wiki/Tet_Offensive.
385   Wikipedia, "Vietnam War casualties," last modified January 8, 2019, https://en.wikipedia.org/wiki/Vietnam_War_casualties.
386   Wikipedia, "Vietnam War," last modified January 13, 2019, https://en.wikipedia.org/wiki/Vietnam_War. 378 "Oil Embargo, 1973–1974," US Office of the Historian, https://history.state.gov/milestones/19691976/oil-embargo.
387   Michel Crozier, Samuel P. Huntington, an Joji Watnuki, *The Crisis of Democracy* (New York: New York University Press, 1975), 65.
388   Wikipedia, "Marxism-Leninism," last modified January 16, 2019, https://en.wikipedia.org/wiki/Marxism%E2%80%93Leninism.
389   Palash Ghosh, "How Many People Did Joseph Stalin Kill?" International Business Times, March 5, 2013, https://www.ibtimes.com/how-many-people-did-joseph-stalin-kill-1111789.
390   History.com Editors, "Fall of the Soviet Union," History, last modified January 3, 2019, https://www.history.com/topics/cold-war/fall-of-soviet-union. 382 Wikipedia, "Russian oligarch," last modified January 13, 2019, https://en.wikipedia.org/wiki/Russian_oligarch.
391   Wikipedia, "Mikhail Khodorkovsky," last modified January 11, 2019, https://en.wikipedia.org/wiki/Mikhail_Khodorkovsky.
392   Stanley Reed, "$50 Billion Rewarded in Breakup of Yukos," New York Times, July 28, 2014, https://www.nytimes.com/2014/07/29/business/international/yukos-shareholders-awarded-about-50-billionin-court-ruling.html.
393   Thomas P. M. Barnett, *The Pentagon's New Map: War and Peace in the Twenty-First Century* (New York: G. P. Putnam's Sons, 2005), 5.
394   Wikipedia, "Carter Doctrine," last modified December 7, 2018, https://en.wikipedia.org/wiki/Carter_Doctrine.
395   "Jimmy Carter State of the Union Address 1980," The Jimmy Carter Presidential Library and Museum, https://www.jimmycarterlibrary.gov/assets/documents/speeches/su80jec.phtml.
396   "General Charles Wald: Dial 1-800-The U.S. Military to solve

your oil dependency issues," Peak Energy and Resources, Climate Change, and the Preservation of Knowledge, energyskeptic, January 18, 2016, http://energyskeptic.com/2016/general-charles-wald-dial-1-800-the-u-s-military-to-solve-your-oildependency-issues/.

397   "Peak Oil - 2000-2004," GlobalSecurity.org, accessed February 27, 2020, https://www.globalsecurity.org/military/intro/oil-1.htm.

398   Ron Patterson, "JODI Data and Giant Field Depletion," Peak Oil Barrel, September 23, 2015, http://peakoilbarrel.com/jodi-data-and-giant-field-depletion/.

399   Ron Patterson, "A Closer Look at Saudi Arabia," Peak Oil Barrel, May 27, 2014, http://peakoilbarrel.com/closer-look-saudi-arabia/.

400   James Cordahi and Andy Critchlow, "Kuwait Oil Field, World's Second Largest 'Exhausted,'" Resilience, November 15, 2005, http://www.resilience.org/stories/2005-11-15/kuwait-oil-field-worlds-secondlargest-exhausted.

401   "The Strategic Importance of the Caspian Sea," Stratfor Worldview Video, May 19, 2014, https://www.stratfor.com/video/strategic-importance-caspian-sea.

402   Zbigniew Brzezinski, *The Grand Chessboard: American Primacy and its Geostrategic Imperatives* (New York, Basic Books, 1997).

403   Zbigniew Brzezinski, "a Geostrategy for Eurasia," Foreign Affairs, September/October 1997, https://www.foreignaffairs.com/articles/asia/1997-09-01/geostrategy-eurasia.

404   Zbigniew Brzezinski, *The Grand Chessboard: American Primacy and its Geostrategic Imperatives* (New York: Basic Books, 1998), 125.

405   Zbigniew Brzezinski, *The Grand Chessboard: American Primacy and its Geostrategic Imperatives*, 39-40.

406   Zbigniew Brzezinski, *The Grand Chessboard: American Primacy and its Geostrategic Imperatives*,Brzezinski, 35-36.

407   Zbigniew Brzezinski, T*he Grand Chessboard: American Primacy and its Geostrategic Imperatives*,Brzezinski, 211.

408   "Rebuilding America's Defenses: Strategy, Forces and Resources for a New Century," The Project for the New American Century, Sept, 2000, http://cryptome.org/rad.htm.

409   "Rebuilding America's Defenses: Strategy, Forces and Resources for a New Century," A Report of the Project for the New American Century, September 2000, https://cryptome.org/rad.htm.

410   Michael C. Ruppert, *Crossing the Rubicon: The Decline of the*

American Empire at the End of the Age of Oil (Gabriola Island, Canada: New Society Publishers, 2004), 573.
411   Justin Lahart, "The Crash of 2002," CNN Money, July 22, 2002, http://money.cnn.com/2002/07/19/news/crash2002/.
412   Wikipedia, "Energy Task Force," last modified October 22, 2018, https://en.wikipedia.org/wiki/Energy_Task_Force.
413   "National Energy Policy: Report of the National Energy Policy Development Group," May 2001, https://www.nrc.gov/docs/ML0428/ML04280056.pdf.
414   Michael Abramowitz and Steven Mufson, "Papers Detail Industry's Role in Cheney's Energy Report," Washington Post, July 18, 2007, http://www.washingtonpost.com/wpdyn/content/article/2007/07/17/AR2007071701987.html?hpid=topnews.
415   Michael C. Ruppert, *Crossing the Rubicon: The Decline of the American Empire at the End of the Age of Oil*, 575.
416   Wikipedia, "Secure Communities," last modified Januaary 12, 2019, http://en.wikipedia.org/wiki/Secure_Communities_and_administrative_immigration_policies.
417   Wikipedia, "Secure Communities," last modified Januaary 12, 2019.
418   The Editorial Board, "The 'Secure Communities' Illusion," New York Times, September 5, 2014, http://www.nytimes.com/2014/09/06/opinion/the-secure-communities-illusion.html.
419   The Editorial Board, "The 'Secure Communities' Illusion," New York Times, September 5, 2014.
420   Ted Hesson, Trump Deportations lag behind Obama levels," Politico, August 8, 2017, http://www.politico.com/story/2017/08/08/trump-deportations-behind-obama-levels-241420.
421   Nick Wing, 12 Unbelievable Things People Have Actually Been Arrested and Thrown in Jail For," Huffpost, December 6, 2017, https://www.huffingtonpost.com/2014/10/04/unbelievable-arrest-jail-crimes_n_5921234.html.
422   Natasha Lennard, "Report: Unpaid rent can lead to arrest in Arkansas," Salon, February 8, 2013, https://www.salon.com/2013/02/08/report_unpaid_rent_can_lead_to_arrest_in_arkansas/.
423   "A Living Death: Life Without Parole for Nonviolent Offenses," ACLU, 2013, https://www.aclu.org/report/living-death-life-without-parole-nonviolent-offenses.

424   "The FBI Can Do What?" Privacy SOS, accessed March 3, 2020, https://privacysos.org/degraded_standards/.
425   J.D. Tuccille, "When Cops Don't Need a Warrant to Crash Through Your Door," Reason, July 31, 2013, http://reason.com/archives/2013/07/31/cops-dont-necessarily-need-a-warrant-to.
426   "National Strategy for Homeland Security," Office of Homeland Security, July, 2002, https://www.dhs.gov/sites/default/files/publications/nat-strat-hls-2002.pdf.
427   Chris Nichols, "MOSTLY TRUE: Odds of fatal terror attack in U.S. by a refugee? 3.6 Billion to 1," PolitiFact California, February 1, 2017, Ibid. http://www.politifact.com/california/statements/2017/feb/01/tedlieu/odds-youll-be-killed-terror-attack-america-refugee/.
428   Wikipedia, "Militarization of police," last modified January 14, 2019, https://en.wikipedia.org/wiki/Militarization_of_police.
429   "What police agencies need to know about Executive Order 13688," PoliceOne.com October 7, 2015, https://www.policeone.com/grants/articles/16020006-What-police-agencies-need-to-know-aboutExecutive-Order-13688/.
430   Peter B. Kraska, "Militarization and Policing – Its Relevance to 21st Century Police," Policing Advance Access, December 13, 2007, http://cjmasters.eku.edu/sites/cjmasters.eku.edu/files/21stmilitarization.pdf.
431   "War Comes Home: The Excessive Militarization of American Policing," ACLU, June, 2014, https://www.aclu.org/sites/default/files/assets/jus14-warcomeshome-report-web-rel1.pdf.
432   Jonathan Wolfe, "Militarization of American police: Skyrocketing SWAT team raids causing needless deaths of innocent suspects," Signs of the Times, April 1, 2014, http://www.sott.net/article/276655Militarization-of-American-police-Skyrocketing-SWAT-team-raids-causing-needless-deaths-of-innocentsuspects.
433   Kevin P. Craver, "Police snatch up military gear: Sparks debate over 'police militarization,'" Northwest Herald, January 8, 2015. http://www.nwherald.com/2014/06/19/police-snatch-up-military- gear/a5e-58gm/?page=3.
434   "War Comes Home: The Excessive Militarization of American Policing," June, 2014.
435   Glenn Greenwald, "The Militarization of U.S. Police: Finally Dragged Into The Light By the Horrors of Ferguson," The Intercept, https://firstlook.org/theintercept/2014/08/14/militarization-u-s-po-

lice-draggedlight-horrors-ferguson/.
436   Faith Karimi, "Dallas sniper attack: 5 officers killed, suspect identified," CNN, July 9, 2016, http://www.cnn.com/2016/07/08/us/philando-castile-alton-sterling-protests/.
437   "What Happened in Ferguson," *New York Times*, August 10, 2015, https://www.nytimes.com/interactive/2014/08/13/us/ferguson-missouri-town-under-siege-after-policeshooting.html?_r=0.
438   Rania Khalek, "8 Stories Buried by the Corporate Media That You Need to Know About," AlterNet, December 15 2011, http://www.alternet.org/story/153455/8_stories_buried_by_the_corporate_media_that_you_need_to_know _about?page=0%2C1.
439   Rich Gardella, "VA Whistleblowers Say They Faced Retaliation for Reporting Problems," NBC News, July 8, 2014, http://www.nbcnews.com/storyline/va-hospital-scandal/va-whistleblowers-say-they-faced-retaliation-reporting-problems-n150626.
440   Tim Wening, "Military body parts found in landfill," NBC 24News, November 10, 2011, http://www.nbc24.com/news/story.aspx?id=684995#.VG5FdckkWdw.
441   Curt Devine, "Bad VA care may have killed more than 1,000 veterans, senator's report says," CNN June 24, 2014, http://www.cnn.com/2014/06/24/us/senator-va-report/.
442   Wikipedia, "Casualties of the Iraq War," last modified January 16, 2019, https://en.wikipedia.org/wiki/Casualties_of_the_Iraq_War.
443   See Book II Ideology, Chapter One on Social Psychology.
444   Timothy B. Lee, "Sen. Obama warned about Patriot Act abuses. President Obama proved him right," Washington Post, August 2, 2013, http://www.washingtonpost.com/blogs/the-switch/wp/2013/08/02/senobama-warned-about-patriot-act-abuses-president-obama-proved-him-right/.
445   "Obama, in Europe, signs Patriot Act extension," MSNBC, May 27, 2011, http://www.nbcnews.com/id/43180202/ns/us_news-security/t/obama-europe-signs-patriot-act-extension/#.XIIC3ahKiUk.
446   Natasha Lennard, "Obama signs NDAA 2014, indefinite detention remains," http://www.salon.com/2013/12/27/obama_signs_ndaa_2014_indefinite_detention_remains/.
447   Natasha Lennard, "Obama signs NDAA 2014, indefinite detention remains."
448   "Cruz: NDAA Does Not Ensure our Most Basic Rights as Amer-

ican Citizensare Protected," US Senator for Texas, Ted Cruz, December 19, 2013, https://www.cruz.senate.gov/?p=press_release&id=733.

449 "New Bill Authorizes Rendition of American Citizens Living Within the United States to Other Countries for Torture," Washington Blog, December 21, 2011, http://www.washingtonsblog.com/2011/12/newbill-authorizes-rendition-of-american-citizens-living-within-the-united-states-to-other-countries-fortorture.html.

450 Naomi Wolf, "Congress Signed Its Own Arrest Warrants," RSN, January 2, 2012, https://readersupportednews.org/opinion2/275-42/9236-focus-naomi-wolf-ndaa-congress-signed-its-ownarrest-warrants.

451 Jim Powell, "Obama's Plan to Seize Control Of Our Economy And Lives," Forbes, April 29, 2012, https://www.forbes.com/sites/jimpowell/2012/04/29/obamas-plan-to-seize-control-of-our-economy-an-our-lives/#6885b)a42eep.

452 Jim Powell, "Obama's Plan To Seize Control Of Our Economy And Our Lives," Forbes, April 29, 2012, http://www.forbes.com/sites/jimpowell/2012/04/29/obamas-plan-to-seize-control-of-our-economy-and-ourlives/.

453 William Rivers Pitt, "Who Needs Republicans?" Truthout, November 14, 2014, https://truthout.org/articles/who-needs-republicans/.

454 William Rivers Pitt, "Who Needs Republicans?" November 14, 2014.

455 Theodore Shoebat, "ISIS Leader Admits: We Are Being Funded By the Obama Administration," Shoebat.com, February 20, 2015, http://shoebat.com/2015/02/20/isis-leader-admits-funded-obamaadministration/.

456 "President Obama, January 26, 2009 Memo to Executive branch officials," http://www.hightowerlowdown.org/node/3402#.VGuirMkkWdw.

457 Thomas Barnett, The Pentagon's New Map: War and Peace in the 21st Century, 42.

458 Patrick Martin, "Capitalism and Global Poverty: Two Billion Poor, One Billion Hungry," Global Research, July 25, 2014, http://www.globalresearch.ca/capitalism-and-global-poverty-two-billion-poorone-billion-hungry/5393262.

459 Patrick Martin, "Capitalism and Global Poverty: Two Billion Poor One Billion Hungry," Global Research, July 25, 2014.

460 See Chapter One: American Capitalists in the Global Economy.
461 As an aside, the debate that raged among the people of Islam as to how to gain their liberty from their enforced subservience gave rise to a controversial book published in 1889 by an Egyptian lawyer, Qasim Amin entitled The Liberation of Women. In his book, Asim argued that emancipation from foreign domination was impossible without the emancipation of women. The book remains controversial to this day, even though it is 100% correct in its premise.
462 Wikipedia, "Sykes-Picot Agreement," last modified January 4, 2019, https://en.wikipedia.org/wiki/Sykes%E2%80%93Picot_Agreement.
463 Wikipedia, "Timeline of Middle Eastern history," last modified December 17, 2018, https://en.wikipedia.org/wiki/Timeline_of_Middle_Eastern_history.
464 Martin Kramer, "Fundamentalist Islam at Large: The Drive for Power," Middle East Quarterly, June 1996, https://www.meforum.org/304/fundamentalist-islam-at-large-the-drive-for-power.
465 Wikipedia, "Third Anglo-Afghan War," last modified December 20, 2018, https://en.wikipedia.org/wiki/Third_Anglo-Afghan_War.
466 Stanley Weiss, "In Egypt, Seeing the Muslim Brotherhood for What It Is," Huffpost, March 2, 2015, https://www.huffingtonpost.com/stanley-weiss/in-egypt-seeing-the-musli_b_6786356.html.
467 Wikipedia, "Muslim Brotherhood in Egypt," last modified December 31, 2018, https://en.wikipedia.org/wiki/Muslim_Brotherhood_in_Egypt.
468 Wikipedia, "Fada'iyan-e Islam," last modified November 8, 2018, https://en.wikipedia.org/wiki/Fada%27iyan-e_Islam.
469 Martin Kramer, "Fundamentalist Islam at Large: The Drive for Power," June 1996.
470 Wikipedia, "Jamaat-e-Islami," last modified Dec. 29, 2018, https://en.wikipedia.org/wiki/Jamaat-eIslami.
471 Martin Kramer, "Fundamentalist Islam at Large: The Drive for Power," Middle East Quarterly, June 1996.
472 Wikipedia, "Jamaat-e-Islami," last modified Dec. 29, 2018.
473 Wikipedia, "Abul A'la Maududi," last modified Jan. 8, 2019, https://en.wikipedia.org/wiki/Abul_A%27la_Maududi.
474 Wikipedia, "Sayyid Qutb," last modified January 14, 2019, https://en.wikipedia.org/wiki/Sayyid_Qutb.."
475 Brian R. Farme, Understanding Radical Islam (New York:

Peter Land Publishing, 2008), 86.

476   Martin Kramer, "Fundamentalist Islam at Large: The Drive for Power," Middle East Quarterly, June 1996.

477   Wikipedia, "National Transitional Council," last modified September 30, 2018, https://en.wikipedia.org/wiki/National_Transitional_Council.

478   Wikipedia, "Muammar Gaddafi," last modified January 3, 2019, https://en.wikipedia.org/wiki/Muammar_Gaddafi.

479   Colin Freeman, "Libya four years on from Colonel Gaddafi's death," The Telegraph, November 5, 2015, http://www.telegraph.co.uk/news/worldnews/africaandindianocean/libya/11976639/Special-report-InsideLibya-four-years-on-from-Gaddafis-death.html.

480   "Seizure of Libyan oil terminals prompts call for military action," The Guardian, accessed March 6, 2020, https://www.theguardian.com/world/2016/sep/12/key-libya-oil-terminals-seized-by-rival-government-sparking-call-for-military-action.

481   Sayyid Ruhullah Musawi Khomeni, "The Form of Islamic Government," Islamic Government: Governance of the Jurist, Al-Islam.org, https://www.al-islam.org/islamic-government-governance-jurist-ayatullah-sayyid-imam-ruhallah-musawi-khomeni/form-islamic.

482   Martin Kramer, "Fundamentalist Islam at Large: The Drive for Power," Middle East Quarterly, June 1996.

483   "Iran-Iraq War (1980-1988)," GlobalSecurity.org, accessed March 3, 2020, https://www.globalsecurity.org/military/world/war/iran-iraq.htm.

484   Wikipedia, "Saur Revolution," last modified January 14, 2019, https://en.wikipedia.org/wiki/Saur_Revolution.

485   "History of Afghanistan," accesssed March 3, 2020, http://www.historyworld.net/wrldhis/PlainTextHistories.asp?ParagraphID=itc.

486   "History of Afghanistan," accesssed March 3, 2020.

487   Wikipedia, "Mohammed Omar," last modified January 8, 2019, https://en.wikipedia.org/wiki/Mohammed_Omar.

488   Wikipedia, "Mohammed Omar," last modified January 8, 2019.

489   Wikipedia, "Hamid Karzai," last modified January 3, 2019, https://en.wikipedia.org/wiki/Hamid_Karzai.

490   Paul Sperry, "We're Training the Taliban to Kill Us and Take Back Afghanistan," New York Post, August 9, 2014, https://nypost.

com/2014/08/09/were-training-the-taliban-to-kill-us-and-take-back-afghanistan/.
491   "Hunting Bin Laden," PBS Frontline, accessed March 3. 2020,https://www.pbs.org/wgbh/pages/frontline/shows/binladen/.
492   Wikipedia, "Faisal of Saudi Arabia," last modified January 15, 2019, https://en.wikipedia.org/wiki/Faisal_of_Saudi_Arabia.
493   Wikipedia, "Abdullah Yusuf Azzam," last modified December 6, 2018, https://en.wikipedia.org/wiki/Abdullah_Yusuf_Azzam.
494   Wikipedia, "Invasion of Kuwait," last modified January 18, 2019, https://en.wikipedia.org/wiki/Invasion_of_Kuwait.
495   Wikipedia, "Bacha bazi," last modified January 14, 2019, https://en.wikipedia.org/wiki/Bacha_bazi.
496   Wikipedia, "Hamid Karzai," last modified January 3, 2019, https://en.wikipedia.org/wiki/Hamid_Karzai.
497   "EYES ON IRAQ: In Cheney's Words: The Administration's Case for Removing Saddam Hussein," New York Times, August 27, 2002, http://www.nytimes.com/2002/08/27/world/eyes-iraq-cheney-s-wordsadministration-case-for-removing-saddam-hussein.html?src=pm&_r=0.
498   "Experts doubt Iraq, al-Qaeda terror link." CBC News, November 1, 2002, http://www.cbc.ca/news/world/experts-doubt-iraq-al-qaeda-terror-link-1.343424.
499   "Post 9-11," see Historical Timeline 2002 War Doubts, http://www.investigatingpower.org/timelines/911/.
500   "President Bush Delivers State of the Union." The White House, January 28, 2003, https://georgewbushwhitehouse.archives.gov/news/releases/2003/01/20030128-19.html.
501   Douglas Jehl, "Report Warned Bush Team About Intelligence Doubts," New York Times, November 6, 2005, http://www.nytimes.com/2005/11/06/politics/report-warned-bush-team-about-intelligence-doubts.html.
502   Martin Chulov and Helen Pidd, "Curveball: How US was duped by Iraqi fanatasist looking to topple Saddam," The Guardian, February 15, 2011, https://www.theguardian.com/world/2011/feb/15/curveball-iraqifantasist-cia-saddam.
503   Angelo Young, "And the Winner For the Most Iraq War Contracts Is ... KBR, With $39.5 Billion In a Decade," International Business Times, March 19, 2013, http://www.ibtimes.com/winner-most-

iraq-warcontracts-kbr-395-billion-decade-1135905.

504   Charles Lewis, "False Pretenses," The Center for Public Integrity, January 23, 2008, https://www.publicintegrity.org/2008/01/23/5641/false-pretenses.

505   Rebecca Leung, "Abuse Of Iraqi POWs by GIs Probed," 60 Minutes, April 27, 2004, http://www.cbsnews.com/news/abuse-of-iraqi-pows-by-gis-probed/.

506   Seymour M. Hersh, "Torture as Abu Ghraib," The New Yorker, May 10, 2004, http://www.newyorker.com/magazine/2004/05/10/torture-at-abu-ghraib.

507   Thomas P. M. Barnett, *The Pentagon's New Map: War and Peace in the Twenty-First Century* (New York, G. P. Putnam's Sons, 2004).

508   Thomas P. M. Barnett, *The Pentagon's New Map: War and Peace in the Twenty-First Century*, 25.

509   Thomas P. M. Barnett, *The Pentagon's New Map: War and Peace in the Twenty-First Century*, 25.

510   Wikipedia, "Timeline of the Iraq War troop surge of 2007," last modified September 25, 2018, https://en.wikipedia.org/wiki/Timeline_of_the_Iraq_War_troop_surge_of_2007.

511   Scott Shane, David Johnson, and James Risen, "Secret U.S. Endorsement of Severe Interrogations," New York Times, October 4, 2007, http://query.nytimes.com/gst/fullpage.html?res=990CE3DD1130F937A-35753C1A9619C8B63&pagewanted=all%20%3E%205753C1A9619C-8B63&sec=&spon=&pagewanted=1.

512   David Barstow, "Behind TV Analysts, Pentagon's Hidden Hand," New York Times, April 20, 2008, https://www.nytimes.com/2008/04/20/us/20generals.html.

513   Tony Capaccio, "KBR gets no-bid contract to support Army in Iraq," Chron, May 6, 2010, http://www.chron.com/business/article/KBR-gets-no-bid-contract-to-support-Army-in-Iraq-1702336.php.

514   "Obama Announces Death of Osama bin Laden," History, accessed March 6, 2020, https://www.history.com/topics/21st-century/obama-announces-death-of-osama-bin-laden-video.

515   Osama bin Laden and others, "Jihad Against Jews and Crusaders," World Islamic Front, February 23, 1998, https://fas.org/irp/world/para/docs/980223-fatwa.htm.

516   Rahimullah Yusufzai, "Face to face with Osama," The Guardian, September 25, 2001, https://www.theguardian.com/world/2001/

sep/26/afghanistan.terrorism3.
517   John Pilger, "Squeezed to death, The Guardian, March 3, 2000, https://www.theguardian.com/theguardian/2000/mar/04/weekend7.weekend9.
518   Anup Shah, "Effects of Iraq Sanctions," Global Issues, October 2, 2005, http://www.globalissues.org/article/105/effects-of-sanctions.
519   Anup Shah, "Effects of Iraq Sanctions," Global Issues, October 2, 2005.
520   Wikipedia, "Bill Richardson," last edited January 24, 2020, https://en.wikipedia.org/wiki/Bill_Richardson.
521   Osama bin Laden and others, "Jihad Against Jews and Crusaders," February 23, 1998.
522   For a full transcript of bin Laden's speech see http://www.aljazeera.com/archive/2004/11/200849163336457223.html.
523   544 "Bin Laden Claims Responsibility for 9/11," Fox News, October 30, 2004, https://www.foxnews.com/story/bin-laden-claims-responsibility-for-9-11.
524   Wikipedia, "September 11, 2007 Osama bin Laden video," last modified May 11, 2018, https://en.wikipedia.org/wiki/September_11,_2007_Osama_bin_Laden_video.
525   Bill Adair, "In 2008, Obama vowed to kill Osama bin Laden," PolitiFact, May 1, 2011, http://www.politifact.com/truth-o-meter/article/2011/may/01/obama-vowed-kill-osama-bin-laden/.
526   Enjoli Francis, Obama bin Laden found in 2009? UCLA Geography Class Project Was on Right Track," ABC News, May 3, 2011, http://abcnews.go.com/US/osama-bin-laden-found-2009-ucla-geographyclass/story?id=13520445.
527   See The Untold Story of Western Civilization, Volume III, pages 238-242 for a description of the origins of the Shia/Sunni conflict.
528   "How were the modern nation-states of the Middle East created?" Global Connections: the Middle East, PBS.org, accessed March 3, 2020, http://www.pbs.org/wgbh/globalconnections/mideast/questions/nations/.
529   Zbigniew Brzezinski, *The Grand Chessboard: American Primacy and its Geostrategic Imperatives*, 25.
530   "Interview with Turabi," Le Figaro, January 25, 1994, https://www.bing.com/news/search?q=turabi&go=S0BF4359344556893CDC939DA3E190.

531   "Unheeded Warnings: The Lost Reports of the Congressional Task Force on Terrorism and Unconventional Warfare, Volume I: Islamic Terrorism and the West," edited by Richard J. Leitner and Peter M. Leitner, (Washington, Crossbow Books, 2007), 485.
532   Norman Byrd, "ISIS Slaughter House Massacre: 'Worst Ever' Video Shows At Least 24 Prisoners Hung From Meat Hooks in Islamic Holy Day Execution," Inquisitr, September 13, 2016, http://www.inquisitr.com/3506406/isis-slaughterhouse-massacre-worst-ever-video-at-least-24-prisoners-hung-from-meat-hooks-in-islamic-holy-day-execution/.
533   Ron Nixon, "US Groups Helped Nurture Arab Uprisings," New York Times, April 14, 2011, http://www.nytimes.com/2011/04/15/world/15aid.html?_r=0.
534   "Tunisia: the protests continue," In Defense of Marxism, January 11, 2011, http://www.marxist.com/tunisiaprotests-continue.htm.
535   Wikipedia, "Islamic Salvation Front," last modified January 14, 2019, https://en.wikipedia.org/wiki/Islamic_Salvation_Front.
536   "Unrest continues in Syria," albawaba news, March 22, 2011, http://www.albawaba.com/mainheadlines/unrest-continues-syria.
537   "Syrian cabinet resigns amid unrest," Aljazeera, March 29, 2011, http://www.aljazeera.com/news/middleeast/2011/03/201132975114399138.html.
538   "Syria: Revolution 2011 - ," Arab Spring: a Research and Study Guide, Cornell University Library, December, 2010, http://guides.library.cornell.edu/c.php?g=31688&p=200753.
539   Wikipedia, "Syrian Democratic Forces," last modified January 15, 2019, https://en.wikipedia.org/wiki/Syrian_Democratic_Forces.
540   Wikipedia, "Southern Front (Syrian rebel group," last modified January 1, 2019, https://en.wikipedia.org/wiki/Southern_Front_(Syrian_rebel_group).
541   "Syrian War: Who are Jabhat Fateh al-Sham?" BBC News, August 1, 2016, http://www.bbc.com/news/world-middle-east-36924000.
542   Wikipedia, "Ahrar al-Sham," last modified January 13, 2019, https://en.wikipedia.org/wiki/Ahrar_al-Sham.
543   Wikipedia, "Salafi movement," last modified January 24, 2020 https://en.wikipedia.org/wiki/Salafi_movement.
544   "The Historical Roots and Stages in the Development of ISIS," Crethi Plethi, Winter, 2014, http://www.crethiplethi.com/the-histor-

ical-roots-and-stages-in-the-development-of-isis/islamiccountries/syria-islamic-countries/2015/.
545	Wikipedia, "American led intervention in the Syrian Civil War," last modified Jan. 18, 2019, https://en.wikipedia.org/wiki/American-led_intervention_in_the_Syrian_Civil_War.
546	David Hudson, "President Obama: "We Will Degrade and Ultimately Destroy ISIL," the White House, September 10, 2014, https://www.whitehouse.gov/blog/2014/09/10/president-obama-we-will-degrade-andultimately-destroy-isil.
547	Martha Raddatz, Luis Martinez and Lee Ferran, "Airstrikes 'Successful' Against ISIS Targets in Syria, US Military Says," ABC News, September 23, 2014, http://abcnews.go.com/International/us-airstrikes-syria/story?id=25686031.
548	"Airstrikes Hit ISIL Terrorists in Syria, Iraq," US Department of Defense, September 30, 2015, http://www.defense.gov/News/Article/Article/621107/airstrikes-hit-isil-terrorists-in-syria-iraq.
549	Gareth Porter, "How America Armed Terrorists in Syria," The American Conservative, June 22, 2017, https://www.theamericanconservative.com/articles/how-america-armed-terrorists-in-syria/.
550	Mike Giglio, "The End of the Free Syrian Army?" Buzzfeed, December 12, 2013, https://www.buzzfeed.com/mikegiglio/the-end-of-the-free-syrianarmy?utm_term=.pnQ0B5RWN#.bkBjaonDg.
551	Elliott Abrams, "Chemical warfare continues in Syria, unpunished," Quartz, May, 26, 2015, https://qz.com/412181/chemical-warfare-continues-in-syria-unpunished/.
552	"Syria's opposition: Down but not yet out," The Economist, October 10, 2015, https://www.economist.com/middle-east-and-africa/2015/10/10/down-but-not-yet-out.
553	Michael D. Shear, Helene Cooper and Eric Schmitt, "Obama Administration Ends Effort to Train Syrians to Combat ISIS," New York Times, October 9, 2015, http://www.nytimes.com/2015/10/10/world/middleeast/pentagon-program-islamic-state-syria.html?&hp&action=click&pgtype=Homepage&module=first-column-region&region=top- news&WT.nav=top-news&_r=0.
554	Murtaza Hussain, Marwan Hisham, "U.S. Strategy To Fight ISIS Has Set Off A New Conflict in Syria," The Intercept, August 31, 2016, https://theintercept.com/2016/08/31/u-s-strategy-to-fight-isis-has-set-off-a-new-conflict-in-syria/.

555   Murtaza Hussain, Marwan Hisham, "U.S. Strategy To Fight ISIS Has Set Off A New Conflict in Syria," August 31, 2016.
556   "Russia graphically warns Obama to stay out of Syria," blastingnews, October 6, 2016, http://us.blastingnews.com/news/2016/10/russia-graphically-warns-obama-to-stay-out-of-syria001166659.html.
557   Wikiedia, "Battle of Raqqa (2017)," last edited April 3, 2020, https://en.wikipedia.org/wiki/Battle_of_Raqqa_(2017).
558   "Launching of Operations to Liberate Final ISIS Strongholds in Syria," Press Release, US Department of State, May 1, 2018, https://www.state.gov/launching-of-operations-to-liberate-final-isis-strongholds-in-syria/.
559   The timeline of the Syrian War from December 2016 to January 2019 was excerpted from Wikipedia, "Timeline of the Syrian Civil War," last modified January 22, 2020, https://en.wikipedia.org/wiki/Timeline_of_the_Syrian_Civil_War.
560   "Syria's opposition: Down but not yet out," The Economist, October 10, 2015, https://www.economist.com/middle-east-and-africa/2015/10/10/down-but-not-yet-out.
561   Wikipedia, "Syrian Civil War," last modified January 24, 2020, https://en.wikipedia.org/wiki/Syrian_Civil_War.
562   Rawan Arar, Lisel Hintz and Kelsey P. Norman, "The real refugee crisis is in the Middle East, not Europe," The Washington Post, May 14, 2016, https://www.washingtonpost.com/news/monkeycage/wp/2016/05/14/the-real-refugee-crisis-is-in-the-middle-east-not-europe/.
563   Rawan Arar, Lisel Hintz and Kelsey P. Norman, "The real refugee crisis is in the Middle East, not Europe," May 14, 2016.
564   Richard Wike, Bruce Stokes and Katie Simmons, "Europeans Fear Wave of Refugees Will Mean More Terrorism, Fewer Jobs," Pew Research Center, July 11, 2016, http://www.pewglobal.org/2016/07/11/europeans-fear-wave-of-refugees-will-mean-more-terrorism-fewer-jobs/.
565   Dan Kopf, "Which Countries Have the Most Immigrants?" Priceonomics, accessed March 3, 2020, https://priceonomics.com/which-countries-have-the-most-immigrants/.
566   Dan Kopf, "Which Countries Have the Most Immigrants?" accessed March 3, 2020.
567   Dan Kopf, "Which Countries Have the Most Immigrants?" accessed March 3, 2020.
568   Elizabeth Scalia, "Witness report: Father Jacques Hamel's last

moments," Aleteia, October 4, 2016, https://aleteia.org/2016/10/04/witnesses-to-martyrdom-father-hamels-last-moments/.
569   Samantha Neal, "Refugee Crisis Fuels European Fears on Terrorism," Huffpost, July 12, 2016, http://www.huffingtonpost.com/entry/refugee-crisis-new-poll_us_5784e754e4b0ed2111d77c7b?.
570   "Fears many of 9,000 refugee children missing in Germany may have been co-opted in crime," The Telegraph, August 29, 2016, http://www.telegraph.co.uk/news/2016/08/29/fears-many-of-9000-refugeechildren-missing-in-germany-may-have/.
571   "Report warns refugee women on the move in Europe are at risk of sexual and gender-based violence," United Nations Population Fund, January 20, 2016, http://www.unfpa.org/press/report-warns-refugee-womenmove-europe-are-risk-sexual-and-gender-based-violence.
572   Liza Ramrayka, "The Quiet Crisis of Europe's Pregnant Refugees," HuffPost, June 13, 2016, http://www.huffingtonpost.com/entry/europe-pregnant-refugees_us_575eba7ce4b0ced23ca88e5e.
573   The following history of Yemen is largely taken from the following article, Brian Whitaker, "Yemen and Saudi Arabia," al-bab.com, March 25, 2015 at http://al-bab.com/blog/2015/03/yemen-and-saudi-arabia#The%20oil%20factor.
574   Wikipedia, "Operation Scorched Earth," last modified January 19, 2019, https://en.wikipedia.org/wiki/Operation_Scorched_Earth.
575   Brian Whitaker, "Yemen and Saudi Arabia."
576   "US State Department approves Saudi Arabia arms sale," BBC News, November 16, 2015, http://www.bbc.com/news/world-us-canada-34838937.
577   Natasha Mozgovaya, "U.S. Announces $60B Arms Sales to Saudi Arabia, Says 'Israel Doesn't Object,'" Haaretz, October 20, 2010, http://www.haaretz.com/israel-news/u-s-announces-60b-arms-sale-tosaudi-arabia-says-israel-doesn-t-object-1.320307.
578   *The US Army Marine Corps Counterinsurgency Field Manual: US Army Field Manual No. 3-24, Marine Corps Warfighting Publication No. 3-33.5* (Chicago: The University of Chicago Press, 2006), xiv.
579   Robert Farley, "50,000 started war without body armor," PolitiFact, February 4, 2008, http://www.politifact.com/truth-o-meter/statements/2008/feb/04/hillary-clinton/50000-started-war-without-body-armor/.
580   Wikipedia, "Mission Accomplished speech," last modified

December 22, 2018, https://en.wikipedia.org/wiki/Mission_Accomplished_speech.

581   Ken Joseph Jr., "Welcome support from Petraeus, Crocker for the Assyrian Christians of Iraq," WayBack Machine, September 13, 2007, https://web.archive.org/web/20090627020733/http://www.assistnews.net/ansarticle.asp?URL=Stories%2F2 007%2Fs07090106.htm.

582   Wikipedia, "David Petraeus," last modified February 27, 2020,, https://en.wikipedia.org/wiki/David_Petraeus.

583   *The US Army Marine Corps Counterinsurgency Field Manual: US Army Field Manual No. 3-24, Marine Corps Warfighting Publication No. 3-33.5*, xix.

584   *The US Army Marine Corps Counterinsurgency Field Manual: US Army Field Manual No. 3-24, Marine Corps Warfighting Publication No. 3-33.5*, Section 1-142.

585   Wikipedia, "Investment in post-invasion Iraq," last modified October 14 2018, https://en.wikipedia.org/wiki/Investment_in_post-invasion_Iraq.

586   Wikipedia, "Ninawa campaign," last modified October 14, 2018, https://en.wikipedia.org/wiki/Ninawa_campaign.

587   Matt Purple, "The military has lost its appetite for overseas nation-building," Rare, October 6, 2016, http://rare.us/story/the-military-has-lost-its-appetite-for-overseas-nation-building/.

588   H. A Goodman, "6,845 Americans Died and 900,000 Were Injured in Iraq and Afghanistan. Say 'No' to Obama's War," HuffPost, February 12, 2015, http://www.huffingtonpost.com/h-a-goodman/6845-americansdied-and-9_b_6667830.html.

589   MintPress News Desk, "Do The Math: Global War on Terror Has Killed 4 Million Muslims or More," MPN News, August 3, 2015, http://www.mintpressnews.com/do-the-math-global-war-on-terror-has-killed-4million-muslims-or-more/208225/.

590   Piero Scaruffi, "Wars and Casualties of the 20th and 21st Centuries," 2009, http://www.scaruffi.com/politics/massacre.html.

591   Halle, "Troops returning to face more struggles back home," PublicSource, April 15, 2012, http://publicsource.org/investigations/troops-returning-face-more-struggles-back-home.

592   Rajiv Chandrasekaren, "A Legacy of Pain and Pride," The Washington Post, March 29, 2014, http://www.washingtonpost.com/sf/national/2014/03/29/a-legacy-of-pride-and-pain/.

593   "A Dead Iraqi is just another dead Iraqi – US Troops," Daily Mail, July 13, 2007, https://www.dailymail.co.uk/news/article-468133/A-dead-Iraqi-just-dead-Iraqi--US-troops.html.
594   Chris Hedges, Laila Al-Arian, *Collateral Damage: America's War Against Iraqi Civilians* (New York, Nation Books, 2008), 89-90.
595   "A Dead Iraqi is just another dead Iraqi – US Troops," Daily Mail, July 13, 2007.
596   Chris Hedges, Laila Al-Arian, *Collateral Damage: America's War Against Iraqi Civilians*, 70.
597   Emily DePrang, "The War Comes Home: Iraq war veterans feel like they are being cast aside," Texas Observer, June 29, 2007, https://www.texasobserver.org/2537-the-war-comes-home-iraq-war-veterans-feel-they-are-being-cast-aside/.
598   Rajiv Chandrasekaren, "A Legacy of Pain and Pride," March 29, 2014.
599   "PTSD: Treatment of Soldiers Returning from the Middle East," Tree Pony, accessed March 6, 2020, http://treepony.com/ptsd-treatment-of-soldiers-returning-from-the-middle-east/.
600   "VA accused of shredding documents needed for veteran's claims," Fox News, April 18, 2016, http://www.foxnews.com/us/2016/04/18/va-accused-shredding-documents-needed-for-veteransclaims.html.
601   Jacqueline Klimas, "Disability appeals process forces some vets to wait for years," Washington Times, Janary 22, 2015, https://www.washingtontimes.com/news/2015/jan/22/veterans-wait-years-for-disabilityappeals-process/.
602   Phil McCausland, "Veterans Affairs Dept. tells Capitol Hill it won't repay underpaid GI Bill benefits recipients," November 28, 2018, https://www.nbcnews.com/news/us-news/veterans-affairs-dept-tells-congressional-staffers-itwon-t-repay-n941491.
603   "Costs of War," Watson Institute, Brown University, November, 2018, http://watson.brown.edu/costsofwar/.
604   Sharon Weinberger, "Windfalls of War: Pentagon's Competition for Contracts Abysmal Compared to Other Agencies," The Center for Public Integrity, September 2, 2011, https://www.publicintegrity.org/2011/09/02/6021/windfalls-war-pentagons-competition-contracts-abysmalcompared-other-agencies.
605   Anna Fifiled, "Contractors reap $138B from Iraq War," CNN

Business, March 19, 2013, https://www.cnn.com/2013/03/19/business/iraq-war-contractors/index.html.
606   "Winning Contractors," The Center for Public Integrity, October 30, 2003, https://publicintegrity.org/2002/10/30/5628/winning-contractors.
607   "Winning Contractors: US contractors reap the windfalls of post-war reconstruction," The Center for Public Integrity, October 30, 2003, https://www.publicintegrity.org/2003/10/30/5628/winning-contractors.
608   William D. Hartung, Stephen Miles, "Who Will Profit From the Wars in Iraq and Syria?" Huffpost, October 1, 2014, http://www.huffingtonpost.com/william-hartung/who-will-profit-from-the_b_5915794.html.
609   "Counter: Total Cost of Wars Since 2001," National Priorities Project, access March 3, 2020, https://www.nationalpriorities.org/cost-of/war/.
610   Leen Abdallah, "The Cost to End World Hunger," The Borgen Project, accessed March 3, 2020, http://borgenproject.org/the-cost-to-end-world-hunger/.
611   Grace Zhao, "How Much Does It Cost To End Global Poverty," The Borgen Project, accessed March 3, 2020, https://borgenproject.org/how-much-does-it-really-cost-to-eliminate-global-poverty/.
612   Annie Lowrey "Homeless Rates in US Held Level Amid Recession, Study Says, But Big Gains as Elusive," New York Times, December 10, 2012, https://www.nytimes.com/2012/12/10/us/homeless-ratessteady-despite-recession-hud-says.html?_r=1&.
613   "Eliminating Illiteracy / Educating Humanity," The World Game Institute, accessed March 3, 2020, http://www.unesco.org/education/tlsf/mods/theme_a/interact/www.worldgame.org/wwwproject/what05.shtml
614   Wikipedia, "List of countries by military expenditures," last modified January 20, 2019, https://en.wikipedia.org/wiki/List_of_countries_by_military_expenditures.
.615   US seeks to enforce global dominance by unleashing war on countries who oppose it – Assad," RT News, October 5, 2016, https://www.rt.com/news/361623-assad-syria-american-hegemony/.
616   Andy Kiersz, "Here Are The Only Ten States That Have More Men Than Women," Business Insider, December 4, 2013, http://www.

businessinsider.com/map-the-states-with-more-men-than-women-2013-12.
617   Robert Briffault, *The Mothers: The Matriarchal Theory of Social Origins* (Whitefish, MT: Kessinger Publishing Co., 2004), 428, Referenced at http://suppressedhistories.net/secrethistory/patriapotestas.html .
618   Wikipedia, "Kathoey," last edited February 2, 2020, https://en.wikipedia.org/wiki/Kathoey.
619   Wikipedia, "History of Homosexuality," last modified December 19, 2018, https://en.wikipedia.org/wiki/History_of_homosexuality.
620   Wikipedia, "Homosexuality in ancient Egypt," last modified January 10, 2019, https://en.wikipedia.org/wiki/Homosexuality_in_ancient_Egypt.
621   Wikipedia, "History of Homosexuality," last modified December 19, 2018.
622   "The Surprising History of Homosexuality and Homophobia," Reflections Asia, September 1, 2017, https://reflectionsasia.wordpress.com/2007/09/01/the-surprising-history-of-homosexuality-andhomophobia/.
623   Wikipedia, "Homosexuality in medieval Europe," last modified January 21, 2019, https://en.wikipedia.org/wiki/Homosexuality_in_medieval_Europe.
624   "Medieval Source Book: Peter Damian: Liber Gomorrhianus," Fordham University, January 26, 1996, http://sourcebooks.fordham.edu/halsall/source/homo-damian1.asp.
625   Wikipedia, "Homosexuality in medieval Europe," last modified January 21, 2019, https://en.wikipedia.org/wiki/Homosexuality_in_medieval_Europe.
626   "Gender Identity," Medscape, March 16, 2015, http://emedicine.medscape.com/article/917990-overview.
627   David Spiegelhalter, "Is 10% of the population really gay?" The Guardian, April 5 2015, https://www.theguardian.com/society/2015/apr/05/10-per-cent-population-gay-alfred-kinsey-statistics.
628   Wikipedia, "LGBT demographics of the United States," last modified January 21, 2019, https://en.wikipedia.org/wiki/LGBT_demographics_of_the_United_States.
629   Lori Grisham, "What does the Q in LGBTQ stand for?" USA Today, June 1, 2015, https://www.usatoday.com/story/news/nation-now/2015/06/01/lgbtq-questioning-queermeaning/26925563/.

630   Jim Edwards, "Goldman Sachs has made a chart of the generations ... and it will make the millennials shudder," Business Insider, December 5, 2015, http://www.businessinsider.com/goldman-sachs-chart-of-thegenerations-and-gen-z-2015-12?r=UK&IR=T.
631   Wikipedia, "Silent Generation," last modified January 24, 2019, https://en.wikipedia.org/wiki/Silent_Generation.
632   Wikipedia, "The Lonely Crowd," last modified April 19, 2018, https://en.wikipedia.org/wiki/The_Lonely_Crowd.
633   "Silent Generation," Life Course Associates, accessed March 3, 2020, http://www.lifecourse.com/about/method/def/silent-gen.html.
634   "The Affluent Society," The American Yawp, accessed March 3, 2020, http://www.americanyawp.com/text/26-the-affluent-society/.
635   "The Growth of Suburbia," Khan Academy, accessed March 3, 2020, https://www.khanacademy.org/humanities/ushistory/postware-ra/postwar-era/a/the-growth-of-suburbia.
636   Elinor Burkett, "Women's movement," Encyclopedia Britannica, accessed March 3, 2020, https://www.britannica.com/topic/womens-movement.
637   Wikipedia, "Me generation," last modified December 23, 2018, https://en.wikipedia.org/wiki/Me_generation.
638   Wikipedia, "Generation X," last modified January 16, 2019, https://en.wikipedia.org/wiki/Generation_X.
639   William Strauss, "What Future Awaits Today's Youth in the New Millenium," Wayback Machine, January 2012, https://web.archive.org/web/20160808195038/https://www.angelo.edu/events/university_symposium/97_St rauss.php.
640   Wikipedia, "Millennials," last modified February 28, 2020, https://en.wikipedia.org/wiki/Millennials.
641   "Employment and Unemployment Among Youth Summary," Bureau of Labor Statistics, August 16, 2019, http://www.bls.gov/news.release/youth.nr0.htm.
642   Hope Yen, "Half of new grads are jobless or unemployed," NBC News, April 24, 2012, http://www.nbcnews.com/id/47141463/ns/business-stocks_and_economy/t/half-new-grads-are-jobless-orunderemployed/.
643   Jana Kasperkevic, "Tired, poor, huddled millennials of New York earn 20% less than prior generation," The Guardian, April 25 2016, https://www.theguardian.com/us-news/2016/apr/25/new-york-mil-

lennialsgreat-depression-economic-crisis.
644   Chris York. "Millennials 'Will Earn Less Than Generation X', And They'll Spend Far More On Rent," Huffington Post, July 18, 2016, https://www.huffingtonpost.co.uk/entry/millennials-screwed_uk_578c7bc7e4b0f4bc59476263?guccounter=1&guce_referrer_us=aHR0cHM6Ly93d3cuZ29vZ2 xlLmNvbS8&guce_referrer_cs=legwVYS4vM9t7D4LwCE-sw.
645   The University of Michigan's "Monitoring the Future" study of high school seniors (conducted continually since 1975) and the American Freshman survey, conducted by UCLA's Higher Education Research Institute of new college students since 1966. Referenced at https://en.wikipedia.org/wiki/Millennials.
646   Tami Luhby, "Millennials say no to marriage," CNN Business, July 20, 2014, http://money.cnn.com/2014/07/20/news/economy/millennials-marriage/..
647   Wikipedia, "Millennials," last modified January 25, 2019, https://en.wikipedia.org/wiki/Millennials. 663 Shiv Malik, Caelainn Barr and Amanda Holpuch, US Millennials feel more working class than any other generation," The Guardian, Mar. 15, 2016, https://www.theguardian.com/world/2016/mar/15/usmillennials-feel-more-working-class-than-any-other-generation
648   Tami Luhby, "Millennials say no to marriage," CNN Business, July 20, 2014, http://money.cnn.com/2014/07/20/news/economy/millennials-marriage/. 665 "Religion Among the Millennials," Pew Research Center, Feb. 17, 2010, http://www.pewforum.org/2010/02/17/religion-among-the-millennials/.
649   "Religion Among the Millennials," Pew Research Center, February 17, 2010, http://www.pewforum.org/2010/02/17/religion-among-the-millennials/.
650   Jacob Pushter, "40% of Millennials OK with limiting speech offensive to minorities," Pew Research Center, November 20, 2015, https://www.pewresearch.org/fact-tank/2015/11/20/40-of-millennials-ok-with-limiting-speech-offensive-to-minorities/.
651   Eric Hoover, "The Millennial Muddle," The Chronicle of Higher Education, October 11, 2009, http://www.chronicle.com/article/The-Millennial-Muddle-How/48772/.
652   Magid Generational Strategies, "The First Generation of the Twenty First Century." April 30, 2012, https://

staticl.squarespace.com/static/56d7388222482e1e2c-87c683/t/56e0cdc2cf80a14684670194/1457573 327672/MagidPluralistGenerationWhitepaper.pdf.

653   "Generation Z Statistics," MediaKix, accessed March 6, 2020, http://mediakix.com/blog/the-generation-z-statistics-you-should-know/.

654   Wikipedia, "Generation Z," last modified January 25, 2019, https://en.wikipedia.org/wiki/Generation_Z.

655   The Room 241 Team, "5 Benefits of Using Cellphones in School: Smartphones as Learning Tools," Room 241, Nove,ber 9, 2012, https://education.cu-portland.edu/blog/classroom-resources/should-students-usetheir-smartphones-as-learning-tools/.

656   "Generation Z Statistics," MediaKix.

657   "Top 10 Gen 10 Questions Answered," The Center for Generational Kinetics, accessed March 6, 2020, https://genhq.com/igen-gen-z-generation-z-centennials-info/.

658   Wikipedia, "Generation Z," last modified January 25, 2019.l

659   News@Northeastern, "'Generation Z' is Entrepreneurial, Wants to Chart Its Own Future," News@Northeastern, Nov. 18, 2014, https://news.northeastern.edu/2014/11/18/generation-z-survey/.

660   Alex Williams, "Move Over, Millennials, Here Comes Generation Z," New York Times, Sept. 18, 2015, http://www.nytimes.com/2015/09/20/fashion/move-over-millennials-here-comes-generation-z.html?_r=0.

661   Stephen DuPont, "Move Over Millennials, Here Comes Generation Z: Understanding the 'New
Realists' Who Are Building the Future," Public Relations Tactics, May, 2015, http://apps.prsa.org/intelligence/Tactics/Articles/view/11057/1110/Move_Over_Millennials_Here_Comes_ Generation_Z_Unde.

662   Mark Abadi, "A millennial 'Shark Tank' entrepreneur who coaches teens for the SAT says adults don't realize what sets Gen Z apart," Business Insider, Sept. 27, 2018, https://www.businessinsider.com/sharktank-millennials-vs-gen-sat-tutor-explains-the-difference-2018-9.

663   J. Maureen Henderson, "Move Over, Millennials: Why 20-Somethings Should Fear Teens," Forbes, July 31, 2013, https://www.forbes.com/sites/jmaureenhenderson/2013/07/31/move-over-millen-

nials-whytwentysomethings-should-fear-teens/#66a1f1eb1d89.
664   Alex Williams, "Move Over, Millennials, Here Comes Generation Z," New York Times, Sept. 18, 2015.
665   Wikipedia, "Generation Z." last modified January 25, 2019.
666   The Annie E. Casey Foundation, "Generation Z Breaks Records in Education and Health Despite Growing Economic Instability of Their Families," Cision PR Newswire, June, 21, 2016, http://www.prnewswire.com/news-releases/generation-z-breaks-records-in-education-and-health-despitegrowing-economic-instability-of-their-families-300287848.html.
667   "Top 10 Gen 10 Questions Answered," The Center for Generational Kinetics. , accessed March 3, 2020.
668   Susie Bearne, "Meet Gen Z: the most progressive, conscientious and connected generation to date," campaign, May 20, 2015, https://www.campaignlive.co.uk/article/meet-gen-z-progressive-conscientiousconnected-generation-date/1347852.
669   "International Convention on the Elimination of All Forms of Racial Discrimination," United Nations Human Rights Office of the High Commissioner, January 4 1969, https://www.ohchr.org/en/professionalinterest/pages/cerd.aspx.
670   German Genealogy Society, "Researching German Speaking Ancestors," Palatines to America, accessed March 8, 2020, https://www.palam.org/links.php.
671   Wikipedia, "Caucasian race," last modified January 22, 2019, https://en.wikipedia.org/wiki/Caucasian_race.
672   Raj Bhopal, Bruce and John Usher, "The beautiful skull and Blumenbach's errors: the birth of the scientific concept of race." BMJ, December 20, 2007, https://www.bmj.com/content/335/7633/1308
673   Wikipedia, "Caucasian race," last modified January 22, 2019
674   Wikipedia, "Craniometry," last modified, November 9, 2018, https://en.wikipedia.org/wiki/Craniometry.
675   Wikipedia, "Pithecometra principle," last modified December 9, 2016, https://en.wikipedia.org/wiki/Pithecometra_principle.
676   David Hurst Thomas, *Skull Wars: Kennewick Man, Archaeology, and The Battle For Native American Identity* (New York: Basic Books, 2001), 38 – 41.
677   Alexander, Charles C. (1962). "Prophet of American Racism: Madison Grant and the Nordic Myth," Phylon 23, No. 1, 73–90, https://

www.jstor.org/stable/274146?seq=1#page_scan_tab_contents.
678 Wikipedia, "Madison Grant," last modified February 12, 2020, https://en.wikipedia.org/wiki/Madison_Grant.
679 Madison Grant, *The Passing of the Great Race* (New York: Arno Press, 1970), 46-55, See http://chnm.gmu.edu/courses/magic/plot/grant.html.
680 Wikipedia, "Madison Grant," last modified January 22, 2019, https://en.wikipedia.org/wiki/Madison_Grant.
681 Kathleen R. Arnold, ed., ABCCLIO *Anti-Immigration in the United States: A Historical Encyclopedia* (Santa Barbara, CA: Greenwood Publishing Group, 2011), 227.
682 "Madison Grant," Abagond, June 10, 2010, https://abagond.wordpress.com/2010/06/10/madison-grant/.
683 Kendra Lechtenberg, "Ask a Neuroscientist: Does a bigger brain make you smarter?" Wu Tsai Neuroscience Institute, Stanford University, May 24, 2014, https://neuroscience.stanford.edu/news/ask-neuroscientist-does-bigger-brain-make-you-smarter.
684 "6 Reasons Why Women Are Neurologically Wired to Be Leaders," The Health Loft, March 26, 2018, https://www.thehealthloft.ca/6-reasons-why-women-are-neurologically-wired-to-be-leaders/.
685 D'Vera Cohn, "Census considers new approach to asking about race – by not using the term at all," Pew Research Center, June 18, 2015, http://www.pewresearch.org/fact-tank/2015/06/18/census-considers-newapproach-to-asking-about-race-by-not-using-the-term-at-all/.
686 "Questions and Answers for Census 2000 Data on Race," United States Census 2000, March 14, 2001, https://web.archive.org/web/20100304131211/http://www.census.gov/PressRelease/www/2001/raceqandas.html.
687 Wikipedia, "White Americans," last modified January 23, 2019, https://en.wikipedia.org/wiki/White_Americans
688 "Working for the Few: Political capture and economic inequality," 178 Oxfam Briefing Paper, January 20, 2014, http://www.oxfam.org/sites/www.oxfam.org/files/bp-working-for-few-political-capture-economicinequality-200114-en.pdf.
689 Joan C. Williams, "What So Many People Don't Get About the U.S. Working Class," Harvard Business Review, November 10, 2016, https://hbr.org/2016/11/what-so-many-people-dont-get-about-the-u-s-workingclass?utm_source=pocket&utm_medium=email&utm_

campaign=pockethits.
690   "Top 26 Signs Than You Are Living in a Bad Neighborhood," Redlink, October 19, 2018, https://reolink.com/signs-you-live-in-bad-neighborhood/.
691   "Manifesto of the Communist Party," MIA: Marxists: Marx and Engels: Library, accessed March 3, 2020, https://www.marxists.org/archive/marx/works/1848/communist-manifesto/ch01.htm.
692   Wikipedia, "Marxian class theory," last modified December 31, 2018, https://en.wikipedia.org/wiki/Marxian_class_theory.
693   Wikipedia, "Progressive Utilization Theory," last modified December 17, 2018, https://en.wikipedia.org/wiki/Progressive_Utilization_Theory.
694   "The Social Cycle," Proutist Universal, accessed March 4, 2020, http://www.prout.org/ChapterTwo.html.
695   Wikipedia, "Elite," last modified November 9, 2018, https://en.wikipedia.org/wiki/Elite.
696   Thomas R. Dye, *Who's Running America: The Bush Restoration* (New Jersey: Prentice-Hall, 2002), 12.
697   "Religious Landscape Study," Pew Research Center, accesssed Marsch 4 2020, https://www.pewforum.org/religious-landscape-study/.
698   "Religious Landscape Study," Pew Research Center, accesssed Marsch 4 2020.
699   "Search Results for War on Women," PoliticusUSA, accesssed March 4 2020, https://www.politicususa.com/?s=war+on+women.
700   Bob Moser, "Anti-Gay Religious Crusaders Claim Homosexuals Mastermind the Holocaust," Southern Poverty Law Center, April 28, 2005, https://www.splcenter.org/fighting-hate/intelligence-report/2005/antigay-religious-crusaders-claim-homosexuals-helped-mastermind-holocaust.
701   Michael Fitzgerald, "Prominent Catholic Cardinal Mocks 'Demonic' Transgender Rights Laws: WATCH," Towleroad, May 26, 2016, http://www.towleroad.com/2016/05/prominent-catholic-cardinal-mocks-demonic-transgender-rights-laws-watch/.
702   See *The Untold Story of Western Civilization*, Volume Four, pages 44 – 54.
703   Herbert Gans, *The War Against the Poor: The Underclass and Antipoverty Policy* (New York: Basic Books, 1995), 1-6.

704   Jeanna Smialek, "Young White America is Haunted by a Crisis of Despair," Bloomberg, April 18, 2017, https://www.bloomberg.com/news/features/2017-04-18/young-white-america-is-haunted-by-a-crisis-ofdespair.

705   Daniel Burke, "5 Facts About Dominionism," Huffpost, September 1, 2011, http://www.huffingtonpost.com/2011/09/01/5-facts-about-dominionism_n_945601.html.

706   "Evangelical Protestants," Pew Research Center, Religion and Public Life, accesssed Marsch 4 2020, http://www.pewforum.org/religious-landscape-study/religious-tradition/evangelical-protestant/.

707   Wikipedia, "Culture of the Southern States," last modified January 22, 2019, https://en.wikipedia.org/wiki/Culture_of_the_Southern_United_States.

708   See pages 168-187 for a discussion of the development of the Torah, and pages 213-238 for a discussion of the New Testament in *The Untold Story of Western Civilization*, Volume 2 on Ancient History.

709   Reinhard Müller, Juha Pakkala, and Bas ter Haar Romeny, Evidence of Editing: Growth and Change of Texts in the Hebrew Bible, Society of Biblical Literature, (Atlanta, GA: Society of Biblical Literature, 2014), 1. Available at https://www.sbl-site.org/assets/pdfs/pubs/060375P-front.pdf.

710   Bruce Nolan, "Changes to the Bible through the ages are being studied by New Orleans scholars," The Times-Picayune, March 27, 2011, http://www.nola.com/religion/index.ssf/2011/03/changes_to_the_bible_through_the_ages_are_being_studied_by_new_orleans_scholars.html.

711   Wikipedia, "New King James Version," last modified November 5, 2018, https://en.wikipedia.org/wiki/New_King_James_Version.

712   Liz O'Connor, Gus Lubin and Dina Spector, "The Largest Ancestry Groups In The United States," Business Insider, August 13, 2013, http://www.businessinsider.com/largest-ethnic-groups-in-america-2013-8.

713   Don Hazen, "Apocalypse Now: Seriously, It's Time for a Major Rethink About Liberal and Progressive Politics," October 25, 2014, AlterNet, http://www.alternet.org/2014/10/apocalypse-now-seriously-its-time-major-rethink-about-liberal-and-progressive-politics.

rk: The Macmillan Co., 1924), https://socialsciences.mcmaster.ca/econ/ugcm/3ll3/commons/LegalFoundationsCapitalism.pdf

715   "The Federal Stimulus," 2008 Financial Crisis and Global Recession, accessed March 4, 2020, http://2008financialcrisis.umwblogs.org/the-federal-stimulus/
716   Philip N. Cohen, "How The American Family Was Affected By The Great Recession," Pacific Standard, February 5, 2015, https://psmag.com/economics/how-the-american-family-was-affected-by-the-greatrecession#.lknmiboa0.
717   Philip N. Cohen, "How The American Family Was Affected By The Great Recession," February 5, 2015
718   "Recession begets family violence," Family Inequality, December 30, 2009, https://familyinequality.wordpress.com/2009/12/30/recession-begets-family-violence/.
719   "Child abuse in the recession," Family Inequality, May, 5, 2010, https://familyinequality.wordpress.com/2010/05/05/child-abuse-in-the-recession/.
720   National Jobs for All Coalition, https://njfac.org/index.php/measuring-unemployment/.
721   Catherine Rampell, "Part-Time Work Becomes Full-Time Wait for Better Job," New York Times, April 19, 2013, https://www.nytimes.com/2013/04/20/business/part-time-work-becomes-full-time-wait-forbetter-job.html.
722   This number is estimated from the Current Population Survey, Bureau of the Census, 8/2016, available at http://www.census.gov/data/tables/time-series/demo/income-poverty/cps-pinc/pinc-05.html.
723   Sarah Kendzior, "Why America's impressive 5% unemployment rate feels like a lie for so many," Quartz, April 20, 2016, https://qz.com/666311/why-americas-impressive-5-unemployment-rate-still-feelslike-a-lie/.
724   David Dayen, "Why Are Voters Angry? It's the 1099 Economy, Stupid." The New Republic, April 6, 2016, https://newrepublic.com/article/132407/voters-angry-its-1099-economy-stupid.
725   Sarah Kendzior, "Why America's impressive 5% unemployment rate feels like a lie for so many."
726   Robert Atkinson, ""Why the 2000s Were a Lost Decade for American Manufacturing," Industry Week, March 14, 2013, https://www.industryweek.com/the-2000s.
727   Robert Atkinson, "Why the 2000s Were a Lost Decade for American Manufacturing," March 14, 2013.

728 Robert Atkinson, "Why the 2000s Were a Lost Decade for American Manufacturing,"
729 Rex Nutting, "The Great Recession is still with us, top forecaster says," Marketwatch, February 11, 2017, http://www.marketwatch.com/story/the-great-recession-is-still-with-us-top-forecaster-says-2017-02-11.
730 Rex Nutting, "The Great Recession is still with us, top forecaster says," February 11, 2017.
731 Jeffrey J. Selingo, "Wanted: Factory Workers, Degree Required," New York Times, January 30, 2017, https://www.nytimes.com/2017/01/30/education/edlife/factory-workers-college-degreeapprenticeships.html?_r=0.
732 Jeffrey J. Selingo, "Wanted: Factory Workers, Degree Required," New York Times, January 30, 2017.
733 Jeffrey J. Selingo, "Wanted: Factory Workers, Degree Required," New York Times, January 30, 2017.
734 Michael J. Hicks and Srikant Devaraj, "The Myth and the Reality of Manufacturing in America," Ball State University: Center for Business and Economic Research, June, 2015, http://conexus.cberdata.org/files/MfgReality.pdf.
735 Michael J. Hicks and Srikant Devaraj, "The Myth and the Reality of Manufacturing in America," June, 2015.
736 Leena Rao, "Here's How Artificial Intelligence Is Going to Replace Middle Class Jobs," Fortune, Octobrt, 2016, http://fortune.com/2016/10/17/human-workforce-ai/.
737 Rob Price, "Stephen Hawking: Automation and AI is going to decimate middle class jobs," Business Insider, December 2, 2016, http://www.businessinsider.com/stephen-hawking-ai-automation-middle-class-jobsmost-dangerous-moment-humanity-2016-12.
738 "Stephen Hawking: 'AI could spell end of the human race'," BBC News, December 2, 2014, http://www.bbc.com/news/science-environment-30289705.
739 Rob Price, "Stephen Hawking: Automation and AI is going to decimate middle class jobs," December 2, 2016.
740 Oscar Williams-Grut, "Robots will steal your job: How AI could increase unemployment and inequality," Business Insider, February 15, 2016, http://www.businessinsider.com/robots-will-steal-your-jobciti-ai-increase-unemployment-inequality-2016-2?r=UK&IR=T.

741   Chuck Jones, "Two Charts Show Trump's Job Gains Are Just a Continuation From Obama's Presidency," Fortune, October 30, 2018, https://www.forbes.com/sites/chuckjones/2018/10/30/two-chartsshow-trumps-job-gains-are-just-a-continuation-from-obamas-presidency/#567813141af3.

742   Robert Reich, "The Truth About the Trump Economy," The American Prospect, October 15, 2018, https://prospect.org/article/truth-about-trump-economy.

743   Bob Bryan, "Trumps trade war is already leading to layoffs and pain for American businesses," Business Insider, August 9, 2018, https://www.businessinsider.com/trump-tariffs-trade-war-layoffs-businesslosses-2018-8.

744   Adam Betz, "Farm bankruptcies are on the rise, and bankers worry that far more are on the way," Star Tribune, November 26, 2018, https/www.startribune.com/farm-bankruptcies-are-on-the-rise-and-bankers-worry-that-far-more-are-on-the-way/501157191.

745   US farmers are going bankrupt at an alarming rate. Trump's trade war is partially to blame," Vox, November 27, 2018, https://www.vox.com/policy-and-politics/2018/11/27/18114566/trump-trade-war-china-farmbankruptcy.

746   Robert Reich, "The Truth About the Trump Economy," October 15, 2018.

747   Tami Luhby, "It's expensive to be poor," CNN Business, April 24, 2015, http://money.cnn.com/2015/04/23/news/economy/poor-spending/.

748   "The Secret Shame of Middle Class Americans," The Atlantic, May, 2016, https://www.theatlantic.com/magazine/archive/2016/05/my-secret-shame/476415/.

749   Tami Luhby, "It's expensive to be poor," April 24, 2015.

750   Editorial Board, "The Middle Class Has a Debt Problem," Bloomberg, May 13, 2015, https://www.bloomberg.com/view/articles/2015-05-13/the-middle-class-has-a-debt-problem.

751   Claire Tsosie and Erin El Issa "2018 American Household Credit Card Debt Study," NerdWallet, December 10, 2018, https://www.nerdwallet.com/blog/average-credit-card-debt-household/.

752   Matthew Frankel, "The Average American Household Owes $90,336—How Do You Compare," The Motley Fool, May 8, 2016, https://www.fool.com/retirement/general/2016/05/08/the-aver-

age-americanhousehold-owes-90336-how-do-y.aspx.

753   David French, "Can America's Divides be Healed?" National Review, January 20, 2017, http://www.nationalreview.com/article/444064/donald-trump-political-polarization-problem-too-big-oneman-fix.

754   "Political Polarization in the American Public," Pew Research Center, June 12, 2014, http://www.people-press.org/2014/06/12/political-polarization-in-the-american-public/.

755   "Political Polarization in the American Public," Pew Research Center, June 12, 2014

756   Seth J. Hill and Chris Tausanovitch, "No, Americans have not become more ideologically polarized," The Washington Post, October 13, 2015, https://www.washingtonpost.com/news/monkeycage/wp/2015/10/13/no-americans-have-not-become-more-ideologically-polarized/?utm_term=.5de7a6ca73ed.

757   Lydia Saad, "Trump Leads Clinton in Historically Bad Image Ratings," Gallup, July 1, 2016, http://www.gallup.com/poll/193376/trump-leads-clinton-historically-bad-imageratings.aspx?g_source=position1&g_medium=related&g_campaign=tiles.

758   Andrew Soergel, "Divided We Stand," US News and World Report, July 19, 2016, http://www.usnews.com/news/articles/2016-07-19/political-polarization-drives-presidential-race-to-thebottom.

759   "Political Polarization," C-Span, June 3, 2016, https://www.c-span.org/video/?410409-5/discussionfocuses-political-polarization.

760   Andrew Soergel, "Divided We Stand," July 19, 2016.

761   David French, "Can America's Divides be Healed?" January 20, 2017.

762   "Exit Polls," CNN Politics, November 23, 2016, http://www.cnn.com/election/results/exitpolls/national/president.

763   Stephanie Pappas, "Trump's Win Uncovers New Deep Divides in America's Social Fabric," LiveScience, November 11, 2016, http://www.livescience.com/56831-trump-win-uncovers-deep-socialdivides.html.

764   Stephanie Pappas, "Trump's Win Uncovers New Deep Divides in America's Social Fabric," November 11, 2016.

765   Stephanie Pappas, "Trump's Win Uncovers New Deep Divides in America's Social Fabric," November 11, 2016."

766   "Who are the three-quarter Americans who didn't vote

for Trump," The Guardian, accessed March 4, 2020, https://www.theguardian.com/us-news/2017/jan/18/american-non-voters-election-donald-trump

767   Justin Gest, "The Two Kinds of Trump Voters," Politico, February 8, 2017, http://www.politico.com/magazine/story/2017/02/trump-voters-white-working-class-214754.

768   Allison Graves, "Did Donald Trump's Carrier deal actually save 'less than half' of jobs headed to Mexico?" PunditFact, December 4, 2016, http://www.politifact.com/punditfact/statements/2016/dec/04/heathermcghee/did-donald-trumps-carrier-deal-actually-save-less-/.

769   Justin Gest, "The Two Kinds of Trump Voters." Politico, February 8, 2017.

770   Melody Wilding, "The communication style that destroys relationships - at work and at home," Quartz, December 1, 2017, https://qz.com/work/1143976/the-communication-style-that-destroys-relationships-at-work-and-at-home/.

771   Derek Flood, "Worlds Apart: Maintaining Personal Relationships As Political Opposites," Life, October 24, 2016, http://www.huffingtonpost.com/derek-flood/worlds-apart-maintaining-_b_12605412.html.

772   "Brain Study looks at why people's political beliefs are so hard to change," CBS News, February 16, 2017, https://www.cbsnews.com/news/mri-brain-study-usc-political-beliefs-challenged/?ftag=CNM-00-10aac3a.

773   Conor Friedersdorf, "Every Racist I Know Voted for Donald Trump," The Atlantic, February 13, 2017, https://www.theatlantic.com/politics/archive/2017/02/every-racist-i-know-voted-for-donald-trump/516420/.

774   Conor Friedersdorf, "Every Racist I Know Voted for Donald Trump," The Atlantic, February 13, 2017.

775   Conor Friedersdorf, "Every Racist I Know Voted for Donald Trump.," The Atlantic, February 13, 2017.

776   "Trans-Pacific Partnership (TPP)," Public Citizen, August 2015, http://www.citizen.org/TPP.

777   "New York Daily News covers of Donald Trump through the years," New York Daily News, November 10, , http://www.nydailynews.com/news/new-york-daily-news-covers-donald-trump-years gallery1.2716080?pmSlide=1.2716053.

778   Jonathan Karl, "Donald Trump Once Proposed the Biggest Tax Hike Ever," ABC News, August 5, 2015, https://abcnews.go.com/Politics/donald-trump-proposed-biggest-tax-hike/story?id=32926722.
779   Corky Siemaszko, "Mass Migration of Muslims to U.S. Mostly a Mirage," NBC News, December 10, 2015, http://www.nbcnews.com/storyline/immigration-border-crisis/mass-migration-muslims-u-s-mostly-miragen477306.
780   Wikipedia, "Guantanamo Bay detention camp suicide attempts," last modified January 22, 2019, https://en.wikipedia.org/wiki/Guantanamo_Bay_detention_camp_suicide_attempts.
781   Alison Parker and Jamie Fellner, "Executive Power after 9-11 in the United States," Global Issues, January 2004, http://www.globalissues.org/article/460/executive-power-after-9-11-in-the-united-states.
782   Julia Ainsley, "Inside's Trump's Guantanamo, where military waits for funding for 'enduring mission,'" NBC News, November 30, 2018, https://www.nbcnews.com/news/us-news/inside-trump-s-guantanamo-wheremilitary-waits-funding-enduring-mission-n941561.
783   See http://www.globalissues.org/article/460/executive-power-after-9-11-in-the-united-states#_ftn55 for a comprehensive analysis the War on Terror.
784   "National Security Letters," Electronic Frontier Foundation, accessed March 4, 2020, https://www.eff.org/issues/nationalsecurity-letters.
785   "National Security Letters (NSLs)," Electronic Frontier Foundation, accessed March 4, 2020, https://www.eff.org/issues/foia/07656JDB.
786   Dan Eggen, "FBI Found to Misuse Security Letters," The Washington Post, March 14, 2008, http://www.washingtonpost.com/wp-dyn/content/article/2008/03/13/AR2008031302277.html.
787   Testimony of Jameel Jaffer Before the House Subcommittee on the Constitution, Civil Rights, and Civil Liberties Oversight Hearing on H.R. 3189, the National Security Letters Reform Act of 2007, April 2008, ACLU, https://fas.org/irp/congress/2008_hr/041508jaffer.pdf.
788   Justin Gardner, "Obama Extends 9/11 "Emergency" War on Terror Powers as US Says Al Qaeda No Longer Target," Activist Post, September 4, 2016, http://www.activistpost.com/2016/09/obama-extends-911emergency-war-terror-powers-al-qaeda-no-longer-target.html.
789   Gregory Korte, "Obama extends post-9/11 state of nation-

al emergency for 16th year," USA Today, September 9, 2016, http://www.usatoday.com/story/news/politics/2016/09/09/obama-extends-post-911-statenational-emergency-16th-year/90004960/.
790   Ashley Gorski, "The Trump Administration is Hiding a Crucial Report on NSA Spying Practices," ACLU, July 12, 2018, https://www.aclu.org/blog/national-security/privacy-and-surveillance/trumpadministration-hiding-crucial-report-nsa.
791   Sarah Lazare, "In Trump's America, 'Felony Riot' Charges Against Inauguration Protesters Signal Dangerous Wave of Repression," AlterNet, January 22, 2017, https://www.alternet.org/2017/01/trumps-america-felony-riot-charges-against-inauguration-protesters-signal-dangerous-wave-repression/.
792   Sarah Lazare, "Law Enforcement Using Facebook and Apple to Data-Mine Accounts of Trump Protest Arrestees," AlterNet, February 22, 2017, http://www.alternet.org/activism/law-enforcement-using-facebookand-apple-data-mine-accounts-trump-protest-arrestees-0.
793   Barton Gellman and Laura Poitras, "U.S., British intelligence mining data from nine U.S. Internet companies in broad secret program," The Washington Post, June 7, 2013, https://www.washingtonpost.com/investigations/us-intelligence-mining-data-from-nine-us-internetcompanies-in-broad-secret-program/2013/06/06/3a0c0da8-cebf-11e2-8845d970ccb04497_story.html?utm_term=.58eb5f0bcd3e.
794   Rachel King, "FBI, NSA said to be secretly mining data from nine U.S. tech giants," ZDNet, June 6, 2013, http://www.zdnet.com/article/fbi-nsa-said-to-be-secretly-mining-data-from-nine-u-s-tech-giants/. 804 Rachel King, "FBI, NSA said to be secretly mining data from nine U.S. tech giants."
795   "The Constitution of the United States," http://constitutionus.com/. 806 Wikipedia, "PRISM (Surveillance Program)," last modified, January 11, 2019, https://en.wikipedia.org/wiki/PRISM_(surveillance_program).
796   Zack Whittaker, "If you have 'nothing to hide', here's where to send your passwords," ZDNet, October 14, 2014, http://www.zdnet.com/article/if-you-have-nothing-to-hide-heres-where-to-send-your-passwords/.
797   "Unrivaled clarity. Actionable intelligence." Interaction Data Intelligence (IDI), accesssed March 4, 2020, http://ididata.com/.
798   David Gauvey Herbert, "This Company Has Built a Pro-

file on Every American Adult," Bloomberg, August 5, 2016, https://www.bloomberg.com/news/articles/2016-08-05/this-company-has-built-a-profile-onevery-american adult?utm_source=pocket&utm_medium=email&utm_campaign=pockethits.

799   David Gauvey Herbert, "This Company Has Built a Profile on Every American Adult,"

800   Mike Adams, New video details how Amazon.com SPIES on your most private thoughts, fetishes and conversations," PrivacyWatch.News, February 10, 2017, http://privacywatch.news/2017-02-10-new-videodetails-how-amazon-com-spies-on-your-most-private-thoughts-conversations.html.

801   "Amazon Echo," Amazon, https://www.amazon.com/Amazon-Echo-Bluetooth-Speaker-with-WiFiAlexa/dp/B00X4WHP5E.

802   Tony Bradley, "How Amazon Echo Users Can Control Privacy," Forbes, January 5, 2017, http://www.forbes.com/sites/tonybradley/2017/01/05/alexa-is-listening-but-amazon-values-privacy-andgives-you-control/#24323f25eed5.

803   Mike Adams, "New video details how Amazon.com SPIES on your most private thoughts, fetishes and conversations," Watch.News, February 10, 2017

804   Sandra Chereb, "Outlawing microchipping humans not so far-fetched, Nevada senator says," Las Vegas Review-Journal, February 13, 2017, http://www.reviewjournal.com/news/politics-andgovernment/nevada/outlawing-microchipping-humans-not-so-far-fetched-nevada-senator.

805   Tim Collins, "Would YOU let your boss implant you with a microchip? Belgian firm offers to turn staff into cyborgs to replace ID cards," Daily Mail, February 8, 2017, http://www.dailymail.co.uk/sciencetech/article-4203148/Company-offers-RFID-microchip-implantsreplace-ID-cards.html

806   Joshua Rhett Miller, "Student-tracking system at Texas schools prompts privacy concerns," Fox News, September 12, 2012, http://www.foxnews.com/us/2012/09/12/texas-school-district-defends-use-student-trackingmart-id-card.html.

807   Sandra Chereb, "Outlawing microchipping humans not so far-fetched, Nevada senator says," Las Vegas Review-Journal, February 13, 2017.

808   Curt Monash, "MythBusters co-host alleges RFID securi-

ty coverup," Network World, Septembr 3, 2008, https://www.networkworld.com/article/2346028/security/mythbusters-co-host-alleges-rfid-securitycoverup.html.

809   Toni, "SPYCHIPPED LEVI'S BRAND JEANS HIT THE U.S." LaLeva.org, April 28, 2006, http://www.laleva.org/eng/2006/04/spychipped_levis_brand_jeans_hit_the_us.html.

810   "Big Brother chips his way into clothing and other consumer goods," Big Government News, December 3, 2015, http://www.biggovernment.news/2015-12-03-big-brother-chips-his-way-into-clothing-and-otherconsumer-goods.html.

811   Lauren Indvik, "Why Luxury Brands Are Putting Microchips in Your Clothes and Accessories," Fashionista, April 14, 2016, http://fashionista.com/2016/04/moncler-ferragamo-rfid-counterfeiting.

812   Rian Boden, "Researchers unveil breakthrough in weaving NFC chips into clothes," NFC World, July 3, 2015, https://www.nfcworld.com/2015/07/03/336391/researchers-unveil-breakthrough-in-weaving-nfcchips-into-clothes/.

813   "Migrant crisis: Migration to Europe explained in seven charts," BBC News, March 4, 2016, http://www.bbc.com/news/world-europe-34131911.

814   "Migrant crisis: Migration to Europe explained in seven charts," BBC News, March 4, 2016.

815   Patrick Kingsley, "One in, one out – the EU's simplistic answer to the refugee crisis," The Guardian, March 7, 2016, https://www.theguardian.com/world/2016/mar/07/one-in-one-out-the-eus-simplisticanswer-to-the-refugee-crisis.

816   Patrick Kingsley, "One in, one out – the EU's simplistic answer to the refugee crisis," The Guardian, March 7, 2016.

817   Helena Smith, "Greeks worry threatened closure of EU border 'would be the definition of dystopia'" The Guardian, January 30, 2016, https://www.theguardian.com/world/2016/jan/30/greece-threatened-closureeu-border-dystopia.

818   "Turkey's Refugee Crisis: The Politics of Permanence," International Crisis Group, November 30, 2016, https://www.crisisgroup.org/europe-central-asia/western-europemediterranean/turkey/turkey-s-refugee-crisis-politics-permanence.

819   Emily Tamkin, "Did Turkey Just Kill the Refugee Deal With Europe?" Foreign Policy, March 14, 2017, http://foreignpolicy.

com/2017/03/14/did-turkey-just-kill-the-refugee-deal-with-europe/.
820   Helen Smith, "Greeks worry threatened closure of EU border would be the definition of dystopia," The Guardian, January 30, 2016, https://www.theguardian.com/world/2016/jan/30/greece-threatened-closure-eu-border-dystopia.
821   Maria Margaronis, "Greece's stranded refugees fear being forgotten," BBC News, July 7, 2016, http://www.bbc.com/news/world-europe-36703503.
822   "Migrants Attacked Around Calais," News 24, February 12, 2016, https://www.news24.com/World/News/migrants-attacked-around-calais-20160212.
823   Joseph Charlton, "Refugee crisis: What life is really like inside the 'Jungle' in Calais," Independent, September 30, 2015, http://www.independent.co.uk/news/world/europe/refugee-crisis-what-life-is-really-likeinside-the-jungle-in-calais-a6674256.html#gallery.
824   David Chazan, Rory Mulholland, Harriet Alexander, "Calais 'jungle' demolition: Hundreds of migrants abandon bus queues and head back to camp after processing delays," The Telegraph, October 24, 2016, http://www.telegraph.co.uk/news/2016/10/24/calais-jungle-demolition-riots-and-chaos-as-police-warn-thatbri/.
825   Anne Guillard, "Refugees start to gather in Calais again, months after camp was closed," The Guardian, April 2, 2017, https://www.theguardian.com/world/2017/apr/02/refugees-gather-calais-campunaccompanied-children.
826   Anne Guillard, "Refugees start to gather in Calais again, months after camp was closed,"
827   Tracy McVeigh, "No money for food, clothing or a home: how asylum seekers are left destitute on UK streets, The Guardian, May 7, 2016, https://www.theguardian.com/uk-news/2016/may/07/homelessasylum-seeker-refugees-forced-red-cross-food?CMP=oth_b-aplnews_d-1.
828   See *The Untold Story of Western Civilization*, Chapter Three on the Warriors
829   Jie Zong and Jeanne Batalova, "Syrian Refugees in the United States," Migrant Policy Institute, Januay 12, 2017, http://www.migrationpolicy.org/article/syrian-refugees-united-states.
830   Jie Zong and Jeanne Batalova, "Syrian Refugees in the United States," Migrant Policy Institute, Januay 12, 2017.

831   Jie Zong and Jeanne Batalova, "Syrian Refugees in the United States," Migrant Policy Institute, Januay 12, 2017.
832   Arnie Seipel, "30 Governors Call For Halt To U.S. Resettlement Of Syrian Refugees," NPR, November 17, 2015, http://www.npr.org/2015/11/17/456336432/more-governors-oppose-u-s-resettlement-of-syrianrefugees.
833   Vivian Salama and Alicia A. Caldwell, "DHS intelligence report disputes threat posed by 7 travel ban nations," Chicago Tribune, February 24, 2017, https://www.chicagotribune.com/news/nation-world/ct-dhsreport-travel-ban-nations-20170224-story.html.
834   Jie Zong and Jeanne Batalova, "Syrian Refugees in the United States," Migrant Policy Institute, Januay 12, 2017.
835   Glenn Thrush, "Trump's New Travel Ban Blocks Migrants From Six Nations, Sparing Iraq," New York Times, March 6, 2017, https://www.nytimes.com/2017/03/06/us/politics/travel-ban-muslim-trump.html.
836   Glenn Thrush, "Trump's New Travel Ban Blocks Migrants From Six Nations, Sparing Iraq," New York Times, March 6, 2017.
837   Anjali Singhvi and Alicia Parlapiano, "Who Would Be Barred by Trump's Latest Immigration Ban," New York Times, March 6, 2017, https://www.nytimes.com/interactive/2017/03/06/us/politics/trumptravel-ban-groups.html?_r=0.
838   Julia Preston, "Number of Illegal Immigrants in U.S. May Be on Rise Again, Estimates Say," New York Times, September 23, 2013, https://www.nytimes.com/2013/09/24/us/immigrant-population-shows-signs-ofgrowth-estimates-show.html.
839   Kelly Lytle Hernandez, "How crossing the US-Mexico border became a crime," The Conversation, April 30, 2017, http://theconversation.com/how-crossing-the-us-mexico-border-became-a-crime-74604.
840   "Attorney General Jeff Sessions Delivers Keynote Remarks at the International Association of Chiefs of Police Division Midyear Conference," The US Dept. of Justice, April 11, 2017, https://www.justice.gov/opa/speech/attorney-general-jeff-sessions-delivers-keynote-remarks-internationalassociation-chiefs.
841   Wikipedia, "Immigration Act of 1924," last modified January 18, 2019, https://en.wikipedia.org/wiki/Immigration_Act_of_1924
842   Kelly Lytle Hernandez, "How crossing the US-Mexico border

became a crime," The Conversation, April 30, 2017.
843   "Dwight Eisenhower on Immigration," On the Issues, accessed March 4, 2020, http://www.ontheissues.org/celeb/Dwight_Eisenhower_Immigration.htm.
844   "Dwight Eisenhower on Immigration," On the Issues, accessed March 4, 2020.
845   Jim Gilchrist and Jerome Corsi, *Minutemen: The Battle to Secure America's Borders* (St. Gardena, CA: World Ahead Publishing, 2006), 32.
846   Jeb Bush and Clint Bolick, *Immigration Wars: Forging an American Solution* (New York: Threshold Editions, 2013), 133-134.
847   Rick Perry, *Fed Up! Our Fight to Save America from Washington* (New York: Little, Brown and Co., 2010), 120.
848   Muzaffar Chishti, Sarah Pierce, and Jessica Bolter, "The Obama Record on Deportations: Deporter in Chief or Not?" Migration Policy Institute, January 26, 2017, http://www.migrationpolicy.org/article/obamarecord-deportations-deporter-chief-or-not.
849   Muzaffar Chishti, Sarah Pierce, and Jessica Bolter, "The Obama Record on Deportations: Deporter in Chief or Not?" Migration Policy Institute, January 26, 2017.
850   "George W. Bush on Immigration," On the Issues, accessed March 4, 2020, http://www.ontheissues.org/Celeb/George_W__Bush_Immigration.htm.
851   Michael D. Shear, "Obama, Daring Congress, Acts to Overhaul Immigration," New York Times, November 20, 2014, https://www.nytimes.com/2014/11/21/us/obama-immigration-speech.html.
852   "What Is President Obama's Immigration Plan?" New York Times, November 20, 2014, https://www.nytimes.com/interactive/2014/11/20/us/2014-11-20-immigration.html
853   Charlie Spiering, "John Cornyn: Obama Executive Amnesty 'Unconstitutional and Illegal,'" Brietbart, November 19, 2014, https://www.briebart.com/politics/2014/11/19/john-cornyn-obama-executive-amnesty-unconstitutional-and-illegal/.
854   "What Is President Obama's Immigration Plan?" New York Times, November 20, 2014.
855   Adam Liptak and Michael D. Shear, "Supreme Court to Hear Challenge to Obama Immigration Actions," New York Times, January 19, 2016, https://www.nytimes.com/2016/01/20/us/politics/supreme-

court-to-hear-challenge-to-obama-immigration-actions.html.

856   A sanctuary city is a name given to a city in the United States that follows certain procedures that shelters illegal immigrants. The term most commonly is used for cities that do not permit municipal funds or resources to be applied in furtherance of enforcement of federal immigration laws.

857   Tal Kopan, "DOJ highlights immigration arrests in statistics report," CNN Politics, March 23, 2017, http://www.cnn.com/2017/03/23/politics/justice-statistics-immigration/.

858   Pia Orrenius, "Benefits of Immigration Outweigh the Costs," The Catalyst, Spring, 2016, http://www.bushcenter.org/catalyst/north-american-century/benefits-of-immigration-outweigh-costs.html.

859   Baher Kamal, "Climate Migrants Might Reach One Billion by 2050," reliefweb, Aug.ust 21, 2017, https://reliefweb.int/report/world/climate-migrants-might-reach-one-billion-2050.

860   Cornell University, "Rising seas could result in 2 billion refugees by 2100," Science News, June 26, 2017, https://www.sciencedaily.com/releases/2017/06/170626105746.htm.

861   Martha Kang, "NOAA: Coastal population boom increases hazard risks, KNKX, March 25, 2013, https://www.knkx.org/post/noaa-coastal-population-boom-increases-hazard-risks.

862   Mathew E. Hauer, "Migration induced by sea-level rise could reshape the US population landscape," Nature Climate Change, April 17, 2017, https://www.nature.com/articles/nclimate3271.epdf?author_access_token=Hvxidg4gL1Q0zWEvyEXiLtRgN0jAjWel9jnR-3ZoTv0NFv3_2_MZIRrCavou7VputY0Z0x-UWFD09j5eSgqBhP56FYSZJPA8_HdSRdIl79npShOcx0Gd16aq4FimtdoF.

863   Marlene Cimons, "Sea-Level Rise Will Send Millions of U.S. Climate Refugees to Inland Cities," AlterNet, May 1, 2017, http://www.alternet.org/environment/sea-level-rise-will-send-millions-us-climaterefugees-inland-cities?akid=15522.1930755.oIeBAa&rd=1&src=newsletter1076131&t=22.

864   See Universal Ideology: the Thought of P. R. Sarkar, Chapter 5 and Nuclear Revolution, Chapter 13 by the authors (San German, Puerto Rico: InnerWorld Publications, 2020), 52.

865   "Ozone Depletion: How is Earth's atmosphere losing its most important layer?" National Geographic, November 14, 2018, http://www.nationalgeographic.com/environment/global-warming/

ozone-depletion/.
866   "Ozone Depletion: How is Earth's atmosphere losing its most important layer?" National Geographic,
867   "Fighting to breathe in the world's most polluted cities," PBS News Hour, February 20, 2017, http://www.pbs.org/newshour/bb/fighting-breathe-worlds-polluted-city/.
868   John Walsh, "Pollution In London Surpasses Beijing: Europe Chokes On Freezing Smog," International Business Times, January 25, 2017, http://www.ibtimes.com/pollution-london-surpasses-beijing-europe-chokesfreezing-smog-2481105.
869   Natasha Maguder, "How to win the fight against air pollution," CNN, August 18, 2016, http://www.cnn.com/2016/08/18/world/ecosolutions-air-pollution-pkg/index.html.
870   Susan S. Lang, "Water, air and soil pollution causes 40 percent of deaths worldwide, Cornell research survey finds," Cornell Chronicle, August 2, 2007, https://www.news.cornell.edu/stories/2007/08/pollutioncauses-40-percent-deaths-worldwide-study-finds.
871   Christina Procopiou, "Air Pollution Claims 5.5 Million Lives a Year, Making It the Fourth-Leading Cause of Death Worldwide," Newsweek, February 12, 2016, http://www.newsweek.com/55-million-deaths-airpollution-worldwide-each-year-426159.
872   Stanley Reed, "Study Links 6.5 Million Deaths Each Year to Air Pollution," New York Times, June 26, 2016, https://www.nytimes.com/2016/06/27/business/energy-environment/study-links-6-5-million-deathseach-year-to-air-pollution.html?_r=1.
873   Heather Amos, "Poor air quality kills 5.5 million worldwide annually," The University of British Columbia, February 12, 2016, http://news.ubc.ca/2016/02/12/poor-air-quality-kills-5-5-million-worldwideannually/.
874   Tom Johnson, "Scorching Summer of 2016 Yields Dozens of Bad-Air Days," NJSpotlight, September 23, 2016, http://www.njspotlight.com/stories/16/09/22/scorching-summer-of-2016-yields-dozens-of-bad-airdays/.
875   "Connecticut officials warn about unhealthy air quality," Associated Press, June 18, 2016, http://newsok.com/connecticut-officials-warn-about-unhealthy-airquality/article/feed/1029065?-custom_click=rss&utm_source=feedburner&utm_medium=-feed&utm_campaign=Feed%3A+newsok%2Fbusiness+%28NewsOK.

com+RSS+-+business%29.
876   Susan S. Lang, "Water, air and soil pollution causes 40 percent of deaths worldwide, Cornell research survey finds," Cornell Chronicle, August 2, 2007.
877   "Excerpts from Silent Spring (1962)," 2, http://www.wheelersburg.net/Downloads/carson_spring.pdf.
878   Ronnie Cummins, "Don't Trust the Feds on GMOs, Pesticides and Chemicals," Organic Consumers Association, October 25, 2016, https://www.organicconsumers.org/essays/don%E2%80%99t-trust-feds-gmospesticides-and-chemicals.
879   Beyond Pesticides, "Over 400 Carcinogens Have Been Found in People's Bodies, According to New Report," AlterNet, June 15, 2016, http://www.alternet.org/environment/over-400-carcinogens-found-peoples-bodies report?akid=14355.1930755.weJRcs&rd=1&src=newsletter1058132&t=23.
880   Marie Gallucci, "TSCA Reform: These Toxic Chemicals Are Still Allowed Under The EPA's Chemicals Law," International Business Times, June 22, 2016, http://www.ibtimes.com/tsca-reform-thesetoxic-chemicals-are-still-allowed-under-epas-chemicals-law-2385455.
881   Felice Stadler, "Pruitt has made environmental injustice the norm at EPA: 5 shocking examples," Environmental Defense Fund, April 5, 2018, https://www.edf.org/blog/2018/04/05/pruitt-has-madeenvironmental-injustice-norm-epa-5-shocking-examples.
882   Environmental News Service, "How Trump's Regulatory Order Jeopardizes the Environment," AlterNet, January 31, 2017, http://www.alternet.org/environment/how-trumps-regulatory-order-jeopardizesenvironment.
883   Joe Romm, "James Hansen: Coal is the single greatest threat to civilization and all life on our planet," Think Progress, February 16, 2009, https://archive.thinkprogress.org/james-hansen-coal-is-the-single-greatest-threat-to-civilization-and-all-life-on-our-planet-8d6f-caa6b85/.
884   "Europe's Dark Cloud," accessed March 4, 2020, https://drive.google.com/file/d/0B61Z9fHPRFJgUktzU3BfRWkzbk0/.
885   "Extremely High Levels of PM2.5: Steps to Reduce Your Exposure," AirNow, accessed March 4, 2020, https://env-health.org/IMG/pdf/dark_cloud-full_report_final.pdf.
886   Jeremy Martin, "Pulling Back the Curtain on a Massively

Polluting Industry," Union of Concerned Scientists, September 14, 2016, http://blog.ucsusa.org/jeremy-martin/pulling-back-the-curtain-on-a-massivelypolluting-industry.

887 Marlowe Hood, "Renewables can't deliver Paris climate goals: study," PHYSorg, January 31, 2017, https://phys.org/news/2017-01-renewables-paris-climate-goals.html.

888 "The Cost of Air Pollution : Strengthening the Economic Case for Action," World Bank, Open Knowledge Repository, 2010, https://openknowledge.worldbank.org/handle/10986/2501.

889 Steve Williams, "Air Pollution Costs Billions of Dollars a Year, and That's Just the Start," Care2, September 11, 2016, http://www.care2.com/causes/air-pollution-costs-billions-of-dollars-a-year-and-thats-just-the-start.html?utm_campaign=feed%3a+c2causes+%28causes%29&utm_medium=feed&utm_source=feedburne.

890 Jess Shankleman, "Eight Fossil Fuel Majors Seen Polluting as Much as the U.S.," Bloomberg, March 8, 2017, https://www.bloomberg.com/news/articles/2017-03-08/eight-fossil-fuel-majors-seen-polluting-asmuch-as-the-u-s?bcomANews=true.

891 Jack Holmes, "It's the Golden Age of Climate Denial," Esquire, March 12, 2017, http://www.esquire.com/news-politics/a53805/climate-skeptics-trump-administration/.

892 "Oil and Gas Threat Map," accessed March 4, 2020, http://oilandgasthreatmap.com/threat-map/.

893 Kevin Kalhoefer, "How Broadcast Networks Covered Climate Change In 2016," Media Matters for America, March 23, 2017, https://mediamatters.org/research/2017/03/23/how-broadcast-networks-coveredclimate-change-2016/215718.

894 Vera Shawiza, "85 Percent of World's Population live in the Driest Half of the Planet," soko directory, March 10, 2018, https://sokodirectory.com/2018/03/85-percent-of-worlds-population-live-in-the-driesthalf-of-the-planet/.

895 Arthur Nelsen, "River pollution puts 323m at risk from life-threatening diseases, says UN," The Guardian, September 22, 2016, https://www.theguardian.com/sustainable-business/2016/sep/22/un-riverpollution-323m-people-risk-life-threatening-diseases?cmp=oth_b-aplnews_d-1.

896 "About guinea-worm disease," World Health Organization, accessed March 4, 2020, https://www.who.int/dracunculiasis/disease/en/.

897	Wenonah Hauter, Melissa Mays, "Too Many U.S. Water Systems Are Falling Apart: Here's the Solution," AlterNet, June 29, 2016, http://www.alternet.org/environment/too-many-us-water-systems-are-falling-apart-heres solution?akid=14399.1930755.T56yiL&rd=1&src=newsletter1059067&t=4.
898	Dr. Mercola, "'Poisoned Waters' — An In-Depth Look at the Sources and Impact of Water Pollution," Mercola, November 5, 2016, http://articles.mercola.com/sites/articles/archive/2016/11/05/water-pollutionsourceseffects.aspx?utm_source=dnl&utm_medium=email&utm_content=art1&utm_campaign=20161105Z1&et_ cid=DM124411&et_rid=1742752912.
899	Wenonah Hauter, Melissa Mays, "Too Many U.S. Water Systems Are Falling Apart: Here's the Solution," AlterNet, June 29, 2016.
900	J. D. Heyes, "SCANDAL: EPA could have issued an emergency order 7 months before Flint water crisis became public knowledge," Natural News, Oct. 31, 2016, http://www.naturalnews.com/055831_Flint_water_crisis_EPA_cover-up.html .
901	"Analysis: Government does not know how much pollution it puts out," American Media Institute, August 13, 2016, https://americanmediainstitute.com/investigations/analysis-government-not-know-muchpollution-puts/.
902	Les Neuhaus, "Miles of Algae and a Multitude of Hazards," New York Times, July 18, 2016, https://www.nytimes.com/2016/07/19/science/algae-blooms-beaches.html See also https://www.washingtonpost.com/news/morning-mix/wp/2016/07/01/floridians-outraged-over-smellyguacamole-thick-toxic-algae-invading-coastline/?utm_term=.322cb98f96be.
903	Samantha Page, "Climate Denier Marco Rubio Tries To Tackle Toxic Florida Algae, Is Baffled By Cause," Think Progress, July 18, 2016, https://thinkprogress.org/climate-denier-marco-rubio-tries-totackle-toxic-florida-algae-is-baffled-by-cause-7daa9e9cfa39#.gkari86yp.
904	"Average sized dead zone forecast for Gulf of Mexico," National Oceanic and Atmospheric Administration (NOAA), June 7, 2018, https://www.noaa.gov/media-release/average-sized-dead-zoneforecast-for-gulf-of-mexico
905	Wikipedia, "Water privatization in the United States," last modified January 12, 2019, https://en.wikipedia.org/wiki/Water_privatization_in_the_United_States.

906   "The Truth About Nestle's Business With Water," Bottles Life, http://www.bottledlifefilm.com/index.php/the-story.html.
907   Phil Lempert, "Is your bottled water coming from a faucet?" Today, October 14, 2016, https:/www.youtube.com/watch?v=czfSwjx4yYA.
908   Claudia Ringler, "What's really causing water scarcity in Africa south of the Sahara?" International Food Policy Research Institute, August 29, 2013, http://www.ifpri.org/blog/what%E2%80%99s-really-causing-water-scarcity-africa-south-sahara.
909   "What is the EPA Clean Water Rule," American Rivers, accessed March 4, 2020, https://www.americanrivers.org/rivers/discover-your-river/why-you-should-care-about-the-epa-cleanwater-rule/.
910   Samantha Page, "The EPA Just Protected Drinking Water For Millions Of Americans," Think Progress, May 27, 2015, https://www.americanrivers.org/rivers/discover-your-river/why-you-should-care-about-the-epa-clean-water-rule/.
911   Natasha Geiling, "New Lawsuit Says Clean Water Rule Threatens 'The Very Structure Of The Constitution'" Think Progress, June 29, 2015, https://thinkprogress.org/new-lawsuit-says-clean-water-rulethreatens-the-very-structure-of-the-constitution-dea1e8bb88ab#.bp9f3mt4r.
912   "About RAGA," Republican Attorney's General Association, http://www.republicanags.com/about.
913   Brad Johnson, "'U.S.' Chamber Of Commerce Is Fueled By Foreign Oil," Think Progress, October 23, 2010, https://republicanags.com.
914   "Inside the $400-million political network backed by the Kochs," The Washington Post, https://www.washingtonpost.com/politics/inside-the-koch-backed-political-donor-network/2014/01/05/94719296-7661-11e3-b1c5-739e63e9c9a7_graphic.html.
915   Ledyard King, "Trump EPA takes aim at Obama-era clean water rules, prompting outcry from environmentalists," USA Today, December 10, 2018, https://www.usatoday.com/story/news/politics/2018/12/10/clean-water-rollback-epas-new-rule-expected-revise-waters-us/2269060002/.
916   "Seven Kings of Environmental Pollution," Sustainable Baby Steps, accessed March 4, 2020, http://www.sustainablebabysteps.com/kinds-of-environmental-pollution.html.

917   Melissa Breyer, "Trash by the numbers: Startling statistics about US garbage," Treehugger, July 1, 2016, http://www.treehugger.com/environmental-policy/trash-numbers-startling-statistics-about-americansand-their-garbage.html.
918   Lorraine Chow, "Fracking Caused 6,648 Spills in Four States Alone, Duke Study Finds," EcoWatch, February 21, 2017, https://www.ecowatch.com/fracking-spills-duke-study-2276074733.html.
919   Theresa Riley, "Honey Bee Die-Off Caused By Multiple Factors Including Pesticides," Moyers, May 2, 2013, http://billmoyers.com/2013/05/02/honey-bee-die-off-caused/.
920   Inhabitat Staff, "Pesticide industry spending 'hundreds of thousands of dollars' to slow U.S. bee protection," inhabitat, accesssed March 4, 2020, http://inhabitat.com/pesticide-industry-spending-hundreds-of-thousands-of-dollarsto-slow-u-s-bee-protection/.
921   "Report: Pesticide industry delaying bee protections across U.S." Friends of the Earth, accesssed June 17, 2016, https://inhabitat.com/pesticide-industry-spending-hundreds-of-thousands-of-dollars-to-slow-u-s-bee-protection/.
922   "UN human rights experts call for global treaty to regulate dangerous pesticides," UN News, March 7, 2017, http://www.un.org/apps/news/story.asp?NewsID=56311#.WMXUMBLytuU.
923   Darryl Fears, "The monarch massacre: Nearly a billion butterflies have vanished," The Washington Post, February 9, 2015, https://www.washingtonpost.com/news/energy-environment/wp/2015/02/09/themonarch-massacre-nearly-a-billion-butterflies-have-vanished/?utm_term=.44ed14669b7b.
924   "Neonicotinoids, Glyphosate & Organophosphates," Friends of the Earth, accesssed March 4, 2020, https://foe.org/neonicotinoids-glyphosate/.
925   Vicki Batts, "Thousands of people now have non-Hodgkin's Lymphoma due to glyphosate (Roundup) exposure, warns legal firm that's suing Monsanto," Glyphosate News, March 23, 2017, https://foe.org/neonicotinoids-glyphosate/.
926   Alanna Mitchell, "The 1,300 Bird Species Facing Extinction Signal Threats to Human Health," National Geographic, August 26, 2014, https://news.nationalgeographic.com/news/2014/08/140825-bird-environmentchemical-contaminant-climate-change-science-winged-warning/.

927   Eric Andrew-Gee, "Bird populations in steep decline in North America, study finds," The Globe and Mail, May 17, 2018, https://www.theglobeandmail.com/technology/science/report-finds-north-americanskies-quieter-by-15-billion-fewer-birds/article31876053/.
928   "Birds, Bees, and Aquatic Life Threatened by Gross Underestimate of Toxicity of World's Most Widely Used Pesticide," American Bird Conservancy, March 20, 2013, https://abcbirds.org/article/birds-bees-andaquatic-life-threatened-by-gross-underestimate-of-toxicity-of-worlds-most-widely-used-pesticide-2/.
929   "The Impact of the Nation's Most Widely Used Insecticides on Birds," American Bird Conservancy, accesssed March 4, 2020, http://abcbirds.org/wp-content/uploads/2015/05/Neonic_FINAL.pdf.
930   Alanna Mitchell, "The 1,300 Bird Species Facing Extinction Signal Threats to Human Health," National Geographic, August 26, 2014.
931   Isabelle Z. "How the Ancient Maya civilization cultivated organic crops using herbal medicine to combat pests," Natural News, July 8, 2016, http://www.naturalnews.com/054596_natural_pesticides_Mayans_agriculture.html.
932   "Traditional Chinese Agriculture and Farming," Facts and Details, November 2011, http://factsanddetails.com/china/cat9/sub63/item1892.html.
933   Eric Andrew-Gee, "Bird populations in steep decline in North America, study finds." 943 Zoetis, Data Shows Growing Prevalence of Diabetes Among U.S. Pets," Cision, November 18, 2015, http://www.prnewswire.com/news-releases/data-shows-growing-prevalence-of-diabetes-among-us-pets300180613.html.
934   Rachel Frazin, "Trump administration stops probing most bird deaths: report," The Hill, December 24, 2019, https://thehill.com/policy/energy-environment/475838-trump-administration-stops-probing-most-bird-deaths-report.
935   "Diabetes in cats and dogs up by 900% over the past five years: Owners giving pampered pets human food partly fueling huge rise in cases, Daily Mail, May 16, 2016, https://www.dailymail.co.uk/news/article-3593935/Diabetes-cats-dogs-900-past-five-years.html.
936   If you are concerned that your pet may have diabetes, check http://www.diabetescare.net/authors/claraschneider/dogs-and-cats-with-diabetes for more information.
937   If you are concerned that your pet may have diabetes, check

http://www.diabetescare.net/authors/claraschneider/dogs-and-cats-with-diabetes for more information.

938   "Now Pets Are Suffering From Bad Flint Water Supplies," The Alternative Daily, January 27, 2019, http://www.thealternativedaily.com/now-pets-are-suffering-from-bad-flint-water-supplies/.

939   Shari Miller, "Dog owners concerned as thousands of dogs dying or suffering," Daily Mail, July 3, 2016, http://www.dailymail.co.uk/news/article-3672378/Thousands-dogs-dying-suffering-severe-reactionsvaccinated-against-bacterial-infections.html?ITO=applenews.

940   "Supplier to Petco and Petsmart captured gassing, freezing and torturing animals to death on secret video, claims PETA," Daily Mail, May 23, 2016, http://www.dailymail.co.uk/news/article-3605076/Fedinspectors-sick-dead-animals-pet-store-supplier.html?ITO=applenews.

941   "ASPCA Research Shows Americans Overwhelmingly Support Investigations to Expose Animal Abuse on Industrial Farms," ASPCA, February 17, 2012, http://www.aspca.org/about-us/press-releases/aspca-researchshows-americans-overwhelmingly-support-investigations-expose.

942   "Factory Farms: Farm Animals Need Our Help," ASPCA, accessed March 4, 2020, https://www.aspca.org/animal-cruelty/farmanimal-welfare.

943   "Factory Farms: Farm Animals Need Our Help," ASPCA,

944   David E. Hoffman, Emma Schwartz, "Sharp Increase Seen in Sales of Antibiotics for Use in Farm Animals," Frontline, October 2, 2014, http://www.pbs.org/wgbh/frontline/article/sharp-increase-seen-in-salesof-antibiotics-for-use-in-farm-animals/.

945   Helena Bottemiller, "Meat Industry Defends Antibiotic Use," Food Safety News, February 25, 2010, http://www.foodsafetynews.com/2010/02/meat-industry-defends-antibiotic-use-on-thehill/#.Vpk_EVMrJE4.

946   Dr. Mercola, "The Antibiotic Apocalypse Advances," Mercola, September 20, 2016, http://articles.mercola.com/sites/articles/archive/2016/09/20/stop-antibiotic-resistantbacteria.aspx?utm_source=dnl&utm_medium=email&utm_content=art1&utm_campaign=20160920Z1&et _cid=DM117506&et_rid=1672279628.

947   Martha Rosenberg, "Our food system is rigged: How the corporate food industry is taking desperate steps to fight animal reforms," Salon, August 23, 2016, http://www.salon.com/2016/08/23/our-

food-systemis-rigged-how-the-corporate-food-industry-is-taking-desperate-steps-to-fight-animalreforms_partner/?utm_medium=email&utm_source=flipboard.

948   Ed Yong, "The Plan to Avert Our Post-Antibiotic Apocalypse," The Atlantic, May 19, 2016, https://www.theatlantic.com/science/archive/2016/05/the-ten-part-plan-to-avert-our-post-antibioticapocalypse/483360/.

949   Kim Bellware, "Scientists Have Found Bacteria Resistant To 'Last Resort' Drug," HuffPost, November 19, 2015, https://www.huffpost.com/entry/antibiotic-resistant-bacteria-colistin_n_564dfbcee4b00b7997f98827.

950   Ashley Welch, "Scientists warn we're moving closer to a "post-antibiotic era," CBS News, November 20, 2015, http://www.cbsnews.com/news/scientists-discover-bacteria-resistant-to-last-line-antibiotics/.

951   "Gray Wolf (Canis lupus)," US Fish and Wildlife Services, December 2011, https://www.fws.gov/midwest/wolf/aboutwolves/biologue.htm.

952   Laura Bies, "House passes legislation to delist gray wolves," The Wildlife Society, November 28, 2018, https://www.congress.gov/bill/115th-congress/house-bill/424/all-info?r=1#cosponsors.

953   "American Black Bear (Ursus americanus)," Untamed Science, accessed March 4, 2020, http://www.untamedscience.com/biodiversity/american-black-bear/.

954   "American Black Bear (Ursus americanus)," Untamed Science accessed March 4, 2020.

955   Katie Herrel, "Ask A Bear: How Many Bear Attacks, Really?" BackPacker, December 1, 2009, http://www.backpacker.com/news-and-events/ask-a-bear-how-many-bear-attacks-really-2.

956   Wikipedia, "Brown bear," last modified January 28, 2019, https://en.wikipedia.org/wiki/Brown_bear.

957   Wikipedia, "Brown bear." last modified January 28, 2019.

958   Stephen Herrero, Bear *Attacks: Their Causes and Avoidance* (Connecticut: Lyons Press, 2002). viii-ix.

959   "Basic Facts About Polar Bears," Defenders of Wildlife, accessed March 4, 2020, http://www.defenders.org/polar-bear/basicfacts.

960   "Threats to Polar Bears," World Wildlife Federation (WWF), accessed March 4, 2020, https://defenders.org/wildlife/polar-bear.

961	Deirdra Lockwood, "Polar Bear Cubs at High Risk from Toxic Industrial Chemicals, Despite Bans," Scientific American, accessed March 6, 2020, https://arcticwwf.org/species/polar-bear/threats/.
962	James O'Hare, "Half of the Species on Earth Could Go Extinct by 2050, Scientists Say," Global Citizen, February 27, 2017, https://www.globalcitizen.org/en/content/half-earths-species-extinct-2050/.
963	Gerardo Ceballos, Paul R. Ehrlich and all, "Accelerated modern human–induced species losses: Entering the sixth mass extinction," Science Advances, June 19, 2015, http://advances.sciencemag.org/content/1/5/e1400253.
964	"How to Save the Natural World on Which We Depend," The Pontifical Academy of Sciences, February 27, 2017, http://www.casinapioiv.va/content/accademia/en/events/2017/extinction.html.
965	"How many species on Earth? About 8.7 million, new estimate says," ScienceDaily, August 24, 2011, https://www.sciencedaily.com/releases/2011/08/110823180459.htm.
966	Rhett Butler, "Calculating Deforestation Figures for the Amazon," Mongabay, January 26, 2017, https://rainforests.mongabay.com/amazon/deforestation_calculations.html.
967	Mark Schwartz, "Selective logging causes widespread destruction, study finds," Stanford News, October 21, 2005, https://news.stanford.edu/news/2005/october26/select-102605.html.
968	Story Hinckley, "Why large animals face a double (or triple) jeopardy," The Christian Science Monitor, June 10, 2016, http://www.csmonitor.com/Environment/2016/0610/Why-large-animals-face-a-double-ortriple-jeopardy.
969	Story Hinckley, "Why large animals face a double (or triple) jeopardy," The Christian Science Monitor, June 10, 2016, http://www.csmonitor.com/Environment/2016/0610/Why-large-animals-face-a-double-ortriple-jeopardy.
970	Chris Mooney, "What the 'sixth extinction' will look like in the oceans: The largest species die off first," The Washington Post, September 14, 2016, https://www.washingtonpost.com/news/energy environment/wp/2016/09/14/what-the-sixth-extinction-will-look-like-in-the-oceans-the-largest-species-dieoff-first/?utm_term=.08920b6cb33c.
971	"How to Save the Natural World on Which We Depend," The Pontifical Academy of Sciences, February 27, 2017.

972   Megan Trimble, "The 10 Species 'Imperiled' by Trump-Era Politics," US News and World Report, December 27, 2018, https://www.usnews.com/news/national-news/articles/2018-12-27/trump-is-putting-species-atrisk-endangered-species-coalition-says.
973   Justin Worland, "How the Endangered Species Act Helps Save Humans, Too," Time Magazine, February 15, 2017, http://time.com/4671860/endangered-species-act-reform-climate-change/.
974   "THE EXTINCTION CRISIS," Center for Biological Diversity, accessed March 4, 2020, http://www.biologicaldiversity.org/programs/biodiversity/elements_of_biodiversity/extinction_crisis/.
975   Eric Chivian and Aaron Bernstein (eds.), *Sustaining life: How human health depends on biodiversity, Center for Health and the Global Environment* (New York: Oxford University Press, 2008), 145–148.
976   Eric Chivian and Aaron Bernstein (eds.), Sustaining life: How human health depends on biodiversity, 18.
977   Holly Dublin, "Endangered Species," Encyclopedia Britannica, accessed March 4, 2020, http://www.britannica.com/EBchecked/topic/186738/endangered-species.
978   Judith D. Schwartz, "There's another story to tell about climate change. And it starts with water," The Guardian, April 3, 2017, https://www.theguardian.com/commentisfree/2017/apr/03/climate-change-waterfossil-fuel.
979   "Earth's Steamy Blanket," NASA Earth Observatory, accessed March 4, 2020, https://earthobservatory.nasa.gov/Features/WaterVapor/water_vapor2.php.
980   "Explaining how the water vapor greenhouse effect works," Skeptical Science, July, 2015, https://www.skepticalscience.com/water-vapor-greenhouse-gas.htm.
981   Willie Scott, "Reducing Greenhouse Gases and Emissions Can Save the Environment," Environmental Science, 2019, http://www.brighthub.com/environment/science-environmental/articles/66073.aspx.
982   Wikipedia, "Carbon dioxide in Earth's atmosphere," last modified January 25, 2019, https://en.wikipedia.org/wiki/Carbon_dioxide_in_Earth%27s_atmosphere.
983   Jay R. Malcolm, Louis F. Pitelka, "Ecosystems and Global Climate Change," Center for Climate and Energy Solutions, Dec.ember2001, https://www.c2es.org/document/ecosystems-and-global-climate-change/.

984   "Earth's temperature is a balancing act," EPA Climate Change Science, City of Philadelphia, June 7, 2017, https://cityofphiladelphia.github.io/climatechangeisreal/climate-change-science/causes-climate-change/.
985   "Earth's temperature is a balancing act," EPA Climate Change Science, City of Philadelphia, June 7, 2017.
986   Rebecca Lindsey, "Climate Change: Atmospheric Carbon Dioxide," NOAA, Climate.gov, September 19, 2019, https://www.climate.gov/news-features/understanding-climate/climate-change-atmospheric-carbon-dioxide.
987   "Volcanoes can affect the Earth's climate," USGS, https://volcanoes.usgs.gov/vhp/gas_climate.html.
988   Anmar Frangoul, "Humans are changing climate 170 times faster than nature, say researchers," CNBC, February 13, 2017, http://www.cnbc.com/2017/02/13/humans-are-changing-climate-170-times-faster-thannature-say-researchers.html.
989   University of Southampton, "Future carbon dioxide, climate warming potentially unprecedented in 420 million years, Science Daily, April 4, 2017, https://www.sciencedaily.com/releases/2017/04/170404124402.htm.
990   "Climate," Bristol University, accessed March 4, 2020, http://palaeo.gly.bris.ac.uk/Palaeofiles/Triassic/climate.htm.
991   Carl Zimmer, "The Planet Has Seen Warming Before! It Wiped Out Almost Everything," December 11, 2018, The New York Times, https://www.nytimes.com/2018/12/07/science/climate-change-mass-extinction.html.
992   Riley E. Dunlap and Aaron M McCright, "Organized Climate Change Denial," In *The Oxford Handbook of Climate Change and Society*, Ed. John S. Dryzek, Richard B. Norgaard, and David (Oxford: Oxford University Press, 2011), 144-160.
993   Naomi Klein, *This Changes Everything* (New York: Simon and Schuster, 2014), 39.
994   Naomi Klein, *This Changes Everything*, 41.
995   "Food Insecurity in The United States," Feeding America, http://map.feedingamerica.org/.
996   Bernadette D. Proctor, Jessica L. Semega, and Melissa A. Kollar "Income and Poverty in the United States: 2015," United States Census Bureau, September 2016, 13, https://www.census.gov/content/dam/

Census/library/publications/2016/demo/p60-256.pdf.
997 Colin Todhunter, "Restoring the Link Between Farmer and Consumer, Challenging the Corporate Hijack of Global Food and Agriculture," Global Research, January 16, 2016, http://www.global-research.ca/restoring-the-link-between-farmer-and-consumer-challenging-the-corporatehijack-of-global-food-and-agriculture/5501709.
998 Source Watch, "Rockefeller Foundation," last modified July 15, 2018, https://www.sourcewatch.org/index.php/Rockefeller_Foundation.
999 Sam Husseini, "Right-Wing Business in Farmer's Overalls," FAIR, September 1, 2000, http://fair.org/extra/right-wing-business-in-farmers-overalls/.
1000 Source Watch, "Rockefeller Foundation," last modified July 15, 2018,.
1001 Source Watch, "Rockefeller Foundation," last modified July 15, 2018.
1002 "THE NSSM 200 DIRECTIVE AND THE STUDY REQUESTED," National Securing Council, April, 24, 1974, http://www.population-security.org/28-APP2A.html. See http://www.population-security.org/11-CH3.html, for cover letter and table of contents.
1003 Brian Clowes, Ph.D., "Exposing the Global Population Control Agenda," Human Life International, February 26, 2014, https://www.hli.org/resources/exposing-the-global-population-control/.
1004 Rasha B. Foda, "Kissinger: Control Food and you Control the People," SHAREeverthing.com, May, 23, 2016, https://shareverything.com/2016/05/23/kissinger-control-food-and-you-control-the-people/.
1005 Arun Shrivastava, "Seeds of Destruction: The Hidden Agenda of Genetic Manipulation," Global Research, June 19, 2008, http://www.globalresearch.ca/seeds-of-destruction-the-hidden-agenda-of-geneticmanipulation-2/9379.
1006 Nigel Morris, "The big five companies that control the world's grain trade," Independent, January 23, 2013, http://www.independent.co.uk/news/uk/home-news/the-big-five-companies-that-control-the-worlds-graintrade-8462266.html.
1007 F. William Engdahl, *Seeds of Destruction: The Hidden Agenda of Genetic Manipulation* (Montreal: Center for Research on Globalization, 2007), 143.
1008 Arun Shrivastava, "Seeds of Destruction: The Hidden Agenda of Genetic Manipulation," June 19, 2008, Global Research, https://

globalresearch.ca/seeds-of-destruction-the-hidden-agenda-of-genetic-manipulation-2/9379.
1009   "Colleges of Agriculture at the Land Grant Universities: A Profile (1995), Chapter: 6 The Shifting Base of Financial Support for Land Grant College Research and Extension, The National Academies Press, accessed March 4, 2020, https://www.nap.edu/read/4980/chapter/7.
1010   Heather Landry, "Challenging Evolution: How GMOs Can Influence Genetic Diversity," Science in the News, Harvard University, August 10, 2015, http://sitn.hms.harvard.edu/flash/2015/challenging-evolutionhow-gmos-can-influence-genetic-diversity/.
1011   Stacy Malkan, "Searle Foundation: Climate Science Denial Network Funds Toxic Chemical Propaganda," US RTK, March 2, 2017, https://usrtk.org/tag/searle-foundation/.
1012   Stacy Malkan, "Searle Foundation: Climate Science Denial Network Funds Toxic Chemical Propaganda, March 2, 2017
1013   Thom Hartmann, "How the Corporate Food Industry Destroys Democracy," AlterNet, July 7, 2016, http://www.alternet.org/food/how-corporate-food-industry-destroys   democracy?akid=14420.1930755.CYkNDH&rd=1&src=newsletter1059359&t=9.
1014   Stephen Dinan, "Obama signs bill overturning Vermont's GMO labeling law," The Washington Times, August 2, 2016, http://www.washingtontimes.com/news/2016/aug/2/obama-signs-bill-overturning-vermontsgmo-labeling/.
1015   David H. Freedman, "The Truth about Genetically Modified Food," Scientific American, September 1, 2013, https://www.scientificamerican.com/article/the-truth-about-genetically-modified-food/.
1016   "GM Crops List," International Service for the Acquisition of Agri-Biotech Applications, accessed March 4, 2020, http://www.isaaa.org/gmapprovaldatabase/cropslist/default.asp.
1017   "Non-GMO Project Verified is North America's Most Trusted Seal for GMO avoidance," NON-GMO Project, accessed March 4, 2020, https://www.nongmoproject.org/.
1018   Brittany Cordeiro, "Do GMOs cause cancer?" University of Texas, MD Anderson Center, June, 2014, https://www.mdanderson.org/publications/focused-on-health/gmos-cancer.h15-1589046.html
1019   Emily Cassidy, "Feeding the World Without GMOs," Environmental Working Group, March, 2015, http://cdn3.ewg.org/sites/

default/files/EWG%20Feeding%20the%20World%20Without%20GMOs%20201 5.pdf?_ga=1.78193172.1609920329.1428230447.

1020   Danny Hakim, "Doubts About the Promised Bounty of Genetically Modified Crops," New York Times, October 29, 2016, https://www.nytimes.com/2016/10/30/business/gmo-promise-falls-short.html?_r=1.

1021   Danny Hakim, "Doubts About the Promised Bounty of Genetically Modified Crops,"

1022   "Do GM Crops Increase Yield?" Monsanto, May 6, 2017, http://www.monsanto.com/newsviews/pages/do-gm-crops-increase-yield.aspx.

1023   "Profile: PG Economics," LobbyWatch.org, accessed March 4, 2020, http://www.lobbywatch.org/profile1.asp?PrId=308.

1024   Danny Hakim, "Doubts About the Promised Bounty of Genetically Modified Crops,"

1025   Danny Hakim, "Doubts About the Promised Bounty of Genetically Modified Crops," New York Times October 29, 2016, https://www.nytimes.com/2016/10/30/business/gmo-promise-falls-short-html?auth=login-email&login=email.

1026   Reynard Loki, "We've Been Sold a Lie for Two Decades About Genetically Engineered Foods," AlterNet, December 1, 2016, http://www.alternet.org/food/genetically-engineered-foods-have-enriched-fewmega-corporations-while-hurtingenvironmental?akid=14985.1930755.Ie9rIN&rd=1&src=newsletter1068037&t=2.

1027   Reynard Loki, "We've Been Sold a Lie for Two Decades About Genetically Engineered Foods" AlterNet, December 1, 2016.

1028   "Vermont's GMO Legacy: Pesticides, Polluted Water & Climate Destruction," Regeneration Vermont, 2016, http://regenerationvermont.org/wp-content/uploads/2015/12/RVT_VermontsGMOaddiction_9.pdf.

1029   "Solutions: Advance Sustainable Agriculture," Union of Concerned Scientists, accessed March 4, 2020, https://www.ucsusa.org/our-work/food-agriculture/solutions/advance-sustainableagriculture#.XFIYMrh7mUl.

1030   "Sustainable Agriculture," Food/Sustainable Agriculture, Union of Concerned Scientists, accessed March 6, 2020, https://www.ucsusa.org/food/sustainable-agriculture#.XFIYMrh7mUI.

1031   James E. Horne, Maura McDermott, *The Next Green Revolu-*

tion: *Essential Steps to a Healthy, Sustainable Agriculture* (New York: The Hawthorne Press, 2001), See the comparison chart between Industrial Agriculture and Sustainable Agriculture on page 261, Available at http://base.dnsgb.com.ua/files/book/Agriculture/Sustainable-Agriculture/The-Next-Green-Revolution.pdf.

1032   "Calories Needed Each Day," Parent Tips, We Can! 2010, https://www.nhlbi.nih.gov/health/educational/wecan/downloads/calreqtips.pdf.

1033   "What is Junk Food," Fat Free Kitchen, accessed March 4, 2020, https://www.fatfreekitchen.com/junkfoods/junkfoods1.html.

1034   Elaine McGee, MPH, RD, "Junk-Food Facts," WebMD, http://www.webmd.com/diet/features/junkfood-facts#1.

1035   Tracey Roizman, "Reasons Eating Junk Food Is Not Good," SFGate, December 7, 2018, https://healthyeating.sfgate.com/reasons-eating-junk-food-not-good-3364.html.

1036   Steve Bradt, "Obesity rate will reach at least 42%," The Harvard Gazette, November 4, 2010, http://news.harvard.edu/gazette/story/2010/11/obesity-rate-will-reach-at-least-42/.

1037   "Health Risks Linked to Obesity," WebMD, accessed March 4, 2020, https://www.webmd.com/diet/obesity/obesity-health-risks#1.

1038   "Food and Mood: Teen Nutrition and Mental Health," Newport Academy, May 10, 2017, https://www.newportacademy.com/resources/empowering-teens/food-mood-nutrition-teen-mental-health/.

1039   Tracey Roizman, "Reasons Eating Junk Food Is Not Good," SFGate, December 7, 2018

1040   Wikipedia, "Super Size Me," last modified January 28, 2019, https://en.wikipedia.org/wiki/Super_Size_Me.

1041   James H. O'Keefe, Neil M. Gheewala and Joan O. O'Keefe, "Dietary Strategies for Improving PostPrandial Glucose, Lipids, Inflammation, and Cardiovascular Health," Journal of the American College of Cardiology, Volume 51, Issue 3, January, 2008, http://www.onlinejacc.org/content/51/3/249?maxtoshow=&HITS=10&hits=10&RESULTFORMAT=&aut

1042   Dr. Mercola, "What Happens to Your Body When You Eat Junk Food?" Mercola, April 29, 2015, http://articles.mercola.com/sites/articles/archive/2015/04/29/junk-food-metabolism.aspx#_edn4.

1043   "More Shocking Fast Food Statistics You Should Know," University Hospitals, July 15, 2016, https://blog.partnersforyourhealth.com/blog/more-shocking-fast-food-statistics-you-should-know.

1044 "More Shocking Fast Food Statistics You Should Know," University Hospitals, July 15, 2016

1045 Katie Wells, "Ten Reasons to Avoid Soda (& How to Kick the Habit)," Wellness Mama, January 23, 2019, https://wellnessmama.com/379/reasons-to-avoid-soda/.

1046 Mark Hyman MD, "5 Reasons High Fructose Corn Syrup Will Kill You," Dr. Hyman, http://drhyman.com/blog/2011/05/13/5-reasons-high-fructose-corn-syrup-will-kill-you/.

1047 "Why Are Foods High in Fructose Corn Syrup So Popular?" Elevation Organic Catsup, accessed March 4, 2020, https://www.elevationgourmet.com/blogs/healthy-eating/why-are-foods-high-in-fructose-corn-syrup-so-popular.

1048 Mark Hyman, MD, "Why You Should Never Eat High Fructose Corn Syrup," Huffpost, January 23, 2014, https://www.huffpost.com/entry/high-fructose-corn-syrup_b_4256220.

1049 Kris Gunnars, BSc, "Nine ways that processed foods are harming people," Medical News Today, August 1, 2017, https://www.medicalnewstoday.com/articles/318630.php.

1050 Wikipedia, "Reward system," last modified January 27, 2019, https://en.wikipedia.org/wiki/Reward_system.

1051 "How Food Addiction Works (And What to Do About It)," HealthLine, accessed March 4, 2020, https://www.healthline.com/nutrition/how-food-addiction-works.

1052 Caroline Davis, "From Passive Overeating to 'Food Addiction': A Spectrum of Compulsion and Severity," International Scholarship Research Notices, Volume 2013, Article ID 435027, May 15, 2013, https://www.hindawi.com/journals/isrn/2013/435027/.

1053 Helen Kollias, "Research Review: A calorie isn't a calorie," Precision Nutrition, accesssed March 4, 2020, https://www.precisionnutrition.com/digesting-whole-vs-processed-foods.

1054 "Food Deserts," Food Empowerment Project, accessed March 4, 2020, http://www.foodispower.org/food-deserts/.

1055 Reynard Loki, "People Who Feel Socially Inferior Eat More and Prefer Unhealthy Food," AlterNet, February 23, 2017, http://www.alternet.org/food/people-who-feel-socially-inferior-eat-more-and-preferunhealthy-food?akid=15261.1930755.Xk8e-J&rd=1&src=newsletter1072793&t=2.

1056   Nichole Tucker, "Obesity And Malnutrition Are The 'New Normal' In Most Countries, Report Says," Inquisitr, June 15, 2016, http://www.inquisitr.com/3206608/obesity-and-malnutrition-are-the-new-normalin-most-countries-report-says/.
1057   "Ag-gag Bills Continue to Flourish in 2015," National Anti-Vivisection Society (NAVS), august 3, 2015, http://www.navs.org/ag-gag-bills-continue-to-flourish-in-2015/.
1058   Nancy Fink Huehnergarth, "Big Agriculture Bullies And Lobbies To Keep Americans In The Dark," Forbes, May 5, 2016, http://www.forbes.com/sites/nancyhuehnergarth/2016/05/05/big-ag-bullies-andlobbies-to-keep-americans-in-the-dark/2/#55539df9329f.
1059   Rick Friday, Facebook, accessed March 5, 2020, https://www.faceook.com/photo.php?fbid=10208214317168718&set=a.1177284905382.27765.1025887983 &type=3&theater.
1060   Laura Kusisto, "Many Who Lost Homes to Foreclosure in Last Decade Won't Return — NAR," The Wall Street Journal, April 20, 2015, https://www.wsj.com/articles/many-who-lost-homes-to-foreclosure-in-last-decade-wont-return-nar-1429548640.
1061   Mark Memmott, "Big Banks Agree To Pay $8.5 Billion To Settle Foreclosure-Abuse Claims," NPR, January 7, 2013. http://www.npr.org/sections/thetwo-way/2013/01/07/168790359/big-banks-agree-to-pay-8-5billion-to-settle-foreclosure-abuse-claims.
1062   David Dayen, "Sorry You Lost Your Home: Americans Deserve More Than an Apology for the Foreclosure Fraud Epidemic," AlterNet, August 9, 2016, http://www.alternet.org/economy/americanforeclosure-fraud-epidemic?akid=14531.1930755.EWdw0M&rd=1&src=newsletter1061833&t=18.
1063   Emily Badger, "How the housing crisis left us more racially segregated," The Washington Post, May 8, 2015, https://www.washingtonpost.com/news/wonk/wp/2015/05/08/how-the-housing-crisis-left-us-moreracially-segregated/?noredirect=on&utm_term=.66584831ff7f.
1064   Emily Badger, "How the housing crisis left us more racially segregated," The Washington Post, May 8, 2015.
1065   Mark Uh, "From Own To Rent: Who Lost The American Dream?," Trulia Research, February 11, 2016, https://www.trulia.com/blog/trends/own-to-rent/.
1066   Bryce Covert, "Surprise funding cuts from the Trump admin-

istration will hit poor New York City residents hard," Think Progress, March 13, 2017, https://thinkprogress.org/new-york-public-housing-trump-cuts-a83399eaa528.

1067   Bryce Cover, "Trump budget cuts amount to 'a homelessness plan,' advocates say," Think Progress, March 16, 2017, https://thinkprogress.org/trump-budget-cuts-hud-housing-d5b7617b9b76.

1068   Bryce Cover, "Trump budget cuts amount to 'a homelessness plan,' advocates say," Think Progress, March 16, 2017.

1069   "Demographic Facts: Residents Living in Public Housing," National Center for Health in Public Housing, May 31, 2016, https://nchph.org/wp-content/uploads/2016/07/Demographics-Fact-Sheet-20161.pdf.

1070   John W. Schoen, "Study: 1.2 million households lost to recession," NBC News, April 8, 2010, http://www.nbcnews.com/id/36231884/ns/business-eye_on_the_economy/t/study-million-households-lostrecession/#.XFJKn7h7mUl.

1071   Charlie May, "Ben Carson is worried that public housing is too good for poor people," May 3, 2017, http://www.salon.com/2017/05/03/ben-carson-is-worried-that-public-housing-is-too-good-for-poor-people/.

1072   "Veteran Homelessness: A Supplemental Report to the 2009 Annual Homeless Assessment Report to Congress," US Dept. of Housing and Urban Development, and Dept. of Veteran Affairs, 5, accessed March 4, 2020, https://files.hudexchange.info/resources/documents/2009AHARVeteransReport.pdf.

1073   "Facts and Figures: The Homeless," PBS, June 29, 2009, https://www.pbs.org/now/shows/526/homeless-facts.html.

1074   "State of Homelessness," National Alliance to End Homelessness, accessed March 4, 2020, https://endhomelessness.org/homelessness-in-america/homelessness-statistics/state-of-homelessnessreport/.

1075   Maria L. LaGanga, "Mortality rate for homeless youth in San Francisco is 10 times higher than peers," The Guardian, April 14, 2016, https://www.theguardian.com/us-news/2016/apr/14/san-francisco-homeless-youth-ten-times-more-likely-to-die?CMP=oth_b-aplnews_d-1.

1076   "Homelessness and Domestic Violence," DomesticShelters.org, January 7, 2015. https://www.domesticshelters.org/domestic-violence-statistics/homelessness-and-domestic-violence.

1077   Crystal Shepeard, "Stigma and High Rents Exacerbate Efforts to House Homeless," Care2, June 11, 2016, http://www.care2.com/causes/stigma-and-high-rents-exacerbate-efforts-to-househomeless.html?utm_source=feedburner&utm_medium=feed&utm_campaign=Feed%3A+c2causes+%28Ca uses%29.
1078   Tim Redmon, "Homelessness: the media's big problem," 48hills, June 29, 2016, http://48hills.org/2016/06/29/homelessness-the-medias-big-problem/.
1079   See what Zillow has to say about housing loss due to rising seas at http://www.cnsnews.com/news/article/joe-setyon/zillow-claims-rising-sea-levels-could-submerge-19million-us-homes-2100.
1080   "Roles of Clothing/Clothing Choices," http://www.uen.org/cte/family/clothing-1/downloads/psychology/option-1.pdf.
1081   In 2017 dollars.
1082   Stephanie Vatz, "Why America Stopped Making Its Own Clothes," KQED News, May 24, 2013 http://ww2.kqed.org/lowdown/2013/05/24/madeinamerica/.
1083   Stephanie Vatz, "Why America Stopped Making Its Own Clothes," KQED News, May 24, 2013.
1084   "Fashion," Bureau of Labor Statistics, June, 2012, https://www.bls.gov/spotlight/2012/fashion/
1085   "Fashion," Bureau of Labor Statistics,
1086   Stephanie Vatz, "Why America Stopped Making Its Own Clothes," KQED News, May 24, 2013.
1087   Robert Pollin, Justine Burns, and James Heintz, "Global apparel production and sweatshop labour: can raising retail prices finance living wages?" Political Economy Research Institute, University of Massachusetts, 7, 2002, https://scholarworks.umass.edu/cgi/viewcontent.cgi?article=1012&context=peri_workingpapers.
1088   "Flawed FabricsThe abuse of girls and women workers in the South Indian textile industry," SOMO - Centre for Research on Multinational Corporations, ICN - India Committee of the Netherlands, October 2014, http://www.indianet.nl/pdf/FlawedFabrics.pdf.
1089   Josephine Moulds, "Child labour in the fashion supply chain, Where, why and what can be done," UNICEF, The Guardian, accessed March 4, 2020, https://labs.theguardian.com/unicef-child-labour/.
1090   Josephine Moulds, "Child labour in the fashion supply chain,

Where, why and what can be done."

1091   Emilie Schultze, "Exploitation or emancipation? Women workers in the garment industry," Fashion Revolution, 2015, http://fashionrevolution.org/exploitation-or-emancipation-women-workers-in-thegarment-industry/.

1092   "Women garment factory workers in India face sexual, physical abuse, new report says," ABC News, June 24, 2016, http://www.abc.net.au/news/2016-06-25/abuse-rife-in-indias-garment-industry/7543498.

1093   Jagg Xxax, "Top Ten Ethical Issues in a Fashion Business," Chron, June, 29, 2018, http://smallbusiness.chron.com/top-ten-ethical-issues-fashion-business-21866.html.

1094   Kevin Liptak, "Trump: 'Nobody knew health care could be so complicated'" CNN, February 28, 2017, http://www.cnn.com/2017/02/27/politics/trump-health-care-complicated/.

1095   Michelle Kulas, "Top 10 Health Problems in America," LiveStrong.com, December 18, 2018, http://www.livestrong.com/article/36536-top-health-problems-america/.

1096   "Heart Disease," National Center for Health Statistics, Centers for Disease Control and Prevention, accessed March 4, 2020, https://www.cdc.gov/nchs/fastats/heart-disease.htm.

1097   "Cancer Stat Facts: Cancer of Any Site," National Cancer Institute, accessed March 4, 2020, https://seer.cancer.gov/statfacts/html/all.html.

1098   "Stroke Facts," Centers for Disease Control and Prevention, accessed March 4, 2020, https://www.cdc.gov/stroke/facts.htm.

1099   "Chronic Obstructive Pulmonary Disease (COPD) Includes: Chronic Bronchitis and Emphysema," National Center for Health Statistics, CDC, accessed March 4, 2020, https://www.cdc.gov/nchs/fastats/copd.htm.

1100   Jo Marchant, *Cure: A Journey into the Science of Mind Over Body* (New York: Crown Publishers, 2016), 254.

1101   David Heath, "Contesting the Science of Smoking," The Atlantic, May 4, 2016, https://www.theatlantic.com/politics/archive/2016/05/low-tar-cigarettes/481116/.

1102   Patricia F. Roberts, "Cigarette Smoking vs Death from Coronary Heart Disease," StatCrunch, accessed March 4, 2020, https://www.statcrunch.com/5.0/viewreport.php?reportid=24348.

1103   "Study Shows Smoking Is A Leading Cause Of Fire Disaster And Death Worldwide, Costing Over $27 Billion Yearly," UCDavis Health, August 4 2000, https://www.ucdmc.ucdavis.edu/publish/news/newsroom/2763.

1104   Ylan Q. Mui, "The shocking number of Americans who can't cover a $400 expense," The Washington Post, May 25, 2016, https://www.washingtonpost.com/news/wonk/wp/2016/05/25/the-shocking-numberof-americans-who-cant-cover-a-400-expense/.

1105   Dan Mangan, "24 million would lose health insurance coverage by 2026 under GOP's Obamacare replacement, new estimate says," CNBC, March 13, 2017, http://www.cnbc.com/2017/03/13/cbo-saysmillions-lose-health-insurance-under-gop-obamacare-replacement.html.

1106   "The History Of Quackery," International Wellness Directory, accessed March 4, 2020, http://www.mnwelldir.org/docs/history/quackery.htm.

1107   Elora Hilmas, "Prescription Drug Abuse," Teens Health, October, 2018, http://kidshealth.org/en/teens/prescription-drug-abuse.html. While this article places the onus of prescription drug abuse on the patient, doctors are often responsible for misdiagnosis of drugs.

1108   Peter Eisler and Barbara Hansen, "Doctors perform thousands of unnecessary surgeries," USA Today, June 19, 2013, https://www.usatoday.com/story/news/nation/2013/06/18/unnecessary-surgery-usa-todayinvestigation/2435009/.

1109   "The History Of Quackery," International Wellness Directory, accessed March 4, 2020.

1110   "Flexner Report...Birth Of Modern Medical Education," MedicineNet, August 5, 2000, http://www.medicinenet.com/script/main/art.asp?articlekey=8795.

1111   "How The Flexner Report Hijacked Natural Medicine," Principia Scientific International, January. 19, 2019, https://principia-scientific.org/how-the-flexner-report-hijacked-natural-medicine/.

1112   "How the Flexner Report hijacked natural medicine," Cancer Tutor, April 20, 2018, https://www.cancertutor.com/flexner-report/.

1113   "New CDC report: More than 100 million Americans have diabetes or prediabetes," CDC Newsroom, CDC, July 18, 2017, https://www.cdc.gov/media/releases/2017/p0718-diabetes-report.html.

1114   "How the Flexner Report hijacked natural medicine," Cancer Tutor, April 20, 2018.

1115   Megan Henney, "US health care system causing 'moral injury' among doctors, nurses," Fox Business, February 7, 2020, https://www.foxbusiness.com/money/us-health-care-system-moral-injury-clinicians.

1116   "IG Farben and Hitler: A Fateful Chemistry," Bloomberg, August 13, 2008, https://www.bloomberg.com/news/articles/2008-08-13/ig-farben-and-hitler-a-fateful-chemistry.

1117   "The Pharmaceutical Racket," accessed March 5, 2020, http://www.bibliotecapleyades.net/sociopolitica/esp_sociopol_brotherhood05.htm.

1118   Scott Glover and Lisa Girion, "Prescription drug-related deaths continue to rise in U.S." Los Angeles Times, March 29, 2013, http://articles.latimes.com/2013/mar/29/local/la-me-ln-prescription-drugrelateddeaths-continue-to-rise-20130329.

1119   Donald W. Light, "New Prescription Drugs: A Major Health Risk With Few Offsetting Advantages," Harvard University, Edmond J. Safra Center for Ethics, June 27, 2014, https://ethics.harvard.edu/blog/newprescription-drugs-major-health-risk-few-offsetting-advantages.

1120   "Trends in Opioid Use, Harms, and Treatment," Pain Management and the Opioid Epidemic: Balancing Societal and Individual Benefits and Risks of Prescription Opioid Use, NCBI Bookshelf, 2017, https://www.ncbi.nlm.nih.gov/books/NBK458661/.

1121   Peter Doward, "Cure: A Journey Into the Science of Mind Over Body review – can illness be 'all in your head'?, The Guardian, February 5 2016, https://www.theguardian.com/books/2016/feb/05/cure-a-journey-into-the-science-of-mind-over-body-by-jo-marchant-review.

1122   Jo Marchant, *Cure: A Journey into the Science of Mind Over Body*, 250-51.

1123   "The History Of Quackery," International Wellness Directory. accessed March 4, 2020.

1124   Dr. James P. Carter, *Racketeering in Medicine: The Suppression of Alternatives* (Newburyport, MA, Hampton Roads Publishing Co., 1993), 51-60.

1125   Wikipedia, "Benjamin Rush," last modified January 19, 2019, https://en.wikipedia.org/wiki/Benjamin_Rush.

1126   "The History of Medicine in America," International Wellness Directory, 2013, http://www.mnwelldir.org/docs/history/history01.htm.

1127   "The History of Medicine in America," International Wellness

Directory, 2013.
1128   "The History of Medicine in America," International Wellness Directory.
1129   Wikipedia, "Willowbrook State School," last modified January 9, 2019, https://en.wikipedia.org/wiki/Willowbrook_State_School.
1130   Wikipedia, "Civil Rights of Institutionalized Persons Act," last modified October 10, 2018, https://en.wikipedia.org/wiki/Civil_Rights_of_Institutionalized_Persons_Act.
1131   "A Brief History of Mental Illness and the U.S. Mental Health Care System," Unite for Sight, accessed March 5, 2020, http://www.uniteforsight.org/mental-health/module2#_ftn6.
1132   "A Brief History of Mental Illness and the U.S. Mental Health Care System," accessed March 5, 2020.
1133   Dennis Thompson, "More Americans suffering from stress, anxiety and depression study finds, CBS News, April 17 2017, https://www.cbsnews.com/news/stress-anxiety-depression-mental-illness-increases-study-finds/.
1134   Dennis Thompson, "More Americans suffering from stress, anxiety and depression, study finds," CBS News, April 17, 2017.
1135   Bill Toland, "How did America end up with this health care system?" Pittsburg Post-Gazette, April 26, 2014, http://www.post-gazette.com/healthypgh/2014/04/27/VITALS-How-did-U-S-employer-based-healthcare-history-become-what-it-is-today/stories/201404150167.
1136   Bill Toland, "How did America end up with this health care system?"
1137   Bill Toland, "How did America end up with this health care system?" Pittsburg Post-Gazette, April 26, 2014.
1138   Alison Kodjak, "Fact Check: 'We Don't Have Health Care In This Country,' Trump Says," NPR, May 18, 2017, http://www.npr.org/2017/05/18/529022011/fact-check-we-dont-have-health-care-in-this-countrytrump-says.
1139   Meg Wagner, "How 'Trumpcare' could cost 24 million Americans their health insurance," Fox6, March 13, 2017, http://fox6now.com/2017/03/13/congress-analyst-14m-lose-coverage-under-gop-healthbill/.
1140   "Why Health Care Eats More Of Your Paycheck Every Year," http://www.nbcnews.com/health/health-news/why-health-care-eats-

more-your-paycheck-every-yearn678051.

1141   "Why Health Care Eats More Of Your Paycheck Every Year," NBC News, November 4, 2016.

1142   Jed Graham, "CBO Will Likely Nullify House TrumpCare Vote Next Week," Investor's Business Daily, May 19, 2017, http://www.investors.com/politics/policy-analysis/cbo-will-likely-nullify-housetrump-care-vote-next-week/.

1143   P. R. Sarkar, Talks on Education: Section H, Prout in a Nutshell Vol. 4 Part 18 (a compilation), (Kolkata, Ananda Marga Publications, 1985). The Electronic Edition of the Works of P. R. Sakar, Version 1.4.0.6, Ananda Marga Publicationss, 2009.

1144   P. R. Sarkar. Suppression, Repression and Oppression, Prout in a Nutshell Vol 4 Part 17 (a compilation), (Kolkata, Ananda Marga Publications, 1989). The Electronic Edition of the Works of P. R. Sakar, Version 1.4.0.6, Ananda Marga Publicationss, 2009.

1145   P. R. Sarkar, Message to Teachers, Discourses on Neohumanist Education (a compilation), (Kolkata, Ananda Marga Publications, 1980). The Electronic Edition of the Works of P. R. Sakar, Version 1.4.0.6, Ananda Marga Publicationss, 2009.

1146   Wikipedia, "Eugenics," last modified January 30, 2019, https://en.wikipedia.org/wiki/Eugenics. 1151 See Volume 4, Chapter 5 under the subhead "How Does State Capitalism Work?" for an in-depth analysis of the role of eugenics in achieving ruling class dominance.

1147   Edward A. Ross, *Social Control: A Survey of the Foundations of Order* (New York, The Macmillan Company, 1901), Last reprint 2009 by Transaction Publishers, New Jersey. https://archive.org/stream/socialcontrolas00rossgoog#page/n4/mode/2up.

1148   The Rockefeller General Education Board, Occasional Letter No.1, 1906, http://www.zhibit.org/diemythographer/die-mythographer-die/occasional-letter-number-one-2006. 1154.

1149   Woodrow Wilson, 28th President of the United States, in a speech to businessmen, and from an address to The New York City High School Teachers Association, January 9th, 1909, http://www.zhibit.org/diemythographer/die-mythographer-die/occasional-letter-number-one-2006.

1150   Ellwood P. Cubberley, Stanford's Dean of Education, Public School Administration, 1916, 338, http://www.zhibit.org/diemythographer/die-mythographer-die/occasional-letter-number-one-2006.

1151   Ivan Illich, *Deschooling Society* (KKEIN Publishing International, 1970), 1-3.
1152   P. R. Sarkar, Problem of the Day, (Kolkata: Ananda Marga Publications, 1959). The Electronic Edition of the Works of P. R. Sakar, Version 1.4.0.6, Ananda Marga Publicationss, 2009.
1153   "A Look at the Shocking Student Loan Debt Statistics for 2018," Student Loan Hero, May 1, 2018, https://studentloanhero.com/student-loan-debt-statistics/.
1154   "Who Got Rich Off the Student Loan Crisis," Reveal News, June 28, 2016, https://www.revealnews.org/article/who-got-rich-off-the-student-debt-crisis/.
1155   "Who Got Rich Off the Student Loan Crisis." Reveal News, June 28, 2016.
1156   "Attorney General Cuomo Announces Settlement With Sallie Mae Over Its Student Loan Practices," Letitia James, NY Attorney General, April 11, 2007, https://ag.ny.gov/press-release/attorney-general-cuomo-announces-settlement-sallie-mae-over-its-student-loan-practices.
1157   "Education Policy: Student Loan," New America, accessed March 5, 2020, https://www.newamerica.org/education-policy/topics/higher-education-funding-and-financial-aid/federal-student-aid/federal-student-loans/federal-student-loan-history/.
1158   Bethany McLean, "The surprising profits of student loans," Fortune, April 16, 2017, http://archive.fortune.com/2007/04/16/news/companies/pluggedin_mclean_sallie.fortune/index.htm.
1159   James B. Steele and Lance Williams, "Who got rich off the student debt crisis?" 23ABC News, June 28, 2016, https://www.turnto23.com/longform/who-got-rich-off-the-student-debt-crisises.
1160   James B. Steele and Lance Williams, "Who got rich off the student debt crisis?" 23ABC News, June 28, 2016.
1161   James B. Steele and Lance Williams, "Who got rich off the student debt crisis"? WTMJ-TV Milwaukee, June 29, 2016, https://www.tmj4.com/longform/who-got-rich-off-the-student-debt-crisis.
1162   "How the Trump Administration is Changing Student Loan Forgiveness Plans," Ernest, September 24, 2018, https://www.earnest.com/blog/trump-administration-student-loan-forgiveness-plans/.
1163   "National Policy Agenda to Reduce the Burden of Student Debt," The Institute for College Access and Success, September 19,

2018, https://ticas.org/initiative/student-debt-policy-agenda.
1164   Terry Arndt, "The Impact of Student Debt on the Daily Lives of Young Americans," College Transition Publishing, June 16, 2016, http://collegetransitionpublishing.com/the-impact-of-student-debt-on-the-daily-lives-of-young-americans/.
1165   "Advocacy," American Student Assistance, accessed March 5, 2020, https://www.asa.org/advocacy/.
1166   P. R. Sarkar, Education, Discourses on Neohumanist Education [a compilation], (Kolkata, Ananda Marga Publications, 1959). The Electronic Edition of the Works of P. R. Sakar, Version 1.4.0.6, Ananda Marga Publicationss, 2009.
1167   "10 Facts About K-12 Education Funding," U.S. Department of Education, accessed Maarch 5, 2020, https://www2.ed.gov/about/overview/fed/10facts/index.html.
1168   "The Federal Role in Education," U.S. Department of Education, May 25, 2017, https://www2.ed.gov/about/overview/fed/role.html.
1169   Stephanie Watson, "How Public Schools Work," howstuffworks, accessed March 5, 2020, https://people.howstuffworks.com/public-schools2.htm.
1170   Bill Chappell, "U.S. Students Slide In Global Ranking On Math, Reading, Science," The Two-Way, December 3, 2013, http://www.npr.org/blogs/thetwo-way/2013/12/03/248329823/u-s-high-school-students-slidein-math-reading-science.
1171   T C Topp, "No (White) Child Left Behind: The American Education Apartheid," Hamilton, September 23, 2014, https://www.hamilton.edu/news/story/no-white-child-left-behind-the-american-education-apartheid.
1172   T C Topp, "No (White) Child Left Behind: The American Education Apartheid,"
1173   "In NYC, Demography Is Still Destiny," Schott Foundation for Public Education, November 9, 2012, http://schottfoundation.org/blog/2012/11/09/nyc-demography-still-destiny.
1174   Liz Dwyer, "Why America's Education System Is Like Apartheid," The Daily Good, April 19, 2012, https://www.good.is/articles/why-america-s-education-system-is-like-apartheid.
1175   Cory Turner, "Why America's Schools Have A Mon-

ey Problem," NPR School Money, April 18, 2016, http://www.npr.org/2016/04/18/474256366/why-americas-schools-have-a-money-problem.

1176   United States District Court, Northern District of Alabama, Northeastern Division, "INDIA LYNCH, a minor who sues by her parent, SHAWN KING LYNCH, et al., Plaintiffs, vs. THE STATE OF ALABAMA, et al., Defendants," https://www.gpo.gov/fdsys/pkg/USCOURTS-alnd-5_08-cv00450/pdf/USCOURTS-alnd-5_08-cv-00450-3.pdf.

1177   T C Topp, "No (White) Child Left Behind: The American Education Apartheid," Hamilton, September 23, 2014.

1178   Paul Street, *Segregated Schools: Educational Apartheid in Post-Civil Rights America* (New York; Routledge Taylor and Francis Group, 2005), quoted in Adam Sanchez, "Educational Apartheid in America," International Socialist Review, Issue 67, http://isreview.org/issue/67/educational-apartheidamerica.

1179   Adam Sanchez, "Educational Apartheid in America," "Educational Apartheid in America," International Socialist Review, Issue 67.

1180   "Jonathan Kozol Speaks on 'Educational Apartheid' in U.S. Public Schools," University of Rochester, March 9, 2006, http://www.rochester.edu/news/show.php?id=2463.

1181   "Zogby 9/11 poll receives no press," October 8, 2004, http://911blogger.com/news/2004-10-08/zogby-911-poll-receives-no-press.

1182   See http://www.nytimes.com/2009/11/15/us/15ksm.html?_r=0 for an account of Khalid Sheikh Mohammed who was also tried as a conspirator in 9/11.

1183   Wikipedia, "Bojinka plot," last modified January 16, 2019, https://en.wikipedia.org/wiki/Bojinka_plot.

1184   Michael C. Ruppert, *Crossing the Rubicon* (Canada: New Society Publishers, 2004), 577.

1185   Terry McDermott, Josh Meyer and Patrick J. McDonnell, The Plots and Designs of Al Qaeda's Engineer," Los Angeles Times, December 22, 20002, http://articles.latimes.com/2002/dec/22/world/fg-ksm22.

1186   Luke Hunt, "Former Warlord Primed For Afghan Presidency," The Diplomat, September 24, 2013, http://thediplomat.com/2013/09/former-warlord-primed-for-afghan-presidency/.

1187   "Complete Time Line," History Commons, accessed March

6, 2020, http://www.historycommons.org/timeline.jsp?other_alqaeda_%20operatives=khalidShaikMohammed&timeline=complete_911_timeline&startpos=0.
1188 Michael C. Ruppert, *Crossing the Rubicon*, 577.
1189 Wikipedia, "Opposing force," last modified December 22, 2018, https://en.wikipedia.org/wiki/Opposing_force.
1190 Wikipedia, "Sibel Edmond," last modified November 16, 2018, https://en.wikipedia.org/wiki/Sibel_Edmonds#cite_note-independent2004-10.
1191 Nafeez Mosaddeq Ahmed, "Why was a Sunday Times report on US government ties to al-Qaeda chief spiked?" Ceasefire, May 17, 2013, https://ceasefiremagazine.co.uk/whistleblower-al-qaeda-chief-u-s-asset/.
1192 Wikipedia, "Operation Gladio/B," last modified January 7, 2019, https://wikispooks.com/wiki/Operation_Gladio/B.
1193 Prof Peter Dale Scott, "US Government "Protection" of Al-Qaeda Terrorists and the US-Saudi "Black Hole", Global Research, August 14, 2015. https://www.globalresearch.ca/us-government-protection-of-al-qaeda-terrorists-and-the-us-saudi-black-hole/5344934.
1194 "Putin: Russia Is Ready To Show Proof That 9/11 Was An Inside Job," News Punch, January 15, 2016, http://yournewswire.com/putin-russia-is-ready-to-show-proof-that-911-was-an-inside-job/.
1195 Deborah Danan, „Saudi Press: U.S. Blew Up World Trade Center To Create 'War On Terror,'" Breitbart, May 22, 2016, https://www.breitbart.com/middle-east/2016/05/22/saudi-press-u-s-blew-upworld-trade-center-to-create-war-on-terror/.
1196 Michael C. Ruppert. *Crossing the Rubicon*, 580.
1197 Philip Marshall, "Want Answers? Who Trained The 9/11 Hijackers To Fly Boeing Jetliners," The Big Bamboozle, Januart 18, 2013, http://thebigbamboozle.tumblr.com/post/40856537710/want-answers-whotrained-the-911-hijackers-to.
1198 "September 11 - US Government accused," Welfare State, March 8, 2002, http://www.welfarestate.com/wtc/flight-skills.txt.
1199 "September 11 - US Government accused," Welfare State, March 8, 2002.
1200 Michael C. Ruppert, *Crossing the Rubicon*, 583.
1201 Michael C. Ruppert, *Crossing the Rubicon*, 574.
1202 "Bin Laden says he wasn't behind attacks," CNN, September 11, 2001, http://www.cnn.com/2001/US/09/16/inv.binladen.denial/.

1203   "Pakistan to Demand Taliban Give Up Bin Laden as Iran Seals Afghan Border," Fox News, September 16,
1204   "September 2001 Interview with Osama bin Laden. Categorically Denies his Involvement in 9/11," Full text of Ummat, Pakistani paper's Sept 2001 "exclusive" interview, September 28, 2001, pub. Global Research, https://www.globalresearch.ca/interview-with-osama-bin-laden-denies-his-involvement-in-9-11/24697.
1205   Wikipedia, "Al-Jazeera," last modified February 2, 2019, https://en.wikipedia.org/wiki/Al_Jazeera.
1206   "Transcript of Bin Laden's October interview," CNN, February 5, 2002, http://edition.cnn.com/2002/WORLD/asiapcf/south/02/05/binladen.transcript/.
1207   Wikipedia, "Responsibility for the September 11 attacks," last modified January 21, 2019, https://en.wikipedia.org/wiki/Responsibility_for_the_September_11_attacks.
1208   Michael C. Ruppert, *Crossing the Rubicon*, 580.
1209   Mark Schone, "9/11 Perpetrators: Where Are They Now?" ABC News, September 11, 2010, https://abcnews.go.com/Blotter/scenes-planners-911-attacks/story?id=11610817.
1210   "Has someone been sitting on the FBI?" Newsnight," BBC News, June 11, 2001, http://news.bbc.co.uk/2/hi/events/newsnight/1645527.stm.

Illustration Credits

The authors have made every effort to contact the owners of illustrations reproduced in this book. In the few cases where they have been unsuccessful, they invite copyright holders to contact them at cpaprocki@gmail.com

Fig. 5-1: Interest and Certain Government Programs
Description: Historical and projected US Federal Government revenues and spending from 2018 GAO financial report
Date 28 March 2019
Source: https://www.fiscal.treasury.gov/reports-statements/financial-report/current-report.html
Author: US Government Accountability Office
This work is in the public domain in the United States because it is a work prepared by an officer or employee of the United States Government as part of that person's official duties under the terms of Title 17, Chapter 1, Section 105 of the US Code

Fig. 5-2: Shrinking Middle Class
Graphic was originated by the Pew Research Center. According to the PRC and their Terms of Use, the graphic is available for public use.

Fig. 5-3: $20 Gold Certificate, series 1928
Date: June 3, 2014
Source: Goddot13
Author: The Bureau of Engraving and Printing (National Museum of American History
Use of this image should give credit to the National Numismatic Collection at the Smithsonian Institution.
This work is free and may be used by anyone for any purpose. If you wish to use this content, you do not need to request permission as long as you follow any licensing requirements mentioned on this page.

Fig. 5-4: IMF/World Bank Protest Sign
Could not find the owner of this illustration. Since it appears on multiple websites; it is assumed to be available to the public.

Fig. 5-5: Interconnectedness of Corporations
Contacted site for permission on March 19

Fig. 5-6: State and Local Debt Per Capita
Contacted site for permission on March 20, but received no response.

Fig. 5-7: Density of World Population in 2019
Description: World map of countries and territories by population in 2019
Date 21 November 2019
Author: Getsnoopy
I, the copyright holder of this work, hereby publish it under the following license: This file is licensed under the Creative Commons Attribution-Share Alike 4.0 International license.

Fig. 5-8: Recent Federal Debt
Description: US National Debt public/intergovernmental
Date: 27 February 2018
Source: https://www.treasurydirect.gov/NP/debt/search?startMonth=03&startDay=31&startYear=2005&endMonth=02&endDay=23&endYear=2018
Author: US Treasury
This work is in the public domain in the United States because it is a work prepared by an officer or employee of the United States Government as part of that person's official duties under the terms of Title 17, Chapter 1, Section 105 of the US Code.

Fig. 5-9: Home Owners Equity in Real Estate: 2000-2010
Contacted MarketWatch for permission on March 20, but received no response.

Fig. 5-10 Map of Global Green parties in national and local governments throughout the world. Contacted site for permission on March 20, but received no response.

Fig. 5-11 Afthanistan Before and After
Could not find original source of this photograph. It appears on multiple websites so it is assumed to be available to the public.

Fig. 5-12 Arabian Peninsula
Contacted Encyclopedia Brittanica on March 21 for permission, but received no response.

Fig. 5-13 Map of the Middle East
Description: Map of the Middle East for use
Date: 1 August 2008
Author: Cacahuate, amendments by Globe-trotter and Joelf
This file is licensed under the Creative Commons Attribution-Share Alike 4.0 International, 3.0 Unported, 2.5 Generic, 2.0 Generic and 1.0 Generic license.

Fig. 5-14 US Warefare Expenditures vs Other Countries
Description: Military Expenditures by Country in US$ billions, 2018 according to Stockholm International Peace Research Institute in a pie chart.
Date: 10 May 2019
Source: data from Stockholm International Peace Research Institute Military Expenditure Database https://www.sipri.org/databases/milex
Author: Barnhorst
I, the copyright holder of this work, hereby publish it under the following license: This file is licensed under the Creative Commons Attribution-Share Alike 4.0 International license.

Fig. 5-15: Ratio of Men and Women in the Fifty States
Description: Population Distribution by Gender
Date 2017
KFF materials may be reprinted, in whole or in part, without written permission, as long as they are not altered, and as long as your readers will not be charged for access (with the exception of tuition or course pack fees). Permission listed at https://www.kff.org/permissions-citations-reprints/

Fig 5-16: Comparison of Skulls
Description: Primate skulls provided courtesy of the Museum of Comparative Zoology, Harvard University.
Date: 13 May 2010
Source: Primate_skull_series_with_legend.png Molecular Insights into Human Brain Evolution, Jane Bradbury, PLoS Biology Vol. 3, No. 3, e50 doi:10.1371/journal.pbio.0030050
Author: Primate_skull_series_with_legend.png: Christopher Walsh, Harvard Medical School
I, the copyright holder of this work, hereby publish it under the following licenses: This file is licensed under the Creative Commons Attribution 2.5 Generic license.

Fig. 5-17: Questions of Race in the 2000 Census
Graphic was originated by the Pew Research Center. According to the PRC and their Terms of Use, the graphic is available for public use.

Fig. 5-18: National Ancestry
Chart located at Wikipedia.org at: https://en.wikipedia.org/wiki/Race_and_ethnicity_in_the_United_States
Last modified on March 14, 2020.

Fig. 5-19: Federal Debt By President & Political Party
Chart found at truthfulpolitics.com at http://www.truthfulpolitics.com/ http:/truthfulpolitics.com/comments/u-s-federal-debt-by-president-political-party/ in an article entitled, "U.S. Federal Debt by President/Political Party.
According to the truthfulpolitics website: Original truthfulpolitics.com articles and charts may be reprinted or distributed, without charge, and in any media. We ask that the editorial integrity of the article/chart be preserved with full attribution. Please give credit to truthfulpolitics.com.

Fig. 5-20: What Democrats and Republicans Say About Each Other
Graphic was originated by the Pew Research Center. According to the PRC and their Terms of Use, the graphic is available for public use.

Fig. 5-21: Top Ten Origins of People Applying for Asylum in the EU Chart found at BBC News Report at https://www.bbc.com/news/world-europe-34131911 in an article entitled "Migrant crisis: Migration to Europe explained in seven charts." The chart was provide by Eurostat. According to Eurostat's website, the statistical data are available free of charge via the Eurostat's website.
Source: https://ec.europa.eu/eurostat/help/first-visit/content.

Fig. 5-22: New Orleans After Hurricane Katrina
Description: View of flooded New Orleans, Louisana in the aftermath of Hurricane Katrina
Date: 11 September 2005
Author: Commander Mark Moran, of the NOAA Aviation Weather Center, and Lt. Phil Eastman and Lt. Dave Demers, of the NOAA Aircraft Operations Center
This image is in the public domain because it contains materials that originally came from the U.S. National Oceanic and Atmospheric Administration, taken or made as part of an employee's official duties.

Fig. 5-23: Emissions from Oil Extraction and Refining for Petroleum Products Used in the US (CO_2e) Compared to CO_2 Emissions from the Use of Major Transportation Fuels in the US. Source: Energy Information Administration and Oil Climate Index.
Chart found in article of Union of Concerned Scientists entitled: "Pulling Back the Curtain on a Massively Polluting Industry" at https://blog.ucsusa.org/jeremy-martin/pulling-back-the-curtain-on-a-massively-polluting-industry#.XmQ1rahKiUk.
Chart was created by the Energy Information Administration whose reuse policy states: U.S. government publications are in the public domain and are not subject to copyright protection. You may use and/or distribute any of our data, files, databases, reports, graphs, charts, and other information products that are on our website or that you receive through our email distribution service. However, if you use or reproduce any of our information products, you should use an acknowledgment, which includes the publication date, such as: "Source: U.S. Energy Information Administration (Oct 2008)."

Fig. 5-24: Rise in Greenhouse Gases Over Last Two Thousand Years
Contacted GlobalGreenhouseWarming for permission to use graphic on March 22, but received no response.

Fig. 5-25: Ingredients in a Typical Protein Bar
Illustration found on bing images for a specific protein bar.

Index

Symbols

1% 302, 492, 624
9/11 22, 159, 160, 162, 164, 165, 262, 289, 294, 296, 339, 340, 343, 344, 347, 407, 411, 440, 515, 516, 518, 696, 697, 698, 700, 701, 702, 703, 704, 705, 706, 707, 708, 709
2016 Election 502

A

Abraham Lincoln 27, 33, 198, 388, 715
Adolph Hitler 263, 272, 445, 446, 450
Air Pollution 550, 551, 557
Al-Afghani 315
Alan Greenspan 27, 53, 152, 166
Allende 62, 63
al-Qaeda 275, 323, 333, 334, 335, 339, 341, 342, 358, 364, 365, 366, 386, 388, 392, 394, 697, 698, 699, 700, 701, 703, 707, 708
American revolution 16, 382, 420
Andrew Jackson 27, 33, 53, 712
Arab Spring 23, 253, 255, 325, 357, 358, 361
Ayatollah Khomeini 318, 326, 329, 355

B

Bailout 44, 114, 122
Bancor 56, 57
Baptists 187, 193, 194, 195, 196, 197, 199, 215
Barak Obama 145, 148, 165, 247
Barry Goldwater 146, 245, 246, 502
Bechtel 161, 162, 163, 164, 408
Big Pharma 636, 638
Bilderberg Group 29, 465
Bill Clinton 111, 145, 148, 155, 166, 246, 657, 699
Bob Dole 154
Brandt Report 92, 93
Bretton Woods 54, 56, 57, 70, 79, 123, 147
Brundtland Report 96
Bubble 110, 113, 166
Bush/Cheney 22, 159, 289, 342, 344, 346, 347, 348, 387, 696, 698, 700, 701, 709

C

capitalism 3, 6, 18, 22, 25, 26, 28, 30, 59, 66, 78, 80, 81, 87, 101, 108, 116, 127, 137, 140, 141, 172, 173, 180, 181, 183, 184, 205, 211, 215, 220, 222, 225, 235, 239, 240, 242, 272, 274, 278, 306, 308, 309, 310, 312, 315, 329, 355, 359, 380, 406, 423, 479, 481, 490, 590, 622, 634
Capitalist 5, 8, 13, 130, 133, 301
cartel 29, 33, 34, 35, 44, 144
Catholic Church 3, 200, 218, 220,

227, 233, 236, 307, 427, 466
Celts 2
Charismatic Christianity 21, 205
Chile 61, 62, 63, 67
Christian Dominionism 211
Christian Reconstructionism 21, 211, 213
Christian Voice 21, 200, 201, 202
CIA 26, 61, 62, 63, 66, 73, 142, 164, 179, 288, 322, 330, 334, 347, 350, 373, 391, 392, 409, 697, 698, 699, 700, 701, 703, 704, 707
class 2, 3, 4, 6, 7, 8, 9, 10, 11, 12, 13, 15, 16, 17, 18, 19, 20, 21, 23, 25, 26, 38, 39, 50, 54, 65, 66, 80, 81, 91, 102, 103, 108, 113, 115, 118, 119, 120, 126, 129, 136, 137, 139, 140, 141, 143, 166, 167, 173, 177, 178, 180, 182, 189, 194, 205, 213, 217, 220, 225, 226, 227, 231, 232, 234, 239, 246, 247, 248, 253, 261, 263, 274, 283, 302, 309, 327, 351, 356, 385, 394, 401, 406, 415, 419, 423, 426, 427, 431, 438, 443, 450, 454, 455, 456, 457, 458, 459, 460, 461, 462, 463, 464, 465, 470, 471, 477, 478, 480, 481, 485, 487, 488, 495, 496, 497, 498, 499, 503, 504, 505, 507, 508, 509, 520, 623, 625, 652, 653, 655, 656, 664, 667, 668, 670, 672, 673, 677, 678, 679, 690, 699, 728
Clean Break 160
Climate Change 98, 99, 127, 556, 583
Clothing 105, 623, 624
Cold War 22, 56, 58, 69, 86, 156, 244, 245, 262, 266, 269, 270, 271, 274, 275, 276, 280, 281, 293, 343, 344, 345
conservative 15, 21, 125, 127, 128, 137, 140, 160, 161, 162, 184, 186, 187, 188, 189, 190, 191, 199, 200, 201, 202, 203, 204, 206, 207, 211, 214, 215, 216, 217, 220, 221, 224, 225, 227, 228, 229, 230, 234, 235, 236, 244, 246, 258, 273, 369, 377, 379, 443, 486, 498, 499, 501, 502, 503, 505, 510, 533, 545, 583, 591, 623
"containment" 281
Corporate Spying 521
Council on Foreign Relations 21, 26, 29, 111, 139, 141, 142, 143, 144, 145, 146, 147, 152, 170, 173, 465, 599, 699
Crisis of Democracy 21, 60, 140, 172, 180, 247, 272, 290, 413, 697

D

Daniel Luban 158, 161
debt 20, 23, 28, 30, 31, 32, 33, 34, 35, 37, 38, 39, 41, 42, 43, 44, 45, 46, 47, 48, 49, 50, 52, 58, 61, 68, 74, 76, 77, 78, 80, 91, 103, 105, 107, 109, 114, 115, 120, 121, 122, 124, 126, 128, 133, 134, 136, 148, 150, 151, 152, 153, 163, 178, 180, 183, 185, 189, 208, 209, 214, 223, 257, 266, 407, 430, 436, 437, 440, 442, 443, 444, 456, 478, 479, 480, 481, 486, 495, 497, 498, 503, 523, 633, 656, 657, 659, 660, 661, 676, 678, 694
Debt Roll-Over Play 41, 42

Declaration of the Occupation of New York City 253, 693

Democrats 7, 14, 15, 16, 18, 24, 103, 141, 163, 197, 198, 214, 223, 225, 236, 245, 246, 248, 252, 266, 273, 282, 302, 303, 305, 345, 498, 499, 500, 501, 502, 503, 504, 505, 506, 507, 508, 539, 542, 659

Department of Homeland Security 135, 291, 294, 539

Department of Veteran Affairs 403

Devotees of Islam 318, 352

Dick Cheney 152, 156, 161, 286, 287, 288, 289, 341, 407, 413, 705, 706, 715

divide and conquer 5, 7, 16, 18, 23, 24, 140, 141, 180, 182, 260, 302, 315, 416, 422, 674

domestic police 298, 413

Donald Rumsfeld 162, 286

Dr. Richard Furman 196

E

Earth Summit 99, 100

Education 10, 11, 13, 105, 190, 210, 232, 432, 439, 479, 634, 649, 650, 652, 653, 654, 656, 657, 658, 660, 661, 666, 667, 668, 669, 728

Education Reform 657

Ellwood Cubberley 11, 654

empire building 3, 21, 677

environment 12, 20, 23, 25, 46, 51, 67, 69, 95, 97, 100, 106, 118, 182, 215, 224, 229, 230, 249, 253, 261, 296, 305, 311, 343, 390, 397, 407, 416, 419, 431, 437, 444, 452, 459, 462, 463, 464, 471, 506, 509, 521, 548, 549, 552, 553, 564, 567, 576, 581, 594, 598, 600, 627, 628, 629, 636, 640, 643, 650, 652, 662, 676, 678, 690, 691

Evangelicals 192, 469, 470, 472, 473

Executive Order 13603 22, 300, 301

F

Federal Reserve Bank 20, 25, 26, 27, 28, 29, 30, 31, 33, 34, 35, 40, 44, 46, 47, 48, 52, 54, 55, 56, 58, 70, 76, 81, 115, 120, 121, 122, 168, 176, 184, 185, 245, 424, 479, 495, 659

Federal Reserve Notes 30, 31, 36, 114

FEMA 135, 706

Field Manual 388

Flexner Report 633, 634, 636, 644

food 9, 23, 32, 52, 53, 77, 80, 93, 104, 129, 131, 132, 134, 163, 176, 209, 241, 258, 283, 301, 362, 367, 416, 420, 431, 443, 457, 458, 481, 484, 488, 495, 497, 498, 523, 547, 549, 553, 559, 563, 565, 566, 567, 569, 570, 573, 575, 576, 577, 578, 582, 586, 593, 594, 595, 596, 597, 598, 599, 600, 601, 602, 603, 604, 606, 607, 608, 609, 610, 611, 612, 613, 614, 615, 616, 626, 628, 629, 635, 636, 639, 647, 649, 663, 676, 693, 711, 722, 723, 724, 725, 727

Fractional Reserve Banking 36

Franklin D. Roosevelt 242, 265, 645, 712

Friedrich A. Hayek 32

Function and Sources of Nutrients 722

Fundamentalist 198, 199, 325, 471, 747, 761, 762

G

GATT 78
G. Edward Griffin 33, 38
General Assembly 69, 82, 83, 92, 93, 95, 96, 321, 695
Generation 429, 430, 431, 434, 435, 436, 437, 438, 439, 440, 441, 442, 443
Genetically Modified Organisms 600
George H. W. Bush 145, 148, 152, 154, 155, 157, 205, 206
George Lakoff 184, 229
George Shultz 152, 162
George Wallace 149
George W. Bush 75, 145, 156, 184, 286, 291, 407, 465, 503, 543, 545, 659
Germans 2, 86, 445, 446, 450, 472, 710
globalization 20, 26, 28, 29, 50, 68, 70, 73, 101, 149, 253, 254, 281, 286, 306, 309, 343, 344, 345, 445, 677
Global Reach 64
Goldman Sachs 28, 44, 110, 111, 117
Grace Commission 31, 730
Great Awakening 192, 193, 194, 195
Great Depression 121, 126, 128, 140, 242, 243, 264, 430, 451, 714
Great Recession 50, 51, 113, 119, 121, 126, 166, 243, 358, 437, 440, 443, 458, 479, 481, 482, 486, 491, 618, 619, 620, 643, 667, 676
Green Revolution 597, 598, 600

Greens 21, 222, 224, 225, 229, 249, 250, 252
Group of 77 83, 84, 89
Guaranteed Payment Play 41, 45

H

Halliburton 156, 157, 161, 162, 163, 164, 342, 391, 407, 408
Health Care 191, 233, 622, 628, 631
health insurance 181, 301, 438, 631, 643, 644, 646, 647, 694
Henry Ford 33, 119, 710
Henry Kissinger 63, 151, 166, 598, 699
Homelessness 126, 620, 622
Houthi Rebellion 385

I

IMF 27, 43, 44, 54, 57, 62, 68, 75, 76, 77, 78, 82, 94, 95, 146, 148, 176, 825
Immigrants and Refugees 528
Industrial Agriculture 596
Initial Public Offerings (IPOs) 111
intellectual 3, 4, 11, 20, 24, 81, 100, 130, 142, 143, 146, 153, 159, 163, 169, 172, 173, 174, 180, 210, 219, 225, 227, 232, 237, 257, 308, 315, 317, 322, 353, 419, 446, 448, 463, 464, 465, 498, 652
Intergovernmental Panel on Climate Change (IPCC) 98
International Bank for Reconstruction and Development (IBRD) 71
International Centre for Settlement of Investment Disputes (ICSID) 71

International Development Association (IDA) 71
International Finance Corporation (IFC) 71
International Monetary Fund 20, 27, 29, 43, 54, 69, 70, 73, 76, 729
International Panel on Climate Change 127
IOU 34, 35, 36, 46, 114, 134
Iraq 23, 61, 88, 153, 154, 157, 158, 159, 160, 161, 162, 163, 164, 165, 180, 221, 278, 287, 288, 297, 298, 304, 306, 309, 316, 321, 323, 324, 326, 328, 329, 335, 341, 342, 344, 346, 347, 348, 349, 350, 352, 353, 358, 360, 361, 364, 365, 366, 367, 371, 376, 382, 383, 387, 388, 390, 391, 394, 396, 397, 398, 399, 402, 403, 404, 405, 406, 407, 408, 409, 410, 411, 413, 518, 528, 529, 532, 538, 539, 600, 675, 715
Islamic Fundamentalism 22, 262, 313, 314, 351, 355

J

Jamaat-e-Islami 319, 320, 334
James A. Garfield 27
James Glattfelder 116, 119
Jimmy Carter 21, 145, 148, 149, 151, 159, 178, 201, 204, 271, 283, 304, 542
John D. Rockefeller 11, 633, 653
John F. Kennedy 27, 33, 647, 710
John Maynard Keynes 30, 56, 242
John McCone 62
John Perkins 72
Jonathan Edwards 192, 194
Joseph E. Stiglitz 167

JP Morgan 140, 633, 636, 660
Judicial Watch 161, 163, 289

K

Kent State University 59, 248
Korean War 268, 270, 396, 637
Kuhn Loeb 28
Ku Klux Klan 197, 510
Kyoto Protocol 98

L

Land Pollution 563
Lazard Brothers 28
League of Nations 139, 142, 143, 316
left 6, 7, 8, 13, 15, 18, 19, 42, 45, 47, 49, 61, 66, 87, 105, 111, 118, 126, 128, 129, 136, 138, 139, 140, 146, 161, 166, 173, 180, 182, 183, 192, 201, 206, 220, 222, 223, 224, 225, 228, 236, 238, 242, 254, 259, 260, 261, 273, 277, 279, 299, 300, 321, 327, 337, 338, 349, 359, 366, 375, 380, 381, 390, 395, 400, 404, 409, 414, 433, 434, 442, 454, 456, 478, 501, 505, 510, 516, 528, 529, 534, 538, 547, 559, 564, 573, 584, 612, 618, 646, 648, 663, 676, 678, 708
legal tender 46, 47
Lehman Brothers 28, 71
Lester Maddox 149
liberal 11, 15, 21, 81, 118, 125, 127, 128, 129, 137, 140, 153, 157, 161, 188, 198, 199, 207, 213, 218, 219, 220, 222, 224, 226, 227, 228, 229, 230, 233, 234, 235, 236, 237, 238, 239, 240, 244, 245, 246, 278, 280, 286, 315, 358, 377, 389, 475, 498, 499, 501, 502,

505, 510, 514, 640, 653
Liberal Christians 228, 234, 235
Liberalism 21, 218, 227, 233, 241, 259
Loss of Large Mammals 578
Loss of Plant Species 582
Loss of Species 565
L. Paul Bremer 162
Ludwig von Mises 32, 242

M

Mao Tse-tung 60
matriarchal society 2
Meeting Basic Needs 593
Mental Health 640, 642
Methodists 193, 195, 215
Mexican Immigrants 539
Micro Chipping 525, 526
militarism 22, 62, 139, 142, 148, 157, 235, 262, 263, 264, 272, 295, 296, 306
Militarization of the Domestic Police 293
military-industrial complex 22, 23, 165, 239, 262, 268, 273, 282, 293, 390, 407, 413, 517
Moral Majority 21, 200, 201, 202, 203, 204, 205, 213
Muammar Qaddafi 324
Multilateral Investment Guarantee Agency (MIGA) 71
Murray Rothbard 32
Muslim Brotherhood 316, 317, 318, 322, 334, 359, 362

N

National Defense Authorization Act 22, 299
national origin 419, 477, 678
national security 23, 28, 62, 133, 153, 262, 266, 299, 301, 307, 341, 342, 345, 346, 411, 478, 515, 518, 519
nation-building 388, 390, 391, 392, 394, 395, 412
Neo-Cons 286, 287, 288, 339, 343, 346, 387, 397, 406, 413
neo-conservatives 160, 286
Neo-Liberals 224, 238
New Left 21, 59, 140, 172, 173, 174, 222, 225, 229, 247, 248, 273
Noam Chomsky 146, 229, 300
North-South Dialogue 83
NSA 73, 135, 185, 209, 291, 292, 299, 346, 518, 520, 521
Nurturant Parent 229

O

Obama 14, 22, 44, 125, 130, 145, 148, 165, 166, 167, 169, 207, 210, 247, 258, 261, 290, 291, 292, 294, 298, 299, 301, 302, 303, 304, 305, 306, 332, 346, 347, 350, 361, 367, 368, 378, 395, 405, 410, 411, 483, 484, 485, 490, 491, 492, 494, 502, 504, 508, 515, 516, 517, 518, 531, 537, 543, 544, 554, 561, 602, 631, 647, 660, 710
Occupy 17, 21, 222, 225, 229, 253, 254, 255, 256, 257, 258, 296, 302
OECD 84, 85, 90, 465, 489
OPEC 84, 88, 89, 94, 147, 148, 153, 162, 323
Operation Desert Shield 154
Operation Iraqi Freedom 159, 342

Osama bin Laden 23, 332, 333, 334, 336, 340, 344, 347, 348, 350, 352, 699, 700, 707, 708

Our Common Future 96, 97

Ozone 549

P

patriarchal society 2, 259, 351

Patriot Act 135, 294, 298, 299, 346, 515

Paul Wolfowitz 75, 286

Peak Oil 282, 756

Pentagon's New Map 305, 339, 342, 360, 370

Perpetual Debt Play 41

Political Polarization 498, 503

politicians 4, 5, 6, 10, 14, 15, 16, 17, 21, 27, 36, 46, 48, 50, 52, 53, 54, 77, 81, 108, 118, 136, 143, 146, 163, 176, 181, 185, 210, 221, 245, 246, 260, 266, 273, 305, 322, 409, 422, 457, 471, 481, 487, 490, 498, 500, 501, 506, 507, 508, 522, 529, 561, 584, 590, 592, 593, 602, 622, 659, 665, 675, 677, 678, 694

poverty line 9, 51, 103, 458, 595, 667

Presbyterians 195

Prescott Bush 154, 157

processed food 607, 609, 612, 629, 636, 639

Profit Motive 655

Progressives 21, 224, 239, 292

Protect the Public Play 41

Protestant Reformation 3

Puerto Rico 19, 226, 265, 545

R

Rabbi Lerner 14

race 4, 19, 23, 87

Race 9

Refugee Migration 376

religion 4, 19, 23, 64, 170, 187, 190, 192, 193, 194, 202, 207, 214, 216, 217, 218, 219, 227, 236, 240, 244, 259, 309, 310, 311, 314, 315, 351, 355, 419, 423, 427, 438, 439, 443, 466, 467, 471, 472, 475, 477, 505, 548, 652, 655, 677, 678, 679

Renaissance 3, 219, 236

Republicans 7, 14, 15, 16, 18, 24, 48, 103, 134, 141, 149, 163, 164, 165, 201, 210, 273, 282, 302, 303, 305, 345, 493, 494, 498, 500, 501, 502, 503, 505, 506, 507, 508, 514, 537, 542, 544, 557, 562, 616, 657, 659

Rescheduling Play 41, 43

reserve currency 56, 57, 133, 148

right 6, 7, 8, 10, 15, 16, 17, 19, 35, 37, 46, 61, 73, 75, 84, 91, 112, 126, 128, 129, 136, 138, 140, 141, 146, 149, 154, 160, 168, 173, 179, 180, 181, 182, 183, 184, 186, 190, 191, 192, 193, 196, 199, 200, 201, 202, 205, 208, 220, 222, 223, 227, 228, 231, 233, 236, 239, 240, 241, 246, 259, 260, 261, 262, 273, 276, 279, 296, 297, 299, 300, 302, 307, 309, 349, 357, 359, 377, 395, 400, 402, 403, 413, 414, 415, 430, 441, 454, 458, 472, 473, 478, 484, 489, 501, 507, 508, 513, 516, 517, 521, 523, 527, 529, 530, 531, 533, 544, 547, 560, 580, 590, 591, 593, 595, 613, 634, 645, 649, 664, 665, 676, 678, 693, 694, 695, 706

Right Livelihood 593
Right to Food 595
Robber Barons 25
Rockefeller 11, 28, 58, 65, 130, 139, 143, 144, 146, 147, 148, 149, 151, 156, 157, 169, 240, 597, 598, 600, 632, 633, 636, 653
Ronald Reagan 31, 87, 145, 148, 151, 201, 204, 205, 246, 503, 542, 675, 712
Ron Paul 31, 146, 207, 299, 406
Rothschild 28

S

Saddam Hussein 153, 160, 221, 287, 329, 335, 341, 342, 346, 348, 349, 365, 382, 383, 392
Samuel P. Huntington 60, 172
Sayyid Qutb 322, 334
Secular Liberals 236
Secure Communities 22, 290, 291, 292, 294
sex and gender 424, 426, 427, 428
Shelter 617
Shiite/Sunni Conflict 366
Slavs 2, 85
social psychology 2, 455
state monopoly capitalism 30, 59, 141, 205
Steve Berkman 74
strict father 184, 185, 186, 187, 188, 189, 190, 215, 229
structural adjustment policies 76
student loan borrowers 661, 662
supranational sovereignty 130, 169
sustainable development 96, 98, 100

Syria 23, 160, 287, 304, 308, 316, 317, 321, 322, 326, 328, 335, 358, 359, 360, 361, 362, 363, 364, 365, 366, 367, 368, 369, 370, 371, 372, 373, 374, 375, 376, 390, 394, 395, 406, 411, 414, 528, 529, 532, 538, 675, 715

T

Taliban 160, 275, 323, 329, 330, 331, 332, 337, 338, 340, 357, 413, 444, 697
Tea Party 21, 184, 185, 207, 208, 209, 210, 258
Ten Key Values of the US Green Party 690
The Creature from Jekyll Island 33
The Establishment 59, 172, 247
The Grand Chessboard 22, 283, 286
The Militarization of the Domestic Police 293
Theodore Roosevelt 30, 712
Third World 20, 60, 74, 91, 97, 355
Thomas Jefferson 32, 195, 237, 238, 715
Timothy Geithner 168
Tories 194
Trans-Pacific Partnership 130, 168, 303, 514
Treasury Note 35
Trilateral Commission 21, 29, 60, 139, 144, 145, 146, 147, 148, 149, 150, 151, 152, 155, 156, 157, 166, 170, 172, 173, 174, 225, 247, 281, 283, 340, 465, 699
Trilateralist 21, 22, 145, 149, 152, 156, 157, 165, 166, 169, 172, 174, 179, 180, 181, 221, 247, 272, 285, 286, 290, 343,

360, 375, 391, 397, 598
Trump 10, 14, 15, 17, 19, 21, 46, 51, 68, 106, 107, 115, 120, 129, 130, 137, 149, 169, 178, 181, 182, 213, 214, 215, 291, 292, 303, 304, 305, 306, 374, 378, 395, 405, 411, 424, 476, 481, 483, 484, 485, 487, 489, 490, 491, 492, 493, 494, 501, 502, 503, 504, 505, 506, 507, 508, 511, 514, 517, 519, 531, 537, 538, 539, 544, 551, 552, 553, 554, 557, 558, 563, 566, 569, 581, 587, 588, 590, 618, 619, 628, 631, 648, 661, 675, 716
Trump Economy 490

U

unemployment 9, 10, 23, 32, 50, 103, 105, 108, 109, 114, 135, 178, 242, 246, 411, 419, 437, 442, 478, 480, 481, 482, 483, 484, 485, 488, 489, 490, 491, 494, 532, 676
Union of Soviet Socialist Republics 85, 274
United Nations 54, 69, 82, 83, 86, 89, 90, 93, 95, 96, 97, 99, 100, 131, 139, 143, 150, 153, 166, 268, 269, 308, 321, 342, 349, 376, 445, 566
Up-The-Ante Play 41, 42

V

Veterans for Common Sense 163
Vietnam War 148, 248, 270, 271, 273, 302, 387, 396, 637, 716

W

Warburg 28
War on Terror 133, 135, 165, 281, 340, 377, 379, 412, 413, 517, 518, 674, 709
warrior 2, 3, 4, 20, 21, 227, 256, 257, 261, 262, 298, 455, 463, 464, 465
Water Pollution 558
Woodrow Wilson 11, 141, 653
World Bank 20, 27, 29, 54, 62, 68, 69, 70, 71, 72, 73, 75, 76, 78, 82, 94, 95, 131, 146, 148, 150, 156, 176, 465, 532, 557, 597
World Commission on Environment and Development (WCED) 96
World Trade Organization 79, 107
World War II 6, 21, 26, 30, 263, 266, 268, 269, 272, 318, 320, 321, 431, 432, 541, 634, 637, 646, 673, 711, 712
WWII 2, 3, 13, 19, 20, 22, 26, 27, 54, 56, 58, 60, 64, 69, 79, 82, 85, 122, 136, 140, 143, 165, 253, 262, 264, 265, 266, 268, 272, 288, 305, 307, 329, 344, 396, 430, 431, 464, 481, 618, 636, 646, 674, 677

Y

Yemen 23, 87, 287, 313, 321, 324, 332, 333, 335, 358, 380, 381, 382, 383, 384, 385, 386, 387, 390, 406, 411, 528, 675

Z

Zbigniew Brzezinski 144, 149, 150, 159, 281, 283

About the Authors

Charles Paprocki has spent many years working with troubled teenagers, prison inmates, welfare recipients, and migrant workers in the human services system. He also owned a graphics and advertising agency in New York City where he combined his skill and knowledge to create social marketing campaigns. He was one of the core leaders to create the Universal Pre-K program in New York State and the local food movement in Illinois. His last work was to manage an organic farm in southern Illinois. He has consulted with international NGO's on management strategies and participated in the Earth Summit in Brazil and the Social Summit in Denmark. He is now retired and living in Carbondale, Illinois.

Tom Paprocki has worked several years in social services, including starting a preschool and daycare center in rural southern Illinois and serving as an administrator for a drug education and crisis center. After receiving a Masters in Public Administration, he was hired by the NASA Goddard Space Flight Center as a Presidential Management Intern. He served thirty years at Goddard, which included positions as head of Personnel, Procurement, and Institutional Resources. He spent the next seven years as Director of Management Operations, which included facilities, acquisitions, environmental and health services, security, and logistics for the research and launch facilities at Greenbelt, Maryland and Wallops Island, Virginia. He is now retired living in Dunkirk Maryland.